Originally from Southampton, UK, Jon Gorvett left home for a holiday in Spain in 1990 and conspicuously failed to return. Since then he has lived and worked in a variety of places around the Mediterranean. For the last nine years he has been based in İstanbul where he works as a stringer and correspondent for a variety of newspapers and magazines, including *The Boston Globe*, *The Business*, *Al Jazeera*, *The Express*, *The Middle East* and the *Washington Report on the Middle East*. His articles have been published in journals as varied as *The New Yorker* and *Pensions International*, *Private Eye* and *Tobacco Reporter*.

A collaborator on the *Time Out Guide to Istanbul* and *The Rough Guide to Turkey*, he is a Fellow of the Royal Geographical Society.

Mediterranean Handbook
This first edition: August 2004

Publisher
Trailblazer Publications
The Old Manse, Tower Rd, Hindhead, Surrey, GU26 6SU, UK
Fax (+44) 01428-607571, info@trailblazer-guides.com
www.trailblazer-guides.com

British Library Cataloguing in Publication Data
A catalogue record for this book is available from the British Library

ISBN 1-873756-72-0

© **Jon Gorvett**
Text (except pp24-36) and photographs

Maps; text (pp24-36) © Trailblazer Publications

The right of Jon Gorvett to be identified as the author of this work has been
asserted by him in accordance with the Copyright, Designs and Patents Act 1988

Editors: Henry Stedman, Patricia Major, Anna Jacomb-Hood
Series editor: Patricia Major
Typesetting and layout: Henry Stedman
Cartography: Nick Hill
Index: Jane Thomas

Important note
Every effort has been made by the author and publisher to ensure that the information
contained herein is as accurate and up to date as possible. However, they are unable
to accept responsibility for any inconvenience, loss or injury sustained by anyone as a
result of the advice and information given in this guide.

Printed on chlorine-free paper by
D2Print (☎ +65-6295 5598), Singapore

MEDITERRANEAN HANDBOOK

JON GORVETT

WITH ADDITIONAL MATERIAL BY HENRY STEDMAN,
PATRICIA MAJOR & ANNA JACOMB-HOOD

TRAILBLAZER PUBLICATIONS

Acknowledgements

Many, many thanks to the dozens of people around the Mediterranean who helped out in the making of this book – consciously or otherwise – and thanks in particular to the following: Buket Cengiz, Bill Sellars, David O'Byrne, Melis Kanik, Andrew Tabler, Chris de Oliveira, Amparo Castell, David Glass, Harry Christopopolous, Alper Çeker, Ferhat Uludaglar, Issandr el Idris, Nabil Shahadi, Tim Gorvett, Andrea Maretti, Claude Simone, and the staff of the EOT office, Hanía, Crete.

At Trailblazer thanks to Bryn Thomas, Patricia Major, Henry Stedman, Anna Jacomb-Hood, Nick Hill and Jane Thomas.

Last but not least – thanks to my Mum and Dad.

A request

The author and publisher have tried to ensure that this guide is as accurate and up to date as possible. Nevertheless, things change. If you notice any changes or omissions that should be included in the next edition of this book, please write to Jon Gorvett at Trailblazer (address on p2) or email him at jon.gorvett@trailblazer-guides.com. A free copy of the next edition will be sent to persons making a significant contribution.

Updated information will be available on the Internet at
www.trailblazer-guides.com

Front cover: Ilıca Beach, Çeşme, Turkey © Jon Gorvett

CONTENTS

INTRODUCTION

With two and a half million square kilometres of water, several major sub-seas and thousands of islands, not to mention thousands of kilometres of coastline, the Mediterranean is a world in itself. In terms of history, culture, art, science and just about every aspect of life, it's vast.

All the older European civilizations developed along its shores and the area was the cradle of religions and philosophy. Springing from ancient myths and legends the history of the Mediterranean is that of the individual countries bordering its shores and from their interaction, the one on the other, and later with adjacent other countries so that the whole has become the history of the Western World.

The sea itself provided the means by which its peoples made contact, usually in order to trade and discover but sometimes to try to conquer what lay on the other side of the water. Their sea routes were the links between places, peoples and hence their cultures; many still exist, the last visible survivors of those ancient patterns of communication which have often now been adopted by air travel routes.

But it is still possible to rediscover the magic of sea travel though in more comfort than those ancient mariners. Obviously shipping has changed since the Phoenicians sailed these routes and now, criss-crossing the Med are hundreds of ferries, hydrofoils and catamarans, most of which offer pleasant and relatively speedy ways of getting around. Capable of taking vehicles as well as passengers, they're generally inexpensive.

In this guide we've approached the subject first and foremost as what it is – a sea – and thus have concentrated not on whole countries but on the mainland and island ports, the main sights within easy reach of them, the ferry routes between these ports and the historical background that links them all together.

Planning your trip

If you could afford the time and the money the ideal would be to spend several months covering the routes in this guide, travelling the entire Mediterranean: there is so much to see, so many places to visit. More realistic for most travellers will be several shorter visits. Highlights and some suggested routes are listed at the start of each section.

One way to extend your time in the Med is to get a job here. There are many opportunities for casual work in the summer. Options include working in hotels, restaurants and bars as well as crewing on yachts. Crewing (see box, p17) is particularly feasible in the Aegean (though seldom between Greece and Turkey) and between France, Corsica and Sardinia, where the sheer volume of boats in summer boosts demand not only for qualified crew but also for deckhands, cooks, cleaners and general companions.

While every effort has been made to ensure the information contained in this book is accurate, schedules do change, boats break down, services get cancelled and restaurants and hotels go bust. With this in mind, planning your trip should involve plenty of room for flexibility. This book gives comprehensive coverage of the possibilities but you should confirm the realities as close as possible to the time you set off. It's more than likely that everything will go smoothly but be prepared to alter your plans as you go along. Some of the most interesting and adventurous travel experiences come out of a serendipitous change of plans.

Using this guide

The section on planning your trip outlines some suggested routes and costs and gives ideas about when to go, what to take and on booking your trip. Part 2 is an overview of the geography, flora and fauna, and history of the region. Part 3 gives basic information (visas, when to go, where to get information, national holidays etc) on all the countries included in the guide. The next five parts comprise the guide itself, each beginning with some more detailed route plans. We have divided the Mediterranean into five sections (**Western Mediterranean**, **Tyrrhenian Sea**, **Adriatic Sea**, **Aegean Sea** and **Eastern Mediterranean**), each roughly corresponding to one of the Med's interior 'seas'. Details are given about the main ports in each sea, including all you need to know about the place's history, what to see, how to get around (by ferry and overland), practical information, where to stay and where to eat. Only basic ferry details (destinations and local contact details) are given in these parts; full details are in the appendix.

The appendix includes a list of the main ferry companies with their contact details and general route information; details (frequency, duration and sample fares) about most ferry services in the Mediterranean (these are shown graphically in the route maps at the start of each section); and, finally, some useful phrases.

Map key

		☆	Police	©	Mosque
⇧	Place to stay	🏛	Museum	Ⓜ	Metro Station
O	Place to eat	📖	Library	Ⓑ	Bus Station
⊠	Post Office	ⓘ	Tourist Information	⛴	Ferry
⌁	Internet	✝	Church / Cathedral	Λ	Campsite
$	Bank / Exchange	✡	Synagogue	●	Other

Routes and costs

Planning a route using ferries in the Mediterranean is not easy. Firstly, because there are so many possibilities, and secondly because the possibilities (the actual services) may be cancelled or changed at any time. Generally, however, there are enough services to make a holiday or travel in the region a memorable and hassle-free experience. The least frequent services tend to be those that travel the furthest, where services may be limited to a single weekly or monthly boat, which makes checking in advance the golden rule of ferry travel.

If time is limited, certain regions are more advisable than others. Top of these is the Aegean, which has frequent services year-round, with the height of summer sometimes seeing bizarre gridlocks in harbour entrances. Also good for regular boats is the Adriatic, particularly the Croatian coast, and the Western Med between Morocco and Spain and to/from the Balearics.

To help you plan your Mediterranean journey, the following provides the briefest of outline to each of the five regions (which, as explained in the introduction, correspond roughly to the Med's five 'interior seas'). For further details of each region and some suggested two- or three-week itineraries, turn to the relevant part later on in the book; while for more extensive information on the ferry services see the appendix on p438.

WESTERN MEDITERRANEAN

For the purposes of this guide, the Western Mediterranean has been divided into two regions, with Barcelona and the Balearics to the north and the Andalucian–Moroccan coasts to the south. The two are connected by frequent air, bus and train services but, unfortunately, not by ferry. Likewise, the North African coast is regrettably devoid of ferries travelling east–west or vice versa these days.

Nevertheless, the existing ferry services do make it easy to bounce back and forth between the ports of Spain and Morocco. The southern coast of Spain and the northern coast of Morocco form a historical and geological bridge between the northern and southern shores of the Med and for centuries have seen armies, traders and migrants passing back and forth.

Nowadays the Western Med's northern coast is a major tourist destination, with the beaches of the **Costa del Sol** among the first in the world to see the development of mass tourism. This makes it a mecca for mainly north European holidaymakers along the coast, while inland the cities of Granada, Cordoba and Seville are major World Heritage sites. **Andalucía** has an ambience all its own, too, home of the flamenco and the classic Spanish *sol y sombre*, the light and

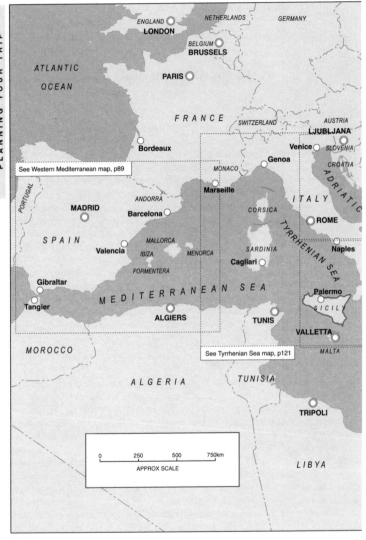

See Western Mediterranean map, p89

See Tyrrhenian Sea map, p121

The Mediterranean Sea

POLAND UKRAINE RUSSIA

PLANNING YOUR TRIP

HUNGARY ROMANIA

See Adriatic Sea map, p205

ZAGREB BUCHAREST BLACK SEA

BOSNIA & HERZEGOVINA BELGRADE

SARAJEVO SOFIA BULGARIA

SERBIA & MONTENEGRO

ALBANIA SKOPJE MACEDONIA ISTANBUL TURKEY

See Aegean Sea map, p283

TIRANA

Brindisi See Eastern Mediterranean map, p397

CORFU Izmir

GREECE CHIOS

AEGEAN SEA Bodrum Alanya SYRIA

Patras ATHENS KOS Nicosia LEBANON

RHODES CYPRUS BEIRUT DAMASCUS

Iraklio ISRAEL TEL AVIV AMMAN

CRETE GAZA STRIP WEST BANK

MEDITERRANEAN SEA JORDAN

Alexandria EGYPT

LIBYA CAIRO

★ TRAILBLAZER

> **Ideas for longer itineraries**
> If you have more time, it may be a good idea to stick some of the routes suggested together. For example, you could do the two-week Italy to Corsica and Sardinia trip (see p122), but in reverse, starting in Rome and ending in Genoa. Then take a train over to Venice before embarking on a slow hop down the Adriatic to Dubrovnik. In this, the Dalmatian coast is likely to be the star performer. While it is gradually returning to the tourism map after the long and painful death throes of Yugoslavia, it isn't quite there yet. It is also a region with an astonishing variety, from sugar-mountain-style islets to long, wooded hills and deserted coves — an amazing setting for some truly historic cities and settlements.
>
> Alternatively, start out in Tangier, Morocco, take a boat to Gibraltar, go overland to Valencia, from where you can go to the Balearics, and then on to Barcelona. From Barcelona take the ferry to Genoa from where you can start the Italy to Corsica and Sardinia route outlined on p122.
>
> The Aegean trips outlined on p281 could be made longer by starting with the Adriatic route (Italy to Albania to Greece, see p206) but going overland from Igoumenitsa to Piraeus, rather than back to Bari. This would offer everything from intriguing Albania to the northern Greek mountains to the dazzling shores of the Aegean's most sun-soaked islands.

shadow of burning hot days in dusty, whitewashed villages.

Across the water from the British colony of **Gibraltar**, the Moroccan city of **Tangier** is a major draw, with its international past and its memorable Medina. Beyond, the Rif Mountains mark a coastal ridge before the rest of the country, the westernmost land of Islam, and the desert beyond. Also along the coast are the Spanish enclaves of **Ceuta** and **Melilla**, remnants of Spain's long role on the southern shores of the Mediterranean.

Further north, the Mediterranean curves gently to the Gulf of Lions and the coast of Provençal France, passing by the **Balearic Islands**, like the Costa del Sol a byword for mass tourism, and the port city of **Barcelona**, one of the sea's greatest venues. Barcelona is also the link to the Tyrrhenian Sea through its ferry connection to another great northern Mediterranean maritime city, Genoa.

TYRRHENIAN SEA

With no shortage of fast, regular ferry services, the Tyrrhenian Sea is an easy place to explore and an area that possesses great variety since its shoreline includes four different countries, each of which contains many different regions. Access by air is fairly straightforward to any of the major cities, while road and rail links to France and Italy are also excellent from the rest of Europe.

The long peninsula of Italy, paralleled by the islands of Corsica, Sardinia and Sicily, is a natural geological and cultural dividing line, separating the eastern and western halves of the Mediterranean. Yet it's also a natural pathway from north to south, Europe to North Africa, a factor which leaves the sea between Malta, Tunis, Sicily and southern Italy something of a crossroads. Unsurprisingly, therefore, the region contains some of Western Europe's most important historical ports, including Columbus' home town of **Genoa**, the French industrial harbour of **Marseille**, **Naples** with its nearby volcano of Vesuvius, **Civitavecchia**, the main port for the Eternal City, **Rome**, and the vibrant North African capital and port of **Tunis**, situated on the site of historic Carthage. Yet just as compelling are the islands of the Tyrrhenian, each rich in history, from the rough-edged yet starkly beautiful **Corsica** and **Sardinia** to **Sicily**, home to the Med's most spectacular volcanoes – particularly in the Aeolian Islands. It also has brilliant beaches and, despite a certain infamy as the home of the mafia, friendly people. And finally there's **Malta**, a real gem, a self-contained world of wonderful architecture, history and industrious organization.

ADRIATIC SEA

In many ways one of the Mediterranean's most under-visited areas, the Adriatic offers one of the most beautiful coastlines anywhere, with its picture-postcard towns and offshore islands. On its western side, the Italian peninsula runs down from the medieval powerhouse and tourism mecca of **Venice** to the eastern Calabrian coast. On the other side of the water, most of the Adriatic coast belongs to **Croatia**, one of the most determinedly European of Yugoslavia's former territories, including the walled delights of **Dubrovnik** and **Korčula** and well-preserved **Poreč** and **Rovinj**. There is, however, one blip along the way, the tiny Bosnian enclave at **Neum** and, further south, **Montenegro**, an ancient kingdom increasingly at odds with Serbia, its partner in what is now left of Yugoslavia. After that comes **Albania**, a much-maligned yet deeply fascinating country. With many warned off the place, you'll receive one of the warmest welcomes in the Med. The capital, **Tirana**, is the main sight here. Also within the boundaries of the Adriatic are the western ports of **Greece** and the intriguing island of **Corfu**.

AEGEAN SEA

The Mediterranean contains many of the world's most spectacular ancient sites, as well as many of its most significant. Nowhere is this more evident than in the Aegean, with the colossal Roman city of **Ephesus**, near Kuşadası, a clear winner for sheer size. In that region, too, you'll find almost every island has a clutch of temples, every harbour an astonishing past. For beauty, the headland temple of **Sounion** near Athens is well known, but the temple to Athena at **Assos**, north of Ayvalık, is also in that league. Near here, too, lies **Troy**, a ruin now none-too spectacular but infused with some of the greatest myths of all time. In fact, touring down the Anatolian side of the Aegean gives credence to the oft-stated belief that most of ancient Greece's best ruins are in Turkey. And many of ancient Rome's best are there too. So, if it's rubble you're after, come to the Aegean.

The Aegean is also, of course, a great place simply to relax and have some fun. Brilliant beaches, rocky coves, crystal-clear waters and a jumping nightlife are here, with well developed bar and club scenes in **İstanbul** and **Athens**, on some of the larger islands such as **Rhodes** and **Crete** and in the larger resorts.

The number of ferry services in the Aegean means there's a vast choice of routes. One international route and one domestic (ie within Greece) are suggested (p281) but it's worth reading the Aegean section and looking at the route possibilities in the appendix (pp453-60) to get an idea of what's available.

EASTERN MEDITERRANEAN

With the **Turkish** coast to the north, **Israel**, the **Palestinian Territories** and **Syria** and **Lebanon** to the east, **Egypt** to the south and **Cyprus** in the middle, the Eastern Mediterranean holds a fascinating range of cultures and peoples. Whether it's the faded glory of places such as **Alexandria** or the hectic nightlife of **Beirut**, it's a region encompassing a wide range of possibilities.

In terms of ferry routes Cyprus is the focal point; today, its old strategic importance as the gateway between Europe and the Middle East is nowhere more evident than at sea. Divided since 1974, the southern Greek/Cypriot part has until recently acted as the entry point from Rhodes and the Aegean – and it is hoped that it will do so again very soon – while the northern Turkish/Cypriot section remains isolated except from Turkey. Yet, limited though the ferry services may be, there are ways of travelling overland through the Eastern Med, and though you'd need a long sabbatical to really explore the region's vast history and cultural variety, it would be an inspiring yet humbling experience to do so.

COSTS

Generally speaking, how much it all costs is largely up to you. With a range of onboard accommodation available, from deck class to a luxury cabin, and a wide range of destinations to choose from, you pay your money and take your choice. However, several factors are worth thinking about.

First, if your budget is tight, try to take night ferries. This way, you pay for your bed for the night and your travel costs simultaneously. Second, try to dovetail arrivals and departures as neatly as possible. Hanging around for a week

---

Ferry discounts for rail-pass holders
    With an Inter-Rail (🖳 www.interrailnet.com), Global or Zone G pass, or a Eurail pass you can travel for free on certain lines/services as long as you travel deck class. However, port taxes are still payable and a supplement must be paid for upgrades eg to a Pullman (reclining chair) or a cabin. High-season supplements may also be payable.

    Hellenic Mediterranean Lines (HML) and Blue Star Ferries accept the above passes on services between Italy (Bríndisi) and Greece (Patras, Igoumenitsa and Corfu). Superfast Ferries accept them on services between Ancona and Patras and Bari and Patras/Igoumenitsa.

    A Eurodomino pass (a train pass that's valid for three or eight days in a month in one European country) is also accepted on HML and Blue Star ferry services between Bríndisi and Patras and on Superfast ferries between Ancona/Bari and Patras.

    Discounts are also offered on SNCM sailings to and from Corsica (30%) and also on Trasmediterránea ferry services (30%).

Deck class survival guide

With the days of slavery now largely at an end and 'stowage class' (a bunk down in the bilges) a thing of the past, the cheapest passage on a Mediterranean ferry is now a deck class ticket.

With this you get to travel just like all the other passengers, just without any of the creature comforts like a bunk or a seat. On some vessels, you'll also be denied access below deck, so onboard entertainment, cafés, bars and restaurants will also be closed to you. In other words, deck class usually means just that: the chance to sleep on an iron and steel deck plate beneath the stars ... or rain, of course, which is why if this is to be your mode of travelling, it's as well to take a few precautions.

First of all, always bring a good roll of foam padding, the sort widely available from camping shops, as ferry decks clearly have a lot less give in them than the bare ground. Many have fixed wooden or plastic benches though, which are generally preferable. It's also worth asking if you can kip in the corridors inside, as these are often carpeted. Earplugs may also be a good idea, as you may find yourself right next to the smoke stacks or generators, or inside with a large party of raucous Italian schoolkids determined to play Beatles' songs till 5am. Above all, bring your own food and drink, as onboard these are much pricier than on land. If you're on a day crossing, plenty of sun cream is also a good idea, as you'll be out beneath the ozone hole all day.

One advantage with deck class is, of course, that if the boat starts sinking, you can easily jump for it. That said, it can be a lot less painful to spend a couple of extra euros and take a Pullman seat...

waiting for a boat out can be expensive, not to mention a trifle dull if you end up in some small, out-of-the-way port. Thirdly, shop around. This applies to everything, from getting to the Med to how and when you travel once there – for example, ferries are cheaper than catamarans or hydrofoils; travelling mid-week and getting a return ticket will also save money. Reductions are often given for children, students and senior citizens, and it is worth looking out for 'family specials', eg two adults and two children.

Ferries crossing international frontiers are often more expensive than you might anticipate, particularly between Greece and Turkey where travelling a few hundred metres can set you back $30. If you fancy doing the Anatolian coast, it is better to make one crossing at the start – say, Ayvalık–Lesbos, then go down the Greek islands to Rhodes before crossing to Marmaris and taking buses, or a Blue Cruise (see p337), back up the Turkish side.

Taking a vehicle, other than a bicycle which is usually transported for free, obviously adds to the cost of a ferry ticket but may minimize your overall travel costs. Some companies have a set rate for motorbikes, others charge according to the engine size (cc); cars are generally charged according to size and caravans generally cost up to three times the cost of a car. If you are travelling with a caravan look out for companies that offer camping on board (see box p16); also look out for special deals for two or more passengers in a car.

Choosing the right season can also make a difference to the cost of the trip. Some companies have just two seasons, some three, some four, so check when making a booking; travelling in the low season is often quite a bit cheaper.

Camping on board

If you are travelling with a caravan it is possible to 'camp on board' on some services. This means that for the price of a deck ticket per person you can sleep in your own caravan and use the ship's power/shower/WC and other facilities for free, though cooking is not permitted. Camping on board must always be booked in advance as there is limited availability and it applies only in the Adriatic Sea for routes between Italy and Greece operated by Blue Star, and between April and October on routes offered by Superfast, Minoan and ANEK on services from Ancona (Italy).

The places to stay and eat listed in this guide are for those on a budget. Prices in Western European countries are generally much higher than in North Africa or the Middle East. For example, average *pension* prices in Spain, France and Italy are around €30 (US$37) a night, with the price halving the further east or south you go. Camping therefore represents a good economic alternative, with many excellent quality campsites available.

Food costs in the Mediterranean can be kept low by avoiding too many restaurants and taking advantage of the widespread institution of corner-store sandwich-making. Supermarkets often also go in for this, with the guy behind the meat and cheese counter only too happy to make you a sandwich for a couple of euros. Also, many of the pensions listed here have shared cooking facilities, which can make a big difference budget wise; always ask about this when you arrive. Eating and drinking on board is often costly so come prepared with your own food and drink.

Travelling modestly, you should be able to get around for €40-50 (US$49-61) a day, including transport costs. This would rise to €60-80 (US$73-98) in Spain, France and Italy, but could drop to €30-40 (US$37-49) in places such as Turkey and Egypt.

When to go

Most ferry companies operate a winter and summer schedule, with services expanding greatly during the season. This is roughly May–September, though there may be some regional variations. During these summer months, the Mediterranean is at its most populated, with July–August being peak times as most of Europe heads to the coast.

Temperatures are also at a peak then, too. Expect it to be hot everywhere, though also watch out for occasional severe thunderstorms, which can bring a relief to the humidity once they've finished but which can also deluge the streets. Sea temperatures are probably at their most tepid in August, when the shallower, tideless coasts can feel more bath-like.

Spring and autumn may therefore be the best times to visit, as the sun isn't quite as strong. In April, the landscape is greener, while in October the sea is still warm enough for swimming, and the crowds thinner.

Check out the temperature chart for each country in Part 3.

Information and bookings

ROUTE AND TIMETABLE INFORMATION

The appendix (see pp438-61) and ferry route maps (see relevant sections) give information about the main routes that operated at the time of writing. Since services are in a constant state of flux, we've included ferry companies' websites (see pp433-7) and general ferry information websites (see p433) but be warned, these may not have been updated for a while and sometimes give contradictory information. However, companies whose websites are updated regularly are generally pretty reliable. When it comes to companies in Greece, it is more in the lap of the gods, though in compensation, there are a lot of boats running, so if one company's service is suspended another company may fill the slot.

If you don't have access to a computer when travelling, the best way to get route and timetable information is to go to the port authority office, local tourist information office, ferry company office or a travel agency. Where relevant, these are listed in this guide.

> ### Crewing
> Crewing means working your passage on one of the hundreds of boats that sail the sea's waters, either for pleasure or commerce, and thus it is possibly the most ideal way of travelling the Med if you have time but a small budget. Yachts are the transport of preference, naturally enough, though perfectly acceptable passage can be had on a fishing smack or cargo ship.
>
> The deal is, they take you wherever they're going and in return you work. You can be employed as a cook, cleaner, deckhand, companion or general odd jobber. Good places to start looking are marinas – particularly yacht clubs and other gathering places for boat owners as they often have message boards where you can advertise your services. Experience isn't always necessary, though obviously it's a plus. Mostly, it's down to a face-to-face interview with the boat captain or owner, and it's up to you to impress them. They don't want extra baggage and will require some hard work.
>
> You may also be asked to pay something towards your keep on longer journeys. Be extra careful with this, and make sure the numbers add up – is it really going to work out cheaper? Also, make sure you are both clear and in agreement about what your duties are before you set off.
>
> Most yachts follow fairly obvious routes between tourist destinations, with the Mediterranean's temperate climate meaning there are boats going at most times of the year – though obviously summer gives you the best chance of finding a passage. It also pays to keep an eye on wind and weather, as captains will be looking at this in determining when and where to go.

PLANNING YOUR TRIP

MAKING A BOOKING

Booking a ferry ticket can be done at most ports at pretty short notice, though it's advisable to turn up at least an hour before and two hours or more if you have a car. In the height of summer, hydrofoil services in Greece often run out of seats, so it pays to get your tickets as early as possible. Also, waiting until the last minute to make a booking is often not worthwhile in terms of saving money as ferry companies rarely offer last-minute reductions. Remember that if your journey is an international service, you may have to submit your passport to the police and customs the night before your journey.

On most ferries there is a variety of ticket options ranging from deck class to a Pullman seat (an aircraft-style seat often with audio-visual entertainment), dorms, inside cabins for two to four people with or without WC/shower and the ultimate, an outside cabin, again for two to four people with or without WC/shower. Hydrofoil and catamaran services generally offer Pullman-style seats only. If you want a cabin but are told there are none available, one trick is to book a Pullman seat or deck-class ticket then, once on board, ask for an upgrade. Cabins that have been booked by people who have failed to turn up are usually handed out just after the ship leaves dock.

Most ferries and many hydrofoils mentioned in this book carry bicycles, motorbikes, cars and caravans, so taking your own transport is feasible. See p19 for further information. If you plan to take a vehicle or want a cabin, making an advance booking is particularly recommended.

Apart from booking at the port or online (see below), it is possible to book through agencies; some are mentioned in the ferry companies list on pp433-7 but most travel agents in your home country will be able to advise.

Wherever you book expect to be asked your name, surname, sex, age and if you are not a citizen/resident of the EU, your nationality, passport number and expiry date, and place of birth. This information is required under the International Directive, SOLAS (Safety of Life at Sea). If you are travelling with a vehicle you will have to state its type and give its registration number.

Booking online

If time is limited and you know where you want to go, it is probably worth booking as many of your trips in advance as possible. Many companies now accept online bookings; this also often means you can take advantage of reductions, such as mid-week or mid-day discounts (10%), or special offers such as supersaver or 'jackpot' fares. Minoan offers a five-ticket bonus; one free ticket is given for every five journeys booked in a six-month period. Book only through websites where you can see the company's details such as address and phone number, and through sites that offer a secure booking.

Once your booking is confirmed the company will probably either send an 'email ticket' or 'fax ticket'; these are valid documents and will be exchanged for a proper ticket at the port. Make sure you always read the terms and conditions of any booking carefully because discounted or special offer tickets can rarely be changed or reimbursed.

> ### EasyCruise
> Due to be launched in spring 2005, easyCruise is, according to their website (⌨ www.easyCruise.com), a whole new concept in the world of cruising. The idea behind easyCruise is to 'eliminate the frills and unbundle the package'. By this they mean that they hope to create a whole new cruising market by offering rooms on a ship on a night-by-night basis, so that customers can cruise for as many or as few days as they wish.
>
> Furthermore, everything is charged separately, so travellers can purchase as much or as little as they want. For example, meals and drinks are paid for separately, as are toiletries and even bedding – so if you don't need something, then, simply put, you don't buy it. Even the cleaning of the rooms is charged separately: do it yourself, or pay £20 to have somebody else do it for you. The accommodation itself is made up of prefabricated fibreglass units, each with a shower unit, a lavatory and Japanese tatami-style mattresses. And the cost? From £29 per cabin a night, depending on how early you book and the season. It will be interesting to see how this new concept turns out.

Visas, documents and money

VISAS

For EU, US, Canadian, Australian and New Zealand citizens, visas are not a major issue for most of the countries covered here. Either they're visa free or you can pick one up on arrival though there's generally a charge. Turkey, which used to charge a swingeing US$100 for US citizens, has recently reduced this visa fee to US$20. The most problematic place is Lebanon, which needs sorting out in advance.

For citizens of other countries it is worth checking visa requirements at the relevant country's embassy in your country or on the internet. Further details are given in the Visa section for each country in Part 3 of this guide.

DOCUMENTS

All the countries included in this guide require you to have official identification on you at all times. For EU citizens with ID cards, these are enough in EU countries and Turkey but if you're not an EU citizen you should carry your passport at all times. Have a photocopy of the ID pages available; this will cut out a lot of hassle if you lose your passport and have to get your consulate to issue a new one.

If you are taking a vehicle ensure you have the relevant insurance documents and a Green Card, your driver's licence and/or an International Driving Permit, and proof of ownership. Before you leave, check the regulations for the countries you are visiting with a motoring organization. Also take your travel insurance details and emergency contact numbers.

MONEY

Since the introduction of the euro, travelling in the Med has become a lot simpler, with no expensive and time-consuming currency-changing necessary between Spain, France, Italy and Greece. The euro looks almost certain to replace the US dollar as the international currency for the region.

ATMs are widely available and if your ATM card belongs to one of the international networks such as Visa, Cirrus or Maestro, you should have no difficulty accessing cash in the local currency deducted from your home bank account at that day's official rate. Many banks charge a service fee for this, which is worth finding out about before you leave home. The advantage of the ATM is that you don't need to carry your entire holiday money supply with you, though you have to be extra careful guarding your plastic.

Credit cards such as Visa, MasterCard and Amex are widely accepted, though of the three, Visa is the most recognized and Amex the least. However, replacing a lost Amex is much easier, as local American Express offices should issue a new one within 24 hours.

Travellers' cheques give good security against loss provided you have kept a record of the cheque numbers and of the ones you have cashed; always keep this information separate from the cheques themselves. However, travellers' cheques are less popular since the boom in ATMs. Some banks charge a fee for cashing the cheques, though it can depend on what currency they are in. Ask about this first, as it may vary from bank to bank. Amex, Visa and Thomas Cook are the most widely accepted travellers' cheques.

Money can also be transferred from an account back home to a Western Union agent; there are agencies in most large towns and cities. However, the charge for this services (about US$40) makes it an expensive way to get money.

What to take

The Med can get pretty hot in summer, so light clothes are clearly a must, along with swimming gear and a good hat – sunstroke can be a really unpleasant experience. Sun block and sun cream are also essential during May to October, though they're also pretty widely available. It can also get quite windy at times, not to mention rainy, so it's also advisable to pack a lightweight anorak-type jacket.

If you're planning on a lot of deck-class travel, a foam mat is vital as well as a sleeping bag. A torch is also essential for camping trips. However, by and large the Med is pretty well equipped and it should be easy to pick up anything you've forgotten – and often for a cheaper price than back home.

Since many of the places included in this guide are easily discovered on foot it is recommended that you take a comfortable pair of walking shoes, or good walking boots if you plan to climb any mountains or volcanoes such as Mt Etna.

Health, insurance and safety

While there are no major life-threatening diseases in the Mediterranean region, it's always advisable to check with your doctor before leaving to see if there are any warnings on particular countries. It's also vital to get a good travel insurance policy that will cover you while you're out there. Check that it covers watersports and sea-based activities as well, particularly if you expect to take part in any of these.

The most likely medical problems you'll encounter are variations on the sickness theme. Dietary changes can induce both constipation and diarrhoea, with the latter also a problem from eating food that hasn't been cleanly prepared. Be wary of eating fruit and vegetables that you can't peel and also check the caps on bottled water, particularly in North Africa and the Middle East, to make sure it hasn't been opened before and filled up from a tap. It's worth packing some anti-diarrhoea pills, and if you do get struck by this, remember to keep drinking plenty of water, as dehydration can develop into a far more serious problem. Also, there is a reason why the locals may seem to put a lot more salt on their food than you're used to. If travelling in the summer, do the same, as you lose a lot of salt from sweating and this can make you tired and lethargic.

Onboard, it's a good idea to check out the safety procedures, which are usually posted up alongside maps of the boat in the corridors, or on the backs of cabin doors. Make sure you know where your cabin or seat is in relation to the muster station – the place where you should go in an emergency. Larger boats will also give a safety lecture on arrival – go along, as you never know when it might come in useful. A couple of other tips are: never chuck a lit cigarette over the side – it could blow back somewhere else and set something alight; take care with wet staircases – they can be extremely slippery – and always hold on to the rail.

Avoiding seasickness
With much of your travelling on the water, seasickness may be a concern. However, it is unlikely to be a problem for even the most confirmed land-lubber on most modern ferries. Seasickness is a variety of motion sickness, so with most ferries now possessing elaborate stabilizers, the sensation of motion may be hard to perceive at all, particularly on the Med's normally calm surface.

However, on smaller boats or in rough seas the roll of the ship can take its toll. There are numerous cures for this, with a number of pills and even a Sea Band – a bracelet that covers pressure points on the wrist – available from pharmacists. One other tip is to get up on deck, take a lot of deep breaths and try and focus your eyes on the far horizon. It may also help to try and stand right in the centre of the boat, where the rocking will be less apparent. If you lie down, also lie along the centre line of the boat, rather than side to side, to reduce the sensation of motion.

Geography

At around 2200 miles long at its longest and 488 miles wide at its widest, the Mediterranean can often seem more like a huge lake than a sea. There are minimal tides, while the two small entrances — the Straits of Gibraltar in the west and the Bosphorus/Dardanelles in the east — are so narrow there is very little mixing between the Med and its Black Sea or Atlantic neighbours.

Given this, it takes around 150 years for the water to make a complete circuit, something to consider if you've just flicked a cigarette butt into it. The surface currents largely flow in an anti-clockwise direction from Gibraltar eastwards. However, because the Med is saltier than either the Atlantic or the Black Sea, there is also a counter current going the opposite way along the bottom.

If a giant was to suddenly stick his thumbs in either end of the Med and block them off, the high temperature of the air overhead would soon lead to the evaporation of most of the water. What would be left would be two salt pans, separated by the land bridge (currently submerged) between Italy and Tunisia.

Meanwhile, at the Straits of Gibraltar, this giant might also be able to wade about on the subterranean ocean floor beneath the shallow sea. But he wouldn't be able to go out too far, as quite rapidly the shelf on which Europe and Africa sit plummets away, leaving the Med, in effect, higher than the Atlantic. The Black Sea at the other end is higher still, creating a strong surface current from there through the Bosphorus and into the Marmara and Aegean beyond.

There's not much depth to the Med either, except in a few places. West of Crete is one of the world's deepest underwater faults, at 14,400 feet, while just off southern Sardinia a pot hole of 10,200 feet has been recorded.

Most of the time too, the sea seems pretty passive — unlike its stormier neighbours. Yet it's also notorious for sudden storms, 'black squalls' being heralded by brooding distant clouds, while 'white squalls' can come out of nowhere in the Aegean, suddenly blowing down from island mountain tops. Elsewhere, the Barbary coast — from Gibraltar along to Tunis — is subject to terrific gales at times, a factor accounting for many a wreck, as well as the destruction of an entire Spanish invasion fleet off Algiers in 1541. The Strait of Messina, between Sicily and Italy, can also still give small craft trouble, as its narrows throw up whirlpools thanks to a tidal difference between the two ends.

Yet despite all this, there's little call for alarm crossing this sea today. It's probably the most heavily charted, explored and navigated on Earth. Your roughest encounter is more likely to be with the cafeteria whisky than with the elements, or perhaps with some of the cheesier onboard entertainment, which can certainly be a greater source of queasiness...

Flora and fauna

While a glimpse into the harbours of Piraeus or Barcelona may quickly convince you that most living creatures would have little chance of survival in the Med, in fact the sea is home to an abundance of marine life.

Just as the sea was created over five million years ago by a sudden surge of Atlantic water bursting through at Gibraltar, so many of the species found in the Med also owe their pedigree to the cold Atlantic waters. Yet the Mediterranean has also evolved a distinct ecosystem of its own and a clutch of species are unique to its waters. In more recent times a number of species from the Red Sea and Indian Ocean have established themselves here. Swimming up the Suez Canal, these immigrants are known to biologists as 'Lessepsian' migrants, after the canal's great architect (see p425).

The Med's geology is also a factor in its animal and plant life, with the Western basin – from Gibraltar to Malta – much richer in terms of variety than the Eastern basin, from Malta to the Levant. Much of this has to do with the extra saltiness of the Eastern half, along with its warmer waters, which are not congenial to many Atlantic species.

However, most famous amongst the Med's indigenous and unique species is the Eastern basin's Mediterranean monk seal, unfortunately now threatened with extinction. Also endangered are the green and loggerhead turtles, which now enjoy the protection of many conservation projects. The striped dolphin is also a feature of the sea that is not as common as it once was; nonetheless, in the Aegean and Eastern Med, they can still be occasionally seen following a ferry or swimming along the coast in pods of three or four.

As for fish, shallower areas of the Med, such as those immediately off many of its beaches, provide a home to quite an array. Watch out for weaver fish, skates and rays, along with sand urchins and starfish. In rockier areas there are peacock and rainbow wrasses, two-banded bream, blennies and gobies and tiny parrot fish, along with bearded red mullets. The cavernous and crenellated coasts of the Aegean are also good places to find anemones, gorgonia and lace coral.

Further out, go down below 10m and across much of the sea you'll find something called the Posidonia Meadows – acres of seafloor covered with this flowering plant. These subterranean fields provide a vital habitat to hundreds of sea creatures, including breams, groupers, sea perches and the bullnose ray.

Go out a little further, and at 15-20 metres everything changes again. Posidonia fades out and the fields turn to green algae – *Caulerpa prolifera* – amongst which some of the sea's most amazing shell life can be found.

Different areas also have their specialities. Malta is good for seahorse spotting, while Gibraltar, Southern Spain and Morocco have fine collections of larger Atlantic fish, along with some impressive octopus. Barracuda and large tuna are often to be found around Cyprus and Turkey.

THE MEDITERRANEAN

As for the more spectacular – and dangerous – denizens of the deep, these are pretty few and far between. You may get lucky and spot a whale, however, with these occasionally seen as far east as the Aegean. There are also sharks, though these are now very rare. Incidents of them attacking humans here are even rarer.

More likely to give you some worries are the jellyfish. These have been phenomenally successful in many parts of the sea, with thousands of these whitish, semi-transparent blobs washing up on shore in late summer. At most though, you're likely to get only a light sting from even the most ferocious of them. Stingrays and weaver fish can be a lot more dangerous but are usually scared away from beach areas by all the tourists. If you are unfortunate enough to step on one, bathe your foot in hot water and seek medical help immediately.

Chronology

The following potted history is not meant to be comprehensive but is designed to provide a basic framework. We hope that it will aid a better understanding of the sea and the relationships between the countries that border it.

c12,000BC First human settlement in the region on the Eastern Mediterranean coast in what is now Palestine, Israel and Lebanon.

c3800BC Temples are constructed on Malta, the Megalithic era's oldest.

Environmental damage
After a quick scan of recent environmental headlines from the Mediterranean, you might be forgiven for feeling a little reluctant to plunge head first into its waters. For starters, just think how many people live around its shores and how many giant cities and harbours there are. Furthermore, with its narrow entrances and exits, changing the Mediterranean bath water takes around 150 years. Meanwhile, the city of İzmir alone pumps some half a million cubic metres of sewage straight out into the Aegean, while several factories in Israel have their discharge pipes directly on public beaches.

These are just drops in the eco-catastrophe ocean, too. In southern Italy, for example, the 'waste mafia' have a powerful grip on many ports, illegally disposing of toxic wastes brought in from other countries. In France's Gulf of Lions, petrochemical plants have turned many of the *étangs*, coastal lagoons, into containers for chemical soups, while in Lebanon, barrels of toxic waste too dangerous to dump in Western countries have been washing up on the beach. Oil tankers also often leave a trail of sticky black tar on many of the Med's once pristine beaches. In short, the Mediterranean has been the subject of appalling pollution for decades.

It's not a new issue either. Back in 1975, the countries of the Mediterranean met in Barcelona to agree an action plan for a general clean-up. According to Greenpeace none of the signatories has completed all the obligations under the Barcelona Convention, while many have still to sign up to all its protocols. *(Cont'd opposite)*

c3500BC Semitic tribes from Arabia arrive on the shores of the Eastern Mediterranean. Foremost amongst them are the Phoenicians who, while not interested in conquering the Med by force, nevertheless wield enormous influence over the area thanks to their abilities as seafarers and talent for trade.

c3100BC The warring kingdoms of Upper and Lower Egypt are united by the Upper Egyptian ruler Menes, heralding the start of the pharaonic age and the prosperous Old Kingdom era (2686–2181BC). The first great Mediterranean empire, they conquer many of the Semitic tribes in Syria and Palestine (see above) as well as constructing the Pyramids at Giza.

c3000BC The mysterious Minoans, possibly originally from Anatolia (modern-day Turkey) inhabit Crete and establish a culture every bit as sophisticated and intriguing as the Egyptians. At around the same time the Cycladic (based on the islands of the Cyclades) and Mycenaean (mainland Greece, possibly originally Minoan colonists) cultures flourish. The latter are most probably the historic basis for the Greek heroic myths.

c1570BC The New Kingdom era (1570–1070BC) begins in Egypt which manages to eclipse in grandeur, influence and power that of the Old Kingdom. The boundaries of the Egyptian Empire now stretch to the Euphrates, and yet more astonishing monuments are built, this time mainly in Upper Egypt near Luxor.

c1500BC Mycenaeans invade and conquer Minoan Crete.

c1400BC Supposed date of the Trojan War.

THE MEDITERRANEAN

❑ **Environmental damage**
(Cont'd from p24) Tourism is also causing major environmental damage. Many rivers and streams have been diverted around the sea to provide fresh water to new resorts, a process which has led to the North African desert crossing the Straits of Gibraltar to southern Spain.

Meanwhile, the impact of pollution on a sea noted for its wide variety of plants and animals continues. The island of Lesbos alone is home to around 279 species of birds, while even small whales sometimes swim the Mediterranean's waters. The case of the monk seal is probably one of the worst: there were once thousands of them in the Aegean but now only around 200 remain. Sea turtles and dolphins are also in very real danger of vanishing from the Med.

Green sea turtles, known locally as the *careta careta*, use beaches for laying eggs. Mass tourism has meant many of these breeding grounds have turned into resorts, scaring off the turtles. Placed on the list of endangered and threatened species back in 1978, recent estimates put their global population at only around half a million. Also, almost everywhere stocks of fish are reaching new lows due to overfishing.

Campaigners such as Greenpeace (🖳 www.greenpeace.org) are still trying to draw attention to the Med's environmental plight, but they face a huge task. At the same time, it is perhaps a testimony to the Mediterranean's strength that it is still possible to find great stretches of it that are relatively pollution free. Yet without action soon, it's not likely to stay that way for too much longer.

c1100BC The Dorian Greeks, possibly from the north, invade the mainland and sweep aside the Mycenaeans.

c900BC The Etruscans inhabit the southern part of Italy, their skill at jewellery-making rarely surpassed in the subsequent 3000 years.

c800BC The emergence of Greek city states, of which Corinth, Sparta and Athens are the most powerful. *Graecia Magnia* (Greater Greece) is formed, which includes southern Italy.

THE MEDITERRANEAN

Mediterranean shipping – from reed boats to hydrofoils

As the ferry you're on churns across the water, more often than not as apparently unaffected by wind, tide and current as a No 11 bus, it may be sobering to pause for a moment and reflect that the piece of metalwork on which you're now sailing represents the culmination of millennia of Mediterranean seafaring.

Casting an eye back to the first boats to ply these waters, you'll find that around 2500BC, the Egyptians were braving the waves with ships made from papyrus reeds tied together and rigged with a steering oar and a single sail. Later, reeds were replaced with wooden planks but navigation away from land remained a business of limited appeal, the Egyptians sticking largely to the Nile or short journeys along the coast.

Propulsion back then was often by rowing, with ancient Egyptian reliefs showing as many as 30 men at the oars in a typical Egyptian Red Sea vessel. If a sail was used, it was usually only if there was a stern wind — pushing the boat from behind — as a method of changing sails around had yet to be discovered. This was fine for any Egyptian who wanted to head south down the Red Sea, as the winds were almost always headed in that direction, but was clearly useless for trying to sail north off the Egyptian coast into the Med. The rudder was not invented until the 14th century AD. Instead, steering was by large paddles strapped to the sides of the stern.

With oars the key to a boat's speed, naturally enough the more oars the better. By 700BC, the Phoenicians had built a vessel with two banks of oars, giving it greater velocity and — due to the extra weight — greater momentum. This bireme was also vital for naval warfare, as the only way ships could fight was firstly to ram each other, followed by boarding. However, such a design wasn't so suitable for trading, with the oarsmen taking up so much space that there was no room for goods. This led to the development of two distinct types of vessels by the trade-loving Phoenicians — the 'round ship' or merchantman and the 'long ship' or war galley.

Both varieties were well in advance of the boats Homer's Achaean Greeks used to attack Troy. These 'hollow ships' had a single bank of oars and were painted with tar, an early protection against the teredo worm, a sea-dwelling wood-chewer that could decimate an unprotected vessel. The Greeks did not supersede the Phoenicians in boat-building and design until much later, the start of the 5th century BC in fact, when the Corinthians came up with the trireme — a galley with three banks of oars.

This set a familiar pattern of escalation, with Carthaginians and then Romans developing the quinquireme — a boat of no less than five banks of oars — by the time of the Punic Wars. Thus the speed, power and size of Mediterranean navies escalated still further. The increasing number of oars also meant the end of the era in which those rowing were all volunteers; slavery became the lot of most oarsmen now.

(Continued opposite)

490BC The Persians led by Darius launch an attack on Athens but are repelled at Marathon before reaching the city.

480–479BC Second invasion by the Persians, this time led by Xerxes. Athens is taken but the invasion is stopped at Salamis where the Persians are defeated in a naval battle. The battle has significant repercussions for the entire Med. Not only are the Persians now finished as a force in the region but their allies, the Carthaginians, who supplied the Persians with both ships and support, lose their markets and influence as a result of the defeat. They are now forced to look for

---

❏ **Mediterranean shipping – from reed boats to hydrofoils**

(Continued from p26) The Roman era also saw the development of massive merchant ships, with boats of 1000 tons being common by the 2nd century AD. These would also carry a top sail, along with the main, traditional square sail on a central mast, now supplemented by additional masts and sails fore and aft. Larger ships would also often tow a small skiff behind to act as a tug boat when manoeuvring into and out of harbour.

Advances in navigation, however, were much more gradual, with position and orientation worked out as it always had been — using the sun, stars and winds. That was until the arrival of the Arabs, who, in the 13th century, introduced the *beit el-ibrah*, the 'house of the needle', to the Mediterranean. This was a primitive compass, based on a magnetized needle that pointed north. The Arabs also introduced the lateen sail — a manoeuvrable rig that finally got round the problem of how to sail towards the wind. With a lateen sail, a boat could 'tack' — moving forward via a series of zig-zags. When this was added to a banked, oared ship, the Mediterranean galley, which was to dominate the sea till the end of the 16th century, was more or less complete.

That domination came to an end abruptly in 1587. In 36 hours, the English admiral, Sir Francis Drake, sent to the bottom a large part of the Spanish fleet moored in Cadiz harbour without any loss to his own, heavily-armed sailing ships. Convention had it that such vessels would be no match for war galleys, of which there were dozens in Cadiz. The key was in the ability of the sailing ship to mount banks of cannons where the galley mounted banks of oars, shooting up the galleys before they could get close enough to ram. The galley's days were now numbered and the sailing ship began its period of dominance, lasting up until the arrival of steam in the 19th century.

The arrival of the industrial age really began in 1845, when the British ship *Rattler* was fitted with a screw propeller powered by steam — a descendant of which is most likely powering the ferries on which you'll be travelling today. Wood was also replaced by iron, the size of the ship grew enormously and, in military terms, the smooth-bore cannon was replaced by the rifled gun, enabling warships to shoot accurately at each other from long range. Modern vessels are usually diesel driven, with huge propellers revolving behind the ship and pushing it through the water. Ferries built more recently also have computer adjusted stabilizing fins on each side to balance the boat, and thrusters — jets mounted at the front to enable the boat to go into reverse and undertake delicate manoeuvres, removing the need for tug boats. The technology for navigation, now involving satellites and advanced radar systems, is also awesome in comparison to Homer's Odysseus, who peered into the heavens for the twinkle of the Pole Star, or felt for the wind on his cheek. Some of the adventure has undoubtedly been lost with these advances, with ferries at the upper end beginning to resemble shopping malls at sea. Yet it is still possible sometimes to get a little of that early spirit; at night perhaps, up on the empty decks by the bows with the wind blowing in off the darkness beyond.

THE MEDITERRANEAN

new markets further away from Carthage and thus for the first time find it necessary to establish new colonies, where previously, like their Phoenician ancestors, they were happy merely to trade. Furthermore, with the Persians vanquished, a new confidence imbues the Greek city states leading to the Great Fifty Years, a glorious flowering of Greek arts, philosophy and science.

However, with no great foreign rival threatening the Greek states, they now begin to squabble amongst themselves:

431BC   The Peloponnese Wars between Athens and Sparta, two ex-allies, begins, with the latter (along with the Corinthians) attempting to prevent Athens from becoming the foremost city state.

404BC   Athens surrenders to Sparta.

338BC   The Greek states are finally united under Philip II of Macedonia, whose dream it is to invade the lands of their erstwhile enemies, Persia. The conquest of Greece by Philip marks the end of the Classical Age and the beginning of what is known as the Hellenistic era. Philip dies on the eve of embarking on his quest. His 20-year-old son, Alexander the Great of Macedonia, takes over and in the space of ten years (333–323BC), builds an empire stretching to the Indian subcontinent, Baghdad and Egypt, where he founds the port and city of Alexandria.

323BC   On Alexander's death at the age of 32, his empire is divided amongst his generals, with Seleucus and Ptolemy sharing the territories of the Eastern Med. In Egypt, the Ptolemites are so influenced by the pharaonic culture (as Alexander was before them) that a curious Graeco-Egyptian state is established, with the Greek rulers emulating the pharaohs of a previous age.

c300BC   Rome overwhelms the Etruscans and now dominates the Italian states.

264BC   First Punic War fought between Rome and Carthage, along with their allies, the Greeks. Carthage loses Sicily, Corsica and Sardinia thanks to Roman naval supremacy, and Rome now controls the central Mediterranean. Hamilcar, leader of the Carthaginians, realizes that, to re-establish themselves, they need to establish colonies and trading posts in the Western Med and Spain, still largely beyond Rome's influence: Cartagena, on Spain's southern shore, is founded.

218BC   Hamilcar's son, Hannibal, deliberately provokes Rome into a second Punic War. Because of Rome's perceived naval superiority, Hannibal attempts to attack Rome overland by marching over the Pyrenees with his elephants. The march enjoys its successes but while he's away Spain is invaded. Hannibal is forced to return home (**201**BC) and the Second Punic War is lost.

149BC   Rome besieges Carthage after the latter starts a war with their Libyan neighbours – in contradiction of a treaty signed between Rome and Carthage in which the latter agreed to ask permission from Rome before launching fresh invasions.

146BC   Once again Carthage is defeated – and is now completely destroyed. In the same year, Corinth is also defeated and Greece now comes under Roman rule.

66–63BC Pompey invades and conquers the Near East for Rome.

51BC Cleopatra ascends the throne of Egypt following the death of her father, Ptolemy XIII, with dreams of rebuilding the Graeco-Egyptian Ptolemaic Empire that thrived 200 years previously. She becomes co-ruler along with her brother who, in typical pharaonic style, is also her husband.

48BC Caesar defeats Pompey at the Battle of Pharsalus. General Pompey arrives in Alexandria and is almost immediately killed.

47BC Caesar arrives in Egypt and is supported by Cleopatra against her brother. The two become lovers and Cleopatra bears him a son.

44BC Caesar is murdered in Rome by conspirators including Brutus, whom he'd brought up as his son; Cleopatra flees back to Egypt. A new power struggle begins in Rome between Octavian and Mark Antony. The latter is given control of the Eastern Med and meets Cleopatra (**c41BC**). The two become lovers.

32BC Mark Antony is deposed by the senate in Rome.

31BC Battle of Actium. Cleopatra flees the battle and Mark Antony, neglecting his duty, follows. The two return to Egypt.

30BC Octavian invades Egypt. Mark Antony, under the misapprehension that Cleopatra had killed herself as part of a pact made between them, commits suicide as well. Cleopatra attempts to seduce Octavian but is rejected and finally kills herself too by holding an asp to her breast. Rome annexes Egypt. Octavian (later Augustus Caesar, **27BC**) is now the overall controller of Rome's territories, heralding the end of the Roman Republic and the start of the Roman Empire.

AD117 The Roman Empire reaches its greatest extent under Trajan.

3rd century AD Goths and other invaders from the north begin to arrive in the Med, heralding a troubled, turbulent period for the region.

263 Athens, Corinth and Sparta fall to the Goths. The Artemis Temple at Athens is burnt to the ground.

c284–306 The reign of Diocletian strengthens and unites the Roman Empire after 50 years of military anarchy. Realizing his empire is too big and unwieldy, Diocletian divides it in two, moving his new (eastern) capital to Nicomedia (now Izmit in Turkey) while Maximilian, his second in command, rules from Rome.

324 Emperor Constantine establishes a new eastern capital, the city that is later named after him: Constantinople. Briefly the two halves of the empire are reunited under him.

364 Once again the Roman Empire has two emperors, Valentinian in the east, Valens in the west.

425 Vandals invade and conquer Spain.

439 The Vandals under Gaiseni conquer Carthage; they now effectively control the Western and Central Med.

445 The Vandals attack and sack Rome.

476 Romulus Augustus is deposed by the Barbarians. It's the end for the Western Roman Empire.

527 Justinian the Law-giver ascends the Byzantine throne to become emperor. Becomes arguably Byzantium's greatest ruler.

533 The Vandals in Carthage and Visigoths in Italy are overthrown by Belisarus, Justinian's greatest general.

540 For a while the Central and Eastern Med was, once more, back under Byzantine control. But then the Lombards, the last of the waves of attackers from the north, attack and take Italy.

627 Byzantium finally defeats Persia.

632 The founder of Islam, the Prophet Mohammed, dies in Arabia. His followers, however, known as the Muslims ('Surrendered Men', as they have surrendered themselves to God), continue the spread of his religion and in **636** conquer Syria before arriving in **639** at the border of Egypt.

642 Muslims conquer Alexandria.

644 The followers of the new religion of Islam split into Sunni and Shi'ite.

647 The Arabs take Cyprus.

692 Ummayad caliphs reunite Muslims temporarily to continue the expansion of their territory.

711 The Moors, an Islamic force from North Africa, invade and occupy Spain, overrunning the land in a few years.

716 The Islamic Arab hordes arrive at İstanbul but fail to capture the city.

722 The first defeat of the Moors in Spain, at Covadonga, Asturias, heralds eight centuries of the *reconquista*.

732 The Muslims are defeated on the battlefield of Poitiers, having crossed over the Pyrenees from Spain. It's the end of their western European conquests.

823 The Muslims begin a period of conquest of the main Mediterranean islands, including Crete (**823**), Sicily (**878**) and Malta (**870**).

1054 The First Papal Schism, with the Catholic Church headed by the Pope in Rome and the Greek Orthodox Church under the patriarchs in Byzantium, Alexandria and Jerusalem.

1057 The Normans, another group of invaders from the north, arrive on Sicily and proceed to conquer Muslim-held lands, backed by the blessing of the Pope.

Most of southern Italy falls under their sway in **1071** before they finally take the strategically vital island in **1090**. With them now providing a protective shield for trade, ports such as Genoa, Venice, and Pisa thrive.

1076 The Muslim Arabs take Jerusalem.

1081 The Seljuks, a Turkish tribe, defeat the Byzantines at Manzikert – a devastating defeat for the Eastern Roman Empire that resulted in the loss of control of Asia Minor.

1096 The loss of Jerusalem and Asia Minor leads directly to the First Crusade. Inspired by the Byzantines, who requested help in recapturing previously Christian-held lands from the invading Arab 'infidel', and with the backing of the Pope in Rome, the First Crusade does much to restore Asia Minor to Byzantium and is easily the most successful of the Crusades. Antioch (modern Antakya) is captured in **1098**, and the following year the big prize, Jerusalem, is taken. Their subsequent mistreatment of the city's inhabitants and the religious persecution that follows is in stark contrast to that of the Muslim conquerors of four centuries previously, who were renowned for their tolerance of other faiths.

1186 The Sultan of Egypt, the charismatic Saladin, unites the Muslim forces against the Crusaders and in **1187** recaptures Jerusalem.

1191 The Third Crusade (in which Richard the Lionheart is one of the main players) recaptures Acre and the rest of the Holy Land's coast, and takes Cyprus, too, but they are unable to regain Jerusalem.

1204 A Fourth Crusade is organized with the intention of invading Egypt. The port of Venice supplies their shipping and food but the Crusaders are unable to pay for all their provisions and are held captive in the city. The ruler of the Venetian Republic, the doge, asks the Crusaders to sack Zara, a rival port, in order to gain enough money to pay for their supplies. However, though the sacking is successful, the Crusaders still find that they have insufficient funds to pay their Venetian hosts.

Simultaneously, the son of the deposed ruler of the Byzantine Empire arrives in Venice and asks for help in regaining the throne for himself. As a result, incredibly, the knights of the Fourth Crusade sail for Constantinople, the largest Christian capital in the world at that time, and sack it! The destruction of Constantinople is monstrous, the city never recovers and the Byzantine Empire is fatally weakened. Venice, on the other hand, which is finally paid by the Crusaders with Mediterranean ports, become the foremost Italian city state. It is, however, no longer trusted by the Pope in Rome, who instead throws his support behind Genoa, Venice's rival. A Crusader knight is also, for 57 years, placed on the throne of Byzantium.

There is one other important result of this action by the Crusaders: Byzantium is no longer there to act as a buffer between Europe and the various invaders from the east.

1245 Tatar Mongols invade Asia Minor and the eastern Med from the north.

1260 Baybars, the Mameluke sultan of Egypt, drives the Crusaders out of his homeland.

1261 Genoa helps the Greeks to take back the throne of Byzantium from the Crusaders and thus earns 'most-favoured-nation' status from Constantinople.

1291 The last Crusader stronghold, Acre, falls to the Arabs. The Knights Hospitaller, one of the Crusader organizations founded in Jerusalem, head first to Cyprus then, in **1309**, to Rhodes, where they become Christian corsairs.

1373 The Genoese seize Famagusta on Cyprus from Venice; the two city states are thus now officially at war. Unfortunately for Genoa, where Venice has a stable government, the Genoese are ruled by several feuding, powerful families.

1379 Genoa defeats Venice and blockades the city, but Venetian ships are summoned from the Eastern Med and, in turn, blockade the blockading Genoan ships. Genoa is decisively defeated. Two years later in 1381 the Peace of Turin is signed.

1453 Mehmet the Conqueror, leading the Othman (later Ottoman) Turks, the latest in a series of tribes to sweep across Anatolia from the plains of Central Asia, invades and conquers Constantinople. The capital of the new Ottoman Empire is established. Greece is conquered soon after.

1469 Isabel, heir to the Castilian throne, marries Ferdinand, the heir to the Aragonese crown, thus uniting the two most powerful states in Spain.

1488 While trade routes overland from the Orient and across the Med were being lost because of Turkish hegemony and the rise in piracy, the two great Catholic maritime powers, Portugal and Spain, were losing interest in the area, the former after the discovery by Bartholomew Diaz of the route round the Cape of Good Hope, the latter after the 1492 discovery of the New World by Christopher Columbus. These developments ensured that the Med is, for the first time, something of a backwater in world affairs. Venice is especially affected, and over the next century loses its overseas territories to the Ottomans.

1492 Isabel and Ferdinand capture Granada, the last possession of the Moors. They also begin the Spanish Inquisition and expel all the Jews and Muslims of Spain, with many of the former settling under Ottoman protection in İstanbul.

1493 Pope Alexander VI, on the hypothesis that all heathen land, both known and unknown, came under his jurisdiction, fixed the Meridian Line. The idea behind it was to avert trouble between the two great Catholic maritime powers, Spain and Portugal, by dividing up the world between them. Those lands to the west of the line went to Spain, while those to the east were granted to Portugal.

1494 Spain and Portugal sign the Treaty of Tordesillas, ratifying the legality of their rights of trade and colonization in the known and unknown world, India and the Far East. Importantly, it led to a reduction in the trading interest in the Mediterranean area, leading to a depression in the Mediterranean economy.

1497 Following Diaz's explorations in 1497, Vasco de Gama discovers a route to India via the Cape of Good Hope, further damaging the economy of the Med.

1500 The Portuguese under Cabral take possession of Brazil which, though west of Pope Alexander's Meridian Line, they are allowed to keep.

1508 The League of Cambrai – an alliance between France, Spain and the Holy Roman Emperor Maximillian – is formed, designed to break the power of Venice.

1509 The Battle of Agnadello, between the League of Cambrai and Venice, rages just outside Milan. Venice is defeated and their subject territories lost. The Cambrai League breaks up after this.

1522 The Ottomans take Rhodes, forcing the Knights of St John to leave. They arrive eight years later **(1530)** at Malta, which is given to them by Charles I of Spain (aka Charles V of the Holy Roman Empire).

1534 Barbarossa becomes head of the Ottoman Navy and conquers numerous Italian ports. He also defeats the combined forces of Christian nations at Preveza (1538), hence his sobriquet 'King of the Sea'.

1565 The Ottoman sultan Süleyman the Magnificent launches the unsuccessful Siege of Malta.

1570 The Ottomans take Cyprus from the Venetians.

1571 The Battle of Lepanto takes place in which elements of Genoa, Venice, the Knights of Malta and a squadron of the Papal states defeat the Ottomans under Barbarossa. The battle is commonly seen as the decisive moment in the struggle between the Ottomans and Europeans. Yet the purpose of the European efforts – to save Cyprus, Venice's last major overseas outpost – fails as the Ottomans capture it. The Ottomans also manage to regroup and rebuild their fleet. Nevertheless, this is the first significant blow to their expansionist empire.

1574 The Ottomans take Tunisia and continue to progress through North Africa to West Algeria.

1669 The Ottomans take Crete, the Venetians' last major foreign possession.

1700 The accession of the Bourbons to the Spanish throne starts the War of Spanish Succession as the Hapsburgs argue that they, too, had a reasonable claim to the crown. Much of the battle takes place in Italy, with the Bourbons taking Rome (1724) and much of southern Italy over the next few decades. They hold on to much of the territory until Italian independence in 1860.

1704 Gibraltar is taken from Spain by the British, who thus now control the strategically vital entrance to the Med.

1713 Following the War of Spanish Succession, control of Italy passes to the Austrians and the Hapsburg Empire.

1796 Napoleon frees Italy from Austria, sounding the death knell for the Venetian Republic.

1798 Napoleon heads to Egypt, where his fleet is destroyed by the British. He does, however, capture Malta.

1805 The Battle of Trafalgar sees Britain reassert naval dominance over Napoleon and his Spanish allies.

1807 France and Spain agree to divide Portugal, Britain's ally, amongst themselves. As a result, Napoleon's troops move into Spain, where they remain and, one year later, are an occupying force.

1809 Britain takes Kefalonia.

1812 Napoleon's forces in Spain are harrassed by the British and, with their focus now on Russia, the French withdraw from the country.

1814 The Maltese, aided by the British, rise up against Napoleon. Britain ends up with the island.

1815 Napoleon meets his Waterloo.

1821–32 The Greeks throw off the Ottoman yoke in their War of Independence.

1827 The Battle of Navarino, where Britain, France and Russia combine to defeat the Ottomans' naval fleet.

1830 France takes Algiers to try to stop the pirates of the Barbary coast and to establish a colony.

1832 Taking advantage of the Ottomans' weakening position, Mohammed Ali, who ruled Egypt for them, took control of the country, charged up the Near East, and was prevented from storming Constantinople only by the European powers, who forced him into sharing power with the sultan.

1853–56 Russia pressurizes the Ottomans to guarantee the safety of Orthodox subjects in Turkish territory. Widely seen as a mere pretext for imperial Russian ambitions to increase their influence over the Mediterranean, it leads to the Crimean War, pitching Russia against the Ottomans and their French and British allies.

1861 Following increasing support for Italy's unification movement, or *Risorgimento*, the Kingdom of Italy is declared with King Vittorio Emanuele as the first ruler.

1859–69 The Suez Canal is built by the French.

1871 France finally completes its conquest of Algeria.

1874 The British prime minister Benjamin Disraeli buys shares in the Suez

Canal off an almost bankrupt Egyptian government and now owns almost half of the canal. Thus it is Britain who, despite initial hostility to the project, benefits most from the canal.

1877 Cyprus becomes virtually a British possession after an agreement with the Ottomans. Britain now has a chain of territories through the Med from Gibraltar to Malta, Cyprus and Port Said at the mouth of the canal.

1881 France expands into Tunisia following cross-border raids into their territory in Algeria.

1882 Following riots, Britain lands troops in Egypt and goes on, reluctantly, to govern the country in order to protect the canal – the main transport link to their possessions in India.

1911 Italy invades and occupies Libya, previously an Ottoman possession.

1912 Morocco becomes a French protectorate except for those parts already in Spanish hands.

1914–18 World War I is fought largely away from the Mediterranean, the main action taking place in Northern Europe. Following Turkey's decision to ally themselves with Germany, British, French, Australian and New Zealand forces attack the Dardanelles with the aim of moving on İstanbul and opening up a supply line to the beleaguered Russians. British and French ships are bombarded by Turkish guns on the Gelibolu (Gallipolli) peninsula, beginning a drawn-out and bloody campaign on the peninsula in 1915. Though the Turks repel the invasion, the Ottomans lose the war. Greece occupies the Aegean coast of Anatolia, while the former Ottoman territory of Palestine becomes a British protectorate, Syria and Lebanon a French colony.

1922 Following relentless protests, the British appoint a descendant of Mohammed Ali, Fuad, to be the first King of Egypt.

1923 With all foreign forces out of Anatolia, and the Greeks defeated, Turkish leader Atatürk declares himself the leader of the Independent Republic of Turkey. This marks the end of the Ottoman Empire, with the last Sultan fleeing Atatürk's supporters for exile in Malta. A brutal population swap between Greece and Turkey takes place (see p284).

1936–39 The Spanish Civil War sees the Nationalists led by General Franco defeat the Republican government.

1939–45 The Med becomes one big battlefield during World War II, with only Turkey and Spain remaining neutral. Greece falls to Germany in **1941**. In France, the southern spa town of Vichy becomes the capital of the German puppet state. Italy under Mussolini enters the war in **1940** but is invaded by the Allies in **1943** and surrenders. In North Africa, the German general Rommel enjoys significant successes but is eventually defeated by the Allies at El-Alamein and is forced to surrender in Tunis in 1943. Greece, Albania and Yugoslavia are occupied by

German and Italian troops in 1940, with the Germans taking over completely in 1943. They eventually withdraw from Greece in 1944, and Yugoslavia in 1945, following the victory of the Yugoslav resistance movement, led by Marshal Tito. British troops occupy Athens and a civil war begins.

1946 Following their defeat, the constitutional monarchy in Italy is abolished and the republic established.

1948 The UN split the Holy Land in three, with the Arabs given the West Bank, Gaza, Jaffa and parts of Galilee, Israel receives most of the rest of the country, and Jerusalem becomes an international city. Britain leaves, and in the fighting that ensues Israel and neighbours Jordan and Egypt appropriate Palestinian land, leaving its people landless.

1949 The bloody civil war in Greece leaves a quarter of a million dead.

1955 Monaco wins its independence from France.

1956 France and Britain invade the Sinai following Nasser's decision to nationalize the Suez Canal. They are forced to back down and leave by the UN.

1957 Tunisia wins independence from France following years of unrest. The following year it becomes a republic.

1960 Cyprus becomes independent from Britain, though the latter maintains two sovereign bases on the island.

1962 Algeria wins its independence from France after a referendum following years of bloody fighting.

1964 Malta becomes independent, though at the islanders' request Elizabeth II is styled Queen of Malta — an indication of the close bond between the two nations. British forces finally leave in 1979, after 180 years.

1967 The Six Day War sees Israel expand its territory at the expense of Egypt, the Jordanians and, once again, the Palestinians.

1975 The Lebanese Civil War begins. Starting off as just a Muslim versus Maronite Christian scrap for power, it soon descends into more secular squabbles. By **1992** the Syrians and the Lebanese army have restored order.

1991 War breaks out after Slovenia and Croatia declare their independence. Macedonia and Bosnia-Herzegovina follow suit.

1992 Elections in Albania end 47 years of communist rule. In the former Yugoslavia, Serbia and Montenegro declare their independence but with no mention of 'autonomous' provinces the long-suffering Albanians in Serbia are angered and in **1998** violence in Kosovo erupts. The Serbian leader Milosevic is ousted in **2000**.

2004 Ten more countries join the European Union, bringing the number of members to 25. Malta, Cyprus (The South) and Slovenia are amongst those joining long-standing members such as France, Spain and Italy.

PART 3: COUNTRY GUIDES

While it is not within the scope of this book to look in great detail at the countries bordering the Mediterranean, a brief overview of the practicalities of visiting each of them *is* necessary, and this is the purpose of this chapter. Beginning on p38 we look at each of the countries in turn. Some of the details may change over the lifespan of this book and we would, of course, be grateful to hear of any changes or omissions that you notice; an address is given on p2.

GENERAL WEBSITES

🖥 **www.mediterraneanco.com** A directory for sites relevant to Mediterranean countries

🖥 **www.embassyworld.com** Lists embassies and consulates for each country and within each country

🖥 **www.weatheronline.co.uk** Climate charts for most countries and cities

🖥 **www.xe.com/ucc** Possibly the most useful exchange rate website, with a calculator that enables you to convert from one currency to another in moments.

TIME

Of the countries in this book, most are on Central European Time (**CET**), which is an hour ahead of GMT (**UTC**). These countries include Albania, Algeria, Bosnia-Herzegovina, Croatia, France, Italy, Malta, Serbia and Montenegro, Slovenia and Spain. Of the other countries, Morocco is on GMT, and Greece, Cyprus, Turkey, Egypt, Lebanon and Israel are on GMT +2.

In addition, most of these countries practise Daylight Saving Time (DST), which means the clocks go forward one hour in summer, usually from the end of March to the end of October. For example, Spain, which is on CET (and thus is one hour ahead of GMT) in winter, is two hours ahead in summer.

In summary:
● Morocco = GMT
● Albania, Algeria, Bosnia-Herzegovina, Croatia, France, Italy, Malta, Serbia and Montenegro, Slovenia, Spain and Tunisia = CET (GMT+1); GMT+2 in summer for most countries.
● Cyprus, Egypt, Greece, Israel, Lebanon, Turkey = GMT+2; GMT+3 in summer for most countries.

ELECTRICITY

Most countries listed in this guide use 220 volt, 50Hz, standard European two round-pin so UK and US appliances will need an adaptor. The exceptions are Malta which uses the UK-style three flat-pin plugs (and the voltage is 240) and Cyprus where some of the sockets are three round-pin rather than two.

DIALLING ABROAD

To ring abroad, first dial the international access code of the country you're in (usually 00 in Europe) followed by the country code of the country you are ringing. Then dial the area code omitting the first zero (if there is one) and then the actual number. The country code is given under the respective countries below.

You can usually dial abroad from phone boxes. It's obviously a lot easier to use a phonecard phone as opposed to a coin-operated one, as with the latter you will have to keep on feeding coins into the phone. If you can't find a phone box, go to the post office, where there is often a telephone exchange nearby.

Albania

PRACTICALITIES

Visas
No visa is required for EU, US, Australian, New Zealand or Canadian citizens for visits of up to three months. Everyone has to pay an entry tax, the amount varying depending on your nationality though expect to pay around US$10. US dollars are the preferred currency; attempts to pay in another currency will probably be met with expressions of disbelief, but persevere and they'll accept it – rounding up the total charge, of course.

Flying to Albania
Direct flights are possible from some cities in Europe but mostly you'll be stuck with a connecting flight. Flights are usually expensive because of the lack of choice and are not recommended as arriving by land (via Greece) or sea is much cheaper.

Information and maps
There is no official tourist information service, and what maps there are are often out of date. Lonely Planet's *Eastern Europe* has a section on Albania but probably the best guide is *The Blue Guide to Albania* by James Pettifer.
   Useful websites include:
🖳 **www.albinfo.com** General links on Albania
🖳 **www.albanian.com** General information about Albania, history, culture etc

Embassies and consulates in Albania
Bosnia-Herzegovina Themistokli Germenji, 5 Tirana (☎ 42-230454)
Canada Pallat 2, Apt 1, Rruga Brigada VIII (☎ 42-57275)
UK/Commonwealth 12, Rruga Skënderbeg, Tirana (☎ 42-34973)
USA 103, Rruga Elbasanit, Tirana (☎ 42-47285)
Serbia and Montenegro Rruga Durrësit 192-6, Tirana (☎ 42-32089). Open 0900-1200 weekdays only; the staff were slow and inefficient and did not speak English when I visited.

Money and banks

The currency is the *lekë*. Credit cards are accepted in major hotels but otherwise Albania is still mostly a plastic-free zone. However, ATM machines are slowly being introduced. Changing cash is a straightforward process at the American Bank of Albania or the Greek National Bank (Banka Kombetare e Greqise). The American Bank may accept credit cards for cash but don't count on it.

By and large, Albania is one of the cheapest countries in the Mediterranean, with food and transport very good value.

❏ Exchange rates	
For the latest rates visit 💻 or www.xe.com/ucc or www.oanda.com/convert/classic.	
£1	AL186
€1	AL125
US$1	AL101
Can$1	AL77
Aus$1	AL72
NZ$1	AL66

Communications

● **Phone** Albania country code = +355

● **Internet** Access is good, with plenty of internet cafés in the main towns. However, remember to keep saving your work as power cuts are frequent.

Post offices

Mail is cheap and fairly reliable but posting letters and cards from a post office rather than a post box is recommended; even then, expect delays and/or theft.

Post offices are open from around 0900 until evening but shut at weekends.

Opening hours and holidays

Albania has a siesta culture; most shops open early (0700/0800), shut for lunch at noon and reopen around 1600, closing for the day at around 1900. These hours fluctuate greatly though, depending on the shopkeeper.

As many Albanians are Muslim, Ramadan and the sacrifice Bajram are celebrated. Ramadan (15 Oct to 14 Nov 2004, 4 Oct to 3 Nov 2005, 24 Sep to 23 Oct 2006, 13 Sep to 12 Oct 2007) and Eid al-Fitr (15-17 Nov 2004, 4-6 Nov 2005, 24-26 Oct 2006, 13-15 Oct 2007) are observed. The festival falls 10 or 11 days earlier every year on a 33-year cycle. Other national holidays are New Year's Day (1 January), Easter (March/April), May Day (1 May), Independence and Liberation Day (28/29 November) and Christmas (25 December).

Albania is on Central European Time so it's one hour behind Greece and Turkey and one hour ahead of the UK.

Media

Unfortunately, there is no local English-language press, but you should be able to get day-late UK and US papers in Tirana, though delivery is patchy.

Health and safety

Foreign citizens can use the state health service for a small fee but this is not exactly state of the art so you are strongly advised to take out a good travel insurance policy before you go.

Many travellers report being surprised by how friendly and welcoming Albanians are, particularly since they have usually been warned to expect the

COUNTRY GUIDES

worst, from mugging to assassination. Albania is not a rich country by any means and many people have suffered a lot from the recent economic problems. For this reason, it is advisable to keep an extra watchful eye on your belongings, particularly on crowded buses, but don't become paranoid.

Accommodation
Finding somewhere to stay is much easier than a few years ago. The best option for budget travellers is to stay in a private home; just ask at the port or bus or railway station. Privately run hotels are now found in most towns and cities and can be recommended; expect to pay at least US$40 per person. Former Stalinist -style places still exist and cost about US$10-20.

Eating and drinking
For anyone who's travelled in Turkey, Albanian cuisine will be familiar. *Qofte* and *shishqebap* are staples while in Durrës the seafood is similar to that of the Aegean.

Coffee is served small and strong and frankly is often better than across the water in Italy. Albanian wine is also worth a try; the white is generally better than the red. For aperitifs, try *uzo* (the Albanian version of *ouzo*) or *Fernet*, the herbal spirit that you'll find in one variety or another all the way from here to Prague.

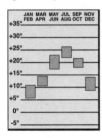

DURRES

When to go
Albania has both a Mediterranean and a Balkan climate, meaning that Durrës and the coast are warm and sunny for most of the year, though cool off in winter, especially since many places cannot afford heating. The central areas are freezing in January/February, particularly towards the mountainous Greek border.

Religion
In the old days, Albania was the world's only officially atheist country. Since the political system has become more relaxed there has been something of a religious revival. Many Albanians are Muslim but most still drink and, while respectful of their religion, aren't too restricted by its rules.

Bosnia Herzegovina

PRACTICALITIES

Visas
No visa is required for EU, US, Australian, New Zealand or Canadian citizens for visits of up to three months.

Embassies and consulates in Bosnia Herzegovina
Canada 7, Logavina, Sarajevo 71000 (☎ 033 447 900)

UK 8, Tina Ujevica, Sarajevo (☎ 033 444 429)
USA 43, Alipasina, Sarajevo (☎ 033 445 700)

Flying to Bosnia
Turkish Airlines fly three times a week from İstanbul to Sarajevo; Bosnian Airways has services from several European cities. Flights here are not cheap, however.

Information and maps
The tourist office in Sarajevo has general information as well as a good recent map; large-scale versions of city plans, including the surrounding areas, are on sale at local bookshops. Unfortunately, most plans don't show the current state of the sights featured on them and, with many closed, expect some disappointments.

Useful websites include:

🖳 **www.webguidebosnia.com** Links on Bosnia Herzegovina

🖳 **www.bhtourism.ba** The official site of Bosnia and Herzegovina Tourism, promotional rather than practical.

Money and banks
Bosnia has moved to the KM (the convertible Mark) which is tied to the euro. Euros are accepted in some places though having KMs is recommended.

There are ATMs all over Sarajevo and in other large towns, with banks working feverish hours, sometimes till 2000 and beyond. Converting currency is easy, with many banks acting as exchange bureaux.

❏ Exchange rates	
For the latest rates visit 🖳 or www.xe.com/ucc or www.oanda.com/convert/classic.	
£1	KM2.91
€1	KM1.96
US$1	KM1.60
Can$1	KM1.20
Aus$1	KM1.13
NZ$1	KM1.03

Communications
● **Phone** Bosnia Herzegovina country code = +387. Phone cards are available from post offices for pay phones, which allow international calls.

● **Post** The postal service is reliable and efficient.

● **Internet** Internet cafés are now a feature of every major town; connections are good.

Opening hours and holidays
On weekdays normal opening hours are 0800-2000; most places close at 1300 on Saturday and all day on Sunday. Monday is generally a bad day for trying to visit galleries and museums.

Public holidays include: New Year's Day (1 January), Orthodox Christmas (6, 7 January), Independence Day (1 March), Easter (March/April), May Day (1 May), Statehood Day (30 May), National Uprising Day (22 June), Feast of the Assumption (15 August), All Saints' Day (1 November), National Day (25 November) and Christmas (25 December).

COUNTRY GUIDES

Ramadan (15 Oct to 14 Nov 2004, 4 Oct to 3 Nov 2005, 24 Sep to 23 Oct 2006, 13 Sep to 12 Oct 2007) and Eid al-Fitr (15-17 Nov 2004, 4-6 Nov 2005, 24-26 Oct 2006, 13-15 Oct 2007) are observed. The festival falls 10 or 11 days earlier every year on a 33-year cycle.

Bosnia Herzegovina is on Central European Time so it's one hour behind Greece and one hour ahead of the UK.

Media

English-language dailies are relatively easy to find in the major towns and cities; most of the international agencies produce their own English-language local magazines and bulletins. These are largely propaganda, but interesting all the same.

Health and safety

While the war caused a vast amount of damage to Bosnia's health infrastructure, this has been largely rebuilt in the country's urban areas. State hospitals provide most services, though there are no reciprocal health agreements so travel insurance is essential. Payment must be made in cash at the place and time treatment is received. In addition, there are still some half a million landmines in rural areas; although most are identified and well signposted, trekking is certainly not an option. Stay on the roads.

Accommodation

The minute you arrive, expect to be met by a cluster of Bosnian women with apartments to rent, or more often than not a room in their apartment. These are usually good value, though may be some distance from the centre of town. *Pansions* (pensions) are found in most large towns; these are generally more friendly and cheaper than staying in a hotel.

Eating and drinking

While Bosnia has never really shone as a culinary capital, it is good for Turkish-influenced food such as *baklava* (a honey and pastry sweet) and *borek*, a cheese- or meat-filled pasty.

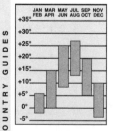

SARAJEVO

When to go

The country has a classic Balkan climate of hot summers and very cold winters; Sarajevo is usually under snow in January or February though it's milder at the coast.

Religion

Around 40% of the population is Muslim, 30% Christian Orthodox, 15% Catholic and 15% 'other'. However, given the ethnic cleansing of the recent conflict, these religious groups are much more dominant in certain areas than in others. In Sarajevo, the population is predominantly Muslim, while in the territory between the capital and Dubrovnik there is a large Croat Catholic population. Orthodox Serbs are concentrated to the north both around and in the capital of the Republik Serbska, Banja Luka.

Whichever religious group you encounter it is good to show respect and dress modestly when visiting their sites. Women should also cover their heads when entering mosques and shorts should not be worn when entering Orthodox or Muslim holy places.

Croatia

PRACTICALITIES

Visas
No visa is required for EU, US, Australian, New Zealand or Canadian citizens for visits of up to three months. Citizens of other countries should check entry requirements on 🖳 www.mvp.hr.

Embassies and consulates in Croatia
Australia Hotel Esplanade, 1, Mihanoviceva, Zagreb (☎ 01 456 6617)
Canada 4, Prilaz Gjure Dezelica, Zagreb (☎ 01-484 8058)
UK 121/III, Vlaska, Zagreb (☎ 01 455 5310); consulate; 10/III, obala Hrvatskog Narodnog Preporoda, Split (☎ 021 341 464) and 1, Atlas Pile, Dubrovnik (☎ 020 412 916)
USA 2, Thomas Jeffersona, Zagreb (☎ 01 661 2200)

Flying to Croatia
Croatian Airlines has frequent flights from other European cities; charter flights operated by various companies serve Split and Dubrovnik during the summer season.

Information and maps
The Croatian National Tourist Office has branches in most main towns and cities; offices have good brochures and maps, along with a lot of stuff on local events and sights.

Useful websites include:
🖳 **www.croatia.hr** Main Croatian national tourism authority site
🖳 **www.visitcroatia.co.uk** Includes lists of useful addresses
🖳 **www.hznet.hr** Croatian railways' website
🖳 **www.dalmacija.net** Website for the Dalmatia region (including Split, Brač, Hvar)
🖳 **www.istra.com** Website for the Istria region (including Poreč, Rovinj and Pula)
🖳 **www.kvarner.hr** Website for the Kvarner region (including Rijeka)
🖳 **www.zadar.hr** Website on Zadar region (including Zadar and Brbinj)
🖳 **www.tzdubrovnik.hr** Website for the Dubrovnik region

❏ **Exchange rates**
For the latest rates visit
💻 or www.xe.com/ucc
or www.oanda.com/con
vert/classic.

£1	Kn10.92
€1	Kn7.33
US$1	Kn5.97
Can$1	Kn4.51
Aus$1	Kn4.25
NZ$1	Kn3.86

Money and banks

Croatia's currency is the kuna, which is divided into 100 lipa.

ATMs are available in most large towns and Visa, MasterCard and Amex are widely accepted. You can change money at post offices and banks at a fixed rate. Banks usually open early, around 0730, as do post offices.

Communications

● **Phone** Croatia country code = +385; international access code = 99. Phonecards widely available for payphones, which allow international calls.

● **Post** The postal service is reliable and efficient.

● **Internet** Internet cafés are a feature of every major town, with good connections.

Driving

To hire a car or scooter you will need to show a current driving licence. Average costs for car rental are around €100 a day. Speed limits are 60km/h in town, 80km/h out of town and 100km/h on motorways.

Opening hours and holidays

Opening hours for shops are 0800-2000 Monday to Friday and 0800-1300 on Saturday. Monday is generally a bad day for trying to visit galleries and museums.

Public holidays include: New Year's Day (1 January), Orthodox Christmas (6, 7 January), Easter Monday, May Day (1 May), Statehood Day (30 May), National Uprising Day (22 June), Feast of the Assumption (15 August), All Saints' Day (1 November) and Christmas (25 December).

Croatia is on Central European Time.

Media

English-language dailies are relatively easy to find in the major towns and cities; the Italian-language *La Voce del Populo* is published in Rijeka.

Health and safety

EU citizens in possession of an E111 have access to free care in state hospitals. Tap water is safe to drink though mineral water is readily available. Generally you are unlikely to have problems travelling around Croatia but it is always best to keep an eye on your possessions.

Accommodation

Most bargain accommodation is provided by local families who rent out rooms in their apartments or sometimes the whole apartment. You don't need to find them as they will find you; prospective landladies greet most arrivals at ports, bus and train stations. Campsites often open only during the summer months.

Eating and drinking
Seafood and fish is what Dalmatia is all about, with a local speciality being *brodet*, a fish stew served with rice. Croatia also has some fine wine and a selection of brandies, from the lethal plum *sljivovica* to the herbal *travarica*.

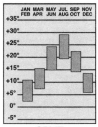

SPLIT

When to go
The coast is fine at any time of year, enjoying a hot, Mediterranean climate during summer and mild winters. The sea temperature is such that you can swim until November, though the water can be quite cool until late May.

Religion
Most Croats are Christian Catholic, the conflicts of the 1990s having seen the departure or destruction of the Orthodox and Muslim minorities. Religion is a serious part of most Croats' national identity and should be dealt with sensitively.

Cyprus

PRACTICALITIES – THE SOUTH

Visas
No visa is required for EU, US, Australian, New Zealand or Canadian citizens for visits of up to three months. However, do not attempt to enter if you have a Turkish Cyprus stamp in your passport and, for that matter, do not attempt to enter from the north, as you will be arrested and charged by the Greek Cypriots with having originally entered Cyprus illegally. Obviously, this does not apply if you've just been over to the north for a day trip.

Please note that all this may change because of Cyprus' accession to the European Union in May 2004. Visitors should check the latest situation with their embassy or on the Cyprus government website.

Embassies and consulates in South Cyprus
Australia 4, Annis Komninis St, 2nd Floor, Nicosia (☎ 02-473001)
Canada 1, Lambousa St, Nicosia (☎ 02-77508)
UK Alexandro Pallis St, Nicosia (☎ 02-286 1100)
USA Gonia Metochiou nd Ploutarchou, 2407 Engomi (☎ 02-277 6400)

Flying to Cyprus
There are dozens of direct and connecting flights to all major European, North American and Australasian cities from Larnaca Airport. There are also flights to

COUNTRY GUIDES

Middle Eastern airports (eg Beirut, Damascus and Cairo) and regular Olympic Airways flights to Athens, Thessaloniki, Rhodes and other island destinations.

Information and maps

The Cypriot Tourist Information Office (CTO) is a well-equipped and experienced government information service. Branches stock good maps, though these are also available from bookstores and souvenir shops on the island. Useful websites include:

🖳 **www.cyprustourism.org** Official Greek Cypriot site with background info
🖳 **http://visitcyprus.org.cy** Practical information for visiting Greek Cyprus.

❏ Exchange rates	
For the latest rates visit 🖳 or www.xe.com/ucc or www.oanda.com/convert/classic.	
£1	C£0.88
€1	C£0.59
US$1	C£0.48
Can$1	C£0.36
Aus$1	C£0.34
NZ$1	C£0.31

Money and banks

The currency is the Cyprus pound, divided into 100 cents.

Cyprus is not a cheap place but is still well below the cost of similar destinations in the Western Mediterranean.

The banking system is state of the art, with plenty of ATM machines and banks more than willing to give you cash advances on Visa and MasterCard. Most major establishments accept credit cards.

Bank opening hours are 0830-1200, Monday to Friday.

Communications

● **Phone** Cyprus country code = +357
● **Internet** Access is good and there are lots of internet cafés in the main towns.

Post offices

The postal system is very efficient and reliable; you can use post boxes with a reasonable assumption that what you put in will be collected in the not too distant future.

Opening hours and holidays

Cyprus has a siesta culture, meaning that shops generally shut for lunch and don't reopen till late afternoon, usually around 1700, before closing for good around 2100/2200. Weekends are pretty strictly observed; almost everything is closed on Sunday.

The main national holidays are: New Year's Day (1 January), Epiphany (6 January), Greek Independence Day (25 March), EOKA Day (1 April), Easter (March/April), Labour Day (1 May), Assumption (15 August), Cyprus Independence Day (1 October), Ochi Day (ie 'No' day, celebrating the day on which the Greeks rejected Mussolini's ultimatum to surrender in 1940; 28 October) and Christmas (24-26 December).

Cyprus is two hours ahead of the UK, one hour ahead of Central European Time and the same time as Greece and Turkey.

Media
There are a number of local English-language papers; the *Cyprus Mail* is the most widely distributed. You can also get the Greek weekly *Athens News*, as well as UK, international and European papers a day late.

Health and safety
Cyprus has reciprocal health-care agreements with the UK and Ireland, entitling their citizens to use the state system. Tap water is safe to drink.

South Cyprus enjoys something of a party reputation these days, with villages such as Agia Napa turned into major international party venues. While boosting the local economy, this has also meant a rise in organized crime. The police are likely to come down hard on anyone caught with illegal substances. Be careful.

Accommodation
Southern Cyprus has a few campsites and HI hostels but finding a guesthouse (offering bed and breakfast) should be straightforward. However, it is worth booking in advance, especially in the summer months.

Eating and drinking
Cypriot cuisine is much like Greek or Turkish, with *mezedes* (a selection of appetizers), followed by fish, grilled meat or kebab and salad, and finished off either with a plate of fruit or a trip to the *zacharoplasteion*, the patisserie. In the winter months *kleftiko*, a lamb stew, and *afelia*, pork cooked in wine and coriander, are popular.

Cypriot wines are also worth a shot, as is the local brandy, but look for the top of the range if your budget will allow it as the lower levels can hurt like hell the morning after. The very sweet dessert wine, *Commandaria*, is also worth a sip as it has an ancient pedigree, having been made originally by the Knights of St John.

When to go
Cyprus has good weather almost all year, with summer starting around the end of April and carrying on into October. However, in the mountains it can get chilly after dark, particularly if you're visiting out of season. The sea temperature is at its best between June and October.

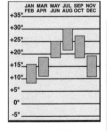

LIMASSOL

Religion
Given Cyprus's history of Turkish–Greek conflict, religion is still a major issue. Most of the population is Greek Orthodox, with a tiny Muslim Turkish minority still remaining, along with some Maronite Christians. Etiquette dictates no shorts in church and modest dressing, while a generally respectful air is strongly advised.

COUNTRY GUIDES

PRACTICALITIES – THE NORTH

Visas

No visa is required for EU, North American or Australasian citizens. However, make sure customs' officials do not stamp your passport; a North Cyprus stamp will complicate attempts to enter Greece and will rule you out entirely from visiting the South.

The thing to do is to get a blank visa paper (usually kept on the counter at passport control), fill it in and hand it to the Customs official with your passport. They then stamp the piece of paper and hand both back to you. On leaving, hand both the paper and your passport to passport control, and they will stamp your exit on the piece of paper as well.

Please note that the rules may change following South Cyprus' entry into the European Union. Visitors should check the latest situation before travelling.

Embassies and consulates in North Cyprus

As the Turkish Republic of Northern Cyprus is not officially recognized by anyone except Turkey, there are no official diplomatic or consular missions here. In an emergency US travellers might get help from government representatives at 6, Saran Sokak, K Kaymakli, Lefkosa (☎ 227 8295); Brits from 23, Mehmet Akif Caddesi, Lefkosa (☎ 227 4938/228 3861) and Australians from 20, Güner Türkmen Sokak, Lefkosa (☎ 227 7332).

The American Centre at 20, Güner Türkmen St (☎ 227 2443/227 3930) may help with visa issues.

Flying to North Cyprus

The only direct flights to Ercan Airport, Nicosia, are from Turkey; Cyprus Turkish Airlines and Turkish Airlines both fly from İstanbul and Ankara. Package flights are available from the UK flying via İstanbul; try President Holidays (☎ 020-7249 4002), 542, Kingsland Rd, London E8 4AH.

Information and maps

Maps and general information can be picked up from the larger hotels or local newsagents. Tourist information offices tend not to be well stocked but are friendly and may offer accommodation lists. Printed information is also rare outside Turkish Cyprus.

There are, however, a number of websites carrying tourist information, including the following:

💻 **www.turkishcyprus.com** Official Turkish Cypriot website
💻 **www.cypnet.com** General information about Turkish Cyprus
💻 **www.tourism.trnc.net** General tourist information about Turkish Cyprus

Money and banks

The currency is the Turkish lira. Prices are also sometimes quoted in British pounds, particularly in Girne/Kyrenia. Bound to the Turkish economy, Turkish Cypriots have gone through the same rollercoaster of high inflation over the last decade, so don't be surprised if prices jump while you're there. **Note that prices in this guide are quoted in US$ as it's less susceptible to change.**

There are several banks; Turkish ones are the most reliable. Ak Bank, Is Bank, and HSBC have branches with ATMs, and most banks will advance cash on a Visa or MasterCard. Opening hours are 0830-1230, 1330-1730, Monday to Friday.

Communications
● **Phone** Turkish Cyprus country code = +392.

Phone cards are widely available and can be used to dial internationally from call boxes.
● **Internet** There are plenty of internet cafés in all towns and even most villages.

Post offices
Post letters from post offices rather than post boxes as the service is more rapid. The system works fine; delivery times are much the same as in other countries.

❑ **Exchange rates**
For the latest rates visit 🖥 or www.xe.com/ucc or www.oanda.com/convert/classic.

£1	TL2,638,651
€1	TL1,771,296
US$1	TL1,442,224
Can$1	TL1,088.233
Aus$1	TL1,027,053
NZ$1	TL933,732

Note that in this guide-book Turkish prices are quoted in the generally more stable US dollar. At the current rate of exchange:

US$1 = UK£0.55 / €0.82
C$1.32 / A$1.40

Opening hours and holidays
While government offices still keep to the old British colonial siesta hours of 0800-1200 and that's it, the rest stay open in the afternoon and even into the evening as well. Shops stay open until 2000/2200 in summer.

The main holidays are: New Year's Day (1 January), National Sovereignty and Children's Day (23 April), Labour Day (1 May), Youth and Sports Day (19 May), Peace and Freedom Day (20 July), TMT Day (TMT were the Turkish Cypriot equivalent of EOKA, a pro-partition Turkish nationalist guerrilla group; 1 August), Victory Day (30 August), Turkish National Day (29 October), Independence Day (15 November) and Christmas Day (25 December).

North Cyprus is two hours ahead of GMT (the UK) and one hour ahead of countries on Central European Time.

Media
The north has its own English-language weekly, *Cyprus Today*, which comes out on a Friday. Otherwise, the main British papers are available a day late, along with some international and German titles. The *Turkish Daily News* is also available a day late.

Health and safety
Turkish Cyprus has no reciprocal health agreements so travel insurance is particularly important. Emergency treatment is free at state hospitals but visitors have to pay to see a doctor.

Travel off the main highways in north Cyprus often involves bone-shaking rides along tracks that only approximate to the word 'road'. Be prepared for tough driving conditions if you hire a jeep; don't attempt to hire anything else. Take plenty of water with you as you may be some distance from the nearest settlement once you get into the hills.

Accommodation

Northern Cyprus has a few campsites but at present no HI hostels. Guesthouses and hotels charge from US$15/20 (single/double) but prices can rise a lot in season, especially at coastal resorts. It's worth booking in advance.

Eating and drinking

Girne/Kyrenia has some of the best food in the eastern Mediterranean, with a wide variety of international cuisines including Chinese, Indian, French and Italian. Local dishes are much the same as in the south, though of course there's no pork (though there are plenty of places that do bacon and eggs!). Alcoholically speaking, the choice is limited, though Salamis brandy isn't bad.

When to go

As in the South, North Cyprus enjoys a warm climate with summer stretching from late April to late October. The sea temperature is good from June to November. See temperature chart for Limassol, p47.

Religion

Unlike their Greek Cypriot neighbours, Turkish Cypriots are much more Western in their approach to religion and it does not play a particularly big role in most people's lives. The vast majority of the population are Sunni Muslim, with small Maronite Christian and Greek Orthodox populations along with a number of Anglican and Protestant British, Dutch and German residents. However, Islam is more significant for the many Turkish settlers who have moved to the island since 1974.

Egypt

PRACTICALITIES

Visas

Everyone has to have a visa but the good news is that most nationalities can buy one on arrival as long as their passport is valid for at least six months, though it is generally best to get one in advance from the embassy or consulate in your home country. The cost of a tourist visa (valid for six months from the date of entry) depends on your nationality and whether you want single or multiple entry but is generally between US$24 and US$40.

Visas can be extended (US$12) by going to any police station or passport office in Alexandria, Cairo or Port Said as long as you have receipts showing that you have changed at least US$200 into Egyptian currency during your stay, so keep hold of any tabs from the exchange bureaux, banks or ATM machines.

Embassies and consulates in Egypt

Australia 1191, Corniche en-Nil, Bulaq, Cairo (☎ 02-575 0444)
Canada 26, Kamel El Shenawy, Garden City, Cairo (☎ 02-794 3110)

Lebanon Embassy: 22, El-Mansur Muhammad St, Zamalek, Cairo (☎ 02-332 2823); Consulate: 63, El-Huriyy St, Alexandria (☎ 482 6589)
UK Embassy: 7, Ahmed Ragheb St, Garden City, Cairo (☎ 02-794 0850); Consulate: 3, Mena Street, Kafr Abdou Rushdi Ramley, Alexandria (☎ 03-546 7001)
USA 5, Latin America St, Garden City, Cairo (☎ 02-797 3300)

Flying to Egypt

Cairo Airport is connected to just about every major city on the planet, as well as to other Egyptian cities such as Alexandria and Luxor. EgyptAir is the national carrier, which also uses Alexandria Airport, as do Lufthansa and Olympic Airways for flights to Germany and Greece respectively.

Information and maps

The tourist offices are usually very helpful, with English-speaking staff, maps and brochures.

In addition, Egypt must surely be the most written-about African and/or Middle Eastern country there is, so there should be no difficulty finding useful maps and guides in your local bookstore.

Useful websites include:

💻 **www.touregypt.net** Official Egyptian tourist board site
💻 **www.interoz.com/egypt** Links to sites on everything Egyptian
💻 **www.intoegypt.com** Useful for those travelling down to Abu Simbel
💻 **www.alexandra-dive.com** Diving to Alexandria's submerged antiquities

Money and banks

The currency is the Egyptian pound (E£). Changing large amounts of cash can leave you with brick-like wads of notes, so be sparing. Remember to collect your receipts from moneychangers as you will need them if you want to extend your stay beyond one month. Also, you are not allowed to take more than E£20 out of the country. Euros are becoming increasingly accepted in Egypt.

Egypt is a comparatively cheap country, though trying to live a Western lifestyle here can be considerably more costly.

There are plenty of ATMs in major cities such as Alexandria and Port Said, but elsewhere there are very few. Likewise, credit cards are accepted only in the main cities. Banks open Sunday to Thursday 0830-1400, though branches of some foreign banks stay open till 1500.

❏ Exchange rates	
For the latest rates visit 💻 or www.xe.com/ucc or www.oanda.com/convert/classic.	
£1	E£11.35
€1	E£7.62
US$1	E£6.21
Can$1	E£4.68
Aus$1	E£4.42
NZ$1	E£4.02

Communications

● **Phone** Egypt country code = +20. Telephone cards are available from post offices for pay phones. International calls can also be made from government telephone offices; however, these can get very crowded in the evenings.

● **Internet** Internet cafés are now a feature of every major town, though connections are often slow and prices high.

Opening hours and holidays

Egypt follows the Islamic week meaning that the weekend is Friday/Saturday, with all government offices, banks and official establishments closed for those two days. However, many shops appear to be open almost all the time, particularly in summer when darkness means it's a degree or two less sweltering. Archaeological sites usually open 0800-1700.

Ramadan (15 Oct to 14 Nov 2004, 4 Oct to 3 Nov 2005, 24 Sep to 23 Oct 2006, 13 Sep to 12 Oct 2007) is widely observed, meaning many restaurants close during the daylight hours of the fast. The festival falls 10 or 11 days earlier every year on a 33-year cycle. Egyptians also observe other Islamic holidays including Eid al-Fitr (15-17 Nov 2004, 4-6 Nov 2005, 24-26 Oct 2006, 13-15 Oct 2007) at the end of Ramadan, and Eid al-Adha, the Feast of Sacrifice (March).

Secular holidays include Sinai Liberation Day (15 April), Revolution Day (23 July), Armed Forces Day (6 October), Suez and National Liberation Day (24 October), Victory Day (23 December).

Egypt is two hours ahead of GMT (UTC).

Media

Egypt has long had a major English-language press, with *Al Ahram Weekly* the international version of the respected government broadsheet.

Health and safety

Egypt has no reciprocal health agreements so travel insurance is particularly important. Chemists (some open 24 hours) are worth trying for help with minor complaints but clinics and hospitals are also open to tourists.

One word of warning: Egypt in summer can be very, very hot, particularly inland and in cities such as Cairo. It is therefore strongly advised that you drink plenty of water (preferably mineral) and take regular salt and sugar tablets if you're travelling at this time. You can get anti-dehydration sachets at a chemist.

Accommodation

There's a youth hostel in most major cities and tourist destinations as well as a range of hotels so finding some accommodation to suit your budget should not be difficult.

Eating and drinking

Egyptian food is a vegetarian's delight, with plenty of pulse-based food on offer. *Fuul* is the local classic, a fava bean paste, along with falafel, going under its Egyptian name of *ta'amiyya*. Another bargain staple is *kushari*, a pasta and vegetable mix served in cardboard cups.

One of the features of Egypt is the variety of food available from street vendors (deep-fried canaries is one speciality) while also look out for plenty of syrupy desserts, *ba'laweh* being the local baklava. However, the food does range in quality and taste.

Eat fresh fruit and vegetables only if you can peel them or feel happy about the cleanliness of your surroundings; there are dire stories about water melons being grown in highly dubious circumstances, so steer clear of them.

As for drinks, Egypt is full of reminders why Islam has such a low opinion of alcohol. The local beer is Stella; it's not unknown for the hangover to begin before you've finished the bottle. Other bootleg spirits with slightly twisted names abound, such as Beeftweeter gin or Smolnov vodka; these should be avoided as people have gone blind and worse from drinking them. In Alexandria you may be greeted by offers from local youths to drive you to the airport so that you can buy them a bottle of the real stuff at the duty free. It's usually a genuine offer and can lead to an interesting view of young Alexandrians at play. The water from taps is heavily chlorinated but not lethal, while water from the street probably is. Check the seals on bottled water.

When to go

Egypt is extremely hot in summer and pretty mild the rest of the year. The Mediterranean coast is the more moderate region, though humidity is high. Technically the desert can be hotter but its dryness makes it easier to move around in. Sea temperatures are usually good for swimming from May to the end of October.

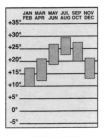

ALEXANDRIA

Religion

Most of Egypt's population is Sunni Muslim, while there is a strong minority of Coptic Christians, along with smaller Shiite, Greek Orthodox, Catholic and Protestant communities. Religion is a major part of most people's way of life and it is likely that you will find yourself in conversation about God very soon after you meet your first Egyptian. Be very respectful of these beliefs; don't go into a religious building if you are wearing shorts or a T-shirt. In addition, women should cover their head before entering a mosque.

France

PRACTICALITIES

Visas

No visa is required for EU, US, Australian, New Zealand or Canadian citizens. EU citizens also have the right to live and work here without permits or additional visas.

Embassies and consulates in France

UK/Commonwealth 24, ave de Prado, 6e, Marseille (☎ 04 91 15 72 10)
USA 12, blvd Peytral, 6e, Marseille (☎ 04 91 54 92 00)

COUNTRY GUIDES

Flying to France

Almost every airline flies to Paris but both Marseille and Nice also have international flights. From the UK, try easyJet (☎ 0870 600 0000, 🖥 www.easyjet.com), who often offer cheap deals to Nice.

Information and maps

Both information and maps are readily available from tourist information bureaux on the ground or from good booksellers back home.

Useful websites include:

🖥 **www.tourisme.fr** French national tourist board

🖥 **www.franceguide.com** Wide information base on France

🖥 **www.francetourism.com** Official US site for the French tourist office

Money and banks

The currency is the euro, divided into 100 cents. ATMs are widespread, and most hotels and restaurants take credit cards.

❏ Exchange rates	
For the latest rates visit 🖥 or www.xe.com/ucc or www.oanda.com/convert/classic.	
£1	€1.49
US$1	€0.81
Can$1	€0.61
Aus$1	€0.58
NZ$1	€0.53

Standard banking hours are Monday to Friday 0900-1200, 1400-1630; the Banque Nationale de Paris gives the best rates for currency exchange. In Ajaccio, on Corsica, the only bank that will change money is the Credit Agricole (see Corsica pp136-50).

France is generally better value for money than Italy, but is more expensive than Spain, though the differences are gradually being ironed out by the introduction of the euro and general economic development.

Communications

● **Phone and internet** France country code = +33. Note that in France you need to dial the area code even when phoning from within that area. You can dial internationally from call boxes, with phone cards available from *tabacs* and post offices, some of which also offer internet services, accessed by buying pre-paid cards from the nearby window.

Post offices

Opening hours are generally Monday to Friday 0900-1900, Sat 0800-1200. Post is very reliable; using a post box is just as quick as mailing from a post office.

Opening hours and holidays

Working hours for offices and shops are generally 0800-1200, 1400-1900 Monday to Friday/Saturday; museums and galleries usually open on Saturdays and close on Mondays.

National holidays are: New Year's Day (1 January), Easter (March/April), May Day (1 May), 1945 Victory Day (8 May), Ascension Day (May), Whit Monday (May/June), Bastille Day (14 July), Feast of the Assumption (15 August), All Saints' Day (1 November), Remembrance Day (11 November) and Christmas (25/26 December).

France is on Central European Time, meaning it's one hour behind Greece and Turkey and one hour ahead of the UK.

Media
There's no local English-language press, but international editions are available often late the same day.

Health and safety
Foreign citizens can use the state service, but must pay upfront unless it's an emergency. You'll be given a *Feuille de Soins* (a statement saying what they've done to you) which you must keep for any claim on your insurance. However, EU citizens should have an E111.

Car theft and pickpocketing (particularly for women) are a problem in France but generally travelling here is safe.

Accommodation
France has everything: campsites, youth hostels (private and HI affiliated), *chambres d'hôte* (B&Bs) and every kind of hotel from budget to five star. Finding a place to stay should not be difficult but booking in advance in the summer is always advisable; expect prices to rise then as well.

Eating and drinking
France is the home for gastronomes. Nowhere else is food invested with quite the same artistry, or, indeed, pretension, and clearly a large part of any visit to the country will involve food and drink. This could be simply the discovery of a small patisserie for a mid-morning snack, or a delicious three-course meal in a crowded restaurant served by the snottiest waiters in Europe. In Marseille, *bouillabaisse* is the major speciality, yet there are plenty of other dishes, including fusion food with a North African slant.

Cafés are a major institution, but be careful about pricing as this rises the further you are away from the barman/woman: sitting at the counter costs less than on a seat inside, which is less again than a seat outside.

Naturally, wine is the main drink; the beer in France is usually rather uninteresting German or Danish lager, though more feisty Belgian ale is sometimes available. These days it's even apparently acceptable to drink your wine, whether red or white, with ice cubes in it.

When to go
Southern France has a typical Mediterranean climate of long hot summers and mild winters. One thing to watch out for, though, is the Mistral, a north-westerly wind that cannons down the Rhône valley and out into the Bay of Lions, sometimes chopping up the sea as far south as Mallorca. Southern France is a major tourist magnet, so high season should be avoided if possible, along with French public holidays, when millions of people usually head south.

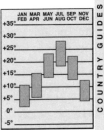

MARSEILLE

Religion

Largely a Catholic country, France is officially secular. Religion is not as powerful a force socially as it is in most Mediterranean countries, though one should obviously be respectful in any holy place. Islam is also a presence in many cities thanks to the large immigrant community from North Africa.

Greece

PRACTICALITIES

Visas

No visa is required for EU, US, Australian, New Zealand or Canadian citizens for visits of up to three months. All EU citizens who have an ID card can travel to Greece just using these, meaning that UK citizens must bring their passports. Everybody, regardless of nationality, should consider bringing their passport, as often banks require a passport rather than an ID before they will exchange money.

Embassies and consulates in Greece

Australia 24, Tsoha/Dimitriou Soutsou 37, Athens (☎ 0210-645 0404)
Canada 4, I Yennadhiou, Athens (☎ 0210-727 3400)
Ireland 7, Vasselios Konstandinou, Athens (☎ 0210-723 2771)
New Zealand 268, Kifissias Ave, Athens (☎ 0210-687 4701)
UK Embassy: 1, Ploutarhou, Kolonaki, Athens (☎ 0210-727 2600); Honorary Consul for UK/Commonwealth citizens: 8, Venizelou, Thessaloniki (☎ 02310-278006); Consulate for UK/Commonwealth citizens: 23, 25th Martiou St, Rhodes (☎ 02410-27247/27306)
USA Embassy: 91, Vassilsis Sofias Ave, Athens (☎ 0210-721 2951); Consulate: 43, Tsimiski, Bldg A, 7th floor, Thessaloniki (☎ 02310-829210)

Flying to Greece

Scheduled flights to Athens are a feature of just about every international airline. There are also dozens of cheap charter flights to Greece from most major European cities, some of which fly direct to an island, particularly to Kos, Crete and Rhodes.

Information and maps

The National Tourism Organisation of Greece (EOT) publishes many maps and brochures to specific islands and towns; these are distributed free through its local information offices. Maps and guidebooks are also available from good bookshops worldwide.

The official site of the Greek National Tourist Office is 🖥 **www.gnto.gr**.

Money and banks

The currency is the euro. Banks open only Monday to Thursday 0800-1400 and Friday 0830-1330, so make sure you do any transactions in the morning. The bank to use for getting money on a Visa card is the National Bank. Otherwise, all the islands have ATM machines accepting Cirrus, Maestro, Visa and other international systems; only Alpha Bank ATMs take Amex though.

Currency conversion transactions usually carry a €2-3 commission. Compared to Turkey, there are hardly any exchange shops, banks being the main places to change money.

❏ **Exchange rates**

For the latest rates visit 🖥 or www.xe.com/ucc or www.oanda.com/convert/classic.

£1	€1.49
US$1	€0.81
Can$1	€0.61
Aus$1	€0.58
NZ$1	€0.53

Communications

● **Phone** Greece country code = +30; note that in Greece you need to dial the area code even when phoning from within that area. So, for example, if phoning a Thessaloniki number from within Thessaloniki, you need to dial the area code (231) first.

For an international telephone operator dial 151 or 161. Phone cards are available from street kiosks and from OTE telephone offices. All public phones accept phone cards and the system is efficient.

● **Internet** All the islands featured in this guide have internet cafés in their main towns. Connections are generally good.

Post offices

Post offices open Monday to Friday 0730-1400. A stamp for a postcard costs around €0.50 for EU countries, €0.75 to the US or Australasia. Post offices also sell phone cards for public phones.

Driving

To hire a car or scooter you will need to show a driving licence; usually a photocopy will do, or a fax from home if you've forgotten to bring one. Average costs for car rental are around €300 a week with unlimited mileage and all taxes included. Speed limits are 50km/h in town, 80km/h out of town and 100km/h on motorways.

Opening hours and holidays

Greece, like most of the northern Mediterranean countries, has a siesta culture, so shops generally open early, close for lunch and then reopen from about 1730 to 2030. Government offices and banks don't usually open again after lunch.

There are a vast number of public holidays, with each region, town, village or island having its own special ones. The main national ones are New Year's Day (1 January), Epiphany (6 January), the first Monday of Lent and Easter (March/April), Independence Day (25 March), Labour Day/Spring Festival (1 May), Whit Monday (May), Feast of the Assumption (15 August), Okhi Day (28 October) and Christmas (24-27 December). Don't expect anything to be open or running on these days.

Greece is two hours ahead of GMT.

Media
Foreign-language newspapers are usually available a day late in the main island towns. In addition, the *International Herald Tribune* comes with a supplement of translated articles from the authoritative Greek daily, *Kathermerini*. There is also the *Athens News*, a weekly English-language newspaper published on Friday, though it's pretty hard to find outside Athens. *Rodos News* (in English) is available from the Rhodes tourist information office.

Health and safety
EU citizens can use the Greek national health service provided they have an E111. However, a good travel insurance policy, one which includes emergency repatriation, is recommended; don't climb on a scooter without one.

Greece is generally safe but as always when travelling it is best to keep an eye on your belongings, especially in crowded places.

Accommodation
Campsites in Greece generally have good facilities and some are in excellent locations. There are some youth hostels in the main cities and on larger islands but not all are affiliated to the HI. Bed and breakfast accommodation/pensions are available almost everywhere as are hotels (budget to five star). Booking in advance in the summer months is recommended.

Eating and drinking
In Greek restaurants a meal generally includes a starter, main course and a drink. The usual custom is to change venue for dessert, going to a café or pastry shop. Greece is known for its *meze* (selection of starters such as hoummus, taramasalata, tsatziki) which can be a meal in itself. Other well-known dishes include moussaka and kebabs; almost everything comes with a salad.

Though there are some Greek (and non-Greek) beers, most people drink wine, particularly retsina. If you like the taste of aniseed try *ouzo*. Soft drinks and bottled mineral water are available everywhere. Coffee is more common than tea.

When to go
The islands are generally cooler than the mainland, with temperatures varying from around 17°C in April or November to 27°C in July/August; they quite often rise above these though. Athens in mid-summer is noted for the desperation with which its citizens try to leave; there are places near at hand to cool off; see the Athens section (pp290-304) for details.

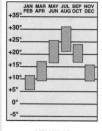

ATHENS   **RHODES**

The sea temperature in the Aegean is lower than the Mediterranean average; swimming is really pleasurable only from late May, unless you enjoy more Atlantic temperature ranges. In terms of temperature the best time to go is between June and the start of October but this is also the time when millions of others will be doing exactly the same thing. Rhodes has the most hours of sunshine on average of the islands covered in this guide.

Religion

Greece is a mainly Orthodox Christian country, with religion a serious part of most people's lives. When entering a church or monastery you are required to show due respect by covering bare legs, so no shorts or beachwear.

Israel

PRACTICALITIES

Visas

No visas are required for US, EU, Australian, New Zealand or Canadian citizens. Remember, though, that getting an Israeli entry stamp in a passport means that you will not be able to visit many other Middle Eastern or North African countries. You should get passport control to stamp you in on a separate piece of paper, which you should carry in your passport while in Israel.

Currently, it is impossible to cross from Israel to Lebanon and vice versa. The only way is to travel via Jordan and Syria, a feat requiring plenty of visas. You will not be able to obtain a Syrian visa in Israel, so this must be obtained before arrival. It is possible to cross into Jordan, via either the Beit Sh'an bridge in northern Israel or via Eilat in the south. Visas for Jordan can be bought at the border crossing (US$4 for Australians and New Zealanders, US$10 for US and Canadian citizens, US$6 for UK citizens). Crossing to Egypt is also possible from Eilat to Taba; see Egypt (p50) for Egyptian visa information.

Accessing the Palestinian territories is, at the time of writing, somewhat dangerous. Currently, for example, the Israeli army requires foreign journalists to sign a waiver absolving the military of any responsibility if they are killed or wounded in the territories. Since almost all foreign journalists killed or wounded in the territories have been victims of Israeli fire, this is not encouraging. Borders are regularly closed and regularly violated by Israeli military raids. If you wish to cross, contact your consulate or embassy for the latest information.

Embassies and consulates in Israel

Australia 4th Floor, Beit Suropa, 37 Shaul Hamelech, Tel Aviv (☎ 03-695 04510)
Canada 3/5 Ninm St, Tel Aviv (☎ 03-636 3300)
UK 6th Floor, Migdalor Bldg, 1 Ben Yehuda St, Tel Aviv (☎ 03-510 0166)
USA 71 Hayarkon St, Tel Aviv (☎ 03-519 7457)

Flying to Israel

All international flights go to Ben Gurion Airport, outside Jerusalem, but given Israel's small size, this isn't a problem; there are regular buses from the airport to Jerusalem, Tel Aviv and Haifa.

The main Israeli airline is El Al, which has extra security checks, so allow more time for checking in and boarding. Many other airlines also fly to Israel.

Information and maps
Tourist offices in Israel are well provided with both brochures and maps, and the staff are always friendly and helpful. There are also many guides and maps available outside the country from good bookstores. The official US tourism website for Israel is: 🖥 **www.goisrael.com**.

❏ Exchange rates
For the latest rates visit 🖥 or www.xe.com/ucc or www.oanda.com/convert/classic.

£1	NIS8.16
€1	NIS5.48
US$1	NIS4.46
Can$1	NIS3.36
Aus$1	NIS3.18
NZ$1	NIS2.88

Note that in this guide-book Israeli prices are quoted in the generally more stable US dollar. At the current rate of exchange:

US$1 = UK£0.55/€0.82
C$1.32/A $1.40

Money and banks
The currency is the New Israeli Shekel (NIS); this divides into 100 agorot. ATMs are widely available and all major credit cards are recognized countrywide. **Note that prices in this guide are quoted in US$ as it's less susceptible to change**.

Communications
● **Phone** Israel country code = +972. Telephone cards can be bought at post offices and give international access from call boxes. You can also call from telephone booths in the post offices.

● **Internet** Internet access is excellent, with plenty of internet cafés around.

Post offices
The postal service is generally reliable but it is best to post letters and cards from a post office rather than a post box. Post offices also change money and cash travellers' cheques.

Opening hours and holidays
Most shops and businesses work 0830-1900 (to 1400 on Friday), with Shabbat (Saturday) the day of rest. In Muslim areas, many shops shut on Friday, the Islamic day of rest, and reopen on Saturday.

There are also a range of Jewish religious holidays: Pesah/Passover (13-19 April 2005, 13-19 April 2006, 20-26 April 2007); Holocaust Remembrance Day (5 May 2005, 25 Apr 2006, 15 April 2007); Memorial Day and Independence Day (2 May 2005, 2 May 2006, 22 April 2007); Rosh Ha-Shana, the new year (16-17 Sep 2004, 4-5 Oct 2005, 22-23 Sep 2006, 12-13 Sep 2007); Yom Kippur (25-6 Sep 2004, 13-14 Oct 2005, 1-2 Oct 2006, 21-22 Sep 2007); Sukkot (30 Sep-6 Oct 2004, 18-24 Oct 2005, 6-13 Oct 2006, 26 Sep-2 Oct 2007); Chanuka (9-16 Dec 2004, 26 Dec-2 Jan 2005, 16-23 Dec 2005, 5-12 Dec 2007).

Israel is two hours ahead of GMT.

Media
The *Jerusalem Post* is a local English-language newspaper. Most European and US papers are also available from kiosks in the bigger towns and cities. There's plenty of English-language radio and TV too.

Health and safety

For minor ailments, try a local pharmacist as they often offer help and advice and usually speak English.

Make sure your travel insurance specifically covers you for Israel and also for the Palestinian Territories if you intend to visit that area. Be prepared to pay a higher premium, but with the current situation it would be inadvisable to go there without adequate cover.

Accommodation

In addition to campsites, hostels (both HI and independent) and B&Bs it is possible to stay on a kibbutz (🖳 www.kibbutzimmer.co.il); many kibbutz permit guests to use their facilities such as swimming pools and sports centres as well as the chance to join in activities; however, they are generally rather more expensive than staying in a hostel or B&B.

Eating and drinking

Israel offers a variety of cuisine from Arab staples such as hoummus and falafel through to Central European *schnitzels*. Food is often *kosher*, ie prepared in keeping with the Jewish religious code. You'll also find a range of meze-style salads and bean dishes along with Turkish-style pastries known as *boureks*.

Neither shellfish nor pork is eaten by strict Jews or Muslims, but both can still be found.

When to go

Israel enjoys much the same climate as its neighbours, Lebanon and Egypt, which have hot summers and mild winters.

Haifa is blessed with sea breezes, though it can also be humid in high summer. In recent years, there has been some snow in winter, so if you're here then, bring warm jumpers and jackets.

HAIFA

Religion

Religion is a huge issue in Israel. Which supermarket you shop at, which side of the road you live on, what kind of clothing you wear and dozens of other factors all give out signals to the initiated as to which religious label should get stuck on you. Religion is also highly politicized. As a visitor, you'll be spared some of the grief that goes with this, but be prepared. Respect all religions so don't wear shorts, T-shirts or beachwear in any house of worship; women should cover their heads in mosques.

Currently, most houses of worship allow in only co-religionists, and many have very tight security. The main faiths are Judaism, Islam and Christianity.

Italy

PRACTICALITIES

Visas
No visa is required for EU, US, Australian, New Zealand or Canadian citizens. EU citizens also have the right to live and work here without a permit or additional visa.

Embassies and consulates in Italy
Australia 25c Corso Trieste, Rome (☎ 06-85 2721)
Canada 27, Via G B De Rossi, Rome (☎ 06-445981)
New Zealand 28, Via Zara, Rome (☎ 06-440 2928)
UK/Commonwealth 80a, Via XX Settembre, Rome (☎ 06-482 5441)
USA 119a-121, Via Vittorio Veneto, Rome (☎ 06-46741)

Flying to Italy
With many flights available to Rome, Venice, Florence, Naples and Milan, Italy is easily accessed by air from almost anywhere in the world. From the UK, budget airlines such as easyJet (🖳 www.easyjet.com) and Ryanair (🖳 www.ryanair.com) are worth trying. Getting to Genoa is less straightforward, though Alitalia has flights there from several places and the Lufthansa subsidiary, Dolomite Airlines (🖳 www.airdolomiti.com) flies from Munich.

Information and maps
Tourist information offices in Italy have good supplies of maps, guides and leaflets. There are also information offices in London (☎ 020-7355 1557, 1, Princes St, W1R 9AY), New York (630 5th Ave Suite 1565; ☎ 212-245-5095) and Sydney (Level 26-44, Market St, NSW2000, ☎ 02-9262 1666). CIT offices, the Italian national travel agency, can also provide information.

Useful websites include:
🖳 **www.enit.it** Italy's tourism authority site
🖳 **www.trenitalia.com** Italian train timetables and online booking
🖳 **www.initaly.com**; **www.travel.it** General information on all aspects of travel in Italy

Money and banks
The currency is the euro. ATMs are widespread and most hotels and restaurants accept credit cards. Standard banking hours are Monday to Friday, 0830-1330, 1430-1630.

Italy is generally worse value for money than Spain or France; eating out is considerably more expensive here unless you stick to first courses,

❏ Exchange rates	
For the latest rates visit 🖳 or www.xe.com/ucc or www.oanda.com/convert/classic.	
£1	€1.49
US$1	€0.81
Can$1	€0.61
Aus$1	€0.58
NZ$1	€0.53

snacks and sandwiches. However, transport costs are lower than in other Western EU countries.

Communications

● **Phone** Italy country code = +39. You can dial internationally from call boxes; phone cards are available from *tabacchis* and post offices. The process seems way too easy, so just to make it difficult, the cards don't work unless you break off the corner before putting them in the machine.

● **Internet** Internet cafés are fairly common, though often they really are cafés rather than computer banks so shut at the same early hours, around 9pm. In Rome things stay open a bit longer; some of the ones in backpacker territory are situated in laundrettes so you can soap and surf simultaneously.

Post offices

Opening hours are generally Monday to Saturday 0800-1830. Post is reliable, and using a post box is just as quick as mailing from a post office. Stamps can also be bought from tabacchi and newspaper kiosks.

Opening hours and holidays

Northern Italian cities keep to northern European working hours (0900-1700) but the further south you go, the more the siesta culture creeps in; in Sicily, opening hours are 0800-1300 and 1600-2000. Apart from cafés, restaurants, *pasticcerias* (for cakes and sweets) and bars almost everything in Italy is closed on Sunday.

National holidays are: New Year's Day (1 January), Epiphany (6 January), Easter (March/April), Liberation Day (25 April), May Day (1 May), Feast of the Assumption (15 August), All Saints' Day (1 November), Feast of the Immaculate Conception (8 December) and Christmas (25 and 26 December).

Italy is on Central European Time, meaning it's one hour behind Greece and Turkey and one hour ahead of the UK.

Media

There's no local English-language newspaper, but the *International Herald Tribune* has a four-page *Italy Daily* supplement, which is produced in collaboration with one of Italy's most reputable papers, *Corriera della Serra*, and provides a round-up of Italian news.

International editions are often available late the same day in Rome and Venice.

Health and safety

EU citizens with an E111 can use the national health system.

Pickpocketing on crowded streets and in trains or buses is something all travellers should be aware of; also motorcyclists who can zoom up very quickly and swipe bags. Apart from these Italy is a safe country to travel in.

Accommodation

Free camping is forbidden but there are plenty of official campsites though the range and standard of facilities on these varies. There are hostels (€10-20 including breakfast) and guesthouses in most cities and large towns. Hotel accommodation is generally overpriced for the standard, particularly in Rome. If you can, book a bed way in advance when visiting the Eternal City, regardless of the time of year. The same is true for Venice if you aim to stay anywhere in the historic part of town.

Eating and drinking

Italian food is quite likely the most familiar 'foreign' food in the world, with a richly deserved reputation for creating a vast variety out of a few basic ingredients. The subject of eating Italian could fill volumes, so for the sake of brevity we provide only a few pointers here.

Moving from small to large, the *cornetto* is not an ice cream here but a stuffed croissant available for breakfast. A lunch staple for any budget traveller is likely to be the *panini* (a sandwich) available from cafés, bars and special sandwich bars. Pizza, of course, needs little introduction, and can be found everywhere. Full meals are served in *trattoria* or *ristoranti*, the difference between the two largely blurred these days, though ristoranti are supposed to be more expensive. You'll probably find neither cheap, though. A full meal usually consists of a starter, then a pasta course followed by meat or fish, plus a dessert. However, most places don't mind if you just stick with the pasta course.

Italy is justly famous for its wine (you can get a reasonable bottle for €4) and for its coffee, particularly espresso (strong and best drunk without sugar), and cappuccino (served with a good thick froth of milk).

When to go

Italy's climate ranges down the peninsula from the sub-Alpine to the sub-Saharan. Summers are hot almost everywhere, but in the south can get sweltering. However, you're never too far from the sea, plus the mountainous nature of the place means it's also possible to cool off by heading upwards. Genoa and Venice can both be a touch windswept in winter, with snow and rain not uncommon. Once again, the best times to visit are spring and early autumn.

Religion

Italy, in particular the Vatican City in Rome, is the home and centre of Catholicism, and Christianity still plays an important part in many people's lives. As such, due respect should be shown around religious buildings.

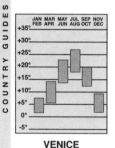

VENICE

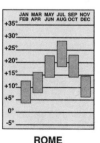

ROME

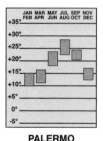

PALERMO

Lebanon

PRACTICALITIES

Visas
Everyone needs a visa to get into Lebanon (contact your local embassy or consulate for details). UK, US, Canadian and Irish citizens can buy visas on arrival at the airport or other official entry point; these cost US$35 for single entry, US$70 for multiple entry and are valid for three months. However, it is probably a good idea to get a visa in advance. For this, you'll need a passport photo, the application form (contact your nearest Lebanese consulate), a contact address in Lebanon, which can be a hotel, the cash and your passport. Applications can be made in person or by post. There's usually no trouble in getting a visa but if you have an Israeli stamp in your passport, forget it, you're not coming in.

Embassies and consulates in Lebanon
Australia Bliss St, Farra Building, Beirut (☎ 01-37 47 01)
Canada 434, Autostrade Jal-el-Dib, 1st Fl, Coolrite Bldg, Beirut (☎ 04-71 39 00)
UK 8th St, Rabieh, Beirut (☎ 04-41 70 07)
USA In Awkar, north of Beirut. Head for Dbayye; from there get a taxi to the embassy (☎ 04-54 36 00).

Flying to Lebanon
The national carrier, Middle East Airlines, has flights from other places in the Middle East as well as some from northern Africa and Europe to Beirut International Airport. Some other airlines operate direct scheduled flights to Beirut but it is possible you will have to get a connecting flight.

Information and maps
The government-run tourist information offices are very good, particularly in Beirut. You'll get maps as well as advice, though be careful with the former. With Beirut undergoing such major construction work, maps are constantly going out of date. However, the locals are almost always kind enough to point you in the right direction.

For information on the civil war, try Robert Fisk's *Pity the nation: Lebanon at War*. Fisk was perhaps the only foreign journalist to live through the entire conflict in the city without either being kidnapped or killed.

Useful websites include:
💻 **www.lebanonpanorama.com** Good Lebanese tourism site
💻 **www.dailystar.com.lb** Lebanon's English-language newspaper
💻 **www.destinationlebanon.com** A useful site with practical information

Money and banks

Lebanon's currency is the Lebanese lira/pound though US dollars are welcomed everywhere. **Note that prices in this guide are quoted in US$ as it's less susceptible to change**.

The city is well provided with ATMs and there are many banks that will advance cash on a Visa or MasterCard. Bank opening hours are Monday to Saturday 0830-1230. Exchange shops are found everywhere and generally offer good rates.

> ### ❏ Exchange rates
> For the latest rates visit 🖥 or www.xe.com/ucc or www.oanda.com/convert/classic.
>
> | | |
> |---|---|
> | £1 | L£2766 |
> | €1 | L£1860 |
> | US$1 | L£1514 |
> | Can$1 | L£1142 |
> | Aus$1 | L£1078 |
> | NZ$1 | L£980 |
>
> Note that in this guide-book Lebanese prices are quoted in the generally more stable US dollar. At the current rate of exchange:
> US$1 = UK£0.55/ €0.82 / C$1.32 /A$1.40

Communications

● **Phone** Lebanon country code = +961. Telephone cards are widely available for pay phones, which allow international calls.

● **Post office** The postal service is reliable and efficient.

● **Internet** Internet cafés are a feature of every major town, usually with good connections.

Opening hours and holidays

Government offices work Monday to Saturday 0830-1400 (Friday 0800-1100). Muslim shops and businesses close on Fridays, others on Sunday. Lebanon does not have a siesta culture, so shops are usually open 0800-1800.

The national holidays are: New Year's Day (1 January), St Maroun's Day, (9 February; St Maroun was the founder of the Maronite Church), Orthodox Good Friday and Easter Monday (March/April), Labour Day (1 May), Martyrs' Day (6 May), Feast of the Assumption (15 August), All Saints' Day (1 November), Independence Day (22 November), Christmas (25 December).

In addition, the Islamic holidays are followed: Ramadan (15 Oct to 14 Nov 2004, 4 Oct to 3 Nov 2005, 24 Sep to 23 Oct 2006, 13 Sep to 12 Oct 2007), Eid al-Fitr (15-17 Nov 2004, 4-6 Nov 2005, 24-26 Oct 2006, 13-15 Oct 2007) and Eid al-Adha, the Feast of Sacrifice (March).

Media

The main local English-language daily is the *Daily Star*. There are also a number of local French-language newspapers. European and North American dailies are usually a day late, sometimes longer for US editions.

Health and safety

The standard of health care in Lebanon is good but it has no reciprocal health agreements so travel insurance is essential. Local chemists are a useful resource and may also prescribe drugs for you.

If you visit south Lebanon take extra care to follow signed roads and paths only. While life has largely returned to normal since the withdrawal of Israeli forces there is still quite a lot of unexploded ordnance around. Local militias can also be sensitive, particularly if you try to take photos; even in Beirut, be careful not to pull out a camera anywhere near military bases or checkpoints.

Accommodation
Finding accommodation is not usually a problem in the larger cities and main tourist destinations though budget places can be hard to find.

Eating and drinking
Lebanon is an expensive place for food and drink, with bars and clubs charging top of the range Western prices, often in US$.

Lebanese cuisine is a blend of Arab and Mediterranean cuisine, from mezes to falafel, and probably the cheapest food you will find. The national dish is *tabbouleh*, a bulgur wheat, parsley, tomato and onion mix, while pita bread is a staple and acts as a serving implement; many dishes are eaten with this delicious bread. It's a good place for vegetarians with plenty of lentil-based dishes on offer, including *mujeddra*, a spicy lentil stew.

For a different drink try *araq*, the Lebanese version of ouzo, or raki, an aniseed-based liqueur which is usually served with water and ice.

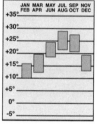

When to go
Lebanon has a typical southern Mediterranean climate, with long hot summers and mild winters. If you're visiting out of season it's best to take something warm as nights can be very chilly and many establishments do not have very good heating arrangements.

BEIRUT

Religion
Intermarriage between members of any of the many religious communities in Lebanon is prohibited. Family issues such as marriage, divorce and inheritance are governed by religious courts. Elections to the government, and the composition of the government itself, is on the basis of religion, with the president always a Maronite Christian, the prime minister a Sunni Muslim and the parliamentary speaker a Shia Muslim. There are also Greek Orthodox Christians and some Catholics, plus the Druze, a 10th-century breakaway group from Islam.

It's not a good idea to ask people what they did in the civil war or to ask them their religion; let them reveal it themselves should they choose to do so. Religious sites should be given great respect, so dress appropriately whatever the site. In addition, women should cover their heads before entering a mosque.

COUNTRY GUIDES

Malta

PRACTICALITIES

Visas
No visa is required for EU, US, Australian, New Zealand or Canadian citizens. Malta is now a member of the EU.

Embassies and consulates in Malta
Australia Ta'Xbiex Terrace, Ta'Xbiex MSD 11 (☎ 338201/05)
Canada 103 Archbishop St, Valletta (☎ 233121-6)
UK 7, St Anne St, Floriana (☎ 233134/37)
USA Development House, 3rd floor, St Anne St, Floriana (☎ 235960/65)

Flying to Malta
Air Malta flies from most European capitals with discount flights often available in the low season. Otherwise, during summer some charter companies offer cheap trips.

Information and maps
Maltese tourism is well developed, so the tourist information bureaux have good stocks of maps and brochures and the staff are helpful.

The official Maltese tourism website is: 🖳 **www.visitmalta.com**

Money and banks
The currency is the Maltese Lira (LM), divided into 100 cents. ATM machines are widely available and most places take Visa, MasterCard and Amex. Banks generally charge a lower commission and give a better exchange rate for changing money than hotels. Out of season (1 Oct-15 June) bank opening hours are Monday to Friday 0830-1230, Saturday 0830-1200; in season, they're Monday to Friday 0800-1300, 1500-1730, Saturday 0830-1300.

At the time of writing, Malta was the best-value place in the Mediterranean for food and accommodation; a three-course meal with wine in a smart restaurant could be had for around €7.50, while a good *pension* would set you back much the same for a night's lodgings.

> ❏ **Exchange rates**
> For the latest rates visit
> 🖳 or www.xe.com/ucc
> or www.oanda.com/
> convert/classic.
>
> | | |
> |---|---|
> | £1 | LM0.64 |
> | €1 | LM0.43 |
> | US$1 | LM0.35 |
> | Can$1 | LM0.26 |
> | Aus$1 | LM0.25 |
> | NZ$1 | LM0.23 |

COUNTRY GUIDES

Communications
● **Phone** Malta country code = +356. International calls are possible from phone boxes, some of which are still old, red British ones, and phone cards for use with these can be bought from TeleMalta offices and post offices.

● **Internet** Internet access is good, with fast connections from internet cafés.

Post offices

The postal system is fast and reliable. Opening hours for post offices are: Monday to Friday 0800-1800, Saturday 0800-1200.

Opening hours and holidays

Malta has a siesta culture, so most offices and shops open around 0900, close around 1300 and reopen around 1600, finally closing at around 1900.

There are plenty of public holidays, on which everything shuts: New Year's Day (1 Jan), St Paul's Shipwreck (10 Feb), St Joseph's Day (19 Mar), Easter (Mar/Apr), Freedom Day (31 Mar), Labour Day (1 May), Commemoration of the 1919 independence riots (7 June), Feasts of St Peter and St Paul and Harvest Festival (29 June), Assumption (15 Aug), Feast of Our Lady of the Victories (8 Sep), Independence Day (21 Sep), Immaculate Conception (8 Dec), Republic Day (13 Dec), and Christmas Day (25 Dec).

There are also *festi*, village or town fiestas; everywhere on the island has one, usually in summer. Celebrations include drinking, eating and fireworks, and they are well worth going to; check at the tourist office for details.

Malta is on Central European Time, meaning it's one hour behind Greece and Turkey and one hour ahead of the UK.

Media

Malta has two English-language newspapers, the daily *Times* and the weekly *Malta Independent*. Both are widely available and good for listings. International papers are also available, usually a day late.

Health and safety

UK citizens who have an E111 and Australians can use the excellent local state health service for free. Malta is a safe country but as always it is best to be careful.

Accommodation

There are no campsites (camping is not permitted) but it is usually possible to find a hostel, guesthouse or cheap hotel.

Eating and drinking

Malta offers an unusual combination of cuisines, from Brit favourites such as eggs and bacon, to Italian pastas and pizzas, with a North African influence also on hand. Local Maltese cuisine includes *pastizzi* (cheese pasties), *timpana* (a macaroni and cheese pie), and *fenech* (a rabbit dish).

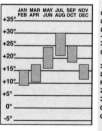

VALLETTA

When to go

Malta enjoys hot summers and mild winters, the main difficulty being the hot sirocco wind which can blow in during July and August from North Africa. Otherwise it's warm enough to swim from about May on, though

COUNTRY GUIDES

few locals go into the water until June/July. In mid-summer it can get pretty muggy, with temperatures soaring into the high 30°s.

Religion
Malta is Catholic and, as in Italy, the church is a major factor in people's lives. The British influence does, however, make a bit of a difference in terms of social mores, with younger people less tied to religious traditions.

Morocco

PRACTICALITIES

Visas
No visa is required for EU, US, Australian, New Zealand or Canadian citizens, who receive a 90-day stamp in their passports on arrival. Melilla and Ceuta operate the same visa rules as Spain.

Embassies and consulates in Morocco
Canada 13 rue Jaafar as-Sadiq, Agdal (☎ 037-67 2880).
UK Embassy: 17, blvd de la Tour Hassan, BP45, Rabat (☎ 037-23 8600); Consulate: 41, blvd Mohammed V, Tangier (☎ 039-94 1557)
USA 2 ave de Marrakesh, Rabat (☎ 037-76 2265)

Flying to Morocco
There are frequent Air Maroc flights from most European capitals and major North African and US cities. These can be expensive though so you may find it cheaper to get a charter flight to southern Spain and get the ferry across.

Information and maps
The Moroccan National Tourism Board (ONMT) has offices in all the major cities and tourist sights. These are usually fairly well stocked with brochures and the staff can also sort out guides and provide accommodation lists. Major ONMT offices usually have someone who speaks English, though French may be the only foreign language spoken. Maps are hard to get hold of, either in Morocco or back home. Michelin publishes the most useful road maps for the country. Useful websites include:
  🖥 **www.tourism-in-morocco.com** Morocco's official site
  🖥 **www.morocco.com** General information and links to a variety of sites

Money and banks
The currency is the dirham (DH), divided into 100 centimes. The dirham is largely a 'soft' currency meaning it's generally unavailable outside the country and cannot be changed back either.
    There are ATMs in Tangier and other major cities and large hotels and restaurants take credit cards (Visa and MasterCard). Bank opening hours are

Monday to Friday 0800-1400 in summer, changing in winter to Monday to Thursday 0815-1130, 1415-1630, Friday 0815-1115, 1445-1645. Banque Marocaine du Commerce Exterieur (BMCE) does cash advances on credit cards.

Morocco is cheaper than Spain and is probably better than Tunisia too for value for money.

❏ **Exchange rates**	
For the latest rates visit 🖥 or www.xe.com/ucc or www.oanda.com/convert/classic.	
£1	DH16.37
€1	DH11
US$1	DH8.95
Can$1	DH6.75
Aus$1	DH6.38
NZ$1	DH5.80

Communications

● **Phone** Morocco country code = +212. You can dial internationally from call boxes; phone cards are available from *tabacs* and post offices.

You can also call from *cabines* inside post offices though bizarrely these are sometimes more expensive.

● **Internet** Internet access is straightforward, with most Moroccan towns having a number of internet cafés.

Post offices

Opening hours are generally Monday to Thursday 0830-1215, 1430-1830, Friday 0830-1130, 1500-1830. Post letters from post offices as collection from post boxes is not reliable.

Opening hours and holidays

Morocco does not have a siesta culture, with shops open almost 24hrs except on Friday when many close for the Muslim day of rest. Offices and museums generally close on Fridays; the latter sometimes close on Sunday and Monday as well. Mosques are out of bounds to non-Muslims at any time.

Morocco observes the Islamic holidays: Ramadan (15 Oct to 14 Nov 2004, 4 Oct to 3 Nov 2005, 24 Sep to 23 Oct 2006, 13 Sep to 12 Oct 2007), Eid al-Fitr (15-17 November 2004, 4-6 November 2005, 24-26 Oct 2006, 13-15 Oct 2007), and Eid al-Adha, also known here as Eid al Kebir, the Feast of Sacrifice (January). During the month of Ramadan immediately preceding Eid al-Fitr there is fasting during daylight hours; the beginning is announced by drums and the end by sirens or flares. During this time it is possible to eat and drink but it's very much behind closed doors; don't be seen smoking or eating on the streets. There are also the holy days of Moharrem, the Muslim new year, and Mouloud, the birthday of the prophet Mohammed.

In addition, Moroccans celebrate several national holidays. These are: New Year's Day (1 Jan), Independence Manifesto (11 Jan), Feast of the Throne (3 Mar), Labour Day (1 May), National Day (23 May), Youth Day (9 July), Feast of the Throne (30 July), Revolution of the King and People (20/21 Aug), Anniversary of the Green March (6 Nov), and Independence Day (18 Nov).

Morocco is on GMT.

Media

There is no local English-language press but international editions are available in Tangier a day late.

COUNTRY GUIDES

Health and safety

Morocco is very hot in summer, so keep hydrated by drinking plenty of water and taking sugar and salt supplements, particularly if staying for any length of time or doing anything particularly arduous. You can get these from chemists, who are also a good source of other medicines.

In Tangier be particularly careful of street hustlers who will try and grab you (sometimes literally) on arrival and drag you off to their pension/restaurant etc. Also keep an eye on your belongings, though upcountry they'll generally be safe, and watch out for rip-offs with dope. As in the rest of North Africa, smoking *kif* is a normal part of most Moroccans' lives, though there are draconian penalties if you're caught. Bribing cops to look the other way is a widespread practice but must be done discreetly. In Tangier, you're likely to be offered several varieties of camel dung or henna if you try and buy some off anyone in the street, and you'll pay a high price. If you really want some kif wait a while until you've got to know some locals from whom you can get the real thing. But it would be wiser to avoid drugs altogether.

Accommodation

Finding somewhere inexpensive to stay should not be a problem as there are plenty of official campsites, as well as youth hostels (*auberges de jeunesse*) and cheap hotels (often in the older parts of town). Paying a bit more often makes it possible to stay in a very atmospheric hotel.

Eating and drinking

Morocco is justly famous for its *couscous*, a giant bowl of steamed semolina and vegetables, usually served with lamb, and for its *tajine*, a stew cooked in a earthenware pot with a chimney in the lid. Also worth a shot is *harira*, a thick chick-pea soup, and any of the sweet desserts. In Tangier, you'll also find plenty of French restaurants and a few Spanish.

Moroccans are often extremely welcoming and you may find yourself invited for dinner if you're there for a while. Upcountry and in some more traditional places, you may have to eat with your hand; use the right one only. It's also considered bad manners to show the soles of your feet, so tuck them under you.

The big drink is mint tea (*thé a la menthe*); this is very sugary and really refreshing on a hot day. Alcohol is forbidden under Islamic law; big tourist hotels are usually the only places serving any, or certain bars in Tangier's Ville Nouvelle.

When to go

In summer Morocco is very hot and dry though it's a bit cooler by the coast and in the Atlas Mountains. As with many countries described in this book the best times to go are spring and autumn.

Religion

By and large, Moroccans take their religion, Islam, very seriously. Mosques are out of bounds to non-Muslims

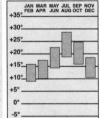

TANGIER

and other religious sites should be treated with great respect. Women should always wear clothes that cover their arms and legs, while shorts for men are really only a beach option.

Serbia and Montenegro

PRACTICALITIES

Visas
No visa is required for EU, US, Canadian, Australian, New Zealand and some other citizens entering Serbia and Montenegro for a period of up to 90 days. Other citizens require a visa which should be obtained from the Serbia and Montenegro (S&M) embassy or consulate in your home country: Australia (11 Nuyts St, Canberra, ACT 2603, ☎ 06 295 1458), Canada (Ottawa ☎ 613-233-6289) and the UK (5-7 Lexham Gardens, London W8 5JJ, ☎ 020-7370 6105). For further details see 💻 www.mfa.gov.yu/visas. See Albania (p38) for details about the embassy in Tirana.

Embassies and consulates in Serbia and Montenegro
Australia 13, Cika Ljubina, Belgrade (☎ 624655)
UK 46, Generala Zdanova, Belgrade (☎ 645087)
USA 50, Kneza Milosa, Belgrade (☎ 645655)

Flying to Montenegro
Montenegro Airlines fly from certain cities in Europe to Tivat and Podgorica airports. Yugoslav Airlines (JAT) fly to the same airports in Montenegro from Belgrade. Belgrade is connected to Montenegro by frequent trains and buses, most of which head for Podgorica. However, arriving this way is expensive so it is recommended that you try alternative routes from neighbouring countries.

Information and maps
Both information and maps are hard to come by, with borders and territories still a hot issue in many respects. The state tourist offices will give some leaflets and information but much of it may be out of date. Try travel agencies or the Montenegro tourism website: 💻 **www.visit-montenegro.com**.

Money and banks
The official currency in Montenegro is the euro and in Serbia the novi dinar. Serbia/Montenegro is largely plastic free, though the bigger hotels in Belgrade may accept Visa or Amex.

Banks and exchange shops will change foreign currency easily, but travellers' cheques are not accepted.

❏ **Exchange rates**
For the latest rates visit 💻 or www.xe.com/ucc or www.oanda.com/convert/classic.

	Euro	Novi Dinar
£1	€1.49	ND109.50
€1		ND73.52
US$1	€0.81	ND59.87
Can$1	€0.61	ND45.17
Aus$1	€0.58	ND42.64
NZ$1	€0.53	ND38.74

COUNTRY GUIDES

Communications
● **Phone** Serbia and Montenegro country code = +381, international access code 99. Telephone cards are widely available and can be used to dial internationally. Since mailing anything more than a postcard out of the country requires a form to be completed you have no choice but to use a post office; the system is also slow.
● **Internet** The internet is ubiquitous, with plenty of internet cafés in Belgrade, Podgorica and Bar.

Opening hours and holidays
On weekdays, banks are open 0700-1900, while shops generally open 0900-1200 and 1600-2000. On Saturdays they shut early (1400) and don't reopen till Monday morning.

National holidays are New Year (1, 2 January), Orthodox Christmas (6, 7 January), Serbia Constitution Day (28 March), Constitution Day of the Federal Republic of Yugoslavia (27 April), Orthodox Easter (March/April), Labour Day (1 and 2 May), Victory Day (9 May), Partisan Day (4 July), Uprising Day (in Montenegro on 13 July, Serbia on 7 July) and Republic Day (29, 30 Nov).

Serbia and Montenegro are on Central European Time.

Media
International English-language publications are becoming available again in Belgrade but usually only in major hotels.

Health and safety
State healthcare is cheap but as always it is best to have a good travel insurance policy. Areas such as Kosovo still have landmines but generally travel in Serbia and Montenegro is safe.

Accommodation
However you arrive expect to be approached by people offering a private room; if not ask at a local travel agency or just wander round the streets looking for signs for 'rooms'. Failing that there are some campsites and also budget hotels.

Eating and drinking
Serbia and Montenegro have a cuisine that is very mixed, from the Turkish *kajmak* of Montenegro (a cheesy cream) and *corba* (in Turkey, soup, but here a more filling stew) to Balkan staples such as *raznjici* (pork shish kebab) and *musaka*. The food here is usually pretty meat-centred, though cheese-based pastry dishes are available.

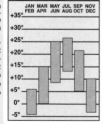

PRISTINA

The best beer is Niksicko, from the brewery of the same name in Montenegro, while coffee is served in the Turkish silt-and-boiling-water style.

When to go
The Montenegrin coast has a Mediterranean climate, though inland it can get chilly in winter in Belgrade.

Religion

Serbs and Montenegrins are by and large Christian Orthodox and their faith plays a major role in their concept of national identity. Be respectful of their churches and monasteries, dressing modestly when entering.

Slovenia

PRACTICALITIES

Visas

No visa is required for EU, US, Australian, New Zealand, Canadian and some other citizens for visits of up to three months. Information about entry requirements is available from 🖳 www.gov.si/mzz/eng/.

Embassies and consulates in Slovenia

Australia 3/XII Trg Republike, Ljubljana (☎ 01-425 4252)
Canada 19, Miklosiceva, Ljubljana (☎ 01-430 3570)
UK 3/IV, Trg Republike, Ljubljana (☎ 01-425 7191)
USA 4, Prazakova ulica, Ljubljana (☎ 01-230 1427)

Flying to Slovenia

Adria Airways, the Slovenian national airline, has regular flights between most European capitals and Ljubljana. In addition, there are a growing number of package flights to the coastal resorts.

Information and maps

Slovenia's tourist information offices are generally helpful and well stocked with maps and other material. The staff may also help find accommodation. There are also some excellent small-scale maps published by the Slovene Alpine Association (🖳 www.pzs.si).

Slovenia's National Tourist Association website is: 🖳 **www.ntz-nta.si**.

Money and banks

Slovenia's national currency is the tolar (SIT), divided into 100 stotini, though the euro is sometimes accepted.

The country is completely plastic friendly; there are plenty of ATMs and most places accept the main credit cards. Banks usually give cash on a credit card too.

Bank opening hours are usually Monday to Friday 0830-1200, 1400-1700, with mornings only on Saturdays. Post offices also change money, as do many travel agents.

❏ Exchange rates	
For the latest rates visit 🖳 or www.xe.com/ucc or www.oanda.com/convert/classic.	
£1	SIT361
€1	SIT242
US$1	SIT198
Can$1	SIT149
Aus$1	SIT141
NZ$1	SIT128

COUNTRY GUIDES

Communications

● **Phone** Slovenia country code = +386. Public pay phones take telephone cards, available from kiosks and post offices, which you can use to dial internationally.

Post offices

Post offices open 0800-1800 on weekdays and 0800-1200 on Saturdays. The postal service is reliable and efficient.

Driving

To hire a car or scooter you will need to show a driving licence (usually a photocopy or a fax from home will do if you've forgotten to bring one).

Average costs for car rental are around €75 a day with unlimited mileage and all taxes included. Speed limits are 50km/h in town, 90km/h out of town and 100km/h on motorways.

Opening hours and holidays

Slovenia has a Central European culture, so shop opening hours are Monday to Friday 0800-1900 and morning only on Saturday (though tourist shops are usually open all weekend). Banks usually open till 1600 or 1700.

Public holidays are: New Year (1, 2 January), Preseren Day (8 February), Easter (March/April), Insurrection Day (27 April), Labour Day (1, 2 May), National Day (25 June), Feast of the Assumption (15 August), Reformation Day (31 October), All Saints' Day (1 November), Christmas (25 December) and Independence Day (26 December).

Slovenia is on Central European Time.

Media

Most international and European papers are available the next day in major towns.

Health and safety

Slovenia has no reciprocal health agreements between the UK, US, Australia, Ireland or New Zealand; healthcare can therefore prove expensive if you do not have travel insurance. There is little crime but it's always advisable to take care of your belongings.

Accommodation

Finding a room in a private house should be easy; if you are not approached by anyone go to a local travel agency or tourist office. Alternatively there are campsites, guesthouses and budget hotels almost everywhere.

Eating and drinking

In keeping with its location at a historical crossroads, Slovene cuisine has many influences, with *bureks* (cheese- or meat-filled pastries) much in evidence, alongside the Central European sausage culture, with the *klobase* coming in many varieties. The typical diet is very meaty so *ocvrti sir* (deep-fried cheese) is likely to be a familiar part of any vegetarian's time here.

Slovenia produces excellent beer and wine, along with the knockout brandy, *sadjevec*.

When to go
Slovenia is not too far from the Alps so expect a climate more in keeping with Austria than the Aegean. In summer, the coast is warm and the sea good for swimming, but from December to March it's skiing weather only.

Religion
The population is 80% Catholic, making Slovenia the most religiously homogeneous of all the former Yugoslav republics. Their approach is pretty easygoing though, with Slovenes taking a more Central European approach to things than a Mediterranean one.

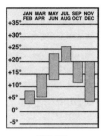

PIRAN

Spain

PRACTICALITIES

Visas
No visa is required for EU, US, Australian, New Zealand, Canadian and many other citizens. EU citizens also have the right to live and work here without permits or additional visas. The same is true for Gibraltar. For further details contact the embassy or consulate in your home country.

Embassies and consulates in Spain
Australia 98, Gran Via Carles III, Barcelona (☎ 93-330 9496)
Canada 10, Carrer Elisenda de Pinos, Barcelona (☎ 93-204 2700)
Ireland 94, Gran Via Carles III, Barcelona (☎ 93-491 5021)
New Zealand 64, Trav de Gracia, Barcelona (☎ 93-209 0399)
UK 477, Avda Diagonal, Barcelona (☎ 93-366 6200); see 🖳 www.ukins pain.com for details of the consular offices in Malaga, Palma, Ibiza, Menorca and other Spanish cities
USA 23, Passeig de la Reina Elisenda, Barcelona (☎ 93-280 2227)

Flying to Spain
There are flights to Spain from just about everywhere. From the UK, try easyJet (☎ 0870 600 0000, 🖳 www.easyjet.com), who often offer cheap deals to Barcelona. There are also plenty of charter flights to Malaga, while Gibraltar is also an option from the UK.

Information and maps
Most towns have a tourist information office with a good supply of brochures and maps as well as helpful staff. Look out in Barcelona for red-coated tourist guides, and in Marbella for yellow-coated ones; these guys speak English and offer helpful advice for free. Maps and guidebooks are available in major bookstores in Spain and in your home country.

COUNTRY GUIDES

Useful websites include: 🖳 **www.spainalive.com** Good 'what's on' section
🖳 **www.andalucia.com** Information about southern Spain
🖳 **www.gospain.org** Loads of links for the peninsula

Money and banks

The currency is the euro, divided into 100 cents. ATMs are widespread and credit cards widely accepted. Standard banking hours are Monday to Friday, 0830-1400. There are two types of bank: the standard *bancos* and the *cajas*, which are a little like building societies; both offer the same services. You can also change money at larger travel agents or at branches of El Corte Ingles department stores.

Spain is still relatively good value. It is cheaper generally than France or Italy, though a touch more expensive than Greece.

> **❏ Exchange rates**
> For the latest rates visit
> 🖳 or www.xe.com/ucc
> or www.oanda.com/
> convert/classic.
>
> | | |
> |---|---|
> | £1 | €1.49 |
> | US$1 | €0.81 |
> | Can$1 | €0.61 |
> | Aus$1 | €0.58 |
> | NZ$1 | €0.53 |

Communications

● **Phone** Spain country code = 34. When calling within the country you need to use the local code even when making a local call.

You can dial internationally from call boxes (phone cards are available from *tabacs* and post offices), or from Telefonica phone centres.

● **Internet** Internet access is widespread and generally fast.

Post offices

Opening hours are generally Monday to Friday 0830-1400, Saturday 0900-1200. Post is very reliable and using a post box is just as quick as mailing from a post office; stamps are available from tobacconists, known as *tabacs*.

Opening hours and holidays

Spain has the original siesta culture, with offices and shops closing around 1400; shops reopen around 1730, finally closing at around 2030. This also means people go out late. Most restaurants will not see any locals till 2100 or later, with clubs and bars staying open till the small hours, if not all night. Museums shut on Sundays and/or Mondays.

Spain also has a fiesta culture, with every village, town and city having its own local festival at some point during the year, together with regional and national celebrations (though national Spanish holidays don't tend to be much of an event in Catalunya). These local fiestas are well worth looking out for as they can be pretty wild and in certain cases continue for days, if not weeks.

Easter is also a major event, particularly in the south. Semana Santa (Holy Week) is celebrated with major processions of cross-bearing penitents, 10-ton floats and masses of candles. Seville, Granada and Cordoba are the main places where this is celebrated and accommodation in those cities at this time is simply unavailable unless booked months in advance.

National holidays are: New Year's Day (1 January), Epiphany (6 January), Easter (March/April), May Day (1 May), Feast of the Assumption (15 August),

National Day (12 October), All Saints' Day (1 November), Constitution Day (6 December), Feast of the Immaculate Conception (8 December) and Christmas (25 December).

Spain is on Central European Time so it's one hour behind Greece and Turkey, and one hour ahead of the UK.

Media

There is no local English-language press but international editions of newspapers are available often late the same day.

Health and safety

EU citizens are covered by reciprocal health agreements; you'll need an E111 as well as a photocopy of it. The standard of health care in Spain is high and there are both private and state-run hospitals. Anyone needing emergency treatment will be looked after irrespective of their ability to pay. However, it is always best to have travel insurance.

Barcelona's Barri Gótic is notorious for bag snatchers and pickpockets. Things have improved a little in recent years but be extra careful when wandering round.

Accommodation

All kinds of accommodation (campsites, HI and private hostels, *pensiones* and hotels) are available though the standard and range of facilities can vary a lot, so if comfort is more important than price check what you are getting before you book in. Prices can increase a lot in tourist areas in the summer months.

Eating and drinking

Eating and drinking are Spanish specialities. While the food in Catalunya is often quite different from that in Andalucia, both are excellent. Naturally, there are the more famous dishes such as paella to try, but there is a vast variety of other dishes on offer. Spanish wine tends to be harsher than French or Italian, but still has a worthy pedigree; the beer tends to be served cold, either bottled or from a tap.

Breakfast is usually light, a croissant or pastry along with a milky *café con leche*, or a stronger *cuartado*, while lunch is a major feast. Look out for the *menu del dia*, a lunchtime institution which involves a three-course meal for as little as €5-6. The better value ones are those furthest from the seafront and main tourist areas. For a menu del dia, you'll have a choice for *primero*, *segundo plato* and *postres* (first course, second course and dessert) with the first often a salad and the second meat, served without any accompanying vegetables. The evening meal is generally less important than lunch.

A way to get by on a small budget is to stock up on *tapas*; these bar snacks can often be a meal in themselves and are particularly good value in the south. In Andalucia, you sometimes get given a free tapas, usually a small one, if you order a drink. Municipal markets are also good sources of food for a budget meal.

There are a number of different places to eat and drink, though the differences are becoming more blurred. A classic *bodega* specializes in wine: some serve only wine and some offer refills for free. Cafés usually serve food, par-

COUNTRY GUIDES

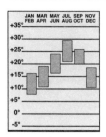

ALMERIA

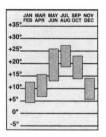

BARCELONA

ticularly tapas and *bocadillos* (bread rolls with a variety of fillings, usually ham and cheese). Bocadillos also come hot, or *caliente* with grilled pork or beef fillings. Restaurants are quieter, more formal places and usually more expensive.

When to go
Southern Spain has a hot, dry climate, with Almeria reputedly the hottest place in the country. Barcelona and the north are wetter and colder, particularly in winter so bring a jumper or coat. The best times to go for both are probably spring and autumn as the prices fall along with the number of tourists.

The sea is warm enough for swimming from about May onwards, though don't be surprised to find bunches of pink-skinned Brits swimming in February, despite pitying looks from the wrapped-up locals.

Religion
A mainly Catholic country, religion is still a major factor in many people's lives, though less so in the north and Barcelona. Most places of worship are open and used to visitors, who should, of course, show proper respect for what are often very much working churches.

Tunisia

PRACTICALITIES

Visas
No visa is required for a three-month stay for EU, US, and Canadian citizens but Australians and New Zealanders have to buy one on arrival (US$3).

There may be trouble if you have an Israeli stamp in your passport, and Israeli nationals are not allowed in. If you have an Israeli stamp, lose your passport and get another one: it's expensive but necessary if you wish to visit almost any North African or Middle Eastern country.

Embassies and consulates in Tunisia
Australia, Canada and New Zealand 3, rue du Senegal, Tunis (☎ 796577)
UK Embassy: 5, place de la Victoire, Tunis (☎ 341444); Consulate: 141, ave de la Liberté, Tunis (☎ 793566)
USA 144 ave de la Liberté, Tunis (☎ 782566)

Flying to Tunisia
In terms of tourism, Tunisia has developed as a winter destination for

Europeans, with charter flights available to Tunis Airport and to Jerba and Monastir. Check out bargain offers, particularly in spring and autumn.

Information and maps

The tourist information office in Tunis is a useful source of maps, though it often runs out of English versions. General maps of the country are widely available back home. Most official information is in French and Arabic, so a passing knowledge of either is handy.

The Tunisian Tourism Board website is: 💻 **www.tourismtunisia.com**.

Money and banks

The Tunisian currency is the dinar, or TD. This is divided not into 100 but 1000 mills; a price such as 1.800 meaning one dinar 800 milles. Foreign currency can be changed only at banks, major hotels or post offices; it is illegal to change money anywhere else.

Generally, Tunisia is an inexpensive country, though if you stick to the major tourist hotels prices will soar dramatically.

Bank opening hours are Monday to Thursday 0800-1100, 1400-1600, Friday 0800-1100, 1300-1500, though during the summer they shut in the afternoon. There are some ATM machines in Tunis but few elsewhere and only major tourist hotels and restaurants take credit cards.

❑ **Exchange rates**	
For the latest rates visit 💻 or www.xe.com/ucc or www.oanda.com/convert/classic.	
£1	TD2.49
€1	TD1.67
US$1	TD1.36
Can$1	TD1.03
Aus$1	TD0.97
NZ$1	TD0.88

Communications

● **Phone** Tunisia country code = +216. International calls are possible from phone boxes, though most are still coin only, so you will need pockets full of dinar coins if phoning any distance or for any time.

● **Internet** Internet access is available from cafés and some post offices, where it is known as Publinet.

Post offices

It's better to post cards and letters from a post office than a post box. Post office opening hours are Monday to Thursday 0730-1330, Friday 0730-1230 from 1 July to 30 September, 0800-1800 in winter. For weekend postage in Tunis, try the central office on ave Charles de Gaulle as it opens every day.

Opening hours and holidays

Tunisians take the afternoon off during summer, which is sensible given the temperatures. Many places also shut on Friday afternoons regardless of the time of year. Otherwise, offices and businesses are open Monday to Friday 0830-1300, 1500-1745. Restaurants also close early; hardly anything is open in central Tunis after 2100.

Public holidays include the Islamic holidays: Ramadan (15 Oct to 14 Nov 2004, 4 Oct to 3 Nov 2005, 24 Sep to 23 Oct 2006, 13 Sep to 12 Oct 2007), Eid al-Fitr (15-17 Nov 2004, 4-6 Nov 2005, 24-26 Oct 2006, 13-15 Oct 2007), and

COUNTRY GUIDES

Eid al-Adha, the Feast of Sacrifice (March). Others are: New Year's Day (1 January), Independence Day (20 March), Youth Day (21 March), Martyrs' Day (9 April), May Day (1 May), Republic Day (25 July), Public Holiday (3 August), Women's Day (13 August), Evacuation Day (15 October) and Ben Ali's presidential anniversary (7 November).

Tunisia is on Central European Time so it's one hour behind Greece and Turkey and one hour ahead of GMT.

Media

Tunisia has two daily French-language newspapers, *Le Temps* and *La Presse de Tunisie* and a weekly English-language paper, *Tunisia News*. They're quite tightly controlled but good for some listings and general news.

The major international dailies are usually available a day late in larger hotels or at major tourist sites.

Health and safety

Currently there are no health alerts for the country but check out the latest with your local health service before departure if planning to visit the more up-country places.

Be advised that in summer it is necessary to drink a lot more water than you're probably used to; plus it's advisable, if you're here for any more than a few days, to take salt and sugar anti-dehydration supplements. These are widely available from chemists.

Accommodation

There are some official campsites in coastal resorts but hotels and pensions may also permit you to camp in their grounds. Hostels are also available in the main towns as are, of course, hotels to suit all budgets.

Eating and drinking

Tunisia has a wide variety of local dishes plus a strong French presence in its more Western restaurants. The specialities are the *Magreb* (couscous, usually served with a lamb or beef stew), *lablabi* (a chick-pea broth with bread), *kammounia* (a cumin-flavoured beef stew) and *tajine* (like an egg flan). In addition, there are a growing number of fast-food outlets and pizza restaurants, useful for their air conditioning and toilets if not for the cuisine.

Most Tunisian places do not serve alcohol; for this, try the French restaurants or tourist hotels.

When to go

In summer, things get very hot, with 30°+C temperatures not uncommon. Further south things get even hotter but also drier, which can make a pleasant change from the humidity of Tunis. As a result, the best time to visit is spring or autumn when it is cooler, the number of tourists thins out and prices fall.

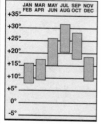

TUNIS

Religion

Tunisia is a Muslim country, with 99.5% of the population Sunni. There are also small populations of Catholics and Jews, mainly in Tunis. When entering Muslim religious sites visitors should dress modestly, with any bare arms or legs covered; women should also wear something on their head. It is also wise to avoid drinking alcohol in any public place, particularly during Ramadan when even non-Muslims should not smoke or eat in public during the hours of the fast, ie dawn till dusk.

Turkey

PRACTICALITIES

Visas

A visa is required for US, Australian and UK citizens and can be obtained on arrival. The cost is US$20 for US citizens, £10 for UK citizens, and A$20 for Australians for a three-month, multi-entry tourist visa; this must be paid in cash. Other EU, New Zealand and Canadian citizens get the same three-month allowance on presentation of a valid passport. German citizens can visit just using their ID cards.

Embassies and consulates in Turkey

Australia 58, Tepecik Yolu, Etiler, İstanbul (consulate; ☎ 0212-257 7050)

Canada 75, Nenehatun Cad, Gaziosmanpasa, Ankara (☎ 0312-436 1275)

Ireland Visnezade Mhl, Acisu Sokak, Cinerli Apt No 5, D4, Macka, İstanbul (☎ 0212-259 6979)

New Zealand 13/4, Iran Cad, Kavaklidere, Ankara (☎ 0312-467 9056)

UK Embassy: 46A, Sehit Ersan Cad, Ankara (☎ 0312-4553444); (honorary) consulates at: 34, Mesrutiyet Cad, Tepebasi, Beyoğlu, İstanbul (☎ 0212-334 6400); 49, 1442 Sokak, Alsancak, İzmir (☎ 0232-463 5151); 401/B, Kibris Sehitleri Cad, Konacil Merkii, Bodrum (☎ 0252-319 0093); and finally, Marmaris (☎ 0252-412 6486). The consulates also serve Commonwealth citizens.

USA 23, Sehit Halil Ibrahim Cad, Istinye, Beyoğlu, İstanbul (☎ 0212-251 3602).

Flying to Turkey

There are dozens of cheap charter flights to Turkey (including to İzmir, Bodrum, Antalya and Dedemen) from all the major European cities and scheduled flights to İstanbul are a feature of just about every international airline. So it pays to shop around before buying a ticket.

If you end up in İstanbul, you can either take advantage of the domestic air schedules to fly direct to İzmir, Bodrum, Dedemen or Antalya or you can cross town to the bus station for a coach.

Information and maps

All the main towns in this book have tourist information offices, though maps

COUNTRY GUIDES

and brochures are often in short supply. Useful websites include:

🖥 **www.tourismturkey.org** Useful info on travelling to and around Turkey

🖥 **www.turkey.embassyhomepage.com** Visa information

Money and banks

Turkey's currency is the lira, which comes in some unusual sizes. The smallest note is TL250,000 (just less than US$0.17), the largest TL20,000,000 (slightly over US$13). This makes calculations difficult, though a very rough rule of thumb is to just forget about the millions, divide the main number by 10 and multiply by four to get British pounds, or divide by three and multiply by two to get dollars. A TL10 million note then becomes roughly four pounds, or around 6.66 dollars.

Inflation is a big problem in Turkey so be prepared for sudden price hikes, even if exchange rates stay stable: *Zam geldi* is what the locals say, usually with a despairing shrug, to announce a new price rise. Naturally, those with their money in the right places make a killing out of such jumps, which is why expensive nightclubs continue to be full even in the midst of a recession. **Note that prices in this guide are quoted in US$ as it's less susceptible to change.**

To change money always use a *Doviz* (exchange shop); these are everywhere in Turkey and don't charge commission. Banks are only for Visa transactions (Garanti Bank does them without commission) or for ATMs, of which there are dozens in all the main towns mentioned in this book. Bank opening times are Monday to Friday 0830-1200 and 1330-1700.

> ❏ **Exchange rates**
> For the latest rates visit 🖥 or www.xe.com/ucc or www.oanda.com/convert/classic.
>
> | | |
> |---|---|
> | £1 | TL2,638,651 |
> | €1 | TL1,771,296 |
> | US$1 | TL1,442,224 |
> | Can$1 | TL1,088.233 |
> | Aus$1 | TL1,027,053 |
> | NZ$1 | TL933,732 |
>
> Note that in this guidebook Turkish prices are quoted in the generally more stable US dollar. At the current rate of exchange:
> US$1 = UK£0.55 / €0.82/ Can$1.32 / Aus $1.40

Communications

● **Phone** Turkey country code = +90. You can buy telephone cards for call boxes at PTT offices. These are also sold by street vendors, who set up a small stall or table next to wherever there are some phone boxes. For the international telephone operator dial 115 or 161.

● **Internet** All the towns featured here have a number of internet cafés and connections are generally good.

Post offices

Post offices, the PTT, are open Monday to Friday 0800-1700; central city offices open on Saturday as well. Use these for posting letters; hand them in at the window marked 'Pul'. Leaving letters in post boxes is not so reliable.

Driving

To hire a car or scooter you will need to show a driving licence; usually a photocopy, or a fax from home, will do if you've forgotten to bring it. Average costs for car rental are around US$400 a week with unlimited mileage and all taxes included. Speed limits are 50km/h in town, 100km/h out of town.

Opening hours and holidays

Turkey differs from other European Mediterranean countries in that there is no siesta. Hours here are more Middle Eastern, meaning shops can open around 0800 and not shut till midnight. Government offices tend to open 0900-1700. Many shops close on Sundays and museums on Mondays. The main religious festivals are Ramadan (15 Oct to 14 Nov 2004, 4 Oct to 3 Nov 2005, 24 Sep to 23 Oct 2006, 13 Sep to 12 Oct 2007), followed by Seker Bayram/Eid al-Fitr (14-16 Nov 2004, 4-6 Nov 2005, 24-26 Oct 2006, 13-15 Oct 2007), and Eid al-Adha (January/February).

Banks and post offices also shut on secular holidays, which fall on New Year's Day (1 January), National Sovereignty Children's Day (23 April), Spring Day (1 May), Atatürk Commemoration and Youth and Sports Day (19 May), Victory Day (30 August), Republic Day (29 October) and Atatürk's Death (10 November).

Turkey is two hours ahead of GMT.

Media

Foreign-language newspapers are usually available a day late in the main towns. There is also the *Turkish Daily News*, a daily English-language newspaper, and its newer rival, the *Turkish News,* also daily. In Bodrum, the *Bodrum Guide*, an English-language magazine, is published during the summer months and contains a ton of handy information. In İstanbul, *Time Out* appears once a month, in Turkish but with an English-language insert giving the lowdown on places to go and things to see in the city.

Health and safety

Turkey has no reciprocal health agreements, so travel insurance is essential. However, treatment at clinics and hospitals in not usually expensive though it is best to find a private rather than a state-run place. Chemists can usually help with minor problems.

Turkey is one of the safest countries in the Mediterranean for travellers, though some extra care should be taken if travelling to the south-east and the Iraqi border region, where a ceasefire between the army and Kurdish separatist militants ended on 1 September, 2003.

Accommodation

Pensions (B&B-style accommodation) and hotels are available everywhere and can often be excellent value for money; hostels are mostly found only in cities. Accommodation in cities such as İstanbul and İzmir is often proportionately more expensive and less easy to find than in other less-touristy towns.

Eating and drinking

Turkey has a cuisine that combines Greek, Arab, Balkan and Central Asian but is still distinctly different. This may not be so apparent to begin with, as most restaurants serve the same standard *doner* or *sis kebabs*, making the search for variety on a longer stay an absolute must. While İstanbul has a vast number of restaurants from every corner of the world, on the country's Aegean and Mediterranean coasts it is a good idea to order fish, which is usually fresh (*taze* in Turkish) and served grilled (*izgara*) or fried (*tava*). Restaurant owners usually don't mind if you have a look at the fish first; they may even insist that you do. The way to check if it is fresh is to bend the head back at the gills: the redder the gills are, the fresher the fish.

In fish restaurants and *meyhanes*, which are often indistinguishable, there is also a wide variety of *meze*; these are small entrée dishes like the Greek *mezede*, which can often be a meal in themselves. Ask to see the meze first; usually they are brought on a large tray for you to choose from. If not, go to the refrigerator, usually by the cash till, and have a look at what is on offer.

One other type of restaurant is the *lokanta*, which is a canteen-like place, with various pre-cooked dishes on view. You take a tray and point to what you want, normally receiving quite small portions. While these are generally not good value, they are sometimes a chance to sample some more unusual Turkish dishes.

An *Ocakbasi* is a place specializing in grilled meats. Ocak means 'hearth' and this is where you sit. The food is cooked on a long charcoal grill, usually topped by a grand old copper chimney cover. Go for the *cop sis* (pronounced 'chop shish'), small pieces of beef or lamb served on long, lethal-looking skewers.

The usual custom is to change venue for dessert, going to a café or pastry shop.

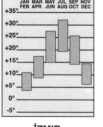

İSTANBUL

İZMIR

When to go
The mainland is generally hotter than the islands, with temperatures varying from around 20°C in April or November to 37°C in July/August. The main season runs from June to the start of October.

In İstanbul and Thrace snow is common between December and February, and rain for the two months either side of that cold spell. The weather is hot from mid-May to the end of October in these northern areas.

Religion
Turkey is a mainly Sunni Muslim country, with religion a serious part of most people's lives. When entering a mosque or other holy place you are required to show due respect by covering bare legs or shoulders; so no shorts, skimpy T-shirts or beachwear. You will also be asked to remove your shoes before entering such places. Women are also required to cover their hair; shawls for this purpose are usually available.

It is extremely bad manners to pass in front of someone while they are praying, so keep discreetly to the back of the mosque.

COUNTRY GUIDES

Introduction

It is indeed a grand entrance, the short strait that links the Mediterranean and the Atlantic. The Pillars of Hercules, for centuries believed to mark the end of the world, are two vast rocks, Gibraltar and Ceuta, either side of the strait between Europe and Africa. The ancient Greeks called them Calpi and Abyla and believed that they were joined until the demi-god Hercules tore them apart. It is likely that the first great seafarers, the Phoenicians, set tall columns on them as markers, hence their name. Beyond the Pillars in that wilder ocean the flat Earth rapidly ran out of ground and ceased to be; yet the early sailors followed the coastline north and south, the Phoenicians getting as far as Britain and, more remarkably, circumnavigating Africa; while Plato put the lost kingdom of Atlantis way out amid the Atlantic's giant rollers. In general, however, a certain darkness enveloped the ancient Mediterranean consciousness when thought went too far beyond the Strait. The Arab geographers later largely concurred, believing that the final edge was Cape Bojador, south of the Canary Islands on the west coast of Africa. According to Ibn Said, beyond that lay the Sea of Obscurity, where the world came to an abrupt end.

Yet, on the other side of the Strait, the Mediterranean world was immediately and triumphantly a place of great civilization and new beginnings. The southern coast of Spain and the northern coast of Morocco form a historical and geological bridge between the northern and southern shores of the sea and for centuries have seen armies, traders and migrants passing back and forth. The Phoenicians settled most of the present-day ports, followed by Carthaginians and then Romans. Later, one of the world's most advanced civilizations, Moorish Al-Andalus, controlled both sides of the Strait, giving the world a host of scientific and cultural treasures.

Today, the Western Mediterranean is in many ways a place of striking contradiction. It is both one of the sea's most developed regions for tourists and one of its poorest: an estimated three million north European holiday-homers now live along its Spanish shores, while Andalucía remains one of Europe's poorest regions. The barrier there between Europe and North Africa is also now greater than it has ever been, yet this is the region that owes most to its southern Moorish neighbours. You'll also come across fusion, in the cuisine and the music, the way of life and the history, making for a great cultural vibrancy. In the north, Barcelona and the Balearics are some of the liveliest places in the Mediterranean with a rich entertainment scene alongside world-class artistic achievements.

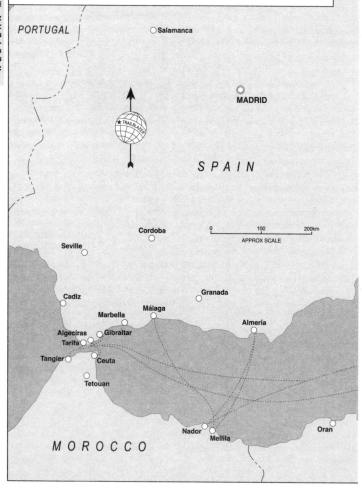

The Western Mediterranean

FERRY ROUTES

PORTUGAL

○ Salamanca

○ MADRID

S P A I N

TRAILBLAZER

Cordoba
○

0   100   200km
APPROX SCALE

Seville
○

Cadiz
○

○ Granada

Marbella   Málaga
Algeciras ○ Gibraltar   ○   ○   Almería
Tarifa ○○   ○
Tangier ○   Ceuta
○
Tetouan

Nador   Oran
○   ○
Melilla

M O R O C C O

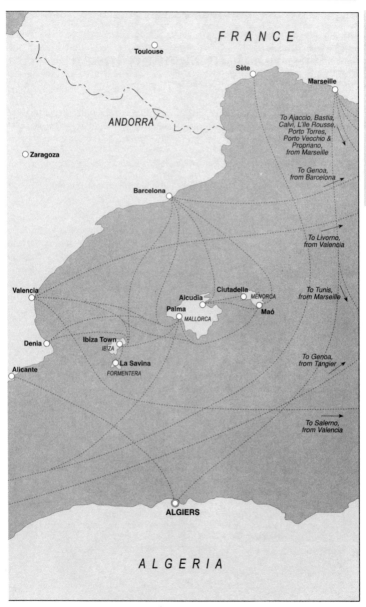

WESTERN MEDITERRANEAN

TRAVELLING THROUGH THE WESTERN MEDITERRANEAN

While regrettably there are no ferries these days linking Barcelona to the southern ports of Spain and Morocco, the journey between them is still fairly straightforward when going overland by frequent trains or buses. Likewise, with the civil conflict in neighbouring Algeria, there is no link between Morocco and Tunisia except by air, or via a lengthy journey south, through subequatorial Africa and then north again through Libya.

If you wish to combine your tour of the Western Med with a visit to some of the ports of the Tyrrhenian Sea, the best sea connection is from Barcelona to Genoa (see p439).

SUGGESTED ITINERARIES

Note: where two times are quoted below the shorter one is for the fast ferry service and the longer one for the ferry.

Exploring the Balearics
A trip like this round the Balearics combines good nightlife with opportunities to chill out. Barcelona, a world-class city offering an architectural feast and non-stop nightlife, provides an interesting contrast with Menorca (capital Maó/Mahón, and Ciutadella), the quietest of the larger Balearic Islands. Palma on Mallorca is most notable for its cathedral whilst Ibiza Town is another place for nightlife, though it still has a few old streets worth wandering down. Formentera has several walking trails so, like Menorca, it provides an excellent chance to recover from any excesses.

The following is merely a suggested itinerary for a tour around the

---

❏ **Western Mediterranean — the highlights**
● **Rock of Gibraltar** – Dramatic views from an astonishing piece of geology; look out at both Africa and Europe from a town that's both British and Spanish.
● **Tangier** – A strange and evocative mixture of Europe and North Africa. The Medina is a must, while the interzone city of some of the 20th-century's most important writers and artists still lurks in the shadows.
● **Barcelona** – Sprawling, hectic, an architectural feast and an entertainment Mecca. Long since a favourite for northern European weekenders, it is also a cool place to set out from on any Mediterranean grand tour.
● **Las Fallas** – Valencia's manic fiesta, a pyrotechnic feast that comes close to an arsonist's idea of heaven. Massive bonfires light up this jumping Spanish city every 12-19 March, for reasons long lost, making Las Fallas the Med's most spectacular festival.
● **La Semana Sancta** – Holy week in Andalucía is a stunning mixture of eerie, hooded gothic and spectacular celebration. Cross-bearing penitents crowd the streets of Seville, Granada, and elsewhere for this Easter festival, while local neighbourhoods try to outdo each other in lugging 10-ton floats of the Virgin through the winding streets. One of the world's grandest pageants.

Balearics. Timetables of ferry services can be found in Appendix B, pp438-41. *Barcelona to Ciutadella (5 per week, 3hrs) or Maó/Mahón (daily, 5-9hrs); Ciutadella to Alcudia (daily, 60 mins), or Maó/Mahón to Alcudia (2-3 per week, 90 mins); overland to Palma; Palma to Ibiza Town (daily, 2-4$^{1}/_{2}$hrs); Ibiza Town to La Savina (daily, 25-60 mins); back to Ibiza Town (daily, 25-60 mins); Ibiza Town to Valencia (daily, 3hrs) or back to Barcelona (6 per week, 2-4hrs).*

Criss-crossing from Spain to Morocco
Málaga, birthplace of Picasso and Spain's most popular tourist destination, is a convenient starting point. Almería is dominated by its Moorish fort and has managed to stay relatively undeveloped. Melilla also has a fort worth seeing and is a good entry point to Morocco. Gibraltar, known for its rock, offers the British experience and easy access to Tangier, with its intriguing Medina and air of faded glamour. Ceuta, like Melilla, is a Spanish enclave on the North African coast and its Castilian streets and plazas provide a contrast to the jumble of most Moroccan towns.

The following is a suggested itinerary for a tour around southern Spain and Morocco. Timetables of ferry services can be found in Appendix B, pp438-41.

(Málaga to) Almería overland; Almería to Melilla (6 per week, 6-9$^{1}/_{2}$hrs); Melilla to Málaga (daily, 4-8hrs); overland to Gibraltar; Gibraltar to Tangier (daily, 80 mins); overland to Ceuta; Ceuta to Algeçiras (daily, 40-90 mins); overland to Málaga.

Western Mediterranean – ports and islands

Barcelona

AREA CODE: ☎ 93 **POPULATION**: 4 MILLION (METROPOLITAN AREA)

Barcelona has a buzz about it that no other city on the Iberian Peninsula can match. Sprawling, hectic, an architectural feast and an entertainment mecca, it has grabbed a reputation in the last 10 years as a premier European destination and a world-class city. Yet it has always been up there with the continent's greats, generating an enormous amount of creativity and energy, from Picasso to Gaudi.

Once the capital of Spain's short-lived revolutionary republic, the city is still the capital of Catalunya, the richest province of the Spanish kingdom, while also home to a nation seeking more autonomy of its own — the Catalans. One of the Mediterranean's greatest 'submerged' nations, they are historically quite distinct from the Castellanos, the Castilian Spanish. The language here is similar but different, forming closer bonds between Barcelonans and their neighbours in Languedoc and Provence to the north than to Madrid and Seville. Catalan nationalism is an obvious factor, though not as pronounced as Basque, lending the city an extra quality of individuality from the rest of the peninsula.

HISTORY
Legend has it that the city was founded by the Carthaginians, with the name coming

WESTERN MEDITERRANEAN

from the wealthy Barca family, whose scion, Hamilcar, was one of Carthage's greatest leaders and an ancestor of Hannibal. After the Roman victory in the Punic Wars (see p28), it was known as Colonia Faventia Julia Augusta Pia Barcino, a settlement making up in names for what it lacked in buildings. It remained little more than a fortified village until Emperor Augustus had a temple to himself built here, on the top of Mons Taber, now the Catalan Excursionist Centre.

Next came the Visigoths, who renamed the city Barcinona and kept control until the Moorish Islamic invasion of AD717. The Moors called the city Barjelinah. The Christian Emperor Charlemagne retook it in 801, setting the frontier of his Carolingian Empire at the River Ebro, well south of the city, with Barcelona being run by an appointed count. The Ebro was for long the frontier, too, between Moorish Islamic Spain and the Christian kingdoms of the north, though the border did shift back and forth as fortune changed. In 985, the city was sacked by al-Man-ir, the chief minister of the Umayyad caliphate of Cordoba, yet this proved a temporary loss as the counts of Barcelona regained control and began building Barcelona into a major Mediterranean

The corsairs

Along with the empire builder, the philosopher and the navigator, one of the central characters of Mediterranean history has undoubtedly been the corsair: long the scourge of the sea's shipping lanes, these buccaneers and pirates were the terror of many coastal communities, with Mediterranean raiders venturing at one point as far as Iceland in search of plunder.

These corsairs were also slave traders seldom operating completely alone but in groups. Many were given the active protection of particular governments or religious orders, making it largely a well-organized business with a multinational background.

It was also enormously successful: in Roman times, pirates were such a menace that corn supplies to Rome itself became difficult, prompting the Senate to commission Pompey in 67BC to lead a major sweep of the whole sea — from Gibraltar to Egypt. However, with the collapse of the Western Roman Empire, things reverted to the old ways. The Barbary coast, the stretch of North Africa incorporating modern-day Morocco, Algeria, Tunisia and Libya, became one of the most notorious havens for corsairs. Plenty of colourful characters operated out of Algiers, Tunis and Tripoli against Christian shipping lanes and territories. One of these was a Flemish captain, who took the Arabic name Murad Reis and led a famous slaving expedition to far off Baltimore, Ireland, in 1631.

The corsairs took full advantage of the conflict between Christians and Muslims, giving them new flags to sail under. Indeed, in many instances, by attacking the supply of only one faith they were assured the support and protection of the other.

Piracy became a little like terrorism today — a label used more often than not to describe one's enemies, while one's friends, who might be doing much the same thing, were given much more heroic-sounding titles. The Barbarossa brothers, two 16th-century Ottoman Greeks, one of whom ended up an admiral in the Sultan's navy, were known throughout the Christian world as ruthless pirates and renegades but are hailed to this day in Turkey as great naval strategists and commanders. Similarly, the Knights of St John, whose ships raided Muslim villages up and down the Anatolian and Middle Eastern coasts for slaves and plunder, are seen as glamorous and chivalrous heroes in Europe but as ruthless, bloodthirsty pirates in the Muslim world.

With this conflict dominating events throughout the Middle Ages and beyond, piracy continued to plague the Mediterranean right up to the 19th century, when the French invaded Algeria, sending the last of the Barbary pirates to the bottom in 1830.

port to rival Genoa and Venice. This was helped considerably to begin with by the 1137 union between Catalonia and Aragon, though not when the Catalan-Aragonese capital switched to Naples in 1442.

In 1469, however, through the marriage of Ferdinand of Aragon and Isabella of Castille, the rulers of the main kingdoms, Christian Spain emerged as a major European country before whose power the Moors gradually retreated until in 1492 their leader handed over the keys of Granada to Isabella of Spain (and Castille).

Catalunya made a major mistake in 1705 by backing the wrong horse in the War of the Spanish Succession. The Catalans supported the Austrian Archduke Charles III's claim to the Spanish throne, which led to an angry Philip V of Spain besieging Barcelona and abolishing Catalan independence on the city's fall in 1714.

A century later and the Peninsular War saw the city once again occupied, from 1808 to 1813, by the French. Napoleon's forces having been driven out by the British under Wellington, the city and the region underwent something of a rebirth. Barcelona became a centre for industrialization with a booming textiles sector. The population also soared, as did radical politics. The city became a hot bed of communist and anarchist agitation, with major uprisings occurring in 1835, the mid-1850s and in 1909. Semi-autonomy was granted by the Madrid government in 1913, which lasted until 1923. The Catalan question was a major factor in the lead-up to the Spanish Civil War, with Barcelona proclaiming an independent Catalan republic in 1931, after which Madrid granted even more autonomy to the region. With the fascist coup in 1936 and the start of the civil war, Barcelona rapidly became the most radical city in the world, largely controlled by massive anarchist and communist unions and political groups. The fall of Barcelona in 1939 marked the end of the war and victory for the fascist forces under General Franco.

Under his dictatorship, Catalunya lost almost all its independence, even the language itself being banned. It was not until Franco's death and major reforms in the Spanish state that such rights were returned, under a series of agreements signed in 1979 that secured Catalan self-government. Ironically, it has since been the Catalan nationalist conservatives who have run things, with the radical movements of the past now all but disappeared. Catalan parties have also played a 'king-maker' role in Spanish politics, while the region continues to dominate the Spanish economy. The Olympics came here in 1992, and the city is now fully established as a global arts capital.

WHAT TO SEE

Right at the bottom of La Rambla at the harbour front is a statue to **Christopher Columbus**, the great explorer. To the west are the medieval shipyards, the Drassanes, which now house the **Maritime Museum** (daily 1000-1900, €5). Inside is an excellent collection of naval memorabilia plus an entire 16th-century galley.

From here, head on up La Rambla and you'll be walking on one of the world's most famous streets. A mix of the grimly seedy and the wonderfully quaint, this pedestrianized avenue cuts straight through the heart of the **Ciutat Vella**, the old city. In the side streets off here lies another realm all its own — the **Barri Gòtic**, or Gothic Quarter. Best explored by day (at night it can get pretty dodgy), this area contains many fine 18th- and 19th-century apartment houses, cafés, restaurants and shops and is worth spending some time just wandering round. On the eastern flank, look out for the Gothic **cathedral** (daily 0830-1330 and 1700-1930), and the **Museu d'Història de la Ciutat** (Mon-Sat 1000-1400 and 1600-2000, Sun 1000-1400, €4); this is housed in the Palau Reial, the former residence of the counts of Barcelona. A little further east, near the Jaume metro stop, is the **Picasso Museum** (Tue-Sat 1000-2000, Sun 1000-1500, €4.50), 15-19, Carrer de Montcada. This houses an extraordinary collection of the artist's work, showing its development from figurative work to more abstract and including dozens of preliminary sketches for his most famous work, *Guernica*.

Come out of here and at the south end of the street you'll see the Gothic **Church**

WESTERN MEDITERRANEAN

of Santa Maria del Mar (daily 0900-1330, 1630-2000), one of the city's best loved. Towards the water from here, you'll stumble into a major dockland redevelopment complex, Maremagnum, which houses the usual collection of revitalization stalwarts, from multiplex cinemas to over-priced restaurants. There is, however, a quick exit: the cable-car (Téléferic) to Montjuïc. This leaves from Torre Sant Sebastia and crosses the harbour to the Torre Miramar, running from 1000 to 1800 and costing €3.50.

Montjuïc is a sprawling park and museum area, the site of the 1929 Barcelona International Fair. The centrepiece of this long-gone exhibition is the Palau Nacional, which now houses the Museu Nacional d'Art de Catalunya (Tue-Sat 1000-1900, €4.50). This has collections from a variety of historical periods; the Romanesque fresco section is excellent. Next door is the Museu d'Arqueologia (Tue-Sat 0930-1900, Sun 1000-1430, €3), which has a few Carthaginian relics worth looking out for, along with Roman and Etruscan artefacts. Also worth a look is the Fundació Joan Miró (Tue-Sat 1000-1900, Sun 1030-1430, €6.50), a museum dedicated to another of Catalunya's great artists. Inside are paintings and sculptures, many donated by Miró himself.

The Olympic Stadium from 1992 is also up here, along with its own museum (Tue-Sat 1000-1400 and 1600-1900, Sun 1000-1400, €2.50). Getting down can be a reasonable walk, but if your feet are beginning to ache, try the funicular railway, which takes you down to the Paral.lel metro station for €2.

From here, get into the metro and head for the Sagrada Família stop, well to the north. There you'll find one of the most bizarre cathedrals in all creation, La Sagrada Família (daily 0900-1800, €6), designed by Antoni Gaudi. Begun in 1882, it's still not finished, with its lumpy walls and inside-out arrangements way ahead of its time, while its tile and stone decorations and multiple rocketing towers give it a kind of seaside-sandcastle-meets-death-metal-album-cover kind of appeal. A narrow staircase leads to the top of one of the towers,

while a lift (an extra €2) will also get you there. Not one for vertigo sufferers.

If this has made you curious about Gaudi (it's unlikely anyone wouldn't be after this), there's a Gaudi Museum inside the cathedral showing how this sacred space was once used as a machine-gun range during the Civil War, and you should also head for the Parc Güeli (daily 1000-1800, free, nearest metro Lesseps) far to the north. There, Gaudi tackled landscaping, with varying degrees of success.

PRACTICAL INFORMATION
Orientation
Ferries arrive at the Estació Marítima at the bottom of Barcelona's most famous avenue, La Rambla. From here it's a short walk to the main budget accommodation areas and quite a number of the sights. From the airport, a frequent and rapid train service takes you to Barcelona Estació Sants, the main railway station, which is a metro hub.

The Barcelona metro is very efficient and has wonderful air conditioning, a reason in itself to use it on a sweltering, humid summer's day. However, on weekdays the metro shuts early (about 2300) though on Friday and Saturday nights it's open until 0200.

The main inter-city bus terminal is at Estació del Nord, near the metro Arc de Triomf station; another train arrival point for some European lines and inter-city connections is Estació de França (nearest metro Barceloneta, Line No 4).

Getting around the city is straightforward, with walking a good idea around the central area. However, be extra careful of bags and belongings, particularly in the Barri Gòtic and surrounding areas. Professional gangs of thieves work the tourists in these areas. If possible, carry only what you can fit in your pockets.

Services
The tourist information office (☎ 906 301 282) beneath Plaça de Catalunya is open daily 0900-2100. The staff dish out maps and are helpful. The major stations and the airport also have useful information bureaux. Look out too for red-coated infor-

mation officers in the main tourist areas; they should be able to answer most queries. Useful websites include 🖳 www.barcelonat urisme.com and www.barcelona-on-line.es.

The Book Store, 13, Carrer la Granja, or Itaca, 81, Rambla de Catalunya, has some **books** in English. The **left-luggage office** at Estació Marítima is open 0900-1300, 1600-2300, and charges a minimum of €2. The two main railway stations also have left-luggage lockers.

If you're interested in art, some of the best exhibitions are held at **MACBA** (Museu d'Art Contemporani) an impressive complex just west of La Rambla.

Ferries   [see p439 for full details]
Balearics Trasmediterránea (☎ 443 2532), Estació Marítima, operates a daily service to **Palma** and **Maó/Mahón**. Between June and September Umafisa offers a daily service to **Ibiza** and Baleària has one to **Maó/Mahón**.

Genoa Grandi Navi Veloci (☎ 443 9898) have their agent at Moll de Penont, next to Estació del Port (the port railway station). The boat goes twice a week in January, three times a week in February and March, four times a week the rest of the year.

Trains
Barcelona is a major rail centre. Trains run regularly to France for connections to the rest of the continent; there are also frequent services to Madrid, including overnight sleepers. Trains to the south are also available via Valencia, with sleepers recommended as the service can be slow, though it's comfortable. Tickets are available from the main stations or travel agents.

Buses
The Estació del Nord bus station information desk (☎ 265 6508) is open daily 0700-1900. There are daily buses to most cities in Spain and some international services. A bus to Granada takes 13-15 hours and costs €50.

Planes
Barcelona Airport is 14km south-west of town. Trains link it to Barcelona Sants railway station or Catalunya metro station, at the top of La Rambla, every half-hour. Tickets cost €2.50. The Aerobus also does the trip from Plaça de Catalunya in 15 minutes for €3.50. A taxi costs around €15.

Where to stay
Youth Hostel Barcelona Mar (☎ 324 8530; 🖳 www.youthostel-barcelona.com), 80 Carrer Sant Pau. New place: clean and modern. Range of rooms from singles to 16-bed dorms; dorm beds €18-23. Open 24 hrs.
Kabul Hostel (☎ 318 5190; 🖳 www .kabul.es), 17 Plaça Reial, Barri Gòtic, just off La Rambla so excellent location. Dorm beds €15-20. Open 24hrs and very popular.
Gothic Point (☎ 268 7808; 🖳 www.gothicp oint.com), 5 Carrer Vigatans. Sgl/dbl modules in dorms; €21; popular; located 30m from Jaume 1 metro station.
Pensión Europa (☎ 318 7620), 18 Carrer Boquiera. €18/30 sgl/dbl, showers extra.
Hostal Lausanne (☎ 302 1139), 24 Avda Portal de l'Angel, near Plaça de Catalunya. €23/40 sgl/dbl.
Hostal Nuevo Colon (☎ 319 5077), 19, Avda Marqués de l'Argentera, near Estació de França. Good sgl/dbl €20/35.
Hostal Sofia (☎ 419 5040), 1-3, Avda de Roma. Near Barcelona Sants and thus good for late-night arrivals; €25/50 sgl/dbl.
Hostal Gat Raval (☎ 481 6670; 🖳 www.gat accommodation.com), 44 Joaquín Costa. Hip hotel near MACBA. €39/60 sgl/dbl.

For **camping** try *Masnou* (☎ 555 1503), some 200m from Masnou station, which is a 15-minute ride from Sants or Plaça de Catalunya.

Where to eat
Eating is a real pleasure here, with a wide variety of wholesome fare on offer. Most cafés and older-style bars serve *tapas* (small snacks or dishes) that can be a meal in themselves, while the *menu del día* (menu of the day: three courses with wine) is excellent value. Available only at lunchtime from certain restaurants and cafés it's usually advertised outside on a blackboard. The cheapest should be about €6.50. In Barcelona, as in the rest of Spain, people eat out late in the evenings — a not untypical time for dinner might be 2200.   *(Continued on p98)*

WESTERN MEDITERRANEAN

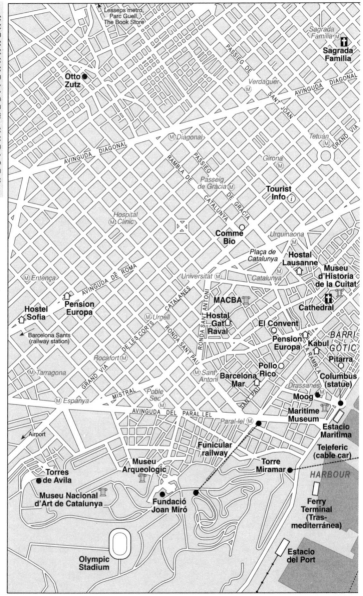

Lesseps metro,
Parc Guell,
The Book Store

Otto
Zutz

Sagrada
Familia

Sagrada
Familia

PASSEIG DE

Verdaguer

AVINGUDA

DIAGONAL

SANT JOAN

AVINGUDA DIAGONAL

Diagonal

Tetuán

GRAN VIA

RAMBLA DE CATALUNYA

PASSEIG DE GRACIA

Girona

Passeig
de Gràcia

Tourist
Info

Hospital
Clínic

Comme
Bio

Urquinaona

Plaça de
Catalunya

Hostal
Lausanne

Museu
d'Historia
de la Cuitat

AVINGUDA DE ROMA

Entença

Universitat

Catalunya

MACBA

Hostel
Sofia

Pension
Europa

CATALANES

RONDA SANT ANTONI

Cathedral

Urgell

Hostal
Gat
Raval

El Convent

BARRI
GOTIC

DE LES CORTS

RONDA SANT PAU

Barcelona Sants
(railway station)

Pension
Europa

Kabul

Pitarra

Rocafort

Pollo
Rico

Columbus
(statue)

Tarragona

GRAN VIA

Sant
Antoni

Barcelona
Mar

Drassanes

MISTRAL

Poble
Sec

SANT PAU

Moog

Espanya

AVINGUDA DEL PARAL.LEL

Paral-lel

Maritime
Museum

Estacio
Maritima

Funicular
railway

Teleferic
(cable car)

Airport

Torre
Miramar

HARBOUR

Museu
Arqueologic

Torres
de Avila

Ferry
Terminal
(Tras-
mediterránea)

Museu Nacional
d'Art de Catalunya

Fundació
Joan Miró

Estacio
del Port

Olympic
Stadium

WESTERN MEDITERRANEAN

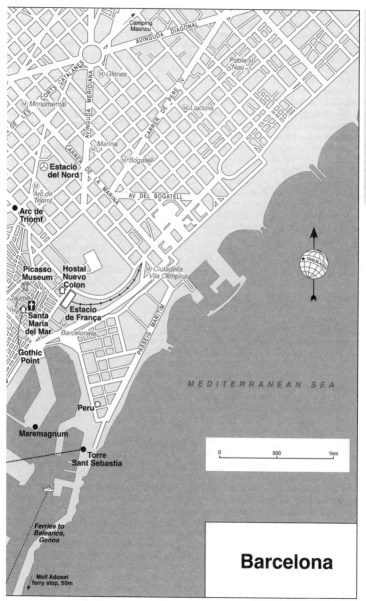

Camping Masnou

AVINGUDA DIAGONAL

CORTS CATALANES

Poble Nou Ⓜ

Ⓜ Glories

AVINGUDA MERIDIANA

Ⓜ Monumental

CARRER DE PERE IV

Ⓜ Llacuna

CARRER DE LA MARINA

Marina

Ⓜ Bogatell

Estació del Nord

Ⓜ Arc de Triomf

AV DEL BOGATELL

● Arc de Triomf

Picasso Museum

Hostal Nuevo Colon

Ⓜ Ciutadella Vila Olimpica

Jaume I

Estacio de França

Santa Maria del Mar

Ⓜ Barceloneta

Gothic Point

PASSEIG MARITIM

★ TRAILBLAZER

MEDITERRANEAN SEA

Peru ○

● Maremagnum

● Torre Sant Sebastia

0   500   1km

Ferries to Balearics, Genoa

Moll Adosat ferry stop, 50m

Barcelona

(Cont'd from p95) There are also many street and municipal markets offering high-quality budget food. The Mercat Sant Josep, off La Rambla, is a classic example. The following prices are per head for an evening meal.

El Convent, 3, Carrer Jerusalem. Quality Catalan food for around €15.

Llar del Filador, 13, Carrer Cortines. In an old workshop in the Barri Gòtic, open till 0130 with a full meal for around €13.

Pollo Rico, 31, Carrer de Sant Pau. Chicken specialities and budget prices; €5.

Peru, 10, Passeig de Bourbon in Barceloneta. A good range of seafood; €12.

Pitarra, 56, Carrer d'Avinyó in the Barri Gòtic. Serving Catalan specialities since 1890; €13, closed Sundays.

Comme Bio, Via Layetana in Barri Gòtic. A veggie staple, with good fills for €12.

Bars

Barcelona has a wide variety of nightlife, with more bars than can possibly be mentioned, along with hundreds of clubs. Good places to look are the Spanish-language listings magazine *Guía del Ocio*, which comes out weekly, or *Time Out*.

Otherwise, *Moog*, 3, Arc del Teatre, is good on Sundays and Wednesdays for techno, *Otto Zutz*, 15, Carrer Lincoln in Gracia, is a huge bar that turns into a club at 0200, (open Tue-Sat), while *Torres de Avila*, Avinguda Marqués de Comillas in Montjuïc, is a cosmopolitan joint (open Thu-Sat). The list goes on but one of the pleasures of Barcelona is finding a good place by chance, and there are plenty of other bars and cafés around if one doesn't appeal.

The Balearics

AREA CODE: ☎ 0971 **POPULATION:** 702,770 + 3 MILLION TOURISTS IN SUMMER.

For long almost synonymous with mass tourism and the blueprint for holiday resorts the world over, Mallorca (Majorca),

---

Crossing to the Balearics

It takes three hours forty five minutes for the Trasmediterránea fast ferry to make the trip from Palma to Barcelona, cutting at true *alta velocidad* through the normally calmish waters of the north-western Med.

Inside, its designers have tried to fashion something between an airplane and a cruise ship, with the usual mixed results. In the Aegean, there's the Greek, Soviet-era rocket boat, its large afterburner giving it the look of something that might have been dropped there by *Thunderbird-2*. From Malta to Sicily, there's the dawn hydrofoil, roaring across the straits in a confident burst of efficiency and well-labelled Maltese smartness, only to have to get down and dirty in the tatty side docks of a Sicilian harbour.

Yet here, between Barcelona and the Balearics, the high speed cutter remains somehow king. Never mind the blurry, too-many-bars-the-night-before fog that sometimes accompanies a crossing, nor the annoyingly twee Hollywood romantic comedies dubbed into Catalan playing in the movie hall (the Maltese seem to favour bloody historical epics for their fast ferry, while the whole concept of onboard movies has yet to penetrate the Eastern Med), this ferry is the business.

Perhaps, it's the hot milky coffee they serve, a life saver after an all-nighter on the island. Or just the fact that soon, you realize, you're going to be in what many consider the most exciting city in the world. Well, perhaps you can strike out that last bit, but Barcelona is good. Very good.

Coming into the harbour, with the city spread out ahead, get to a window because the first sight of the city, especially in the early hours, is not to be missed. Something special there, and even right out on the water, you can sometimes feel the city stir, that buzz on the horizon line. And next thing, you've arrived.

Menorca, Ibiza and Formentera have suffered the slings and arrows of outrageous development for much of the last 30 years; despite all this they've maintained a certain distinctiveness and even charm. Yet let there be no doubt, apart from Mallorca, which is just about large enough to come up with something other than beach bars, this is Mediterranean mass tourism at its most in-your-face. Everything, even if marketed as places the 'tourists don't know about', is part of the package.

HISTORY

The talayots, ancient stone towers that gave their name to a prehistoric period, are the earliest evidence of human habitation on the islands. This native civilization goes back around 2600 years but was superseded by Phoenicians, Carthaginians and then Romans. The Vandals got here in AD526, followed by the Byzantines in 534. The Moorish invasion then followed, with the islands coming under the rule of the Islamic crescent by 903. The Moors stayed till 1229, when the Aragonese took the islands, though they later granted them autonomous status in 1298, with the islands' Catalan population enjoying the benefits of the Catalan-Aragonese joint kingdom. In 1349 though, the autonomy was revoked and the Balearics became part of Aragon itself.

Not much of world-shattering import happened after that until the War of the Spanish Succession, when the British captured Mahón, the largest town on Menorca, in 1708. Under the Treaty of Utrecht the island was given to Britain, with rule from London lasting nearly a century, till 1802. Passed around during the Napoleonic wars, the islands were all finally taken by Spain in 1833. It was not until some 150 years later that they regained their autonomous status, having been tied to the Catalan nationalist and republican Spanish causes for most of the 19th and 20th centuries.

Tourism developed rapidly during the 1970s, though people had been visiting the islands since the 19th century. Until then, the islanders had shunned the beaches and coastal areas as they were too susceptible to attacks by pirates. Now, the reverse is the case, with most people living on the coast. Many of these are British or German residents who have moved en masse to the islands, buying their place in the sun.

WHAT TO SEE
Mallorca (Majorca)

The major urban sprawl here is the bay of **Palma**, the island capital, which is solid concrete for most of its length, punctuated by tarmac. The city of Palma does have something going for it though, particularly the **cathedral**, which houses a small **museum** (open daily 0930-1900, €3). Gaudi (see Barcelona p94) designed some of the internal features. Nearby is the **Museu de Mallorca** (same hours, €2.50), which has a good collection of items outlining the island's history, one episode of which is still visible in the Banys Árabs — the Moorish baths in Carrer de Can Sera.

That done, head for the hills, or more precisely, the **Serra de Tramuntana**. These mountains run along the island's north-west coast up to Cap Formentor and are accessible by the Palma–Soller train, which departs from Plaça España station. Soller is worth a stay and is a centre for hiking on the island. Look out for the brochure covering walking routes there, available from the tourist office.

As for **beaches**, the village of Cala Mondrago is a good option, though Ses Arenas and Es Trenc, near the tourist resort of Colonia San Jordi, are better.

Ibiza

Ibiza Town is the island's most picturesque place, with streets of old houses to wander through, although most of them are now selling stuff to the tourists. Frankly, this is not an island for sightseeing, but for entertainment, with a typical day starting late on the beach at Es Cabellet or the nearer Figueretas, the latter next to town, the former a short bus trip away. It's then off for a bit of shopping, with souvenir places open till late, followed by a meal, then on to the first bar.

The port area is hip and immensely expensive, while other areas are less hip but still immensely expensive. Clubs open only at around midnight. Spanish and Catalan towns are used to epic clubbing sessions,

WESTERN MEDITERRANEAN

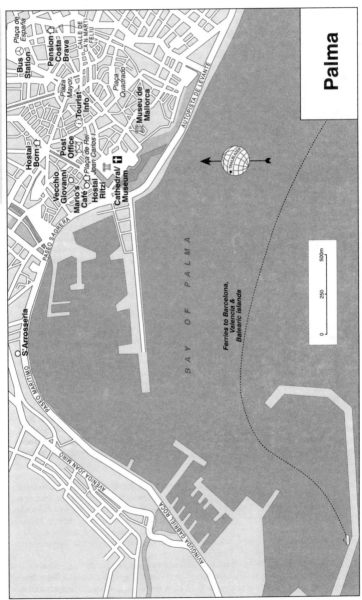

WESTERN MEDITERRANEAN

Palma

Plaça de España
Bus Station
Pension Costa Brava
CALLE DE CAN MARTI FELIU
Hostal Born
Plaça Mayor
Tourist Info
Plaça Quadrado
Museu de Mallorca
Post Office
Vecchio Giovanni
Mario's Café
Plaça de Rei
Hostal Jean Carlos
Ritzi
Cathedral/Museum
AUTOPISTA DE LEVANTE
TRAIL BLAZER
PASEO SAGRERA
S'Arrosseria
PASEO MARITIMO
AVENIDA JOAN MIRO
AVINGUDA GABRIEL ROCA

BAY OF PALMA

Ferries to Barcelona, Valencia & Balearic islands

0   250   500m

with the very civilized custom of opening some cafés around 0500 so that hot chocolate and sweet doughy pastries can revitalize the revellers. Particularly hard nuts can, of course, order more drinks for breakfast. If budget is a problem, probably you shouldn't be here to start with, but if you are, getting a few cans and sitting on the beach is your main option. You'll still be able to dance, with the Ibiza beat deafening till way into the early hours.

Menorca
Much the quietest of the larger islands, Menorca is a banana-shaped land with Mahón (Maó) the capital at one end and Ciutadella at the other. Mahón is an odd combination of styles, with the century of British occupation leaving some strangely cast-up Georgian mansions among the Mediterranean mansions. Centred on Plaça España, the town has some interesting staircased streets and good views as it rises up above the harbour. Also useful is a harbour boat trip, which usually takes in the Xoriguer gin distillery and its free samples.

Exploring the rest of the island isn't so easy as bus services run infrequently between Mahón and Ciutadella and hardly at all to anywhere else. Hitching could be your best option. The central Monte Toro mountain is a good place to size up the land and, if the weather's right, to catch a glimpse of Mallorca, off in the distance. Around the interior you'll also find plenty of examples of the ancient talayotic stone towers.

You really need a car to get to the beaches, with La Vall, near Ciutadella, a good stretch, along with the sands surrounding Santa Galdana.

Formentera
Across a short strait from Ibiza, Formentera has tried to resist the spread of mass tourism with greater success than the other islands, though partly this is because it is almost completely barren. Nevertheless, as a day trip from Ibiza it provides a more beautiful setting for the post-bar/club detox. The 2km hiking path from the La Savina–Es Pujols highway finishes with a swim across to the islet of S'Espalmador, with some excellent

stretches of sand. There are numerous other paths too, with a walking guide available from the tourist office.

PRACTICAL INFORMATION
Orientation
Boats from Barcelona arrive at **Palma** harbour, which is some 3.5km west of town. Bus No 1 takes you back and forth. On Ibiza, the ferry docks at **Ibiza Town** ferry terminal, a more impressive arrival as the town walls and streets are right ahead as you dock. On Menorca, you'll arrive in **Mahón** harbour, again right in the heart of town. Ibiza–Formentera boats dock at **La Savina**, a tiny harbour with a correspondingly tiny village attached. Travel between the islands is over priced, as is accommodation, food and entertainment.

Getting around is straightforward enough on Mallorca and Ibiza, with bus services between the major towns, along with just about every other conceivable mode of transport, from paragliders to donkeys. Walking can also be a pleasure in the spring and autumn. Travelling on Menorca and Formentera is a bit trickier, with few services. On these, hiring your own transport is advised, or hitching.

Services
There are **tourist offices** on each island: **Mallorca** (☎ 7720 251, 🖳 www.mallorcao nline.com), 2, Plaça de la Reina, in the heart of Palma, has loads of maps, accommodation lists and timetables; **Ibiza** (☎ 301 900; 🖳 www.total-ibiza.com), 13 Vara de Rey; **Menorca** (☎ 363 790; 🖳 www.e-menorca. org), on Plaça de la Esplanada, Mahón; **Formentera** (☎ 322 057) on the harbour side in La Savina.

Ferries [see pp438-40 for full details]
Barcelona Trasmediterránea (national enquiry service ☎ 902-454645), Estación Marítima, 2, Muelle de Paraires, Palma, offers a daily service (both ferry and fast ferry) from **Palma** and **Maó/Mahón**.

Between the islands Baleària has daily fast ferries between **Palma and Ibiza** (Baleària also has a ferry service). Trasmediterránea has a weekly ferry between **Palma and Mahón**. Baleària has daily ferry and fast-ferry services between **Ibiza and La Savina**, Formentera.

Valencia Baleària and Trasmed also have regular services from Ibiza and Palma to Valencia; Trasmed has a weekly service from Maó/Mahón via Palma.

Buses
The main bus station in **Palma** is on Plaça d'España, with regular services to Inca, Soller, Deia and other larger settlements. The tourist office also hands out bus timetables in English.

Avenida d'Isidoro Macabich is the main street for bus stops in **Ibiza Town**; a timetable is available from the tourist office. Services run to major settlements only.

TMSA, the bus company on **Menorca**, operates several services a day between Mahón and Ciutadella, connecting to the major coastal tourist resorts.

Infrequent services connect the main towns on **Formentera**; an alternative is to consider cycling. A bike can be rented for €4-8 a day from any agency in La Savina.

Planes
In summer, the skies are thick with charter planes descending from northern European destinations. On Mallorca, the airport is connected to Plaça d'España in Palma by the half-hourly bus No 17 (€3), while a taxi is around €18. On Ibiza, buses run every hour to the airport and cost around €1, while a taxi would be €12. On Menorca the only way to town is hitching or grabbing a cab for around €9.

Where to stay
On all the Balearic Islands, accommodation is difficult to find in season and expensive. The season is also fairly long, often from Easter to the end of October. The upshot is, book ahead if at all possible, or try **camping**.

Mallorca *Hostal Ritzi* (☎ 714 610), 6, Carrer Apuntadores, Palma. Good rooms with sgl/dbl for €15/30.
Pensión Costa Brava (☎ 711 729), 16,

Carrer Marti Feliu, Palma. An old favourite; €10/20 sgl/dbl.
Hotel Born (☎ 712 942), 3, Carrer de Sant Jaume, Palma. For a little more opulence; €45/75 sgl/dbl.
Camping Club Picafort (☎ 537 863), on the north coast, 9km south of Port d'Alcudia. A good option.

Ibiza *Hotel Montesol* (☎ 310 161), 2, Paseo Vara de Rey. A good choice in Ibiza Town; sgl/dbl for €25/45.
Hostal Sol y Brisa (☎ 310 818), 15, Avda de Bartomeu Vicent Ramón. Sgl/dbl €20/50.
Casa de Huéspedes Navarro (☎ 310 825), 20, Carrer de la Cruz, Ibiza Town. Some harbour views; €15/30 sgl/dbl.
Cala Nova Campsite (☎ 331 774), 500m north of Cala Nova and near a good beach.

Formentera *Hostal La Savina* (☎ 322 279), 23, Avda Mediterránea, La Savina, overlooking the lake. The town's only practical choice; €40/80 for sgl/dbl.
Hostal Tahiti (☎ 328 122), Playa Pujols. Popular; €35/65 sgl/dbl.
Camping is not allowed.

Menorca *Hostal la Isla* (☎ 366 492), 4, Carrer Santa Catalina, Mahón. Sgl/dbl €35/65.
Hostal Orsi (☎ 364 751), 19, Carrer de la Infanta, Mahón. A welcoming atmosphere; €30/45 sgl/dbl.
Campers should try *Cala Galdana*, 10km south of Ferreries but it is open only in the summer.

Where to eat
Mallorca *S'Arrosseria*, 13, Passeig Marítimo, Palma. Good local dishes and classics for €10.
Vecchio Giovanni, 1, Carrer Sant Joan, Palma. Good for lunchtime menus and other deals; €10.
Mario's Café, Carrer de la Mar, Palma. Pizza and pasta from €6.50.

Ibiza *Ca'n Costa*, 19, Carrer de la Cruz, Ibiza Town. Good wholesome fare; €10.
Comidas Bar San Juan, 8, Carrer Montgri, Ibiza Town. Good value servings; €6.

Menorca Mahón is the home of mayonnaise, a factor in many of its tastier tapas.
Ca'n Sintes, Carrer Cami des Castell, Mahón. Good Catalan dishes; €10.
Roma, 295 Andén de Levante, Mahón. Good pizzas and pastas; €5.

Formentera *Casa Rafal*, Sant Francesco Xavier, La Savina, has good stuff for €7.50 on an island with few culinary delights beyond standard international hotel cuisine.

Valencia

AREA CODE: ☎ 96 POPULATION: 800,000
Overlooking a broad gulf and surrounded by hills, Valencia has a well-deserved reputation for holding one of the most spectacular – and maddest – festivals in the Mediterranean, Las Fallas. It's also well located for trips to and from the neighbouring Balearic Islands. With a lively nightlife, it also has a good spread of museums and cultural events, making it a city of growing importance on Spain's Mediterranean coast – with northern rival Barcelona well in its sights. The city's Ciudad de las Artes y de las Ciencias, a complex containing interactive museums, an IMAX cinema, an oceanographic park and an arts centre, is also a major international venue.

HISTORY
Established by the Romans in 138BC, Valencia later fell to the Visigoths and then the Moors, becoming the capital of the Moorish kingdom of Valencia in 1021. A few decades later, enter El Cid, one of Spain's most famous medieval figures, who captured the city for Christendom in 1089. He was to rule it until his death in the city in 1099. The Moors recaptured the place three years later.
In 1238, however, Jaime 1 of Aragon arrived to take over, though the kingdom of Valencia remained more or less independent until the end years of the *Reconquista* – the Spanish reconquest of the Iberian Peninsula from the Moors.

It became part of the unified Spanish and Portuguese kingdom in 1479. Emerging as an important Mediterranean entrepôt during the era of Spain's global empire, it then fell seriously out of favour at the dawn of the 18th century when it supported the losing side in the War of Spanish Succession.
Valencia always had something of a rebel streak though, something that featured again during the Spanish Civil War, when it became capital of the republican government from 1936-37.
Many Valencianos today see themselves as quite a distinct breed, with their own language, Valenciano, which is closer to Catalan than Castilian Spanish. The region has its own autonomous status, and autonomous character.

WHAT TO SEE
Instituto Valenciano de Arte Moderno (IVAM) focuses on 20th-century art and has permanent collections as well as temporary exhibitions. It includes the Julio González Centre, opened in 1989, and the Sala de la Muralla ('Wall Room'), with remains of the city's old medieval fort. **La Ciudad de las Artes y de las Ciencias**, open daily 1000-2100, is also a must. Look out for **L'Hemisfèric**, which has a planetarium, IMAX cinema, laser show, and the **Museo de las Ciencias Príncipe Felipe** (☎ 974 500), 48, Piazza de la Alameda. There's also the Parque Oceanografico and the Palacio de las Artes, also worth taking in. Entry charge: adults €9-19, children €7-13.
Forget Indiana Jones. It's claimed that the much-coveted Holy Grail, the cup Christ drank from at the Last Supper, and which is thought to have miraculous powers, is actually right here and on view to the public (but see also p133). The chalice is in the Gothic Capilla del Santo Caliz, with the **Cathedral and Diocesan Museum** lying beyond this.
The cathedral itself is a mix of styles, while there are also some important paintings in the chapel La Capilla de San Fransisco de Borja, which includes two strong canvases by Francisco de Goya, painted in 1799, of Saint Francis de Borja taking leave of his family and attending a

WESTERN MEDITERRANEAN

dying man. The museum is open daily 1000-1300, 1630-1930, entrance €1.50.

PRACTICAL INFORMATION
Orientation
The main part of the city is bordered to the north by the Antiguo Cauce del Rio Turia ('Old Course of the River Turia') and to the south by the Nuevo Cauce ('The New course'). The port is to the east of the old course, down Avenida del Puerto. The walls of the Old Quarter were demolished in order to make way for a ring road (Calle Guillem de Castro, Calle Xativa and Calle Colon).

Both the main railway station (Estación del Norte) and the bus station border the old riverbed to the north. The former is on Calle Rivelles la Trinidad, the latter is further west on Avenida Menéndez Pidal. The tram connects the port with the city centre and Las Arenas. A bus runs every 15 minutes (06.30-22.45, Mon to Fri) from the airport to the centre; the journey takes 45 minutes, the fare is €1.

Services The main **tourist information office** (☎ 398 6422, open Mon to Sat) is at 48, Calle de la Paz but the branch at 1, Plaza del Ayuntamiento may be more convenient. A website worth looking at is 🖳 www.turisvalencia.es.

The main **post office** (24, Plaza del Ayuntamiento) is open weekdays 0830-2030, and 0930-1400 on Saturdays.

Ferries   [see p441 for full details]
Trasmediterránea (☎ 902-454 645), Estación Marítima, has frequent services to **Mahón** and **Palma** and a weekly service to **Menorca**. Grimaldi (☎ 306 1300), 310-1, Avda del Puerto, has a weekly ferry to **Livorno** and **Salerno**.

Trains
Trains go from Norte station to Almería, Málaga, Barcelona, and most other cities in Spain. For details of services visit the Renfe website (🖳 www.renfe.es).

Buses
EMT (🖳 www.emtvalencia.com) operates local bus services.

Planes
Manises Airport (☎ 159 8500) is 8km from the city centre. There are both charter and scheduled flights from many destinations; however, not all scheduled flights go direct to Valencia.

Where to stay
Hotel Alkazar (☎ 351 5551), 11, Mossén Femades. Sgl for €40, dbl €60 in this basic, air-conditioned, one-star stopover.
Alberge Ciudad de Valencia (☎ 392 5100; 🖳 www.alberguedevalencia.com), 17, Balmes. Well-placed, near the heart of town, this friendly youth hostel has beds for €12 a night and cooking facilities.
Alberge Juvenil La Paz (☎ 369 0152, 🖳 alberguecmlapaz@planalfa.es) 69, Avda del Puerto. Located in a pretty seedy part of town, it is nevertheless run by very welcoming and multi-lingual staff. Rates are €10-20 a bed.
Camping y Bungalows Puzol (☎ 146 5806, 🖳 www.campingpuzol.com), Playa de Puzol, off the main Barcelona highway, north of Valencia; €4 per person and €4.60 per tent. Next to the beach, with two pools of its own. Also offers 4-person mobile homes for €70 a night.

Where to eat
The Valencian paella, with rice, chicken, rabbit and green vegetables, is the typical local dish. Go to Las Arenas area for this.

Nightlife
Plaza de Xuquer and Avenida de Aragon are the areas for bar life, along with Canovas, El Carmen and Juan Llorens. These have a variety of venues opening till late, but for later still, try Avenida Blasco Ibanes. It's there that the big clubs operate, going till morning. Valencia prides itself on its nightlife, and is *muy movida*, as the saying goes – basically, 'jumping'.

However, if you have any chance at all of being there between 12 and 19 March, take it. This is the time of Las Fallas de San José, for many the most outstanding fiesta in the Mediterranean. It is certainly one of the most crazy, with neighbourhoods competing to build giant bonfires – often in the form of enormous papier-mâché figures — which are then set on fire on the final day to the accompaniment of an awesome fireworks display. Meanwhile, the whole town parties, except for the fire brigade, who every year end up trying to minimize the damage to surrounding buildings.

Almería

AREA CODE: ☎ 0950 **POPULATION:** 125,000
Capital of Spain's hottest region, Almería sits sweltering on the coast while inland the landscape is so desert-like it was an obvious candidate for the filming of *Lawrence of Arabia*. Long a powerful city of the kingdom of Al-Andalus (see p106), it is still dominated by a massive Moorish fortress. The Moors named Almería al-Mariyah, meaning Mirror of the Sea, and its coast and beaches do sometimes still live up to such a name. The region's relative lack of tourist development and long summers also mean visiting in spring or autumn is a pleasant experience, away from the nearby Costa del Sol.

HISTORY
Originally Phoenician, then Carthaginian, its Roman name was Urci, or Portus Magnus. In the mid-8th century it fell to the Moors, becoming part of the Caliphate of Cordoba. Rebuilt and fortified, it withstood repeated Castilian Spanish attempts to take it until 1489, when it fell to *Los Reyes Catolicos*, Ferdinand and Isabella, the two Spanish rulers who were to complete the final destruction of Moorish Spain, the Moorish leader handing over the keys of the city of Granada to Isabella of Castille in 1492.

However, centuries of Spanish rule have not entirely done away with the town's Moorish flavour, with a distinctly Moroccan feel to many of the streets and alleys, a feature perhaps enhanced in recent years by the large numbers of Moroccan immigrants who now live here. In modern times, the region's lack of irrigation has kept out the
· developers, with only recent moves being made to expand the tourist economy into

the Costa de La Luz ('The Coast of Light'), of which Almería forms the centre.

WHAT TO SEE
Almería's principal draw is the **Alcazaba** (daily 1000-1400, 1730-2030, €1.50), built in 773 on the orders of the Emir of Cordoba and later refortified in the 10th century. From its battlements, the whole coast can be seen, with good views out over the town as well. Head back down and the Gothic **cathedral** (Mon-Fri 1000-1700, Sat 1000-1300, Sun services only, €1.80) is probably the next port of call. It was built in the form of a fortress between 1524 and 1543, a testament to the town's continued vulnerability to attack from the sea.

Elsewhere, worth a wander round is the **Barrio de la Chanca**, where there are a number of cave houses and storerooms.

To get further afield the best bet is to head for the bus station. There are frequent services to **Mojácar**, a wonderful town of whitewashed cubic houses gathered round a rocky outcrop a few kilometres inland to the east of Almería. Around here you'll also find the best **beaches**, between Carboneras and La Garrucha. If planning to stay in Mojácar, try *Pensión La Luna* (☎ 478 032), 15, Calle Estación Nueva, in the town; singles/doubles for €35/60. *Bahía* (☎ 475 010), down at the beach on Paseo Mediterraneo, charges €20/40 singles/doubles. In summer, **camping** is permitted on the beach at Mojácar Playa. *Restaurante El Viento del Desierto* can provide a good meal for €10.

Some 25km inland from Almería in the desert is **Mini-Hollywood** (€3), a Wild West film set used to shoot a number of spaghetti westerns back in the 1970s, including *A Fistful of Dollars*. Gunfights are held regularly on its main street.

PRACTICAL INFORMATION
Orientation
The harbour for Morocco ferries is close to town, with the main **Paseo de Almería** heading up from here to the central **Puerta de Purchena**. Streets largely run parallel to the coast, with the *pensión* district between the **train station**, **bus station** and town centre. Getting around Almería is easy on foot.

WESTERN MEDITERRANEAN

Al-Andalus

Of all the Mediterranean's lost kingdoms, Al-Andalus must surely be one of the most widely lamented. During its golden age, it produced some of the most beautiful architecture and most important medical and astronomical discoveries in the world, as well as classic works of geography and some of the best medieval travel writing anywhere. In the 11th and 12th centuries the Moors of Andalus journeyed the lands of the Mediterranean, the Balkans and North Africa, keeping alive much of the ancient knowledge of the Roman and Greek worlds, and the Arabic too.

A result of the Islamic conquest of Spain in the 7th century, Al-Andalus came into its own under 'Abd ar-Rahman III in 929. Originally, it covered the entire Iberian Peninsula, though it shrank back over the centuries through successive military defeats in the process of Christian reconquest. By the time it came to an end in 1492, only the city of Granada and its surrounding hills remained.

However, it did produce an impressive hall of fame. Among the favoured sons of Cordoba, Al-Andalus' capital, were 'Abbas ibn Firnas, who preceded Leonardo da Vinci, testing out a flying machine 600 years before the Italian. Ibn Firnas also put together a working planetarium which could reputedly simulate thunder and lightning. Then there was Al-Zarqali, known to the West as Arzachel, who built a famous water clock and compiled some of the greatest astronomical tables. Al-Andalus' astronomers gave us many of the terms we still use for the stars – such as zenith and nadir – while their systematic cataloguing of the heavens gave us the names of stars such as Altair, Deneb and Betelgeuse.

Much of this was due to the fact that in Al-Andalus there flourished an ethos of intellectual and cultural life almost completely absent from Christian Europe at the time. While many vital Greek and Roman pre-Christian texts were proscribed as heresy by the medieval church, translations were widely available in the cities of Al-Andalus.

These thereby excelled in science, with Ibn al-Nafis, for example, discovering the pulmonary circulation of blood. Abu al-Qasim al-Zahrawi, known in the West as Abulcasis, wrote the *Tasrif*, which when translated into Latin became the leading medical text book in European universities for many centuries afterwards. Meanwhile, Ibn al-Khatib did pioneering work on infectious diseases, while Ibn Hazm discovered the importance of clinical hygiene. And there were many more.

Elsewhere, pre-dating modern political and social science by some centuries, was Ibn Khaldun, with his theory that history was not a series of random events but a scientific process with laws that could be determined. The philosopher Ibn Rushd had a major impact on the whole development of philosophy; known as Averroes in the West he introduced many in Europe to the work of Aristotle, translated by Muslim scholars.

Ibn Battutah wrote an immensely rich travel book, based on 28 years of wandering the Mediterranean seaboard, which complemented Al-Idrisi's geography text, known as the *Book of Roger* – after his Christian patron, Roger II of Sicily; this was inscribed on a silver 'planisphere', a disc-shaped map that was one of the wonders of the medieval world.

Yet for all their achievements in the world of philosophy and science, it is probably for their distinctive architecture that they are more generally known today. Granada's Alhambra, Cordoba's Mezquita and Seville's Alcazar and Giralda are probably the most famous, but in many Spanish towns and cities, there is some reminder of this magnificent past. All are well worth trekking up from the coast to see during your time in Andalucía.

Services
The **tourist information office** (☎ 274 355), 4, Calle Hermanos Muchado, open Mon-Fri 0900-1900, Sat-Sun 0900-1400, has maps and accommodation lists.

Ferries [see p439 for full details]
During the summer months Trasmediterránea (☎ 236 155), Estación Marítima, operate six services a week to **Melilla**, the Spanish colony on the Moroccan coast. Tickets are available in Estación Marítima, or from any of the travel agencies around town.

Trains
Almería is on the railway line to Granada, from where there is an overnight sleeper to Madrid, and regular services operate to Cordoba and Seville.

Buses
For Mini-Hollywood take a Tabernas bus; the ride takes about 30 minutes. Otherwise, there are regular buses (from the bus station) to Mojácar and the Cabo de Gata, as well as long-distance services to Cordoba, Granada, Algeçiras and beyond.

Where to stay
Hostal Maribel (☎ 235 173), 153, Avda Lorca. Decent sgl/dbl for €15/30.
Hostal Universal (☎ 235 557), 3, Puerta de Purchena. Backpacker haunt. €12.50/25.

Campers should try *La Garofa*, a campsite 5km west of Almería on the Aquadulce and Roquetas de Mar bus routes.

Where to eat
Hunt around near the station for the cheaper *menu del dias*. Otherwise, plenty of snack bars and cafés offer *bocadillos* and sandwiches off the central Paseo de Almería.

Melilla

AREA CODE: ☎ 956 **POPULATION:** 70,000
With its powerful medieval fortress, Melilla is the more interesting of the two Spanish colonies on the Moroccan coast and the longest established. Built on the eastern side of the Cap des Trois Fourches, it juts out into the Mediterranean to form a natural strategic landfall between Europe and North Africa.

Much of its interest lies within the walls of its old fortress, where the streets and plazas are more Madrid than Moorish. There's also a strong military presence to remind you of its garrison town basis. For much of its life, Melilla has been under siege, with its status still very much disputed by Morocco, though the inhabitants, 70% of whom are Spanish, seem determined to maintain their special status.

The port is also a useful gateway, with frequent ferries over to Almería and Málaga, while it is relatively easy to cross the frontier from here into Morocco, with the port of Nador close by. Up behind, the Rif mountains loom, squeezing the roads out to the coast, with Tangier the most common destination, though some buses also bounce across country to Fes and beyond.

HISTORY
It was the usual succession of Phoenicians, Carthaginians and Romans who settled here in ancient times, when the port was known as Rusaddir. Vandals and Byzantines then passed through, along with Arab and Moorish rulers, before the Spanish took over in 1497, fortifying the city to withstand repeated sieges. In 1909, the colony expanded, moving out from behind the giant walls of the fortress to build new avenues to the west. The port was developed at that time, enabling Melilla to function as an important military base for Spanish Morocco.

During the Rif War of 1921, an early bid for Moroccan independence, the town was almost captured by Abd el-Krim, the commander of the Berber Rif tribesmen. Garrisoned by the élite Spanish foreign legion, it was also one of the first garrisons to join Franco's fascist uprising against the Spanish government in 1936, triggering the Spanish Civil War. With Moroccan independence in 1956, Melilla was retained as a Spanish enclave, and in 1995 was granted the status of an autonomous administration by Madrid. Morocco occasionally raises the issue of getting it back, but with little result.

WESTERN MEDITERRANEAN

WHAT TO SEE

The main item is undoubtedly the fortress, the **Melilla la Vieja**, or Old Melilla. The 15th-century fortifications have been rebuilt and strengthened over the years, with the result now indeed impressive. The town has several huge fortified gateways, including the **Puerta de la Marina** by the harbour and the **Puerta de Santiago**, complete with drawbridge. There are also good views from the summit. Spend time wandering within the fortress walls, before going to the cathedral, **Iglesia de la Concepción**. Nearby is also the **town museum** (1000-1300, 1430-1800, €1.50), with a display of artefacts from the locale.

PRACTICAL INFORMATION

Orientation

The Estación Marítima is right next to town and a short walk from the fortress.

The town consists of an old, medieval walled town and a new town, sprawled out to the east. The main street is Avenida de Juan Carlos I, which runs from the Plaza and contains most of the shops and banks.

Services

The **tourist information office** (☎ 675 444), Palacio de Congresos at the junction of Calle de Querol and Avda General Azipuru, has maps and brochures, along with accommodation lists.

Ferries   [see p440 for full details]

Trasmediterránea (☎ 690 902) has its office on Plaza de España, though you can get tickets for Spain at the ferry terminal or at any travel agent. There are six ferries a week to **Almería** and regular ferry/fast ferry services to **Málaga**.

Buses

Catch a local bus to the Moroccan border from Plaza de España. After crossing over, Moroccan buses leave regularly for Nador, Tangier and Fes.

Where to stay

Hostal Rioja (☎ 682 709), 10, Calle Ejército, Español. Good sgl/dbl for €15/30.

Pensión del Puerto (☎ 681 270), off Avda General Macias. Has bunks for €7.50 but coming here can be quite an adventure due to the odd mix of fellow residents, from legionnaires to would-be desert explorers.

Where to eat

Barbacoa de Muralla, Melilla la Vieja. Great stuff for €7.50.

Bodegas Madrid, Calle Castelar. Good for snacks and drinks. Around Calle Castelar is a good area in general for budget food.

Málaga

AREA CODE: ☎ 095 POPULATION: 455,000

Known to its Moorish rulers as a 'terrestrial paradise', Málaga today is perhaps not quite what it was, yet is still a city with a powerful presence. Birthplace of Pablo Picasso and capital of the Costa del Sol, Spain's most popular tourist destination, it is also a major port of access for cruise ships 'doing' the Granada, with easy connections up to the old city of the Alhambra. Málaga has an impressive citadel and some equally impressive fish restaurants, while on the edge of town there are still some echoes of old Spain, away from the hotels and summer apartments.

HISTORY

Founded by the Phoenicians in the 12th century BC, Málaga followed the usual passage of Andalucían and Moroccan coastal towns of Carthaginian, Roman and Vandal rule before falling to the Moors in AD711. From then on, it rose to be one of the most important cities in Spain, part of the Caliphate of Cordoba until that disintegrated, when it briefly became an independent Moorish kingdom. The port flourished as the outlet to the sea for Granada, which gave Málaga the strategic importance necessary for the Castilian Spanish to covet it. After several attempts, it fell to Ferdinand and Isabella's *reconquista* in 1487.

Málaga never really got back this past

greatness and is today one of Spain's poorest cities. Around it, tourism boomed in the 1960s and 1970s, with much of this glorious coast swallowed up by unappealing concrete constructions. The Costa del Sol has become something of a byword for package holidays, with many major environmental errors being made in the rush to accommodate the influx from northern Europe (see box on p24).

WHAT TO SEE
Looming over the town is the 170m **Mt Gibralfaro**, with a Moorish fortress (daily 0900-1800, free) on the summit. Nearby is the other grand Moorish building, the **Alcazaba fortress** (Wed-Mon 0930-1800, free). This has been partly restored and contains a museum and garden. From here, the emirs of Málaga once ruled their independent kingdom. There is also a Roman amphitheatre under excavation, testimony to Málaga's ancient past.

Back down in the town, the **cathedral** on the site of the city mosque was begun in 1528. The second tower still hasn't been finished; the first was completed in 1782. Another notable church is **Santo Victoria**, which contains the tombs of the counts of Luna, decorated with some bizarre engravings.

Picasso's birthplace, Casa Natal, 16, Plaza de la Merced, is now a house-museum (entry free) and is open daily 1100-1400, 1700-2000 (1800-2100 in summer, closed on Sunday afternoons).

PRACTICAL INFORMATION
Orientation
While ferries come in close to town, the bus and train stations, which are close together, are a bus ride from the centre; the No 3 or No 18 should get you there. The main places to visit are mostly uphill, though no great distance apart. The better restaurants and seaside places are also a bus ride away; the No 11 from Paseo del Parque should get you to Pedregalejo or El Palo.

Services
The municipal **tourist office** (☎ 240 7768; 🖳 www.malagaturismo.com), 1, Avda de Cervantes, (in summer daily 0930-1500, 1700-2000, in winter Mon-Fri 0830-1500, 1630-1900, Sat 0930-1330) has lots of maps and information, including accommodation lists. There are also information booths at the bus and railway station and at other points around the city. The Andalucían tourist office is at 4, Pasajes Chinitas (☎ 221 3445) and at the airport.

Ferries   [see p440 for full details]
Between July and September Trasmediterránea (☎ 206 1218), Estación Marítima, has a regular ferry and fast ferry service to **Melilla**; tickets are available from the Estación Marítima or any travel agent.

Trains
The **train station**, 1km west of the centre, has frequent services to major Spanish cities including sleepers to Madrid and beyond.

Buses
The **bus station** is round the corner from the train station. As Costa del Sol's hub, there are frequent services to Granada, Seville, Madrid, Córdoba, Barcelona and beyond.

Planes
Málaga is a major airport for package holidays to the 'costa', with frequent and relatively inexpensive flights more or less throughout the year. The airport is on a rail line to the centre of town, with trains leaving every half hour. The train continues west to Torremolinos and Fuengirola.

Where to stay
Hostal Castilla (☎ 221 8635), 7, Calle Córdoba. Has good sgl/dbl for €15/30.
Pensión Córdoba (☎ 221 4469), 9, Calle Bolsa. A fine choice, €12.50/20 sgl/dbl.
Hostal La Palma (☎ 222 6772), 7, Calle Martinez. Similar prices and standards.

Where to eat
Málaga is known for its food, particularly its fish and drink; the local, sweet Málaga wine has star status. The area around the Alameda is the place to look.

Antigua Casa de Guardia, 18, Alameda Principal. Reputed to be the oldest *bodega* (wine cellar) around and serves good tapas with the local brew.

El Jardin, Calle Cister. Has a good-value selection and a fine *menu del dia*, €10 a head come evening.

Otherwise, head for Pedregalejo on the No 11 bus from Paseo del Parque for some fine waterfront fish restaurants, most charging €10-15 a head.

Gibraltar

AREA CODE: ☎ 956 FROM SPAIN, +350 FROM ELSEWHERE POPULATION: 28,843

With its famous rock Gibraltar is a rare and slightly oddball experience. Mixing Spanish with old-fashioned English, yet with a population also boasting Maltese, Genoese and Jewish ancestry, it has recently come back into the headlines as a bone of contention between Britain and neighbouring Spain. The town is 5km long and 1.5km across at its widest, little more than the size of the Rock itself; it's festooned with Union Jacks and mass displays of the inhabitants' desire to remain British.

Yet not so far over the water is Africa, with Gibraltar a handy port for Tangier. Since the border with Spain was reopened, it's also relatively straightforward to cross back and forth, linking the colony to the European road and rail networks. It's also easy to get to from Britain, with plenty of cheap flights on offer. It is, however, outside the euro zone, sticking to the Gibraltar pound, a currency equal to the British pound. Euros can be used, but the exchange rate isn't good so it's worth changing some money at one of the many banks or bureaux de change on offer.

The Rock, at 426m high, is also a place of immense atmosphere and history. Tunnelled through almost to the point of becoming a massive slice of Emmental cheese, it has recently begun to crumble a little round the edges. Yet its daunting presence at the mouth of the Mediterranean remains a grand starting point for any journey round the inland sea.

HISTORY

The Rock has been inhabited since prehistoric times, with evidence of this discovered during excavations of the rock in the form of primitive artefacts and skeletons. Yet the imposing cliffs of Gibraltar are not exactly a natural base; but, dominating the narrowest point, they saw plenty of armies pass through, with Romans and Visigoths heading south, while Carthaginians and Moors headed north; the last of these establishing a settlement here in 711, known as Jabal-al-Tarik, 'Mount of Tarik' after the Moorish commander who took the place and built its first fortifications.

The Moors lived here until 1462, when Castilian troops finally seized it, annexing it to Spain in 1501. However, two hundred years later the Rock was stormed by an Anglo-Dutch force, with the Rock being ceded to Britain in 1713. This state of affairs has never been fully accepted by Spain, with repeated attempts being made to get it back. Between 1779 and 1783, there was the Great Siege, while during the Napoleonic Wars Gibraltar was similarly surrounded. In 1830 though, the Rock was made into a British Crown Colony, while the 1869 opening of the Suez Canal further strengthened Gibraltar's importance to the British Empire as a guardian of its sea lanes through the Med to India and beyond.

In WWII, Gibraltar acted as a vital naval base and a refuge for many fleeing fascism in Spain and Europe. The Franco dictatorship also stepped up the pressure on the colony, closing the land frontier in 1969. In 1967, a referendum among Gibraltarians had turned out 12,138 votes to 44 in favour of continued British rule. A new constitution then gave self-government to the colony in all matters except defence. However, Franco's death and the return of civilized government to Spain made Madrid's case for the Rock's return stronger and negotiations between Britain and Spain on this issue have been ongoing ever since. Gibraltarians were given full British citizenship in 1981, while Spain lifted its border blockade in 1985.

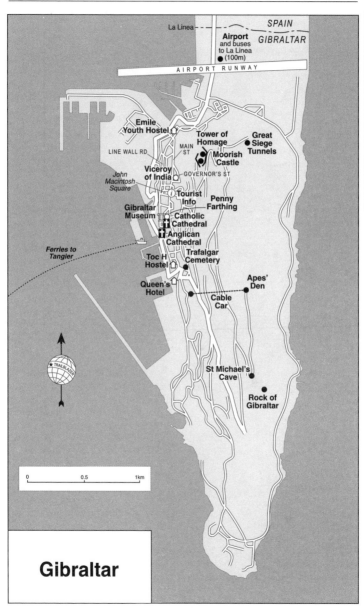

WESTERN MEDITERRANEAN

Gibraltar

Talks in 2002 reached the point where Britain seemed to have no objections to the return of Spanish rule after 300 years (a longer period than Spain itself has ever ruled the Rock) as long as Gibraltarians approved the change in a referendum. Currently, it seems such a vote would produce a similar result to that in 1967.

WHAT TO SEE

The harbour road, Queen's Way, heads south to curve up inside the walls to the **Trafalgar cemetery**, where many of those killed in the decisive 1805 naval battle, fought not far off in the Atlantic approaches, are buried. The British commander in the battle, Admiral Nelson, was also killed, but his body was shipped home preserved in a barrel of rum. Here you'll also be at the southern end of Main St, which runs down the centre of the town to the northern gates. However, continue on south along Europa Road for the continent's Land's End, Europa Point. From here, the Rif mountains of North Africa loom large.

Also round here is the **Apes' Den**, where you'll find some cheeky examples of Europe's only wild primates – except, that is, for the humans; these Barbary macaques are just as used to tourists and think little of ripping them off too, so watch out for any loose cameras or wallets. From here, head for **St Michael's Cave**, a massive limestone cavern sometimes used as a venue for concerts, then on to the **Great Siege Tunnels**. These are 18th-century gun emplacements hacked out of the rock by the British during Spain's unsuccessful 1779-83 attempt to get Gibraltar back. From here, a steep staircase, the Mediterranean Steps, takes you back down to the south-eastern corner of the Rock.

Main St is worth a wander, taking you past the **Catholic** and **Anglican cathedrals**, and with a **Moorish castle** perched at its north-eastern end. This contains the 1333 **Tower of Homage**, which itself withstood a lengthy Spanish siege in the 15th century. At 18-20 Bomb House Lane, about halfway along Main St, is **Gibraltar Museum** (Mon-Fri 1000-1800, Sat 1000-1400, £2) with a good display on the town's chequered history, including a Moorish bathhouse.

PRACTICAL INFORMATION
Orientation

Ferries arrive under the colossal cliffs of the Rock. Nowhere is far from here, though it can be a steep ascent. There is a cable-car to the summit, which takes in the Apes' Den, the Upper Rock Nature Reserve and St Michael's Cave for £5 return, open Mon-Fri 0930-1800. Otherwise, trust your feet; there are plenty of places to stop for a breather on your way up.

Services

The main **tourist office** (☎ 74950, 💻 www.gibraltar.gi), Duke of Kent House, Cathedral Square, is open Mon-Fri 0900-1730, Sat 1000-1400, and has handy maps and brochures. There are branches at the border and the Gibraltar Museum.

Ferries   [see p440 for full details]

Ferrys Ràpidos del Sur operate daily ferries to **Tangier**. Some travel agents also advertise day trips, which might be good value if you're short on time and not planning to travel on further into Morocco.

Buses

Buses from Spanish towns and cities go to La Linea rather than directly to Gibraltar. From there, you can walk across the border into town (20 mins), or take the No 3 or No 9 bus.

Planes

Several budget airlines do deals to Gibraltar from the UK; there are also some flights from Tangier. The airport is right on the sandy strip at the neck of the peninsula, with the frontier road crossing the tarmac.

Where to stay

Availability can be limited in season; try booking in advance if at all possible.
Toc H Hostel (☎ 73431), 36a Line Wall Rd. A backpacker staple that tests spartan resolve at £11 per bed.
Emile Youth Hostel (☎ 51106), Line Wall Rd. In the Montagu Bastion; £11 per bed.
Queen's Hotel (☎ 74000), 1, Boyd St. More distinguished rooms; £35/45 sgl/dbl. Discounts for students.

Where to eat

Brits dying for home cooking won't have far to look as there's no shortage of 'greasy spoon' cafés or fish & chip shops. There are plenty of pubs, too, all with the added advantage of not keeping British opening hours.

Viceroy of India, 9-11 Horse Barrack Court. Gibraltar's premier Indian restaurant, offers a good spread for £6 a head.

The Penny Farthing, Kings St. English food and international dishes.

The Piazza, 156 Main St. Has budget pizzas for £4.50

Algeçiras

AREA CODE: ☎ 956 **POPULATION:** 86,042

No great shakes as a tourist attraction, Algeçiras nevertheless has a long history and an important maritime role, with plenty of ferries heading out from here across the narrow strait to Morocco.

The town's importance is also based on its position, mirroring Gibraltar, the British colony across the bay. Much of the country's commerce with North Africa and beyond passes through here, making it a busy, workaday place.

HISTORY

Algeçiras was founded by the Moors in 713 as al-Jazirah al-Khadra, from which the present name derives. Fought over for centuries, it was taken by the Castilian Spanish in 1344, but recaptured by the Moors 24 years later. In the process, much of it was destroyed, and it never regained its former glory until the British occupied Gibraltar in 1704, sending many of the Spanish inhabitants there into exile; these outcasts largely refounded Algeçiras, with the core city built

in 1760 on the orders of Charles III of Spain.

In 1906 the Algeçiras Conference was held in its town hall. This was a major meeting of Great Power diplomats to try to avert war. The cause was France's attempts to take over all of Morocco, which led to strong protests from the emergent German Empire, the Kaiser himself landing at Tangier to support Moroccan independence. The conference was called on the initiative of US President Theodore Roosevelt, with Germany largely forced to back down by the same coalition of powers that would later be involved in WWI: Britain, France, Russia and the USA.

Since then, Algeçiras' main role has been as a busy port expanding as the Spanish economy developed and Gibraltar was closed off. Now it handles both transatlantic and transmediterranean shipping, with a tourism sector also beginning to take off.

PRACTICAL INFORMATION
Orientation

The **Estación Marítima** is right beneath the town, while local buses depart from along the waterfront for La Linea, the border town before Gibraltar. There is also a **train station** near the harbour for other destinations. Algeçiras hasn't any real sights, so it's likely all the walking you'll do is enter town one side and go out the other.

Services

The **tourist information office** (☎ 572 636), Calle Juan de la Cierva, has plenty of maps and information.

Ferries   [see p438 for full details]

Both Trasmediterránea (☎ 651 755), at the Estación Marítima, and Euroferrys operate five ferries a day to **Ceuta**, the Spanish colony on the Moroccan coast. Baleària,

---

Formalities on ferries to Morocco

On ferries from Spain to Morocco you must present your passport to the Moroccan officials on board as without their stamp you will be turned back at the port. There is usually a tannoy announcement about this and anyhow you should see people queuing but ask what to do to avoid any problems once you have arrived.

Comanav, Euroferrys, Ferrys Rápidos del Sur and Trasmediterránea operate frequent services to **Tangier**. Tickets can be bought from the ticket agencies on the waterfront.

Trains

Algeçiras has train connections inland to Bobadilla, the junction for trains to Granada, Madrid, Córdoba and Seville. Spanish trains are reliable and reasonably priced but a little slow. There are also sleepers to Madrid.

Buses

Local buses run every half-hour to La Linea for the frontier with Gibraltar, while less frequent buses go direct to the Rock. Ask the travel agents on the waterfront for details.

Where to stay and eat

There are plenty of budget *pensións* and restaurants around the harbour but you'll probably prefer to leave Algeçiras as soon as possible.

Ceuta

AREA CODE: ☎ 0956 POPULATION: 69,000
Built on a narrow strip of land between the main Moroccan coast and Mt Hacho the Spanish enclave of Ceuta is both the *bête noire* of many a Spanish military conscript and a major free port.

As with Melilla, its twin colony, it is a strange dot of Spain glued to the North African coast, with its predominantly Catholic population and Castilian streets and plazas a big contrast to the jumble of most Moroccan towns. It also has an impressive number of ferry connections across the strait to Algeçiras, while it's easy enough to move on into Morocco from here, with Tetouan, Tangier and Chefchaouen a straightforward bus ride away.

HISTORY

Originally a Phoenician settlement, in ancient times Carthaginians, Greeks and Romans occupied this strategic point on the narrow Straits of Gibraltar. Later, it fell to the Byzantines, though their governor, Count Julian, decided to run it as his own independent city state. This didn't last, with the arrival of the Arab and Moorish conquests in the 8th century. Ceuta, known as Sebta in Arabic, became a major bridging point between North Africa and Europe, as well as a key naval base. With the Moorish occupation of Gibraltar, for the best part of 500 years the western entrance to the Mediterranean was in their hands.

In 1415, all that changed. The Portuguese, under the command of Henry the Navigator's father, arrived and seized the place, shocking the Moors, and establishing Portugal's first major overseas colonial adventure. Ceuta stayed under Lisbon's rule until 1580, when the Portuguese kingdom was absorbed by Spain through dynastic marriage. A century later, in 1688, it was formally declared Spanish territory, a status it has had ever since.

Ceuta then began to act in much the same way it had for the Moors, only in reverse: as a bridgehead for Spanish intervention in North Africa. This role switched again in 1936, when Spain's future dictator, General Franco, used it as a base for his invasion of republican Spain.

As with Melilla, since Moroccan independence in 1956 Morocco has periodically tried to get the enclave back, without much success. This was most recently illustrated by the July 2002 fracas over the Parsley Islands, a nearby group of offshore islets also considered part of Spain but suddenly occupied by Moroccan troops. After a nasty diplomatic exchange, the islets were taken back by the Spanish and the crisis dissolved. In 1995, Ceuta was made an autonomous province of Spain, with its own assembly.

WHAT TO SEE

Ceuta is not big on sightseeing, though there are some excellent views across the strait to Gibraltar, particularly from the convent, **Ermetia de San Antonio**. Otherwise, the museum in **Paseo de Colon** (Mon-Sat 1000-1400, Sat only 1400-1800, free) is a tribute to Spain's élite colonial troops, the *Legion Extranjero*, or foreign legion.

PRACTICAL INFORMATION
Orientation
The ferry terminal is west of town, with the Puerto-Centro bus taking you to the Plaza de la Constitución. This is also where the buses to Morocco arrive and depart. The town itself is not any great size, with the sights easily reached on foot from the town centre.

Services
The **tourist information office** (☎ 501410; 🖥 www.turiceuta.com), in Plaza de la Constitución, is open Mon-Fri 0800-1500, and has maps and accommodation lists.

Ferries   [see p439 for full details]
Both Euroferrys and Trasmediterránea at 5, Muelle Canoñero Dato (☎ 505390), have five ferries a day to **Algeçiras**; tickets are available from Estación Marítima or from any travel agent in town.

Buses
Buses for Morocco go from Plaza de la Constitución, the No 7 leaving every 15 minutes and costing €0.45. At the border, there are plenty of *grands taxis* (shared taxis) to take you to Tetouan, from where buses go to most other Moroccan destinations.

Where to stay
Pensión Bohemia (☎ 510 615), 16, Paseo de Revellín. Good clean sgl/dbl for €15/25.
Casa de Huéspedes (☎ 517 756), 3, Plaza Teniente Ruiz. Similar standards and prices to the Bohemia.

Where to eat
Calle Real is the cheapest area, though you'll find plenty of budget options around the harbour, with snacks and tapas on offer.

Tangier

AREA CODE: ☎ 039 **POPULATION:** 521,731
Another great emblematic city, Tangier has long been a coveted prize, lying at the Atlantic entrance to the Mediterranean. Almost every European empire has made a grab for it at some time, leaving it a strange mixture of North African and southern European in appearance. It also has a great deal of faded glamour stemming from its one-time role as the international zone, a city outside boundaries that belonged neither to Morocco nor anyone else for many years, being run instead by a gaggle of Western diplomats. In the process, it gave literary birth to a distinguished group of American writers, including William Burroughs and Paul Bowles. Their sex and drugs exploits wove first a beatnik, then a hippy chic around Tangier, an image that still persists in the West, even if it has always been largely irrelevant to the vast majority of Moroccans.

The city also boasts an intriguing Medina, or old town, complete with walled kasbah, and some of the most persistent street hustlers in the cosmos. Don't let them put you off, though, as wandering the streets here is a fascinating business. Tangier is also an excellent starting point for exploring the rest of Morocco and for ferries with good connections across the strait to Gibraltar and Algeçiras.

HISTORY
The first recorded settlement here is once again Phoenician, with the city then following the path of many western Mediterranean settlements from Levantine rule to Carthaginian and then Roman. Known as Tingis, it became a free port in AD42 and was then capital of the Roman province of Mauretania Tingitana.

The Vandals and Byzantines both passed through following the collapse of the Western Roman Empire, with rule then passing through the Arab invasions to a succession of Moorish Islamic dynasties. These lasted until 1471, when the Portuguese and Spanish took it, later passing it on as part of the dowry of Catherine of Braganza on her marriage to Charles II of England in 1662. Tangier thus became one of England's first overseas colonies, an affair so deeply embarrassing that it has been largely blotted out of the national consciousness ever since. Suffice to say that the episode ended with the colonists accidentally burning down their

WESTERN MEDITERRANEAN

own town before giving up and handing the whole place over to the Moroccans. The English did, however, leave one thing, the city walls, which stand to this day.

That was largely how things stood until the 19th century, with Tangier an important port city in the independent kingdom of Morocco. However, the French invasion of Algeria, followed by the rest of Morocco in 1912, left the city with a bizarre status. The European powers were not prepared to leave such an important port to the French, but couldn't agree on anyone else having it; therefore in 1923 Tangier was declared an international city. From then until 1956, a commission of British, French, US, Spanish, Portuguese, Italian, Belgian, Dutch and Swedish diplomats ran the place, along with one representative of the Moroccan sultan, appointed by the French.

With Moroccan independence this arrangement ended, as did the city's fringe status for many Westerners, who had come here in large numbers to live out the last days of the colonial fantasy. Since then, Tangier's hybrid status has faded rapidly, with the European population of the Ville Nouvelle shrinking fast. Instead, Tangier has developed a major tourism industry as well as important port facilities. The king of Morocco also spends his summers here, away from the swelter of the capital.

WHAT TO SEE

Out of the port entrance, the Medina is easily reached, with the **Great Mosque** just ahead. This is strictly closed to non-Muslims. From here, turn left and you'll come to the **Petit Socco**, or Zoco Chico, the central square and long the heart of the Medina. It's both seedy and picaresque, filled with cafés and restaurants, some of which go back to the days of the international city, when this was Tangier's sleaze central. Off here, rue des Almohads runs north to become rue Ben Raisouli. Off this stands the **Bab el-Assa**, the gateway to the **Kasbah** — the city within a city that has been home to the city's rulers since Roman times.

Inside the kasbah is the 17th-century **Dar el-Makhzen**, the Sultan's Palace (Wed-Mon 0900-1300, 1500-1800, 10dr). This is now a museum with some excellent items on display in the Treasury, the Bit el-Mal, and in an archaeological annex.

Back in the Medina, in the southern-most corner stands the **American Legation**. This 18th-century building housed officials of the American republic soon after its foundation, Morocco being one of the first countries in the world to recognize the USA after its War of Independence from Britain. It now functions as a museum (open irregular hours; hammer on the door and see what happens, entrance usually free).

From here, head back for the rue es Siaghin and turn left; this takes you through the Medina walls to the **Grand Socco**, the large souk, once the city's main market but now rather empty in its post-independence incarnation as the place du 9 Avril 1947.

PRACTICAL INFORMATION
Orientation

Tangier is divided like most large Moroccan towns into the ancient Medina and the French colonial-era Ville Nouvelle, which sprawls around to the south. The **ferry terminal** is immediately below the Medina, at the northern end of town. The **CTM bus station**, for connections to places elsewhere in Morocco, is right outside the port entrance, while from here you can also get a *petit taxi* (a normal, metered cab) to **Tangier Morora station**, the train stop for Morocco's few railway connections. Most places to stay are either in the Medina around the Petit Socco or in the Ville Nouvelle on rue el-Antaki or rue Magellan. The sights can all be reached on foot.

You should change some money on arrival; there are bank branches at the ferry, bus and train terminals. Don't change money before arriving in Morocco as the exchange rate in southern Spain or Gibraltar is usually very bad, that is if you can find anywhere that has dirhams.

Services

The **tourist office** (☎ 938 239), 29, blvd Pasteur, is open Mon-Thu 0830-1200, 1430-1830, Fri 0830-1130, 1500-1830, and has maps and a few brochures.

Internet access is available at Cyber Café Adam, which is located on the corner of rue Ibn Rochd and rue de Prince Moulay Abdallah in the Ville Nouvelle.

Ferries   [see p441 for full details]
Baleària, Comanav, Euroferrys, Ferrys Rápidos del Sur, and Trasmediterránea (office in rue du Prince Moulay Abdallah, but tickets available from the port or any travel agent) operate frequent ferry and fast ferry services to **Algeçiras**. There are also daily boats to **Gibraltar** and **Tarifa** and some services to **Genoa** and **Sète**.

Trains
The train station is at Tangier Morora, or Moghogha, some 4km from the Medina to the west. From here there are rail links to Fes, Rabat, Casablanca and Marrakesh. ONCF (🖳 www.oncf.org.ma), the national rail company, provides easily the most comfortable way to get between these destinations. Couchettes (beds) are available on certain trains to Marrakesh and Fes.

Buses
CTN, the main state bus company, operates around the country from the station just outside the port entrance. Other, private buses go from the *gare routiére*, 1.5km from the Medina near the Syrian Mosque down blvd Mohammed V. The Moroccan bus network is relatively inexpensive and comprehensive.

Grands taxis
These are shared, stretch taxis that go when full. For many destinations in Morocco they're easily the best option, with prices a little more than the bus but worth it for the extra leg room. Of course, the disadvantage is there's no timetable, so you may find plenty of time to read your *War and Peace* if you're heading for an unpopular outpost.

WESTERN MEDITERRANEAN

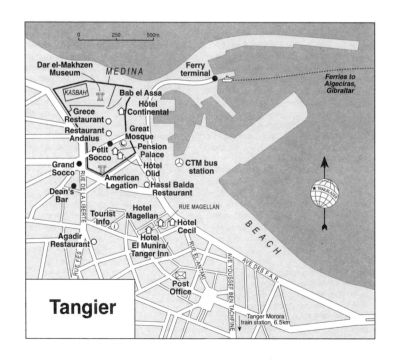

WESTERN MEDITERRANEAN

If there's a group of you all heading for the same place you can usually bargain with the driver for a reduced fare.

Petits taxis
These are normal city cabs, which can be a cheap enough way to get around. In Tangier, they're all metered according to distance rather than time, though there's still scope for bargaining.

Planes
Tangier's international airport is 15km out of town, connected by *grands taxis* to the gare routiére, the main private bus station around 1.5km south of the centre. From there, get a *petit taxi* into town. The airport has many flights to Europe, as well as along the North African coast to Tunis and Cairo.

Where to stay – Ville Nouvelle
Hôtel el-Munira/Tanger Inn (☎ 935337), 1, rue Magellan. Where William Burroughs wrote *Naked Lunch*. The bar is also an institution, with pictures of the famous patrons of the international-zone era on the walls and an expat clientele; 100/150dr sgl/dbl.
Hôtel Magellan (☎ 372319), 16, rue Magellan. A little cheaper than the above.
Hôtel Cecil (☎ 931087), on the corner of rue Magellan and rue el-Antaki. Good sgl/dbl for 150/300dr.

Where to stay – Medina
Pensión Palace (☎ 936128), 2, ave Moktar Ahardan. Decent sgl/dbl without bathrooms for 50/100dr; showers extra.
Hôtel Olid (☎ 931310), at No 12 just opposite Pensión Palace. Offers much the same as the above.
Hôtel Continental (☎ 931024), on the harbour front. Was used for some of the scenes in Bertolucci's film of Paul Bowles' *The Sheltering Sky*; 300/500dr sgl/dbl.

Where to eat
Many of the best budget places are in the Medina, around the Petit Socco.
Grece Restaurant, north of the square. Good wholesome stuff for around 50dr.
Restaurant Andalus, rue de Commerce. Small but popular, with good fish for 50dr.

Where to eat – Ville Nouvelle
Agadir, 21, rue Prince Heretier Sidi Mohammed. French and Moroccan dishes for 100dh.
Hassi Baida, 85, rue Salah Eddine al-Ayoubi. Moroccan specialities for 75dr.

Bars
Alcohol is not available outside the main tourist hotels and expat bars in the Ville Nouvelle. If you fancy a beer, try the famous bar at *Tanger Inn* (Hôtel el-Munira, see above), or *Dean's Bar*, rue Amerique du Sud, south of the Grand Socco.

PART 5: TYRRHENIAN SEA

Introduction

The waters of the Tyrrhenian Sea, and in particular the Strait of Messina that separates Sicily from the Italian mainland and joins the two halves of the Med, are amongst the most hazardous in the entire Mediterranean. Different tidal levels cause a surface current that flows south from the Tyrrhenian to the Ionian, while the northern sea's slightly warmer and less salty content creates a countercurrent flowing north. It's a dangerous combination that accounted for many an early mariner – as well as a few present-day sail boats. The North African coast is also known to be treacherous thanks to the strong westerly and north-westerly gales that sometimes blow along its length, making large stretches into graveyards for ancient ships. Both factors seem to be conspiring to erect a barrier between east and west here, with the apocalyptic earthquakes and volcanoes of the Arc of Fire between Sicily and Calabria another major obstacle to voyagers sailing between the two halves of the Med.

Yet the two seas, Ionian and Tyrrhenian, are still massively interrelated, sharing the same history and the same spread of civilizations. Greek cities on Sicily were once as numerous and powerful as on Euboea or Crete, while it was the Levantine Phoenicians who first set up an effective port in Marseille. With the arrival of Islam on the North African coast, the political divisions changed, with the opposite shores now enemies, hostile to each other for many centuries.

Travelling in the Tyrrhenian region now, many echoes of this undoubtedly remain, yet the exchange and flow of people and ideas has never really halted, either north–south or south–north. On this route you will, however, experience one relatively recent development: the effective ending of borders between Italy and France and their replacement with a more subtle, regional transition. It's a development that stands in marked contrast to what happens further south, where the walls of 'Fortress Europe' now appear to be higher than ever.

TRAVELLING THROUGH THE TYRRHENIAN SEA

The passage of **ferries** in the Tyrrhenian Sea is very much north–south, with little traffic along the North African Barbary coast. Thus the traveller progresses either from the richer, developed north of the region, namely southern France and the industrial north of Italy, to the poorer south, or vice versa; and plenty of ferries ply these routes.

When it comes to travelling beyond the boundaries of the Tyrrhenian, the Italian ports are well connected to the neighbouring regions. Travelling east, a short rail or road journey from Genoa brings you to Venice and the start of the

TYRRHENIAN SEA

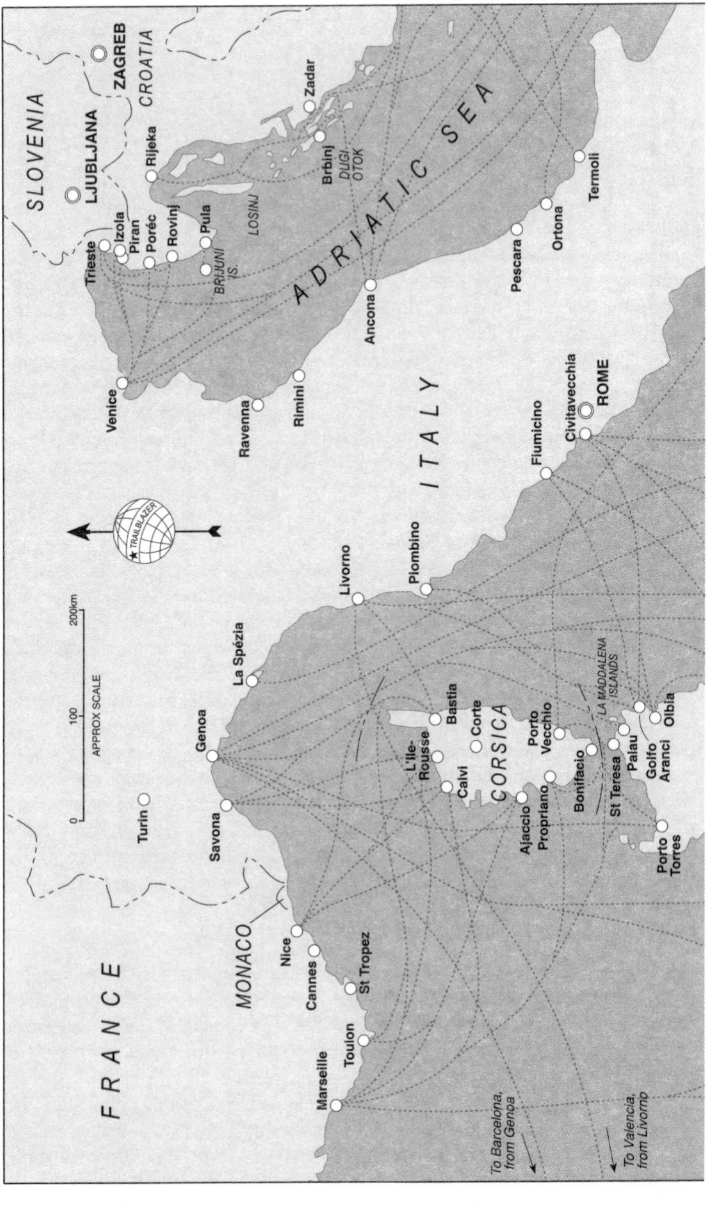

The Tyrrhenian Sea
FERRY ROUTES

TYRRHENIAN SEA

Villa San Giovanni
Reggio di Calabria
Messina
Naples
Salerno
Sorrento
CAPRI
ISCHIA
STROMBOLI
PANAREA
SALINA
FILICUDI
ALICUDI
LIPARI
VULCANO
Milazzo
Catania
Cefalu
SICILY
Palermo
Trapani
Mgarr GOZO
Cirkewwa
Sa Maison
MALTA VALLETTA
TYRRHENIAN SEA
TUNIS
SARDINIA
Arbatax
Cagliari
TUNISIA
ALGERIA
Annaba
To Algiers, from Marseille
To Tangier, from Genoa
To Valencia, from Salerno

Adriatic route from the north; from Messina you can go to Bari or Bríndisi and start it from the south. The latter also allows a hop over to Igoumenitsa or Patras for the Aegean routes and the eastern Med.

Genoa also has good connections with the Western Mediterranean, with regular ferries to Barcelona. Unfortunately, with the ending of Barcelona–Tunis ferries there's no way to do this from the south of the Tyrrhenian region for once again the North African side of the sea is badly served with no sea links to the Western Mediterranean – the Air Maroc plane from Tunis to Tangier being the only way – nor indeed to the Aegean, Adriatic or Eastern Mediterranean. It is to be hoped that a land route may reopen soon when Algeria's current woes finally come to an end.

SUGGESTED ITINERARIES

Italy to Corsica and Sardinia

Starting out in one of the Med's most important historic ports, this itinerary leads you first to Corsica, where Bastia is a great introduction to the Corsican *différence* and Bonifacio a dramatic place to leave the island. In landscape and scenic terms, Sardinia is in many ways Corsica's brother. However, even though few of its towns are great tourist destinations, La Maddalena and its archipelago should not be missed. Cágliari has some of the island's best Roman remains as well as a citadel and medieval quarter. Civitavecchia, meanwhile, on the Italian mainland, has some worthwhile sights but is mainly a good base for exploring the Eternal City, Rome – its more famous neighbour.

Genoa to Bastia (daily, 4¹/₂hrs); overland to Bonifacio via Corte, Ajaccio and Propriano or down the east coast via Porto Vecchio; Bonifacio to Santa Teresa di Gallura (daily, 30 mins); overland to Palau from where there is regular access to La Maddalena; overland direct to Arbatax, or overland to Olbia and then take the twice-weekly ferry to Arbatax (3-5hrs); Arbatax to Cágliari overland, or on the twice-weekly service (5¹/₄hrs); Cágliari to Civitavecchia (4-7 per week, 13-17hrs) for Rome.

(Mainland) Italy to Sicily, Malta and Tunisia

This route takes you to some of the Med's most famous volcanoes on the Aeolian Islands. Arriving in Palermo by sea is a memorable experience while Catania is a gateway to Mt Etna and has a range of historical and religious sights of its own. Travelling to Malta, you dock at Valletta, one of the most perfect late medieval towns anywhere. Tunis is perhaps the real place to finish, though, with its vibrant North African, Islamic culture situated on the land of historic Carthage.

(Naples to) Palermo (daily, 4-11¹/₂hrs); overland to Milazzo from where there are regular services to the Aeolian Islands; explore the Aeolian Islands; Milazzo to Catania via Messina; Catania to Valletta (4 per week, 3hrs); Valletta to Tunis (weekly); and finally Tunis to Naples (2 per week, 19-21hrs). Alternatively, those with more time could take a ferry from Tunis to Genoa (3 per week, 20-24hrs).

❑ **Tyrrhenian Sea – the highlights**
● **The Aeolian Islands** – Volcanic cauldrons, hellfire and brimstone amongst wonderful scenery and a lively town in Lipari. Just off the Sicilian coast, these rumbling lava cones form a spectacular maritime ring of fire.
● **Bonifacio (Corsica)** – A stunning setting, perched along the crest of towering limestone cliffs. With the old town a classic of winding streets and gorgeous wholesome food, Bonifacio provides a great gateway to a marvellous island.
● **Rome** – Where all roads lead, and quite a few ferries too. Boasting a curriculum vitae of ancient empires and monuments that's hard to beat anywhere – and the ice cream's not bad either.
● **Malta** – A marvellous world within a world, the best-organized Mediterranean island in existence with one of the best-preserved medieval towns, Valletta, anywhere. With a giant-sized history packed into a tiny scale on the ground, it has an astonishing – and easily accessible – richness.
● **Sidi Bou Said (Tunisia)** – A wash of blues and whites by the bay of Tunis, this hilltop village seems to have been designed for postcards. With the ruins of ancient Carthage just down the road and the not to be underestimated Tunis itself not too far away, this is a great place for a mint tea and a hookah pipe.

Tyrrhenian Sea – ports and islands

Marseille

AREA CODE: ☎ 04 **POPULATION:** 807,071
Sprawling, sometimes seedy, often exhilarating and never dull, Marseille is France's premier Mediterranean port. In recent years its waterfront has been given a tidy up, with the focal point the old harbour, home to yachts, trendy warehouse cafés and the mother of all fish stews: *bouillabaisse*.

The city authorities have also made an effort to turn Marseille into a tourist venue, highlighting the many important historical and cultural sights in the city. While this has added another good reason to visit, it still hasn't made too much of an impact on the city's distinctly shady side. Marseille has been a base for the ultra-right in recent times with the neo-fascist Front National a strong presence, not only among disaffected white youth but also among the respectable white bourgeoisie.

The other side of the coin has been the city's eminent status as a capital of Rai, the vibrant French/North African fusion music popular amongst the city's large Algerian and Moroccan immigrant population.

HISTORY
Marseille's story goes back more than 2500 years to its probable foundation as a Phoenician port. The Greeks were established there by 600BC, calling it Massalia. These early inhabitants were adventurous sailors, establishing trade routes across the Western Mediterranean and beyond. The Massalian captain Pytheas got as far as Britain and the Baltic in the 4th century BC, while his colleague Euthymenes made it as far south as Senegal.

The city also backed the winning side in the Punic Wars between Rome and Carthage, though blundered badly in the Roman Civil War, backing Pompey against Julius Caesar. In 49BC, Caesar's troops took the city, though it kept its free port status. Nevertheless it declined rapidly and by the 10th century was little more than a village.

However, in times of depression a good Crusade is an excellent restorative; a handy port for shipping off Europe's armies to the Holy Land, Marseille came back from the dead under the counts of neighbouring Provence.

A sacking in 1423 by Alfonse V of Aragon did little did to stop the boom. Rene I of Provence came to the rescue, installing his winter palace in the city and thereby resurrecting the old port. In 1481 though, Provence became a province of France, and Marseille along with it. Many were deeply unhappy about this and the city began a protracted period of revolt and rebellion against central authority, whether that be against the previously Protestant Henry IV (Marseille was fiercely Catholic) in the 16th century, Louis XIV in the 17th or the whole principle of monarchy in the 18th. It's not for nothing that the great anthem of the French Revolution was the *Marseillaise*, composed in 1792 by Rouget de Lisle, the marching song of the 500 volunteers from the city who joined the revolutionaries in Paris. It is now the French national anthem.

With the Reign of Terror, however, initial enthusiasm waned. Marseille's rebellion against the ruling National Convention was crushed and it was designated 'the city with no name'. The Revolutionary Wars became the Napoleonic Wars and because of the crippling blockade of the port by the British Navy, Marseille became fiercely anti-Napoleon. But France's imperial ambitions in North Africa gave the city a new boost as the 19th century went on. The French conquest of Algeria in 1830 made Marseille the natural transit for imperial cargo, and the opening of the Suez Canal also boosted traffic.

Marseille was badly hit in WWII. A centre for the French Resistance to both French Vichy collaboration and, after 1943, subject to direct German occupation, large parts of the historic but working class and rebellious Panier district and the old port were dynamited by Nazi troops.

Post-war, rebuilding was priority number one, with the city expanding massively outwards while the centre depopulated and began to collapse. This process has begun to reverse in recent years, with more attention and cash going into reviving the central districts. Long run by the French Socialist Party whose mayor, Gaston Defferre, officiated from 1953 to his death in 1986, a degree of institutional corruption seems to have also afflicted the city, while giving rise to political disaffection and the growth of the far-right Front National. As France's premier port for North Africa, the country's former colonial territory, it has also seen a large number of North African immigrants alongside thousands of *pied noirs* (French colonial settlers who left Algeria after it won its independence). This makes for a great mix of cultures but the relations between them have not always been good.

WHAT TO SEE

The entrance to the Old Port is fronted by some heavy fortresses, **Fort St Jean** on the north side, **Fort d'Entrecasteaux** and **Fort St Nicolas** on the south. Regrettably, these are not open to the public so head for the **Jardin du Pharo** in front of the south side forts for the best harbour views. From here, back along ave de la Corse, is the **Abbaye Saint-Victor** (daily 0830-1830, €2). Monks have lived on this site since the 4th century, while in the crypt are sarcophagi from even earlier. Most of the fortifications are the work of the 14th-century abbot, Guillaume de Grimoard, who later became the rival Pope Urban V in Avignon. On 2 February there's also a candlelight procession of the Black Virgin.

Further south still, on Montée de Notre Dame de la Garde is the **basilica** of the same name (daily, winter 0700-1900, summer 0700-2000, free). This stands on the city's highest point (154m), and was originally a fort, the remains of which can still be seen around the church's base. The current structure was commenced in 1853 and finished 11 years later. While no great work, it does command an excellent view of the city.

Head on back down to the Old Port from here though, and the boulevards going north take you through some of the city's more fashionable districts, including a

T Y R R H E N I A N S E A

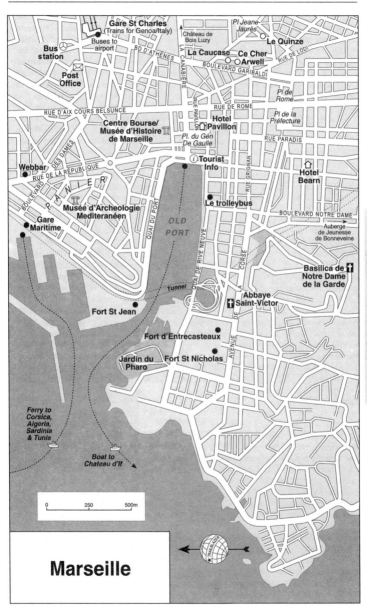

Gare St Charles
(Trains for Genoa/Italy)

Pl Jeane-Jaurès

Château de Bois Luzy

Le Quinze

Bus station

Buses to airport

BD D'ATHÈNES

La Caucase

Ce Cher

RUE DE LODI

Arwell

BOULEVARD GARIBALDI

Post Office

LA CANEBIÈRE

RUE D'AIX COURS BELSUNCE

RUE DE ROME

Pl de Rome

Centre Bourse/
Musée d'Histoire
de Marseille

RUE PAVILLON

Hotel Pavillon

Pl de la Préfecture

RUE PARADIS

DES DAMES

Pl. du Gén De Gaulle

Webbar

RUE DE LA RÉPUBLIQUE

Tourist Info

Hotel Bearn

P A N I E R

Musée d'Archeologie
Mediteranéen

RUE GRIGNAN

Le trolleybus

BOULEVARD

QUAI DU PORT

OLD PORT

BOULEVARD NOTRE DAME

Gare Maritime

Auberge de Jeunesse de Bonneveine

TYRRHENIAN SEA

QUAI DE RIVE NEUVE

Basilica de Notre Dame de la Garde

Tunnel

AVENUE DE CORSE

Abbaye Saint-Victor

Fort St Jean

Fort d'Entrecasteaux

Jardin du Pharo

Fort St Nicholas

AVENUE DE

Ferry to
Corsica,
Algeria,
Sardinia
& Tunis

Boat to
Chateau d'If

0   250   500m

Marseille

TRUE-MER

trendy docklands area off the quai de Rive Neuve. Head east and up La Canabière to the Centre Bourse shopping mall for the **Musée d'Histoire de Marseille** (Mon-Sat 1200-1900, €1.50). Inside are the remains of a 2nd-century AD merchant ship and many Roman relics recovered during the construction of the mall itself. The neighbouring Jardin des Vestiges has more.

Going back west from here brings you to the Panier district, a hilly area of winding streets and poor families which is now also the home to the **Musée d'Archeologie Méditerranée** (Mon-Sat 0900-1200, 1330-1645, €2.50). This has ancient Egyptian, Greek, Roman, Etruscan and Phoenician relics on display in a number of rooms around an arcaded courtyard, and also organizes special shows and forums on all aspects of the ancient Med. Watch out in the Egyptian room for the various eyes of the god Horus.

You must visit **Château d'If**, perched on an island just south-west of the Old Port entrance. This was the famous prison island of *The Count of Monte Cristo*, by Alexandre Dumas; an escape-proof jail reached by boat from the quai des Belges (departing every two hours, 20-minute trip, €7.50 return). Built in 1513 as a fortress to defend the harbour approaches, it never saw battle, but did witness the grislier side of French history. Many political and religious prisoners were killed here, while many more went insane. The Man in the Iron Mask (unending speculation as to his identity includes a suggestion that it was Louis, son of Louis XVI and Marie Antoinette) and the Marquis de Sade were held here, the former for life, the latter temporarily. Nonetheless, it is darkly atmospheric, with a courtyard plaque commemorating the 3500 Protestants kept here during the Counter Reformation and political prisoners sent here following the abortive revolution of 1848.

PRACTICAL INFORMATION
Orientation
As far as the visitor is concerned almost everything is within walking distance, and the Panier district, the Old Port and the avenues off it are the areas to stay in, eat and look around. Ferries arrive further north in the Basin de la Grande Joliette. The Gare Maritime discharges its passengers into a twilight world of harbour-front expressways, with quite a hike involved to the Panier (about 15 mins) or the Old Port (25 mins) to the south.

The square-sided Old Port is the main focus, running inland from the sea to a square at the eastern end off which the main boulevards run. The first stretch up the grandest, La Canabière, takes you past the old market area to the right. The train station, Gare St Charles, is to the north-east with the airport, 28km to the north-west, connected by frequent buses to the train station.

Services
The main **tourist information office** (☎ 91 13 89 00; 🖳 www.marseille-tourisme.com, in French only) is in the Old Port at the bottom of La Canabière. It's open Mon-Sat 0900-1915, Sun 1000-1700. The office will book accommodation.

The main **post office** is at 1, place de l'Hôtel des Postes. For an **internet café** try Webbar in rue de la République, or Infocafé, 1, quai de Rive Neuve. **Virgin Megastore**, 75, rue St Ferréol, has both fiction and non-fiction titles in English.

Ferries [see p445 for full details]
Algeria Algerie Ferries and Société Nationale Maritime Corse-Méditerranée (SNCM) have boats to **Algiers** and other destinations in the country but getting a visa is not easy and the political situation is still unstable so check before you even think about making a booking.

Corsica Ferries to Corsica (**Ajaccio, Bastia, Calvi, L'Île Rousse, Propriano** and **Porto Vecchio**) are run by SNCM and include the best boat in the Mediterranean, the *Napoléon Bonaparte* (see box, p143). Even if you've no desire to go to Corsica this is worth going on: a luxury floating hotel complete with a Jacuzzi-surrounded swimming pool, several classy restaurants and excellent cabins, all for fairly normal prices. Tickets for the SNCM (France ☎ 0891 70 18 01) ferries are on sale at most travel agents or try their office at 61, boulevard des Dames (☎ 91 56 30 10; Mon-Fri 0800-2000, Sat 0830-1200 and 1400-1730).

Sardinia SNCM operates ferries to **Porto Torres** daily between May and September and three times a week the rest of the year.

Tunis The Tunisian ferry company CTN operates the service but ticketing is dealt with by SNCM (see above).

Trains
Trains run from the main station, **Gare St Charles**, north-east of the Old Port. Buy your tickets at the station or in the French railways (SNCF) shop on the ground floor of the Centre Bourse. You can also reserve tickets online at 🖳 www.sncf.fr.

There are nine trains a day to Nice (1½ hours, €25), where you should change for the connection to Genoa. The through trip takes about six hours, costing €42. There are also many regular connections to other cities in France, and internationally.

Buses
The **bus station** (☎ 91 08 16 40) is on place de Victor Hugo. There are regular connections to Nice, Avignon, Arles, Orange and Cannes, but try the train as it's more or less the same price and much more comfortable.

Planes
The airport (☎ 42 14 14 14) is 28km north-west of the city. There are TRPA buses to/from Gare St Charles every 20 minutes (€7, 25 mins). The first to the airport leaves at 0530, the last one back is at 2220.

The airport is fairly well connected, with Air France routing you through other French cities if there's no direct link.

Where to stay
The area around the bottom of La Canabière is thick with hotels, most of which offer deals, so shop around.
Hôtel Caravelle (☎ 91 48 44 99), 5, rue Guy-Mocquet. Sgl/dbl for €20/30.
Hôtel Pavillon (☎ 91 33 76 90), 27, rue Pavillon. Similar and with a good location; €25/40 sgl/dbl.

Hôtel Bearn (☎ 91 37 75 83), south of the Old Port, 63, rue Sylvabelle. A good choice at €17.50/30 sgl/dbl.

There are two hostels, both about 5km from the centre. Set in a château, *Auberge de la Jeunesse Château de Bois Luzy* (☎ 91 49 06 18), is on allée des Primevères. *Auberge de la Jeunesse de Bonneveine* (☎ 91 17 63 30), is off avenue Joseph Vidal. Both charge around €9-11 for dorm beds.

Where to eat
Marseille is known for its garlic- and saffron-flavoured fish stew, *bouillabaisse*. This is best mixed with the local ouzo equivalent, the aniseed-flavoured *Provençal pastis*. However, finding a bouillabaisse you can afford is not easy, with the best varieties served around the Old Port, usually only to a minimum of two people. Expect to pay at least €15 a head, though it will probably be worth it. Cheaper eats are to be had around place Jeane-Jaurès, while North African and Middle Eastern snacks are on offer in rue des Feuillants. *Le Quinze*, 15, rue des Trois Rois, parallel to Cours Julien, has good Provençal stuff for €12 a head. *Ce Cher Arwell*, 96, cours Julien, has more general French offerings at similar prices. *La Caucase*, at No 62 in the same street, has Armenian specialities ranging from €12 to €17 a head.

Nightlife
Cours Julien still has some life in it, while rue de la République features a trendy bar, *Webbar*, which turns into a free-entry club venue on Friday/Saturday. Also try *Le trolleybus*, 24, quai de Rive Neuve, for a variety of music from funk to techno.

Nice

AREA CODE: ☎ 04 POPULATION: 1.1 MILLION
No longer the select Côte d'Azur prerogative of jet-set movie stars and dodgy aristocrats, Nice is now a major city with an urban sprawl to prove it. Nonetheless, the old centre still has a major charm factor,

TYRRHENIAN SEA

with the ochre beauty of the surrounding coast a major draw. With its famous cafés along the promenade des Anglais and the Baie des Anges, it also has a spectacular Mardi Gras carnival in late February or early March. It's also a handy place to explore the rest of the coast, with Monte Carlo and Cannes close by, as well as the wonderful coastal railway running from Marseille along to Genoa.

HISTORY

Founded by ancient Greek colonists from neighbouring Marseille in around 350BC, Nice most likely gets its name from the Greek word *nike*, meaning victory. An important trading station under the Romans, it was ransacked by the Moors in 813. They controlled much of the coast of Provence until being driven off by the Provençal Count Guillaime in 974. It stayed part of the kingdom of Provence until 1382, when it went to the counts of Savoy.

Beating off a Turkish attack in 1543, it remained under the control of Savoy up until 1860, when it finally passed into French hands. In the late 19th and early 20th century it developed its reputation as a playground for the rich of Europe and North America, a status it still enjoys to some degree, with film stars and tabloid princesses often in situ.

WHAT TO SEE

While thin on ancient sights, Nice has an excellent collection of modern art museums. These begin with **Musée Chagall (Museum of the Biblical Message)** in ave du Docteur Ménard (☎ 93 53 87 20; July to Sep, Wed-Mon 1000-1800, Oct to Jun, Wed-Mon 1000-1700, €6, €2.75 for students and free for under 18s). This contains 17 paintings by the master based on Biblical texts, as well as hundreds of etchings and other works on the same theme. This was the culmination of many years' study of Jewish religious themes by the painter, and was opened by Chagall himself in 1972. Take bus No 125 and get off at the Chagall stop.

More modern art can be found at the **Musée Matisse** at 164, ave des Arènes de Cimiez (☎ 93 81 08 08; Apr to Sep, Wed-Mon 1000-1800, Oct-Mar 1000-1700, €4, €2.50 for students and free for under 18s). Matisse lived in Nice for much of his life, with this a collection of his paintings, sketches and bronzes. Take bus no 15 from the Chagall Museum.

Finally, there is the **Musée d'Art Moderne et d'Art Contemporain** on promenade des Arts (☎ 93 62 61 62, Mon & Wed-Sun, 1000-1800, €4) with works by Andy Warhol, Roy Lichtenstein and a gallery of pieces from the Fluxus group.

PRACTICAL INFORMATION
Orientation

The port is right in the heart of the city, which spreads around a curving coastline, ringed by the promenade des Anglais. The main train station is back inland, left at the end of the main ave Jean Medecin. The airport is some 6km to the south-west, connected by the half-hourly bus No 23 to the train station (Gare Nice Ville), main bus station (Statione Centrale) and city centre (promenade des Anglais).

Sunbus (☎ 93 16 52 10), 10, ave Félix Faure, operates a service throughout the city, with tickets a flat €1 from the driver or you can buy a one-, five- or seven-day bus pass (€3.80/13/17). The long-distance bus station is on blvd Jean Jaurès with regular links along the coast and into Italy.

Services

There are **tourist information offices** at 5, promenade des Anglais (☎ 92 14 48 00, Oct-May, Mon-Sat 0999-1800; June-Sept, Mon-Sat 0800-2000, Sun. 0900-1800); one next to the train station in ave Thiers which keeps the same hours and another at Nice Côte d'Azur Airport – Terminal 1 (open daily 0800-2200).

The **post office** is at 23, ave Thiers.

Ferries   [see p446 for full details]

The port of Nice has around 500 mooring berths, making it a potentially useful place to volunteer your services for crewing.

Both Corsica Ferries (☎ 92 00 42 93) and SNCM (☎ 93 13 66 66 or 93 13 66 99), Gare Maritime, quai du Commerce, sail to **Ajaccio**, **Bastia**, **Calvi** and **L'Île Rousse**.

Trains
Nice lies on a major east–west rail link with frequent services to Genoa, Milan and other Italian destinations and to elsewhere in France such as via the Trans Europe Express to Paris (6¹/₂hrs). Fast TGV trains also link to Lyon and Marseille several times a day and there is a car-train service between major French cities: vehicles are conveyed at the same time as their owners who travel in 'couchettes'. Check out the railway website ▣ www.sncf.fr for timetables and online purchases/reservations. For TGV trains you must make a reservation and don't forget to frank your ticket in one of the yellow or orange coloured punch boxes by the main platform entrance before boarding the train.

The station is the Gare SNCF at avenue Thiers, ☎ 92 14 82 52/53. There is also the smaller Chemins de Fer de Provence with rail services between Digne and Nice, headquartered at 40, rue Clément-Roassal, ☎ 97 03 80 80, ▣ www. trainprovence.

Buses
Services go to most towns along the coast as well as inland.

Planes
Nice's Côte d'Azur Airport, the second largest airport in France, is a major international hub. There are two terminals, one for international flights and the other for domestic. Nice has also become a major destination in recent years for budget airlines from northern Europe. Check easyJet and Ryanair for some bargain offers from the UK.

Where to stay
The train station area is the best place to look for budget deals. *Les Mimosas* at 26, rue de la Buffa (☎ 93 88 05 59) has rooms for €20-25. The **youth hostel** is 4km out of town on the way to Forestière du Mont Alban (☎ 93 89 23 64, €10-15 shared dorms). The nearest **campsite** is *Camping Terry*, 768, Route de Grenoble (☎ 93 08 11 58), 6km north of the airport and difficult to reach.

Where to eat
One area not to be missed for Provençal food at its best is the Marché aux Fleurs, the flower market, which is lined with good, if a little pricey, eateries.

Regional gastronomy in the Provence-Alpes-Côte d'Azur is very distinctive, with a Mediterranean influence blending hot spices and seafood with cuisine from the rest of France. Niçois cooking is special, well-respected and unique. It uses very little milk and goat cheeses are predominant. Garlic, olive oil and olives are the leitmotif, along with abundant *herbes de Provence*.

For one local speciality, the chick-pea flour pancake known as the *socca*, try *Chez Rene Socca*, 2, rue Miralheti.

Genoa (Genova)

AREA CODE: ☎ 010 **POPULATION:** 706,754
While one of the greatest cities of Mediterranean maritime history, Genoa has changed since its days as a contender with Venice and the Ottomans for supremacy of the world's seas. But while its glory days as an independent maritime republic may be over, the city still has a grandeur and a character like no other. From its shabby ancient arcades to its stunning renaissance streets and warren-like old town, Genoa is a much overlooked gem, rough cut and unpolished but somehow all the more interesting for it.

The port is also a major routeway for boats across to Barcelona and the Western Mediterranean, as well as south to Sardinia, Sicily and Tunis. There are excellent road and rail links too: west into France, east to Venice and south-east to Rome and beyond.

HISTORY
Genoa has long been an important natural port for the region, Liguria, while also benefiting from being an important east–west road junction along the coast. A Roman town, it suffered badly during invasions of Ostrogoths and Lombards when the empire collapsed, but by the 10th century had begun to return to its former glory. Although raided and sacked by an Arab fleet around 934, the

TYRRHENIAN SEA

Genoa

TYRRHENIAN SEA

PORTO VECCHIO

PORTO ANTICO

Ferries to Tunis, Valetta, Tangier, Barcelona, Sicily, Sardinia, Corsica

Stazione Principe (trains to France) & buses to airport

Stazione Marittima

Hotel Lausanne

VIA BALBI

VIA ANTONIO GRAMSCI

ALDO MORO

VIA VENEZIA

VIA MILANO

Airport, 1km

Aquarium

Ugo II Pirata (pirate ship)

Columbus sculpture

Tourist Info

Maritime Museum

CITTÀ DEI BAMBINI

Ostello Genova, 1km

Flowers Hotel

La Taverna di Colombo

VIA SAN LUCA

SOTTORIPA

VIA DELLA MADDALENA

VIA GARIBALDI/STRADA NUOVA

Municipal Art Gallery

Funicolare di S Anna

Piazza delle Fontane Marose

Hotel Major

Hotel Doina

Britannia Pub

Palazzo Ducale

Piazza Matteoti

Piazza de Ferrari

Doge Bar

Hot Vibes

VIA S BERNADO

Cathedral of San Lorenzo Treasury Museum

VIA XXV APRILE

VIA XX SETTEMBRE

Liquid Café, 500m

To Stazione Brignole (trains for Italy), 200m; bus station, 200m; Piazza della Vittoria, Trattoria Lombardi, Trattoria da Peppino & Ugo II Pirata, 750m

0   250   500m

city came back fast as an independent commune run by a number of elected consuls.

During the 12th and 13th centuries success on the high seas allowed Genoa to grow into a city state of 100,000, with interests and colonies stretching as far afield as the Caspian Sea. Rivalling Venice for control of the Eastern Mediterranean trade, it also dominated many of the overland routes through Western Europe. Most of Liguria, Corsica and northern Sardinia were run directly by the Genoese, while trading posts and colonies spread around the whole Mediterranean, the Genoese generally favouring local trade monopolies to direct colonization. One of these trading posts was Galata, on the eastern shores of the Golden Horn in Byzantium, a trading colony which eventually outstripped Byzantium itself (see İstanbul pp380-93).

Genoa was by this time run by a group of ruling families, with the Spinola, Fieschi, Grimaldi and Doria being the most influential. They ran the city state as a corporate venture, social policy being entirely based on what was good for their individual profit margins. By the 13th century these merchant nobles dominated Genoa without needing recourse to such unbusinesslike ventures as elections.

At first they enjoyed some remarkable success. In 1284, their largely privatized navy won a crushing victory over Italian city-state rival Pisa, followed by an impressive showing against the Venetians in 1298. This was the time when the city became known as *La Superba* ('The Proud') for its mighty wealth. Genoa had a pre-eminent place in Mediterranean trade, a position that soon proved fragile. Political strife between the ruling families soon undermined the gains won by Genoa's sailors, traders and soldiers, with a general depression in trade during the 14th and 15th centuries further undermining the city's power. The strong Ottoman expansion in the east was something Genoa was in no position to withstand, and this dramatically altered patterns of commerce. Outposts such as Cyprus lost value, while a resurgent Venice also stripped Genoa of many of its trade links. Eventually, the Genoese attempted a political system based on elected *doges*, as in Venice, but by then it was too late.

Neighbouring France, and Milan (also then an independent state), grew to dominate Liguria, the Genoese sheltering behind a lengthy series of walls inland from the port. Meanwhile, a series of rebellions by the Corsicans drained Genoa of manpower and resources. Sardinia was then lost to the Spanish Aragonese, while by the mid-1400s,

Columbus

It is generally accepted that Christopher Columbus was born c1451 in Genoa, though many places in the area lay claim to the great navigator, colonizer and discoverer of America. Greeks in Chios and Corsicans in Calvi both claim him as their own, the link being that once they were all Genoese territories.

Convinced that the world was round and that by sailing west across the Atlantic he would reach India and all the spices and wealth of the Orient, Columbus strove for many years to raise money for his enterprise. His fellow Genoans and others including Henry VII of England refused him but Ferdinand and Isabella of Spain, impressed by this deeply religious man and anticipating a wealth of gold and converted souls, gave sufficient funds to equip and crew three vessels, the *Santa Maria*, the *Cristina* and the *Nina*. In 1492 he sailed from Palos in Andalucia and after a difficult voyage made landfall on the Bahamas; he had discovered the New World and he returned 33 weeks later to a hero's welcome at the Spanish Court. With increased help he led an expedition to colonize the island of Hispaniola. This proved a disaster; he was recalled to Spain in chains and accused of misrule. His last voyage ended in shipwreck off Jamaica in 1504, after which he was *persona non grata* at the Spanish Court. He died in poverty in 1506.

all Genoa's eastern Mediterranean colonies had been taken by the Ottomans or Egyptians. Spain's star was now rising, however, and Genoa sought alliances with Madrid. Genoese captains such as Columbus (see box on p131) headed for Spain to get the more lucrative new contracts. In 1528, a new Genoese leader, Andrea Doria, instituted a new system of governance and established Genoa's status as a Spanish satellite, reasoning that this might give Genoa some of the booty from Spain's growing empire in the New World. The reasoning was good, and in the 16th and 17th centuries the city went through a boom on the back of much stolen Inca gold.

However, tying the city's fortunes to Spain ultimately saw Genoa also follow the Spanish Empire into decline. By 1768, Genoa was broke, handing over its last outpost, Corsica, to France. With the advent of Napoleon, Genoa and Liguria were annexed by France in 1805, but with Napoleon's defeat, the region was given to Savoy. Trade recovered and continued to blossom when Italian unification made Genoa the new kingdom's greatest port. During the unification struggle it was from Genoa that Garibaldi set off with his 'Thousand' in 1860 to open the campaign for unity.

In WWII, Genoa suffered greatly from Allied bombing but the city was the first in the north to rise up against fascism and liberate itself before the arrival of Allied troops in May 1945. Post-war there was a boom as northern Italy's industrial centres expanded and the region's trade flooded through Genoa. However, by the 1960s it had dried up, with Genoa reaching one of its lowest points. Political unrest also added to the port's woes in the 1970s, as did ongoing corruption scandals and Mafia assassinations in the 1980s and '90s. However, recent years have seen a revival, thanks partly to injections of EU cash and also central government money released to mark the 500th anniversary of Columbus' voyage in 1992. The waterfront has new museums, shops and office complexes, and the atmosphere now is far from the grim decay of previous decades. In 2004, the city was made European Cultural Capital, a just reward for its great historical contributions, as well as for its recent recovery.

WHAT TO SEE

Three areas are well worth a visit, the first being the old harbour, Port Antico. On the eastern side you'll find the **Aquarium**, the largest in Europe (Mon-Fri 0930-1730, Sat & Sun 0930-1830, €11.60). Inside, huge tanks hold a variety of marine animals, including sharks, dolphins and 'joking seals'. Moored outside is the replica corsair ship built for Roman Polanski's swashbuckling epic, *Pirate*. Further south still is a huge **sculpture** of masts and rigging built to commemorate the 500th anniversary of Columbus' discovery, along with a dome further down the pier that quite effectively celebrates the great 1492 voyage.

Head on round, though, for the **Maritime Museum** (Padiglione del Mare a della Navigazione) housed in the renovated warehouses of the Città dei Bambini (daily 1030-1930, €7). It's above a shopping mall and there are escalators to it. You'll find much on the two local heroes Columbus and Andrea Doria, all with tri-lingual labels (Italian, English and Genoese). There's a walk-through mock-up of a ship's chandlers from the 13th century, a model of the *Rex*, Mussolini's 51,602-ton, 268.2m luxury liner built in 1930 to compete for the Blue Riband Atlantic crossing, and a final, sobering reminder of the risks involved in all this, a mock-up shipwreck beached on a dark and foreboding shore.

Heading east from here, under the harbour-front highway, you enter the second area of exploration, the jumble of old town streets leading up the hill. This is the older, more sleazy side of town, with hustlers and street types a plenty, so be cautious but take some time just to wander. Along the harbour front is the medieval arcade, the **Sottoripa**, which was once night by the water. On Via S Lorenzo you'll pass the Gothic **Cathedral of San Lorenzo**, with its black-and-white striped façade. In here, the **Treasury Museum** (Mon-Sat 0900-1200, 1500-1800, €5.50) keeps a casket containing St John the Baptist's ashes and also allows you to fulfil a quest handed down through the ages from King Arthur to Harrison Ford: a green glass basin held here is said to be the Holy Grail (but see p103).

Eventually, you should make Piazza Matteotti and the **Palazzo Ducale**, the seat of the Genoese doges from 1384 to 1515 (daily 0900-1930, €5). Regular exhibitions are put on here, usually for an extra charge, while sights include dungeons and the Grimaldina Tower, the only real survivor from the original medieval palace, the rest being a 17th-century update. Head north from here across Piazza de Ferrari and up Via XXV Aprile to Piazza delle Fontane Marose, the eastern end of Via Garibaldi. This street is one of the most remarkable in Europe, being chock full of medieval palazzos. This started out in the 1500s as the Strada Nuova and all the important, immensely wealthy families of the city state lived here. Most are now banks or municipal offices but the Palazzo Rosso and Palazzo Bianco, both once owned by the Brignole Sale family, now form the **Municipal Art Gallery** (Tue, Thu & Fri 0900-1300, Wed & Sat 0900-1900, Sun 1000-1800, €4). There is a good collection of Flemish art here, including some Van Dyck and Rubens (the latter once sketched the street outside).

To get a good idea of the city's overall look, just north of the Via Garibaldi is the terminal for the **Funicolore di S Anna**, in Piazza del Portello. Use a normal bus ticket and take a ride on this up the hill.

The third area of interest is east of Piazza de Ferrari, where the grand arcaded avenues of a more contemporary city head out. Via XX Settembre is a porticoed shoppers' delight, heading through a monumental arch to the Piazza della Vittoria beyond. North of here, in the streets around Piazza Colombo, look out for some excellent shops selling freshly-made pasta and the bustling municipal market.

PRACTICAL INFORMATION
Orientation
Ferries still leave and arrive from the old harbour, **Porto Vecchio**, a narrow bay to the west of the old town. Currently, international boats leave from the western side of the

harbour, with the actual **Stazione Marittima** more for cruise ships.

Most of the sights are to the east of the harbour, around the old town. Genoa is a very vertical city, though, with plenty of hills and sometimes staircases instead of streets. The main roadway around the harbour is Via Antonio Gramsci, which is more expressway than elegant harbour corniche. The eastern side of the harbour is where much of the redevelopment has taken place, with museums and classy tributes to Columbus and the city's maritime golden age. Back up behind this is the jumble of narrow streets and dark arcades that constitute the old town, a sometimes very seedy venue, but during the daytime a bustle of small traders, in keeping somehow with its medieval feel. Up behind here the streets get grander; this is where most of the hotels, museums and other sights are located.

The **airport** is no real distance away, having been built on reclaimed land off the seafront just west off the harbour. There are two **train stations**: Stazione Principe just north of the harbour and Stazione Brignole to the east of town. Getting around town is easily done on foot, though there are frequent buses; tickets are available from *tabacchi* (small newsagents).

Services
The main IAT **tourist information office** (☎ 248 711; 🖳 www.apt.genova.it), on the waterfront of the Porto Antico in Palazzina Santa Maria, is open daily 0900-1830. There are also smaller offices at Piazza Giacomo Matteotti (☎ 557 4000, daily 0900-2000) and next to Magazzini del Cotone (☎ 248 5611, same hours). There are also information offices at the airport (☎ 601 5247) and at Stazione Marittima (☎ 530 8201, Mon-Sat 0800-2000).

The main **post office**, 4a, Via Dante, is open Mon-Sat 0815-1940.

Bar Superba, an **internet café** at Salita San Giovanni, just outside Stazione Principe, is a handy venue, though it shuts around 2000. Internet Point Il Faro at 17r, Via Polleri shuts at 1900.

There are several **bookshops**: try Libreria Monadori at 210r, Via XX

Settembre for general books in English, or the Touring Club Italiano in Piazza Matteoti for travel and tour stuff. A good second-hand/rare book venue is Libreria di Piazza delle Erbe, at 25, Piazza delle Erbe.

Ferries [see p443 for full details]

Genoa is a lynchpin port for the Western Mediterranean ferry system, with boats from here to:

Barcelona Grandi Navi Veloci, or GNV (☎ 25465), 51, Via Milano, part of the Grimaldi group, an ancient Genoese family, run services twice a week in January, three times a week in February and March, four a week the rest of the year.

Corsica From June to September, Moby Lines (☎ 254 1513) at Terminal Traghetti, run between **Bastia** and Genoa.

Sardinia Tirrenia has a service to **Arbatax** and **Cágliari**; GNV (see above for contact details), Moby and Tirrenia to **Olbia**; GNV to **Porto Torres**, and Enermar to **Palau**.

Sicily GNV operates services to **Palermo**.

Tangier Comanav services operate approximately every four days between June and September.

Tunis Compagnie Tunisienne de Navigation (CTN)/Tunisia Ferries, GNV and SNCM operate on this route. CTN boats dock at Quay Doria. Contact Tunisia Ferries (☎ 25 80 41) via any travel agent.

Valletta GNV's Tunis service goes via Valletta from Genoa but directly back to Genoa from Tunis.

Trains

Genoa has two stations: Stazione Principe (☎ 274 2150), just north of the harbour in Piazza Aquaverde for most trains to and from France; and Stazione Brignole (☎ 543 070) to the east of town in Piazza Giuseppe Verdi, mainly for trains to Italy.

There are frequent trains to Nice (3 hours, €15), with several direct but most

involving a change at Ventimiglia on the border. For Marseille change at Nice. This coastal line is one of the most scenic in Europe. Going the other way are frequent trains to Rome (5½ hours, €29) and on to Naples (7½ hours, €40). There are also regular trains to Turin (1½ hours, €12) and Milan (1¾ hours, €12). For Venice, change at Milan.

Buses

The main bus station is in Piazza della Vittoria, which deals with international and Ligurian services, as well as some other Italian destinations. Try Pesci Viaggi e Turismo (☎ 564936) in the piazza for tickets. There is a Eurolines bus from the UK to Genoa: for details call ☎ +44 870 514 3219 or try ⌨ www.eurolines.it. The train, though, is generally faster and more comfortable.

Planes

Genoa's airport (☎ 60151, ⌨ www.airport.genova.it) is 6km west of the main harbour. Bus No 100 calls at the airport, Stazione Principe, Stazione Brignole, and Piazza de Ferrari. The service runs twice an hour and costs €2. Use regular city-bus tickets, on sale from the nearest newsagent kiosk. Currently the last bus leaves the airport at 2345; the first one goes there at 0615.

Air Dolomiti (in partnership with Lufthansa), and Alitalia are the main carriers from the airport. Connecting flights via German and Italian airports link Genoa to most of the rest of the planet, so it should be possible to get there without encountering too much trouble.

Where to stay

Ostello Genova (☎ 242 2457), 120, Via Costanzi in Righi, north of the old town. The official HI hostel; take bus No 40 from Stazione Brignole; €14 per bunk including breakfast.
Flowers Hotel (☎ 246 1918), 1, Via Lomellini, just off Via del Camp; €40/65 sgl/dbl.
Hotel Doina (☎ 247 4278), 2, Vico dei Garibaldi, in a tucked-away location; €32/45 sgl/dbl.

Hotel Major (☎ 247 4174), 4, Vico Spada, in the heart of the old town. €22/32 sgl/dbl in basic accommodation.

Hotel Lausanne (☎ 261 634) Near Stazione Principe off Via Balbi, reached by a lift from street level. €32/45 sgl/dbl.

Where to eat

Eating breakfast and lunch represents little difficulty for the budget traveller in Genoa as there are dozens of cafés selling all types of pastries and *panini* (sandwiches). However, in the evening you may be limited to one course at a restaurant or trattoria, or something from a fast-food chain.

Trattoria Lombarda da Peppino, 26, Via Finocchiaro Aprile Camillo. Good local fare for €10 a head.

Doge Bar, 5, Piazza Giacomo Matteotti. Good views and fine *panini* for €1.90; closed evenings.

Ugo Il Pirata, 34, Via Finocchiaro Aprile Camillo. Some excellent local variants served in mock pirate-ship surrounds; €8 at lunch, €12-18 evenings.

La Taverna di Colombo, 6, Vico della Scienza. A popular choice in the old town; €12 or a first course only at €3.90.

Nightlife

Hot Vibes, 26, Salita Pollaiuoli. A bit off the beaten track but a good place to check out the posters for other clubs.

Liquid Art Café, 35r, Piazza Cavour. Good hours and DJs, turning clubby after 2200.

Britannia Pub, 76, Vico della Casana. For a Guinness fix.

Livorno

AREA CODE: 0586 **POPULATION**: 175,000

Long known in English, bizarrely, as Leghorn, Livorno is now a thriving and bustling port city, with a mass of ferry and rail connections. Not known for its beauty, it does, however, have an impressive artistic past and still boasts some pleasant back streets and picturesque neighbourhoods, once you venture out of the city centre. It's

unlikely you'll be staying long, with regular boats leaving for Corsica and Sardinia, but if the ferry times are out of sync, there's still enough to make a stop worthwhile.

HISTORY

Livorno began to feature on the historical map in the Middle Ages, becoming first a Pisan port in the 14th century. Shuffled round between the Pisans, the Genoese and the Florentines, it was the latter, under the reign of Cosimo I, the Medici ruler of Florence, who began the major construction of the harbour in 1571. Ferdinand I then began transforming it from a provincial centre into a Mediterranean one, bringing in different ethnic and religious groups from across the sea. This was continued by Leopold II in the 18th century, who enlarged the city still further. This policy of encouraging many of Europe and the Med's outcast communities — Jews, Greeks, Spanish Muslims and English Catholics — to settle here continued into the 19th century, when it became a venue for many northern artists and poets, with Shelley foremost among them.

By the time it became part of the Kingdom of Italy in 1860, Livorno was rapidly expanding. It was a major port city by World War II, which meant it suffered badly from Allied bombing. This also explains the less-than-graceful rebuild of much of the city centre and port area since 1945.

WHAT TO SEE

Livorno is not strong on museums, cathedrals or other visitor staples, with the **Museo Civico Giovanni Fattori** (☎ 808001, open Tues-Sun 1000-1300, 1600-1900, €6.50) a somewhat solitary museum. Located 1km south of Via San Jacopo at 65 Acquaviva on the No 1 bus route, it has a collection of Italian impressionist paintings.

There's also the Jewish museum, the **Museo Ebraico** (☎ 893361, open daily except Sat 1000-1700, free) at 21, Via Micali. Housed in the Marini Oratory, this was converted into a synagogue in 1867 and came to house many of the Jewish community's treasures, many of which are now on display.

TYRRHENIAN SEA

PRACTICAL INFORMATION
Orientation
The Stazione Marittima in the central Porto Mediceo is 500m south-west of the city centre, behind the Fortezza Vecchia and the politically dubious Quattro Mori, a 16th-century statue of Ferdinand I lording it over four Moorish slaves.

Check ferry departure points when you buy the ticket, though, as some depart from the Varco Galvani, west of town, connected to the Piazza Grande in town by a regular port bus (☎ 800 371 560).

The train station is 2km east of Piazza Grande, on city bus No 1 or 2 from the square, while Piazza Manin is the place for intercity buses.

Services
The main **tourist information office** is at 6, Piazza Cavour, ☎ 204611, open Mon-Fri 0900-1300 & 1500-1700, Sat 0900-1300.

Ferries   [see p445 for full details]
Corsica Ferries (CFSF; ☎ 881380), Nuova Stazione Marittima, Calata Carrara, and Moby (☎ 826822/23/25), Via V Veneto, 24, operate services to **Bastia**. CFSF also goes to **Golfo Aranci**, and Moby and Linea dei Golfi to **Olbia**. Linea dei Golfi also has services to **Cágliari**.

GNV (☎ 409804), Darsena 1, have services to **Palermo** and **Valencia**. Other companies with offices in Livorno are Corsica Marittima (☎ 210507), with services to **Porto Vecchio**, at Via dei Carabinieri, 28 Palazzo Centrale; Saremar and Tirrenia to **Golfo Aranci** (☎ 424730), Calata Addis Abeba, Varco Galvani, and finally Toremar (☎ 896113), Porto Mediceo.

Trains
Livorno is on the main north-south west-coast line and on the network heading across Italy via Pisa. Thus it has regular connections to destinations throughout Italy – with Florence and Siena only an hour or so away.

Buses
ATL buses to Piombino go from the Piazza Grande, while inter-city buses to Florence, Pisa and Lucca use the Piazza Manin.

Planes
Pisa airport (🖳 www.pisa-airport.com) is around 20km from the city, connected to Pisa by CPT bus which leaves every 20 minutes (€0.80). The bus goes to Pisa central station, from where trains to Livorno depart. It's easier, however, to catch a train straight from the airport, with tickets purchased at information in arrivals. There are regular trains to Pisa, where you change for Livorno or keep going for Florence.

Where to stay
Try the *Milano*, (☎ 219 155) at 48, Via degli Asili, in the main cheap hotels and pensions region around the harbour.

The **campsite** is *Miramare* (☎ 580 402, 🖳 www.campingmiramare.com) at 220, Via del Littorale, though it closes October–April.

Where to eat
Seafood is the Livorno speciality, with the *cacciucco* – a seafood stew – world renowned. Try *Antico Moro* at 59, Via Bertelloni for a reasonably priced version. Otherwise, try the **Piazza Cavour** for other options.

Corsica

AREA CODE: ☎ 0495 **POPULATION:** 250,000
This place has it all, from stunning beaches to towering mountains, from wondrous cooking to the birthplace of Napoleon. On Corsica, it's possible to combine just about every type of holiday going, from diving to potholing to lounging around doing absolutely nothing, all within fairly easy distance of each other.

It's also one of the least French parts of France there is. Come here from the south, from Sardinia, and the difference is barely noticeable at first, particularly since EU membership and the euro zone mean there's no customs and the currency is the same. It's more the case of a subtle change of tone, rather than the completely new colours marked by a national frontier. If it weren't for a change of postage stamps, you'd think you were still in the same country, just in a different region.

Which, psychologically speaking, is true. Corsica has spent most of its existence outside France, a fact that still resonates in the strong Corsican nationalist movement. As with Provence, Langue d'Oc and Catalunya, there is a sense here of being in one of the great buried medieval kingdoms of the north-western Mediterranean, and of there being a great deal of life left in these grand old nations.

HISTORY

It's generally thought the first Corsicans probably came over from the Italian mainland. They created *menhirs*, giant standing stones, many of which can still be seen about the island. Around 1100BC, though, the island was invaded by a different race, the Torréens, so called after the *torri* (stone towers) they built alongside and even occasionally amongst the old menhirs. The Torréens were also present on Sardinia, where they built the characteristic conical stone towers known as *nuraghi*.

In the 6th century BC the Greeks founded the city of Alalia at what is now Aleria, on the eastern coast. The name change came when the Romans invaded to gain a useful base in their conflict with the Carthaginians. Roman rule was highly unpopular and its Western Empire collapsed on the arrival of the Goths and Vandals. The Eastern Empire, Byzantium, took over Corsica in the 6th century but as a distant province Corsica was vulnerable to attacks from the Moors of North Africa, who launched repeated slaving expeditions to the island.

The protection of the Papacy, who acquired the island in 774 from the Franks, did little to prevent the attacks. Sending the bishop of Pisa to reassert papal authority, the island became de facto Pisan territory for the next 50 years, though the Pisans' enduring struggle with the Genoans forced Pope Innocent II, in 1133, to divide the island between the two Italian city states. Genoa didn't stop there, though, and expanded its control, taking the whole island after defeating Pisa at the naval battle of Meloria (near Livorno) in 1284.

This began a period of Genoese rule that was to last five centuries. The island was divided up between Corsican feudal lords and Genoese administrators, who fortified the island and developed it as a resource for Genoa. Little love was lost between anyone here, with Vincentello d'Istria, the leader of the Corsican lords, finally striking a deal with Alfonso V, the king of Aragon, in 1420 to try to evict the Genoese. Alfonso was an ally of Genoa's great rival of the time, Venice. However, the Aragonese attack on the island was largely a failure, d'Istria doing what many a Corsican has done over the centuries and taking to the hills. His campaign against the Genoese continued from there until he was caught and executed in 1434.

The rebellious Corsicans were proving expensive, though, so in 1453 the Genoese privatized their administration of the island by contracting it out to the Banco di San Giorgio, one of the world's top Renaissance financial houses. They pacified the island through a policy of summary executions, until the French took an interest in 1553. Anxious to weigh in on turmoil in Italy at the time, a French force, with the Turkish corsair Dragut as second in command, rapidly took the island. However, the French then just as quickly lost it, a bad outcome for the many Corsicans who had given their support to the losing side when the Genoese returned to take command.

This sorry state of affairs continued until 1730 when a tax revolt turned into an armed rebellion that lasted 40 years. Genoa was aided by the Austrian Empire. A number of pitched battles occurred, one of them, the Battle of Calenzana in 1732, a notable success for the Corsican rebels. In 1735 the Corsicans drew up a constitution for an independent sovereign state. Desperate for some international legitimacy, the Corsicans then made a visiting German aristocrat-cum-con-man, Theodor von Neuhof, constitutional monarch — a position von Neuhof found well to his liking before he vanished with much of the rebels' gold.

The Genoese, meanwhile, had enlisted

TYRRHENIAN SEA

the support of the king of France, Louis XV. Despite an initial defeat at the Battle of Borgo, the French seemed to have finally put down the rebellion by 1741. However, their administration pleased neither the Genoese nor Corsicans, and the French troops pulled out in 1753. Within two years the rebellion had broken out again. This time the Corsican leader was Pascal Paoli, still venerated to this day. Paoli designed an ahead-of-its-time constitution and succeeded in pressing the Genoese so far that once again they called in French assistance: having beaten Paoli's forces at the Battle of Ponte Nuovo in 1769, they annexed Corsica.

The French Revolutionary Wars seemed at first to offer Corsica another chance. Paoli, who had been in exile in London, was allowed to return and lead a revolutionary army against neighbouring Sardinia. The campaign failed and the Paris government ordered Paoli's arrest.

It was known that Napoleon, Corsica's most famous son, and now a captain in the French Army, had encouraged Paoli's Sardinian venture and, on his arrest, he was ordered back to France. Taking with him his mother and brothers, in danger because of their recent close association with Paoli, Napoleon left Corsica forever. Henceforth the island became a mere pawn in the Napoleonic Wars.

Paoli's supporters sought British aid against the French and the British Navy under Nelson rapidly gained control, overwhelming a series of French garrisons and finally Calvi (where Nelson lost the sight of one eye). The Anglo-Corsican kingdom soon broke up, the bitterly disillusioned Paoli dying in London in 1807. Corsica as a British base rapidly became strategically untenable, and the British abandoned it to the French in 1796, after having apparently considered giving it to the Russians.

The 19th century saw mass emigration from Corsica, leaving a semi-feudal rural structure dominated by Mafia-style families and grotesque traditions such as the vendetta of their homelands. This strong reputation for resistance, however, served the island well in WWI and WWII.

Post-war the nationalist struggle resurfaced. The Front de Libération National de Corse (FLNC) was set up in 1976 to demand independence, and bomb attacks became a daily occurrence. The FLNC then proceeded to split into various groups in the 1980s and 1990s, each often more intent on killing each other than independence. The violence has calmed down a great deal since then, though political assassinations have continued. Meanwhile, the French administration has veered from granting more autonomy to cracking down on dissent, a process that continues to this today. By and large, though, while visitors will most likely find themselves in discussion over these issues at some point, there is little danger posed to tourists themselves.

ORIENTATION

Your point of arrival by sea on Corsica is likely to be either Bonifacio in the south, if you're coming from Sardinia, or Ajaccio, Bastia or Calvi if you're coming from mainland France or Italy. The main island airport is at Ajaccio, though there are also smaller airports at each of the towns listed above. There are no flights between these airports.

Getting around on public transport is not always easy. There are buses, though these are often only once a day between the major cities and towns. There's also a train network including the marvellous light railway through the heart of the mountains from Ajaccio to Corte, yet there aren't many services elsewhere. Your best bets may therefore be either hitching or hiring.

Topographically, Corsica is a real mixture. Most of the island is national parkland, with towering granite mountains, forests and some of the clearest highland streams throughout the central areas that I have ever seen. The east coast, though, is mainly flat marshland, while there's even a bona fide desert in the north-west, the **Désert des Agriates**. Meanwhile, the coast around Bonifacio is like southern England's, all high chalky cliffs and wild, eroded sea stacks.

BASTIA

AREA CODE: ☎ 0495 **POPULATION:** 38,728
After Calais, Bastia is France's busiest port for passenger traffic, being the shortest route

over to the mainland and nowadays a tourist destination in its own right. North of it runs the mountainous **Cap Corse** Peninsula, while the Désert des Agriates is a short way to the north-west. There's also a train south which eventually leads across the island's central peaks and down to the capital, Ajaccio. The town's citadel makes a good place for a wander, and the whole is a great introduction to the Corsican *différence*.

History
In 1372 the Genoese established Bastia, its name deriving from *bastiglia*, the Genoan word for 'fortress'. It rose in importance to become the capital of the Genoese-controlled island in 1452, a status that led to further expansion and the construction of the Terra Nova district.

In 1764, though, the island passed into French hands, only for it then to be taken away by the British in the early years of the Revolution following a two-month siege by the Royal Navy under Nelson. Passing back to the French in 1791, Bastia then lost its status as capital to Ajaccio, largely because of Bastia's reputation for rebelliousness. It remained the island's military capital, though, and today it is capital of Haute Corse, one of the island's two *départments*.

What to see
The **statue of Napoleon** in place St Nicolas is probably as good a place as any to start a tour, the great man looking out east towards the island of Elba on which he was exiled in 1814, escaping in 1815 to make his final gamble and meet his Waterloo.

Head south from here, down rue Napoléon, and you'll find the Terra Vecchia, Bastia's oldest district, and two baroque chapels, **Chapelle St Roch** and **Oratoire de l'Immaculée Conception**. The latter is of note both for the Genoese sun motif and for being the venue for the short-lived Anglo-Corsican parliament. Inside, there's the throne intended for George III.

Turn left here for **place de l'Hôtel de Ville**, the town hall, which usually serves as a market. In the south-west corner is **Église St Jean Baptiste**, the town's largest church, built in 1666. Towards the sea from here are a number of tightly-grouped streets containing some of the older houses, many being 17th- and 18th-century Genoese constructions. There might have been more, were it not for a tragic WWII 'friendly fire' incident in which Allied bombers mistakenly flattened the area during celebrations by the locals to mark the fact that the occupying German troops had just withdrawn.

From here a walk back around the old harbour brings you to the Citadel, or Terra Nova district on the south side. The main entrance leads you to **place Donjon**, with the **Palais du Gouverneurs** on the right. From here, wander along to see the houses that have been largely restored and are a delight to investigate. You should go also into **Église Ste Croix** and look out for the much venerated Black Cross, discovered at sea by local fishermen in 1428.

Practical information
Orientation   Ferries dock at the Gare Maritime right next to place St Nicolas in the centre of town, with the fortress and Terra Nova to the south. The *place* is also

---

Désert des Agriates
This mysterious region north-west of Bastia was until relatively recently a fertile agricultural zone. Repeated fires and bad land-use put paid to that and now it's a stony, barren wasteland. Strangely, this desert is where you'll find several of the best beaches in the Mediterranean.

Getting to them can be tricky without your own transport but you can take a Calvi bus, getting off at Casta on the D81 to hitch north from there, or just hitch all the way: hitching is fairly easy on Corsica. Or you can go to St Florent and take a 30-minute boat trip from the harbour (€9 return). The beaches to head for are Plage de Saleccia, Plage du Loto and Plage de l'Ostriconi.

NOUVEAU PORT

South Ferry Terminal

Buses to Ajaccio & Corte

Hôtel Riviera

Post Office

BLVD GENERAL GRAZIANI

Train station

AVE MARECHAL SEBASTIANI

AVE F. PIETRI

Hotel de l'Universe

Tourist Info

Place St Nicholas, bus stops

BLVD GEN DE GAULLE

BOULEVARD PAOLI

Napoleon statue

Hotel Central

RUE MIOT

RUE NAPOLÉON

Chapelle St Roch

QUAI DES MARTYRS DE LA LIBERATION

Ferries to Marseille, Livorno, Savona, Toulon, Nice & Genoa

Chapelle de l'Immaculée Conception

BLVD GEN GIRAUD

RUE CESAR CAMPINCHI

BOULEVARD PAOLI

Place de l'Hotel de Ville (market)

Eglise St Jean-Baptiste

A Scaletta

U Marinaru Restaurant

TERRA VECCHIA

OLD HARBOUR

TYRRHENIAN SEA

QUAI DU SUD

Tunnel

0   100m

Palais des Gouverneurs

CITADEL

Eglise St Croix

TERRA NOVA

Camping du Bois de San Damiano, 8km

Bastia

where buses arrive, using a few spare parking spots at the bottom of rue du Nouveau Port in the north-west corner. The train station is also just inland from the north-western corner, up ave Maréchal Sébastiani. The rest of the town runs roughly north–south along the coast, with the more historical bits at the southern end. Nowhere's very far away, though, with everything within easy walking distance.

Services The **tourist information office** (☎ 95 54 20 40), on the northern side of place St Nicolas, is open daily, in summer 0800-2000; in winter 0900-1200, 1400-1800. It has plenty of free handouts, including maps, and organizes free walking tours.

For a **bookshop** try Libraire Jean-Patrice Marzocchi, 2, rue du Conventionnel Saicetti. **Car hire** is available at ADA , 35, rue Caesar Campinchi, though it shuts on Sundays. Most of the international companies also have branches here.

Cycles can be hired out from Objectif Nature, 3, rue Notre Dame de Lourdes, for €15 a day.

Ferries [see p442 for full details] SNCM (office Nouveau Port; Mon-Fri 0730-1900, Sat 0800-1200; national enquiries, France ☎ 0891 701801) operate daily boats to **Marseille**; both SNCM and CFSF (☎ 32 95 95, 5 bis, rue Chanoine Leschi) have services to **Nice**.

From June to September, Moby Lines (☎ 34 84 94), Sarl Colonna d'Istria et Fils, rue Commandant, sails daily to **Genoa**. Both CFSF and Moby go to **Livorno**, and CFSF also goes regularly to **Savona** and **Toulon**.

Trains Chemins de Fer de la Corse (CFC) operate two trains a day from the train station (☎ 32 80 61) to Calvi (3 hours, €15), and seven to Corte (1½ hours, €9.50), with five of these continuing on to Ajaccio (4 hours, €19). There may still be delays on the Corte–Ajaccio section as work continues on the light railway line through the mountains. Look out for signs in the stations announcing the expected delays. The journey is magnificently scenic.

Buses Eurocorse (☎ 21 06 30) operate a service to Ajaccio (Mon-Sat, 5 hours, €16). Autocortenais (☎ 46 02 12) go three times a week to Corte (2½ hours, €9).

Where to stay As with any destination in France, finding accommodation in the high season can be tricky. Avoid the island altogether during public holidays (see p54). Otherwise, there are plenty of characterful and relatively inexpensive places.
Hôtel de l'Univers (☎ 31 03 38), 3, ave Maréchal Sébastiani. Right in town; sgl/dbl for €25/35 with shared bathrooms.
Hôtel Riviera (☎ 31 07 16), 1, rue du Nouveau Port. A long-standing haunt, €30/55 sgl/dbl.
Hôtel Central (☎ 31 71 12), 3, rue Miot. A range of rooms and prices but try for €38/50 sgl/dbl.
Camping du Bois de San Damiano (☎ 33 68 02), Plage de la Marana, 8km to the south. Shuttle bus; camping costs €5 a person, €2 extra for a car.

Where to eat *A Scaletta*, in the old port. A top fish and seafood place; €10-15 for a full meal.
Restaurant U Marinaru At 2, rue de Pontetto in the Old Harbour, is similarly located and has similar fare; closed Sundays.

CORTE
AREA CODE: ☎ 0495 POPULATION: 6329
This is the Corsican heartland, the one-time capital of nationalist rebel leader Pascal Paoli, now the seat of the island's only university and a mountain redoubt dominated by a medieval citadel.

It's also at the centre of some simply beautiful countryside, with the light railway up from Bastia running down to Ajaccio through here and on the way passing by some wonderful mountain villages and halts, snow-covered for much of the year. Far from the sea it may seem, but it is here that much of the island's soul is held.

History
A settlement since the earliest times and a fortress town by the 11th century, the story of

the town is also largely the story of Corsica's historical rebellions. Vincentello d'Istria, the Corsican lord who fought the Genoese, built a small fortress here in 1419; its strategic position was lost on no one. Almost every battle in the island's history seems to have been settled around here, while Pascal Paoli briefly made it the centre of his independent Corsican state from 1755 to 1769.

With Paoli's defeat, the French occupied the town and fort, continuing to garrison it until 1962 with the Foreign Legion. It continued as a seat of protest by Corsican nationalists, especially around the university, which Paoli had founded but which was closed until the 1980s. Today it has a certain small-town feel, high in the hills and remote from the flashier Corsica of the coast.

What to see
The main target for any visitor is usually the **citadel**. This is perched high above the River Tavignanu, and while much of what you see now is French 18th- and 19th-century development, the original fort here dates from 1419. Inside, the Caserne Serrurier, the former legion barracks, houses the **Musée de la Corse** (Mon-Sat 1000-2000, closed Mon in winter, €5). The focus is very much on the cultural and commercial artefacts of the Corsican people. It's well laid out and with an English language cassette available for touring around.

Paoli's government was installed next door at the **Paluzzu Naziunale**, the former Genoese governor's residence. Now it holds some university departments and a ground-floor exhibition area. From the battlements of the citadel have a good look around as the views are magnificent. This done, there's not a lot else here to see but Corte can be a good base if you fancy some outdoor pursuits such as walking or horse riding in the valleys and hills around. Otherwise, get back on the train and go down to Ajaccio.

Practical information
Orientation You'll need to be fairly fit, as the town is built on a series of crags. The place is pretty much split in two by Cours Paoli, with an upper and lower town on either side of this. The train station is about

1km east of the town and someway downhill. Buses arrive and depart from the Bar Majestic. Corte is a small place though so getting around on foot is easy.

Services The **tourist information office** (☎ 46 26 70), located in the Padoue barracks at the entrance to the Citadel, is open during summer Mon-Sat 0900-1300, 1500-1900, Sun 1000-1300, 1500-1900; the rest of the year, weekdays only 1000-1800. Has some material, such as maps and local guides in French (and of course, Corsu) and accommodation lists.

Trains The station (☎ 46 00 97) has six trains a day to Bastia (1½ hours, €9.50), five to Ajaccio (1¾ hours, €19). See Bastia section (p141) for the note on delays.

Buses Eurocorse runs a daily service to Ajaccio (2 hours, €9) and Bastia (1½ hours, €9). Autocars Cortennais also run 3 buses a week to Bastia from their office on Cours Paoli, with similar prices and times.

Where to stay *Hôtel HR* (☎ 45 11 11), 6, allée du 9 Septembre. Spacious and has a sauna; €20/30 sgl/dbl.
Hôtel de la Poste (☎ 46 01 37), 2, place Padoue. An old favourite; €28/40 sgl/dbl.
Camping Alivetu (☎ 46 11 09), allée du 9 Septembre, about 1km south-west of the train station. Apr-Oct only, €7.50 for a tent and one person.

Where to eat *Le Gaffory*, place Gaffory de l'Église. Has an excellent wild boar lasagne; €15 a head.
U Paglia Orba, ave Xavier Luciani. Menus for €8-10, with plenty of local produce.
Auberge de la Restonica, 1km out of town on the D623. Best for a splurge, an old hunting lodge by a waterfall with most of the dishes caught rather than bought; €20.

CALVI
AREA CODE: 04 95 POPULATION: 5000
With its yacht-filled harbour lying beneath a 15th-century citadel, Calvi is another hugely popular destination for beach-lovers, with a fine, sandy strip running

along pine-covered shores. Located in the north-west of the island, it also has good ferry links to France and rail and road links to other places on the island. These include the mountainous interior which rises rapidly inland behind the town.

History

Settled by Greeks in ancient times, they are said to be responsible for introducing the olive trees to the region, which became known as Balagne, or 'olive grove'. Never much more than a village, though, Calvi became Pisan territory, then Genoan, with the Genoese building the impressive citadel. Calvi remained faithful to Genoa for many years, launching an uprising, led by Pietro Baglioni, against the Spanish Aragonese who had taken the town in 1420.

It also stayed loyal to Genoa during the famous Pascal Paoli rebellion of 1755. Calvi is also one of the many Mediterranean venues to lay claim to Christopher Columbus, who was allegedly born in the citadel around 1436.

Several attempts to take the town were made in the 16th century by the Franco-Turkish coalition of the day, though these proved unsuccessful – miraculously so, according to the local legend. The city then grew to become capital of Corsica for a while, before the 1768 treaty joined the whole island to France. The British then besieged the town in 1794, a battle that involved the naval action in which Admiral Nelson lost an eye. During the 19th century Calvi developed further thanks to the new train line and the development of tourism.

The ferry Napoléon Bonaparte

As its name suggests, the Napoléon Bonaparte is not just a prince among ferries, but an emperor. When I first saw it, towering above the dock side in Ajaccio, this 171m-long floating hotel seemed as far removed from the tired old Aegean ferries I was used to as the space shuttle is from a Montgolfier balloon.

For the budget traveller, SNCM's Napoléon Bonaparte is about the closest you're likely to get to a cruise liner during your Mediterranean travels. With its indoor and outdoor swimming pools, Jacuzzis, choice of restaurants and bars – hell, it even has electronic key cards for your cabin – it can be a welcome piece of luxury after many a night on deck, or trying to get comfy in a Pullman seat. It's also no great expense, either, thanks to the booming holiday traffic between France and Corsica, and doubtless too a useful subsidy from Paris, worried about its troubled island drifting off.

So, make sure you've remembered your swimming costume as you board via the space-age terminal at Ajaccio, entering through a transparent, umbilical-cord-like covered walkway high above the quayside. While the ship design is of the up-ended skyscraper variety so beloved of contemporary liner architects, once inside, its boxy shape undeniably gives it a feeling of space. In fact, it gives a feeling of being inside anything but a ferry. Shopping centre, perhaps, or hotel, but where is the smell of the sea, the cramped bulkhead, the rattling and thudding of the propellers? There is scarcely a vibration as the ship puts out to sea, which seems too far below us from the well-scrubbed deck, or the 212-seat Piano Bar La Vigie, towering up beyond that still.

Arriving in Marseille the next morning, the great ship parks against the quay thanks to a spread of side jets and box and stern propellers that your average Greek ferry skipper would die for. Even disembarkation, that usual moment of pushing and shoving down crowded, pitching staircases, seems almost graceful, along another, airport-like connecting corridor.

While it's not the adventurous battle with the elements some might wish for during a sea crossing, that's clearly the point here – and it's a point that may be very welcome after too many traditional Mediterranean ferries.

TYRRHENIAN SEA

The latter has continued into the present, with Calvi receiving the most visitors of any Corsican resort.

What to see
Calvi's ochre-walled 15th-century citadel, built by the Genoese, contains most of the town's treasures. The entrance is just above place Christophe Colomb at the top of blvd Wilson. From the square, a cobbled alley winds up into the citadel and the 13th-century **Cathedral de Saint Jean Baptiste**. A classic baroque building, it was heavily restored in 1570.

Uphill along rue Colomb lies the ruined house locally known as the birthplace of Christopher Columbus. A plaque on one wall attests to this, though the jury has long been out on the veracity of Calvi's claims to the discoverer of the New World.

Otherwise, looking around is a major attraction in Calvi, with spectacular views on offer at Chez Tao, over the marina; while the **Chapelle de Notre Dame de la Serra**, perched on a ridge high above Calvi, has other, finer vistas. To get there, walk from Hôtel La Villa, following the lane uphill until you see a path forking to the left into the *maquis*, the rocky landscape of shrubs and small, wiry bushes that characterizes much of the Mediterranean coast. While the present chapel dates from the 19th century, there has been some form of shrine here since at least the 1400s.

The excellent white-sand beach is on the south side of the marina and curves for more than 4km around the bay. This stretch can still seem a short one in the height of summer, when it gets packed out, but, as usual, the further you walk away from town, the better it gets.

Practical information
Orientation The port is just below the citadel, with a short walk along quai Landry to the train station. The main street, blvd Wilson, links place Christophe Columb with La Porteuse d'Eau, the small square in front of the train station. Buses from Bastia arrive there. The airport is Ste-Cathérine, 8km south-west of the centre, which has no bus connection to town. A

taxi should cost around €15.

Services The **tourist office** (☎ 65 16 67 or 65 36 74) is open mid-June to end Sep, daily 0900-1930; Oct to mid-June, Mon-Sat 0845–1200, 1400-1800. It stands in Port de Plaisance, just above quai Landry. Check bus times there or better still at the travel agent on La Porteuse d'Eau.

Useful websites are ⌨ www.calvitravel.com and ⌨ www.tourisme.fr/calvi/e-index.htm.

Ferries [see p443 for full details] Both SNCM (☎ 65 17 77) and Corsica Ferries (☎ 65 43 21) operate ferries to **Marseille**, **Nice** and **Savona**.

The ticket booths on quai Landry for boat trips and ferries open two hours before departure; tickets are also available from Agence Tramar (☎ 65 01 38).

Trains There are two to three trains a day, on the Trinighellu, to L'Île Rousse (30-40 mins) and Ponte Leccia (80-100 mins), with connections to Ajaccio and Bastia.

Buses As well as local services, buses also run regularly to L'Île Rousse and Bastia.

Planes There are few direct flights to Calvi from anywhere other than places (such as Paris, Nice and Marseille) in France, and fewer airlines serve Calvi than Ajaccio and Bastia, so it's cheapest to come by ferry.

Where to stay
BVJ Corsotel (☎ 65 14 15, ⌨ bvj@wanadoo.fr), 43 ave de la République, is opposite the train station. It charges €22 per bed in a dorm of 4-8 beds, with attached bathrooms, or €25 per person in a double room including breakfast.
Hôtel du Centre (☎ 65 02 01), 12-14 rue Alcase-Lorraine, has rooms with attached showers for €30-45.

Where to eat
Finding somewhere to eat will not be a problem, though expect to pay more at places along quai Landry.

AJACCIO

AREA CODE: ☎ 0495 POPULATION: 59,000
The island capital, birthplace of Napoleon, major port and a town some of the inhabitants would rather see compared to Nice or Cannes than Bastia or Bonifacio, Ajaccio seems the most Gallicized Corsican town. It's also got some fine streets and buildings, good restaurants and several great museums. For Napoleonic buffs, it also has some regular re-enactments of parades from the bad old, good old days of the Grande Armée, while for others it's a relaxing connecting point for boats on to France.

History

Ajaccio's story starts some 3km north of the present town as a Roman settlement called Ajax. Things never really got anywhere until 1492, however, when the Genoese took over and decided to move here to escape the mosquito- and plague-ridden eastern coast. Briefly under the Turkish sailor of fortune, Drago, who ran the town along with his Corsican and French allies from 1553 to 1559, it stayed Genoese until the final French takeover in 1768.

The transfer of the capital from Bastia to Ajaccio during the Napoleonic Wars was part of the French emperor's overall strategy for dominating Europe; Bastia was strategically placed and well fortified and he cleared it for war by moving the capital. The Napoleonic tradition has had its ups and downs over the years — after defeat at Waterloo, the locals celebrated by throwing Napoleon's statue in the harbour — yet Ajaccio now seems distinctly proud of its most famous son. And it has a lot to thank him for in helping to maintain the town's importance and fair prosperity.

What to see

Regrettably, the town's most imposing structure, the citadel, is not open to the public. Instead, sightseeing in Ajaccio is really a matter of museums. This has recently become better value as the town launched its *Ajaccio pass musée* in 2002. For €10, you can use the pass to enter any or all of the town's museums. Valid for seven days,

it's on sale at the tourist information office. The place to start is the pedestrianized rue Cardinal Fesch, running inland parallel to the western side of the harbour, as it's here you'll find the Musée Fesch, at No 50. This is a clear contender for the Most Confusing Opening Hours in the Mediterranean Award. Here goes: July & Aug, Mon & Tue 1330-1800, Thu 0900-1830, Fri 0900-1830, 2100-2400, Sat & Sun 1030-1800; April-June and Sept, Mon 1300-1715, Tue & Sun 0915-1215, 1415-1715, closed Wed-Sat; Jan-March, Tue & Sat 0915-1215, 1415-1715. If you're fortunate enough to be there when it's open, expect to pay €5.25 to get in.

Cardinal Fesch was Napoleon's ambassador to the Vatican, a position perhaps helped by the fact that he was also one of Bonaparte's uncles. Fesch had a notable first secretary with him at the Vatican, Chateaubriand, and between them they famously persuaded the Pope to go to Paris in order to crown Napoleon emperor — although perhaps most famously of all, Bonaparte seized the crown from the Pope's holy fingers and crowned himself at the last minute.

Over the years, a diplomat may find he accumulates the odd trifle, and Fesch was clearly no exception. The Musée was in fact specially built to house his private collection of paintings, antiques and other treasures, including Botticellis, Titians, Bellinis and a whole host more. Next door is the Imperial Chapel which contains the remains of some of Napoleon's relatives, though the man himself is entombed at Les Invalides in Paris. There's also the Bibliothèque Municipal, a 70,000-volume library built in 1868 but commissioned way back in 1801 by Lucien Bonaparte, Napoleon's brother. Entrance is free and it is quite an impressive sight. Many of the books were originally confiscated by the revolutionary government from fleeing aristocrats and passed on to these new aristocrats.

The Napoleonic trail continues, with the Musée National de la Maison Bonaparte on rue Saint Charles (April-Sept, Tue-Sun 0900-1200, 1400-1800; Oct-Mar, 1000-1200, 1400-1645, €4). The museum contains the room in which Bonaparte was born,

TYRRHENIAN SEA

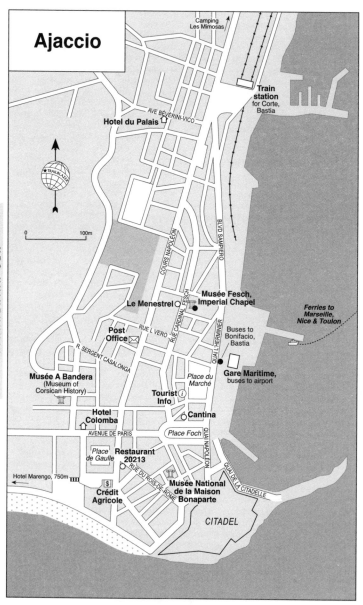

Ajaccio

Camping
Les Mimosas

Train station
for Corte, Bastia

AVE BEVERINI-VICO

Hotel du Palais

★ TRAILBLAZER

0   100m

COURS NAPOLÉON

BLVD SAMPIERO

Musée Fesch, Imperial Chapel

Le Menestrel

RUE CARDINAL FESCH

Ferries to Marseille, Nice & Toulon

RUE L VERO

Post Office

R. SERGENT CASALONGA

QUAI L'HERMINIER

Buses to Bonifacio, Bastia

Musée A Bandera
(Museum of Corsican History)

Place du Marché

Gare Maritime,
buses to airport

Tourist Info

TYRRHENIAN SEA

Hotel Colomba

AVENUE DE PARIS

Cantina

Place Foch

QUAI NAPOLÉON

Place de Gaulle

Restaurant 20213

RUE DU ROIS DE ROME

Hotel Marengo, 750m

Musée National de la Maison Bonaparte

QUAI DE LA CITADELLE

Crédit Agricole

CITADEL

on 15 August 1769. There are many exhibits of period weapons, furniture and documents, the house being occupied by the Bonaparte family from 1682.

Perhaps the best museum, however, is the **Musée a Bandera**, also known as the Museum of Corsican History, on rue du General Levie, further inland (1 July to 15 Sept, daily 0900-1900; 16 Sept to 30 Jun, Mon-Sat 0900-1200, 1400-1800, €3.80). Here you'll find a much broader spread of history, covering the whole island story up to and including WWII. There are plenty of dioramas, including one of the decisive 1769 Battle of Ponte Nuovo when the French finally gained control of the island. Look out, too, for the cap badges of the Royal Corsican Rangers, the British regiment raised from among King George III's loyal islanders. The museum also has a collection of nasty-looking knives used in vendettas, along with models of famous, Jesse-James-style 19th-century bandits.

Practical information

Orientation Ferries come and go from the Gare Maritime, a space-age construction by Mediterranean ferry standards, with an airport-like docking arm to take you on and off the plush SNCM ferries; the gare is on the western side of the harbour, just below the town centre. The train station is also on this side of the harbour but a little further north, on place de la Gare. The Gare Maritime is also the main bus station (*terminal routière*).

The town is spread around the harbour, with most of the sights immediately up behind the Gare Maritime, with the coast road leading south to the citadel before curving round to head west past some mediocre beaches. You'll have no need for the town's bus service, as everything is easily reached on foot.

Services The **tourist information office** (☎ 51 53 01), 3, blvd du Roi Jerome, is open July and August, Mon-Sat 0800-2030, Sun 0900-1300; and Sept-Jun, Mon-Fri 0800-1800, Sat 0800-1700. The office has good maps and brochures.

Changing money is not easy. While the town has plenty of ATM machines and

everywhere will accept credit cards, there's only one place, the Credit Agricole Bank on place de Gaulle, that will change money.

Internet access is available at Salle des Jeux on ave Ramaroni; it stays open until midnight.

Ferries [see p441 for full details] SNCM (quai L'Herminier, open Mon-Fri 0800-2000, Sat 0800-1200; national enquiries ☎ 0891 70180) has daily ferries to **Marseille** and services to **Nice**. CFSF (☎ 50 78 82) operates to **Nice** and **Toulon**.

Trains There are five trains a day to Corte (2 hours, €9.50), all of which continue on to Bastia (3¼ hours, €19).

Buses Eurocorse goes from the Gare Maritime to Bonifacio (4 hours, €19) twice a day. Note that this is the only way to get there by public transport. There are also two buses a day to Bastia, (5-6 hours, €18). The tourist information office should help with the latest schedules.

Planes Campo del'Oro Airport (☎ 23 56 56) is 8km east of town, with TCA bus No 8 making the trip from Gare Maritime, taking 20 minutes and charging €3.50. The half-hourly buses start to the airport at 0620, (last at 1810), while the last to the town is at 2245.

Where to stay *Hôtel Colomba* (☎ 21 12 66), 8, ave de Paris. Has sgl/dbl for €28/38. *Hôtel Marengo* (☎ 21 43 66), 2, rue Marengo. €35/55 but closes Dec to Feb. *Hôtel Palais* (☎ 22 73 68), 5, ave Bévérini Vico. Up another notch at €45/65. *Camping Les Mimosas* (☎ 20 99 85), 3km from the town centre on route d'Alta. €7 but shut in winter.

Where to eat *Restaurant 20213*, at 2, rue du Roi de Rome, for good local food at €15-25 a head. *Le Menestrel*, 5, rue Cardinal Fesch. Local music; the food's around €10 a head. *Cantina*, 3, blvd du Roi-Jérôme. Good local snacks for cool prices, €5.

BONIFACIO

Area code: ☎ 0495 Population: 1874

Arriving here by ferry from Sardinia is one of the more spectacular entrances of the Western Med, with the towering limestone cliffs seeming to present a solid wall as you approach. At the last minute, though, the curtain parts and a narrow inlet leads in below the Genoese town, which watches sternly from its hilltop perch.

Bonifacio is the island's most Genoese outpost, its connections across the short, 12km strait to Sardinia more frequent than its links to the rest of Corsica. Up in the old town you'll also find some of the island's most picturesque streets and remarkable views, the wind- and sea-sculpted coast around rippling with inlets, coves and sea caves, roaring against a wave-torn sea. In winter, hunkered down in one of its tiny cafés or restaurants, it's a place of seaside desertion, while in summer, the queue of traffic up the road from the marina to the old town can stretch inland for miles. Yet take time here whatever the season and from its City of the Dead, the Cimetière Marin, you'll see a town that long stays in the memory, a place at once familiar yet different.

History

Bonifacio was founded around AD833 by Boniface, Count of Tuscany, as a defensive bastion against attacks by pirates and Moors, a conflict that resulted in the town coming under the control of Pisa from 1050. The other Italian state contesting rule over Corsica, Genoa, then arrived in 1187, attacking while the Pisan defenders were attending a wedding. The Pisans regained it briefly in 1195, the Genoese returning the following year.

In 1215 St Francis of Assisi moved into a cave near the convent of St Julian. By this stage Bonifacio was a major Genoese settlement with its own governor. The fortress on the headland was supplied with its own underground cistern and generally fortified to withstand long sieges. The first of these began in 1420 when Corsican feudal lord and nationalist hero Vincentello d'Istria joined forces with the Spanish king, Alphonso V of Aragon, in an unsuccessful five-month bid to take the town and the rest of the island.

By 1528 the town's population had risen to 5000. This was, however, reduced to 700 by the plague in that same year. Barely recovered from that, a second siege began in 1553 when a similar alliance of Corsican nationalists and foreign powers saw local hero Sampiero join up with French Maréchal de Thermes and the corsair Dragut, now the Turkish sultan's greatest leader. This time it was all over in 18 days, with the town surrendering to far superior forces.

However, Genoese rule soon returned, the 1559 Treaty of Cateau-Cambresis undoing all the gains of the Franco-Turkish invasion. The Genoese further strengthened the defences, gradually expanded the old town and secured Bonifacio as a primary port for trade between Corsica and Sardinia. The town doesn't feature much again until after the island had been handed over to the French in 1768. Then in 1793 Captain Napoleon Bonaparte launched his ill-fated expedition against Sardinia's La Maddalena Island from here. On his return he was also nearly beaten to death by rebellious mutineers in one of the town's backstreets. The town sunk largely into oblivion following that, until recently undergoing a revival as a tourist destination.

What to see

The steps of the Montée Rastello lead you up to the **Porte de Gênes**, a tunnel of an entrance that gives you a good idea of the thickness of the fortification walls. This is the **Citadel**, a wonderful example of medieval architecture, a Renaissance Death Star with quaint meandering streets and beautiful squares. This gate dates from 1588, though the next door Bastion de l'Etendard ('Fortress of the Standard') is on an even older site. There you'll find the history museum, the **Memorial du Passe Bonifacien** (daily 1000-1230, 1330-1700, €1), which holds the remains of one of Bonifacio's earliest inhabitants, an 8000-year-old neolithic woman. There's also a fossilized Turkish soldier from the 1553 siege and some bizarrely misshapen waxwork Genoese guards.

Continue on to the rue des Deux Empereurs, which shows the houses where both Napoleon and Emperor Charles III stayed at various times, while in the street parallel to the south, rue du Palais de Garde, you'll find the small **Sacred Art Centre** (same hours as the Memorial, €1). In here are examples of the capes and crosses worn by the town's five brotherhoods, who parade on holy days and particularly at Easter, when cross-bearing penitents flank sacred reliquaries, iron and gold floats, which are manoeuvred up the town's steep steps. One of these, that of the white-caped and red-hooded San Bartolu brotherhood, weighs a hefty 800kg.

The main church of the Haute Ville is the **Église Ste Marie Majeure**, a Pisan job finished in the 14th century. Next to it is the old cistern, built by the Genoese and in use as a place for collecting rainwater until relatively recently. From here, walk south-west to the **Escalier du Roi d'Aragon**, a 45° cut of 187 steps sliced down through the limestone cliffs straight to the sea below. Local legend has it that this al-fresco staircase was built in one night by the besieging Spanish in the 1420 siege. However, hearing the doubtless not inconsiderable noise created by the army of Aragonese making the steps, a local woman, Marguerite Bobbia, raised the alarm and saved the town.

Out on the end of the Haute Ville Peninsula is the **Cimetière Marin**, the marine cemetery, composed in the high-Catholic style of houses of the dead, arranged in streets and squares within a walled enclosure. It's well worth spending some time wandering around, with the mausoleums and tombs of many of the town's inhabitants located here. Out beyond, the concrete emplacements of wartime defences edge the cliff-top, while the view along the coast is quite spectacular.

For a closer look at some of those dark **marine caves** eaten into the limestone cliffs, take a boat trip from the harbour — the **Port de Plaisance** being the place, at the marina end of the inlet. A **boat trip** will cost around €10 and will take you to some of the highlights of what is now a marine

park, a protected zone of the Bouches de Bonifacio, the narrow straits between here and Sardinia. There are also numerous coastal paths to the north and south, with the 1½-hour amble to Capo Pertusato, Corsica's southernmost point, a distance of 5.6km away south, a pleasant cliff-top stroll. As for beaches, the nearest is Plage de Sotta Rocca, at the end of a steep path down from the Montée St Roch.

Practical information

Orientation Bonifacio divides into two, both horizontally and vertically, with the old town on the headland — the **Haute Ville** — a quite separate world from the harbour and marina down below. Ferries arrive right beneath the cliffs of the old town, from where there's a five- to ten-minute walk to the bus station and the main group of hotels and restaurants at the harbour's end. To get up to the old town, prepare yourself for quite a climb, up steep steps from the harbour side — the **Montée Rastello** — or the much longer road — ave Charles de Gaulle — that winds round behind the town and up to the old town entrance. Apart from the puff that's required to get up there, you won't have to walk far to catch all the sights.

Services The **tourist information office** (☎ 73 11 88, 🖳 www.bonifacio.com), 2, rue Fred Scamaroni, opens in summer daily 0900-2000; the rest of the year Mon-Fri 0900-1200, 1400-1800, Sat morning only. It has maps and literature.

Internet access is available at Boniboom, on quai Jérôme Comparetti, next to the harbour. **Europcar** (☎ 73 10 99) has a branch on quai Noel Beretti.

Ferries [see p442 for full details] There are frequent ferries between Bonifacio and **Santa Teresa di Gallura**, Sardinia. CFSF and Moby Lines (☎ 73 00 29). Saremar lines (☎ 73 00 96) and Happy Lines (☎ 73 00 96) also operate but their services were suspended at the time of writing.

Ferries use the ferry terminal below the Haute Ville in the harbour, which is where you'll find the above companies' offices.

TYRRHENIAN SEA

Buses Eurocorse buses run from the large car-park area east of the harbour's end to Ajaccio, via Porto Vecchio, Roccapina, Sartene, Propriano and Olmete. Services operate Monday to Saturday twice a day in low season (early morning and lunchtime) and four times a day in summer. Be advised that afternoon boats from Sardinia will arrive too late out of season to get a bus to Ajaccio — or anywhere else en route.

Where to stay Nowhere in Bonifacio is exactly cheap though quality is generally good. If you're stuck and don't fancy camping, you may be in trouble, particularly if you've missed the last bus. Try the tourist office or hitching to Ajaccio, or grinning and bearing it with one of the below. In the off-season, prices can be lower.

Hôtel des Étrangers (☎ 73 01 09), ave Sylvère Bohn. Down in the harbour area, with sgl/dbl for €35/60.

Hôtel du Roi d'Aragon (☎ 73 03 99), 3, quai Jérôme Comparetti. Has a variety of rooms, the cheaper ones at the back being €45/70 sgl/dbl.

Le Royal (☎ 73 00 51) 8, rue Fred Scamaroni, in the old town. Has 14 rooms with prices from €39 for the smallest in winter to €68 for the same space in summer.

   Camping l'Araguina (☎ 73 02 96), ave Sylvère Bohn, is north of the marina and close to town. It charges about €8 for one person and a tent.

Where to eat Look out at lunchtimes for decently priced menus, particularly along the harbour-front road. *Cantina Doria*, 27 rue Doria, up in the Haute Ville, is an excellent, small-sized Corsican eatery with plenty of good quality local nosh for around €9 a head. *U Castille*, rue Simon Varsi, in the citadel, has good local fare for €8-10.

Sardinia

AREA CODE: ☎ 0789 **POPULATION:** 1.6 MILLION
Off the beaten track for many years, despite being the second largest of the Mediterranean islands, Sardinia has recently come back into favour as one of the more forgotten regions of this well-visited sea. This is especially true of its interior, where wild mountains and scrub-covered hills are home to some of the Med's rarer species, the griffon vulture and the albino donkey among them. Proximity to the Roman port of Civitavecchia does mean a fair crowd of tourists in the summer months for the beaches, yet some of the offshore islands can still be relative havens even in August. The island is also becoming more well known for its festivals, particularly the spectacular Feste of Sant Efisio in Cágliari over the first four days of May, while the 15 August Feast of the Assumption is a major mover all over the island.

HISTORY
Just looking at Sardinia's landscape is enough to give you a good idea of the ancient nature of human settlement on the island. The stone towers and 'giants' tombs' of the nuraghic culture date back to around 1500BC but there is evidence of habitation going back even further, the earliest discoveries being even from the paleolithic era.

   While little can be certain about these ancient civilizations, it seems that the nuraghic culture went through several phases, the last of which, from around 1200-900BC, saw the tombs and towers evolve into considerable settlements, the most famous of these being at Su Nuraxi. Their culture was highly stratified and produced some remarkable bronze work, through which it is possible to trace Sardinia's growing role in Mediterranean trade. Phoenician sailors established a number of colonies here around the 9th century BC, while from the 6th century onwards it was the Carthaginians, operating out of their capital on the Tunisian coast, who began to exert a strong influence over the island.

   The Carthaginians' main rivals, at least initially, were the Greek colonies of the Western Mediterranean but by the 3rd century BC the big emerging power was Rome. In Carthage's life and death struggle with the Romans, the Sardinians fought alongside the Carthaginians, following them into defeat in 232BC, after which the island became a Roman province. Subsequent rebellions against Roman rule failed, thinning out the population as reprisals led to massacre, the survivors fleeing into the island's rugged mountainous interior. In consequence, there was little love lost between Sardinians and Romans, with the latter building relatively few of the impressive cities and public monuments they are famous for elsewhere.

This pattern of neglect was to continue in one way or another for much of the following millennia. With the Western Roman Empire gone, the island came under Byzantine rule, yet the forces of the Eastern Empire were unable to offer much assistance to the locals trying to withstand more and more frequent attacks by pirates and other raiders operating from the North African coast. Many of the island's coastal regions were depopulated by slaving raids, with the resulting collapse in the local economy bringing disease and famine in its wake. In 1015 the Moors of southern Spain landed and began to occupy the island in force, a move that finally brought aid — but in the form of conquering Christian armies from Genoa and Pisa.

These two city states quickly began to vie for control. Pisa was strong in Torres and Cágliari, while the Genoese based themselves in Castelsardo. By the 13th century Genoa had the upper hand, at least until 1326 when the King of Aragon tried to take the island, defeating the Pisans in Cágliari. After this there was continuous low-level fighting between the Aragonese, Genoese, Pisans and Sardinians, the latter being led for a while by Eleanora d'Arborea, Sardinia's Boudicca and Jean d'Arc all rolled into one. However, following her death in 1404, Aragon gained mastery of the whole island at the battle of Sanluri in 1409.

There then followed some three centuries of Spanish rule. A Catalan and Aragonese nobility lorded it in true feudal fashion but failed to avert the continuing pirate attacks along the coast. From the latter half of the 15th century, however, Spain's main focus of interest was Latin America and the Atlantic routes; interest in Sardinia waned but with the decline of the overseas empire, Spain's involvement in European affairs revived. Sardinia suffered accordingly. In 1708, during the War of the Spanish Succession, an English fleet bombarded Cágliari and occupied it briefly, before turning it over to Savoy, an Italian kingdom in the Piedmont region. While under the king of Savoy, rebellions broke out as the old Spanish aristocracy fought the new Italian one. This was a period of great *Banditismo*, a time when many took to the hills to earn a living raiding and thieving. In 1793 the French, in support of the king of Savoy, ordered Paoli, the Corsican leader (see p138), to raise an army in Ajaccio to take Sardinia. Captain Napoleon Bonaparte, together with a French contingent, advised taking La Maddalena Island to form a base for its conquest but the expedition failed.

Rebellion remained in the air, however, and during a popular revolt in 1794 Giovanni Maria Angioy's insurrectionists enjoyed some early successes. By 1796, however, he had been beaten and later died in exile in Paris. Rule by Savoy was to last until 1861 and the unification of Italy — a struggle in which Sardinia was to play a major role, supplying the Kingdom of Italy with its first king, Vittorio Emanuele II. Yet the new state did little to reverse the pattern of neglect in its largest island. Banditismo continued to be a major employer, while radical Sardinian nationalist ideas took hold, principally with the creation of the Partito Sardo d'Azione, which called for autonomy, in 1920.

The rise of fascism in Italy ushered in a period of high investment for the island from a central government anxious to produce grandiose projects for the newsreels. Unfortunately, this was followed by industrial failure and a devastating war. Cágliari was bombed to bits by the Allies, losing around 75% of its buildings.

Post war, things did begin to change a little. A degree of self-rule was granted and the malaria problem of the coastal flats, a constant thorn in the island's side since nuraghic times, was finally cleared up.

TYRRHENIAN SEA

Tourism was introduced, as were petro-chemical plants and a US nuclear submarine base. Thus while all this has brought cash and jobs, progress has perhaps been a touch double-edged.

ORIENTATION

Sardinia has both a rail and bus service between all its major towns and ports, though away from these main routes things can get a little ropy. ARST is the main coach company, while the railways are split between three different operators. Only the state-run FS takes Inter-Rail cards, the other two, FMS and FdS, being privately-owned operations. Fewer services operate on Sundays so check in advance if you plan to travel on that day.

Getting there in the first place is relatively straightforward. There are airports at Cágliari, Olbia and Alghero, with most international flights headed for Cágliari. There are also very good regular ferry services across from Bonifacio in Corsica, Civitavecchia near Rome, Palermo and Trapani on Sicily and on up to Genoa too.

The island splits into a number of provinces, with the eastern half generally more mountainous. There are also groups of offshore islands in the north-east and south-west corners, both of which are easily reached by local ferries and well worth a visit. Otherwise, travelling round off the beaten track is best undertaken with hired transport or hitching, the latter probably best done in pairs.

GOLFO ARANCI

AREA CODE: ☎ 0789 POPULATION: 2000
The most likely reason for finding yourself in Golfo Aranci is because this is where the ferry from Civitavecchia arrives, dovetailing nicely with the bus and railhead. Most likely, too, you'll stumble bleary-eyed in the early morning through the large Stazione Marittima to the bus or train and be whisked straight through this largely late 20th-century settlement without ever looking back.

That would be a small shame, though, as the town does nestle amongst some good beaches, the best lying to the south around the Golfo degli Aranci. Try the Cala Banana

for a good sandy stretch or Cala Sassari, a string of small coves. All are well within walking distance. There's also a nuraghic well, the Pozzo Sacro Milis, next to the train station in town.

Practical information

Ferries [see p444 for full details] There are Corsica Ferries Sardinia Ferries (CFSF ☎ 46780), Molo Sud for services to **Livorno** (daily) and **Civitavecchia**. Tirrenia operates daily to **Civitavecchia** and to **Fiumicino**.

Trains and buses These are very frequent to Olbia, where the main network continues. Some services come straight into the port terminal, others depart from the railway station, but there's little difficulty in catching either. Bus tickets can also be bought from the ticket office in the train station and must be validated when you board the bus.

Where to stay Sardinia is not cheap but try *King's* (☎ 46075), a small hotel on Via Liberta, which has sgl/dbl for €40/60. *La Cugnana* (☎ 33184), the nearest campsite to Golfo Aranci, is north of town, near Porto Rotondo. To reach it, take the bus to La Cugnana.

Where to eat 14 August is a good day to be in town for a meal as that's the day of the annual fish festival, the *sagra di pesce*, when the locals serve up heaving tables of free fish dishes and generally make merry. At other times, head for the harbour, next to which you'll find *Manzoni* doing more fish for around €10.

OLBIA

AREA CODE: ☎ 0789 POPULATION: 40,600
The north-east's main port of call, Olbia has an ancient pedigree and an international clientele, albeit mainly of the US squaddie variety, mingling in its none-too-attractive streets, with much passing traffic heading for the island's other destinations from the busy mainland Italian ferries.

This is a working town and harbour, with all that that implies, so if time is short you're probably better off doing what most arrivals do and depart as soon as possible: La Maddalena archipelago is just to the north and the rest of the island is well connected by train and bus services.

History

Olbia was a Sardinian-Carthaginian town when the Romans took it in 259BC, with the Carthaginian general Hanno going down in the fighting. After several centuries as Rome's principal east coast Sardinian port, it declined with the fall of the Western Empire and the frequent bouts of malaria that swept in from the surrounding marshes. The Pisans rebuilt it in 1198, renaming it Terranova Pausania, only to then have it taken by the Aragonese in their conquest of the island. It was then ransacked in 1553 by the Turkish corsair-cum-maritime-hero, Dragut, in alliance with France against the Aragonese, but was rebuilt, only to then be occupied by the English in 1711.

In 1717, one of the city's more bizarre episodes occurred, when Olbia was occupied by the Austrians. The Hapsburg army intended to take the rest of the island but, according to local legend, they were led into a trap by a local priest hired as a guide. They surrendered and were taken prisoner by the Sardinians.

In the 20th century, massive doses of DDT shot into the local marshes and the construction of a railway brought some prosperity back, as did the US Navy, who maintain a large base locally. The development of the nearby Costa Esmerelda as a tourism resort by the Aga Khan also helped the revival.

Today Olbia is one of the island's busiest ports, serving most of the ships between Sardinia and the Italian mainland.

What to see

This won't take long. Basically, the Pisan-era Romanesque **Church of San Simplico**, north-west of the train station, is the sightseeing; really you'd do better heading out than staying in Olbia for any length of time.

TYRRHENIAN SEA

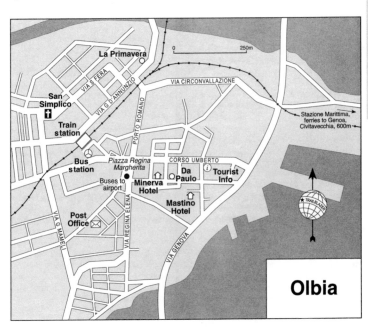

Olbia

Practical information
Orientation Ferries dock at the Stazione Marittima, which is at the end of a 2km causeway from the town's mainland. You won't have to walk as buses come right up to the Stazione, a large facility containing ticket offices for all the ferry companies and for the buses. There's also a railway station here, though most services of use to the visitor go from the station in town, off Corso Umberto. This street also has most of the hotels and restaurants gathered around it, along with the town's few sights, and runs straight inland from the main harbourside square at the end of the Stazione Marittima causeway.

The nearest airport, Aeroporto di Costa Esmerelda (☎ 23721), is connected to town by the No 2 bus, which leaves every half hour from Piazza Regina Margherita (€1, last one out 2000). A taxi costs around €17. There are also two buses a day directly to S Teresa di Gallura and Palau.

Services The **tourist office** (☎ 21453) on Via Piro is open mid-June to mid-September, Mon-Sat 0830-1300, 1600-1930; for the rest of the year it's mornings only.

Try the train station or the FS office at the Stazione Marittima for **left-luggage** facilities.

Ferries [see p446 for full details] Grandi Navi Veloci at Stazione Marittima (☎ 200126), Moby Lines at Via Principe Umberto (☎ 23572) and Tirrenia operate daily services to **Genoa** in summer. Moby Lines and Tirrenia also have services to **Civitavecchia**.

Trains There are regular daily trains to Cágliari (€18) which chunter the whole 300km stretch of the island, via Oristiano. The line also forks west to Sassari (€12) and Porto Torres. Train information (but not the station) is on ☎ 147-888088.

Buses The bus station (☎ 22477) is next to the train station, with services run by ARST — the Azienda Regionale Sarda Trasporti. There are regular services every two hours to Palau for the La Madallena

ferry, plus services to S Teresa di Gallura for the Corsica boat six times a day. Buy tickets from the office in the train station.

Planes There are easyJet flights to Olbia from London Gatwick, along with BA and Monarch. From Europe, Lufthansa have regular links, as do Alitalia from Rome and Milan. From Nice, a clutch of bargain airlines fly, along with state carrier Air France.

Where to stay *Minerva Hotel* (☎ 21190), 7, Via Mazzini. Good, clean accommodation in the town centre; rates €40/60 sgl/dbl.
Mastino (☎ 21130), Via Vespucci. Lowest price accommodation (€25/45 sgl/dbl), with a central location.

The nearest **campsite** is the one mentioned in Golfo Aranci (see p152).

Where to eat The main restaurant area is around Piazza Margherita in the heart of town. Cheaper options are *La Primavera*, 16, Via d'Annunzio, which has a good choice in relaxed surroundings for €10 a head; and *Da Paulo*, 18, Via Garibaldi, €12 a head but shut on Sunday nights.

PALAU
AREA CODE: ☎ 0789 POPULATION: 1750
Like Golfo Aranci, Palau has little to offer for a long stay, being largely a transit station for La Maddalena archipelago, just offshore. However, plenty of ferries from mainland Italy now come here, so it may well be your first sight of Sardinia. If it is, don't worry, things improve dramatically further on.

Practical information
Orientation Ferries arrive at the Stazione Marittima, where you can buy tickets for all the ferry and bus services. Buses stop at the Stazione Marittima, too. The town is a short walk up the main road from the Stazione.

Ferries [see p446 for full details] Enermar (at Stazione Marittima, ☎ 760002) runs boats to **Genoa** between June and August and operates a frequent service to **La Maddalena**.

Buses There are frequent buses during the day from Palau to Olbia (€2) and to S Teresa di Gallura (€3) for the Corsica ferry. However, the latter service reduces to three or four a day on Sundays.

Where to stay If you need to stay here, try *Serra* (☎ 709519), 17, Via Nazionale, where sgl/dbl go for €30/50. Otherwise, there's a **campsite**, *Baia Saraceno* (☎ 709 403), open May to October. It's about a kilometre east of town near Punta Nera and has a great beach.

LA MADDALENA

AREA CODE: ☎ 0789 **POPULATION:** 11,826
La Maddalena archipelago is a scattered drift of islands and islets just off the Sardinian coast with a sense of unearthliness that is heightened by the surreal rocky coasts and bays, all dotted with odd holiday villages seemingly transported from other planets. The only town has a lively nightlife year-round. The archipelago, consisting of Maddalena, Caprera, Santo Stefano, Spargi, Budelli, Santa Maria, and Razzoli, is a preferred place to make for when arriving in the north of Sardinia. Accommodation isn't cheap but there are some handy campsites.

History
Ancient Roman wrecks dredged up from the seabed nearby indicate that this area had some role in imperial trade, but there's little evidence of any really ancient habitation. The first major mention of the islands is in 1793, when France ordered a Corsican assault on Sardinia and the young Napoleon advised making a base at La Maddalena. Ten years later, British Admiral Horatio Nelson used the archipelago as his headquarters for some 15 months. He was waiting for the French fleet to sail out from Toulon on the coast to the north, while trying unsuccessfully to persuade Britain to invade Sardinia, largely because he reckoned if they didn't, the French would.

In 1856, Italian nationalist leader Giuseppe Garibaldi moved here in his twilight years, dying on Caprera in 1882. In the 20th century, La Maddalena became an important naval station for the Italian kingdom

Garibaldi had helped to found, leading to major Allied air attacks in WWII after fascist Italy under Mussolini had joined Nazi Germany. After the war, the US Sixth Fleet used the islands' strategic position, maintaining a permanent support facility, largely on Santo Stefano, for its nuclear submarines.

What to see
Walking up from the ferry port, you'll quickly enter the narrow main street which winds through the town to a series of small piazzas and the church, **Santa Maria Maddalena**, in which you'll find some silver candlesticks left as a gift by Nelson. At the end of this main roadway is Cala Gavetta, the old harbour, which still bobs with a few fishing boats and yachts. The only real sight is the **Museo Archeologico Navale** (Mon-Sat 0900-1330, free), which has a cross section of the hull of a 120BC Roman trading vessel, raised off Spargi in the 1950s.

Heading out east from the ferry stop brings you into some less-inspired architecture, the naval barracks spreading along the coast road all the way to the causeway to Caprera. It's worth a stroll though, as Caprera itself is quite a find, not least for the **Garibaldi Museum**, in the hero's house, Casa Bianca (daily 0930-1330, €3). This is something of a shrine to him. He was born in Nice and spent a large part of his life outside the frontiers of modern Italy. After ending up in Uruguay, he led 60 of his 'redshirts' back home to fight in the Risorgimento, Italy's war of independence against the French, Austrians and Spanish. Garibaldi also went on to make Sicily and Naples a part of Italy. (Cavour and Mazzini are just as important historically but Garibaldi, being a romantic, Byronic figure, was the one who captured popular imagination). Success in these struggles was not entirely to Garibaldi's benefit, however, for he was widely feared by Italy's new rulers for his popularity and military prowess. Exiled, he was finally allowed to return home in 1854, buying part of Caprera and building this South-American-style house. Inside you'll find a *camicia rossa* (red shirt) and the bed where he died, a stopped clock and wall calendar

TYRRHENIAN SEA

perpetual reminders of the hour and day.

Otherwise, La Maddalena is all about **beaches**. A 5km walk north of town takes you to one of the best, Cala Lunga, while closer in you can dive off the flat rocks of Punta Tegge, 2km south-west. On Caprera, head for Cala Coticcio on the east coast, about a kilometre from Garibaldi's house.

Practical information

Orientation Boats from Palau arrive at the small quay in front of La Maddalena town. Ferry services are frequent, except on Sundays, so it's worth checking out how they match up with bus departures from Palau if you're leaving on a Sunday; the times are posted at the tourist office.

One of the pleasures of the islands is that everything is easily reached on foot. The second largest island, Caprera, is connected by a causeway, making it an easy walk from La Maddalena.

Services The **tourist information office** (☎ 736321), Cala Gavetta, on Piazza Baron des Geneys, is open Mon-Fri 0800-1400, 1600-1900, Sat 0800-1400. Out of season it's not much use but it does have timetables and maps. To **hire a bike or scooter** try along the seafront between the ferry stop and Cala Gavetta.

Ferries [see p444 for full details] **Enermar** runs boats between Palau and La Maddalena roughly every half an hour. Buy tickets at the quayside.

Buses Island buses leave from the end of XX Settembre near Banco di Sardegna. Departures are around every hour for a tour round, as there aren't that many places to go.

Where to stay *Hotel Archipelago*, at 2 Via Indipendenza (☎ 727328), is open year-round (€35/55 sgl/dbl) but is 15 minutes out of town. From the ferry stop turn right through the naval area. Head out for the traffic lights, turning up the hill to the left, then immediately right until you see a sign; the hotel's next to a small supermarket. Phone ahead in season. Likewise, *Hotel Gabbiano* (☎ 722507), 20, Via Giulio

Cesare is another 15-minute slog, this time in the opposite direction beyond Cala Gavetta. It charges €40/60 sgl/dbl.

Campsites worth trying include: *Il Sole* (☎ 727727), to the east of town, open mid-June to Oct; *Maddalena* (☎ 728051), also to the east, facing Caprera Island.

Finally, *Abbatoggia* (☎ 739 173), in the north of La Maddalena, is more of a walk but is close to some good beaches.

Where to eat The seafront road in La Maddalena has plenty of restaurants and trattoria, while back along the main street you'll find cafés galore selling sandwiches during the day. *Sottovento*, 1, Via Indipendenzia, has some good pasta dishes for around €10 a head. For a drink, *The Penny Drops*, opposite the main church, has Guinness for €5 a pint.

SANTA TERESA DI GALLURA
AREA CODE: ☎ 0789 POPULATION: 5000

A town with something of a split personality, Santa Teresa can be a beach holiday centre surrounded by some of the choicest bays and inlets in all Sardinia if visited in summer, while for the rest of the year it's more likely to seem the kind of place you always arrive far too early for the ferry or bus out.

That said, most of the time it's a pleasant enough place for a stroll around, particularly the small harbour at the head of a yachting-village type inlet beneath the headland on which the town spreads out. From here, regular and frequent ferries make the short hop over to Corsica and back, with the cliffs around Bonifacio clearly visible on the horizon.

Buses from Palau and beyond drop you west of the harbour, on Via Eleonora d'Arborea, where there's the main ARST and FdS bus stop. This is below the headland, meaning that there's a bit of a walk up and down hill.

The town itself centres on Piazza Vittorio Emanuele, where there is a string of restaurants and cafés, almost all shut in winter. That's also the case for the town's singular monument, the **Torre Aragonese**, a 16th-century Aragonese watchtower with good views over the straits. To the west is the main town **beach**, the Spiaggia Rena Bianca. However, the real strands are a minibus ride away from the main bus stop, with La Marmorata and Capo Testa local favourites.

Practical information

Services The **tourist information office** (☎ 754127), Piazza Vittorio Emanuele, is open June-Sept, daily 0830-1330, 1520-2000; for the rest of the year weekdays only, 0900-1300, 1530-1830. The office has maps and bus timetables.

You can **leave your bags** in the ferry ticket office in the harbour, though it is locked between sailings, opening only half an hour or so before departures or arrivals.

Ferries [see p447 for full details] CFSF, Moby Lines (☎ 751449), Saremar and Happy Lines operate between Santa Teresa and **Bonifacio** in Corsica.

Buy tickets at the small harbour office in Santa Teresa or in advance at any of the island's travel agents. If at the latter, you'll have to pay a small commission.

Buses There are regular, if not so frequent, ARST buses between Santa Teresa and Palau and from there on to Olbia, Cágliari and other destinations. The main bus stop is on Via Eleonora d'Arborea. You buy your tickets onboard.

If you plan to leave town soon after arriving, head straight west from the harbour without going up the hill into town and you'll cross Eleonora d'Arborea after about 5-10 minutes.

Where to stay Accommodation in summer is almost impossible to get and in winter very expensive as all the budget options close. *Hotel Scano* (☎ 754447), 4, Via Lazio, on the west of town, gets booked up early but is a reasonable €30/50 sgl/dbl. *Hotel Bellavista* (☎ 754162), near Rena Bianca Beach, is shut from November to the end of April but if open is a good bet at €30/50 sgl/dbl.

The nearest **campsite** is 6km away at Capo Testa: *La Liccia* (☎ 755190) is shut mid-Oct to the end of April and reached by minibus.

Where to eat *Central Bar 80*, on the corner of the main square, has sandwiches and panini along with good ice-cream. The main square is good for other snack bars too, though daytime only for food. *Due Palmi*, on Via Capo Testa, is open year-round and has a decent menu; a full meal will set you back €15 a head.

CÁGLIARI

AREA CODE: ☎ 070 **POPULATION:** 219,096
Island capital and dominated by its old citadel and medieval quarters, Cágliari contains some of the island's best Roman remains and grandest cathedrals. It's also a key port for the Tyrrhenian Sea, with ferry connections over to the Italian mainland and, more importantly, south to Sicily and Tunis. If you're fortunate enough to visit at the beginning of May you'll be here for one of the Med's classic festivals, the four-day Festa di Sant'Efisio.

History

The Phoenicians are thought to have founded the port, as Karalis, after which it became the main Carthaginian city on the island. That was until the Second Punic War when the Romans came along and took over in 238BC. Then known as Caralis, it became one of Rome's most important Western Mediterranean ports. In those days all the roads on this island led here, while the Roman Sardinian Governor had his palace in the town.

With the Western Empire's collapse, however, the town fell to the Vandals and Goths, was taken back by the Byzantines, then looted by the Arabs. With the Pisan takeover, the citadel was built and fortified enough to withstand a two-year siege by the Aragonese, though the Pisans were eventually forced out in 1326.

Bombarded by an English fleet and then handed over to Austria in 1708, it then went to the House of Savoy in 1718. The 'Sardinian Revolution' broke out here in 1793, in imitation of the more successful French version, the revolutionaries here being butchered by Savoyard troops. The city continued to expand, however, spreading out beyond the walls and joining the rest of Sardinia in 1861 in becoming part of the new Kingdom of Italy (see p151).

In common with many Italian ports, it took heavy bombing during WWII by Allied aircraft, which destroyed almost half the city. Since then it has been rebuilt, without too much damage to the overall appeal.

What to see

From **Piazza Constituzione**, a flight of steps forms the most impressive entrance to the Castello, through the huge **Bastione**

San Remy. The view of the town from here is particularly good, though you can get another good vista by ascending the **Scalette S Chiara** up from Piazza Yenne to the **Torre dell'Elefante** (Tue-Sun 0900-1630, free). This was designed by a local architect, Giovanni Capula in 1307 and was a kingpin in the town's defences, hastily strengthened by the Pisans in expectation of an Aragonese attack — thus the open rear of the tower, which seems unfinished.

The **Cattedrale Santa Maria del**

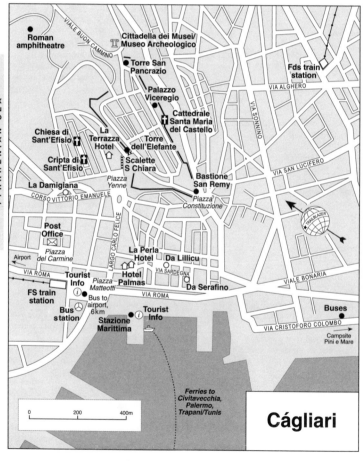

Cágliari

Castello, in Piazza Palazzo (daily 0800-1230, 1600-1800), is a 13th-century original with a 1933 façade. Look out for two massive stone pulpits on the inside, made in 1160 originally for Pisa Cathedral, and a painting — the *Trittico di Clemente VII*, which is thought to be the work of several Flemish artists working on it at different times. The result is surprisingly excellent, a view shared by a bunch of Catalan sailors who stole it from Pope Clement VII's private apartments in Rome during the 1527 sack of the city. The sailors brought it here, whereupon the archbishop returned it to the Pope, along with a number of other possessions; the Pope handed it back in thanks for its recovery.

Next door is **Palazzo Viceregio** (Tue-Sun 0900-1300, 1500-1900, €4). This was the city and island's main governmental centre under the rule of Savoy and is now the meeting place of the provincial assembly. It is also used for exhibitions and your ticket gets you in to whatever's showing.

Heading north, you'll come to the **Torre San Pancrazio** (Tue-Sun 0900-1300, 1500-1900, free but closed to under-12s). This had a similar purpose and history to the Torre dell'Elefante and has similarly good views. First a military bastion, it later became a prison then an observatory. On the Porta di San Pancrazio down below, look out for a small plaque commemorating the visit of Miguel de Cervantes to the town in 1573. The author of *Don Quixote* came here briefly before his capture and imprisonment by Moorish pirates. Further on, you'll see the entrance for the **Cittadella dei Musei**, an area containing the **Museo Archeologico** (daily 0900-1400, 1500-2000, €4). The museum has a good collection of artefacts from the nuraghic culture, including a series of bronze statues of amazing cast. There are also notable collections of Phoenician, Carthaginian and Roman finds.

You can visit more spectacular Roman remains further up Viale Buon Cammino, the road down the western side of the museum complex. The **Roman amphitheatre** (daily 0900-1300, 1600-2000; winter 0900-1700, free) is from the 2nd century AD, its 10,000 seating capacity illustrating

the size and importance of the city at that time. Returning to the Stampace quarter, look for the **Cripta di Sant'Efisio** (Tue-Sun 0900-1300, 1700-2000, free). This crypt takes you down into the remains of the old Roman city and is the place where Sant Efisio, a Roman soldier, and a Christian from modern-day Turkey, were imprisoned before being killed at Nora. This calvary is re-enacted in the yearly Festa di Sant'Efisio, when an effigy of the saint is carried from the nearby **Chiesa di Sant'Efisio** to Nora — some 40km — and then returned during the four-day festival.

Practical information
Orientation The ferry port is right in front of the town, the **Stazione Marittima** lying on the main harbour-front road, Via Roma. From Piazza Matteotti at its western end, the Largo Carlo Felice leads inland for the citadel, the Castello and the Stampace quarter with its churches, beyond which most of the principal Roman sights are situated.

The main **FS train station** is just west of the Stazione Marittima on the waterfront, while the narrow-gauge **FdS train station** is north-east of the harbour in Piazza Republica, a good 20- to 25-minute walk away. **Buses** come and go from a stop on Via Cristoforo Colombo, the eastern extension of Via Roma, a good 15-minute hike from the Stazione Marittima.

Otherwise, everything you're likely to want to see is within walking distance around the Castello.

Services The main **tourist information office** (☎ 60231), 97, Via Mameli, is open daily mid-May to Sept 0800-2000; Oct-Nov and mid-Feb to March, Mon-Sat 0900-1900, Sun 0900-1400; Dec to mid-Feb, Mon-Fri 0930-1730, Sat 0930-1330; April to mid-May, daily, 0900-1900.

This office has heaps of information on the whole island as well as Cágliari.

Ferries [see p442 for full details] Tirrenia (☎ 666 065, office in Stazione Marittima) operates a weekly service to **Palermo**, **Trapani** (the boat continues to Tunis), and daily to **Civitavecchia**. CFSF (Molo

Catitaneria Ichnusa, ☎ 684 8638) has a service to **Civitavecchia** from June to
September.

Trains The main FS train station is on

Piazza Matteoti, while private FdS trains go
from Piazza Republica.

Sardinia isn't flush with train services,
the main lines going between Cágliari and
Arbatax on the east coast, Olbia/Golfo

Su Nuraxi

Try to visit this place, the largest and one of the best-preserved
nuraghic sites on the island. It dates from around 1500BC and consists of a tight mesh
of lanes, houses and temples, all built from the same dark grey stone. Very little is
known about it despite decades of ongoing archaeological research. One thing that is
certain is that the local Sardinians and their Carthaginian overlords completely buried
it when the Romans invaded the island. Given that the central tower was around 21m
high, this seems quite a feat of engineering.

Regrettably, guided tours are compulsory, though at least they're usually informative. It is a site that breathes atmosphere so try and get away from the group for a
moment to look around. Most likely this was once the capital city of a complex and
prosperous culture, well protected by massive curtain walls and forts.

Sadly, Su Nuraxi is quite difficult to get to. It's around 60km north of Cágliari
and the only bus options are the two ARST services a day to Desulo and Samugheo,
via Barumini, the nearest stop to Su Nuraxi. From there, you'll have to walk the last
few kilometres to the site, which is open 0900-dusk, price €4.10. Remember to check
return times ... or bring a tent.

Nora

Closer in to Cágliari than Su Nuraxi and easier to get to, Nora is another deeply
atmospheric ancient site, this time partly covered by sea.

Built right on the headland by the Phoenicians, then enlarged by the
Carthaginians, it later became a Roman centre. From its time under Carthage right
through to its erosion by tide and wind in the 3rd century AD, it was a major city and
capital of the entire island. Its strategic position at the end of the Capo di Pula
promontory made it a natural place for trading with Sicily, the mainland of Italy and
the North African coast.

Today the site is open daily April-Oct, 0900-2000, Nov-March 0900-1800 (€4,
€6 including the museum in the neighbouring town, Pula). For a close-up view of
much of this you need a wet suit and diving equipment. However, what is visible
above ground is worth a look, though it's mostly Roman. The few Carthaginian and
Phoenician remains are limited to a ruined Punic temple to Tanit, the goddess of fertility, and a few loose stones. The mosaics in one Roman villa are good and the whole
site is well marked with Italian and English explanations.

North of the site is a good beach, the Spiaggia di Nora, though it gets rather
crowded in summer. If you head still further north, round the bay, you'll find the 11th-
century Church of San'Efisio, built on the site where the saint was martyred by the
Romans in the 3rd century AD. The procession of the Festival of San'Efisio arrives
here on foot from Cágliari before returning, also on foot, for the end of the festival.

Getting to Nora involves a change of bus. Two services, Nos 1 and 2, run
between Nora and Pula; Pula is on the ARST route from Cágliari (see p157).

TYRRHENIAN SEA

Aranci in the north-east, and two branch lines over to Iglesias and Carbonia in the south-west. Trains are on the whole dependable but a bit slow.

Buses The main **bus station** serves all the ARST buses. There is also a private long-distance bus company called PANI. Buy tickets at the kiosks next to the bus stops. Cágliari is the main destination of most services; buses to most destinations are frequent.

Planes The airport is 6km north-west of the centre (information desk ☎ 240 200). It's a 15-minute bus ride on the service bus to and from Piazza Matteoti, the first bus leaving at around 0600, the last around midnight.

Cágliari is the main international airport so is relatively well connected, and linked into Alitalia routes.

Where to stay *Hotel Palmas* (☎ 651 679), 14, Via Sardegna, near the harbour. Good sgl/dbl for €25/38.
La Terrazza Hotel (☎ 668 652), 21, Via S Margherita. Further from the water but with similarly priced rooms to the Palmas.
La Perla Hotel (☎ 669 446), 18, Via Sardegna. Much the same as the Palmas; €28/40 sgl/dbl.
Pini e Mare (☎ 803103), the nearest **campsite**, is a 45-minute bus ride away at Quartu Sant'Elena — try the bus station at Piazza Matteoti.

Where to eat The area round Via Sardegna is a good place for local dishes and popular venues, while Via Roma has good cafés for coffee and panini.
La Damigiana, 115, Corso Vittorio Emanuele. A decent no-frills local trattoria, with a full menu for around €15 a head.
Da Lillicu, 78, Via Sardegna. May need booking in season as it's popular. Strong on fish and local Sardinian goodies; expect to pay €10-15.
Da Serafino, 109, Via Sardegna. A popular choice with no-frills service and a young crowd; €10.

Civitavecchia

AREA CODE: ☎ 0766 POPULATION: 50,832
Founded by Emperor Hadrian in AD106, Civitavecchia has long been known as the Port of Rome. Today, at only 70km from the Eternal City and with a direct link by fast train, it's clearly also the port of choice for those starting out from Leonardo da Vinci Airport, or heading home that way.

While not a major tourist attraction, it does have some worthwhile sights and is a good place to stay if you fancy looking round Rome. Accommodation here is much cheaper than the extremely overpriced rooms in the capital. It also has good rail links if you're going north (to Livorno, Pisa or Genoa) and is good for ferries over to Sardinia and down to Sicily.

HISTORY
Civitavecchia (originally Centumcellae) was built on Emperor Hadrian's specifications as a port that could take up where the ancient harbour of Rome, built at the mouth of the Tiber, left off. Under the Christianized Empire it became an episcopate in AD314 until occupied by the Byzantines in 537. In the 8th century it came under Vatican rule, though in 828 it was taken by the Arabs.

They stayed until 889, when the port was reoccupied by its original inhabitants, who had largely fled to found the nearby settlement of Leopoli. Legend has it that the decision to return was thanks to one Leandro, who persuaded the town elders to up and go back under the shade of a large oak tree, still a prominent symbol in the town's coats of arms. They gave the place a new name, Civita Vetula, which then became Civitavecchia.

From then on the port was controlled by the counts of Civita Castellana, the Farfa Monastery and the prefects of Vico, who ruled until 1432 when it became part of the

TYRRHENIAN SEA

pontifical Vatican state. After that, things were pretty stable, with the pontiffs ordering a major strengthening of the port's defences — including the solid bastion of Fort Michelangelo. In 1515, Leonardo da Vinci visited to draw what remained of the old fortifications before they were pulled down to make way for the new walls.

In 1798, the Napoleonic Wars, the French took over the base, withdrawing in 1815 after Waterloo. From 1820 to 1870 the struggle for the unification of Italy led to the gradual expulsion of the various foreign rulers who controlled different states; most of them, including France, had troubles enough at home after the 1848 Year of Revolution, thereby facilitating the work of Cavour, Mazzini and Garibaldi. Thus, while Rome was becoming the capital of Italy under King Vittorio Emanuele II in 1870-1, Paris, besieged by Germany, was eating rats and baking bread on its hot pavements.

As with almost all Italian ports, the global conflicts of the early 20th century were highly damaging, with much of the town and harbour area, including most ancient monuments, destroyed by Allied bombing in WWII.

WHAT TO SEE

Little remains of the Roman town except in museums, so the sights that remain are largely from the period of pontifical rule in medieval times. First off, the **Forte Michelangiolo**, lynchpin of the harbour defences, is worth a look, and is in fact unavoidable if you arrive or depart by ship as you'll have to walk right past it. Built in 1535, it bears the coat of arms of Pope Paul III and its construction was a solid demonstration of Civitavecchia's refound role as Rome's chief port. From here, head northwards along the land side of the harbour and you'll pass the 17th-century walls constructed

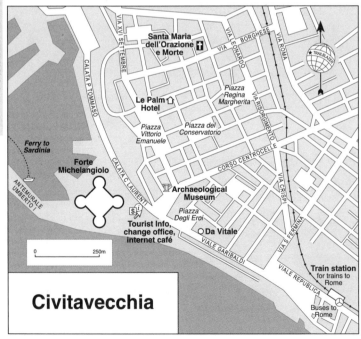

Nothing quite as nice

Italy undoubtedly possesses some of the best ice cream in the world, with thousands of cafés and snack bars from the Alps to Mt Etna serving up millions of tons of the stuff every year to a vast army of eager customers.

Italians often claim, too, that their country is the home of ice cream, being introduced to the Western world in the 13th century via Marco Polo, who brought back the recipe from China. Yet, for something so cool and refreshing, the debate over where ice cream actually comes from and how it evolved is in fact pretty heated.

There are indeed records showing an Italian predilection for flavoured ices going back at least to the 4th century BC. Later, the Emperor Nero apparently had snow specially imported to Rome, where it was dunked in fruit juices and honey and served as a refreshment between bouts of bloodletting at the Colosseum.

Yet ice cream itself, made from cream or butterfat, milk, sugar, and flavourings, probably started out much further east. Records from China's Tang dynasty (AD618-907) show a kind of yoghurt being developed that was thickened and cooled before being served up to King Tang of Shang by his 94 professional, full-time ice-men.

But the ice cream's arrival in the Mediterranean had to wait until someone cracked the secret of how to prevent water from freezing at 0°C, in order that the various ingredients could mix properly. It was a conundrum finally solved by the Arab medical historian Ibn Abu Usaybi sometime in the mid-1200s. He mixed salt with ice to reduce the freezing point to around −14°C.

However, given the almost continuous state of warfare between Christians and Muslims at the time, while Arabs, Moors and Ottomans could cool themselves with a medieval Magnum, it wasn't till 1503 that the secret finally got out to Europe, when it arrived in Italy.

From then on, the Italians became the undisputed masters of the ices. The famous Buontalenti, chef to Catherine de Medici, prepared such things for the French court, while in 1664, ices made with sweetened milk first appeared in Naples. Six years later, a Sicilian by the name of Francisco Procopio opened the first café in Paris to sell ices and sherbets. By 1676, there were 250 ice cream makers in the French capital alone.

How to make the stuff remained a closely guarded secret though, with the first recipe in English not appearing until 1718. Once it did though, it soon got scooped up in the Industrial Revolution. The first ice-cream machine was invented in 1843, leading to the rapid development of an ice-cream industry in the British Empire, run mainly by Italians. The need for skilled ice-cream labourers drew many poorer workers from southern Italy and the Ticino area of Switzerland to Britain. In London they lived in dreadful conditions, working the huge ice-house pits built near Kings Cross by Carlo Gatti in the 1850s. In these he stored the ice shipped to England from Norway that was used to freeze the vanilla, chocolate and strawberry delights exported throughout the industrialized world.

Revolutionary waves throughout Europe and the growth of the trade union movement did eventually improve the lot of the ice cream workers, yet even today ice cream selling is a tough and fiercely competitive business that can often turn violent.

Nonetheless, such thoughts are likely to be far, far off when you contemplate the dazzling array of ices on display in your average Italian café. The flavours there are unlikely to include garlic, avocado or sweet corn, all of which have been popular at one time or other, yet somehow it's not so hard to make do with some of the others.

TYRRHENIAN SEA

under Pope Urban VIII and an 18th-century **fountain** dedicated to Pope Benedetto XIV.

A small entrance ahead leads into the old inner harbour, which still has walls around it built in the classic medieval star-fort pattern, with pointed bastions at each corner designed for that new weapon of mass destruction, the cannon.

Back towards town, the **Church of Santa Maria Dell'Orazione e Morte** is interesting to wander around. The dome was painted in 1788 by Giuseppe Errante. The 18th century also produced the building in Largo Plebiscito, just back from the Forte

Michelangiolo, that now houses the **archaeological museum** (daily 0930-1300, 1530-1900, €3). Inside you'll find a modest collection of Roman, Etruscan and medieval finds from the town and local area.

PRACTICAL INFORMATION
Orientation
Ferries dock in the harbour, alongside the **Antemural Umbert I**, a long battlement jetty that reaches out protectively around the boat pool from the imposing walls of Forte Michelangiolo. Outside the ferry gates, turn right and then go left up the main inland

---

The rise and fall of the Roman Empire
What have the Romans ever done for us? Plenty, of course, as their ruined monuments stretching from Syria to Scotland reveal. Unlike the ancient Greeks, they pushed the frontiers of their empire much further inland, making them not just rulers of the entire Mediterranean seaboard but of most of Western Europe and the Middle East too.

And everything else they did was on a grander scale. Visit any ancient city that started out Greek and ended up Roman and you'll see the difference. More often than not, the ancient Greek part is a huddle of buildings up on the hill, or acropolis. The Roman part, on the other hand, usually stretches for acres, with vast boulevards, streets and even the first apartment blocks all their doing.

Rome also contributed enormously to the development of the arts and technology. Many of their inventions, lost in the Dark Ages that followed, would not see the light of day again for centuries. A cursory look around the museum at Alexandria, for example, shows an astonishing sense of realism in the paintings and sketches, while Roman sculpture, such as the giant head of Emperor Constantine in Rome, seems to have been heading towards the abstract by the 4th century AD.

All this started out c750BC with the founding of Rome, as legend would have it, by Romulus and Remus, who were raised by a she-wolf. In the early days, Rome was a republic, run by a powerful senate. By the 3rd century BC it had decided to expand and headed south for Sicily, then held by the Carthaginians. Three Punic wars later, the Carthaginians were defeated and Rome controlled the Western Med.

The next stage came with expansion northwards, with the Roman armies led by Julius Caesar conquering Gaul, modern-day France, and even launching an unsuccessful invasion of Britain. Rivalry between Julius Caesar and Pompey, the other surviving member of a triumvirate appointed by the senate, then led to the first of many Roman civil wars. Caesar won, only to be stabbed to death in 44BC, having been suspected of imperial ambitions.

Following his death, another civil war broke out between the members of the new triumvirate: Mark Antony, Octavian and Lepidus. Enter Cleopatra, queen of Egypt, who'd earlier been Julius Caesar's lover and then fell for Mark Antony. Octavian, fearing the ambitious power of Egypt and Mark Antony, defeated Antony and Cleopatra's forces in 31BC, the latter killing herself with a poisonous snake, the asp. *(Continued opposite)*

(Continued opposite)

TYRRHENIAN SEA

road, Corso Centrocelle, for the town centre, or carry on south-east along Viale Garibaldi, which then becomes Viale Republica, for the waterfront station and trains to Rome. The whole slog takes about 10 minutes with a backpack. Most of the sights are around the harbour area and easily reached on foot.

Services

For **tourist information** try Eurotrade SAS (see Buses, p166) which has **internet** services and an **exchange office** but closes at around 2000 out of season. The station has a **left-luggage** section.

Ferries   [see p443 for full details]

Sardinia CFSF at Calata Laurenti (☎ 500 714) operates to **Golfo Aranci** on Sardinia between May and October and to **Cágliari** from June to September. Tirrenia has a daily service to **Cágliari** via **Arbatax**. Both Tirrenia and Moby Lines (☎ 35245), at Agenzia TMA, 20, Calata Principe Tommaso, run ferries to **Olbia**.

Trains

There are frequent trains from Civitavecchia to Rome Termini, taking about 40 minutes. There's also a daily train

---

❏ The rise and fall of the Roman Empire

(Continued from p164) Octavian declared himself emperor, changed his name to Augustus and finally overthrew the ancient Roman republic. He expanded Roman power to new limits, beginning a dynastic rule that wasn't to end until Emperor Nero in AD68, who was famously said to have fiddled while Rome burned. He blamed the fire on the Christians who were by then a powerful underground movement throughout the empire. From then on, persecutions became a regular affair, with an untold number of early believers slaughtered.

Meanwhile, despite these setbacks, the empire itself continued to expand. The first non-Italian emperor, the Spanish-born Trajan, pushed the empire out east into Mesopotamia. His successor, Hadrian, set a number of important boundaries, with Hadrian's wall in northern England marking the northern frontier, and the River Euphrates the south-eastern. The whole thing was beginning to become unmanageably large. As a result, Diocletian (see p231) divided it in AD284, moving his own capital (and thus the main Roman capital) to Nicomedia (now Izmit in modern-day Turkey) while his second-in command, Maximillian, continued on in Rome as the head of the Western Roman Empire.

Not unexpectedly, this resulted in a period of almost continuous internal warfare — until the arrival of the Emperor Constantine. By AD330 he had managed to unify most of the empire again, and also moved the main centre of the empire from Nicomedia to Byzantium. Renamed Constantinople in his honour, this city continued as official capital of the Eastern Roman Empire until the fifteenth century, with Constantine also converting to Christianity, from then on the empire's official religion.

Constantine's reign proved to be no more than a brief renaissance, however, and by AD395 the two halves of the empire were being run entirely independently; and in the western half, things weren't going so well. Successive waves of invasions by tribes from the north and east resulted in its collapse. And though the Eastern Empire nearly succeeded in restoring the supremacy of Rome under Emperor Justinian in the 6th century AD, it was little more than the last gasp of a single, unified Mediterranean world under Roman domination. With the arrival of a radically new force, Islam, from the east, the days of the Roman Byzantine Empire were numbered, though their capital staggered on until 1453.

After defeating the Carthaginians, the Romans took to calling the Med *Mare Nostrum* (Our Sea). For years that was justified; and their legacy remains with us today.

TYRRHENIAN SEA

to Genoa (about four hours), to Livorno (around two hours), and to Pisa (two hours).

Buses

Buses for Piazzale Tiburtina in Rome leave from outside the railway station, though some services also run to the port. Check services with Eurotrade SAS (☎ 220391), an agency at the entrance to the port at 7, Via Cadorna.

Where to stay

Le Palm Hotel (💻 www.civitavecchia.com/lepalme), 15, Via Guastatori del Genio. A decent B&B with beds at around €25 per person.

Villa Chiara (☎ 370158), 68, Via San Gordiano; close to the station and similarly priced.

Where to eat

Viale Garibaldi is the place to go, with some reasonable local restaurants along the front – most offering a hearty meal for around €15 a head.

Da Vitale, 26/28, Viale Garibaldi. Open all year, a full meal here will set you back €20, while having only a pasta course will cost €5-7.

Rome

AREA CODE: ☎ 06 POPULATION: 450,000

It is not the remit for a guidebook such as this to include detailed information about the Eternal City. And more has probably been written about Rome over the millennia than any other metropolis on earth.

However, it's likely you've come to Civitavecchia for what lies beyond, so here are a few hints about travelling to Rome, in no way to be taken as more than a meagre drop in the Trevi fountain of Roman travelogues.

PRACTICAL INFORMATION

Rome is some 17 miles north-east of the northern end of the River Tiber. Since 1870 it has been the capital of Italy.

Services

The main **tourist office** (☎ 488 991), 5, Via Parigi, is open Mon-Sat 0900-1900. Alternatively, in backpacker land — the block between Via Marsala and Via Pretorio next to Termini station — is Enjoy Rome (☎ 4451843), a private tourist information centre at 8a, Via Marghera; it has a useful free guide to the city and its nightlife.

The warren of streets around Termini station contain a multitude of **internet cafés**, particularly in the block between Via Marsala and Via Pretorio. The one at the bottom of Via Vicenza is handy as it's also a laundrette, enabling you to surf as you soak. It's open until 2200.

The **left-luggage office** at Stazione Termini is open 0700-midnight, charging €3 for five hours, then €0.60 for every hour after that.

To **book flights** or other travel try CTS (☎ 462 0431), 16, Via Genova, or the Termini station information and booking office.

Trains

Trains to/from Civitavecchia run from Roma Termini station, often from platform 25, which is a 10-minute walk at least from the ticket offices, so allow plenty of time. The trains are usually pretty packed too.

From this terminal, just about everywhere with a railway station in Italy and Europe is accessible.

At the station information centre, next to platform No 5, there are some friendly if stressed-out staff available to help with bookings and you can also buy ferry and plane tickets, book accommodation and get some decent maps.

Be warned: the queues at the info office — as for everything else in Rome — can make you feel as if you'll be there forever. You won't be though — they chuck you out at 2100.

Buses

The main inter-city terminal is in Piazzale Tiburtina, next to Stazione Tiburtina on metro line B. There you'll find all the main bus company offices and services are available to all the main Italian cities and regions.

TYRRHENIAN SEA

Planes
Rome's main international airport, Leonardo Da Vinci, is connected to Rome Termini by a fast and frequent rail service which takes about 20 minutes and costs €9. After 0100 the train goes only to Tiburtina, from where night bus No 42 goes to Termini.

Rome has another airport, Ciampino, which deals mainly with charter flights. From there, Cotral buses run to Anagnina, on metro line A, which also goes to Termini. A taxi from either place costs €40-50.

Where to stay
Accommodation in Rome is a major difficulty. Book well ahead and/or be prepared for overpriced, low-quality rooms. The main hunting ground for *pensions* is the area next to Stazione Termini between Via Marsala and Via Pretorio, though many of these get booked up.

VR Hostel (☎ 445 4385), run from the snack bar at 65, Via Palestro, charges €20 for a bunk in a crowded dorm out of season. In season the price jumps according to demand. It's one of the cheaper options and a good place to compare the snoring of other cultures. *Fawlty Towers* (☎ 445 4802), 39, Via Magenta, has risen above its name and is near Termini station; expect to pay €25/50 sgl/dbl or €20 for a bed in a dorm.

Hostel Alessandro (☎ 446 1958), 42, Via Vicenza, is in a wonderful house also near Termini station; it charges €35/50 sgl/dbl but book in advance.

M&J Place Hostel (☎ 446 2802), 9, Via Solferino, also near Termini, has internet access and charges €30/50 sgl/dbl.

If you want to **camp** try *Camping Tiber* (☎ 3361 0733), Via Tiburina Km1400, which operates a free shuttle service from Prima Porta station, which is connected by train F1 to Piazzale Flaminio station in town. Otherwise, try *Camping Flaminio* (☎ 333 2604), in Via Flaminio Nouva, on bus routes No 202, 204 and 205, 8km north of the city centre.

You can also catch the tram from Piazzale Flamino on metro line A to Piazza Mancini for bus No 200, which drops you off at the site.

Where to eat
The list is almost endless, but if you're in a hurry there are plenty of budget places around the Termini hostel area. Try the *restaurant* at the top of Via Vicenza for a pasta course for €5, a full meal for €15.

Naples

AREA CODE: ☎ 081 **POPULATION:** 1,000,050
Raucous, dirty, way beyond the law yet somehow getting deep under the skin, Naples is southern Italy at its rawest. Crowded round the bay, with Mafia hotels sprawling down the coast to the west, it's not hard to see why many northern Italians see this city as belonging to quite a different country. Plenty of the inhabitants would happily agree with them, being fiercely proud of their city, for all its obvious faults. To the south looms Mt Vesuvius and the spectacular ruins of Pompeii, the ancient Roman city buried by one of the mountain's volcanic eruptions. Expect more of the same from many a local Neopolitan, these southerners not exactly being known for their reserve. For all its hassles though, Naples delivers a vibrant culture, strong in the arts, nightlife and religious ritual at its most baroque.

HISTORY
There has been a settlement here for around 3000 years, with the first city being known as Parthenope. Later, Greek colonists arrived to establish the colony of Cumae, located to the north-west of Naples. This *polis* established an outpost in the bay area known as Neapolis around 750BC.

The city prospered for centuries as part of the Greek territory of Magna Grecia – the area now covered by southern Italy and Sicily. Later becoming part of the Roman Empire, it continued to grow until that empire too vanished, leaving it independent from 763 to 1139, when it was taken by the Normans. From then on its history grew more turbulent as it passed between the Angevins and Aragonese and back again

TYRRHENIAN SEA

during the medieval conflicts between the two, with the Aragonese establishing Spanish rule over the city in 1422. The War of Spanish Succession at the start of the 18th century left the city in the hands of the Bourbons via a brief period of Austrian rule. This collapsed into chaos by the end of the century, with a period of revolutionary upheaval as the Parthenopean Republic was ended by British troops led by Admiral Horatio Nelson, who was simultaneously, and famously, conducting an affair with Lady Hamilton, the wife of the British Ambassador in Naples.

The 19th century saw much emigration from both the city and the region to the New World, while the grip of the Camorra – the Mafia – also tightened. Organized crime still has a major role in almost every aspect of city life today, from town hall politics to the local police department, and from the carving up of European Union aid to the local bar scene. Efforts have been made to tidy this up and change the reputation of the town, with many recent festivals and campaigns to promote the city and stressing its many cultural and historical highlights.

WHAT TO SEE

With so many museums, those planning a longer stay should think about a **Campania artecard** (☎ 800-600-601, 🖳 www.napolia rtecard.it, www.campaniartecard.it), which offers free access to two museums and 50% off on four others over a 60-hour period, plus free public transport. The cards come in 3-day (€18 for 18-25 year olds, €25 for over-25s) and 7-day (€21 for 18-25 year olds, €28 for over-25s) varieties. You can purchase the cards in the larger hotels and newsagents, travel agencies, the airport and port, as well as the main railway stations.

Top sights are the Museo Nazionale Archeologico, the Museo Nazionale di Capodimonte, the Museo Nazionale di San Martino, Castel Sant'Elmo, and the Palazzo Reale – all of which are covered by the arte-card.

Museums

The **Museo Nazionale Archeologico** (Mon & Wed-Sun 0900-1930, €6.50) in the Piazza Cavour is a treasure house of finds from the ancient Roman cities of Pompeii and Herculaneum. Here you'll find the largest single piece of classical sculpture in existence – the Farnese Hercules – along with some superb mosaics and a collection of once banned Roman erotica. To see the latter, you must take an extra 'timed' ticket, which is free but which somewhat limits your time in the company of delights such as Pan humping a goat, or of the remarkable collection of ancient phalluses. Upstairs are some excellent wall paintings taken from the two cities so spectacularly destroyed by volcanic eruptions on 2 August, AD79. Beyond these are finds from the cities, with some petrified food, laid out for eating on that fateful day and frozen in time since then, particularly telling.

Some way out of the centre on the hilltop north of the archaeological museum is the **Museo Nazionale di Capodimonte** (Tue-Sun 0830-1930, €7.50; No C40 bus from Piazza Garibaldi). This was once the royal residence of the Bourbon king Charles III and now houses the city's picture gallery. Built in 1738, the royal apartments are also on view, though the paintings are more of a draw. You'll find a major Renaissance collection, including work by Botticelli and Titian, along with Flemish masters such as Brueghel. Outside, the parklands of the Palazzo Reale di Capodimonte are also excellent; they're open from 0900 to an hour before dusk and are free.

The **Museo Nazionale di San Martino** (Tue-Fri 0830-1930, Sat & Sun 0900-1930, €6) is also a hilltop venue, west of the port. Set in the 14th-century Certosa San Martino Monastery complex, it is also next to the Castel Sant'Elmo (Tue-Sun 0900-1900, €1), Naples' highest point. The Castel was formerly a prison, built in the 14th century, and is now a military building, though open to some public inspection. The Museo building, which underwent major restoration in the 17th century, divides into sections exploring the city's historical and artistic development. Mainly, though, this is a place for views, with the terrace a chance to see the whole city spread out below.

TYRRHENIAN SEA

The **Palazzo Reale** (Thu-Tue 0900-2000, €4) was built in 1602 to give Philip III somewhere to stay on a royal visit to the city. In this, it is illustrative of Naples' history of absentee kings, ruling from overseas and generally neglecting the locals. With more fine views of the city, the palazzo contains a particularly fine chapel, while a collection of statues of the city's foreign rulers is also informative.

Churches

Situated in the Forcella quarter north of the port, the **Duomo** (daily 0830-1230, 1630-1900, free) is a 13th-century Gothic construction with a 19th-century neo-Gothic façade. Naples' main cathedral, it is dedicated to the city's patron saint, San Gennaro, who was martyred nearby during the persecution of Christians ordered by the Roman Emperor Diocletian in AD305. The saint still has a major role in the city thanks to a thrice-yearly miracle which takes place on the first Saturday in May, 19 September and 16 December. A large crowd packs the church on these days and, if you wish to be there too, start queuing well before the 0900 Mass. Two phials of dried blood, supposedly from the saint, are said to miraculously liquefy on these days, an occasion for much rejoicing.

The Duomo itself contains a 1305 reliquary holding the phials and the saint's skull, while the basilica of Santa Restituta is the oldest structure in the city, erected on the order of the Emperor Constantine in AD324.

The **Church of San Lorenzo Maggiore** on Via Tribunale is also worth a look, for under this Gothic structure an archaeological dig has revealed part of the Roman forum and Greek agora (April-Oct, Mon-Sat 0900-1700, Sun 0900-1300; Nov-March, Mon-Sat 0900-1300 and 1500-1700, Sun 0900-1300, €4).

Around Naples

The must-sees are undoubtedly the cities of **Pompeii** (April-Oct, daily 0830-1930, gates close at 1800; and Nov-Mar, daily 0830-1700, gates close at 1530, €10) and **Herculaneum** (Mar-Sept, daily 0830-1930; Oct-Feb, daily 0830-1830, €10), which both lie east of Naples near the still-active volcano, Vesuvius. A combined ticket to both ancient cities is available (valid for 3 days, €17.50). Access is best via the Circumvesuviana, the train from the station on Corso Garibaldi, which stops first in the town of Ercolano, the modern adjunct to Herculaneum, then right by the Pompeii entrance.

Both cities were destroyed by an eruption of the volcano on 2 August AD79, an event recorded vividly by Pliny the Younger. Buried in ash for centuries, Pompeii was rediscovered in around 1600, and Herculaneum a century later. Since the mid-18th century they have both been under almost continuous excavation, revealing more about the Roman world to us than any other ancient sites.

To ascend Mt. Vesuvius, which last blew its top in 1944, take the Circumvesuviana to Ercolano and from there take the Transporti Vesuviani (☎ 559 2583) bus which leaves more or less hourly between 0910 and 1410, costing €5 return. This takes you up to a car park near the crater. From there, it's a walk on foot, with a charge of €6, which includes a talk in English from a guide. Another way is to take a taxi, which costs around €6 per person but waits for you to take you back. Otherwise, the last bus down is around 1600 Apr-Oct, 1500 rest of the year.

PRACTICAL INFORMATION
Orientation

Most long-distance ferries arrive at the Stazione Marittima; local ferries dock just south-west of this at Molo Beverello. These are both near the historical heart of Naples. Buses to Pompeii leave from just outside the Stazione Marittima while the main bus station is at the western end of Piazza Garibaldi. The main Stazione Centrale is at the eastern end of Piazza Garibaldi.

From the airport take a taxi or bus: the 3S departs about every ten minutes for Piazza Garibaldi (for the main train station). Alibus departs every 30 minutes between 0630 and 2330 for Circumvesuviana rail station and the port. Tram Nos 1 and 4 go from the port to the city centre and Circumvesuviana stations.

TYRRHENIAN SEA

To get around the city on public transport it is best to buy a GiraNapoli ticket (€0.77 valid for 90 minutes, or €2.30 valid for a day). Both allow you to travel on any bus, tram, funicular, train or metro in the area of Naples.

A Unico ticket (💻 www.unicocampania.it) is similar but valid in a wider area, for 100 mins (€1.29) or for a day (€2.58). A weekend ticket costs €2.07. All tickets must be punched before the start of the first journey. A normal ticket costs €1.55.

Services

The main **tourist office** is at the Stazione Centrale (☎ 268779). Other branches are at Piazza dei Martiri (☎ 405311) and Stazione Mergellina (☎ 7612102).

Useful websites include 💻 www.ept. napoli.it and 💻 www. inaples.it. Look out for the free monthly *Qui Napoli,* which has tourist info and listings in English and Italian.

Ferries   [see p445 for full details]

Naples is a major port and both ferries and fast ferries leave for a wide variety of destinations. The main central harbour, the Molo Beverello, serves major destinations such as Sardinia and Sicily, while the Mergellina is good for hydrofoils to Capri and other local destinations.

From Molo Beverello   Medmar Linee Lauro (☎ 552 283811, or 761 1004) has departures to **Ischia**, **Palau**, **Porto Vecchio**, and **Tunis**. Caremar (☎ 551 3882) operates daily to **Capri**, **Ischia**, and **Procida**. LMP (☎ 552 7209) has daily departures to **Sorrento**.

Tirrenia Navigazione (☎ 251 4711/720 1111), Stazione Marittima, Molo Angioino, has services to **Cágliari**; TTT has ferries to **Catania** and Ustica Lines runs to **Ustica**.

From Mergellina Harbour   Alilauro runs services to **Ischia**, **Positano**, **Sorrento** as well as to **the Aeolian Islands**. Call them on ☎ 761 1004.

SNAV(☎ 761 2348) operates to **Capri**, **Procida**, **Palermo**, **Milazzo** and the **Aeolian Islands**.

Other   Metro del mare (💻 www.metrode lmare.com) operates services in and around the **Bay of Naples** in the summer months. Check for details when in Naples. The port authority is on ☎ 206133.

Trains

It is possible to get to most cities in Italy from Napoli Centrale; services to Rome are the most frequent, while there are also regular services south to Reggio di Calabria and the Sicily crossing. The main rail information line is ☎ 848 888 088. There is also the local, out-of-town Circumvesuviana (☎ 772 2111), which goes down the coast from the station of Curso Garibaldi and is good for Herculaneum, Pompeii and Vesuvius. Naples also has an underground railway, the metropolitania, with the Piazza Dante a useful stop for the archaeological museum. Tickets are available for this and the three funicular railways from stations and *tabacchi*, with a flat-fee ticket of €0.77 valid for an hour and a half.

Buses

There are services from the main bus station in Piazza Garibaldi to many places including Salerno, Bari and Bríndisi. For information phone ☎ 801 5420 or 801 6376. Local buses also leave from here for the city centre and the ports. Flat-fee tickets from stations and tabacchi cost €0.77.

Planes

Capodichino Airport is 7km north-east of the city centre, 48km to Sorrento and 50km to Salerno. Several charter airlines fly to Naples and most scheduled ones too so it is possible to fly almost anywhere.

Where to stay

As with most cities the area around the train station and Piazza Garibaldi is the best for cheap accommodation. Places to try include: *Ginevra* (☎ 283210; 554 1757), 116, Via Genova, *Potenza* (☎ 286330), 120, Piazza Garibaldi and *Sayonara* (☎ 554 0313), 60, Piazza Garibaldi. There's also the *HI Hostel Mergellina* (☎ 761 2346), 23, Via Salita della Grotta, with dorm beds from €14, but it gets busy so book or turn up early. To get there take the metro to the Mergellina stop and then walk, following the signs.

Where to eat
In the city that is credited with inventing the pizza, the 'what to eat' in Naples is definitely either *panino napoletano*, *pizza napoletana* or *pasata napoletano*, but of course the full range of pizza and pasta dishes are available. The old city is the venue for bars and most decent clubs.

Sorrento

AREA CODE: 081 **POPULATION**: 17,000
A well-placed base for the Amalfi coast, as well as Pompeii and Mt Etna, Sorrento has long had a reputation as a holiday resort. Back in Roman times it was already known as the place for a weekend break, while in the 19th century it proved a fine hang-out for many poets and writers escaping cold, grim northern Europe. In this guise, Sorrento was a welcome temporary retreat to the Nordic likes of Goethe, Nietzsche, Wagner and Ibsen.

Nowadays, there's less quality to the visitors, yet while Sorrento is very much a package-holiday resort, it does still manage somehow to defy the worst ravages of mass tourism. Some 20km from Naples and lying on the headland on the southern side of the Bay, it still has plenty to offer the more independent traveller while also providing an easy access point for local islands Capri and Ischia.

HISTORY
Known to the Romans as Surrentum, the settlement here was most likely ancient Greek in origin, as suggested by the grid layout of the streets in the city's historical centre. Run for a while by the Byzantines and sacked by the Lombards, it came under the rule of the Normans in 1137. Much later still, in 1558, it was sacked again, this time by the Ottomans, with the city then fading out until the late 18th and early 19th centuries when

it underwent a rebirth thanks to tourism and the age of the Grand Tour. It was during this time that it became a stop on the soul- and body-improving trips abroad undertaken by north European aristocrats.

Sorrento's favourite son is the poet Torquato Tasso, who was born here in 1544. Widely thought to be the greatest Italian bard of the Late Renaissance, he also became the subject of a play by Goethe. His classic work is *Jerusalem Delivered*, an epic poem which later helped earn him the title as the Pope's poet laureate – an honour he was tragically unable to receive as he died the day before the award ceremony.

WHAT TO SEE
Museo Correale di Terranova (☎ 878 1846, open Mon & Wed-Sun 0900-1400, €6) at 50, Via Correale has a collection of paintings by the Neopolitan school as well as various archaeological artefacts unearthed locally. The building itself is one of the more impressive parts of the museum, being a former palace of the counts of Sorrento.

Elsewhere, in the Palazzo Pomarici Santomasi, at 28, Via S Nicola is the **Museum-Workshop of Wooden Tarsia** (open Tues-Sun 0930-1200, 1700 to 1900, €8). This is a good chance to look at a local speciality, inlaid wooden *intariso* work. Further on, there's the **Antiquarium Aequano — Silio Italico** (☎ 801 5668, open Mon, Wed and Fri 0900-1300, Tue and Thu 1530-1830, Sat and Sun 0930-1230, free) in the Palazzo Comunale-Vico Equense, Corso Filangieri. Here you'll find archaeological discoveries dating back to Etruscan, Greek and early Italian times.

In the west wing of the Imperial Hotel Tramontano, at 1, Via Vittorio Veneto, are two rooms remaining from the house where Torquato Tasso was born. This hotel, while well out of the price range of this book, is also where many of the town's literary visitors in the 19th century stayed, with Goethe, Byron, Scott, Shelley, Musset, Lamartine, Keats, Leopardi, Longfellow and Fenimore Cooper all stopping here at various stages.

The 14th-century **Church of San Franscesco** is known for its 14th-century 'paradise cloister', an impressive floral

TYRRHENIAN SEA

inner courtyard, while Sorrento's Roman-esque, 15th-century cathedral houses paint-ings by artists from the Neapolitan school of the 1700s, with much wooden inlaid work also on view.

PRACTICAL INFORMATION
Orientation
The port, Marina Piccola, is about 500m from the centre of town. Walk along Via Marina Piccola to reach Piazza Tasso, the main square. Corso Italia is the main street running west–east. The train station (Stazione Circumvesuviana) is to the east along Corso Italia. Capodichino Airport is the nearest airport to Sorrento (50km). Curreri operates six buses a day (one hour, €5) from the airport to Piazza Tasso. Alternatively take a bus or taxi to Naples and go either to Beverello port for a hydrofoil or ferry to Sorrento, or to the Circumvesuviana station to take a local train to Sorrento.

Services
The **tourist information office** (☎ 807 4033; 🖳 www.sorrentotourism.it) is at 35, Via Luigi De Maio, a short walk from the port. Another useful website is 🖳 www.visi tsorrento.com.

Ferries   [see p447 for full details]
Linee Marittime Partenopee (LMP; ☎ 552 7209), Navigazione Libera del Golfo (NLG; ☎ 551 3882), and Alilauro have daily departures to **Naples Beverello**.

LMP, SNAV and Caremar also have frequent departures to **Capri**), and LMP and Alillauro sail to **Ischia**. Tickets for most services can be bought from the many travel agencies in Sorrento.

Trains
There are frequent departures to Pompeii, Herculaneum and Naples. The journey to Naples takes about an hour but trains can often be crowded so you may prefer to go by boat.

Buses
There's a daily bus from Piazza Tasso to Rome (4 hours) via Pompeii (45 mins) and Naples (90 mins).

Both Circumvesuviana (orange buses) and SNTA run frequently to places around the Amalfi Coast.

Planes
Both chartered and scheduled airlines have flights to Capodichino Airport, Naples.

Where to stay
Hostel Le Sirene (☎ 801 2925, 🖳 www. hostel.it), 160, Via degli Arance, 300m from the railway station; dorm bed with bath and breakfast from €16.

Two **campsites** worth considering are: *Nube d'Argento* (☎ 878 1344, 🖳 www. nubedargento.com), 21, Via Capo, open Mar-Nov, per person €6-€9, tent €8-13; and *Santa Fortunata – Campogaio* (☎ 807 3579; 🖳 www.santafortunata.com), 41, Via Capo, open Mar to Nov, per person €4-9, per tent €3-€7.

Where to eat
There is a wide selection of places to eat for all budgets. Try around Piazza Tasso and the railway station.

Sicily

POPULATION: 5.1 MILLION
The Mediterranean's largest island, Sicily bestrides the great old land bridge that once joined Europe and Africa and cut this sea into two large lakes. Calamitous floods, volcanic outbursts and millions of years later, that land bridge lies submerged beneath the waves under the chopping seas of the Sicily–Malta channel, nowhere more than 100 fathoms deep.

Yet in many ways, Sicily remains both a land of fire and a bridge between at least two continents and cultures, if not many more. Most widely known as the birthplace of the Mafia and one of Italy's poorest regions, it also contains some of the Mediterranean's most spectacular volca-noes, brilliant beaches and friendly people. Its strategic position between the western and eastern halves of the sea has also made it a coveted land, fought over for millennia by rival empires and colonists who have all left their mark on the island's rocky landscape, and on its culture and language.

Sicily is also a main stopping-off point for ferries from Sardinia and the Italian mainland, and on to Malta and Tunis. There are good rail links across the narrow straits of Messina that separate the island from the toe of Italy and the Adriatic ports beyond.

HISTORY

In caves and tight valleys hidden away in the island's interior, archaeologists have uncovered evidence of Sicily's ancient role as a land highway between Italy and Africa: elephant bones and 10,000-year-old neolithic settlements indicate habitation from both north and south. Yet recorded history begins with the Phoenicians settling colonies on an already inhabited island. By the 8th century, the Greeks had taken over at Catania, Messina, Syracuse, Megara and a dozen other places, including colonies across southern Italy. Sicily flourished as a Greek island, as important to Athens and Corinth as Crete or Rhodes.

The emerging rival to these Greek city states was Carthage, which attempted unsuccessfully to take the island in 480BC, its army losing badly at the battle of Chimera. Yet Carthaginian pressure continued, with an eventual take-over by the middle of the following century. In the course of the three epic Punic Wars fought on water over most of the Western Mediterranean and Tyrrhenian Sea, the Romans overthrew the Carthaginians, their occupation of Sicily beginning in the 3rd century BC after the first Punic War.

Under Rome the island was treated largely as a bread basket. When the Western Empire collapsed, things didn't get much better. Vandals and Goths respectively gained control of the northern and southern coastline areas. In AD553, however, Belesarius, the great general of Emperor Justinian (the lawgiver) drove out the Vandals (North Africa) and the Goths (Italy), temporarily restoring the whole empire. But by the 9th century (AD823) Sicily had become an Arab province.

The Arabs stayed for around 300 years, leaving a major mark on every part of Sicilian life, including its language. It was the Normans who replaced them, a people more known in northern climes who brought with them another quite alien culture. The rule of Norman Charles of Anjou, who was given Naples and Sicily by the Pope, was characterized by extravagance and brutality, leading to the Sicilian Vespers in 1282, when the Sicilians rose up and 2000 French citizens were massacred in Palermo in one evening.

With the Angevins gone, the Sicilians chose as his successor Peter III of Aragon. However, the Count of Anjou remained the Pope's nominee and the papacy and various Italian states contested the take-over, though the Aragonese retained control until the first half of the 18th century.

After this, complex European power politics saw the island passed around between the Savoyards (1713–20), Austrians (1720–34) and, after them, the Bourbons, who held the island until Napoleon arrived in 1806. After his downfall in 1815 the Bourbon king Ferdinand was returned by the British to the throne of the so-called Kingdom of Two Sicilies, though his decision to use Naples as his capital led to Sicily becoming something of a backwater.

Garibaldi's campaigns in Sicily led to it becoming part of the new Italian Kingdom in 1861, though this made little difference to many Sicilians who continued to live in a semi-feudal poverty. The Mafia families that grew up on the island could stretch their roots down deep into the Sicilian soil, exploiting many real grievances and the inefficient and corrupt authorities to institute their own system of 'justice'. Major emigration, chiefly to the USA, helped spread the Mafia westwards among the poor of the New World. In the 1990s the Mafia were put onto the back foot with a string of arrests, but their ability to intimidate local politicians, union leaders and ordinary citizens into acquiescence has regrettably continued. Meanwhile, there are also demands for more autonomy, if not outright independence, from an Italy seen as foreign by many locals.

TYRRHENIAN SEA

Volcanoes

'*He was now so close to the mountain that the cinders, which grew thicker and hotter the nearer he approached, fell into the ships, together with pumice stones and black pieces of burning rocks ...*'

So wrote the Roman Pliny the Younger, describing the fatal last journey of his uncle towards the erupting Mt Vesuvius in AD79. It's a vision that's been repeated many times around the Mediterranean since then, volcanic activity being a major part of the region's character, because the sea is constantly being squeezed and shoved by the movements of the Eurasian plate to the north and the African plate to the south, with one going underneath the other. The result is known as a subduction zone, a region prone to earthquakes and volcanic explosions.

Volcanoes themselves are formed when hot, molten lava shoots up through a fissure in the Earth's crust. This produces a cone as the lava cools and forms rock around the central fissure. Sometimes, the top of the cone blows off in a particularly violent eruption, producing a crater, or caldera. The Med is dotted with examples of this. Sometimes, the caldera-creating big bang is so big that the whole cone is blown apart, the sea then breaking back in to flood the crater. A good example of this is Santorini in the Cyclades, whose beaches are of black volcanic sand. Eruptions can also be extremely rapid and entirely new islands can be created in a matter of hours and days: Vulcanello, next to the island of Vulcano in the Lipari Islands off Sicily, was blasted off the seabed in a single eruption in AD21.

Volcanoes often go hand in hand with earthquakes, though sometimes the latter make an appearance all on their own. Tremors can be far more devastating and affect a much wider area, with the most recent in the region, the August 1999 quake in north-western Turkey, leading to the deaths of around 20,000 people. This particular tremor was the result of movements in the North Anatolian fault, which runs along the Black Sea coast, up the Gulf of Izmit and under the Marmara Sea. Further west, faults under the Aegean make this another region prone to earthquakes.

Given the destructive power of such phenomena, it's no surprise that the ancients saw them as clear proof of some very angry gods. Poseidon, the Greek god of the sea (Neptune to the Romans), was also thought responsible for 'earth-shaking' in its various forms. Nowadays, it's all science, with plate tectonics and seismology explaining much about the movements of the Earth's crust and the havoc caused. Nevertheless, on a small boat at night, heading for Stromboli, Europe's only continuously erupting volcano, or crunching along amidst the clinker of rocks in Vulcano's crater, its sulphurous gases steaming off in all directions, it's perhaps not too difficult to hear the thump of Poseidon's trident, still shaking the very earth around.

ORIENTATION

The island's two main airports are Palermo and Catania, both of which are well served by international flights and Alitalia flights from other parts of Italy.

As for ferries, the main port for Malta is Catania, for Tunis, Trapani, and for Sardinia, Trapani and Palermo, with both served by a boat to and from Cágliari. There are also regular ferries between Palermo and Naples, and Palermo and Genoa, plus frequent and regular ferries across the narrow straits between Messina and Reggio di Calabria on the mainland. There are also regular local ferries from Milazzo to the Aeolian Islands, and Trapani to the Egadi Islands.

Settlement — and therefore transportation — on the island itself is mainly around the coast, with rail and road links following the shoreline from Catania to Messina, then back west to Palermo and on to Trapani, before doubling back along the south coast east to Agrigento and finally Syracuse. The system is reliable, if slow. Even along the coastal strip, which the railway line clings to most of the time, whole stretches are through tunnels and over mountains. Allow most of the day, for example, for a train ride from Milazzo to Trapani. Several direct rail services are also available over the straits and on up to Rome.

Buses run by SAIS also cruise up to the Eternal City from Catania and Syracuse, connecting through to Palermo, while Segesta run coaches straight through. These companies, and others, also run services between the major cities.

Hitching is relatively straightforward, though women travelling alone are strongly advised against it. Cars and scooters are also widely available for hire.

PALERMO

AREA CODE: ☎ 091 POPULATION: 694,000
Sicily's 'Golden Shell' is a great bowl of a city, set beneath some grand hills that run sharply down through an ancient medieval core to a sweeping bay. It's one of the most memorably-situated places in the Med, best appreciated by arriving by sea.

While WWII bombing caused considerable carnage in its tightly-packed old streets, much still remains of Palermo's ancient heart, which has been beating since Phoenician times. Depressed, often battered, and a Mafia capital, it nonetheless has a distinct buzz to it, an eclectic mesh of styles and cultures from Arab *medresse* (college) to Normandy cloister.

History

A Phoenician colony by the 7th century BC, Palermo's great strategic position and natural harbour made it rapidly a place of conflict as the Greek colonists of Syracuse made repeated grabs for it. Under Carthaginian rule it resisted one siege by the Romans in 258BC before finally falling to them in another in 254BC.

Carthaginian attempts to reconquer it were seen off, and with Rome's triumph in the Punic Wars (see box, p192), the city became known as Panormus, meaning 'All

harbour'. It was certainly all go from then on, with the port flourishing under Roman rule. With the collapse of the Western Empire, though, the city suffered the same invasions by Vandals and Goths as the rest of the island. The Byzantine period lasted until 831, when the Arabs began a period of rule now seen as a golden age. The city became the seat of an emirate, with lavish new building work undertaken as the cash flowed in from Palermo's pre-eminent position as the trading post between Muslim North Africa and Christian Europe.

All that came to an end though with the Norman invasion in 1060. By 1072, these northerners, under Robert Guiscard, had taken the whole island, with Palermo as their capital. Until the end of the 12th century the Normans controlled things, building many grand cathedrals, monasteries and churches under Germanic rule and then under the Count of Anjou. From then on, the city's story was much the same as the rest of the island, with Spanish rule up until Napoleon's arrival in 1806. After the unification of Italy, Palermo continued as the island capital and was heavily bombed in WWII and fought over as Allied troops battled with German occupiers in its narrow streets. Post war it has continued as the cultural and artistic centre of Sicily, while clearly still one of Italy's poorest, yet most vibrant, cities.

What to see

The historic centre is focused on Quattro Canti, the junction of Via Maqueda and Corso Vittorio Emanuele, marked by a 1611 Spanish façade on each of the four corners of this square, adorned by four statues. Immediately south-east of here is a cluster of fine churches and the Palazzo dei Municipio, the town hall. Head for the Norman Church of Santa Maria dell' Ammiraglio, otherwise known as **La Martorana** (Mon-Sat 0930-1330, 1530-1700, Sun 0830-1300), which was founded in the first half of the 12th century. The façade is a 16th-century baroque addition, with an excellent belltower. Inside, look out for a mosaic on the right wall in which Roger II humbly puts himself in the picture

TYRRHENIAN SEA

❏ **Safety in Palermo**
Palermo can be quite dangerous for tourists at night with mugging and petty theft a
problem for all, and sexual harassment and/or assault for women. Take extra care of
yourself and valuables, particularly after dark.

TYRRHENIAN SEA

with Christ. You'll notice, too, a feature of
many Sicilian churches, the combination of
Greek and Latin styles and even languages
in the sacred art. This was mainly because
many of the builders, locals and architects
were part of a strong Greek community that
still exists to this day.

The neighbouring **Church of San
Cataldo** is also 12th-century, yet a lot
quirkier, with Arabic crenellations and
small Byzantine-style red domes on the
roof of this Norman church. Inside is a fine
mosaic floor and a bare but evocative feel.
Nearby, the **Church of San Giovanni degli
Eremiti** is even more Arabic, and in fact
was built on the site of a mosque.

The main **cathedral** (Mon-Sat 0700-
1900, Sun 0800-1330, 1600-1900), west up
Corso Vittorio Emanuele, is another
Norman-era work, though with an 18th-
century dome. Begun in 1184, it also stands
on the site of an old mosque. There's also
plenty of Catalan Gothic here, particularly
in the 14th- and 15th-century façade and
porch. Inside are the tombs of a number of
the island's rulers, including Frederick II
and the Empress Constance, as well as a
number of chapels, including that of Santa
Rosalia, the city's patron saint, whose
remains are in a niche-mounted silver urn.

The **Palazzo dei Normani** in Piazza
Indipendenza is another building that owes
its origins to the Arab period. Under the
Normans it became the royal palace and is
now the seat of the Sicilian Regional
Assembly. Part of it is open to the public,
however, with the **Palatine Chapel** a must
(Mon-Fri 0900-1145, 1500-1645, Sun
0900-1000, 1200-1300). Begun in 1130 and
finished 13 years later, its best artworks are
the mosaics carried out by Byzantine
artists. There are two stunners — *Christ the*

Pantocrator with Archangels and Angels,
and *Episodes from the Life of Christ*.

The regional **Archaeological Museum**
(Mon-Sat 0900-1315, Sun 0900-1300,
€4.50) is back over Via Roma and has an
impressive collection of Greek and Roman
artefacts from across the island and from
Selinunte in particular. This notably fine
ancient city on the south-west coast dates
from the 7th century BC.

Another must-see lies some way out of
town. **Convento dei Cappuccini** (daily
0900-1200, 1500-1700, €2) is reached by
bus No 327 from Piazza Indipendenza,
which goes south-west to Via Pindemonte, a
25-minute walk away. Beneath this
Cappuccin church is a maze of catacombs
containing some 8000 mummified corpses,
preserved in the Cappuccin manner – that is to
say they're left lying about on the floor.

It's certainly an experience to remember, the kind of place that leaves you praying the lights don't fail, rather than for the
souls of the long departed.

Practical information
Orientation The train station, **Stazione
Centrale**, is at the junction of Via Roma
and Via Abramo Lincoln. Ferries dock to
the north-east, with **Stazione Marittima**
off Via Francesco Crispi, the main harbour-
front road. The **airport** is 30km west at
Punta Raisi; the blue city-buses go there
from the Stazione Centrale every 40 minutes from around 0600 to 2130 (€4.50).
Getting around the city on foot is easy and
highly recommended; the town is spread
along the bay and inland and the main roads
either run parallel to the coast (Via Roma
and Via Maqueda) or at right angles (Corso
Vittorio Emanuele, Via Cavour, Via
Abramo Lincoln).

Most of the *pensions* are in the district off Via Roma between the train station and Corso Vittorio Emanuele. Piazza Rugerro Settimo (the main square) is known as Piazza Politeama locally.

Services The main **tourist office** (☎ 583 847, 🖥 www.palermotourism.com – in Italian only) is at 35, Piazza Castelnuovo, though there's another office at Stazione Centrale. Both are open Mon-Fri 0830-1400, 1430-1800, Sat 0830-1400). The

offices supply maps and brochures as well as accommodation lists. The **tourist police office** (☎ 210111) on Piazza della Vittoria is open 24hr.

There's an **internet café** at 64, Via Cala and in Via Candelai.

Ferries [see p446 for full details] SNAV and Tirrenia (at the Stazione Marittima, Calata Marinai d'Italia, ☎ 602 1111) have services to **Naples**; Tirrenia also has a weekly service to **Cágliari** on Sardinia.

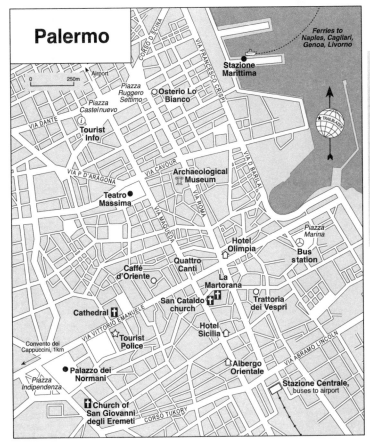

Between June and December, GNV (also at Calata Marinai d'Italia, ☎ 587404) operates to **Genoa** and **Livorno**.

Trains There are 11 trains a day to Messina with several of these heading across by boat to the mainland before continuing to Rome, Florence, Bologna and beyond. There are also regular services to Trapani and round to Catania. Prices are generally good, though journeys are lengthy.

Buses Inter-city buses leave from around Via Paolo Balsamo, with the SAIS coach company office (☎ 616 6028) at No 16 and Segesta (☎ 616 7919) at No 26. Both have services to the mainland. Inner-city buses operate a flat €0.80 fee or you can get a day pass for €3.10. Buy these from kiosks and/or *tabacchi* at the bus stops.

Planes Air Malta fly regularly to Palermo, while Ryanair provide a cheap way to get there from London Stansted. There are also regular connections to Tunis, Rome, Milan, Venice, Barcelona and Paris.

Where to stay The area around the Stazione Centrale is the budget accommodation zone, with Via Maqueda and Via Roma the best hunting grounds.
Hotel Orientale (☎ 616 5727), 26, Via Maqueda. An atmospheric location and sgl/dbl for €25/50.
Hotel Olimpia (☎ 616 1276), Via Roma, just before the Corso Vittorio Emanuele. Some rooms with Piazza views; regular sgl/dbl €25/50.
Hotel Sicilia (☎ 616 8460), 99, Via Divisi, on the corner with Via Maqueda. A touch more upmarket; rooms in the €35/60 sgl/dbl range.

The main **camping** centre is 13km north-west at Sferracavallo, on the No 616 bus route from Piazza Vittorio. There you'll find two sites, namely *Campeggio Internazionale Trinacria* (☎ 530590) and *degli Ulivi* (☎ 533021).

Where to eat *Trattoria dei Vespri*, Piazza Santa Croce dei Vespri. Has outdoor dining and is good value at around €17 a head for

the works, though a simple pasta dish should be no more than €5.
Caffè d'Oriente, Piazza Cancellieri. North African food, with a fine couscous at €12.
Osterio Lo Bianco, Via E Amari, off Via Roma. Some fine local dishes; a full spread costs around €12.

Bars are to be found around the Teatro Massima and the area behind the Church of Sant'Ignazio All'Olivella. **Cafés** are ten a penny, particularly off Via Roma towards the harbour.

TRAPANI

AREA CODE: ☎ 0923 POPULATION: 72,000
Built on a long finger of land heading out towards Spain from the western tip of Sicily, Trapani lies in the slopes of giant Mt Erice, with the Aegadian Islands, the Isole Egadi, out in front. Nowadays it's the main stopping-off point for an important ferry route (the Sardinia–Sicily–Tunis boat), while also providing Sicily with the only maritime link to its more distant offshore islands, Pantelleria and Lampedusa, the most southerly and solitary outposts of the European Union.

It also has some fine old churches and streets in the area west of the station that hooks round the harbour. Unpretentious and workaday, it may not mark itself out for a grand stay but is more than enough for a between-journeys sojourn.

History

The area around Trapani is one of the oldest inhabited on the island. Homer had it that Mt Erice was the home of the one-eyed Cyclops, one of whom, Polyphemus, imprisoned Odysseus who blinded him while escaping.

Its origins are shrouded in mystery, though legend has it that Elyx, king of the Elymians and son of Venus and Butes, founded the place. They set up the mountain settlement of Eryx (now Erice), after their king, which was fought over for years before the Carthaginians captured it in 260BC and destroyed the Elymian temple. Down below, the Greeks had established more permanent premises, founding Drepana, later Drepanum, after the Romans

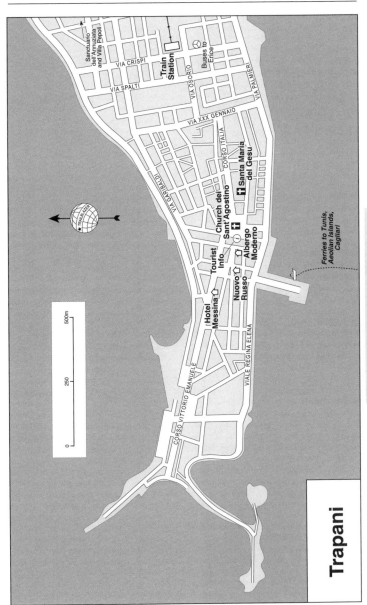

Trapani

TYRRHENIAN SEA

Ferries to Tunis, Aeolian Islands, Cagliari

Santa Maria del Gesù

Church del Sant'Agostino

Albergo Moderno

Tourist Info

Nuovo Russo

Hotel Messina

CORSO ITALIA

VIA XXX GENNAIO

VIA GARIBALDI

VIA SPALTI

VIA CRISPI

VIA OSORIO

VIA PALMIERI

Train Station

Buses to Erice

Sanctuario dell'Annuziata and Villa Pepoli

CORSO VITTORIO EMANUELE

VIALE REGINA ELENA

TRAILBLAZER

0   250   500m

had driven out everyone in 241BC.

The port found some prosperity in medieval times, particularly under the Aragonese, with Charles I of Spain (aka Emperor Charles V) investing considerably in the port defences in the 16th century. The port rebelled from within, however, against the later rulers and instead joined the movement in the nineteenth century for Italian unification. Allied bombers once again levelled much of the place in WWII and since then rebuilding has left it rather like a photocopy of many other post-war reconstructions, though much of the old town around the harbour remains intact. The port continues to be the major source of revenue, with Trapani now the seat of its own regional government.

What to see

The main venue in town is the **Sanctuario dell'Annunziata**, at the eastern end of town opposite the **Villa Pepoli Gardens**. Begun in 1315 and finished in 1332, what you see now is largely a 1760 refit, save for the original façade. In here you'll find the Madonna of Trapani, appropriately enough in the **Chapel of the Madonna**. Elsewhere, try the **Church of Santa Maria del Gesu**, a Romanesque 15th- or 16th-century work, or the 14th-century **Church dei Sant' Agostino**, which has a remarkable 16th-century Fountain of Saturn.

If you have more time, a trip to **Erice** is worthwhile. Some 10km north-east of Trapani, right on Mt Erice, with its spectacular views out across the waters, this settlement has long been a very holy site. Known in ancient times as Eryx, the Phoenicians built a temple here to Astarte, their goddess of love, starting a long-standing trend. When the Greeks took over, the temple was rededicated to Aphrodite (Venus when the Romans arrived). Later, the Normans built Castello di Venere on the same site, inside which can still be found some remains of the Temple of Venus. More of these can be found in the **City Museum** (daily, 0930-1300, 1400-1730, €2), including a head of Aphrodite. You should also walk around the medieval town which is more complete than Trapani, and with more impressive

views between the narrow streets and tight-packed houses.

Practical information

Orientation
The **railway station** is back inland from the peninsula and the harbour, but most avenues lead straight east–west, so once out of the station go straight ahead and after about 10 minutes you'll be in the old town area. Head towards the harbour and you'll soon see signs for *pensions* and other places to stay. The old quarter is next to the harbour and consists of a number of parallel streets, the main roads being Corso Vittorio Emanuele and Viale Regina Elena. Many streets here are pedestrianized and all are easily reached on foot.

Services
The main **tourist information office** (☎ 29000), on Piazza Saturno, is open daily 0930-1300, plus in summer 1400-2000.

Ferries [see p447 for full details]
Tirrenia (☎ 545433, office in the Stazione Marittima) has a weekly service from Trapani to **Cágliari** on Sardinia. The same boat also does the Trapani–Tunis run. Be advised that Trapani–Tunis is a day voyage, Tunis–Trapani a night one. Buy all tickets at the Stazione Marittima. Medmar Linee Lauro also runs to **Tunis**.

Trips to Tunis involve some cackhanded customs procedures, with ample time to observe the multitude of lavish uniforms and cool sunglasses available to the Italian police, along with plenty of clues as to why they're so useless at combatting the Mafia. Allow plenty of time to pass through the hoops before getting on board.

There are also ferries to the Island of **Pantalleria**, the closest point between Europe and Africa, leaving at 23.59 daily, arriving at about 05.30, returning midday to arrive back at Trapani at 16.30. The fare is €18.58/22.44 low/high season, one way.

Finally, there are also nine hydroferries a day to the **Egadian Islands** (Marsala, Favignana and Lavanzo), run by Ustica Lines. The first leaves at 07.30, the last at 19.30. They go on a circular tour, Trapani-Marsala-Favignana-Lavanzo-Trapani, taking about

20 minutes for each leg. The cost is €5. Ustica Lines can be found at Via Amm Staiti, (☎ 22200, 🖹 23289).

Trains The main station is some 15-minutes' walk from the port east along the promontory. From here there are regular trains to Palermo, from where the rest of the island network comes into play.

Where to stay *Albergo Moderno* (☎ 212 47), 20, Via Ten Genovese. Handy for the port and the main old town streets; sgl/dbl for €23/40.
Hotel Messina (☎ 21198), 71, Corso Vittorio Emanuele. Clean and central, €18/35 sgl/dbl.
Nuovo Albergo Russo (☎ 22166), 4, Via Tintori. Three star but more reasonable priced at around €25/50 sgl/dbl.

Where to eat Along the harbour-front road are a clutch of fairly priced restaurants and trattoria. Try the unnamed one at the end of Vittorio Emanuele by the port for a hearty €10 meal. Otherwise, the old town is good for panini snack bars and breakfast.

CATANIA
AREA CODE: ☎ 095 **POPULATION:** 375,000
For a long time this sprawling port city was known after the giant volcano in whose shadow it lies. Mt Etna looms large to the north-west, a truly eerie sight visible far and wide and particularly other-worldly if you're flying down here; through the wisps of low cloud, you'll see its distinctive cone from miles away, slowly puffing out its own cloud of sulphurous vapour.

Living under the volcano has left Catania very different from other Sicilian cities. With its grand public buildings largely composed of black volcanic stone, it has an austere look, added to by a certain industrial grubbiness. Yet it's a vibrant enough place with a range of historical and religious sights you'll find nowhere else on Sicily outside Palermo.

But it is mainly for the volcano that people come. From here, the ascent is easiest and most popular by road or rail. It's also here that the hydrofoil from Malta puts in, making it the only place on Sicily for travelling to that great Mediterranean island. Catania also has good rail and road links up to Messina, Malazzo and, round the corner, on to Palermo and Trapani.

History
In 729BC Greek colonists from Chalcis in the Euboea landed and founded the city. The rival Greek city state of Syracuse took over in the 5th century BC, renaming it Aetna after the volcano. Following the Punic Wars it went to Rome in 263BC and later received colonial status under Emperor Augustus. Many a Christian martyr died here in the jaws of the lions, including St Agatha, nowadays the city's patron saint.

With the collapse of the Western Roman Empire, the city followed the course of the rest of Sicily: prey to Goths and Vandals until taken by the Byzantines, then the Arabs and finally the Normans. Catania also took an ill-advised stance against the Normans' successors, the Swabian Germans, who sacked it twice, first under Henry VI and then under Frederick II.

Under Aragonese and Spanish rule the port prospered, despite repeated outbreaks of the plague and pirate attacks. Things did not get any better in 1669, when an eruption by Etna levelled a lot of the surrounding area, the subsequent 1693 earthquake hardly helping matters. The place became a seat of rebellion from then on, including a major uprising in 1837 that took place during a cholera epidemic and was brutally suppressed. Nonetheless, Catania joined the 1848 revolutionary movement sweeping Europe at that time, demanding independence for Sicily, an uprising that was brutally put down. In WWII, much of the town was flattened by Allied bombing and by street-fighting during the liberation of Sicily in 1943.

Since then, things haven't been quite so bad, and the port is now one of the busiest in Italy. It has also expanded greatly from the old town area around the harbour and is a major metropolis, still largely built on the solidified lava flows of the growling monster to the north.

TYRRHENIAN SEA

What to see

Starting from the Piazza Duomo, the first thing to look at is, naturally enough, **the elephant**. This 17th-century fountain is a knock-together job consisting of a Roman-era creature with an ancient Egyptian obelisk stuck on its back. Its local name is the Liotru, for reasons somewhat obscure, but which may be either derived from the Carthaginian, or possibly from the name Eliodoro, a legendary character who apparently flew elephants from here to Constantinople.

Right there in the square is the **Duomo**, originally an 11th-century Norman cathedral, though earthquakes have erased all of the original structure except for three apses. What you see now is largely baroque, a rebuild after the 1693 quake. Inside, look out for the tomb of the composer Vincenzo Bellini, just 25 years old when buried here in 1835. St Agatha is also widely commemorated in sculpture and painting, along with her own chapel.

From here, heading south-west takes you rapidly to the **Castello Ursino** (daily 0930-1300, 1400-1900, €3). This is a classic defensive work, built under orders from Frederick II of Swabia. At that time it was surrounded by sea, and remained so up until 1699, when a stream of lava filled the entire area around it, a surreal thought when one looks at the comfortable gardens, streets and apartment houses now so solidly built here.

Inside the Castello is the **Municipal Museum** (same hours and admission as the Castello), which has various collections of artworks donated by Baron Zappala-Asmundo and the Benedictine monks.

The ruins of the 1st-century-AD **Roman amphitheatre**, built over the original Greek one, are on Corso Vittorio Emanuele, back across Via Garibaldi. Next, keep north for Via San Giuliano, where the **church** of the same name was one of the star reconstructions in the city after the apocalyptic events of the late 17th century. Finished in 1751, its interior has a remarkable octagonal centre, and the church is bathed in a wonderful glow. Another church of interest is **S Agata al Carcere**, on Via Capuccini, just to the north; its 16th-century bastion incorporates a much older structure. Tradition has it that this is the Roman prison where St Agatha was incarcerated. Inside you'll find a coffin in which St Agatha's body was apparently transferred from Constantinople, and two lumps of lava in which her alleged footprints can be seen.

Turn right to Piazza Stesicoro and the **Roman amphitheatre**. Holding around

---

Mt Etna

At 3330m high and covering a 160 sq km base, Etna is one of the most spectacular and liveliest volcanoes in the Mediterranean. Four craters are still active, constantly pouring out ash and various vapours; there are also intermittent bursts of red-hot magma sparking out from the summit.

It's usually perfectly safe to climb, however, and in recent years it has taken off as a winter ski resort as well as a summer trekking destination. Getting to the top can be a problem. The AST bus leaves at 0815 every morning from outside Catania railway station; it will take you on a two-hour journey to the end of the road and *Sapienza Refuge* (☎ 911062) at c1980m. The refuge offers some food and accommodation. From there, for around €35 return, a guide will take you in a jeep to as close to the top as is considered safe at the time. The quantity of ash and vapour in the air at this altitude makes it sensible to wear goggles or glasses; a handkerchief or scarf to place over your mouth is essential.

An alternative is to gò on a guided tour: Autocitta (☎ 436569), 29, Viale Regina Margherita, offers a full day trip with lunch for €52 per person.

15,000 spectators, it's the biggest in Sicily and dates from around the 2nd century AD. As with the other Roman sites here it's built from lava, in dark contrast to the white marble inlays of the seats.

Practical information

Orientation The harbour is south of the main bulk of the city, but south-east of the old part of town. Arriving on the Malta ferry, ignore the road signs outside the port exit pointing right to the Centro and turn left instead. After five minutes, cut right inland and soon you'll come to the main road, Corso Vittorio Emanuele. Keep west on this for the Piazza Duomo, the main square. The city branches off to the north, along Via Etnea, and then west. The main railway station is up the coast north-east from the harbour and right by the seafront on Via VI Aprile. All the main sights are within easy walking distance of the Piazza Duomo.

Services The best **tourist information office**, at 172, Corso Vittorio Emanuele, opens daily in summer 0930-1900. and has maps and plenty of useful info and advice. The one to avoid is the office at the harbour, which doesn't open when it says it will. The railway station has a **left-luggage** office.

Ferries [see p443 for full details] Both MA.RE.SI and Virtu Ferries (☎ 535711), Molo Centrale, Porto di Catania, run between Catania and **Valletta**, Malta. Virtu's hydrofoil has a café/bar and decent films on the TV.

Trains There are frequent services up the coast to Messina and over to mainland Italy or round to Milazzo and on to Palermo.

Buses Buses to Etna leave from Piazza Giovanni XXIII in front of the railway station; see Mt Etna (box, p182) for further details. Services to Messina and beyond also depart from outside the railway station; tickets can be obtained from the kiosk or at the AST window inside the train station.

Where to stay *Sicilian Home* (☎ 316 557), 66, Corso Vittorio Emanuele, near Piazza Duomo and the harbour. Located in a fine 18th-century house; sgl/dbl for €20/50.
Hotel Aiello (☎ 387804), 31, Via Vittorio Veneto. A basic one-star hotel but with clean, decent sgl/dbl for €18/30.
Europensione (☎ 531007), 8, Piazza deo Martiri. Good sgl/dbl for €35/60.

Campers should try *Aragosta Rossa* (☎ 712 8669), 25, Via Acque Casse.

Where to eat *Trattorio Sangiuliano*, 207, Via A di Sangiuliano. A quality trattoria with excellent Sicilian dishes for around €15 a head.
Via Coppola Pizzeria, 39, Via Coppola. Good slices and whole pizzas for €10.
I Pitagorici, 59, Via Archimede. A vegetarian place with an esoteric bookshop.

TAORMINA

AREA CODE: ☎ 0942 **POPULATION:** 10,085
Located on the coast halfway between Catania and Messina, Taormina is one of Sicily's greatest ancient sites, partly due to its location on the slopes of Mt Tauro above the long, curving coast, with Mt Etna towering behind. There are three good beaches, connected to the small town of Taormina by cable-car, with the place doubling as a resort with even a little winter skiing available. However, forget staying here during the high season unless you've booked the previous year. Nonetheless, it is still possible to visit as a stop-off between Catania and Messina as it's well placed on the main coastal railway line and roadway.

History

Founded by Greek colonists around the 4th century, Tauromenion soon came under the influence of the island's most powerful Greek city state, Syracuse. With the arrival of the Romans in the 3rd century BC, it continued to prosper, but as Syracuse's fortunes declined, along with those of the Western Roman Empire, Tauromenion's increased and by the time the Byzantine reconquest took Sicily, it was sufficiently grand to become capital of the island. That was until the 10th century and the Arab invasion, after which Taormina never quite recovered

TYRRHENIAN SEA

its earlier significance. From then on, it followed the fortunes of the island as a whole, today being one of Sicily's most visited tourist venues.

What to see

Most visitors head first for the **ancient Greek theatre** (daily 0900 to one hour before sunset, €4.50), mostly for its spectacular views along the coast and back inland to Etna. What you see now is of Roman construction from the 1st century AD, built on an earlier Greek effort from the 3rd century BC. The Romans altered things a little to allow gladiatorial combats to take place; look out for the deep trench before the stage where the combatants and victims would be held before the show began. Next door to the theatre is the **Antiquarium**, holding a collection of rather average archaeological finds.

Most of the rest of the historical sights are back in town. The Piazza Vittorio Emanuele is the location of the ancient **forum**, where the remains of the Roman baths have been partially uncovered. Taormina's medieval gems include the 15th-century **Palazzo Corvia** — site of Sicily's first parliament — and the **Duomo**, a 13th-century original largely reworked in the Renaissance.

If you fancy a swim after all this, head for Via Pirandello and the top of a cable-car (€1.50), which leads down to Mazzaro, a classic curved beach with islet.

Practical information

Orientation The train station — Taormina-Giardini — is a stiff 30-minute walk below the town and the ancient sites, though there is a bus from outside the station that can take you to the town centre. From there the ancient sites are quite clearly marked, and wandering about is also highly recommended as Taormina is a delight of old streets and piazzas shaped around the main pedestrianized street, Corso Vittorio Emanuele. Once you've reached the town, all the sights are within easy walking distance.

Services The **tourist information office** (☎ 23243, 🖳 www.taormina-ol.it), in

Palazzo Corvia on Piazza Santa Caterina, is open Mon-Sat 0830-1400, 1600-1900. It has accommodation lists and maps.

Where to stay Finding accommodation can be very difficult in summer but an alternative is Giardini Naxos, a small seaside resort just south of Taormina. This was the ancient Greek settlement of Naxos, destroyed by the Syracusans in the 5th century BC and never really a major player in the island's affairs since then. Nonetheless, it has a fine beach, is a 20-minute walk from Taormina train station and has a number of *pensions* including *La Sirena* (☎ 51853), 36, Via Schiso, which has sgl/dbl for €25/40. The nearest **campsite**, *San Leo*, is below Taormina and open all year.

Where to eat *Il Baccanale*, in Taormina, is a relatively low-priced trattoria with a full meal costing around €10 a head. *Da Angelina*, in Giardini Naxos, has good views and a fine selection of pizzas for €8 a head.

MESSINA

AREA CODE: ☎ 090 POPULATION: 232,911

A busy, bustling port town, Messina is inevitably described as the 'Gateway to Sicily', a role it has played for millennia. Crossing the narrow straits to the toe of Italy are almost continuous ferry services taking cars, backpackers, coaches, trucks and even trains between the two mountainous landmasses. Messina itself is well placed in the foothills of the Peloritan Mountains and has a wonderful curving natural harbour. It's unlikely you'll stay here unless you're arriving at some godforsaken hour from the mainland. From here, trains depart along the northern coast of the island to Milazzo and the Aeolian Island ferries, and south to Taormina and Catania. Yet you might want to a have a quick look round in transit, as Messina holds many a hidden gem.

History

Settled by Greek colonists from Chalcedon in the 8th century BC, Messina started out as Zancle, meaning 'sickle', a natural epithet given the curving shape of the harbour.

Embroiled in the conflicts between the Dorian and Ionian Greeks, in 493BC it was captured by Anaxilas, the tyrant of Rhegium, who renamed it Messina after his native country Messenia on the Pelopponese. Unlike much of the rest of the island, Messina prospered under Roman rule following their takeover in 264BC thanks to its natural role as the main crossing point to the Italian mainland.

With the collapse of Western Roman rule, it followed the fortunes of the rest of Sicily more closely, passing through Gothic, Byzantine, Norman, Swabian, Angevin, Aragonese, Savoyard, Bourbon, Austrian and finally unified Italian control in 1860.

Mother Nature has not been kind to Messina. Lying in a high-risk earthquake zone, a tremor in 1783 wiped out the whole city. Its surviving inhabitants then bravely rebuilt it by 1908, only to have it levelled again that year by another earthquake, followed by a devastating tidal wave which killed an estimate 80,000 people. WWII also saw carpet-bombing of the strategically vital harbour area by US and British planes.

What to see

The main attraction is the **Duomo**, the cathedral, which was rebuilt following the 1908 earthquake and Allied bombing in 1943. The site was originally occupied by a 12th-century church built on the orders of the Norman King Roger II. Inside, visit the Treasury, which contains a number of 14th-century chalices, 12th-century reliquaries and even a couple of Byzantine paintings. Elsewhere, see the **Church of San Francesco d'Assisi**, which not only suffered from earthquakes and warfare but was also burnt down in the late 19th century. That anything remains is nothing short of a miracle, an event made more remarkable by the fact that this building still looks like a medieval church. The original design was Norman. Outside, there is a simple statue of St Francis of Assisi, looking quizzically at the heavens.

Practical information

Orientation The main **railway station** is above the port area where the ferries from

Italy come in. However, certain trains go to the **Stazzione Marittime**, where they connect with ferries to Villa San Giovanni or Reggio di Calabria. The few local sights are largely within walking distance of each other.

Services The **tourist information office** (☎ 74236), 301, Via Calabria Isol, is open daily 0930-1900 and has maps and accommodation lists.

Ferries [see p445 for full details] Perhaps it's easier to say when there aren't any ferries than when there are, as this is Italy's busiest ferry port, with boats making the 15- to 20-minute trip over to **Reggio di Calabria** and **Villa San Giovanni** every five or ten minutes most of the day. Caronte & Tourist operate a daily service to **Messina** from May to December and SNAV (☎ 364 044), 27, Via della Munizione, has services to the **Aeolian Islands** from here and from Milazzo.

Trains There are direct trains from Messina to a number of mainland Italian cities such as Milan, Florence, Rome and Naples. Ticket prices include the ferry trip across the straits. In addition there are regular services to Milazzo, for the Aeolian Islands, and on to Palermo and Trapani, while trains also head south for Catania, stopping off at Taormina on the way.

Buses Buses for Milazzo leave from the Giuntabus office at Via Terranova 8, on the corner of Viale San Martino.

Where to stay *Hotel Cannata* (☎ 984 3161), 13, Via Umberto I. Some 30m from the sea with a good restaurant; sgl/dbl for €30/60.

Locanda Donato (☎ 393150), 8, Via Carlo Caratozzolo. Decent rooms for €46/61 sgl/dbl.

Hotel Mirage (☎ 293 8844), 1, Via N Scotto, near the railway station. In a handy location; €37/47 sgl/dbl.

Finally, Campers should try *Il Peloritano* (☎ 348496), Fraz Rodia, which charges €4 a head.

TYRRHENIAN SEA

Where to eat As with most Italian cities, restaurants are pricey. Budget alternatives are the pizza and snack bars around the station and the main shopping area.

Lungomare da Mario, 108, Corso Vittorio Emanuele. Reasonable at €20 a head for a full meal; a simple pasta dish can be had for around €5.

THE AEOLIAN ISLANDS

AREA CODE: ☎ 090 **POPULATION:** 12,784

Part of the volcanic arc of fire created by deep geological faults around the southern tip of Italy and eastern Sicily (see box on p174), the Aeolian Islands are a remarkable collection of volcanic peaks blasted up from the seabed by a series of cataclysmic ancient eruptions. The very word 'volcano' comes from here, with the island of Vulcano still smouldering, while Stromboli is Europe's only permanently erupting volcano, the eruptions occurring several times an hour. One, on 5 April, 2003, was large enough to destroy several houses, though thankfully nobody was injured

The islands are all connected by fast ferry boats with the mainland port of Milazzo and each has a distinctive aura, with the capital of the group, Lipari, a lively holiday centre year-round. Most of all, though, this is a place for some trekking, as walking up to the craters is usually possible and affords some spectacular views.

History

Inhabited since neolithic times, it was in the Bronze Age that the islanders first began to get noticed, stringing together trade routes from as far away as the Aegean and Britain, from where they imported tin. Around the middle of the 8th century BC, however, the Ausonians invaded. They were led by Lipari, after whom the largest island is named. Later, his successor, Eolus, built a house there that, according to Homer, Odysseus stayed at during his fraught attempts to go home. The Greeks called the islands the Aeolians as they believed that it was the home of Aeolus, god of the winds.

In 580BC more Greeks arrived, this time exiled from Rhodes, and their pirates grew rich attacking Phoenician and Carthaginian vessels from this strategically well placed haven. This seems to have come to an end with the Carthaginian takeover of Sicily, which resulted in the islanders fighting on Carthage's side in the Punic Wars against Rome. The Aeolians paid dearly for this, Lipari being attacked and sacked by the Romans, who established their rule here until the end of the Western Empire.

There then followed invasions by the Visigoths, Vandals, Ostrogoths and Byzantines, finishing off with an Arab attack in AD836. In the 11th century the Normans arrived and began a period of relative stability. The islands remained loyal to Anjou during the Sicilian Vespers, while in 1337 they let the French fleet in without resistance, securing valuable privileges. Under the Kingdom of the Two Sicilies the Aeolians switched sides and began attacking French ships alongside the Spanish Aragonese. In 1544, though, a major Ottoman fleet arrived under the command of Barbarossa (see box, p92), which sacked the fort on Lipari and enslaved a large part of the population. The Aragonese then largely repopulated the islands with settlers from Calabria and Sicily, while also establishing tighter maritime control.

However, under Bourbon rule, the islands were mainly used as prison colonies for political dissidents, a role reprised in the 20th century by the Italian fascists. After the liberation, the islands sunk back into a pattern much like the rest of Sicily, though in more recent times it has developed a strong tourism base.

What to see

Vulcano With its main settlement, Porto di Levante, lying in the dip between two volcanic cones, Vulcano is the first stop for the Milazzo ferry and a great introduction to the group. To the left of the jetty is a small black beach, while to the right you go down the main street to the SNAV ticket office and further to the hot springs. Don't be surprised to see some aged locals sitting amongst the springs' sulphurous fumes on small wooden chairs: the vapours are thought to be a good cure-all. You can swim in the sea next to these pools even in the dead of winter, as underwater vents shoot out hot gases, warming the water by the narrow shingle beach into a pleasant, milky-white bath. Beyond here to the north is the cone of Vulcanello, which suddenly rose clear off the seabed in AD21 in a spectacular eruption. Subsequent lava flows then joined this islet to the mainland in the 16th century. Walking to the crater rim takes about half an hour: follow the main road out of town for about 750m, then keep straight on up a winding path to the 102m summit.

The main attraction, however, is the Gran Cratere, the **Fossa di Vulcano**, which steams away high up to the south of town. This last got really angry between 1888 and 1890 when 19 months of eruptions caused many deaths and wiped out the local sulphur mines. Since then it has been quiescent but is still officially classified as active. The walk up and back takes around two hours, with the paths marked on local maps deceptive; don't attempt the climb without some good walking boots. Follow the main road out of Porto di Levanta south-west for a good 500m before turning left along a clearly visible path that tacks back and forth up the side of the cone to the crater rim. Once you're up, the view of the island group is spectacular, the landscape first lunar and then hellish, with sulphurous fumes running in great rivers out of the clinker-like rocks. You should take a handkerchief or thin scarf to wear over your mouth, as the air can be pretty thick up there. A path leads down into the crater itself, finishing at the bottom where some intrepid person has dug the Vulcano equivalent of 'John loves Julie' in the soft volcanic ash.

Lipari The capital of the group and the home of its largest settlement, also called Lipari, this will probably be your main base for accommodation and for exploring the other islands. It's also the centre of the Aeolian pumice and obsidian trade, with both being quarried here for millennia. The island is dominated by two extinct volcanoes, Monte S Angelo and Monte Pilato, with the former the higher at 594m.

The town of Lipari is dominated by the headland castle, once the site of an ancient Greek acropolis. For a long time a prison for Bourbon oppositionists, then anti-fascist fighters, it now houses the **archaeological museum** (daily 0930-1900, €4) which contains relics dating from the pre-Greek 'obsidian civilization' based here, along with later Greek and Roman work. There is also the **Museum of Vulcanology** (same hours and prices) which gives the geological lowdown on the Aeolians.

The town is quite a pleasant place to stroll round. The main road is the north–south Corso Vittorio Emanuele, which runs parallel to the coast several blocks inland. North of town, the road leads to Canneto, the island's other significant settlement, with an excellent, long curving beach.

Climbing the volcanoes is much more of an expedition here than on Vulcano and, since they're no longer active, is really only for enthusiasts. For Monte S Angelo you need to take a bus to the village of Varessana, which leaves early in the morning only, or walk the 4-5km to the village. A path leads north-east from there up the side of the cone, finally bringing you to the summit after about another hour's walk. Monte Pilato is reached via Canneto and a twisting road to the north-west which squiggles up to the village of Pomiciazzo before heading more steeply for the 476m top. Again, allow an hour from Pomiciazzo, and a further hour and a half from Canneto.

Stromboli Europe's only permanently erupting volcano, this cone has even given its name to a whole category of volcanic behaviour: 'strombolian activity'. The island is shaped like a pyramid, some 924m high, and descends some 2000m beneath the sea to the Mediterranean floor.

Lava eruptions occur here several times an hour, along the Sciara del Fuocco, the Trail of Fire, and the most dramatic way to see it is at night. This involves joining an organized tour, the boat departing Lipari when there are enough people. Enquire at Lipari tourist office for details. Tours usually cost around €25-35. You can, of course, visit during the day. In either case, you are advised to wear good walking shoes and take something to cover your mouth and nose.

TYRRHENIAN SEA

Practical information

Orientation All seven islands are connected by regular fast hydrofoils to the mainland port of Milazzo and to other destinations (see Ferries, below). None of the islands is of any real size, so walking round them is fairly straightforward: it is even possible to see two or three on a day trip and be back in Milazzo for the Palermo or Messina train. The ferry/hydrofoil routes usually go either from Vulcano to Salina, then Lipari, Filicudi and Alicudi, or from Vulcano to Salina, then Panarea and Stromboli, though there are some interconnecting services such as those from Alicudi to Stromboli.

Services Both the **tourist information office** on Lipari (☎ 988 0095), 202, Corso Vittorio Emanuele, and on Milazzo (☎ 922 2865) in Piazza Caio Duilio, give out leaflets and enjoy long lunches.

Ferries [see p441 for full details] SNAV (☎ 928 7821), on Via Dei Mille, the main harbour-front road, and Navigazione Generale Italiano have regular services to **Milazzo**. Siremar operates to **Milazzo** and **Naples**, SNAV to **Messina**, **Naples**, **Palermo** and **Reggio di Calabria** and Alilauro runs daily between the islands and **Naples**. Check 🖥 www.eolnet.it/eng for further details about reaching the islands.

Trains Milazzo station is the nearest mainland railway stop for the islands but this is a significant bus ride away from Milazzo itself and the ferry offices. Buses go frequently from the car park outside the station, the trip taking 10-15 minutes and costing €0.77. Note that on Sundays and public holidays, bus services diminish to just three a day.

Where to stay Lipari is the centre for accommodation and there's a possibility that you'll be met in season at the quay by people offering rooms, usually for around €15 per head per night. Take them up, as accommodation is otherwise not easy to find in summer. *HI Hostel* (☎ 981 1540), 17, Via Castello, near the castle, has bunks for €12 a night. *Cassara Vittorio* (☎ 981 1523), 15, Vico Sparviero, has singles/doubles for

€25/50. *Hotel-Residence Mendolita* (☎ 981 1002) on Via G Rizzo has a beautiful garden and is well placed in the old town; €35 a double Jan-Mar and Oct-Dec, €55 a double Apr-Sep.

For **campers**, *Baia Unci* (☎ 981 1909) is outside Canneto, 2km north of town.

Where to eat Try the northern end of Corso Vittorio Emanuele for 'tourist menus', which usually cost around €15. *Il Galeone* serves its own wine, while *Trattoria d'Oro* is also recommended.

Tunis

AREA CODE: ☎ 01 **POPULATION:** 1.9 MILLION
From its medieval Medina to its ancient ruins, its French colonial boulevards to its bustling cubist coastal resorts, Tunis is a lot to deal with in a short time. Coming from Europe you'll experience the first rush of North Africa in a very physical way; with dozens of taxi drivers, baggage handlers, customs officials, hawkers and hotel touts literally coming straight at you at the dock. Expect this to be repeated, particularly if you're a woman. Yet, beyond this, you'll find Tunis and, Tunisia, a huge eye-opener and a place of remarkable friendliness.

Tunis is far and away the country's largest city as well as its capital. It's also a major ferry terminal, with boats leaving for Marseille, Genoa, Sicily and Sardinia on a regular basis. The airport is also well connected to European and other North African and Middle Eastern cities, while Tunis is the main centre for the country's bus and rail network. The capital is also well used to tourists, with many locals speaking French, if not English – one of many reminders of the country's colonial past.

HISTORY
Carthage, almost on the site of Tunis, began as a Phoenician trading post in c814BC. By the 6th century BC, however, the Carthaginians had not only overcome their Phoenician ancestors but were dominating

the western half of the Med with their then-unrivalled navy and merchant fleet. They ran much of the Magreb coast, Sicily, southern Italy, Eastern Spain and southern France, engaging in frequent battles with the Greek city states of the region.

During the expansion of the Roman Empire the three Punic Wars (intermittently between 264 and 145BC) brought about the gradual downfall of the Carthaginians, though Hannibal's epic dash across southern Europe and over the Alps, taking over several northern provinces and threatening Rome itself, might have led to victory in the second Punic War had not the Roman general, Scipio, with armies from southern Spain conquered the Carthage area before Hannibal could return to defeat him. Nevertheless, Carthage retained several rights and continued to trade so successfully as to threaten Roman commerce: hence the third Punic War.

Following the lead of the Roman senator Cato, who ended every speech in the senate with *'Delinda est Carthago'* (Carthage must be destroyed!), the Roman army levelled the ancient city of Carthage, selling the entire surviving population into slavery. They now held a great port in a strategically brilliantly location for the pursuit of their imperial ambitions. Roman Carthage thus rose quickly from the city destroyed in

146BC, becoming capital of the province of Africa and later known as Tunis.

Better known for its desert wastes these days than its acres of golden wheat and barley, North Africa then was quite a different place. The 'Bread Basket' of the Roman world, Carthage and its province became one of the most prosperous areas in the empire, though in many respects the 'over-cultification' at this time later contributed to so much desertification.

With the collapse of the Western Empire, the Vandals took Carthage in AD439 and held it until the Byzantine reconquest in 533. Following the advent of Islam and their lightning conquest of North Africa in the seventh century, the Arabs swept in, setting up their capital at Kairouan, some 150km inland. This vast Arab empire soon collapsed too, Tunis then coming under the control of the Morocco-based Almohads. For over three centuries the Hafsid family seem to have governed relatively successfully, at least until the arrival of Süleyman I's Turks in 1534 under Barbarossa (Red Beard; see p92), who took the city and deposed Muley Hassan, the Hafsid ruler.

The Spaniards saw this as a threat to their possessions in Sicily and Sardinia and pre-empted an Ottoman invasion by commissioning the Genoese admiral, Andre Doria, to capture Tunis, which he duly did

TYRRHENIAN SEA

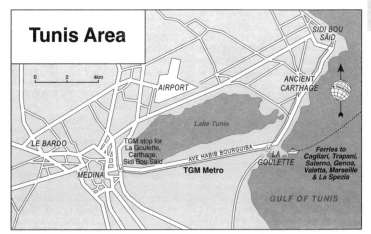

Tunis Area

0   2   4km

AIRPORT

SIDI BOU SAÏD

ANCIENT CARTHAGE

Lake Tunis

LE BARDO

TGM stop for La Goulette, Carthage, Sidi Bou Saïd

AVE HABIB BOURGUIBA

LA GOULETTE

Ferries to Cagliari, Trapani, Salerno, Genoa, Valetta, Marseille & La Spezia

MEDINA

TGM Metro

GULF OF TUNIS

in 1535. The Ottomans, however, then retook it in 1574.

Another period of relative stability ensued, the Turks becoming gradually subsumed into the local population and culture. A Tunisian monarchy began to emerge during this period too, the Huseinids, who, by the 18th century were largely running the country independently of İstanbul. This left them in a precarious position when the 19th century brought a great explosion of imperialism to the north. The French, after invading neighbouring Algeria, then invaded Tunisia in 1881, making the country a protectorate in 1883.

The struggle to oust them was protracted. Habib Bourguiba headed the national liberation movement, Neo-Destour, despite being jailed by the French authorities. During WWII, the Germans occupied Tunis, using it as a main supply base for General Rommel's famed Afrika Korps, which pushed the British and their allies back almost to Alexandria. Bourguiba was also released by the Germans as part of their efforts to undermine French influence, but after Germany's defeat in 1945, the French returned to power and Bourguiba fled to Egypt, from where he orchestrated a long guerrilla war. Finally, in 1955, the French withdrew and in 1957 Bourguiba became first president of the Republic of Tunisia.

Bourguiba continued to rule until 1987, when he was finally ousted by his interior minister, Zine el-Abidine ben Ali, still in control today. The country now has a reputation as a leading 'modernizer' in the Islamic world with a highly developed tourist industry, despite there being considerable political repression. The violence next-door in Algeria has not occurred in Tunisia, a fact which some put down to there being little tolerance of Islamist politics, with a strong emphasis on secularism; witness the large numbers of Tunisian women without a *hijab* (headscarf) on the streets of Tunis.

WHAT TO SEE

The **Medina** is the great magnet at the heart of Tunis, walled off from the splurge of modernity around it and entered through a pseudo Arc de Triomphe in the place de la

Victoire, the Bab Bhar. Now a UNESCO world cultural heritage site, the Medina lies on what was once a major crossroads for North African trading caravans back in Roman times. It then developed further after the Islamic conquest when Hassan ibn Nooman, the conqueror of the Byzantine city, built the **Ez-Zitouna Mosque** here, located now at the top of the narrow rue Jamaa Zitouna, which heads west from place de la Victoire. The street is lined with souvenir shops, old cafés and tea houses, offering *nargiles* (hookahs) and mint tea: excellent places to watch the world go by.

The mosque (*Zitouna* means 'olive') appears abruptly, the narrowness of the street making it impossible to get a full grasp of its size. What you can see now is actually a 9th-century rebuild by Emir Ibrahim bin Ahmed which used the ruins of ancient Carthage as a handy source of supplies: many of the 184 columns in the mosque were moved from there. There's also a 1450 library, while the Ottomans added a gallery around the courtyard in 1653. The Moorish minaret, a square, solid structure, in contrast to the needle-like minarets of further east, was added in 1834.

Around the mosque are the various souks (markets), arranged in order of prestige: the closer to the mosque, the greater the reputation. **Souk el Attarine**, where the perfume-makers' guild is established, is to the right of the mosque entrance, while passing down the **Souk Ettrouk**, along the northern edge of the mosque, you come to the **Souk el Berka**, where members of the jewellers' guild have worked since 1610, when Youssef Dey had it constructed. In the centre of the souk once stood the wooden block on which slaves were also exhibited prior to sale.

On returning to the front of the mosque, go left down rue des Libraires, keep straight on, then turn right into rue du Tresor, then left again down rue Tourbet Bey. Five minutes' walk will bring you to the **Mausoleum of Tourbet Bey** (daily 0930-1700). These rooms are crowded with the tombs of the Huseinids, the dynasty that ruled Tunisia in the 18th and early 19th centuries. This mausoleum is from the era of Ali

Pasha II, who ruled from 1758 to 1782. As with Islamic graves elsewhere, the headstone of the males supports a stone carved headdress, either a turban or a fez depending on the status and occupation of the person buried. The female graves are less embellished, with marble plaques at each end.

Out of here and heading back east along rue Sidi Kacem, the **Dar Ben Abdullah Museum** (Sat-Thu 0930-1700) is on the right. Housed in a 1796-built palace, waxworks recreate scenes from the 19th-century life of the city's rich, with some splendid costumes on show.

Outside the Medina, the city's other major pull is the **Bardo Museum** (Tue-Sun, 0930-1700), a bus or tram ride north-west. Here you'll find a splendid collection of Roman artefacts including mosaic floors, though there is little to speak of in terms of Carthaginian remains.

Carthage

Located on the coast a TGM ride away from Tunis, from the walls of ancient Carthage a great civilization once looked out that is now all but vanished. Legend has it that in 814BC the Phoenician princess, Elyssa, better known as Dido, Queen of Carthage, fleeing Tyre, sought refuge here and persuaded the Libyans to give her as much land as a single

ox hide could enclose. She cut it so very finely into strips that she gained a vast tract of land, the site of her beautiful capital and her great harbour complex.

This also makes visiting the site today quite a task, as it spreads over a considerable area. However, for original Carthaginian (Punic) remains, the hill of Byrsa and the archaeology museum there are the main centres. Take the TGM to Carthage-Hannibal and head straight up the palm-lined ave de l'Amphitheatre. On the left after around 200m there is a small road and off this a dirt track leads steeply up to bring you out by the huge, French-built Catholic **Basilica of St Cyprien**. The site and the museum are next to this. Entry to all the sites (daily 0930-1700) is on one ticket which costs 12 dinars. On a terrace in front of the museum is a viewing point, from where there is an excellent view of the Gulf of Tunis and of the modern city. You can also get a good idea of the ancient Carthaginian port, now two circular lagoons with a central island located to the south-west on the coast. These were once the military and commercial powerhouses of a major Mediterranean empire, with ships at anchor here that regularly journeyed as far north as Britain and south to trading posts on the African Atlantic coast.

TYRRHENIAN SEA

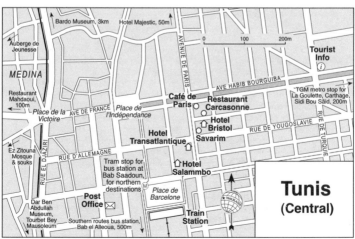

At Byrsa now there is only a small Carthaginian quarter to see, the **Punic Quarter**, which contains some remains of houses from the 3rd century BC. In the **museum** you'll find some more relics of those times but they're rather dwarfed by the later Roman remains. Look out for the Punic symbol, a triangle with a line and a circle at the summit which often appears on the bottom of pots and other ceramics. It is actually the symbol of the goddess Tanit, the triangle representing her robe, the circle her head, with her shoulders represented by the horizontal line between them. It's a signa-

The Carthaginians
Originally a Phoenician colony, the city state of Carthage rose rapidly to dominate the entire western Mediterranean and for a brief period looked like it might overturn the power of Rome itself.

Established in 814BC, the Carthaginian Empire expanded via commerce and colonization to encompass Sicily, Sardinia, the southern French coast and much of Mediterranean Spain within its territory, along with the North African coast both east and west of Tunisia. At its height, in the 3rd century BC, Carthage was the greatest port in the Mediterranean, with an estimated population of around a million. Its great military harbour, the circular Cothon, had room for 150 quinqueremes (an ancient galley with five files of oarsmen on each side), with capacity for around 300 crew each. This harbour was connected by a canal to the commercial harbour, from where Carthaginian traders became some of the richest merchants in the world.

Like their Phoenician ancestors, the Carthaginians were firm believers in the free market. Fighting was contracted out to armies of mercenaries, while alliances were largely at the service of profit and loss. The free market also led to rule by oligarchy — a few rich families dominating the entire business (and therefore political) world.

Protection of trade routes was the reasoning behind Carthage's first great conflict with the ancient Greeks. Greek colonists had begun to set up shop on Sicily, Sardinia and Corsica by the 6th century BC, leading to a lengthy fight for control of the western Mediterranean. Sicily became the main battleground, with the conflict raging for centuries until finally resolved by the emergence of a yet stronger power: the Romans.

War between Carthage and Rome came in three episodes, known collectively as the Punic Wars; 'Punic' was the Roman term for 'Phoenician'. The first of these was largely fought at sea, with the Romans scoring a surprise victory, given that they had no previous record of naval prowess. The secret of their success was in developing new tactics, which involved attaching grappling hooks to the Carthaginian ships, pulling alongside and then boarding, effectively turning naval battles into land battles — an area in which the famed Roman legionaries excelled.

The Second War largely arose from the Carthaginians' thirst for revenge. This time, the Carthaginian general Hannibal marched a considerable army — including a dozen African war elephants — from his base in Cartagena (Spain) all around the western Med and finally across the Alps into northern Italy. A military genius, Hannibal inflicted a number of defeats on the Roman army, yet lacked the equipment to lay siege to Rome itself. Worn down by Roman 'scorched earth' tactics, he eventually sailed back to Carthage, to be confronted by another Roman army outside the city itself. Defeated there, he fled, finally committing suicide. Allegedly he is buried in what are now the Asian suburbs of İstanbul.

Round three proved to be the final contest. Faced once again with a resurgent Carthage, Rome decided to finish its great rival once and for all. A siege of the city began in 149BC and finished two years later with its complete annihilation. Carthage was razed by the Romans, who made sure it would never rise to challenge them again.

ture you'll find echoed in museums all over the Med, a testament to the Carthaginians' great role in this sea's long story.

Sidi Bou Said

Further on along the same TGM line as Carthage, Sidi Bou Said is a hilltop seaside town of whitewashed cubic buildings with blue shutters and doors that is reminiscent of a Greek Cycladean village as well as a classic Magrebian town. Wandering round is a major Sunday occupation for many Tunisians as well as a year-round business for tourists, with a major selection of souvenirs on offer as well as some tea gardens with excellent views. It's a great place to finish a day out, with the TGMs back to town running until around midnight.

PRACTICAL INFORMATION
Orientation

Tunis is situated inland from the sea, with the shallow Lac de Tunis out front separating the city from the coastal strip where La Goulette, the harbour, lies. This means that when you get off the ferry you're still some 9km from Tunis. The distance is easily covered by taxi (around 6 dinars) or by train, known as the TGM. The nearest station is a 10-minute walk from the port and you buy the tickets on board for the 10-minute journey). The TGM is also the train you'll be heading the other way for the coastal suburbs of Carthage and Sidi Bou Said. Remember that it's illegal to change money anywhere except a bank or bureau de change, so if you're arriving late, use the bureau in the ferry terminal.

Getting around Tunis is really straightforward, with the TGM rolling in at the bottom of the main boulevard, ave Habib Bourguiba. At the other end of this is the Medina, the old town, while on the way, off to the left, is the main hunting ground for budget accommodation and the main train station for other Tunisian destinations. Either side of the avenue is the French-built Ville Nouvelle, constructed on land reclaimed from Lake Tunis. There are trams but walking is much more interesting and possible, as all the main sights in Tunis are in range of the ave Habib Bourguiba district except the

Bardo Museum, some 3km away on tram line No 4 or bus No 3 from the avenue.

Services

The **tourist office** (☎ 341077, 🖳 www.tourismtunisia.com), 1, ave Mohammed V, on place de l'Afrique, at the bottom end of ave Habib Bourguiba, has good maps of the city and brochures to major sights.

There is no internet in Tunisia but instead there's **'publinet'**, effectively the same thing, with the café in rue de Grece, just near place de Barcelone, a good option and open from 0830 to midnight.

Ferries   [see p447 for full details]

The Tunisian ferry company CTN (☎ 713 322 802) is at 122, rue de Yougoslavie; otherwise, go to their desk at the ferry terminal in La Goulette. They run regular services to **Marseille** and **Genoa** (also GNV. and SNCM). Tirrenia (contact details same as for CTN) goes to **Cágliari** (Sardinia) and **Trapani** (Sicily). Medmar Linee Lauro also goes to **La Spezia** (Italy) and **Trapani** (Sicily). Grimaldi/GNV has a weekly service to **Salerno** via **Valletta**.

Arriving by ferry in Tunis can be a hassle. Fill in your arrival card before you get off the boat; it's written in French and Arabic only. New Zealand and Australian citizens will need to buy a visa; the visa office is located after passport control in the ferry terminus, so expect to be pulled out by the police. Don't worry, though, they're friendly enough and will escort you through to the visa office.

Trains

Trains for other sights in Tunisia depart from the station on place de Barcelone, near to the main *pension* area and just off ave Habib Bourguiba. The main lines head south down the coast to Hammamet, Sousse, Monastir, El Jem and Sfax, dividing after that to continue south to Gabes or west into the desert for Metlaoui. The other lines head west from Tunis, originally over the border to Algeria, though travellers are strongly advised not to cross over. The train does go to Jendouba in the Bulla Regia, though, while also running close to Dougga.

Buses

For destinations in the north, Gare Routière Nord de Bab Saadoun is the place, next to Bab Saadoun, north-west of the Medina on tram No 4 from place de Barcelone. The southern bus station is Gare Routière Sud de Bab el Alleoua, 10 minutes' walk south of place de Barcelone.

Both stations offer buses and *louages* (shared extended taxis), which offer a more comfortable and only slightly more expensive way of getting around the country. They don't go until full, however, so you may have to wait a while. Otherwise, green and yellow SNTRI buses offer a decent, air-con service to all major towns and cities.

Trams

There are four lines in the city, with No 4 the one you're most likely to need as it goes near the northern bus terminal and the Bado Museum. The tram is known as the *metro leger*, with tickets very cheap.

Planes

Tunis Airport is nowhere near the TGM station marked 'airport', so you're definitely better off taking a taxi, which will cost around 6 dinars from ave Habib Bourguiba. There are regular flights to all European destinations. Tuninter (☎ 701111) also offers domestic flights.

Where to stay

Hôtel Salammbô (☎ 334252), 6, rue de Grece. A well located and friendly place with sgl/dbl for 30/55 dinars.
Hôtel Transatlantique (☎ 240680), 106, rue Yougoslavie. Looks dead from ave de Carthage but try the entrance round the corner. Rates similar to the nearby Salammbô.
Hôtel Bristol (☎ 244836), on rue Lt Mohammed Aziz Taj. Round the corner from the Café de Paris and a popular choice; 25/45 dinars sgl/dbl.
Hôtel Majestic (☎ 242848), ave de Paris, north of ave Habib Bourguiba. A splendid French colonial hotel with tons of faded glamour at 50/90 dinars sgl/dbl.

The best youth hostel, *Auberge de Jeunesse* (☎ 567850) is in an old palace in the Medina, on rue es Saida Ajoula. It has bunks for 7-10 dinars.

Where to eat

Tunis has plenty of fine eateries, with French and Moorish food on offer along with Italian and international cuisine. Most restaurants close early, 2100 being the normal time, and bars are hard to find outside the main international hotel chains.
Restaurant Carcasonne 8, ave de Carthage. Has an excellent three-course lunch menu specializing in French/Italian food for 7 dinars a head, but it shuts around 2100.
Café de Paris on the corner of ave Habib Bourguiba and ave de Carthage. A Tunis institution; a meal costs around 10 dinars a head, with snacks also available.
Savarim, opposite Hotel Bristol. Tunis' only late-night drinking haunt is wall-to-wall with blokes but is friendly enough for women in groups or accompanied. Serves a good lamb couscous for 2 dinars, plus Celtia beer — Tunisia's own — till 0400.
Restaurant Mahdaoui, opposite Ez-Zitouna Mosque in the Medina. Tunisia's oldest restaurant, great for local dishes though open lunchtimes only. No alcohol.

Malta

AREA CODE: ☎ 21 POPULATION: 376,000
Probably the best organized and, at the time of writing, the best-value destination in the Mediterranean, Malta is a giant in the story of this sea, even if only a tiny dot amongst the waves themselves. Located between the western and eastern halves of the Med and not far from both its northern and southern shores, the island's vital strategic value has seen it fought over repeatedly, with two heroic defences — first against the Ottomans and more recently against fascist Italy and Nazi Germany — largely shaping much of its national pride and identity. History is thick on the ground here, with hardly an inch of the place not covered by the scene of some major incident from the past.

In recent years, this has given the place in part a kind of theme-park feel, which is both a plus and a minus. The flurry of 'living-history' museums and 'Malta experiences' that now entice in the tourists undoubtedly gives a well crafted and executed retelling of the island's story, even if the result is more reminiscent of the Museum of London than the Mediterranean. Yet there are few harbours in the world as evocative as Valletta, with generations of maritime and military use building up layer upon layer of fortresses and naval dockyards. The town itself is also a real masterpiece and one of the world's first examples of civic planning.

Given its excellent bus network and small size — 246 sq km for Malta and 67 sq km for neighbouring Gozo — the island is extremely easy to get around. It's also easy to get to, with regular flights to and from most European and North American destinations. There's also the ferry to Catania in Sicily from Valletta, a vital route in connecting the island up to the rest of the Mediterranean ferry network.

History

Malta and the lesser-known Maltese islands of Gozo and tiny Comino have been inhabited for millennia, with the first archaeological findings dating back to 3800BC, when there must have been a thriving population given the number of megalithic temples, *dolmens* and *menhirs* on the main islands. Malta itself has the oldest megalithic structures in the world at Hagar Qim and a half dozen other cliff-top temples.

Much later, the Phoenicians arrived, colonizing the islands around 800BC until superseded by the Carthaginians around 500BC. Signs of Phoenician Malta are still evident, too, in the eye motifs used to decorate the prows of Maltese fishing boats and in the language itself, which apart from the strong Arabic influence also has many Semitic words said to be of Phoenician origin.

Once the Romans had driven out the Carthaginians, the islands became a colony of Rome. In AD60 St Paul was shipwrecked on Malta's rocks while a prisoner on his way to trial in the Eternal City. He is said to have been bitten by a snake but didn't die, thereby convincing the locals of the truth of his creed and making the Maltese early converts to Christianity.

For over 200 years from 870 the Arab occupation greatly benefited the Maltese and their influence is still strong in the language and the location of many of the island's main settlements. The Islamic faith, however, made little impression.

A second attempt by the Normans to take over the islands led to occupation under the Angevin Count Roger II between 1130 and 1194, making them part of the Kingdom of Sicily granted to Roger by the Pope. Malta shared the same succession of ruling houses – Swabians, Angevins and Aragonese – until 1530 when the islanders were abruptly given to the Order of the Knights of St John (see box p322).

Under their previous rulers, the Maltese had developed a brutal reputation as pirates and slavers, locked in combat and commercial competition with their North African slaving and pirating rivals, the corsairs of the Barbary coast (see box p92). The Knights' introduction of the Corso, which gave pirates the protection of this Holy Order so long as they attacked only Muslim shipping, allowed this tradition to continue, much to the annoyance of the principal Muslim Mediterranean power, the Ottomans. They decided in 1565 that enough was enough and attacked Malta, hoping to repeat their success against the Knights on Rhodes (see box p197). After a heroic battle the Ottomans were defeated, and in celebration much of Valletta was rebuilt and refortified.

Yet as time went on, the Knights were increasingly at odds with the mood of the times, particularly after the great schisms in Western Christianity during the Reformation and the later development of nation states which had little truck with their ideas of a global Christendom. The order hung on until 1798, when Napoleon arrived, taking the island without a struggle. An uprising by the Maltese — who had not been consulted over the Knights' surrender — then followed, assisted by the British, who ended

TYRRHENIAN SEA

up taking the island for themselves in 1814.

The island's strategic position was even more vital to the British once the Suez Canal opened and the Mediterranean became the shortest route to Britain's imperial colonies in India and the Far East. The harbour was extensively fortified and garrisoned enough to withstand the second great siege during WWII (see box p197). The island was devastated by air raids during the war, with the island as a whole awarded the George Cross — Britain's highest civilian honour — and a degree of autonomy in 1947. Malta had always had mixed feelings about British rule. A substantial pro-Italian element saw the island as rightfully Italy's while a substantial pro-British camp saw Malta's future as part of the empire. Post war, there also grew up a third camp, which saw Malta as Maltese and belonging to neither. This group came to prominence first under Dr George Borg Olivier, who secured independence in 1964, and later Dom Mintoff, the Maltese Labour Party leader, who established a republic in 1974 and expelled the British military — which had continued to run the naval base — in 1979.

Mintoff then took Malta in a decidedly dangerous direction — forging links with Libya, the Soviet Union and even North Korea, moves which led to Labour's ejection from power in 1987 by the rival Nationalist Party. The main schism in the following decade was over whether Malta should join the European Union (EU), with the Labour traditionalists against this, the Nationalists in favour. Labour returned to power in 1996 but by 1998 the Nationalist Party was back in control. On 1 May 2004 Malta joined the EU.

ORIENTATION

The islands of Malta and Gozo are connected by ferry from Cirkewwa on the former to Mgarr on the latter, which means the fastest way over from the island capital of Valletta is actually by helicopter from the airport, which is around 5km south-west from the town. Most towns are linked by bus, with the main bus station just before the main entrance to Valletta. Taxis are very expensive, making car hire reasonable in comparison, while hitching is an easy and fairly reliable option. The harbour area around Valletta is not so straightforward to traverse: ferries are often the quickest way to get from one part to another, while buses tend to take the long way round. Ferries to Sicily leave from the Grand Harbour in Valletta, just beneath the headland of the main medieval town.

The third member of the group is the tiny island of Comino, also reached by ferry. Named after the cumin herb that grows here, this car-free island is renowned for its wonderful snorkelling and diving, particularly the delightful Blue Lagoon, a sheltered inlet fringed by white-sand beaches.

VALLETTA

One of the most perfect late medieval towns anywhere, Valletta is an entirely planned city, built on the headland between the Grand and Marsamxett harbours and still largely within its 16th-century battlements. The plans were drawn up on the orders of Jean de la Valette, the French grand master of the Order, and work began in 1565. Buses arrive at the circular square before the main city entrance, which leads through to the start of the main road, Republic St. The rest of Valletta is on a grid pattern, skilfully arranged so as to keep shadow on the streets and ventilate the running terraces of beautiful old houses with breezes up from the sea. It's a hilly place, though, with staircases sometimes replacing streets, yet look out at every crossroads for the statue, built into a niche in one of the corners.

At the top of Republic St are the ruins of Valletta's opera house, bombed during the WWII siege and left as a memorial. Continue on to the **Archaeology Museum** (0800-1700 daily, LM1). Inside is an excellent collection of relics from the megalithic sites, including many examples of the frankly overweight goddesses of Hagar Qim and other early temples.

Further down Republic St is Great Siege Square and **St John's Co-Cathedral** (Mon-Fri 0930-1300, 1330-1630, Sat 0930-1330, free). Started in 1573 and finished four years later, it was designed by Gerolamo Cassar, the Order's chief architect, and was the Knights' principal place of worship.

Malta: A tale of three sieges

While these days Malta welcomes overseas visitors with open arms, it has a long and proud history of resistance to those who in the past have had a mind to take the entire island as a souvenir.

Three times since the latter part of 16th century, sieges have formed — each defining moments in Malta's history, and all combining to have a significant place in its present.

Malta's largest siege, and the one that is perhaps best commemorated, is that undertaken by the forces of the Ottoman sultan, Süleyman the Magnificent, in 1565. Many of the island's fine stone fortifications either date from this time or were built afterwards out of fear of a repeat performance by the troops of the Grand Turk following their initial failure. They are monuments to a hard-won victory against overwhelming odds and an architectural celebration of the turning back of the tide of Ottoman conquest in the Mediterranean.

Less than impressed by the piratical activities of the Knights of Saint John, and wanting to gain control of all of the Mediterranean, Sultan Süleyman sent a massive fleet and an army of 40,000 men to capture the rocky thorn in his side. Facing them were a mere 700 knights of the order and about 8000 Maltese hurriedly recruited to defend their homes under the command of the redoubtable 70-year-old grand master of the Knights of St John, Jean de la Valette.

Landing in May, it took the Ottoman forces more than a month to capture the small fortified post of St Elmo guarding the main harbour, at a cost of more than 7000 men. The fort finally in their hands, the Ottomans then concentrated their efforts on the main defences at Birgu and Isla. Though the attackers managed to breach the walls, none of their ten major assaults was able to break into the fortifications.

Though promised aid by the king of Spain even before the siege opened, for months the defenders looked in vain for the sails of the relieving fleet on the horizon. Then, on 7 September, an 8000 strong army from Sicily landed. It was enough for the Ottomans. Weakened by disease, as well as by their heavy losses in battle, they took to their boats. However, seeing the small size of the relieving force, the Ottoman commander, Mustafa Pasha, ordered his troops ashore again. Reluctantly forming up for battle near St Paul's Bay, the Ottomans were routed, the survivors streaming back to their ships and setting sail for İstanbul to face the wrath of the sultan.

Total losses on both sides were horrendous. Of la Valette's defenders, only 600 were still on their feet, while up to 30,000 of the invaders fell. Malta's defences lay in ruins and hardly a house remained standing. However, from the ruins rose present-day Valletta, named in honour of the greatest of the Knight's grand masters.

While the second of Malta's sieges was far less bloody or devastating than the first, it did last much longer, a shade over two years. It was also different from most sieges as it featured the locals as the besiegers and foreign invaders as the besieged.

Within months of Napoleon ousting the Knights of St John on his way to Egypt in mid-1798, the Maltese rose up in rebellion against their new French masters. Rather put off by the French trying to impose revolutionary ideas on their conservative society and incensed by the appalling public relations gaffe of looting the island's churches, the population, led by a senior churchman, who had a vested interest in ending the desecration of Malta's holy places, slaughtered the French garrison in Mdina on 2 September and then laid siege to the rest of the 4,000 French troops in Valletta.

Even with the help of the British Navy, which blockaded the port, it was two years and three days before the French finally threw in the towel, starved into submission rather than beaten by force of arms. *(Continued on p198)*

TYRRHENIAN SEA

❏ **Malta: A tale of three sieges** (*Continued from p197*)
The last and longest trial by fire that Malta underwent was in WWII. Long a major British naval base, serving as it did in the times of the Knights to block both the Eastern and Western Mediterranean, the island also sat astride the shipping routes to Italy's Libyan colonies. A day after Mussolini's Italy entered the war on the side of Germany, Malta suffered its first air raid.

In an effort to subdue the island, Italian and later German bombers pounded Malta, with initial attacks fended off by three antiquated biplanes, *Faith, Hope* and *Charity*. Though repeatedly reinforced by the Royal Air Force, Allied losses in the air and at sea were heavy, and the Axis bombers slowly reduced much of the island to rubble, with more than 40,000 homes being destroyed.

At the height of the bombing campaign in April 1942, in recognition of the island's staunch defence, King George awarded Malta Britain's highest civilian medal for bravery, the George Cross. However, by mid-1942 Malta was at breaking point, close to starvation and, almost as importantly, out of fuel for the island's few remaining aircraft and low on the oil needed to fire the ovens for the population's bread. Though an earlier convoy of ships had been practically wiped out, the British government decided to again try to relieve the beleaguered Malta, sending 14 merchant ships, including the tanker *Ohio*, in a heavily escorted convoy into the Mediterranean from Gibraltar.

The battle to fight the convoy through to Malta was an epic struggle, with nine of the 14 merchant ships, as well as a number of Royal Navy vessels, sunk by attacks from German and Italian aircraft, submarines and warships. The last merchant ship to enter Grand Harbour was the *Ohio*, dubbed the 'Oh 10' by its crew. Badly damaged by both bombs and a torpedo, the sinking tanker was towed into port with two British destroyers tied on either side of its hull, acting as a splint. As the last of the *Ohio*'s vital cargo was unloaded, the tanker sank at its moorings.

Reinforced and reinvigorated, Malta was able to resume its role in cutting the Axis' supply routes to Africa, denying Rommel much needed fuel and equipment ahead of the decisive battle of El Alamein. The subsequent rout of the Desert Fox's Afrika Korps in the October 1942 battle, the first major land defeat for the Axis in the war, owed much to Malta's tenacious defence. Britain's wartime Prime Minister Winston Churchill, never short of a good line, described the island as the 'lynchpin of victory'.

Caravaggio's *Beheading of St John* hangs in the Oratory, while the carvings and tombstone-chequered floor are worth suffering the surging crowds for a look.

Keeping on down Republic St, the very next square, **Republic Square**, holds the national library and, next door, the **Grand Master's Palace**, now housing the island's presidency and parliament. Here you'll also find the **Great Siege of Malta Experience**, the first of several all-singing, all-dancing history shows on the island, which takes you through the battle in 45 minutes (daily 0900 to 1600 for LM3).

Following the street, you eventually come out at the headland tip and **Fort St Elmo**. This is not the heroic, last-stand fort of the Great Siege but part of the later rebuild. To the left of the fort is the **War Museum** (Mon-Sat 0815-1700, Sun 0815-1600, LM2) with an extensive collection of WWII memorabilia including the fuselage of one of the three ancient Gladiator fighter planes, christened *Faith, Hope* and *Charity*, that initially comprised the entire air defence force for Malta. The lone survivor here is *Faith*.

Return round the peninsula on its southern side following Mediterranean St, and you'll come to the second audio-visual show, the **Malta Experience** (hourly from 1100 to 1600, 45 mins, LM3). This gives the whole history of the island, from megalithic to modern, in a custom-built auditorium with

TYRRHENIAN SEA

Valletta

Fort St Elmo

War Museum

Malta Experience

Lower Barakka Gardens

MERCHANTS STREET

REPUBLIC STREET

ST URSULA STREET

ST CHRISTOPHER STREET

Grand Master's Palace

Perfection

Grand Harbour Hotel

ARCHBISHOP STREET

Republic Square

St John's Co-Cathedral

Asti Guest House

OLD THEATRE STREET

Great Siege Square

Upper Barakka Gardens

ST LUCIA STREET

Labour Club

Lascaris War Rooms

Archaeology Museum

Old Opera House

OLD BAKERY STREET

ST JOHN ST STREET

Coronation Guest House

Internet café

Maestro e Fresco

Tourist Info

Ferries for Sicily, Genoa, Salerno, Tunis, Reggio di Calabria & Pozzallo

Bus Station

Boats to Sliema

TYRRHENIAN SEA

0   200   400m

multi-lingual soundtrack and some great pictures. Leaving here, keep along the harbour side for the **Lascaris War Rooms** (Mon-Fri 0930-1630, Sat-Sun 0930-1300, LM2). This complex of underground tunnels formed the island's defence command during WWII and now houses a museum commemorating this with waxwork dummies and blitz soundtracks. Access is tricky, though, as it is through the municipal offices on St Anthony St and under Upper Baraka Gardens. At the far end is one of the Med's more bizarre cafés — the **NAAFI**, named after the British catering corps. This consists of an army tent in which bacon and eggs are served all day to the accompaniment of black and white WWII British propaganda movies, with stiff upper-lips aplenty, along with plenty of shorts and knee-length socks beneath the cruel wartime sun.

Services
The **tourist office** (☎ 23 7747), 1, City Arcade, Valletta, just inside the city gate, has a load of useful brochures and maps.

Try **Sapienza Bookshop** (☎ 23 3621), 26, Republic St, for works in English by local authors such as Francis Ebejer, Malta's most famous novelist and playwright, and Olivier Friggieri, a more modern writer.

There is an **internet café** on the corner of South St and Old Mint St.

Ferries   [see p447 for full details]
Services from Valletta to **Catania** in Sicily are run by MA.RE.SI Ferries and Virtu

Ferries (☎ 23 2522) at Harbour Office, Marina Pinto, Valletta, though the office opens only two hours before departures. At other times, tickets for Virtu's services can be bought from S Mifsud & Sons in Republic St, opposite the ruined opera house. Virtu's hydrofoil is good and even has an 'in-flight' movie, but sets off painfully early, at 0500. Virtu also combines these with organized tours to Mt Etna and other sights on Sicily. There are also services from Valletta to **Genoa**, **Salerno** and **Tunis** with Grimaldi/GNV, **Pozzallo** with Virtu, and **Reggio di Calabria** with MA.RE.SI.

The most direct ferry to **Gozo** goes from Cirkewwa but taking the freight ferry from Sa Maison gives the advantage of seeing the beautiful coastline of Malta and also provides a less crowded and just as comfortable journey.

During the season, other ferry day trips are available that may also be useful ways of getting to Sicily; enquire at S Mifsud and Sons for details.

Buses
Malta's buses are a sight in themselves, with many wonderfully customized ancient British coaches from the 1950s and 60s. Inside, around the driver's seat, you'll find an eclectic collection of Catholic and English Premier League football imagery, with the Virgin Mary often sharing space with a Manchester United scarf. The service is reliable and comprehensive, with useful bus maps readily available from the kiosks

---

Clapham Junction
One of Malta's most enduring mysteries is the dozens of ruts carved into the rock of the island's cliff-tops by what looks to have been an army of road-drill wielding acid freaks. The ruts scar and swirl across the landscape in many places, but the most manic collection of these is near the village of Buskett, on the No 81 bus route near the Dingli Cliffs on the south coast; here they are so complicated they've become colloquially known as 'Clapham Junction' after the main railway line interchange south of London.

Theories abound as to how these tracks were made, ranging from bizarre geology to even more bizarre astrophysics, but the most acceptable indicates that they are man-made, dating from c500BC. Originally lying next to a quarry, these areas were at that time composed of softer rock and clay, the tracks being from the wheels of carts plying to and fro with heavy rocks. Over the centuries the soft ground solidified to stone.

round the Valletta bus station, just outside the main city gate. Fares are low, with travel passes also available.

Don't lose your tickets once you've boarded, as inspectors do come round.

Planes

The airport is some 5km south of Valletta and there is no airport service bus. Instead, go out of the airport building exit by the tourist information office and cross the car park outside. Head for the large, concrete shed carwash, on the other side of which is a roundabout. Keep straight on in the direction of Valletta for around 50m and you'll see a bus stop. Any of the buses stopping here will take you to the main Valletta bus station, outside the main city gate. The walk from airport to bus stop takes 5-10 minutes and the bus trip into town 10 minutes. A taxi will set you back LM5 to the same destination.

Where to stay

Coronation Guest House (☎ 23 7652), 10E, Miriel Anton Vassalli St. Friendly and simple, with good-value budget rooms at LM5 per person per night.

Hibernia House (☎ 33 3859), an official HI hostel, Depiro St, Sliema. Sliema lies to the north of Valletta and is best reached by ferry from Marsamxett Harbour, though the last departure is at 1745. Otherwise, it's a 15-minute bus ride from Valletta bus station. LM4 a bunk.

Hotel Europa (☎ 33 0080), 138 Tower Rd, Sliema. LM6.50/13 sgl/dbl.

Asti Guest House (☎ 23 9506), St Ursula St. Quiet, clean, side-street hotel in Old Valletta with a charming owner. LM6 per person.

Places to eat

Malta is exceptional value food-wise and the wine's not bad either. Some expensive-looking places may actually charge reasonable prices, so don't be afraid to check the menus. There are also plenty of snack and buffet bars for sandwiches and so on, with the cuisine itself an interesting mixture of Italian, North African and local.

Grand Harbour Hotel Looks expensive but in fact does excellent fare for LM4 a

head in its panoramic restaurant overlooking the Grand Harbour from around Battery St.

The Labour Club If ideology is no object, the Maltese Labour Party Club on Republic St does an excellent English breakfast for LM1 and hands out a free glass of wine with lunch or dinner. LM3 a head.

Perfection, Old Theatre St. Has some good-value lunch menus.

Maestro e Fresco, 8, South St. Serves tasty bar food and has a good bar, serving local Blue Label beer, a not half-bad bitter for those missing the real thing. The place is one of the few bar/cafés in Valletta that's open until the small hours out of season.

Nightlife

While Valletta tends to empty at night, Paceville sets the pace. This area lies up the coast north of Valletta and north of Sliema, with buses leaving frequently until midnight from Valletta's main bus station (the last one takes a circular route, turning into the last bus back at 0130). Taxis are expensive, so keep an eye on the time if you're staying in Valletta — if you do miss the last bus and can't rustle up a group to share a cab back, it may be cheaper to stay — *Windsor Guest House* (☎ 31 2232), Schreiber St, has sgl/dbl for LM5/10. Most varieties of club and bar are on offer around St George's Rd.

MDINA

For many years the island capital during the early years of the Knights of St John, Mdina is a warren of medieval streets set within a classic fortified hill town 10km inland from Valletta. Easily reached by bus, it's easy to lose an entire day wandering about here. Known as the 'Silent City', it is still quite eerily quiet at times, despite the coach parties in season, and the view of the rest of the island from the battlements is excellent.

Getting around

Walking is not only possible but is one of the town's particular pleasures. Nowhere is very far from anywhere else, with the No 80 and 81 buses from Valletta's main bus station dropping you off at the walls themselves.

TYRRHENIAN SEA

What to see

The main attraction, apart from the streets themselves, is the **cathedral**, a 1697 reconstruction of the original 11th-century Norman edifice, a rebuild necessary because of the 1693 earthquake which devastated much of the town. The house of the Roman governor, Publius, is thought to have been built on this site. He was converted when the shipwrecked saints Paul and Luke stayed here, and became the first bishop of Malta.

In Mesquita Square you'll also find the **Mdina Experience** (Mon-Fri 1030-1600, Sat 1030-1400, LM2), an audio-visual show giving the whole 3000 years of the town's history with a very good rumbling earthquake simulation to stop you nodding off. In St Publius Square you'll find the **National Museum of Natural History** (daily 0930-1300, 1330-1700, LM1) housed in the Vilhena Palace, with a fine collection of local animal remains.

Underneath the palace are the **Mdina Dungeons** (daily 0930-1700, LM1.50), complete with waxwork victims, while in Magazines St is another tableau, the **Knights of Malta**, (Mon-Fri 1030-1600, Sat 1030-1400, LM2), which also has plenty of ghoulish recreations of medieval barbarism while retelling the story of the Order and their stay on the island.

Where to stay

Xara Palace St Paul's Sq, Mdina's best-known budget choice; sgl/dbl LM6/12 with breakfast.

HAGAR QIM/MNAJDRA

Of Malta's many megalithic temples, these two are probably the finest, with both located on the coast not far from the village of Qrendi, on the No 38 and 138 bus routes from the main bus station in Valletta. They are about 10 minutes' walk from each other and while Mnajdra was closed at the time of writing (though it is said to be opening again in 2004) because of some incomprehensible vandalism, it is still possible to view from the outside and well worth doing so, as in many ways its location makes it the more atmospheric of the two.

History

'Hagar Qim' means 'standing stones' and for much of history all that was visible was the tops of some of the temple megaliths jutting out from a large earth mound. In 1839 the British governor of the island, Sir H F Bouverie, commissioned an excavation, beginning a series of digs, many of the findings of which are in the Archaeology Museum in Valletta. What the excavations revealed was that these were most likely temples rather than burial mounds and dated from between 3800 and 2500BC, making them some of the oldest buildings on earth. During this period many similar sites were constructed around the island, but this seems to have abruptly ceased, along with the race of people who made them. Theories suggest that drought, famine or foreign invasion may have wiped out these Copper Age Maltese; the local story is that Ggantija, the giantess who built them, ran out of beans to eat because of a drought and went off to sulk in a cave below Gozo, never to return.

After this the island may even have been uninhabited for some time, and the next arrivals did not continue their traditions.

The buses from Valletta stop at the bottom of a track leading to Hagar Qim, amongst the drystone walls of Malta's southern coast. Tell the bus driver that's where you want to get off (they all speak English) and he'll make sure you do. A five-minute walk brings you to the entrance, while the temple of Mnajdra is another 5-10 minutes down a coastal path. This leads you past a monument to General Sir Walter Congreve, a British governor of Malta who died in 1927 and is buried here, looking out at the sea and the crushed top hat islet of Filfa, used in the old days by the Royal Artillery for gunnery practice. Around the slab-like gravestone are dozens of small crosses stuck into the rocks of the cliff-top, sometimes with small offerings next to them. These commemorate those Maltese seafarers who have died over the years out on the waters.

On the way back, remember that the bus you want follows a circular route so you must stand on the same side of the road you alighted. The last bus goes at around 1730.

PART 6: ADRIATIC SEA

Introduction

There are a number of possible entry points to the Adriatic – Venice, Trieste, Ancona, Bari, Bríndisi, Dubrovnik, Corfu, Igoumenitsa and Patras – but currently no ferry routes between the Adriatic and the Eastern Mediterranean, Tyrrhenian or Western Mediterranean.

Connecting to the Tyrrhenian Sea requires an overland journey – from Venice/Trieste to Genoa, or from Ancona, Bari or Bríndisi to Rome/ Civitavecchia. This is very straightforward, with frequent rail and coach services.

TRAVELLING AROUND THE ADRIATIC

With much of the attraction of the Adriatic on the Dalmatian side, there are frequent services between the mainland and the dozens of islands and islets that make up its length. Unfortunately, few ferry routes go up or down the coast, the exception being within Croatia, so you frequently have to tack back and forth from one side of the Adriatic to other.

Ferry services operate from the Italian ports of **Ancona**, **Bari** and **Bríndisi** to Greece and the Aegean (see pp280-93), though there is also a ferry service from Venice to İzmir in Turkey.

If you travel south–north, you'll end up with a train or bus ride from Venice to Genoa for the Tyrrhenian Sea (see pp119-202), while heading the other way, you'll have to cross overland from Igoumenitsa or Patras to begin the Aegean section, or go across the toe of Italy for Sicily to enter the Tyrrhenian Sea from the south.

SUGGESTED ITINERARIES

Note: time variations below reflect either whether the journey is direct or not, or whether the route has both ferry and fast ferry/hydrofoil services.

Venice to Dubrovnik

Both Poreč and Rovinj are charming, well-preserved towns while Pula, set on the tip of the Istrian Peninsula, is the main jumping-off point for the Brijuni Islands – where Marshal Tito used to spend his summers. Split is the largest city on the Dalmatian coast and is where the Roman emperor, Diocletian, built his celebrated palace.

Korčula has long been one of the region's most popular destinations and Korčula Town, a classic medieval city, is a convenient base for discovering the

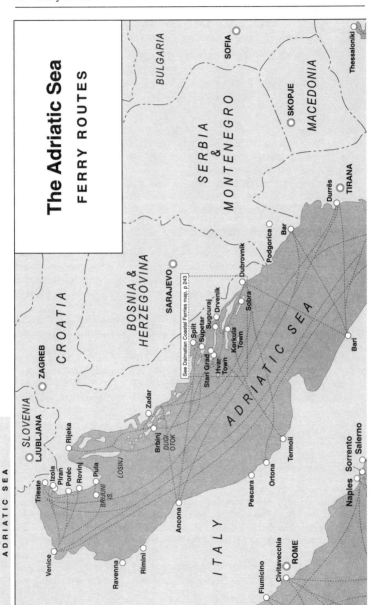

The Adriatic Sea
FERRY ROUTES

GREECE

Patras

Ioánnina

Igoumenitsa

Nidri

Ithaca

LEFKADA

KEFALONIA Pessada Sami

Schinari

ZAKYNTHOS

Corfu Town

CORFU

ALBANIA

To Cesme, from Ancona & Brindisi

To Izmir, from Venice

Brindisi

PALM & AZUR

APPROX SCALE

0   100   200km

Messina

Reggio di Calabria

STROMBOLI

PANAREA

SALINA

Milazzo

FILICUDI

ALICUDI

VULCANO

LIPARI

Cefalu

Catania

ISCHIA

CAPRI

TYRRHENIAN SEA

SICILY

GOZO

MALTA

Mgarr VALLETTA

Cirkewwa

Palermo

Trapani

ADRIATIC SEA

other islands off the Dalmatian Coast. The magnificent walled city of Dubrovnik is surrounded by wonderful beaches. The city also has good transport links with the rest of Croatia and a regular ferry service back to Italy (Bari).

Venice to Poreč/Parenzo (daily, 2¹/₂-5hrs) or to Rovinj (3 per week, 2³/₄hrs); overland from Poreč/Rovinj to Pula; Pula to Rijeka (daily, 3hrs); Rijeka to Split (direct, 2 per week, 10¹/₂hrs, or via Zadar 1 per week, 13hrs); Split to Korčula Town (direct 1 per week, 3¹/₂hrs, via Stari Grad 2 per week, 5-6hrs); Korčula Town to Dubrovnik (direct 3 per week, 3hrs, 1 per week via Sobra, 4hrs).

Italy to Albania and Greece

Ancona has some charms but you will probably come here because of the many ferry services which leave from its port rather than for the city itself. However, Durrës, Albania's chief port, offers a good first taste of this intriguing country and is also only a short distance from Tirana, a city which still retains signs of its Ottoman-, Stalinist- and Maoist-influenced past. If you take the bus from Albania to Greece expect long delays and a fair amount of unpleasantness. The alternative is to return to Durrës and take a boat to Bari. Both Bari's new and old towns have worthwhile sights and Corfu is an interesting introduction to Greece with the strong Italian influence on its architecture. Igoumenitsa has little to attract but does have a bus service to Ioánnina, a city with an astonishing setting and a medieval *kastro* (citadel).

Ancona to Durrës (4 per week, 18hrs); overland to Tirana; overland by bus from Tirana to Athens or by ferry from Durrës to Bari (daily, 8-9hrs); Bari to Corfu (2-3 per week, 8-11hrs); Corfu to Igoumenitsa (daily, 3hrs); overland to Ioánnina and then back to Igoumenitsa; ferry back to Ancona (daily, 16hrs).

Adriatic Sea – ports and islands

Venice

AREA CODE: ☎ 041 **POPULATION:** 277,000
The one-time centre of the eastern Mediterranean's richest trade routes, La Serenissima, the Most Serene Republic of Venice, is a city that never fails — a beautiful, tortuous maze built across some 117 small islands and 150 canals.

It is expensive to stay here but nonetheless attracts a vast army of tourists, particularly in summer. Yet it still keeps enough of itself hidden from tour parties to be a place where you can wander relatively alone, and this is one of its great pleasures: rarely is walking city streets so visually pleasing as in Venice.

Of course, there are also the classic gondolas, with the *traghetto* (public gondola) an essential way to get around. So common are pictures of it that St Mark's Square is familiar to almost everyone but actually to be there is an overwhelming experience.

The *Carnevale*, held in the 10 days leading up to Lent, is also breathtaking. Above all, Venice is one of those few cities that remain ineffably impressive whatever the season, the weather or the time of day.

It is also very much a marine city. Venice's wealth, power and glory all came, and largely still do come, from across the waters that lap constantly along the ends of its streets and the sides of its squares. As you travel east you'll see the Lion of St Mark, the city's emblem, carried down the long Adriatic, via trading posts and walled cities, to Greece, the Aegean and on, out as far even as Cyprus, where one of the republic's final battles was fought. Few cities can claim such an important role in the Mediterranean's history, and none is quite so uniformly beautiful.

HISTORY
Venice began life as a humble refuge for people fleeing the attacks of Lombard tribesman. With the collapse of Roman authority in the West, a succession of barbarian tribes streamed across the Alps and down into northern Italy around the 5th and 6th centuries. Venice began as a relatively protected enclave and part of the territory belonging to the Roman Empire's successor, the Byzantines. However, civil strife between pro- and anti-Byzantine factions within the city finally led to the victory of the anti-Byzantine party by around AD840, when the doge, the city's chief magistrate, began acting independently of Constantinople.

Doge Domenico Flabanico (1032-42) was the first of a series of famous rulers and instituted a system under which, at least in theory, the doge was elected. Doge Domenico Contarini (1043-70) then had St Mark's built (named after the city's patron saint) and expanded Venetian interests along the Adriatic. Victory over the Normans, an early threat to Venetian traders thanks to their control of Sicily and southern Italy, also secured an agreement in 1082 with the grateful Byzantines, who granted Venice freedom to trade in Byzantine waters. This marked the beginning of Venice's long involvement with the Aegean and Levant.

Relations with the Byzantines did not remain good for long. Competition for control of the lucrative Black Sea, Aegean and Middle Eastern trade routes developed into open warfare with a Venetian-led attack on Constantinople in 1204 (aka the Fourth Crusade). Doge Enrico Dandolo led the attack which successfully sacked the city and permanently crippled the Byzantines, leaving them vulnerable to the emerging Ottoman Empire to the east.

The post-Crusade settlement gave the doges control of Crete and parts of Euboea, along with several key trading stations and fortified lookout posts on the Greek mainland. From then on, the doge's title was *Quartae Partis et Dimidiae Totius Imperii Romaniae Dominator* ('Lord of One-Quarter and One-Eighth of the Entire Byzantine Empire') and Venice continued to prosper.

In 1261, however, the Byzantines regained control of Constantinople and granted to Genoa most of the trading privileges previously given to the Venetians,

❑ Adriatic – the highlights
● **The Dalmatian coast** – A string of stunning islands, still largely undiscovered by the package tours. From pine-clad hills to sugar-loaf mountains, the sheer range of landscapes the islands encompass is extraordinary.
● **Dubrovnik** – A star among medieval cities, with its fantastic architectural wealth, great connections and friendly locals making it a must-see of the Adriatic.
● **Albania** – One of Europe's most neglected corners – ignore the tales of doom and expect to be pleasantly surprised by a friendly, much misunderstood people.
● **Sarajevo** – Once a symbol of despair and conflict, the city has been battling to get back on its feet in recent years. A fascinating mix of Ottoman and Serbian, Muslim and Orthodox; expect many preconceptions to be shattered.
● *Slivovic* – A Balkan plum brandy that can change your life or, at least, your ability to walk. A speciality of Bosnia-Herzegovina in particular, one or two 'slivos' from a local, home brewery can be a risky business but also an unmissable one.

while the collapse of the Roman East with the ejection of the Crusaders from the Levant forced more heated rivalry over those trade routes that remained, particularly in the Black Sea where Genoa was strong.

This conflict continued for the best part of 200 years, with a number of campaigns fought across northern Italy by the two rival city states, which finally ended in a Venetian victory with the Peace of Turin in 1381. However, during this time Ottoman power had begun to limit Venetian control in the east, leading to a strategic policy shift that many historians regard as a decisive blunder: Venice's decision to attempt territorial expansion in northern Italy.

A succession of campaigns in the local region against other Italian city states, each backed by one of the more powerful countries to the north who came to help but stayed to hold, led to a dangerous neglect of the overseas empire. In 1470, Euboea fell into Turkish hands, while in 1508 the Spanish, French and Germans, together with the Pope, the Hungarians, the Savoyards and the Ferrarese, united to form the League of Cambria against the Venetians, who were defeated at the Battle of Agnadello. While Spain was becoming the great power in Europe through her riches from the New World, Venice had no such other trade outlet as her eastern markets fell away. Meanwhile, the Ottomans defeated Venice at Prèveza in 1538, and despite the victory at Lepanto (see box on p274), Cyprus still fell to the Ottomans in 1571. In 1669, after a 25-year campaign, Venice lost Crete, her last possession in the eastern Mediterranean.

Despite a successful reconquest of much of Venice's old Greek territory by Francesco Morosini in 1684-8, this proved ultimately of little value and in 1718 the Morea was returned to the Ottomans. In 1797 France's revolutionary republic saw the last doge, Ludovico Manin, deposed on Napoleon Bonaparte's orders. Venice was then given to the Austrian Empire, where it stayed until 1866, when Austria's defeat by Prussia led to it being handed over to the newly united Kingdom of Italy.

Since then, the biggest threat to Venice

has been environmental. Pollution, rising sea levels and the wear and tear of hosting around 20 million tourists a year have all affected the islands' ecology. The city is not sinking, as originally feared, but is still in great danger, as arguments continue over how to protect the Lagoon and its islands.

WHAT TO SEE

Venice is divided into six *sestieri*: Cannaregio, Castello, San Marco, Dorsoduro, San Polo and Santa Croce. Most of the major sights are in San Marco, though all of them have something impressive to offer. Begin with a *vaporetto* (water bus) ride along the Grand Canal, getting off at the San Marco stop, which is right next to St Mark's Square.

Towering up in the centre of the square is the **Campanile** (daily 0930-1600, €4.20), originally a lighthouse but now a reconstruction after the original collapsed in 1902. The view from the 99m-high top is of the entire city and some distance out over the sea. In 1608, in the original tower, Galileo Galilei tried unsuccessfully to demonstrate the military advantages of the telescope to a party of Venetian senators.

To the right, looking inland, is the 1094 **Basilica of St Mark**. Built to house the body of St Mark, brought from Egypt by two Venetian adventurers, it is modelled on the now non-existent Church of the Twelve Apostles in İstanbul (Constantinople). The **Basilica Museum**, the **Museo Marciano** and the **Loggia dei Cavalli** (daily 1000-1730, €1.50) also house the famous Roman equine statues that used to grace the Hippodrome in Constantinople (see p386) until brought to Venice after the Fourth Crusade.

The basilica is decorated with some fine mosaics, the earliest in the narthex: the *Madonna with Apostles and Evangelists* dates from the 1060s. The **Sanctuary** (Mon-Sat 1000-1730, Sun 1400-1600, €1.50), next to the south transept, holds the valuable Pala D'Oro, a 976 altar panel also looted from Constantinople, the source of most of the exhibits both here and in the neighbouring **Treasury** (Mon-Sat 1000-1730, Sun 1400-1600, €3), demonstrating just how wealthy a city Constantinople once was, and indeed how lucrative a Crusade could be.

The **Palazzo Ducale** (daily 0900-1700, €4), next door, was the one-time residence of the doge, along with the Serene Republic's chief bureaucrats and administrators. The building is in parts 9th century, but dates mostly from the 14th. The star attractions are the paintings of Tintoretto and Veronese in the Sala del Maggiore Consiglio, with the latter responsible for the *Apotheosis of Venice*, painted on the ceiling. The Palazzo is also connected to the prison next door by the **Bridge of Sighs**, across which many a sad prisoner, including Casanova, made his way, hence its name.

Try to time your return to the square to see the bronze Moors strike the bells of the 15th-century law court belltower. The Libreria Sansoviniana, on the left as you walk up from the sea, is a fine Renaissance building which houses the **Archaeological Museum** (daily 0900-1900, €4), whose contents are hardly worthy of their setting.

To its east lies the Sestieri of Castello and the **Campo San Zanipolo**, the site of the 13th-century Church of Santi Giovanni e Paolo; building began about 1240 but it wasn't consecrated until 1430. Some 25 doges have memorials here; the 1481 statue of Bartolomeo Colleoni outside is generally considered a masterpiece. Also in Castello is the 16th-century **Scuola di San Giorgio degli Schiavoni** (Tue-Sat 1000-1230, 1500-1800; Sun 1000-1230, €3). *Scuola* were religious confraternities, with this one set up by the city's Slav community. The ground-floor room is decorated by a Vittore Carpaccio cycle from 1502-7 in honour of the confraternity's three saints, George, Tryphon and Jerome.

Wandering back to the north-west you come eventually to the Sestieri of Cannaregio, home to the Ghetto Nuovo, the city's original Jewish quarter. The **Jewish Museum** in Campo Ghetto Nuovo (Sun-Fri except Jewish holidays, 1000-1700, €3, or €7 with a tour of the local synagogues included) tells the story of this area, Europe's first ghetto, which was sealed off every night from the rest of the city.

Elsewhere in the district, Tintoretto is buried in the **Church of Madonna dell'Orto** (Mon-Sat 1000-1730, Sun 1500-1730, €3) which also has two of his paintings, *The Last Judgement* and *The Golden Calf*.

Going back towards the station and turning across the Grand Canal you get to San Croce, then San Polo. On the far side of the Rialto Bridge is the market, a lively reminder that the Rialto was once one of the most important commercial districts in the world: the merchants of Venice would trade everything from stocks to slaves with the Venetian ducat, the dollar of the late medieval Mediterranean. Here, you'll find the **Church of Frari** (Mon-Sat 1000-1730, Sun 1500-1730, €2), begun in about 1330 and finished around a century later. Inside are two paintings by Titian, with one of them, *The Assumption*, often described as the beginning of the high Renaissance in Venice. Painted in 1518, the frame becomes part of the picture, which is itself a dynamic work, full of motion.

There's more fine art behind the church in the **Scuola Grande di San Rocco** (daily 0900-1730, €5). Here, Tintoretto's huge masterpiece, *The Crucifixion*, fills the upstairs Sala dell'Albergo. Some 13m long and 5.5m high, its epic scale reflects the enormity of the fact of the Crucifixion; some of the spectators in the painting are members of the confraternity of the time. The scuola also contains Tintoretto's *Glorification of St Roch*, *The Annunciation*, *Flight into Egypt*, *St Mary Magdelene* and *St Mary of Egypt*.

South of San Polo is Dorsoduro, which contains the **Guggenheim Collection** (Wed-Mon, 1000-1800, Sat 1000-2000, €7). Set in the Palazzo Venier dei Leoni, it contains a more modernist collection once belonging to the American heiress Peggy Guggenheim, who is buried in the garden. Works by Salvador Dali, Max Ernst, Jackson Pollock and Mark Chagall are on display. More traditional is the art of the **Galleria dell'Academia** (Tue-Sat 0900-1900, Sun 0900-1200, €6). A fine collection of European work from the 14th to 18th centuries, it includes more Tintoretto, Titian, Carpaccio and Veronese.

ADRIATIC SEA

0   150   300m

Campo di
Ghetto Nuovo/
Jewish Museum

Casa Gerotto
Calderan Pension

Locanda Antica
Casa Carettoni
Pension

Train Stations
(for Italy, Europe)

Stazione
Marittima

Ferries to
Greece &
Turkey

BACINO DELLA
STAZIONE MARITTIMA

Bus
Station

Piazzale
Roma

Buses to
airport

Domus
Civica

Alle
Oche

Church
of Frari

Bar La
Sosta

Galleria
dell'Academia

CANALE DELLA GIUDECCA

Venice

Madonna dell'Orto

Paradiso Perduto

CANALE DELLE FONDAMENTA NUOVE

Ferries to islands

Fondamenta Nuove

CANAL GRANDE

Trattoria Enoteca all Bomba

Church of Santi Giovanni e Paolo

Rialto Bridge

Post Office

Cip Ciap

Hotel Forestaria Valdese

Scuola di San Giorgio degli Schiavoni

Al Gambero Hotel

Al Volto

Basilica of St Mark

Bridge of Sighs

Campanile

St Mark's Square

Palazzo Ducale

Prison

Tourist Info

Libreria Sansoviniana/ Archaeology Museum

Vaporetto Stop

Hotel Toscana, 500 Casa Mia, 100

CANAL GRANDE

BACINO DI SAN MARCO

Guggenheim Collection

Santa Maria della Salute

↓ Giudecca Island & Ostello Venezia, 400m

ADRIATIC SEA

The nearby **Church of Santa Maria della Salute** (daily 0800-2000, sacristy €2) is also a major art gallery, with a group of Titian paintings in the Sacristy. His *St Mark Enthroned with Saints Cosmas, Damian, Sebastian and Rocco* is joined by Tintoretto's *Marriage at Cana*, which has people he knew painted onto the canvas.

The islands

Shielding the city from the Adriatic storms is the narrow island of **Lido**, reached easily enough by *vaporetto* and once a fashionable beach resort for Europe's wealthy. Today, it's still an expensive resort, venue for the annual film festival and pretty packed out — a long way from when Thomas Mann stayed here at the Grand Hotel des Bains or when Shelley and Byron used to go riding along the strand. The sands are all pay beaches, except at the unswimmable northern and southern ends of the island.

Opposite is the island of **Le Vignole**, dominated by the 1543 Fortress of Sant'Andrea, while closer to Venice itself the island of **San Giorgio Maggiore** has a wonderful Renaissance church in the former monastery of the same name (Mon-Sat 1000-1230, 1430-1630, Sun 0930-1030, 1430-1630). Inside is Tintoretto's famous *The Last Supper* and also *Fall of Manna*.

Closer in still, one of the larger islands is **La Giudecca**, which contains the 1592 Capuchin **Church of Redentore** (Mon-Sat 1000-1700, Sun 1300-1700, €2). On the third Sunday in July, this is the venue for the Festival of the Redeemer, when the church is decked out with the branches of trees and flowers as a reminder of the end of a devastating plague in 1576.

The *vaporetti* provide easy transport from Fondamente Nuove to the northern islands: **Murano** is famous for its glass, the whole process of production on display at the Museo Vetrario (Thu-Tue 1000-1600, €4); **Burano** is the island for lacemaking, with a museum in the Scuola Dei Merletti (Tue-Sun 1000-1600, €3); while **Torcello** is the site of Venice's first cathedral, Santa Maria Assunta (daily 1000-1230, 1400-1700, €2). Inside is a great 12th-century mosaic of the Madonna and Child.

PRACTICAL INFORMATION
Orientation

With the snaking curl of the Grand Canal through its heart, Venice is criss-crossed by dozens of smaller waterways. Access to the city is via a long causeway connecting it with the much larger new city of Mestre on the mainland. Along this runs the railway line and a road, though cars must be parked on the island of Tronchentto or at Piazzale Roma, as Venice is a car-free zone.

The train station, Stazzione Santa Lucia, is on the main island and is well connected to other Italian cities and to Europe in general, while the airport, Marco Polo, east of Mestre, is connected to Venice by boat from San Marco and Lido, or by bus from Piazzale Roma.

Ferries arrive at the Bacino della Stazzione Maritime, the dock of the 'Maritime Station', which is on a branch line from Venice's main railway station and only a few minutes' walk from there.

In town, *vaporetti* (water buses) and *traghetti* (public gondolas), the Venetian equivalent of the bus, are the best and cheapest way to get around over any distance, though walking is also recommended: you'll probably get lost at least once but that's part of the pleasure.

ACTV (No 5, €1) and ATVO (€2) operate bus services from the airport to Piazzale Roma; alternatively take a *vaporetto* (€12) to San Marco or the Lido.

Services

The main **tourist office** (☎ 520 8964) is at 71/f, San Marco. Open daily 0940-1520, the office's staff distribute free maps and will help with accommodation. There are also information offices at the airport and train station. A website worth looking at is 🖥 www.veniceforvisitors.com. The tourist office also distributes the English-language listings magazine *Leo*.

The **tourist police** (☎ 271 5511) are based at 24, via Nicoldi, Marghera.

The main **post office** is at Salizzada del Fontego dei Tedeschi, near the Rialto Bridge. Next door is a **telephone office**, open 0800-1200 and 1600-1900.

Net House Venice, 2958-2976, Campo

San Stefano, is an **internet café** open 24hr.

The **left-luggage** facilities at the train station are open 24hr.

A good **bookstore** is Studium, on the corner of Calle de la Cannonica.

There are several **festivals**: Carnevale is held in the 10 days leading up to the Christian festival of Lent. Venetians wear colourful masks and costumes and join gondola processions; there is zero chance of getting a room anywhere unless booked well in advance.

Regata Storica takes place on the first Sunday in September, a competition between gondoliers with races and regatta events of all kinds. There's slightly more chance of getting a room.

Venice Film Festival (also held in September) is now one of the world's top art-house gatherings, with the chance to combine a visit to this photogenic city with a high number of films.

Ferries   [see p453 for full details]
Venice is connected by regular services to Greece and Turkey.

To Greece Blue Star Ferries (☎ 277 0559) run twice a week in winter, then three times a week June–September to **Igoumenitsa** and on to **Patras**. Minoan Lines also operate this route (3-6 per week).

To Turkey Turkish Maritime Lines (TML) run to İzmir once a week.

To Croatia Venezia Lines has services to **Poreč/Parenzo**, **Pula**, **Rijeka** and **Rovinj** between May and September.

Trains
The Italian railway network (🖥 www.trenitalia.com) is reliable, if a little slow. Trains depart from Stazzione Santa Lucia (☎ 147-888 088, or ☎ 041-238 1560 for the automatic timetable) to Florence (6 per day, 3 hours), Rome (6 per day, $4^{1}/_{2}$ hours), Trieste (hourly, 130 mins), Padua (6 per day, 30 mins) and Bologna (2 per day, 2 hours) from where a connection goes to Ancona and the Adriatic coastline to Bari and Brídisi.

Venice Mestre, across the lagoon on the mainland, has two trains a day to Milan, the best connection for Genoa.

There is now a train all the way from London to Venice, via Paris, Turin, Milan and Verona. Heading east, the trains go to Salzburg and Vienna, or via Trieste to Ljubljana and the rest of the Balkans.

Buses
Piazzale Roma is the main bus station. There are regular inter-city buses for Padua and Treviso, as well as further afield; services for Mestre also depart from here.

Pasta
One of the world's most successful foods, Italian pasta is also one of its most ancient. Carvings in an Etruscan tomb show spaghetti being served in the 4th century BC, while the Greek god Vulcan is widely credited with inventing the world's first pasta-making machine.

Elsewhere, the Chinese were making egg noodles as early as 3000BC, hence the claim that Marco Polo brought the idea back in the 13th century. True or not, Italians have since taken up the noodle with an awesome vengeance. Made from durum wheat flour, pasta has a high gluten content (good for protein) which, combined with a sauce, makes a meal that has everything for a balanced diet.

The wide variety of pasta types includes spaghetti, meaning 'little string', vermicelli ('little worms'), farfalloni ('large butterflies'), lancette ('little spears'), fusilli ('spindles'), and riccioline ('little curls'). Any restaurant or trattoria will serve a good variety, while the best place to buy some is from shops, a little like bakeries, that make their own. Boxes of different types are usually on display, with a range of sauces available too. Municipal markets also usually have a stall selling the best homemade stuff.

ADRIATIC SEA

Planes

Marco Polo Airport (☎ 260 9240) is served by many international airlines; Alitalia flies to Rome and other domestic destinations.

Where to stay

Unless you book accommodation well in advance you are likely to have problems, especially if your budget is tight. Staff in the tourist information offices will help but deal only in hotels and charge a fee. The places below might have a spare room if you're lucky. Cannaregio is the better value district, San Marco the priciest.

Ostello Venezia (☎ 523 8211), 86, Fondamenta delle Zitelle, on Giudecca Island, Vaporetto No 82 from the train station. An official HI youth hostel, with excellent views across the water; bunks for €16 with breakfast.

Domus Civica (☎ 721 103), Calle Campazzo, San Polo. Women-only hostel, with a 2330 curfew; €20 a bunk.

Foresteria Valdese (☎ 528 6797), Castello 5170. At the foot of the bridge at the far end of Calle Lunga; €20 for a bunk, €50 for a double room.

Hotel Toscana Tofanelli (☎ 523 5722), Via Garibaldi 1650. Clean, basic accommodation for €25/50 sgl/dbl.

Casa Gerotto Calderan (☎ 715 361), 283, Campo S Geremia, Cannaregio. Close to the station and good value; €20 for a dorm bed; €35/60 sgl/dbl; more for rooms with attached bath.

Hotel Antica Casa Carettoni (☎ 716 231), 130, Lista di Spagna, Cannaregio. €25/40 sgl/dbl.

Al Gambero (☎ 522 4384), 4587 Calle dei Fabbri. About the best value in San Marco; €45/70 sgl/dbl.

Where to eat

Venice is known for rice dishes, with risotto a popular choice, but the city is no friend to those on a tight budget so try the local cafés or *pasticcerie*, where you can grab a sandwich or snack while standing at the bar for less than if you sit down. There are also restaurants serving a *menu turistico* (tourist menu), which fall in price the further you get from San Marco and are generally good

quality, if more expensive than their French or Spanish cousins.

Trattoria Enoteca all Bomba, Calle de L'Oca, Cannaregio; €10 menu.

Alle Oche, Calle del Tintor, has a wide variety of pizzas for around €8.

Paradiso Perduto, Fondamenta della Misericordia, Cannaregio. Another €10 restaurant, sometimes has live music, closed on Wednesdays.

Cip Ciap, Ponte del Mondo Novo. Quality pizza by the slice for €1-2.

Bar La Sosta, Campo Santa Margherita. A student hang-out, excellent sandwiches and panini for €1-3.

Casa Mia Calle dell'Oca, Castello, close to Santi Apostoli Church; trattoria and pizzeria.

Al Volto, Calle Cavalli, San Marco. A wine bar, and with over a thousand bottles to choose from, you might get a bargain. Good snack food, €10, closed on Sundays.

Trieste

AREA CODE: ☎ 040 POPULATION: 219,000

Once the main seaport of the Austro-Hungarian Empire, then later a UN administered zone, Trieste is one of Italy's more melancholic places. Lying at the edge of the Istrian Peninsula, and on the coast of a remarkable run of white limestone flats and ridges, it is a West European frontier town nowadays with Slovenia and Croatia only a short distance away.

While it is also undeniably shabby in places, it has its own ambience and historical significance, and though the cosmopolitan glitter is pretty tarnished, it is still a fascinating place to wander round. It also has good ferry connections to the Dalmatian coast and Greece, plus a local airport and train links to the rest of Italy and Europe.

HISTORY

Initially a port and a Roman city, Trieste's harbour and the walls were built c33BC by Emperor Augustus. The collapse of the Roman Empire left it tied to Istria until independence in AD948. Venice took it over in

1202. Rebelling against their new overlords, it got support from Austria, only to become a vassal of Hapsburg Leopold III in 1382.

The Austrian Charles VI made Trieste a free port in 1719, a status which lasted until 1891. By then the city had become the chief base of the Austro-Hungarian navy and the chief port of the dual monarchy's extensive Central European domains. Yet despite this connection to a Central European and Balkan hinterland, around two-thirds of the population looked across to Italy for their ethnic and cultural roots.

Apart from Italians, its still cosmopolitan populace included Germans, Hungarians, Austrians, Croats, Serbs, Slovenes and a large Jewish community. In 1904, James Joyce arrived with a job as an English teacher, staying until 1920. Joyce referred to the city later in *Finnegan's Wake* as 'tarry easty', the meeting place of 'all the ends of Europe'. However, this was not to last. With Italy on the victorious allied side in WWI, the complete dismemberment of the Austro-Hungarian Empire followed and Trieste was handed over to Italy in 1918, a move that satisfied national pride but destroyed the port economically; Trieste was now separated from its natural hinterland by an international border. After WWII, however, Yugoslavia, whose guerrilla tactics had so helped the Allies to victory over the Axis powers, Germany and Italy, wanted Trieste in recompense for fascist occupation. Britain and the US distrusted communist-led Yugoslavia occupying such a strategic port. Therefore the Free City of Trieste was created in 1947, divided into two zones under UN administration. In 1954, however, the Yugoslavs, British and Americans agreed to Trieste becoming part of Italy once again, though this was not ratified until 1975.

The city has since recovered some of its former wealth, but is still very much defined by its proximity to Slovenia and Croatia. Amongst the crumbling neo-classical architecture of a former polyglot empire, Trieste has also seen the regrettable rise of a new Italian nationalism, increasingly paranoid about immigration from the new EU lands beyond.

WHAT TO SEE

Starting from Piazza Liberta, you'll first see the Palazzo del Comune and Palazzo di Governo on either side of the square, while bus No 24 takes you up to the **Castello** (daily 0900-sunset, €1.50). Built in the 15th century on the hill of Monte Giusto by the Venetians, it is still in fair condition and now contains a **museum** (Tue-Sun 0900-1300) with a collection of pikes and muskets. It is also the centrepiece of Trieste's old town, the largely German-populated Triest, which huddled around this hill.

In another example of the city's multi-cultural past, the **Cathedral of San Giusto** (daily 0800-1200, 1530-1930) combines not just two original churches but also part of an ancient Roman temple. It has a Romanesque façade, Gothic windows and, inside, Byzantine columns. The frescos are 13th century and depict the early Christian martyr, St Justus.

The city has two main museums: one a former Italian fascist-era concentration camp and the other a 19th-century Viennese palace. The former is the **Risiera di San Sabba**, 43, Rattodella Pilera, on the No 10 bus route (Tue-Sun 0900-1300, free). It contains an exhibition displaying the unpleasant realities behind Mussolini's gimcrack regime. The latter is the **Museo Revoltella**, 27, Via Diaz (Wed-Mon 1000-1900, €3), has a good modern art collection and is also an interesting place to contemplate the past grandeur of the Austro-Hungarian rulers of the city.

If you're staying a day or two and are interested in caving you should visit the limestone carst country of the Carso. This contains miles of caves and tunnels, with the **Grotto Gigante** the high point. Some 100m high, 65m wide and 280m long, this cave, the largest in the world, is big enough to swallow London's St Paul's Cathedral.

To visit, catch the Opicina tram from Piazza Oberdan in the centre of town; it climbs Salita di Scorcola to reach the village of Opicina, a few minutes' walk from the grotto.

Miramare Castle is also worth a visit; it's down the coast to the south, an easy local bus ride away.

ADRIATIC SEA

PRACTICAL INFORMATION
Orientation
The city of Trieste seems to fit almost perfectly into the bay, the docks running around a headland shore behind which the city sprawls up into the surrounding limestone hills. Most of what you'll want to see is within walking distance of the main square, Piazza dell'Unita d'Italia. Conveniently ferries dock near here too.

Services
The **tourist office** (☎ 679 6111, 🖳 www.trie stetourism.it), 20, Via San Nicolo, on the seafront, is open Mon-Sat 0900-1900, Sun 1000-1300, 1600-1900. The staff will help you find a room but you shouldn't have too much difficulty on your own.

Ferries   [see p453 for full details]
Venezia Lines run weekly between May and September to **Poreč** (Parenzo in Italian) and **Rovinj** (Rovingo) in Croatia.

ANEK Lines (☎ 322 0604) run a daily service to **Igoumenitsa**. Some services continue to **Patras** and **Corfu**.

Grecia Maritime Ltd operates a twice weekly service to **Durrës**, Albania.

Trains

Trieste central station is on Piazza Liberta, north of the centre. Services operate daily to Bologna, Florence, Milan and Rome and twice daily to Venice.

There are also weekly through-trains to Ljubljana, and north to Vienna. Rail enquiries: ☎ 147 88 80 88.

Buses

The main bus station is next to the railway station; services go mainly to the surrounding area though there are some to Venice and also over the border to Ljubljana. Times and frequencies change so check with the tourist information office.

Planes

The airport has flights to many European destinations and connections to just about everywhere.

Trieste's airport, Rouchi dei Legionari, is some 33km out of town. Bus No 51 (€3) goes there from the airport bus stop near the train station. The first departure from Trieste is at 0454, the last at 2240, while the first bus from the airport leaves at 0540, the last at 2350.

Where to stay

HI Hostel (☎ 224 102), 8km from the city at Viale Miramare. Take the No 6 bus from the tourist information office, then change to bus No 36; bunks for €10 a night.

Blaue Krone (☎ 631 882), 12, Via XXX Ottobre. Reasonable rates for good quality accommodation; sgl/dbl €20/35.

Istria (☎ 371 343), 5, Via Timeus. Bit pricier but good standard; €25/45 sgl/dbl.

Take the No 4 bus to Obelisco for the nearest **campsite**.

Where to eat

Da Giovanni, 14, Via Lazzaro. A fine trattoria/restaurant with full meals for around €10 a head.

Caffé San Marco, Via G Battisti. A Trieste institution with snacks served in 80-year-old surroundings.

Pepi Sciavo, Via Casa di Risparmio. Mostly snack food but good panini for €7-8.

Piran

AREA CODE: ☎ 066 POPULATION: 5000

Slovenia's Istrian gem, Piran, has none of the overblown tourism of neighbouring Portorož, and it's rather more attractive than Koper, Slovenia's other coastal settlement. Classically situated on a curving finger of land hooked around its harbour, it's worth spending some time here, particularly if you are interested in caving and hiking, as the countryside offers plenty of possibilities. Ljubljana, the capital, is easily reached by bus.

HISTORY

As an ancient Greek city, Piran got its name from *pyr*, which means 'fire'. On the end of the headland here, large fires were lit as beacons to ships looking for the approaches to Koper, then the Greek port of Aegida. The Romans were also here, and the Venetians, who built most of the old town houses you see today. Most of the hinterland was, like the rest of Slovenia, under various Frankish and then Germanic kings who, by the end of the 18th century, became the Hapsburg Austrian emperors and went on, finally, to take over the coast. The residents of Piran were thus a strange mix of Slavs, Italians and Austrians, along with Hungarians and Croats, all under the rule of the dual monarchy until its collapse after WWI. Piran then joined Yugoslavia, was bombed and occupied during WWII and liberated to become part of Tito's socialist state in 1947.

In 1990, with the writing on the wall for Yugoslavia, Slovenia held a referendum that voted overwhelmingly for independence. A 10-day war against the Serb-dominated Yugoslav federal army followed with Slovenia winning, the result of which being a peace settlement recognizing the present borders. Croatia is not entirely satisfied but on the whole Slovenia was spared the fighting that hit the other former Yugoslav republics and has moved rapidly towards

ADRIATIC SEA

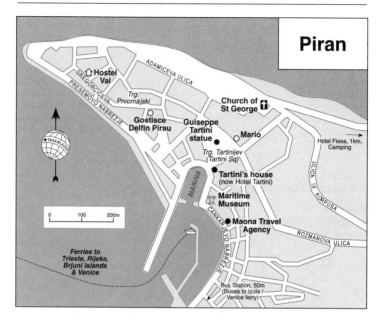

Piran

Hostel Val
GREGORCICEVA
PRESEMOVO NABREŽJE
ADAMICEVA ULICA
Trg. Prvomajski
Gostisce Delfin Pirau
Church of St George
Guiseppe Tartini statue
Mario
Trg. Tartinijev (Tartini Sq)
Hotel Fiesa, 1km, Camping
ULICA IX KORPUSA
MARINA
Tartini's house (now Hotel Tartini)
Maritime Museum
CANKARJEVO NABREŽJE
Maona Travel Agency
ROZMANOVA ULICA
Ferries to Trieste, Rijeka, Brjuni Islands & Venice
Bus Station, 50m (Buses to Izola / Venice ferry)

0   100   200m

EU membership since it was recognized as a country in 1992. It joined on 1 May 2004.

WHAT TO SEE

The main sight here is the house of **Giuseppe Tartini** in Tartinijev trg (Tartini was a violinist and composer born here in the 18th century whose statue stands in the middle of the square), a beautiful town square, worth spending some time in for its own sake.

Just around the corner to the south, at 3, Cankarjevo nabrežje, is the **Maritime Museum** (Tue-Sun 0900-1200, 1500-1800, SIT500). This holds some excellent model ships and figureheads, along with a copy of Tartini's violin. Head north from the square and you'll quickly find the **Church of St George**, on the north side of the headland. This has a 1609 *campanile* (belltower) that is an exact replica of the one in St Mark's Square, Venice. Inside this Romanesque and baroque hybrid are some good frescos and a statue of St George slaying the dragon. The **baptistry** next door holds a 1300 Gothic wooden crucifix in the Tree of Life shape.

PRACTICAL INFORMATION
Orientation

Ferries arrive and depart in the harbour, south of the peninsula. The harbour-side road is Cankarjevo nabrežje, which leads north to the marina and the old town beyond. Most of the sights are north or north-east of here, while the classic winding streets are off to the west. The bus station is due south of the harbour, on Dantejeva ulica. Again, the town is perfectly easy to walk around.

Ferries   [see p452 for full details]

Piran is on Venezia Lines' twice weekly high-speed catamaran service (May to September only) to **Venice**.

In summer a service operates from neighbouring Izola (see Buses, p219) to Venice; get details from the tourist office.

There's also a daily Adriatica ferry from **Trieste**, leaving at 0800 and arriving at Piran 2 hours later. It then goes on to **Rijeka** (80 mins from Piran) and **Brjuni** (1 hour from Rijeka), returning at 1630 via the same route, leaving Piran at 1845 for Trieste. The one-way Piran–Rijeka cost is €8.26, and Piran–Trieste €7.23.

Buses
There are hourly local buses to Portorož (15 mins, SIT100), Izola (20 mins, SIT150) and Koper (45 mins). There are also six buses a day to Trieste (1 hour, SIT2000) and Ljubljana (1¹/₂ hours, SIT1500).

Where to stay
Try one of the private rooms offered on arrival — the going rate should be from about SIT3000/€15 a head a night. Otherwise, try **Maona** (☎ 673 4520), 7, Cankarjevo nabrežje, to make a booking. *Hostel Fiesa* (☎ 746 897), Fiesa. A modest establishment offering sgl/dbl for €18/30. To get to Fiesa head east from the Church of St George; it's 1km on the coastal path but 4km on the road. *Hostel Val* (☎ 673 2555), 38, Gregorciceva. Well located in the old town; €18/30 sgl/dbl.

The closest **campsite** is also at Fiesa (see Hostel Fiesa). *Camping Jezero Fiesa* is close to the beach in a small valley some 4km from Piran; open Jun-Sep only.

Where to eat
Gostisce Delfin Piran, 4, Kosovelova ulica. A local favourite; SIT1500 a head. *Mario*, off Tartinijev trg. Good seafood and fish dishes.

Poreč

AREA CODE: ☎ 052 **POPULATION:** 18,900
Istria's largest tourist resort, Poreč is another charming town on a peninsula jutting out into a beautiful sea. The bustle never takes over, with the old buildings and rambling streets a delight to wander round, even in season.

It's also a stop on both the Trieste and the Venice ferry routes and is close to the Slovenian border, giving it a vantage point on all three countries.

HISTORY
The Romans were the first to make something of this natural harbour and defensive position, laying out the grid pattern of the town much as it exists now. The main square, Marafor trg, is the ancient forum, off which the Dekumanus, the Roman main road, is still the town's main thoroughfare.

After the fall of the Western Empire, the town became another Byzantine possession, with its own bishop. Tustled over by local rival lords, it went to Venice until taken, along with the rest of the peninsula, by the Austrians in 1797.

Under the Austro-Hungarians it became another important port serving the Central European hinterland. In 1918 that ended, and while under Italian, then German and finally, following WWII, Yugoslav control, it turned to other industries to support itself. Principal among these was tourism, which boomed in the 1980s. Now, following the conflicts of the 1990s, it is picking up smartly, being a short hop for many tourists angling for a crystal-clear sea and a picturesque town.

WHAT TO SEE
The star attraction here is the **Basilica of Euphrasius** (daily 0700-2000, free), on the northern side of the peninsula. This 6th-century place of worship has a collection of priceless mosaics both in and around it from different periods. On the north side are scattered remnants of early Christian work and worship from the Oratory of St Maur; Christianity was then an underground religion and the mosaics make use of early symbols of the faith, such as the fish. Inside though, a later, very much above-ground Christianity shows through in the Baptistry, decorated with wonderful Byzantine mosaics commissioned by Euphrasius himself in AD543. Dotted with semi-precious stones, gold and mother-of-pearl inlay, they are frequently compared to those at Ravenna with which they are contemporaneous. Further examples are also on display in the **Bishop's Palace** next door (daily 1000-1830, Kn10), which contains mosaics that previously covered the basilica floor.

ADRIATIC SEA

Elsewhere, **Poreč Museum** (daily 0900-1200, 1600-1900, Kn10) has a collection of Greek and Roman finds housed in the baroque Sincic Palace at 9, Dekumanska. Heading west down this road you eventually come to **Marafor trg**, which contains the remains of Roman temples to Mars and Neptune.

If you want a swim, head back to the harbour and follow obala Maršala Tita round to the Sveti Nikola boat pier. A trip out to this island costs around Kn12 one way and takes you to a less crowded local pebbly beach. Last boat back is at midnight.

PRACTICAL INFORMATION
Orientation
The ferry dock is in the harbour under the peninsula's protective arm, with the main harbour-front road still called obala Maršala Tita after the former Yugoslav leader. The bus station is on Rade Končara, the road alongside the small boat harbour to the south-east. Most of the sights are in the old town and the headland, which has the Dekumanus (now Dekumanska) running down the middle between Marafor trg at the western end and Slobode trg at the eastern. You can easily walk everywhere.

Services
The **tourist office** (☎ 451 458, 🖳 www. istra.com/porec), 9, Zagrebačka, open daily 0800-2200 in summer and Monday to Friday 0800-1500 in winter, has maps and will also help with accommodation.

Ferries   [see p452 for full details]
Poreč is on the weekly Venezia Lines (May to September) service between **Trieste** and **Rovinj**. Services to **Venice** (3-7 per week) go during the same months. There is also an occasional summer-season only day-trip boat service across to Venice. Ask at the tourist information office for details.

Buses
There are two buses a day to Trieste (2 hours, Kn40) and Ljubljana (2½ hours, Kn50), five a day to Rovinj (1 hour, Kn25),

Zagreb (4 hours) and Rijeka (2 hours). There are also hourly buses to Pula (2 hours).

Where to stay
Private rooms go for around Kn60-80 a head; try **Atlas Agency** (☎ 432 273), 11, Bože Milanovica.

Hotel Poreč (☎ 451 811), 1, Rade Končara. Just behind the bus station; sgl/dbl for Kn300/450 though rates can be bargained down out of season.

Hotel Neptun (☎ 451 711), in the old town on Marsala Tita, right on the waterfront by the harbour. Slightly pricier at Kn400/650 sgl/dbl but again, try a bit of bargaining.

Autocamp Zelena Laguna (☎ 451 696), 6km south at Zelena Laguna; buses leave on the hour from the bus station.

Where to eat
Sarajevo Grill, Matije Vlacica. Good for local specialities and big chunks of meat. Kn45 a head.

Istra, on the junction of Bože Milanovica and obala Maršala Tita. Good seafood and fish.

Rovinj

AREA CODE: ☎ 052 **POPULATION:** 12,910
One of Dalmatia's oldest modern tourist resorts, starting out as a much-favoured watering hole and health spa for Austro-Hungarian nobility, Rovinj is today a fine port town with a toe-like peninsula nudging out into an islet-filled sea.

Still a busy harbour, it has managed to avoid any major industrial scarring and the old town is wonderfully preserved, cobbled streets and all. There's a major Italian influence here, not just historically but in the population itself. It's also on the main Istrian ferry route and has good road connections north to Italy or north-east to Slovenia and northern Croatia.

ADRIATIC SEA

HISTORY

Not much is recorded of its ancient history, with the port arriving on the scene only late in the 6th century AD as part of the Byzantine Exarchate of Ravenna. In 788 it became part of Franconia and was dominated by alternating feudal lords for several centuries until Venice took over in 1283. It remained a possession of the doges until the collapse of the Venetian republic in 1797, after which it followed much of the rest of the coast into Austrian control, with railways and roads built to connect it to Vienna and Budapest. As an Austro-Hungarian city it rose in importance in the 19th century with the establishment of various charitable rest homes and health spas, popular with the Viennese gentry, its first holidaymakers.

As with other ports in the area, it became Italian after WWI. The industrial and port areas were heavily bombed in WWII but not the old town. In 1945 it passed to Yugoslavia and finally to Croatia.

WHAT TO SEE

Cresting the old town peninsula is the **Cathedral of St Euphemia**. Built in 1736, this baroque giant is the largest of its kind in Istria. Inside is the tomb of the saint herself. You can climb the tower between 1000-1200 and 1600-1900 for Kn10.

Wandering the streets around the cathedral hill is the best way to see Rovinj. Returning eventually to Marsala Tita trg, you'll come to the **town museum** (summer only, Mon-Sat 1000-1330, 1800-2100, Kn10).

This isn't much to get excited about but **Rovinj Aquarium**, 5, obala Giordano Pallaga, north-east of the centre (Easter to Oct, daily 0900-2100, Kn10) is one of the oldest aquaria in the world, being set up in 1891. The collection includes a wide variety of sea creatures from the prosaic to the poisonous.

If you still have time, visit **Katarina Island**, a pleasant pebbly place to while away a few hours. The ferry (Kn10 return) there leaves half-hourly from a point on the south-eastern coast, half a kilometre from the old town. Ferries to **Crveni otok**, another island, leave from the same place.

PRACTICAL INFORMATION

Orientation

Ferries dock in the harbour south of the old town and its peninsula. You disembark at obala Pina Budicina, behind which are most of the town's sights. You can go everywhere on foot. The bus station, however, is on M Benussija, to the east.

Services

The **tourist office** (☎ 811 566, 💻 www. istra.com/rovinj), 12, obala Pina Budicina, is open daily 0800-1500. A website worth looking at is 💻 www.tzgrovinj.hr.

Ferries   [see p452 for full details]

Rovinj is on the weekly (May to September only) Venezia Lines ferry route to **Trieste** via Poreč. Venezia Lines has three services a week in the same months to **Venice**.

Buses

There are hourly buses to Pula (30 mins, Kn25), 8 a day to Poreč (1 hour), and 2 a day to Ljubljana (4 hours, Kn120).

Where to stay

Try private rooms, hired either from the ubiquitous landladies at the ferry stop or **Natale** (☎ 813 365, 💻 www.natale.hr), 4, Carducci, opposite the bus station.

Hotel Adriatic (☎ 815 088), Marsala Tita trg. Couldn't get more central; sgl/dbl for Kn300/Kn400.

Hotel Monte Mulin (☎ 811 512), 66, A Smareglia. Ten minutes' walk south of the bus station and overlooking the bay; Kn250/Kn350 sgl/dbl.

Campers should try *Polari* (☎ 813 441), 3km south on the Villas Rubin bus route; open May to mid-October only.

Where to eat

Konoba Veli Jože, 1, Svetoga Križa. A good fish and seafood restaurant.

Da Sergio, 11, Grisa. A mainstream pizza and pasta place.

ADRIATIC SEA

Pula

AREA CODE: ☎ 052 POPULATION: 55,000
Once the main harbour of the Austro-Hungarian Empire, Pula has retained a blend of buildings, stories and people that gives it a unique place on the Adriatic. Located at the tip of the Istrian Peninsula, it also has a hinterland of wooded hills and mountains that is well worth a trip in itself.

Offshore are the Brijuni Islands, one-time summer residence of Marshal Tito and a good place for a day trip or longer journey.

HISTORY
Pula really took off as a Roman port, with the legions arriving in 177BC. By the 2nd century AD it had its own bishop, finally passing to Byzantium on the fall of the empire of the West. For the next few centuries Venice, Genoa and the Frankish kings all attempted to secure Pula for themselves, with varying degrees of success, while the plague wiped out most of the population in the 1630s.

Austria arrived on the scene in 1797, and converted the town back to an important naval base and port for their empire, much as it had been for the Romans. The ships of the dual monarchy proved repeatedly that they were more than a match for the neighbouring Italians. As with Trieste, however, Italy took over in the WWI post-war settlement, occupying it in 1920. Heavily bombed and then occupied by the Germans in WWII, Pula was liberated in 1944/45, but didn't pass into Yugoslav hands until 1947. Once again a major naval base, it is also one of Croatia's busiest working ports.

WHAT TO SEE
From the harbour-front road, the **15th-century cathedral** is easily visible. Originally a Romanesque-era basilica, this was built on top of a Roman temple and the altar inside was once a Roman sarcophagus that reportedly used to contain the remains of the 11th-century Hungarian king, Solomon.

A 17th-century **Venetian fortress** rises up on the hill behind. The **History Museum** (daily 0900-1800, Kn10) inside is not very exciting but does offer good views. From here, go down the hill to the east to see a wide range of prehistoric and ancient relics from Pula and Istria in the **Archaeological museum** (Mon-Sat 0900-1500, Kn20).

The Roman-era sights are on the whole the most worthwhile. The best is the 1st-century AD **amphitheatre** (daily 0900-1700, Kn18), on Istarska, north of the centre and set into a hill. This once accommodated crowds of 23,000, making it the sixth largest in the world. The good state of preservation allows a glimpse of the below-ground strong rooms, where wild animals and soon-to-be-martyred Christians would have been kept.

The **Temple of Augustus** in the Forum area west of the fortress was built around AD10 as part of Emperor Augustus' elevation to the status of God. The forum area was once Pula's old town, and before that was indeed the Roman forum. A pedestrianized street east from here, Slavoluk obitelja Sergijevaca, is now the town's main shopping and café area.

PRACTICAL INFORMATION
Orientation
Pula's almost landlocked harbour is lined with both a road and railway, with the shipyards and arsenal, situated on an island out in the bay, connected to land by a causeway. The train station is on the harbour front, north of the customs wharf, while the bus station is on ulica Mate Balote, behind the citadel. Most of the sights are around this area and within walking distance.

Services
The **tourist bureau** (☎ 219 197, 🖳 www.gradpula.com), 13, ulica Istarska, opens mornings and evenings only but does have maps and accommodation lists.

Ferries   [see p452 for full details]
There's a fast catamaran to **Venice** on Saturday, leaving at 0830 arriving 1130, returning from Venice at 1700, arriving back in Pula at 2000. Between 4 July and 30 August, it repeats this schedule on a Monday.

Ferries to
Rijeka, Brjuni,
islands, Trieste
& Venice

★ TRAILBLAZER

SHIPYARDS

*Pula
Harbour*

Train
Station

Hotel
Riviera

SPLITSKA ULICA

Tourist
Info (i)

Roman
amphitheatre ●

RIVA

Delfin

Cathedral

Archaeology
Museum

ULITARSKA

Temple of
Augustus

Fortress/
History Museum

Bus
Station

SERDO
DOBRICA
ST

Gostiona
Korzo

Ulix

Hotel
Omir

0   200   400m

ARSENAISKA ULICA

RADICEVA ULICA

MARULICEVA ULICA

ULICA KATELINICA JERETOVA

RIZZLIEVA ULICA

ULICA VERUDA

TOMASINI EVA ULICA

KRIEZINA ULICA

RIZZLIEVA ULICA

Youth
Hostel

ULICA VERUDA

Valsaline Bay

ADRIATIC SEA

Pula

Excursion boats go to the **Brijuni Islands** (Brioni in Italian) up the Istrian Peninsula. Some stop on the islands and some just tour round so make sure you get the one you want. It's usually a five-hour round trip.

Trains
There are two trains a day to Zagreb (5 hours, Kn120), and two to Divaca, near Trieste, for connecting trains to Ljubljana.

Buses
There are 18 buses a day to Rijeka (1½ hours, Kn60), 8 of which head on for Zagreb; half-hourly buses to Rovinj (20 mins, Kn25), 12 a day to Poreč (30 mins, Kn35) and 3 to Trieste (1½ hours, Kn100).

Where to stay
Private rooms go for around Kn150 a head — if you don't find a good offer, head for **Arenatours** (☎ 218 696), 4, Giardini, near the bus station.
Youth Hostel (☎ 391 133, 🖳 www.whereis thebeach.com), 4, Zaljev Valsaline in Valsaline Bay, 4km south of the centre. An official HI hostel by an excellent beach on bus routes Nos 2 and 7; Kn100.
Hotel Omir (☎ 210 614), 6, Serdo Dobrica. Worth bargaining; sgl/dbl for Kn350/450.
Hotel Riviera (☎ 211 166), 1, Splitska ulica. Around Kn450/650 sgl/dbl.
   Campers should try *Stoja* (☎ 387 144), 3km south-east of town on No 1 bus route.

Where to eat
Gostiona Korzo, at prvog Maja 34, serving local dishes for around Kn70 a head.
Delfin, 17, Kandlerova, near the cathedral. Good seafood and fish dishes.
Ulix, near the Forum and Slavoluk obitelja Sergijevaca. A bar with snacks.

Rijeka

AREA CODE: ☎ 051 **POPULATION:** 150,010
Not in any way the most glamorous of the Adriatic ports but nonetheless a strategic

harbour – which is probably the only reason you'll end up here – Rijeka does have a famous past, though mainly under its Italian name, Fiume. It's a vital stopping-off point for the Istrian Peninsula and for the border crossing into Slovenia. The main railway runs through here too, heading for Trieste and on into the Central and northern European networks. All of which gives it great industrial and commercial significance as Croatia's most important port, which explains the busy harbour and bustling atmosphere, but most likely won't be any incentive to stay.

HISTORY
Rijeka started life as Tarsatica, a Roman town about which we know little except that Emperor Charlemagne sacked it in 800. By the 10th century there was a recognizable settlement on the right bank of its river, the Rječina. The local power here was Austria, which annexed it in 1471. The city then passed between the various rulers of the Hapsburg's polyglot crown, becoming a free port in 1717, a part of Croatia in 1776, and Hungary in 1779.
   The French then took over between 1809 and 1814 before being ejected by the British. They then handed it back to the Austro-Hungarian Empire, which continued to juggle it around between the Croatian, Austrian and Hungarian royal houses until losing it completely in WWI. Meanwhile, in 1845, a railway was finished between here and Budapest, making this Hungary's main port. Also, in 1866, an Englishman called Robert Whitehead, who was working at the docks here, invented the torpedo, a device destined to send many of his countrymen to the bottom of the ocean in the two world wars to come.
   In 1918, following WWI, Rijeka was handed over to the new Yugoslav kingdom but was soon grabbed by the Italians, who were fuming that they hadn't been given more of the dismembered Austro-Hungarian Empire in the post-war peace settlement. In 1919, the Italian nationalist Gabriele d'Annunzio led a freelance invasion of the place, claiming it as an Italian town despite

its negligible Italian population. While forced ultimately to withdraw, he provided a springboard for the official Italian seizure of Fiume in 1924, a rare success for Italy's new fascist ruler, Benito Mussolini.

The port came under German control on Italy's surrender in 1943 during WWII. Allied air raids hit the port and most of the city badly, while a final battle to liberate the city in 1945 culminated in the Germans blowing up what remained in the harbour. This left Tito's post-war government with the immense task of rebuilding, with much of the medieval town gone forever.

WHAT TO SEE

A hike up to **Trsat Castle** (closed Mondays) is worthwhile. It's some half-hour or so north-east on the Zagreb road (I Grohovca), and overlooks the Rječina River from a high promontory. Built in the 13th century, it gives good views over the town and coast as well as inland to the mountain passes. This was once the stronghold of a Croatian noble family known as the Frankopans, the local satraps during Austrian and Hungarian rule. The Doric temple inside is a mausoleum for the family of an Austrian general who occupied the place. On the way up you'll pass the baroque Church of our Lady, marking the spot where, local legend has it, the house of the Virgin Mary and Joseph stood for three and a half years.

There is also the **maritime museum**, behind the town on a hill above Žrtava Fašizma. This may not be open, given the thorny problems of history in these parts, but it's still worth a look as it's housed in the highly ostentatious 19th-century mansion where d'Annunzio installed himself during his troops' occupation of the city.

PRACTICAL INFORMATION
Orientation

The squared-off harbour in Rijeka has Riva as its northern portside road; heading west on this along the railway tracks you reach the railway station after about 10 minutes. On the way you'll pass Žabica trg (Žabica Square); the bus station is tucked just round its north-eastern corner on Adamiceva.

The sights are to the east, with the Korzo, the Italian-style main street, arching east–west.

Services

Tourist information is available from Turistički Savez Općine Rijeka (☎ 213 145), 2, Uzarska. Jadroagent (☎ 211 276), 2, Ivana Koblera trg, is good for **ferry information**. Both the bus and the train station have **left-luggage** rooms.

Ferries   [see p452 for full details]

Rijeka is the northernmost stop for the regular Jadrolinija ferry south to **Dubrovnik** and **Bari** via **Brbinj**, **Zadar**, **Split**, **Stari Grad**, **Korčula**, and **Sobra**. The Jadrolinija office (☎ 211 444), 16, Riva, is on the waterfront.

Trains

Four trains a day run to Zagreb (5 hours, Kn100), seven run over the Slovenian border to Ljubljana (3 hours, Kn50), though some are *poslovni* (1st class only) requiring advanced reservations. There are also daily trains to Budapest, Munich and Salzburg, which effectively means you can reach anywhere in Europe from here.

Buses

There are two buses a day to Dubrovnik (10 hours, Kn300), 12 to Split (8 hours, Kn200) and Zadar (4 hours, Kn120), and a half-hourly service to Zagreb (4 hours, Kn110). Also enquire at the bus station about international routes; these change frequently but there are usually good connections to Central and Western European destinations.

Where to stay

Getting a private room is usually the best deal (the going rate is around Kn80-120 a person) and easily arranged.
Hotel Neboder (☎ 373538), north-east of the centre. Sgl/dbl for Kn200/300.
Hotel Bonavia (☎ 333 744), Dolac St, three blocks in from the north front of the harbour. More central; Kn250/400 sgl/dbl.
Preluk Autokamp (☎ 621 913) at neighbouring Opatja, on the Rijeka highway, 5km west of the port. Bus No 32 from Rijeka train station will drop you there.

ADRIATIC SEA

Where to eat
Express, 14, Riva, near the ferry office. A good cafeteria-style place.
Index, 18, ul Kresimirova, between the bus and train stations. Similar to Express above.

Zadar

AREA CODE: ☎ 023 POPULATION: 60,000
Northern Dalmatia's main port and a much less-visited place than its southern neighbours Split and Dubrovnik, Zadar is nonetheless a fine old town with a unique position between harbour and channel. The finger of land in between was once the capital of Dalmatia and was part of Italy up until 1947. As such, it has a wide variety of influences, and while it lost many of its original buildings to Allied bombing in WWII (and some to Serb rocket attacks in 1991-3), it still manages to combine a rare jumble of architectural styles and a wonderfully shambolic old town.

HISTORY
The first recorded settlement here was in the 9th century BC when it was known as Jadera and inhabited by a group called the Liburnians. Eight hundred years later it was a Roman settlement and thriving centre, a period of prosperity that continued into the Byzantine era when it became the cultural as well as commercial centre of Byzantine Dalmatia. However, as with all the coastal settlements of the Adriatic, Venice was to influence the town's development dramatically. Zadar fought the Venetians on a number of occasions before being sold to them in 1409 by the collapsing Byzantines. The Ottomans then attacked it in 1571, unsuccessfully, after which the Venetians constructed giant fortifications to secure the city from further attacks.

With the collapse of Venice in 1797, Zadar went to Austria, despite a brief period of French occupation between 1808 and 1813. As a town of the Austro-Hungarian Empire, it was also an important base for the navy of those two landlocked countries.

With the post-WWI peace settlement, the city was given to the Italians in 1920 and as a consequence was heavily bombed during WWII by Allied planes, with some 75% of the buildings being destroyed. In 1944 it was liberated and became part of Tito's Yugoslavia. When that collapsed, it came under bombardment once more, this time in the early 1990s by Serb forces. Most of the damage has been patched up now and there is little evidence that a war took place here just a few years ago. The post-war rebuilding under Tito was also remarkably faithful to the original.

WHAT TO SEE
Right on Zeleni trg is the town's main attraction, the **Church of St Donatus**, built in the 9th century in classic, circular Byzantine style on top of the Roman forum. St Donat was an Irishman, who was possibly bishop here.

Opposite, the **archaeology museum** (Tue-Fri 0730-1230, 1800-2030, Sat-Sun 0800-1200, Kn20) has a good collection of Roman and early medieval relics. Next door, the **Museum of Church Art** (same times and entry charges as the archaeology museum) is housed in an old Benedictine monastery and has a fine group of religious paintings and reliquaries. Also on the square is the **Cathedral of St Anastasia**, a 13th-century Romanesque building and the largest of its genre in Dalmatia.

North from here, up Aleksandra III, is the **Narodni Musej** (National Museum; opening hours vary so check before you go). The museum contains a number of dioramas and models showing the history of Zadar along with many pictures and plans. Go out through the sea gate and take a pleasant harbour-front stroll round the peninsula. Look out, too, for the boat-hire people, who can ferry you over to some of the 101 local islets, known as the Kornati, which are uninhabited and real gems. Day trips usually include lunch and cost around Kn80 a head.

PRACTICAL INFORMATION
Orientation
The Zadar Peninsula, where the old town and almost all the sights are located, is very

ADRIATIC SEA

walker friendly, being fairly flat and compact. The ferry dock is in the harbour to the north of the peninsula, while the train and bus stations are next to each other, a 15-minute walk south-east from the old town entrance. Through this, a long street takes you to the central square, Zeleni trg, off which are most of the churches and museums. The main shopping street, and also the location of the official tourist information office, E Kotromanic, which later becomes Široka ulica, is parallel to this to the north.

Services

South of Narodni trg are a string of **tourist information offices** which will give you a hand with accommodation and maps. Turistićka Zajednica (☎ 212 412), 1, Smiljanica, is the official tourist office. A useful website is 🖳 www.zadar.hr.

Ferries   [see p453 for full details]

Zadar lies on the Jadrolinija (☎ 250 555, 7, Liburnska obala) route between **Rijeka** to the north and **Split**, **Stari Grad**, **Korčula**, **Sobra**, **Dubrovnik** and **Bari** to the south. Jadrolinija and Blue Line also have regular services to **Ancona**. Aliscafi operates daily between July and September to **Hvar Town**.

There are also regular small boats to neighbouring islands.

Trains

There is one train a day to Zagreb (11 hours, Kn140) via Knin. The line south to Split may also be open; check at the station or at a tourist information office.

Buses

There are daily buses to Zagreb (7 hours, Kn100), half-hourly buses south to Split (4

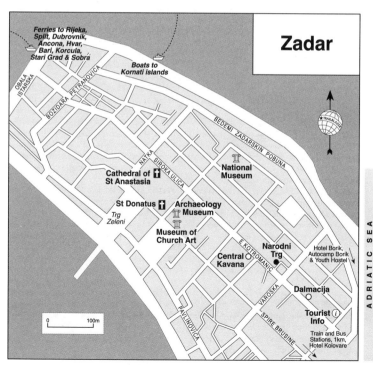

Zadar

Ferries to Rijeka, Split, Dubrovnik, Ancona, Hvar, Bari, Korcula, Stari Grad & Sobra

Boats to Kornati islands

OBALA ISTARSKA

BOŽIDARA PETRANOVICA

BEDEMI ZADARSKIN POBUNA

NATKA

ŠIROKA ULICA

Cathedral of St Anastasia

National Museum

St Donatus

Trg Zeleni

Archaeology Museum

Museum of Church Art

E KOTROMANIC

Central Kavana

Narodni Trg

Hotel Borik, Autocamp Borik & Youth Hostel

VAROŠKA

Dalmacija

PAVLINOVICA

SPIRE BRUSINE

Tourist Info

Train and Bus Stations, 1km, Hotel Kolovare

0   100m

ADRIATIC SEA

hours) and three daily to Rijeka (4 hours).

Where to stay

As usual, that ubiquitous Dalmatian character, the forceful landlady, will make her appearance on arrival. In season, expect to pay Kn100-150 a head.

Hotel Kolovare (☎ 203 200), 14 Bože Peričiča; sgl/dbl for Kn450/700 but off season, you can probably bargain them down.

Borik Youth Hostel (☎ 331 145), 76, obala Kneza Trpimira, Borik. About 5km northwest of Zadar and connected by half-hourly buses; Kn80 a bunk.

Hotel Borik (☎ 332 151), in the neighbouring beach resort of Borik. Kn250/400 sgl/dbl.

Autocamp Borik (☎ 332 014); see Borik Youth Hostel above for details on getting to Borik. The campsite is next to the hostel.

Where to eat

Central Kavana, Široka ulica. A good sample of Zadar café life, with snacks as well.

Dalmacija, end of Kraljiće Elizabete Kotromanic. Seafood and pizza.

Ancona

AREA CODE: ☎ 071 POPULATION: 104,000

While more of a workaday port than a tourist destination, Ancona does have some hidden charms. As ferry services between the Dalmatian coast and Greece no longer operate, it has also emerged as the northernmost passenger port in Italy for ferry connections between the two countries. Services from Ancona also go to Montenegro, Albania and Turkey.

Ancona is capital of the province and the largest city in the Marche region, which spreads down from Italy's Apennine backbone to the Adriatic.

HISTORY

Taking its name from the shape of the promontory that guards the harbour – in Greek *angkon* means 'elbow' – Ancona began life as a colony of Syracuse in about 390BC. Later part of the Roman Empire, the harbour was enlarged by Trajan and became a busy port on the Adriatic coast.

With the Western Roman Empire's collapse, Ancona changed hands several times before regaining its importance under the Byzantine Exarchate of Ravenna as one of the principal cities of the Maritime Pentapolis. However, in the 12th and 13th centuries powerful feudal families emerged in the region known as the Marches (or *Marche* in Italian), such as the Montefeltro of Urbino and the Malatesta of Pesaro (and Rimini). This ushered in a period of violent struggle, with the neighbouring papal states set around Rome also getting involved. After the fall of the Eastern Roman Empire in 1453, control from Rome over Ancona itself was established under a papal decree, though not until 1532, while the duchy of Urbino was finally taken over by the papal states in 1631.

In the Napoleonic period, the French ran things from 1797 to 1816, when control reverted to the papal states. In 1860 Ancona became part of the new Kingdom of Italy. In WWI, the port was bombarded by the Austro-Hungarian navy, while in WWII it was severely bombed by Allied aircraft. Many of its finer old houses were destroyed and the city today still shows its wounds, with a number of new buildings around the small, old-town nucleus. Earthquakes in the 1970s didn't help much either; yet nowadays, restoration work is gradually bringing some colour back to the city's cheeks.

WHAT TO SEE

The entrance to the port is rather grand, with a AD115 marble **Arch of Hadrian**, the port's main ancient benefactor, still standing there. Behind this is the later **Arch of Clementine**, dedicated to Pope Clementine XII, who clearly had grand imperial pretensions too.

Walking uphill from the port to the old town you first reach the Piazzale del Duomo then the 11th- to 12th-century **Church of Santa Maria della Piazza**, famous for its 1210 façade and 5th- to 7th-century mosaics. The church is also built on what was once a Temple of Venus and incorporates a 5th- or 6th-century basilica.

ADRIATIC SEA

Arch of
Hadrian

Arch of
Clementine

LUIGI VANVITELLI

Archaeology
Museum

VIA FERRETTI

Art
Gallery

Ferries to Greece,
Albania, Croatia,
Montenegro & Turkey

Tourist
Info

Santa Maria
della Piazza

San Francesco
delle Scale

Stazione
Marittima

Osteria
del Pozzo

Osteria Teatro
Strabacco,
250m

CORSO G GARIBALDI

VIA LUIGI EINAUDI

CORSO

Pensione
Centrale

STAMIRA

0   250m

VIA XXIX SETTEMBRE

VIA ENRICO CIALDINI

VIA TORRIONI

TRAILBLAZER

VIA GUGLIELMO MARCONI

VIA GIANBATTISTA PERGOLESI

VIA RAFFAELLO SANZIO

Train
Station

VIA FLAMINIA

Hotel
Dorico

VIA ALCIDE DE GASPERI

CORSO CARLO ALBERTO

Albergo Fiore
Hostel

VIA GIORDANO BRUNO

Ancona

ADRIATIC SEA

Another church of note is **San Francesco delle Scale**, with an amazing Venetian-Gothic doorway.

The chief regional archaeological museum, the **Museo Archeologico Nazionale delle Marche** (Tue-Sun 0830-1930, €3) is housed in a fine Gothic building with frescoed ceilings by Tibaldi. There are also some well-executed Roman sculptures, though some suffered earthquake damage back in the 1970s. The town's **art gallery** is at Via Pizzecolli (Mon 0900-1330, Tue-Sat 0900-1900, Sun 1500-1900, €3) and has work by Titian, Lotto and Crivelli.

PRACTICAL INFORMATION
Orientation
Ferries arrive just below the city's most interesting part, with a large, two-building Stazzione Maritime on the quayside selling tickets to Montenegro, Croatia, Albania and Greece. The railway station is further along the seafront on the No 1 bus route from the port. You can easily walk from the port to look round the old town and so are unlikely to need the city's other local bus services.

Services
The **tourist information office** (☎ 358 991, 🖳 www.marcheturismo. it), 4, Via Thaon de Revel, is open daily, Mon-Fri 0900-1400, 1500-1800, Sat 0900-1300, 1500-1800, Sun 0900-1300.

Ferries   [see p448 for full details]
The ferry companies listed below sell tickets at the Stazzione Maritime; some also sell through the many travel agents in town.

ANEK Lines (☎ 207 2275), Blue Star Ferries (☎ 207 1068), Minoan at the Stazione Marittima (☎ 071 56789) and in Via Astagno (☎ 201 708), and Superfast Ferries (☎ 202 805) all operate services to **Igoumenitsa** and **Patras** in Greece.

There are also Adriatica Lines, Blue Line and Jadrolinija (☎ 207 1465) services to **Split** in Croatia. Other Croatian destinations served by Jadrolinija include **Brbinj**, **Korčula**, **Stari Grad** and **Zadar**. Blue Line has a service to **Hvar Town** between July and September (4 per week).

Adriatica also run weekly ferries to **Bar** in Montenegro and four per week to **Durrës** in Albania. Marmara Lines have a weekly service to **Çeşme** between April and November.

Trains
Ancona station (☎ 42574) on Piazza Rosselli has services to Bari (5 per day, 4hrs), Bologna (6 per day, 2hrs), Bríndisi (3 per day, 5 hrs), Milan (5 per day, 4hrs), Rimini (7 per day, 1 hr) and Rome (5 per day, 3hrs).

Where to stay
Pensione Centrale (☎ 54388), 10, Via Marsala near Corso Stamira. €25/35 sgl/dbl.
Hotel Dorico (☎ 42761), 8, Via Flaminia. Near the train station; €25/45 sgl/dbl.
Albergo Fiore (☎ 43390), 24, Piazza Rosselli. Next to the train station; €25/40 sgl/dbl.

Where to eat
Osteria Teatro Strabacco, 2, Via Oberdan, off Piazza Cavour. Good atmosphere and quality food for €10 a head (closed Mon).
Osteria del Pozzo, 2, Via Bondo, off Piazza del Plebiscito. A good seafood place; full meals for €7.

There's also a good market, the **Mercato Publico**, off Corso Mazzini, for DIY meals.

Split

AREA CODE: ☎ 021 **POPULATION:** 210,000
Split is not only the largest city on the Dalmatian coast but also its best connected. For centuries an important city, it was here that the Roman Emperor Diocletian built his celebrated palace-cum-retirement home, a structure that was to stand as pleasure dome, strong room, fortress and architectural inspiration in the centuries to come.

While the modern town has sprawled out around it in most directions, the palace is still the core area of the old town, a place of narrow alleys and evocative passageways breaking into small squares and sudden reminders of the ancient past. The hills around are mainly covered in houses but there are also wooded parks and views out over the long coast of the Adriatic.

HISTORY

The story of Split really began, appropriately enough, with one of Roman history's most famous splitters. Emperor Diocletian picked this spot in AD295 for a palace that would cover seven acres and allow him, so the story goes, to pursue his favourite hobby: growing cabbages. Unfortunately, Diocletian also had a King Lear-like predilection for dividing things up. On his retirement as ruler of an enormous and increasingly unwieldy empire, he ushered in a new era of rule by four, known as the Tetrarchy. The results were disastrous, with a four-way civil war breaking out that reduced Diocletian to suicide.

The palace, thanks largely to its remote location some distance from the nearest large settlement, the city of Salona (now known as Solin), survived both his death and the war that raged through the empire. In 614, though, the Avars sacked Salona and the surviving inhabitants fled, first to the neighbouring islands and then later back to the coast. The old, overgrown palace seemed an excellent place for a base, its high defensive walls and harbour making a better protected settlement than their previous one at Salona. By 812, the new city was a major port in Byzantium's Adriatic possessions.

As such, it began to attract its share of predators. In 998 the Venetians attacked, followed by the Croats in 1069. In 1105 the city was held under the authority of the combined Hungarian-Croatian kingdom, fighting with its rival, the nearby port of Trogir. However, in 1420 the Venetians returned in greater strength, took over once more and stayed for the next 370 years, when the whole of Dalmatia passed to Austria. The French under Napoleon ran the port from 1805 to 1813, before they in turn handed it back to the Austrians. They stayed for a century, before yielding control to Yugoslavia at the end of WWI. The port really took off when the Italians occupied Rijeka

(see p224) in 1924, which had until that time been Yugoslavia's busiest port. In WWII, Split was heavily bombed by the Allies and fought over on the ground by Tito's partisans and Germany's occupying forces.

Post-war rebuilding spread the town along the coast, Split being the fastest-growing town in Yugoslavia during the 1980s. The subsequent break-up of the country and the conflict itself did not cause much physical damage to the place, though it hurt its ability to trade and killed off tourism. Now, however, all that is coming back fast as the harbour picks up business and the tour parties return.

WHAT TO SEE

Signs to **Diocletian's Palace** point you to the row of shops on obala Hrvatskog Narodnog Preporoda, the main northern harbour-front road. However, go up Hrvojeva and you'll see another entrance, through the Silver Gate, next to the market. Entering the palace this way brings you immediately onto what was the east–west road of the palace's basic cross-plan. Through the row of columns to your left you'll also see the **cathedral**, formerly Diocletian's mausoleum (Mon-Sat 0700-1200, 1600-1900, free). This is a fantastically atmospheric place, dark and looming. The emperor's body rested here for some 170 years before its mysterious disappearance. A frieze above its ring of Corinthian columns depicts Diocletian and his wife. It is perhaps a good place to ponder the irony that such a persecutor of Christians as Diocletian should end with his very tomb a church. The point is rammed home by a figure of St Anastasius above the brilliantly executed altar named after him. The saint is shown with a millstone round his neck, the method employed by Diocletian's executioners when they threw the hapless martyr into the sea. It is also a good place to get an idea of the continuity between pagan and Christian forms, with much religious architecture clearly staying the same through the centuries, regardless of the god or gods being worshipped.

Outside, dividing the eastern and western wings of the palace, is the **peristyle**,

ADRIATIC SEA

with a **Temple of Jupiter** on the other side. As the baptistry of the cathedral it is often now shut, but the frequency of tour groups usually means it is easy enough to wander in amongst the crowd. On the ceiling you'll see Hercules and Apollo still in evidence, despite its more recent uses. The font is 11th century and supposedly shows a loyal subject bowing before a Croatian king.

South of the peristyle, the vestibule leads through the empty rooms of the palace before going underground into the central hall. Follow this through and you pass various exhibitions, often for industrial and commercial fairs, with the emperor's rooms on the left and right. At the end you come to the Brass Gate: the harbour-side entrance. Here, double back and head north, past the cathedral and right on Papaliceva for the **City Museum** (June-Sept, Tue-Fri 0900-1200, 1700-2000, Sat-Sun 1000-1200; Oct-May, Tue-Fri 0900-1400, Sat-Sun 1000-1200, Kn20). This has a good collection of mainly medieval relics, including weaponry and historical displays.

Now continue northwards to the **Gold Gate**, the best preserved and, when it was first constructed, most impressive of the gates. Through it you can turn to see an unusually clear view of the palace walls stretching off, and there is the satisfyingly wizard-like **Statue of Bishop Grgur Ninski** (Gregorius of Nin). He it was who harangued the Church of Rome to let the Catholic liturgy be said in Croat, making him an important nationalist figurehead. Now, though, he's better known for his big toe. Rubbed shiny by years of penitential fondling, touching this digit while making a wish has reportedly impressive results.

Opposite here, on the other side of Kralja Tomislava, is the site of the once impressive Museum of the Revolution, now the base for some import-export companies of unknown pedigree (Marshal Tito must be turning in his grave). Now go west, following the wall. The municipal authorities have done well in preserving various ancient relics along the way here, all marked with clear explanatory panels. **Split Archaeology Museum**, 25, Zrinsko Frankopanska, (June-Sept, Tue-Fri 0900-1300, 1700-2000, Sat-Sun 1000-1200; Oct-May, Tue-Fri 0900-1400, Sat-Sun 1000-1300, Kn20) is some 15-20 minutes' walk north-west of the bishop's statue. This contains an impressively thorough collection of artefacts recovered from the nearby Roman site of Salona, along with Greek and Illyrian items. The courtyard outside also has a good collection of gravestones, stellae and sarcophagi. Of the latter, the 4th-century Good Shepherd sarcophagus is particularly interesting, blending the Christian motif of the shepherd with the Greek gods, Eros and Hades, at either end.

If you liked the bishop's statue, the **Meštrovic Museum**, 46, Ivana Meštrovica,

Salona (Solin)

The ruins of ancient Salona (now called Solin) lie only a few kilometres to the north-west, on the Trogir road; catch the half-hourly No 1 bus from Republike trg (15 mins).

The bus puts you down at the Snack Bar Salona, from where a track takes you into the site, now an archaeological reserve (daily 0800-1500) ringed by motorways. The first thing you come across is the Manastirine, once a burial ground for Christians killed in the frequent purges initiated by emperors such as Diocletian. Salona was in its day the most important city on the coast and the capital of the Roman province of Dalmatia. It kept going until AD614 when it was sacked by the Avars and the survivors fled to what is now Split.

Next to the Manastirine is the Tusculum Museum, south of which is the city wall. On the other side are the ruins of a 5th-century cathedral, baptistry and public baths. Follow the walls westwards for the site's most impressive ruin, the 2nd-century amphitheatre.

ADRIATIC SEA

(Tue-Sat 1000-1600, Sun 1000-1400, Kn20) is a must. It is about 20 minutes' walk from the city centre (or bus No 12 from the waterfront heading west). Meştrovic was born in 1883 and died in 1962, the bishop's statue being one of his grander works. The museum does him proud, with many of his smaller statues on display; while his former workshop, 300m up the road, has a wonderful wood-carved interpretation of the Stations of the Cross, one of his most significant works.

For those who've had enough of museums and monuments, the nearest **beaches** are at Bačvice, five minutes' walk south of the railway station, or at Bene, reached by bus No 12 from the harbour front or on foot. The latter is a rocky, cove-like affair on the north side of the Marjan Peninsula, west of town.

This wooded and lightly inhabited area is also worth a walk over in its own right for its views, as well as a number of other, smaller swimming areas.

PRACTICAL INFORMATION
Orientation
Ferries from Italy dock at the eastern side of the harbour, where the main terminal is located. Here you'll find ticket offices for other ferries and the main bus station on the harbour-front road, obala Kneza Domagoja (the railway station is just behind the bus station). Head north up this road, along the harbour side, and you'll come to the old town and Diocletian's palace, the two completely interwoven.

The old town area is built on the grid pattern of Diocletian's palace, which in turn is based on the grid of a Roman army camp. North of this is Kralja Tomislava street and a small park, with roads off into the modern town. Wandering around within the walls of the old town is very pleasant.

Services
The **tourist information office** (☎ 355 088, 🖳 www.visitsplit.com), on the northern waterfront at 12, obala Narodnog Preporoda, is open July-Sept Mon-Fri 0730-2100, Sat 0800-2000, Sun 0800-1300; Oct-Jun Mon-Fri 0730-2000, Sat 0800-1400.

Staff will help with finding accommodation. There is also an office on Peristyle.

Internet Games and Books on obala Kneza Domagoja, north of the train station, offers **internet access**. The **banks** here open early, around 0830, and will change money. The railway station has a **left-luggage** office.

Try website 🖳 www.visitsplit.com for details of the **festivals** here. From mid-July to mid-August the city usually has a festival of opera, drama and ballet.

Ferries   [see p452 for full details]
The main place for ferry tickets and schedules has to be the ferry terminal, where there is a large Jadrolinija office (☎ 355 673), and Adriatica services.

Adriatica, Blue Line and Jadrolinija have services to **Ancona** (Italy).

Jadrolinija also has regular services south to **Dubrovnik** and **Bari** (Italy) via **Stari Grad**, **Korčula** and **Sobra**. The service north goes to **Rijeka** and to **Zadar**.

Local companies operate to **Supetar** on Brač, **Hvar Town** (Hvar) and to other islands along the coast; ask at the ferry terminal or tourist information office.

Trains
Split is on the main Zagreb line with two trains a day (9 hours, Kn110). There are also two a day to Sibenik (2 hours, Kn30).

Buses
There are 16 buses a day to Dubrovnik (4½ hours, Kn110), buses every 30 minutes to Zadar (4 hours, Kn80), 12 a day to Rijeka (8 hours, Kn120), three a day to Pula (10 hours), one a day to Rovinj (13 hours) and **Korčula** (5 hours), and every hour to Zagreb (8 hours, Kn140). All buses depart from the bus station on obala Lazareta.

Planes
Split Airport is 16km west of town but connected by bus from the stop at 3, obala Lazareta, right in the harbour. Buses leave 90 minutes before Croatian Airlines flight times and cost Kn30. There are four flights a day to Zagreb, as well as many package flights to the UK.

ADRIATIC SEA

Where to stay

Once again, expect to be met at the bus/train/ferry stop by landladies bearing private room deals; aim for Kn80 a night and try and get them to show you where the room is on a map before heading off as you may find their idea of a 10-minute walk from the city centre is not yours.

Hotel Slavija (☎ 347 053), 3, Buvinova in the old town. Reasonable rooms for Kn150/250 sgl/dbl.

Hotel Bellevue (☎ 585 655), 2, Bana Jelačića, west of town. Kn200/300 sgl/dbl.

Autocamp Trstenik (☎ 521 971), 5km east of the centre on the No 17 bus route from the market.

Where to eat

Konoba Varo, behind Hotel Bellevue. Good local dishes.

Galija, 2, Matosica. A good pizzeria on the western edge of town.

Sarajevo, 6, Domaldova. Good local cuisine with hearty offerings.

For **bars**, the old town has plenty to offer, with *Bačvice* the place for a dance.

Dubrovnik

AREA CODE: ☎ 020 POPULATION: 40,125

With its old town still walled and magnificent on its coastal headland, Dubrovnik is clearly an important venue on the Adriatic coast, if not on the Med in general. Restored since bombardment by Serbian guns during the bitter war over Bosnia in the mid-1990s, it is also central for other Dalmatian destinations and for nearby Mostar and Sarajevo in Bosnia. The coast on either side of Dubrovnik is some of the finest around, with a gorgeous range of islands and beaches running north to Split and south to Bar. Communications are good, the people generally friendly and food's pretty tasty too.

HISTORY

The name Dubrovnik comes from the Serbo-Croatian word for 'grove', a reference to the forested hills around. It was known as Ragusa until 1918 and records of it date back to the 7th century when Roman refugees fleeing the Slav and Ava sack of Epidaurus set up the Latinate town on a small island separated from the mainland settlement on the opposite bank, a town that was later developed by the Slavs. This symbiotic uniting of Slav and Roman culture brought about the unique character of the town and affected its whole history.

With the fall of the Roman Empire, the city, although nominally under Byzantine control from the 9th to the 12th centuries, was relatively independent until Venice took it on in 1205. Even then the people managed to exercise considerable freedom of action, thanks not only to their excellent strategic location at the head of many land routes through the Balkans but also to their seafaring ability.

By the 15th century they were powerful and rich enough to sign a treaty with the Ottomans, by then the rulers of most of south-eastern Europe. In return for a huge tribute they achieved virtual independence. Such was the flourishing of the arts from the 15th to the 17th centuries that Ragusa was called the 'Athens of the south Slavs' while her traders were known as far off as India and the Americas.

In 1667 a major earthquake devastated the city, killing around 20% of the population. Trade revived a little during the Napoleonic Wars, when Ragusa was the only neutral port on the Dalmatian coast, but instead of reverting to a city state it became part of the Austrian Empire at the 1815 Congress of Vienna.

After WWI Ragusa, now Dubrovnik, became part of the new kingdom of Yugoslavia. As such it was occupied by Italian and German troops in WWII, then continued as a major port and later a tourist attraction in Tito's socialist Yugoslavia. In 1991 the Croat majority of the Dalmatian coastal population set up an independent republic, Dubrovnik becoming part of it. Consequently, the Serb-controlled Yugoslav navy shelled and blockaded the port. Thankfully it is fully rebuilt now and regaining its place as a major Mediterranean tourist venue.

WHAT TO SEE

Going through the angular 15th-century **Pile Gate** in the old town, you pass the **statue of St Blaise** then continue straight down the main road, Stradun, or Placa. Until 1272, this was the channel that divided the Latin island of Ragusa from the Slavic coastal settlement of Dubrovnik. Right in front is **Onofrio's Fountain**, built in 1444 as a kind of disinfectant tank to wash down new arrivals in the city and protect against the plague and lice. You're also likely to see a good number of nuns here as **St Clare's convent** is to the right of the fountain. Built at the end of the 13th century, in 1434 one of the wings was turned into one of the world's first orphanages. Later, Napoleon's troops used it as an arsenal and stables. To the left, the 1520 **Church of St Saviour** was built in thanksgiving for the city surviving an earthquake in the same year; the church also survived the devastating 1667 tremor, unlike much of the town. Behind it is the 14th-century **Franciscan monastery** (daily 0900-1600, free except for the treasury, Kn4), which contains items from a 1317 apothecary collection, claimed to be the oldest in Europe, and many priceless medieval manuscripts in its fine library.

Walking north from here you'll come to the **Minceta Fortress**, the north-western corner tower of the city's defences. Dubrovnik's city walls are some of the most impressive medieval fortifications anywhere; you can walk along them from an entrance on this northern stretch next to the **Church of St Spasa** (daily 0900-1400, Kn10). The walls were built between the 8th and 16th centuries and run for nearly two kilometres, encompassing five bastions, three round and 12 square towers.

Returning to the Stradun and continuing east you'll pass rows of wonderful Renaissance buildings – and flocks of pigeons – before finally arriving in Luza Square, at the street's eastern end by the old harbour. Just before this, on the left, is the synagogue at 5, ulica Žudioska (Tue 1700-1900, Fri 1000-1200, free). To the north of the square is the 1522 **Sponza Palace**, the former Ragusan mint, which now houses the **city archives** (daily 0800-1500, free); some-times there are exhibitions in the courtyard.

Keeping left here you come to the Gothic-Renaissance **Dominican monastery**. The displays in the small museum (daily 0900-1700, Kn10) are mostly of 15th- and 16th-century religious art.

Incorporated into Ploce Gate, the north-eastern exit, is the imposing 16th-century **Revelin Fortress**. Built to ward off a feared Venetian attack, it played a role as both harbour defence and landward kingpin in the city's fortifications.

South of Luza Square, along Priodvorum, you pass the baroque (1714) **Church of St Blaise** on the right, outside of which is **Orlando's Column** (built in 1419). This statue of a knight was used as a rallying point for the city in times of trouble, as a place of execution, and also as a unit of measurement (Orlando's arm being the length of the Ragusan cubit). St Blaise (Sv Vlaho) is the city's patron saint, who saved the city by giving warning of an impending Venetian attack.

Opposite the church is the City Hall, and next to that the **Rector's Palace** (1441). This was the office of the city government in the old days, the rector being elected leader for a monthly term. By a quirk of the Ragusan constitution, he was forbidden to leave the palace unless the city senate gave its permission. Perhaps this explains why its interior is so splendid, with a massive staircase leading up to his old apartments. These apartments, now the **City Museum** (daily, 0900-1800, Kn15), hold a collection of work by Dalmatian artists from the 15th to the 17th centuries.

At the end of the street, the city's main **cathedral** contains a number of interesting artworks plus the skull of St Blaise. A Titian polyptich, *The Assumption*, is a high point, while in the **treasury** (daily 0900-2000, Kn5) St Blaise's head is enshrined in a gold and enamel filigree reliquary. The cathedral was originally built with a cash gift from England's Richard the Lionheart in gratitude to the city which had allowed him asylum following the 11th-century Crusade.

Head east from here, alongside the southern end of the harbour, and you come to the **Fort of St John**, also known as the

ADRIATIC SEA

Dubrovnik

Ferries to Bari,
Split, Zadar, Ortona &
Dalmatian Islands

Ferry
Station

Hotel
Petka

Gruz Harbour

GRUSKA OBALA

Airport,
20km

JADRANSKA MAGISTRALA

Camping
Solitude

Begovic
Boarding
House

Bus
Station

Post
Office

ANTE STARCEVICA

Pile
Gate

OLD
TOWN

Hotel
Lero

HI
Hostel

LAPAD
PENINSULA

Hotel
Zagreb

TRAILBLAZER

ADRIATIC

0   0.5   1km

Dubrovnik Old Town

Minceta
Fortress

Franciscan
Monastery

Revelin
Fortress

Pile
Gate

St Saviour
Church
(Church of
Sv. Spasa)

PRI JEKO

Ploce
Gate

Dominican
Monastery

UDILICA

Onofrio's
Fountain

Tourist
Info

STRADUN / PLACA

Synagogue

Sponza
Palace

ADRIATIC

SIROKA ULICA

Baracuda

Harbour

St Clare's
Convent

Luza
Square

St Blaise
statue

Ferries to
Lokrum
Island

House of
Marin Drzic

St Blaise
Church

City
Hall

PRIODVORUM

ULICA STROSMAJEROVA

Gunduliceva
Poljana
(fruit & veg market)

Rector's Palace/
City Museum

Kamenica

ULICA OD MARGARITE

Mirage

Fort of St John/
Fortress of St Ivan/
Maritime Museum

St Ignatius
Church

Cathedral

TRAILBLAZER

ADRIATIC SEA

0   100m

ADRIATIC

Fortress of St Ivan, containing the **maritime museum** (daily, summer 0900-1800, winter 0900-1300, Kn15) and the **aquarium** (daily, summer 0900-2100, winter 0900-1300, Kn15). The former has some good displays on the city's rich naval history and the latter a diversity of sea creatures, including a fine octopus.

In this southern section of the city, some of the streets rise steeply by means of stepped passages, leading into the maze of closely-built houses. The 1725 **Church of St Ignatius**, on ul Strosmajerova, is a Jesuit building; the steps in front are modelled on Rome's Spanish Steps. The street leads to the site of the weekly fruit and vegetable market in Gundulićeva Poljana. Further on is the **House of Marin Drzic** (daily 0900-1400), a playwright and writer who was a great name in the European Renaissance. The museum employs sound and video to tell his story.

PRACTICAL INFORMATION
Orientation
The city divides into two parts: the dramatically picturesque old walled town, Stari Grad, with its massive defensive bastions, and the newer town that spreads out a considerable distance to the north-west. Unfortunately, the bus station and the ferry port are in the new town, around 3km from the old and the port's on the other side of the Lapad Peninsula, so arriving by ferry can be a little disappointing.

Keep going. From the ferry port, in Gruz harbour, it's a ten-minute walk south-east to the bus station, where frequent buses head for the old town, a kilometre further on. Alternatively, get the No 1 or 3 bus which heads along the main coast road, Grunška obala, from the port. Old town buses stop in the square outside the walls, which you enter through Pile Gate.

The airport is 20km south of the city and the only service buses are those that meet Croatian Airlines' flights. They also take you to the main bus station.

Since cars are not allowed in the old town getting around is done on foot. It is a real pleasure walking among this labyrinth of old medieval houses but it can be a bit of a slog as the streets run up some pretty steep hills; in summer, be sure to take some water.

Services
Staff at a privately-run **tourist information** agency (☎ 426 354, daily 0900-2000), just inside Pile Gate, supply maps for free and will book accommodation, including private rooms. The Dubrovnik *Riviera* magazine has a good amount of information on local ferry and bus times as well as on hotels, restaurants and bars. Pick it up at the above office or in the larger hotels.

The main **post office**, 28, Put Republike, is open Mon-Fri 0800-2000, Sat 0800-1900, Sun 0800-1200. **Phones** are at the same location. **Internet Centar**, 1, Brsalje, is open 0800-midnight.

The bus station is happy to provide **left-luggage** facilities between 0450 and 2100.

Between July and August, the **city festival** (☎ 412 288, 🖳 www. dubrovnik-festival.hr) has a packed programme of music and theatre.

Ferries   [see p450 for full details]
Jadrolinija (☎ 418 000, 40, obala S Radića) run ferries once a week from October to May and five times a week from the beginning of June to end of September to **Bari** in Italy. Adriatic Shipping Company offers a similar but slightly less regular service and also runs twice weekly ferries in the summer months to **Ortona** (Italy).

There are also ferries to many of the islands off the coast; just turn up at the port and hop on the next service. There are daily boats to **Sobra**, on Mljet, **Sugcuraj** on Hvar, **Sipanska Luka** on Sipan and **Kolocep**. There are also regular Jadrolinija services to **Korčula**, **Stari Grad** on Hvar, **Split**, **Zadar** and **Rijeka**. The bus is faster, but this is certainly a better way to see the coast and also more comfortable.

Buses
From Dubrovnik bus station (☎ 357088) there is a three-times-a-week Aurotrans coach service to Sarajevo in Bosnia (4½ hours, Kn200). The bus also goes via Mostar. There's also one a day to Podgorica in Montenegro. Check at the bus station or

ADRIATIC SEA

tourist information on this, as schedules and prices vary.

There are also 16 buses a day to Split (4$\frac{1}{2}$ hours, Kn120), nine to Zadar (5$\frac{1}{2}$ hours, Kn150), seven a day to Zagreb (11 hours, Kn200), and three a day to Rijeka (10 hours). Buses heading north-west along the coast slip through a thin strip of Bosnian territory around the largely moribund port of Neum. There is usually no passport control, however, unless you are heading from here inland to Mostar or Sarajevo. The road narrows thanks to a makeshift roadblock, but otherwise the coach enters and leaves without stopping.

Planes
Dubrovnik airport (known as Cilipi International) is some 24km out of town. From the Croatian Airlines office (☎ 413 777), 9 Brsalje, next to the Pile Gate, a coach connects with Croatian Airlines flights, costing Kn20. A taxi would be about Kn150.

Where to stay
On arrival at the bus station or ferry stop, you're likely to be set upon by some of Dubrovnik's most fearsome residents — the small army of old ladies offering private rooms. These can be bargains, though most likely they will be some distance away from the old town. Do ask how far, though be prepared for the reply to be 'just 10 minutes', even if it's closer to Split than the *stari grad*. The price is usually around Kn50-80 a night per person, though bargaining is advised.
YHA Hostel (☎ 423 241), 15/17, Bana Jelačića. Official HI hostel; bunks: Kn100.
Hotel Petka (☎ 418 008), 38, obala Stjepan Radića. Opposite the ferry docks; Kn300/450 sgl/dbl.
Hotel Zagreb (☎ 436 146), 27, Setaliste Kralja Zvonimara at the city's Lapad Beach, 5km west of Pile Gate, near a number of package hotels; Kn300/500 sgl/dbl.
Begović Boarding House (☎ 435 191), 17, Primorska. Again in Lapad; a few rooms at Kn100/200 sgl/dbl. Popular, so phone ahead.
Hotel Lero (☎ 411455), 14, Iva Vojnovića. Kn280/450 sgl/dbl.
Camping Solitude (☎ 448 166) Vatioslava,

on the Lapad Peninsula; take No 6 bus from the bus station. Kn40 a pitch, depending on season, plus Kn30 per person.

Where to eat
There is no real shortage of places to eat in the old town, though late arrivals at the ferry port or bus station may have their options reduced. Try next to the municipal market on Grunška obala for a couple of unnamed restaurants that stay open until midnight. Generally speaking, Croatia is not an open-all-hours culture, with people rising early and going to bed correspondingly so. Nonetheless, in the old town, try *Baracuda*, a pizzeria on Bozidareviveca (Kn50 a head), or *Kamenica*, 8, Gundulićeva Poljana, for good local fish dishes.

As for bars, the back-streets off Stradun are best. *Mirage*, Buniceva Poljana, is a student hang-out.

Sarajevo

AREA CODE: ☎ 033 **POPULATION:** 350,000
Something of a by-word for violence, tragedy and bitter ethnic rivalry for much of the 1990s, Sarajevo usually comes as a pleasant surprise to those who visit it today. While much damage remains — not least in the psychological pain caused by years of warfare — much has been done to repair things, and a stroll these days down the once notorious Snipers' Alley is more reminiscent of Budapest or Prague than of a war zone. The Sarajevans, always a resilient bunch, are also keen to stress that they are open for business — and thus tourists get a generally warm welcome.

The city is also quite remarkable. Set in a long river valley, the Miljacka, with hills on either side, it is the Balkans' essential crossroads, with mosques and churches clustering the slopes and a mix of architectures that can take you to İstanbul, Vienna or maybe even Moscow in the blink of an eye.

It's also not a divided city. Unlike Nicosia or Beirut, when travelling through the town it is hard to tell sometimes where the ethnic boundaries lie. There are also no roadblocks or soldiers guarding the entrances to districts, and the tram happily trundles from Muslim to Christian areas, from Bosniak to Croat to Serb.

Yet a lot still remains to be done here, and travellers should still be sensitive to the problems and the continuing pain many of the inhabitants still suffer. Many of the areas you pass through on your way here from Dubrovnik — now largely Croat — have been ethnically cleansed, with the problem of returning people to their old homes still a major issue. The countryside also suffers from mines, thousands of which were laid during the war, so travellers are well advised to curtail any desire to hike around.

HISTORY

While this area has been inhabited since neolithic times, it was the Romans who where the first recorded settlers here — at nearby Ilidza, where there are sulphurous spa waters. Later the Goths, then the Slavs, moved in and first developed the city — the latter arriving in about the 7th century. For them, Sarajevo was Vrhbosna, which is how it stayed until the late Middle Ages when the Ottomans arrived, taking the area during the 15th century.

From early on the place was a mix of peoples and styles. Merchants from Dubrovnik built the heavily Latinized Latinluk quarter, while Sephardic Jews built the Cifuthani district. Meanwhile, the Ottomans, who knew this place — and in Turkey still do — as Saraybosna, built a number of mosques, karavansarays and other prestigious buildings as the city grew. This was largely thanks to its position on caravan routes up from İstanbul to the empire's frontiers along the Danube.

When the Ottomans' power started to wane, however, Sarajevo also suffered. In 1697 Prince Eugene of Savoy burnt the place down as his victorious armies pursued the Ottomans south, and this was followed by several bad outbreaks of the plague. Regained by the Ottomans, they then made it the capital of Bosnia-Herzegovina in 1850. However, thanks to some clever diplomatic footwork by the Austro-Hungarians,

in 1878 their army marched in, sowing the seeds for the world war to follow.

Under rule from Vienna, the city became something of a hot bed for Serbian nationalist groups who wanted the Austrians out and for Bosnia to become part of a greater Serbia. One of their number, Gavrilo Princip, then fired the fatal shot in August 1914 that sparked WWI. He assassinated the Archduke Ferdinand of Austria and his wife while they were on an ill-judged drive about in the city's streets. This provoked an Austrian attack on Serbia, which was allied to Russia, thus compelling the Russians to declare war on Austro-Hungaria. Germany, however, was committed to come to Austria's aid in such an eventuality and so it declared war on Russia. Bizarrely thinking this too good a chance to miss, Imperial Germany then also invaded the low countries, bringing Britain and France into the conflict. Within a few months, a war that was to see the deaths of millions of people had begun.

One might have thought, given the catastrophic scale of the carnage that followed, that the assassination would have been something the Serbs would have wanted to pass over hurriedly — but not so. Until the recent fighting, the imprints of Princip's feet at the place where he had fired the fatal shots were preserved as something of a shrine, next to what was then named the Princip Bridge. Nowadays, thankfully, this has been removed, as shrines to Serbian nationalism have become even more misplaced.

At the end of WWI, the city was the venue for the Diet of Sarajevo, which proclaimed union with the new kingdom of Yugoslavia. In WWII, the city was occupied by German troops and was the scene of some fierce battles with resistance fighters. The latter was led by the communist partisans of Marshal Tito, and the fighting here was as bitter as elsewhere in the country.

In Tito's Yugoslavia Sarajevo had considerable importance, with the surrounding mountains being the setting for the 1984 Winter Olympics. Yet with the collapse of the country, and the declaration of independence by Bosnia-Herzegovina in 1992, the city became a battlefield. While the

ADRIATIC SEA

majority of the inhabitants were Bosniak (Slavic, mainly Muslims) and in favour of independence, the large Serb population (Slavic Orthodox) was against such an idea. Backed up by the largely Serb Yugoslav National Army, they laid siege to the city for three and a half years. The fighting did not finish until the Dayton Peace Agreement in December 1995.

Now, a fragile balance has been restored. The new Bosnian republic is divided into a Serb republic in the north around Banja Luka, and a Bosnian-Croat Federation in the south and centre. Certain Bosnian Croat (Slavic Catholic) nationalist groups initially pushed for a break up of this new entity, as did various Serb nationalist groups, yet so far their efforts have proved unsuccessful. The country is also largely now under international control. The Office of the High Representative (OHR) in Sarajevo, backed up by the troops of the Stabilization Force (SFOR), is attempting to stick the political and social structure back together again, and has had some success in doing so — using a combination of stick and carrot. Yet the future remains unclear for this beautiful but fractured country, as it does for this most resilient of cities.

WHAT TO SEE

With most of the city's museums closed since the fighting started, Sarajevo is lacking traditional tourist sightseeing venues. Many of the fine buildings on the river are still boarded up and show war damage. One museum that is open, however, is the **Sarajevo Tunnel**, out under the airport (daily, 0900-1700, KM4). This was the city's lifeline during the siege as Bosniak forces occupied the areas either side of the airport, while Serb guns had the airstrip itself covered. Through this route supplies could be brought in and the wounded evacuated.

In the old town, a walk along the north side of the river brings you to the now-unnamed Princip Bridge and the empty Museum of the Assassination on the corner of Zelenih Beretki and obala Kulina Bana. On the other side is the Emperor Mosque,

built in 1566, while back over the river is the Old Town Hall, built in 1892. Behind this is the Bascarsija district — the Ottoman market area. Here you'll find the usual maze of stalls and a fine mosque, the **Gazi Husrev Bey**, dating from 1531. The tomb — or *turbe* — of the bey is in the courtyard, while outside is a fine clocktower, built to herald the times of prayers. Opposite this is the Kursumlija Medressa, built as part of the mosque complex.

The Serbian Orthodox cathedral is on Mula Mustafe Bašeskije, the eastern end of Marshal Tita — the city's main road to the west. Beyond the Holiday Inn, this was known as Snipers' Alley during the siege, an open, inviting target for Serbian positions across the river. Head for Ferhadija, the pedestrianized street that runs parallel to it and contains many of the city's new cafés and restaurants. The contrast is impressive.

PRACTICAL INFORMATION
Orientation

The city is basically a long ribbon of buildings along the generally straight course of the river into the mountains. At the western end of the ribbon is the airport and the suburb of Dobrinja, while most of the sights are at the eastern end in the old town, *stari grad*.

The bus station is up the eastern end, on the northern bank of the river next to the train station. Public transport is cheap and very good with trolleybuses running most routes until late at night. Buy tickets from kiosks next to the main stops: there's a flat rate of KM0.50 to go anywhere. However, **remember to frank your ticket** in one of the clippers on board the buses as there are frequent inspections and the fine is KM30. Note, too, that getting around the main tourist areas is easily done on foot.

Services

The **tourist office** (☎ 532606), 22a, Zelenih Beretki, is an absolute lifesaver. It has maps, advice on the latest travel developments and a handy pocket-sized listings mag of events in town.

The **post office**, on the corner of Ferhadija and Cemalusa, is open from 0900

ADRIATIC SEA

to 2000 and sometimes beyond. It sells phone cards and stamps, the **phones** being right outside.

Sarajevo's **banks** also open late, with the Volksbank and Turk Ziyaret Bank on Ferhadija open 0900-2000. Under the Dayton System the Bosnian currency was reissued as the Konvertabilni Mark, with one KM equivalent to the German Mark. Now it has parity with the euro. This means that you can use euros in shops but for some reason you can't at the post office. All the banks have exchange offices, however, while there are also plenty of ATMs connected to the main international systems.

Several shops around the Oslobodenja trg, along Ferhadija, provide **internet access**. There are many **bookstores** on Marshal Tita, along its old town stretch, and most have a few English-language tomes, including several on the siege and conflict.

Trains
Services are again irregular; check with the tourist information office or at the station.

Buses
Sarajevo is connected to Dubrovnik by bus three times a week (4½ hours, KM90). There are buses three times a day to Mostar (1 hour, KM4). Other bus services are subject to frequent timetable changes. Check with the tourist office or at the station.

Planes
The airport is on the No 31 and No 36 trolleybus routes. A taxi to the old town would be around KM20. Turkish Airlines fly three times a week to İstanbul (1 hour, KM300), while Bosnian Airlines fly to a variety of European destinations.

Where to stay
By far the best way to stay in Sarajevo is to take up the offer of **a room** from one of the landladies who greet you on arrival at the bus station. The tourist office can also sort something out for you. The price is usually around KM20 a night per person.

Otherwise, **hotel accommodation** can be expensive as you are relying largely on international hotels, with the vast numbers of international civil servants in town (for SFOR, OHR, UN, NATO, ICRC etc etc) keeping prices artificially high.

Where to eat
Ferhadija is the place to head for, with plenty of restaurants along here serving good quality scoffs for around KM20 a head. Street snacks include hot dogs and crêpes, along with boreks (cheese- or meat-filled pastries) around the Bascarsija.

The Dalmatian coast

North-west of Dubrovnik, a string of attractive islands fringes the coast as far as Split and beyond. Connected by ferry, they can provide an island-hopping holiday in themselves. Alternatively, if time is short, just catching the Split–Dubrovnik ferry can be a memorable experience.

What is also remarkable about the islands is their variety of forms, while their towns and villages — often still walled — are more reminiscent of the Italian side of this coast than the Balkans beyond.

HISTORY
The word Dalmatia probably comes from an Illyrian tribe called the Delmata who lived along this coast around 1000BC. Greek colonists then started arriving in the 4th century BC, setting up trading posts on Issa (Vis), Pharos (Hvar), and Corcyra Melaina (Korčula). They also set up shop at Salona (Solin) near Split (see p230). In conflict with the Illyrians, the Greeks eventually brought the Romans in, with a series of wars ending in Roman victory in AD155. With the fall of the Western Empire, the coast then became a battleground for control between the Byzantines and the Goths. They were not alone though, and by the time the Venetians finally established control in 1420 by defeating the Croats, the region had made its way into the medieval book of records by changing hands some 30 times.

ADRIATIC SEA

The Venetians stayed until 1797, for most of that time alternating between conflict and compromise with both their Ottoman neighbours inland and their Croat subjects on the coast. Napoleon's destruction of the Venetian republic resulted in Austrian control of the coast, a situation which continued until 1918 and the post-WWI dismemberment of the Hapsburg Empire. In WWII the islands were occupied by the Italians, then returned to Yugoslavia on the former's defeat. In 1947 they were made part of the Croat Federal Republic, becoming one of socialist Yugoslavia's premier tourist destinations during the 1980s.

On Yugoslavia's dissolution, Dalmatia passed to Croatia proper. In the fighting that followed, some of the islands were shelled, though the conflict was less intense here than elsewhere. The tourism industry is now gradually reviving, unsurprising given the good infrastructure and, above all, the beauty of one of the Med's best coastal strips.

MLJET, LOPUD AND SIPAN
AREA CODE: ☎ 020
What to see
Known as the Elaphites, this group of islands is remarkably free from tourists, despite its proximity to Dubrovnik. All are on regular ferry routes too, with a laid-back atmosphere, pine-covered land and crystal-clear waters lapping mainly rocky beaches.

Lopud (pop: 348) was once the seat of the vice-rector of Dubrovnik and before him a holiday retreat for various wealthy Romans. With only one small settlement on the landward side, it takes all of 20 minutes to walk across, the far side possessing a long, rocky beach. The settlement itself has a strip of imported sand at the front of an old hotel, with a post office and a few shops to its right. Further on, reminders of Yugoslavia's 1980s' tourism boom abound, with several (now largely empty) concrete hotels.

Sipan (pop: 500), also on a daily ferry route, is larger yet no louder. The main town is Sipanska Luka, located at the end of a long inlet. After that there's not much else to see except lots of pine trees and low hills: definitely another place to get away from it all.

The largest island of the group, **Mljet**, (pop: 1237) is one-third national park. Pine-clad, with two inland salt-water lakes, this was most likely once the island of Melita, on which St Paul ran aground on his way to Italy. He was bitten by a viper, not much of a problem these days since a colony of mongooses was imported to deal with them. As is often the way with such things though, mongoose are now a plague in themselves.

Mljet has several settlements. Boats from Dubrovnik dock at Sobra, at the island's eastern end, though this doesn't amount to much except as a good place to find a private room. The main village is Babino Polje, connected by intermittent buses to Sobra and Pomona, where ferries from Split and Korčula sometimes dock. The main business here is day trips, with a typical itinerary taking you to the lake of Veliko Jezero, in the middle of which is an islet with a 12th-century Benedictine monastery on it. A boat will take you out there and it makes a great place for lunch. Swimming in the lake is also refreshing; plus, when the tour parties have gone, you may get the place to yourselves — along with most of the rest of the island. With the forests extending over much of the thin strip of land, it makes a good place for gentle walking and camping too.

Practical information
Orientation All the islands featured here are accessible by regular ferry. Other smaller ones may also be accessed by hunting around local harbours to see what's on offer. In season, tour boats also ply these seas, offering set excursions and operating on a go-when-full basis. As tourism has yet to fully regain its lost ground, this can require some patience. Ferries also tend to go from one island to the next, in a loop, meaning that relatively close islands can take longer to get to than more distant ones. Dubrovnik and Split are the main harbours to set out from.

Ferries　　[see p451 for full details]
See the Dubrovnik section (Appendix p450) for details of ferries to the Dalmatian Islands.

There are also frequent day-trip boats from Dubrovnik and from Korčula, a typical

Dalmatian Coastal Ferries

BOSNIA - HERZEGOVINA

YUGOSLAVIA

CROATIA

Split

Ferries to Zadar, Rijeka

Ferries to Italy

Solta Island

Supetar

Milna

Brac Island

Bol

Sumartin

Stari Grad

Hvar Island

Hvar

Vis Island

Suguraj

Suguraj-Drvenik Ferry

Drvenik

Ploce

Peljesac Peninsula

Sarajevo

Mostar

Ston

Spanska Luka

Sipan Island

Lopud Island

Dubrovnik

Ferries to Italy

Sobra

Mljet

Babino Island

Polje

Polace

Pomena

Orebic

Orebic-Korcula Town Ferry

Korcula Town

Lumbarda

Korcula Island

Vela Luka

Lastovo Island

ADRIATIC SEA

ADRIATIC SEA

50km

25

0

TRAILBLAZER

day out including return fares, lunch and plenty of sunbathing and swimming for around Kn80.

Where to stay On **Lopud** you may get lucky and be offered a private room, probably for around Kn80 a head. Otherwise, you're looking at one of the package holiday venues, which could be pricey. They may also be fully booked in mid-summer, so it may be advisable to see the island as a day trip and push on — or double back — to Dubrovnik. On **Mljet**, the situation is much the same — private rooms are offered for the same prices, or package hotels. **Camping** has more scope, though, with the *Autocamp Sikjerica* just outside Pomena, though camping rough is also very possible.

Where to eat Thankfully, there's little shortage of choices here. On Mljet, try the *restaurant* on the islet, once part of a hotel, which has plans to reopen soon. Expect Kn80 a head for a full meal.

KORČULA

AREA CODE: ☎ 020 POPULATION: 17,038
From the classic medieval walled city of Korčula Town to the wooded slopes of its interior, Korčula was long one of the coast's most popular tourist destinations — a status that seems to be returning rapidly. A long strip of land off the Pelješac Peninsula, it is large enough to accommodate a longer stay and can also act as a base for visiting the other islands. Its southern coast is quieter, though nowhere is exactly loud here, and contains some beautiful coves and isolated beaches. The north side also has its attractions, while the town itself is unmissable.

History

Colonized by the Greeks in the 4th century BC, they knew it as Black Corfu thanks to its dense forests and dark, hilly interior. The Romans came along next, followed by the Goths, Slavs, Byzantines and Genoese and finally the Venetians, who stayed for around 400 years. It is also reputedly the birthplace of the explorer Marco Polo who started life's great journey here in about 1254.

With the Russians, British, French and then Austro-Hungarian forces occupying the place once Venice had lost to Napoleon, it's possible that the Ottomans were the only Mediterranean imperial power not to have run this place at one time or another.

Matters continued in much the same vein after WWI, as the island went to Yugoslavia, then fascist Italy, then Nazi Germany during WWII, before finally being liberated by Tito's communist partisans between 1944 and 1945. Post war it gradually developed a tourism industry in addition to the traditional pursuits of fishing, agriculture and, until recently, wild jackal hunting. All of this was badly damaged by the warfare of the 1990s which ushered in the age of capitalist Croatia. Perhaps as a result of this, things are once again picking up and the island is on the tourism map once more.

What to see

Set on a small headland, Korčula Town seems almost too perfect a Dalmatian town to be true. Built to an expert design to afford shade and cool breezes along its grid of streets, its 16th-century Venetian architects clearly built the place to last.

The town's central square — which is in truth more of a slightly enlarged junction — contains the Cathedral of St Mark, Venice's patron saint. Mainly 16th century, it has various later add-ons but is most remarkable for holding two Tintorettos: *Three Saints* and an *Annunciation*. There is also a display of medieval weaponry, some of which was used in the famous siege of 1571 when the island was attacked by the Algerian king Uliz Ali. The siege was a failure, as a result of which Ali stormed off to butcher everyone on Hvar instead.

Moving on, the **Bishop's Treasury** (summer only, 1000-1200, 1700-2100, never on Sunday; Kn10) in the 14th-century abbey behind the cathedral contains many more artistic offerings of a religious kind, including some Raphael drawings and Carpaccio's *Portrait of a Man*. There's also a carving of Mary Queen of Scots. A Catholic, she was the legitimate heir of Elizabeth I, queen of an increasingly Protestant England.

The **town museum** (Mon-Sat in summer, Mon-Fri in winter, 0900-1200, 1700-2100, Kn10) holds more archaeological stuff including a Greek tablet from the 4th century found at Lumbarda — the primary evidence of them having settled here — and some Roman ceramics. Round the corner is the supposed **House of Marco Polo** (summer only, daily 1000-1300, 1700-1900, Kn10), an old Venetian abode. The case for his hailing from these parts seems to rest mainly on the fact that he was captured by the Genoese off Korčula, thus writing his *Travels* in jail in Genoa. Many Venetian captains and sailors were raised in Dalmatia, so it's not impossible he had some connection here — though there's no evidence for it. Anyway, the house isn't up to much these days, being only a shell — a fate that many of the town's houses suffered after the plague of 1529 when they were deliberately burned out as a way of disinfecting them.

The final sight in town is the **Icon museum** (summer only, Mon-Sat 1000-1300, 1700-1900, Kn5), overlooking the eastern harbour. This is a collection of Cretan holy icons stolen by local sailors after the fall of that island to the Ottomans in the 17th century. A 15th-century triptych of the Passion is the highlight.

Lumbarda/Vela Luka Lumbarda is definitely the place if you're after **beaches**. About 15 minutes out of Korčula Town on the bus, here you'll find two of the island's specialities — the beach of Plaža Pržina and lashings of the local wine, the wonderfully vowel-free Grk.

Right at the western end of the island is the village of Vela Luka, reached by a bus that takes you through the rather uneventful town of Blato, the largest settlement on Korčula. Vela Luka itself isn't much, though it has a beautiful setting with the wooded islet of Osjak, a national park, out in the bay.

Practical information
Orientation Most boats arrive at Korčula town, at the eastern end of the island, right beneath the magnificent walled quarter. However, the car ferry from Orebic on the mainland — but not the passenger ferry —

sets you down at Bon Repos, a couple of kilometres from town. There are then frequent buses from both Bon Repos and Korčula Town down the island's spine-like central road, which runs to Vela Luka at the western end. On the way, there's the town of Lumbarda with its good beach, Plaža Pržina.

Services The **tourist information office** (☎ 715 701), in Korčula Town, opposite the bus station, is open June-Sep, Mon-Sat 0800-2100 and Sun 0800-1500; Oct-May, Mon-Sat 0800-1500.

Ferries   [see p451 for full details]
There is a daily bus/boat service from Dubrovnik to Korčula, the coach boarding the ferry to put you down at Bon Repos, 2km from Korčula town.

Jadrolinija operates a weekly service in the summer months to **Ancona**, **Brbinj**, **Dubrovnik** (4 per week), **Rijeka** (2-3 per week) and **Split** (3 per week). The Jadrolinija office (☎ 715 410) is at Plokata 21 Travnja in Korčula Town.

In summer, there are boat trips around the island and to **neighbouring islets**. Ask at the harbour for details.

Buses There are six buses a day between Korčula Town and Vela Luka (1¹/₂ hours, Kn30), and hourly services to Lumbarda (10 mins, Kn10) except on Sundays, when there are none. Buses go from the station just outside the old town entrance in Korčula Town.

Where to stay Once again, expect to be met with offers of private rooms at the ferry dock, the usual charge being around Kn80 a head. Marco Polo Travel (☎ 715 400), between the bus station and the old town entrance in Korčula Town, organizes rooms too. *Hotel Korčula* (☎ 711 078), on the western harbour, is a local institution at the pricier end but still only around Kn300/400 sgl/dbl. *Hotel Badija* (☎ 711 115), located on the small islet of Badija out in the bay, can be reached by taxi boat from the harbour. Formerly a Franciscan monastery, it offers a bargain at Kn120/200 sgl/dbl.

Campers should try *Autocamp Kalac*

(☎ 711 182), 3km south-east of Korčula Town on the Lumbarda bus route.

Where to eat *Restaurant Grill Planjak*, next to the Jadrolinija office, has plenty of local specialities; expect to pay around €7 for a full meal. *Adio Mare*, round the corner from Marco Polo's house, has legendary offerings, particularly its fish.

HVAR
AREA CODE: ☎ 021 **POPULATION:** 11,459
Rocky Hvar is the longest island in the Adriatic with a splendid Venetian town as its capital and miles of inlets, coves, wooded hills and gorgeous colours that combine to make it a real gem. It also has more sunshine than anywhere else on the Dalmatian coast and regular ferry connections to Dubrovnik, Split and the other surrounding islands. In consequence, it was also one of the coast's most popular tourist destinations during the 1980s' boom, yet the scattering of hotels hasn't really made much of an environmental impact. And while the tourism industry is coming back in leaps and bounds, it's still possible to find plenty of deserted spaces.

History
The first settlement here seems to have been back in neolithic times but it was once again the Greeks who first developed proper towns. In 385BC they founded Dimos (now Hvar town) and Pharos (now Stari Grad). Once again, as with the rest of the coast, the Romans then took over, this time in 219BC. With the fall of the Western Roman Empire the island became Byzantine, but in the 7th century AD was settled by Slavs escaping from the mainland. Other forces then took it in turns to run the place during the Middle Ages, with the Genoans, Hungarians and Ragusans from neighbouring Dubrovnik all having their moment of glory. Eventually, though, it was the Venetians who managed to establish long-term occupancy. Their capital was Stari Grad until 1331, when they moved the administration to Hvar town.

In 1571 the island was sacked by Uliz Ali, the Algerian corsair, and the town was destroyed. It was then rebuilt almost from scratch and stayed as an important staging post for Venetian galleys on their way south to the Aegean and the Levant beyond. With the end of the Venetian republic at the end of the 18th century, ownership once again shifted, with the Austro-Hungarian Empire taking over until its defeat in WWI. After that, Hvar followed the history of the rest of Yugoslavia and, latterly, of Croatia.

What to see
Hvar town is likely to be the place you'll start from. Head north from the Jadrolinija ferry stop along the eastern flank of the harbour toward the main square and you'll quickly find the imposing colonnaded bulk of the Venetian arsenal. This was the town's equivalent of a U-boat pen, housing the doge's warships whenever they needed a refit. The upper part of this building was added later, in 1612, to house **Europe's first municipal theatre** (June-Sept 1000-1200, 2000-2300, Oct-May 1000-1200, Kn10). Rebuilt in the 19th century, it is quite a remarkable place for its baroque interior and cosy design.

From here, head off towards the old town walls that lie strung out amongst the newer surrounding houses. The shell of the Hektorovic Mansion, home of the 15th-century Croat poet Petar Hekterovic, marks the old town entrance. Inside, passing the **Benedictine Convent** on the left, head up the hill to the **Venetian fortress** (June-Sept only, 0800-2000, Kn10). This was state-of-the-art 16th-century defensive technology, built in 1551 to try and keep out the Ottomans, a task it unfortunately failed to perform in 1571. The view from here is spectacular, out over the town and across the water to the neighbouring island of Vis.

The walk up will also have given you a taste of the rambling, close-knit jumble of the old town, which is worth a stroll round in itself. To the west is the town's archaeological museum, housed in the ruins of a Dominican monastery destroyed in the 1571 attack. Regrettably, it's shut, but nevertheless gives a good view of the town. The other monastery worth seeing is the

A D R I A T I C   S E A

Franciscan monastery on the other side of town (Mon-Fri 1000-1200, 1700-1900, Kn10). This 15th-century building holds a number of works by Venetian artists, including a vast *Last Supper* by Matteo Ingoli. On a further ecclesiastical note, the town's 16th-century cathedral is at the head of Sv Stjepana trg, east of the arsenal. The **Bishop's Treasury** here (daily, June-Sept 0900-1200, 1700-1900, Oct-May 1000-1200, Kn10) contains a fine collection of 16th-century religious objects from chalices to embroidery.

Stari Grad also has an old town (indeed, 'stari grad means 'old town' though it now refers to a much larger area than the original town) worth wandering about in, though apart from another house of Petar Hektorovic, it doesn't have much of a tourist trail except from the ferry stop to the bus. The poet's house *is* a fine affair, though, complete with fishpond, while the town's surroundings are pleasant too.

Practical information

Orientation The island is basically a long, thin dash of rock, with Hvar town at the western end, Stari Grad on the north-western and the village of Sugcuraj on the eastern. The ferry stop is right in the heart of Hvar Town, with the Split–Stari Grad and Drvenik–Sugcuraj ferries similarly dropping you in the heart of things. Connecting the three are buses that come out to meet the arriving ferries. Hvar Town and Stari Grad are both smallish places, easily walked around on foot, while there is little to keep you in Sugcuraj.

Ferries   [see p450 for full details]
Jadrolinija has three boats a day between **Stari Grad** and **Split**, going down to two at weekends. Stari Grad is also on the route between **Rijeka**, **Brbinj**, **Zadar** and **Split** to the north and **Korčula**, **Sobra**, **Dubrovnik** and **Bari** to the south. Jadrolinija and Blue Line have services to **Ancona** in the summer months.

Blue Line/SEM have services to **Hvar Town** from **Ancona** between July and September and also to **Split**. Aliscafi has a daily June-to-September hydrofoil service

to **Zadar**. See Drvenik (Appendix p450) for details about **Sugcuraj–Drvenik** boats.

The Jadrolinija office (☎ 741 132) in Hvar Town is opposite the ferry dock.

Buses There are three buses a day between Hvar Town and Stari Grad (20 mins, Kn20) and between Hvar and Sugcuraj. The buses usually coordinate with ferry arrivals and departures. It's also reasonably straightforward to hitch, with the island really containing only one road, running east–west.

Where to stay Again, private rooms are widely offered for around Kn120 per head per night. In Hvar town, the **Mengola** agency (☎ 742 099) on the harbour arranges such things too. Hotels are often package orientated and expensive. In high season, bookings are recommended.
Hotel Delfin (☎ 741 168), on the western side of Hvar town harbour. Sgl/dbl for Kn160/250.
Hotel Dalmacija (☎ 741 120), on the eastern side of Hvar town harbour. A little bland, Kn160/250 sgl/dbl.
Camping Jurjevac (☎ 765 555), right in the old town.

Where to eat *Hannibal*, on the main square. Good quality for Kn80 a head.
Kod Kapetana, next to Hotel Delfin. A great seafood and fish restaurant.

BRAČ
AREA CODE: ☎ 021 POPULATION: 13,824
The fatter of the fish-like islands of this coast, Brač is famous for its brilliant white marble, excellent beach at Bol and rugged, lonely interior. It also has the highest point of the Adriatic Islands, Mount Vidova, at 780m, and is probably one of the least developed for tourists. For its size, the infrastructure is poor, yet is still perfectly adequate for getting around. It is also connected to neighbouring Split by regular ferries.

History
Sharing much the same story as the other Dalmatian Islands, Brač's marble quarries have set it apart in some ways. It was on

ADRIATIC SEA

this island, around Donji Humac, that the stone was quarried for the Roman Emperor Diocletian's palace in neighbouring Split and for the White House in Washington DC. Over the years, most of the great powers of the Mediterranean occupied it, though again it was the Venetians who stayed the longest.

Made part of Yugoslavia after WWI, in WWII it was liberated from German control by Tito's partisans and US and British special forces in 1944.

What to see

Supetar is not notable for much in particular but does contain a bizarre mausoleum, the Petrinovic family tomb, a kilometre west of town. The Petrinovices were a rich local merchant family who reportedly made their fortune by selling British coal to Chile and Chilean nitrates to Britain.

Bol, though, is where most people head for, across the mountains from Supetar. The famous beach, **Zlatni Rat**, is west of the village centre along the coast. Unlike most beaches in Dalmatia, this one is sandy and long, prodding out into the sea and much photographed by the Croatian tourist board for its promotional posters. The beach is also a good place for windsurfing.

Bol itself is a charming place of old houses and winding narrow streets, with a **Dominican monastery** (daily 1000-1200, 1700-2100, Kn10) east of town. The museum holds a well worked *Madonna and child* by Tintoretto.

You can also walk from Bol to the top of **Mount Vidova**, which rises behind the village and takes only a few hours to climb. From the top, summer evenings can be quite breathtaking, the view south from island to island lit up by the setting sun. Further afield is the hermitage at **Blaca**, set up in 1588 and a 12km hike west from Bol itself. It's closed Mondays, but otherwise open 1000-1700. Inside, you'll find an eclectic collection of astronomical instruments and Poussin lithographs left behind by the last monk to live there.

Practical information

Orientation Ferries arrive at the island capital Supetar, which is connected by regular bus to Bol. Supetar itself is no great size, being more of a village enlarged with package hotels, which is also true of Bol, though the latter has a more impressive setting and the Zlatni Rat ('Golden Horn') Beach. The rest of the island is more usefully hitched, as bus services are irregular and infrequent.

Services The **tourist information office** (☎ 630 551, 🖵 www.supetar.hr), 1, Porat, Supetar, next to the ferry dock, is open June-Sep, daily 0800-2200; Oct-May, Mon-Fri 1000-1600. In Bol, the office (☎ 635 638, 🖵 www.bol.hr) next to the bus stop is open daily June-Aug 0800-2200, Mon-Fri 0830-1500 the rest of the year.

Ferries [see p452 for full details]
There are seven ferries per day weekdays between Supetar and **Split** (1 hour, Kn15), going down to five at weekends.

The Jadrolinija office is next to the village bus station.

Buses There are hourly buses between Supetar and Bol (30 mins, Kn15) during the season, dropping to three per day in winter. The bus station in Supetar is next to the ferry stop, and it puts you down in Bol Harbour.

Where to stay Look out for Kn100 a night private rooms, otherwise, in Bol, Boltours (☎ 635 693), 18, Vladimira Nazora, will help arrange a room.
Hotel Britanida (☎ 631 038), 3, Hrvatskih Velikana, in Supetar. Good value at Kn170/250 sgl/dbl.

East of the Supetar ferry dock you'll find two private **campsites**. In Bol, try up the hill east of the village for some similar camping areas.

Where to eat *Vinotoka*, 6, Dobova, in Supetar. A good range of traditional local dishes.
Gust, 14, F Radica, above the harbour in Bol. Good value.

Bar

AREA CODE: ☎ 085 **POPULATION:** 45,000
The main port for Montenegro, or more accurately, the only port of Montenegro, Bar has come on in recent years as the sea outlet for Serbia too, with a rail line through to Belgrade being completed in 1976. While the new town has little to offer save its port, the old town, Stari Bar, 5km inland, is worth a visit, as is the neighbouring resort of Ulqini and the old capital of Cetinje. The new Montenegrin capital, Podgorica, is not too far off either, though it's not recommended as anything more than a place to change buses and trains.

Since the late 1990s, and the end of the war in Bosnia, it has also been quite possible to get buses from either Bar or Podgorica north-west to Dubrovnik in southern Croatia and through to Sarajevo and other Bosnian towns. It's also relatively straightforward to go through to Belgrade and take an international train south as far as İstanbul, or north to Zagreb, Budapest and Vienna.

HISTORY
There's not a lot of history to speak of as far as Bar is concerned, with the port a new development mushrooming up around the rail terminal in the mid-1970s. An earthquake in 1979 did some damage, though this has now long since been repaired. Way back, when this was Ottoman territory, the coastal strip had a reputation for piracy, especially when Moors from the Barbary coast were settled here by the Ottomans to fight Venetian and other attacks on their Balkan possessions. Stari Bar, the nearby old town, has more of a pedigree, with crumbling 19th-century walls alongside restored stone houses. A battle was fought here in 1878, too, between Ottoman defenders and liberating Montenegrin troops.

Historically, what is now Montenegro was once part of the Roman province of Illyria. The Slavs arrived in the 7th century, and the area was incorporated into the Serbian Empire in the late 12th century. Despite the decisive victory by the Ottomans over a Serb-led coalition at Kosovo Polje in 1389, Montenegro managed to stay independent, and after 1516 was ruled by a succession of prince-bishops of the Orthodox Church. Entering into an alliance with Russia in 1711, the Montenegrins gained a fearsome reputation as a thorn in the Ottomans' side.

This tenacity eventually paid off following the catastrophic defeat of the Ottomans in the 1878 war with Russia. Montenegro doubled in size, with Podgorica and the coast — including Bar (known in Italian as Antivari) and Ulcinj (known as Dulcigno) — added after an agreement on the border with Albania in 1880. In the Balkan Wars of 1912-13, Montenegro allied with Serbia against the Ottomans, adding more territory to the north and east and giving it a common frontier with Serbia.

This alliance continued in WWI, with Montenegro joining Serbia against the Austro-Hungarians and Germans. However, a controversial episode then occurred when the defeated Austro-Hungarians withdrew and Serbian troops moved in to occupy Montenegro. A Serb-influenced National Assembly met at Podgorica and dethroned the Montenegrin king, Nicholas, and joined the country to Serbia. In 1923, it became part of the new south Slav kingdom, which from 1929 was known as Yugoslavia.

In WWII, Montenegro was the scene of almost continuous fighting as Italian and German troops sought to establish control over this rebellious and mountainous domain. By 1944 the communist partisans, led by Jospi Broz Tito, had managed to gain the upper hand. The post-war communist Yugoslavia gave Montenegro status as one of the country's six federal republics. When Yugoslavia disintegrated in 1991, Montenegro was the only territory to stay with Serbia, with all the other republics declaring independence. However, since

ADRIATIC SEA

the end of the Bosnian war, during which many Montenegrins refused to fight in the Serb-controlled Yugoslav National Army (JNA) against the Bosnians, and a further refusal to take part in the Serb occupation of Kosovo, Podgorica has drifted further and further away from control by Belgrade. An ambiguous referendum gave independence a further boost and, in 2002, a new constitutional arrangement, giving Montenegro yet more independence, was agreed.

WHAT TO SEE

There's not much to see in Bar, but **Stari Bar** has a few attractions. There is the 12th-century Cathedral of St George and the 14th-century Church of St Nicholas, along with the remains of a Turkish hamam, plus it's quite a nice place to wander round amongst the semi ruins. The walls are in sections impressive, with a number of towers.

Another local haunt worth heading for is **Ulcinj/Ulqini**, which still holds an Ottoman rather than Slavic influence in its ethnic mix and oriental feel. Some 26km south of Bar on a regular bus route (30 mins, €1), the place was founded in the 5th century BC by Greek colonists. The old town has some of their handiwork still remaining in the Cyclopean walls, thought to be the oldest town defences on the Adriatic. In 163BC the Romans took the place over from the Olciniates, an Ilyrian tribe. The port developed a fine seafaring reputation which continued through to medieval and modern times. By the 17th century, Ulqini had a fleet of around 500 two-masters, with the town's sailors often serving in important positions within the Ottoman fleet.

Following the Ottoman defeat at the naval battle of Lepanto (see box on p274), a party of Barbary corsairs who had survived the encounter settled here under the leadership of the Bey of Algiers. They also brought the Black African slave trade; today a few local families are obvious descendants from captives once sold here at Ulqini's very own slave market. There is also quite a noticeable Albanian Muslim population today, adding to the ethnic mix.

Ulqini also has some fine beaches. The best of these is around 5km south-east of town. The best way to get there is on the Ada bus. Take this from Ulqini bus station, some 2km south of Mala Plaža, and stay on the Bar–Ulqini bus until it gets to the bus station itself, rather than getting off in town. The beach is called Velika Plaža and has 12km of good-quality sand.

Podgorica Formerly known as Titograd, the capital of Montenegro is unlikely to become a tourist pull in its own right anytime soon. Its acres of concrete blocks are testimony to the devastation wrought on the town by Italian, German and then Allied bombing during WWII, and to the astonishing lack of imagination of post-war planners. Built hurriedly, it is usually missed out altogether by the guidebooks, perhaps the only capital city in Europe to have achieved this status.

One other reason for its eminent 'missability' is that the bus and rail stations are both a kilometre or so out of town. Thus you can quite easily pass through the Podgorica experience on your way between Bar and Belgrade, or elsewhere, without having to visit the town itself at all.

Cetinje This is more like it — and indeed, this was Montenegro's capital for most of its history and still is, spiritually. Located on a high plateau some 35km north of Bar, it is easily accessed from the port by taking the Podgorica train in the morning and transferring to one of the regular and frequent Cetinje buses, returning in the afternoon.

Attacked unsuccessfully on numerous occasions by the Ottomans, this superb defensive position maintained Montenegrin independence for centuries. Within the fantastic courts a succession of bishop princes held sway, the most famous of which was probably that of Petar Njegos II.

His palace, the Biljarda, is so-called because he had a billiard table dragged up here in 1840. Over 2m tall, Petar was the stuff of romantic legend — fighting off invaders, leading the faithful and rattling off the odd poem in between swordfights. He was also a crack shot — the visiting English aristocrat Sir Gardiner Wilkinson recalling how he would shoot the pips out of a falling lemon at 20 yards – 'a singular accomplishment for a bishop' Gardiner wrote.

Behind the Biljarda is **Saint Petar Monastery** (daily 0700-1400, 1700-1900). Founded in 1484, it was largely reconstructed following another grim siege of the town by the Ottomans in 1785.

Inside is one of the oldest Slavic manuscripts anywhere — the 1494 *Oktoih*, a collection of liturgical songs.

PRACTICAL INFORMATION
Orientation
The main points in Bar are the ferry port and the railway/bus station, with the former only a 5-minute walk from the town centre. The rail and bus terminals are further off — about 2km south-east of the centre. To get to Stari Bar, take a bus to the hospital from outside the port entrance, getting off to walk straight on for a further 20 minutes or so.

Services
The **tourist information office**, located next to the port exit, is mostly closed.

Both the **post office** and the **banks**, off the main square around the port, can change money and give cash for travellers' cheques and on a Visa card. There are no ATMs.

Ferries   [see p448 for full details]
Services from Bar to **Bari** in Italy are operated by the Adriatic Shipping Company, Marlines, Prekookeanska plovidba (☎ 085-312 366, on obala 13 Jula) and, on the same street, Vektar (☎ 085-317 202). Adriatica has a weekly service to **Ancona** in Italy.

Trains
There are currently five trains a day from Bar (☎ 085-312 210) to Belgrade via Podgorica, and ten a day just to Podgorica.

Buses
Bar bus station (☎ 085-314 449) has frequent buses to Podgorica and to all destinations along the coast. There's also a frequent Podgorica–Dubrovnik bus. Bar's main coach company in is Rumijatrans (☎ 085-312 400).

Where to stay
Bar You may find yourself approached with the offer of a private room, which should be no more than €10 a night. The **Putnik Turist Biro**, near the port entrance, can also arrange accommodation for a small fee.
Hotel Topolica (☎ 085-311244), north of the port on the beach. A five-storey block with sgl/dbl for €25/45 with breakfast.
Autocamp Susanj, located 2km north of the port on the beach.

Ulcinj/Ulqini Try **Adriatours** (☎ 086-52057), 18, ulica 26 Novembar, for arranging private rooms. These should be around €6 per person.
   Camping is available at the *Milena* and *Neptun* campsites on Velika Plaža.

Cetinje Intours (☎ 086-21157), next to the post office, will arrange private rooms for around €10.
Grand Hotel (☎ 086-21104), close to the town centre. Has sgl/dbl for €30/45 including breakfast.

Where to eat
In **Bar**, try *Grill Sidro*, between the bus and rail stations, for €7 a head, or *Grill Obala*, near the Putnik office, for similar fare and prices. In **Ulcinj**, ulica 26 Novembar is the street for budget eateries, with *Restaurant Dubrovnik* a clear favourite at €7.
   Stari Bar has better places but prices are much higher. In **Cetinje**, try *Spoleto Pizzeria* near the post office; €5-6.

Durrës

AREA CODE: ☎ 052 POPULATION: 83,000
Albania's chief port and gateway to the capital, Durrës may have seen better days but is still a good first taste of this remarkable and intriguing country. Part Mediterranean, part Balkan, part former Stalinist, part former Maoist, it manages to present a slightly surreal microcosm of some of the weirder moments in world history. It's a role boost-

ADRIATIC SEA

ed now by the presence of a major base for the international soldiers of the Kosovo Force (KFOR). While they peer down on the town from their headquarters in the former palace of King Zog, the main items in the souvenir shops are shoulder patches for the Kosovo Liberation Army, the UCK, and flags to celebrate a Greater Albania.

All of which makes a visit a rarity in mainland European travel — a serious mindbender. Be prepared to have your preconceptions given a serious going over.

HISTORY

Durrës has been a port for close to three millennia, with Greek colonists from Corinth founding Epidamnus here in the 7th century BC. The Illyrian king Glaucias captured it in 312BC. Later it went to the Romans who renamed it Dyrrhachium. While neighbouring Bríndisi in southern Italy marked the end of the Via Appia, — the road east out of Rome to the Adriatic coast — Durrës became the western terminus of the Via Egnatia, which ran on across the south Balkans to Constantinople. This made it a vital transport hub for the Roman Empire, as well as being capital of the province of Illyricum and, by AD449, an archbishopric.

Durrës followed the fortunes of southern Italy in other respects too. Sacked by various invaders when the Western Roman Empire collapsed, it finally went to the Norman adventurer Robert Guiscard in 1082. From him it went to the Byzantines, then in 1185 to King William II of Sicily.

The Venetians also ran the place briefly in the early 13th century, before Sicily restored control in 1258 — only for Charles I of Anjou, king of Naples and Sicily, to take over in 1272. It was then seized by a neighbouring Greek principality, Achaea, in 1333, with the Serbian king Stefan Duõan stealing it from them in 1336.

All pretty confusing, and that wasn't the end of it. When Duõan died in 1355, the Albanian family of Thopias took over briefly before the Venetians came back in 1392, holding it this time for over a century. Their tenure was ended by the Ottomans, who arrived in 1501. They ruled here for nearly four centuries until their defeat in the First Balkan War of 1912-13.

The peace settlement from this war (surely one of the shortest-lived 'peace processes' in history, as the Second Balkan War broke out almost immediately afterwards) made Durrës capital of an independent Albania. However, this independence lasted for even less time than the peace settlements, as the European Great Powers (Britain, France, Austro-Hungaria, Germany and Italy) promptly decided that a German aristocrat called Wilhelm von Wied would be this new independent country's ruler. He took up residence in Durrës, a move greeted by the locals with an uprising that soon forced his departure.

Durrës remained capital until 1920, although it was occupied in WWI by Serbian, then Italian and finally Austro-Hungarian troops. Being a target for so many invasions, the new Albanian government considered it wiser to shift everything to Tirana. The pattern repeated in WWII, when Durrës was again occupied by the Italians, followed by the Germans. While the former used it to supply their invasion of the rest of Albania, the latter saw the port as a potential threat and blew most of it up in 1944. Resistance to the Italian fascist occupation is still commemorated about the city, the first resistance to the invasion occurring here in Durrës.

After the war, Durrës, along with the rest of the country, turned to a bizarre brand of communism with President Enver Hoxa the Albanian ruler. Hoxa had led the wartime resistance and had achieved liberation without much help from anyone. Cold War politics initially left Albania a pro-Moscow state; though, like neighbouring Yugoslavia, it was always something of a loose cannon in the Stalinist ranks. The cannon went off all of a sudden in 1961 when, with the split in world communism between Moscow and Beijing, Hoxa decided to take the country into the pro-Chinese, Maoist camp. Albania was the only place outside South-East Asia to do so.

With the Soviet invasion of Czechoslovakia in 1968, the paranoia of the Albanian leadership then took a new turn. Fear of a similar invasion led to the construction of hundreds of thousands of small bunkers and pillboxes all around the country. Durrës was no exception, with clusters of these concrete bumps dotted around every road turning on the outskirts of town.

Mao's death and the decision by the Chinese leadership that it didn't matter what colour the cat of communism was, as long as it caught the mice, led to a bit of an ideological meltdown in Albania too. Hoxa himself died in 1985, with the country economically still in the stone age. Some liberalization followed, with Durrës' mercantile past making it the forerunner. The collapse of the Soviet Bloc in 1989-90 also led to a more radical change in Albania, with an explosion of popular feeling. However, most of this feeling seemed to boil down to dark despair and a desperate scramble to leave the country. A refugee crisis developed in Durrës as thousands came to the port hoping to get to neighbouring Italy, where another crisis was developing as hundreds of thousands of Albanians began turning up on anything that would float.

The get-rich-quick rip-off of 1996, when almost the entire population was hoodwinked into putting its savings into a dodgy pyramid scheme, led to further chaos. Many of the economic advances of the early 1990s were wiped out overnight. Once again, Durrës suffered greatly from this, with many new businesses going under.

Civil collapse then brought the Italian army back again as a stabilization force. The war in neighbouring Kosovo also brought some significance back to Durrës as it became a major supply port for the international forces, KFOR, deployed over the border.

Today, the port is still active, though the town itself seems unsure where it's going next. Many hope for some arrangement with the European Union, while many others still stand at the dockside, looking with some longing at the boats heading out.

WHAT TO SEE

Outside the ferry port exit, turn left to head along the seafront, past a collection of knock-together bars and restaurants that give some echo of Durrës' former seaside-town past. Head inland after 5-10 minutes to meet up again with sections of the city defences, the walls themselves being a Byzantine attempt to keep out the Visigoths in 481, while the round towers are Venetian. You'll also pass a large mural commemorating the workers from the Stamless tobacco factory here who died fighting the Italian fascist invasion in 1939. The entire town is in fact dotted with memorials such as this, as well as patriotic statues aplenty.

Up the hill a little further is the **Roman amphitheatre**, built around the turn of the second century AD and partly excavated to reveal a small Byzantine-era church in the side of the theatre. Keep heading west, though, and the road leaves the built-up area for woodland as it heads on up the hill. Here is a good place for bunker spotting, with dozens of them lurking in amongst the trees and most of them so badly situated that if an invasion had occurred, they would most likely have shot each other.

Further on up is a small Greek Orthodox church, with a friendly local priest and some good views over the harbour. Continuing on from here, the former **Palace of King Zog** lies nestled at the top of the hill. Nowadays a KFOR base and out of bounds, it nonetheless offers a good view over the town and coast. The archetypal Balkan monarch, Ahmet Zog came to power in a coup d'etat in 1924 which overthrew the vaguely democratic government of Bishop Fan Noli. Zog was backed up by conservative landowners and the Italians, who had been booted out of the country in a series of popular uprisings that were partly led by Noli. Declaring himself King Zog I in 1928, his allegiance to the Italians proved a major liability in 1939 when Mussolini's troops invaded the country.

The king fled to London but only after he'd emptied the Albanian treasury — later using the gold to live in lavish style at the Ritz Hotel.

ADRIATIC SEA

Back in town, Rruga Durrah leads up past the 1502 Sultan Fatih Mosque to a large, Stalinist-style square in front of the Aleksandër Moisiu Theatre. To the right and behind the town hall is an Ottoman hamam, sadly now in some state of disrepair. Taking the right-hand fork at the theatre leads you to the town centre, with banks and a luna park, along with the post office. Notice here the Ottoman influence that has survived in the local cuisine — the ubiquitous *borek*, a pastry stuffed with cheese or minced meat, is on sale at numerous small shops, known in Albanian as a *byrek*.

Take a right at the crossroads and you arrive after about five minutes at the train station, a sad, semi-abandoned affair. Further right from here is Rruga Skënderberg which has the main bus stops, plus some splendid relics of past glory — late 19th and early 20th-century buildings that once housed banks, hotels and shipping agencies but which are now mostly boarded up. Following this along brings you back to where you started at the ferry terminal exit.

PRACTICAL INFORMATION
Orientation
Ferries dock at the bottom of Rruga Durrah, the main street into the town centre. (But note that ferries *leave* from further round, at the north end of the harbour, which is a good 10- to 15-minute walk away.) Outside the port gates, there are lines of ticket agencies for ferries and buses out, while the American Bank of Albania, in the tower block to the left as you exit the port, can change money and give you cash on a Visa card after it opens at 0930. There are no ATMs. Turning left from the port exit along Rruga Skënderberg, the railway station is some 10-15 minutes' walk away, too, and on the way you'll pass the main bus stops for Tirana.

The town lies up Rruga Durrah, while heading left along the seafront will eventually take you up the hill to King Zog's former palace. The sights of the town are all within 10-15 minutes' walk of the ferry port exit.

Ferries   [see p450 for full details]
Regrettably, there are no ferries these days from Durrës to ports further up or down the Dalmatian coast. This means that you're obliged to cross to Italy and then back again to continue along the coast by sea. Ferry tickets can be bought from any of the ticket agencies by the port exit, but for cash only.

The ferry lines operating from here are Adriatica, with ferries four times a week to **Ancona**; and Adriatica, and the Adriatic Shipping Company, which have daily boats to **Bari**. Ventouris also run daily boats to Bari but from July to September only.

Grecia Maritime Ltd operates a twice weekly service to **Trieste**.

Please note that leaving Albania by ferry can be an exacting experience, but an eye-opening one too. Hundreds of Albanians turn out at the port gates, many without tickets, while the local police try to keep them back, sometimes quite harshly. Be prepared for a scramble once you are allowed to start trying to get aboard. Nobody queues and there are at least five checks before you finally get admitted onto the ferry. If you are in a group, try to get just one of you to present all the passports/forms/stamps etc as the space in which to fight for attention is also dangerously narrow. Allow plenty of time.

Trains
There are seven trains a day to Tirana (1½ hours), two to Shkodra (5 hours) and two to Pogradec (6 hours) near the Macedonian border. Shkodra has the connection to Montenegro, with two trains a day over the border to Podgorica, then on to the port of Bar. Check first that the passenger service on this train is running, as mostly it is freight only.

Buses
Catch these either from the huge car park area in front of the train station or from Rruga Skënderberg, just round the corner. Buses to Tirana are frequent and cheap — around €0.25 one way, taking around 45 minutes. From Tirana, a wide selection of bus services is then available to other Albanian and international destinations.

Services
Currently there is no **tourist information office** but the ticket agencies around the

port exit are pretty helpful. The **post office** is to the left at the main crossroads in the town centre.

There are **telephones** in the square besides the theatre, with phone cards sold by the guy with the strange hat who hangs around near them. If you can't see him anywhere, loiter with intent for a while and someone will most likely see you and go fetch him.

There's an **internet café** opposite the phones and the main **souvenir shop**.

Where to stay

People wait at the port exit to offer a room in their home (around €10 a night). *Hotel Durrësi*, next to the post office, charges €15 a night for spartan conditions, while 5km south-east of town on the Tirana road is *Hotel Adriatic* (☎ 23 612) with sgl/dbl for €35/40 in a classic Stalinist construction.

Where to eat

Try either of the two restaurants next to each other on Rruga Skënderbeg, just along from

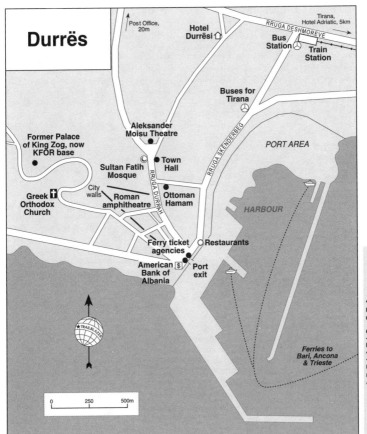

Durrës

the ferry port exit. The furthest one does good fish dishes for a modest €5 a head. Even cheaper eats are provided by the *byrek-to* (small shops selling cheese- and meat-filled pasties) which dot the town centre.

Tirana

AREA CODE: ☎ 042 POPULATION: 400,000
Albania's capital lies along the Ishm River some 27km from the coast and in the shadow of eastern mountains. In truth it was not much more than a village when it took over from Durrës as the seat of government in 1920, and it still retains some of its old, heavily Ottoman-influenced past. However, the main impression is largely of Stalinist-era people's palaces and firmly closed ethnographic institutes, the signature establishments of former Soviet republics.

Easy to get around — it's still really only a large town — it is also the transport hub for land links to neighbouring countries and the rest of Albania. Close to Durrës, it's also convenient for a quick dash between ferries, though quirky enough to deserve a little longer.

HISTORY
Tirana was founded by the Ottoman general Barkinzade Süleyman Pasha in the early 17th century. Lying on a strategic crossing of the river, it developed as a relatively minor caravan stop during the long years of Ottoman rule but sank into obscurity until Albania became independent. In 1920, it was chosen as capital as a more easily defendable site than the traditional centre, Durrës.

The coup in 1928 which made King Zog I ruler led to a flurry of Italianate building due to the king's pro-Italian stance, though the city remained largely hostile to his rule. The Italians themselves also added several buildings during their WWII occupation, an indignity brought to an end largely by the activities of the Albanian Communist Party, which was founded in Tirana in 1941. The city was liberated by a

popular uprising in 1944 from what had by then become German occupation.

Post-war, the city expanded rapidly, with aid from Yugoslavia, Russia and finally China. Unfortunately, a 1950s' urbanization drive also demolished many of the city's older structures to make way for the new, and pretty scary, constructions of the New Albania. The focus is Skënderbeg Square, where the various regimes of the past 70 years have all acted out their first — and final — moments.

WHAT TO SEE
Skënderbeg Square is dominated by the equestrian statue of Albania's national hero, Gjergj Kastrioti. He was born in 1402, the son of an Albanian prince who had given him to the Ottoman sultan, Murat II, as a hostage. Educated in Edirne, he converted to Islam and was given the Turkish name Iskender – which itself derives from Alexander the Great – and the title of *bey* (roughly equivalent to a knighthood in English titles). Played back into Albanian, this then emerged as Skënderbeg. However, he soon revealed his true colours when, during the Battle of Niö in 1443, he deserted the Ottomans to fight alongside his native Albanian Christians.

Between 1444 and 1466 he became a famous defender of Christendom, repelling some 13 Ottoman invasions. Given the title Captain General of the Holy See by Pope Calixtus III, he seemed to lead a charmed life, operating from his castle at Kruje. However, the independent Christian Albania he fought to preserve soon went under following his death in 1468, with Kruje finally falling to the Ottomans in 1478.

On the north side of the square is the **National History Museum** (Tue-Sun 0900-1200, 1600-1900, €2). The façade is covered by a mural entitled *Albania*, while inside, the post-communist era has left its usual fallout with plenty of sections shut — marking, if not the end of history, then at least its temporary suspension. On the other side of the square is the Palace of Culture, another Soviet-era monolith which started out as a gift from Moscow, but ended up

ADRIATIC SEA

being completed when Albania had shifted to the Chinese camp.

Some of the city's older constructions include the 1819 Ethem Bey Mosque to the east of the square and the clocktower, the 1830 Sahat Kule, which stands next to it. South of the square, along Bulevardi Dëshmorët e Kombit, the grand buildings leading eventually to the entrance to Tirana University are primarily interesting for their former status: over the bridge on the left is the former Enver Hoxa Museum, while on the right there is the old headquarters of the Central Committee. On the corner with Rruga Ismail Qemali is Hoxa's house, the personal residence of Albania's long-time dictator.

Continuing south down the boulevard, the **Archaeological museum** (Mon-Sat 0700-1500, €2) has a point to make, providing many examples of ancient Illyrian culture, which Albanians claim as their own, and a rival to Roman and Greek. Beyond here is the main park, Kombetar, with a lake and an impressive view. On the other side of the lake is the zoo and the botanical gardens, the latter well worth a stroll in summer with its good variety of plants.

PRACTICAL INFORMATION
Orientation
Skënderbeg Square is the city's focal point, with the long boulevard heading north from here to the train station now known as Bulevardi Dëshmorët e Kombit, instead of the previous Bulevardi Stalin. The station is also where buses to and from Durrës hang out, while those running to the castle of Kuja are on the corner of Mine Peza and Rruga e Fabrikës së Këpucëve, 1km northwest of the square. Most of the sights are easily walkable from the centre though, with little need to use the city-buses. The river crosses east–west south of the square.

Services
There are no **tourist offices**; try your hotel for local information. **Telephones** are available on Bulevardi Dëshmorët e Kombit, opposite Hotel Arberia. Phone cards are on sale from street vendors hereabouts. Cashing cheques and getting **money** on Visa cards is best done at World Travel, 102 Rruga Durrësit, as there are no ATMs.

Trains
Tirana is connected to Durrës by seven trains a day (1½ hours), two a day to Pogradec — for Macedonia — (7 hours), and two daily to Shkodra (3½ hours). The station is at the top of Bulevardi Dëshmorët e Kombit.

Planes
Tirana International Airport, Rinas, is 23km north-west of town. The airport bus leaves from in front of Albtransport in Rruga Durrësit, off Skënderbeg Square. Costing around €3, it takes half an hour. A taxi should be between €15-20.

Kruja
There are frequent local buses making the 32km journey north from the corner of Mine Peza and Rruga e Fabrikës së Këpucëve to this mountain citadel, the capital of Skënderbeg's kingdom that resisted direct Ottoman assault three times before finally falling in 1478. This spectacular site is well worth a day trip, standing as it does on a ridge above the modern town.

Nowadays, economic crisis and historical confusion have left the castle museum — designed by Enver Hoxa's daughter in order to parallel Hoxa and Skënderbeg's lives — and the ethnographical museum closed. However, there is the Bektashi Tekke in the lower part of the citadel, home to the Bektashi Dervish order during Ottoman times, along with a Turkish bath, or hamam. A reconstructed Ottoman bazaar is also in town, full of souvenir shops. If you fancy staying, try the Hotel Skënderbeg, which is next to the square where the Tirana buses stop. With singles/doubles for €15/18, it's a bargain, and has a good restaurant to boot.

ADRIATIC SEA

Buses

Frequent buses depart for Durrës from outside the train station. Pogradec buses leave from the Dinamo bus station next to the stadium, which is the main place to get buses anywhere except Durrës or to the north of the country.

For the north, try the stop outside Asllan Rusi Stadium, on the Durrës highway. Shkroda buses leave frequently throughout the day.

Daily buses to Ioánnina and Athens in Greece and İstanbul go via the border crossing at Kakavija and leave from the Axhensi bus office near the art gallery off Bulevardi Dëshmorët e Kombit, south of the square but before the river. Another route is to go to Korca (from the Dinamo stop) and then catch a bus to Florina in Greece via Kapshtica. This route is preferred if you're heading for Thessaloniki.

For Macedonia, take the Pogradec bus, which brings you to the south side of Lake Ohrid. From there, cross over on foot. Alternatively, get a direct bus from the stop behind the Palace of Culture.

Getting through to Montenegro and Yugoslavia is more problematic, particularly since the Kosovo crisis. Check with the Axhensi bus office, or at any of the travel agents on Rruga Durrësit, off Skënderbeg Square, for the latest. It may also be possible to get a bus through to Prizren and Pristina in Kosovo too, though this is subject to short-notice changes.

Where to stay

On arrival, you are likely to be met by people offering private rooms. These should be around €10 a night. Or this can be arranged via World Travel for considerably more (€15-20), but is likely to be better quality. *Hotel Dajti* (☎ 33326), Bulevardi Dëshmorët e Kombit. South of the square in an old Italian-era building; €40/60 sgl/dbl. *Hotel Arberia* (☎ 42813), Bulevardi Dësh't e Kombit, north of square; €25/35 sgl/dbl. *Tirana International* (☎ 34185), Skënderbeg Sq. Very pricey place but good quality and includes breakfast in its €80/120 sgl/dbl tariff. Try bargaining, though, as the big hotels sometimes give

big discounts due to lack of demand. Also has a good restaurant, €8 a head.

Where to eat

Skënderbeg Square is once more the centre for things, with plenty of places off here and along Bulevardi Dëshmorët e Kombit. Try the *Berlusconi Bar* behind the Palace of Culture for some Italian food, €5-7 a head. *Qendra Stefan*, near the fruit and veg market east of the square, also has snacks and pizzas for €3-4. *Ujvara*, south of the river near the Dinamo bus station is also good, with fine fare for €7-8.

Bari

AREA CODE: ☎ 080 POPULATION: 355,000
With a more extensive old town than Ancona or Bríndisi and some fine avenues to boot, Bari comes as quite a surprise on the Italian Adriatic coast. While never really advertising itself as a place for tourism, it nonetheless contains more than enough to make stopping here for more than just a change of ferries a sound idea.

The second largest city in Italy's poorer southern region, the *mezzogiorno*, it has good sea and rail connections with Greece, Albania and Croatia on its maritime itinerary. Above all, the old town, still ringed with medieval walls, is a labyrinth of cobbled streets and alleys, leading to some fine churches — one a joint Catholic/Greek Orthodox holding the stolen bones of St Nicholas (Father Christmas).

HISTORY

There is some speculation as to when this site was first inhabited, but it seems it was first settled by the mysterious Illyrians in around 1500BC. The Romans were here by the 4th century BC, under whom it became an important harbour and centre for fishing. With the fall of the Western Empire, the city was then taken by a succession of Goths, Byzantines, Lombards and Arabs. The latter ran it between 847 and 871, making it into an important emirate, before the Byzantines then retook the city to make it the seat for their governor of Apulia in 885. The locals weren't too impressed by this, however, and a famous rebellion against Byzantine rule in 1009 was led by a native of the city, known as Melo. The rebellion was crushed, and Melo fled to Germany where he died a hero.

The Norman adventurer Robert Guiscard then had a go in 1071, booting out the Byzantines. The city's fame then took a boost in 1087, when a group of locals whisked the bones of St Nicholas — today's Father Christmas — away from their resting place in Myra, now near Kale in south-western Turkey (see p333). The sacred relics were then reinterred in a brand new basilica, consecrated by Pope Urban II.

In 1096 Peter the Hermit chose Bari to kick off the First Crusade. Meanwhile, the inhabitants continued to grow uneasy under the Norman yoke and in 1119 declared their independence. This was to prove short-lived, however, as in 1131 the Norman king

Roger II took back the city and put many of the rebels to the sword.

In a later effort to gain independence, the inhabitants appealed to their old foes, the Byzantines, asking Emperor Manuel Comnenus to take back the city in 1156. This had disastrous consequences, as William the Bad of Sicily, Roger II's successor, ransacked the place so thoroughly that it took a decade for any semblance of normal life to return.

But Bari gradually managed to wangle its way out from under Norman and then Swabian control and became an independent duchy under a succession of rulers from the 14th century on. In 1558, though, the ruling Sforza family handed it over to the kingdom of Naples, then largely under the tutelage of Spain. There it stayed until 1707, when the Austrians jumped in, holding Bari until 1734 when they lost it to the Spanish Bourbons. With the exception of a period of French control during the Napoleonic period, the Bourbons ruled Bari

---

All Saints

With churches around Italy and beyond dedicated to a pantheon of different saints, it can sometimes be quite confusing knowing who — or what — is being worshipped where. Certainly, of course, God stands above all, but what about, for example, Saint Martin?

The answer in this case would be that Martin was a mortal who once shared his cloak with a poor man and has thus ended up patron saint of tailors and fashion designers — presumably a high-status sainthood in a country like Italy.

Elsewhere though, you might find Saint Lucy, saint of opticians, or Saint Urbano of Langres, the patron of wine growers. Look out too for Saint Matthew, the apostle who started out as a Roman tax collector and now runs as the patron saint of currency changers, financiers and accountants.

In short, there's a saint for every occasion. Skiers are guided by Bernard of Aosta, while footballers should look to Mauronto of Marseille. If you suffer a fear of flying, try a prayer to Joseph of Copertino, who also doubles as the patron saint of people sitting exams. One to avoid though is Saint Biagio of Sebaste, who's the patron saint of sore throats, though if you play the clarinet, he's also watching over you. Another unpopular one is Saint Gengolfo, the patron of unhappy marriages. The story runs that he was count of Langres in the 8th century, and was murdered by his wife's lover — a clergyman.

One other to look out for, and who was not infrequently invoked during the writing of this book, is Saint Pier Damiani, reputed to work wonders with headaches. But, in case you think this all a little old fashioned, right now the debate is on within the Catholic Church over Saint Isidore of Seville. If all goes well, she could end up patron saint of the internet.

— and the rest of the south — until Italian unification in 1860.

Since then the city has continued to prosper, with a university founded in 1924, and the annual Fiera del Levante — described as an Occidental–Oriental trade fair — beginning in 1930.

While WWII saw some damage from Allied bombing of the docks and railways, the historic old town survived much more intact than at Ancona.

WHAT TO SEE

The western end of the old town is guarded by the **Norman-Swabian-Aragonese castle** (Castello Normano-Svevo; Tue-Sat 0830-1830, Sun 0900-1300, €3). Begun in 1131 and progressively strengthened up until the end of independent Bari in 1557, after that it was used as a prison but now houses the regional cultural ministry, who sometimes open it for art exhibitions and concerts. Behind is the Piazza Federico II di

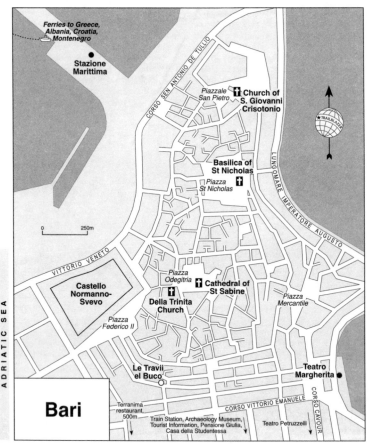

Bari

Svevia, dedicated to the son of Frederick Barbarossa, who was King of Sicily and ruler of Bari in the early 13th century. Passing down the side of the 11th-century Della Trinita Church, you enter the maze of the old town proper. Following your path round down an increasingly narrow street, keep an eye out for the doorway leading into the Piazzale Odegitria in which the 12th-century **Cathedral of St Sabine** looms suddenly upwards. The cathedral is Apulian Romanesque, with many 18th-century baroque additions. Of the two belltowers, only one is standing, rebuilt in the 1950s, while the other collapsed in 1613. Inside, in the crypt, an altar is believed to cover the bones of St Sabine, the second patron saint of the city.

Plunging back into the labyrinth, head roughly north for the other great religious site, the **Basilica of St Nicholas**. Herein lie the sacred bones of the saint more popularly known as Father Christmas, (see p333).

The basilica stands on what was once the Byzantine governor's residence, adding insult to injury since the bones had been stolen from Byzantine territory. Work began in 1087, with the resulting structure something of a mix and match of existing buildings. The basilica was not finally consecrated until 1197, and earthquakes and sackings have taken their toll over the centuries. Yet it still has a powerful atmosphere inside, the holy broken bones held in the crypt where St Nicholas' tomb is thought to exude sacred manna; this gum-like substance is believed by some to perform miracles. For centuries it has been mixed with water and dispensed in small bottles, some of which are minor works of art in themselves. The basilica is also unusual in that there is a small chapel attached dedicated to the Orthodox Christian rite, as St Nicholas continues to be of great importance in Eastern Christianity.

Piazzale San Pietro, at the northern end of the old town, contains another indication of Bari's mixed eastern and western past — the small **Chiesa di S Giovanni Crisostomo**, in which the Orthodox rite is still celebrated, the church dedicated to one of Byzantium's greatest heroes.

The new town of Bari also has some worthwhile sights — starting out on the Corso Cavour and the art nouveau Teatro Margherita in Piazzale 4 Novembre. Continuing down past blocks of sumptuous 19th-century grandeur, further down on the seaward side is the 1903 Teatro Petruzzelli, which still has four rows of boxes and a two-tiered gallery inside. The city's **Archaeological museum**, in Piazza Umberto (daily 0930-1600, €3) is housed in the wonderful Palazzo Ateneo and is good for its exhibits on the Peucetii, the pre-Roman tribes of the area.

PRACTICAL INFORMATION
Orientation
Ferries arrive in the long harbour west of the old town headland. Unfortunately, as with most ports, this one is designed to get round by car, rather than on foot, so you can find yourself walking a good 20 minutes west for the port exit. Try buttering up some of the cops at the earlier exits if you can. The main road, the Corso Vittorio Emanuele, runs parallel to the harbour-front road, the Vittorio Veneto, joining the north–south Corso Cavour by the old port. Most of the sights are on these two roads, or in the old town, on the headland north of the Corso Vittorio Emanuele, and everything is easily walkable. The train station is off the southern end of Corso Cavour, in the Piazzale Aldo Moro. There is a minor airport, Palese, 9km to the west.

Services
The **tourist office** (☎ 524 2361, 🖳 www.pugliaturismo.com/aptbari), on Piazza Aldo Moro, next to the train station, is open Mon-Fri 0800-1400, gives out maps and has some lists of accommodation. For **internet access** try Net Café, 11, Via Andrea di Bari, off Corso Vittorio Emanuele.

Ferries [see p448 for full details]
All the ferry companies below have offices at the Stazzione Maritime.
To Greece Ventouris (☎ 521 7609) has regular services to **Corfu Town**, **Igoumenitsa** and **Patras**. Superfast (☎ 521 1416 or 528 2828) operates daily to **Igoumenitsa** and **Patras**.

ADRIATIC SEA

To Albania Adriatica (☎ 5530 0360) and Adriatic Shipping Company run boats daily to **Durrës**. Ventouris (see p437) runs daily boats to Durrës from July to September only.

To Croatia Jadrolinija run weekly, October to May, to **Dubrovnik**, increasing to four times a week June to September. The Adriatic Shipping Company also goes to Dubrovnik but from July to September only.

To Montenegro Adriatic Shipping Company (☎ 5283 5750) runs two boats a week to **Bar**. Marlines, Prekookeanska plovidba and Vektar also have services.

Trains
From the main station in Piazzale Aldo Moro there are five trains a day to Bologna (6 hours), six a day to Bríndisi (one hour), four a day to Milan (8 hours), five a day to Rimini (5 hours) and seven a day to Rome (5 hours).

Where to stay
Pensione Giulia (☎ 521 6630), 12, Via Crisanzio. Reasonable rates at €25/35 sgl/dbl.
Casa della Studentessa (☎ 521 2414), 58, Via Garruba. €20/28 sgl/dbl.

Where to eat
Terranima, 213-215, Via Putignani. Good local specialities for around €10 a head.
Le Travi i el Buco, Largo Chiurlia, in the old town. A safe bet, though closed on Mondays. Budget on €7.50 a head.

Bríndisi

AREA CODE: ☎ 0831 POPULATION: 92,000
The port with the shortest Adriatic crossing, Bríndisi is seldom out of the news these days as an EU frontier post, the place where the refugees from Africa and Asia receive a far less welcoming reception than Western tourists. The port has had a transit role for centuries and as such hasn't developed much to hold the visitor long. Nonetheless,

there are a few worthy monuments and the old town has something of a crossroads-between-continents feel. Bríndisi also has good rail links to the rest of Italy and Europe and good regular ferry services to Greece. For Albania, Montenegro and Croatia you'll have to head for Bari, though.

HISTORY
According to myth, Bríndisi was founded by one of Odysseus' shipmates, Diomedes. Its name is probably derived from the ancient Illyrian word for 'stag's head', a reference to its Y-shaped harbour and inlet.

Falling under Roman rule in 266BC, it then became a base of operations for the Carthaginian general Hannibal in 216BC during the Second Punic War (see box, p192).

In 19BC the poet Virgil died here after returning home from Greece. By this time, it had become the major Adriatic crossing-point for the Roman Appian Way, the main ancient highway from Rome to the south Balkans and beyond.

As with much of the rest of Italy, the collapse of the Western Roman Empire left Bríndisi and its surrounding region — Puglia — vulnerable to attacks by Goths, Lombards and Arabs. The Byzantines ran the port until it came under Norman sway in 1071, when it served as the departure point for many of the Crusades. Under the Hohenstaffen monarch and Holy Roman Emperor Frederick II, Puglia went through something of a golden age, at least as far as grand building works are concerned, with many of the cathedrals and churches of the city and region constructed during his tenure at the start of the 13th century.

As the Middle Ages progressed, however, Bríndisi suffered from various conflicts for control of the Kingdom of Naples, as well as from a bad earthquake in 1456. The port came under Austrian rule (1707-34), before the Spanish Bourbon kings took over in 1759. With the opening of the Suez Canal in 1869, the British Peninsular and Oriental Steam Navigation Company, then the largest shipping company in the world, chose Bríndisi as a central port for its ships sailing to Bombay in

India, giving it a welcome boost.

Bríndisi has also long had a military role, serving in WWI as the centre for Italian naval operations against the Austro-Hungarians in the Adriatic. In WWII, the defeat of Italian fascist forces by the Allies in 1943 and the subsequent Allied invasion of Italy led to the establishment of the first pro-Allied government of Italy, under Marshall Pietro Badoglio, in Bríndisi. Up until February 1944, Bríndisi was the country's capital.

Nowadays, the city and port are a major focus for trade and communications, as well as the main crossing point for road traffic, via the ferries, to Greece. Tourism thus sits, sometimes awkwardly, next to the less glamorous requirements of industry. While many come here, nowhere near as many stay.

WHAT TO SEE

As a transit place since Roman times, it seems fitting to start a tour of the place at the seafront **Roman column**, which marks the end of the Appian way. Virgil is supposed to have died in a house near here. At the point where the harbour forks into its two branches is the 1933 Italian sailors' monument, built in the shape of a giant rudder. Inside the small chapel at its base is the bell of the battleship *Benedetto Brin*, sunk by the Austro-Hungarians out in the harbour in 1915.

Back up in town, on the Piazza del Duomo, is the 14th-century Palazzo Balsamo, while the square also contains the **Francesco Ribezzo Archaeology museum** (Mon-Fri 0900-1330, with an extra 1530-1830 on Tuesdays, free admission). Inside is a small collection of coins, statues, ancient inscriptions and finds from an underwater excavation of a Roman shipwreck north of Bríndisi harbour.

The port has no shortage of castles, though many are not open to the public. Out guarding the narrow harbour entrance on a small island is the 1491 **Aragonese castle**, also known as the Sea Fortress, currently undergoing restoration. In town, the 1227 **Swabian castle** (Castello Svevo) of Frederick II is largely built from materials

nicked from the old walls and monuments of the city. Expanded in 1488 by the port's Aragonese rulers, the castle has been a naval base for centuries. It also hosted the Italian government during Bríndisi's spell as the capital towards the end of WWII.

Also worth seeing is the **archaeological dig** in the San Pietro degli Sciavoni quarter. Under the new municipal theatre, an area of the Roman town has been excavated, containing houses, streets and some mosaics still in situ. Entrance is free, while it is also viewable from through the glass floor of the theatre.

The 11th-century circular **Temple of St John** is a remarkable Crusader construction with a wooden roof. The **cathedral**, dedicated to St John the Baptist, was originally built between 1098 and 1132 but then almost entirely rebuilt to the original design after the 1743 earthquake. Inside is a fine 1178 mosaic, while a small chapel next to the belltower contains the bones of Saint Theodoro, Bríndisi's patron saint, together with those of St Lawrence.

Further out, the 1300 **Chiesa di Santa Maria del Casale**, some 4km from the harbour towards the airport, is a mix of Romanesque, Gothic and Byzantine styles. Inside are several fine Byzantine frescos.

PRACTICAL INFORMATION
Orientation

The port's two main transit hubs — the Stazzione Maritime and the train station — are connected by the Corso Umberto I, which changes name to the Corso Garibaldi later on. The distance takes no more than 10-minutes to cover on foot, though there are also buses (Nos 6, 9 and 12). Most hotels and restaurants, cafés and bars are on or just off the Corso, while the town's sights are also within easy walking range of this street. Remember that Bríndisi is a major transit place, so car owners may have to add an hour or two onto their journey times, as the traffic into the ferry terminals can be gruesome. Also, this is not the kind of place that looks kindly on shabby travellers sleeping in bus shelters, with immigration a major issue, kept on the boil by local neo-fascists. Be careful.

ADRIATIC SEA

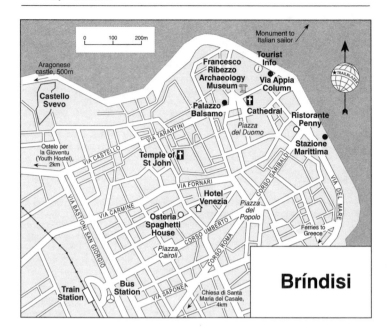

Services

The **tourist information office** (☎ 562 126, 🖥 www.pugliaturismo.com/aptbrindisi), Via C Colombo, is open daily except weekends in summer, 0830-1400, 1500-1900, winter open Sat 0830-1300 only.

Ferries   [see p449 for full details]

Bríndisi has good connections to Greece but for other Adriatic destinations you'll have to take the train north to Bari. Tickets for all the below are available at the Stazzione Maritime.

Services to **Corfu** are operated by Blue Star (☎ 562 200), Fragline (☎ 548 534), Hellenic Maritime Lines (☎ 528 531), Maritime Way, Med Link Lines and SNAV.

Agoudimos Lines (☎ 529 091), Blue Star (see above), Fragline (see above), HML and Maritime Way go to **Igoumenit-sa** – some services are direct and some go via Corfu.

HML, Maritime Way and Med Link Lines have services to **Kefalonia** and also to **Patras**.

Marmara Lines have weekly sailings to **Çeşme** (Turkey) between June and September.

It's worth bearing in mind that all the above offer vast reductions for return tickets — sometimes up to 50% off. This can often make a return the same price as a single.

Trains

From the main station at the top of the Corso Umberto I, there are three trains a day to Ancona (5½ hours), seven a day to Bari (1¼ hours), three to Bologna (7 hours), two to Milan (9 hours), three to Rimini (6 hours) and four to Rome (6 hours).

Buses

From Viale Regina Margherita there are two buses a day to Rome, taking you to the Stazione Tiburtina. Tickets are available from Appia Travel, 8-9 Viale Regina Margherita, price €32.

ADRIATIC SEA

Where to stay
Hotel Venezia, 4, Via Pisanelli. A back-packers' favourite with comfortable sgl/dbl for €15/30.

Ostello per la Gioventú (☎ 413 123), 2, Via Brandi. HI hostel some 2km out of town on bus Nos 3 and 4 from the stop on Via Cristoforo Colombo. However, they occasionally send out a bus to pick you up. Bunks for €12.50. Has internet access.

Where to eat
The Osteria Spaghetti House, 57, Via Mazzini, has good local fare for €10 a head, while *Ristorante Penny*, Via S Francesco 1,

has good seafood for around €15 a head.

Otherwise, the Corso is lined with cafés and restaurants serving the transitory crowds heading for the port — no great cuisine, but good enough if you're just passing through.

Corfu

AREA CODE: ☎ 2661 POPULATION: 89,600
Known as 'Kerkira' in Greek and shaped like a long inverted comma, Corfu is probably one of Greece's best-known islands. This is

Corfu and cricket
Think of Greece and many images may come to mind. Whitewashed villages perched above dark blue seas, strange circle dances and the bozouki, ouzo and grilled octopus. But whatever your image might be, it's unlikely to involve cricket bats, bowlers and googlies. On Corfu, though, the game of cricket is as Greek as a bottle of retsina.

The connection comes via the long forgotten British Ionian Protectorate. Following the Napoleonic wars, in 1815 Corfu and the other Ionian Islands — which had previously belonged to Venice — were put under British rule. They stayed that way till 1864, which was plenty of time to organize a game of cricket, and just about enough time to get a result.

So, on 23 April 1823, a team of British sailors took on an eleven from the local garrison, an event that bizarrely caught the local imagination. Two local Corfiot teams emerged, which on the departure of the British formed the basis of a Corfu cricket league that survives to this day.

Gymnastikos was then the leading club, being formed in 1893 to take on visiting English teams. In 1923, rival Ergatikos was formed, opening its ranks to members of the island's aristocracy and becoming known as the Byron Cricket Club. In those days, the most hotly contested games were often with teams from visiting British navy ships, the 1904 season being particularly good for matches as the British Mediterranean fleet was anchored in harbour. In 1932, the then Prince of Wales himself was also on hand to watch the batting.

After WWII, Corfu cricket was given some good coverage in the British press and many local clubs from England, Australia and New Zealand started touring the place. Corfu had always been a favourite for Brit expats, who were also on hand to give encouragement.

In 1976, a third club was formed — Feax Cricket Club — and Corfiot cricketers began an invasion of Greece proper, with the Hellenic Cricket Association now boasting teams in Thessaloniki, Athens and Patras.

In the old days, games were played in the square in front of the castle in Corfu town, a tradition set to continue after the ground has been given a thorough facelift. Sitting watching a game while sipping a few drinks in the surrounding cafés is a great way to spend a few hours, even if the rules, and what's actually happening, remain way beyond you.

ADRIATIC SEA

certainly true amongst Brits, who flock here every year in droves for its beaches and package-holiday resorts. It has a feel quite unlike the Greek islands of the Aegean, with a strong Italian influence on the architecture, and the influence of more rain than any other island on the vegetation. The result is quite beautiful.

The most northerly of the Ionian Islands, Corfu also has a role as an entry point for ferries and planes, with its airport working overtime in summer to ferry in the tourists, while boats to Italy depart year-round. Corfu town is the main urban area and an excellent place to wander round, with its narrow streets and shuttered 18th- and 19th-century houses. It also boasts one of Corfu's lesser-known attractions — a functioning cricket ground (see box, p265).

HISTORY

Corfu first gets a significant mention in Homer's *Odyssey* as Ulysses' last stop before he returned home to Ithaca, another Ionian island lying some 100 miles to the south. Settlers from the mainland city of Corinth colonized the place in 734BC but, like many colonists to come, they soon found themselves at odds with the homeland and enlisted the Athenians to help them fight Corinth in 435BC, a request that proved instrumental in sparking the Peloponnesian Wars.

Ownership of the island then became rather fluid, with the Illyrians, the mysterious inhabitants of modern day Albania, grabbing it in 229BC. The Romans then took over, using it as a useful naval base at the entrance to the Adriatic.

This strategic position was a blessing and a curse, however, as Goths, Arabs, Lombards, Normans, Sicilians, Genoese and Venetians all made a grab for it over the following centuries. Eventually, it fell to the Venetians in 1401, and remained in their hands until 1797. This made it, and most of the other Ionian Islands, the only present-day Greek territory to have never been under Ottoman rule.

When Venice finally collapsed, the island passed back and forth between French, Russian and finally British control in 1815. Thus began the short-lived British Ionian Protectorate, which lasted until 1864 when the islands were given to Greece.

The next time Corfu got into the headlines was in 1923 when it was bombarded and briefly occupied by Italian forces. In WWII the islands were again occupied by the Italians and then the Germans. The island was liberated from both in 1944.

Since then, Corfu has managed to dodge a major earthquake that flattened much of the other Ionian Islands, and developed its tourist industry to be one of the most extensive in the Mediterranean. Despite this, though, it has retained a great deal of its charm, composed as it is of so many layers of history, if not occupation.

WHAT TO SEE
Corfu Town

Corfu Town is undoubtedly the premier urban experience on the island, with its two fortresses and wonderful combination of Italian, French and even British colonial architecture.

The place to start a walkabout is probably Spianada Square, not least because the area north of this is where the town's cricket club plays. On the north-western side of the square is the **Liston**, a French-built terrace of arcaded houses dating from the brief Napoleonic occupation.

East of here is the imposing bulk of the Old Fortress, the **Palaio Frourio**. Connected to the land by a narrow bridge, this 12th-century guardian was once the site of a temple of Hera, Zeus' notoriously jealous wife (see box on p296). The fortress is open 0830-1500 and costs €3.50 entrance.

Heading north from the square along Kapodistria brings you round to two of the town's museums — the **Byzantine Museum** (Tue-Sun 0830-1500, €2) and the **Solomos Museum** (Mon-Fri 0930-1400, €1). While the former is well known for its collection of Byzantine icons, the latter is the one-time home of the poet Dyinisios Solomos, who lived on the island for 30 years.

Corfu Town

250m

0

Palaio Frourio
(Old Fortress)

Faliraki

Byzantine
Museum

Solomos
Museum

Agios
Spiridon
Church

The
Liston

Restaurant
Arpi

ELEFTHERIAS

DOUSMANI

Splanada
Square

Serbian War
Museum

KAPODISTRIA

Taverna
O Giogas

MOUSTOXIDI
STREET

N ZAMBELI

AKADIMIAS

DIMOKRATIAS

Hotel
Constantinople

VELISSARIOU

ZAVITSIANOU

THEOTOKI

Tourist
Info

Archaeology
Museum

IROMANOU

ALEXANDRAS

MARASLI

Fast Ferries
to Igoumenitsa

Tourist
Police

Plateia
San Rocco

Town
Buses

ZATIROPOULOU

Post
Office

Neo Frourio
(New Fortress)

Slow Ferries
to Igoumenitsa

AVRAMIOU

DIMOULITSA

KOLOKOTRONI

Ferries to
Paxi &
Patras

XENOFONDOS STRATIGOU

Island Bus
Station

Hotel
Ionian

Camping
Kontokali, 5km

Hotel
Europa

ADRIATIC SEA

From here, keep heading west for the New Fortress, the **Neo Frourio**, which is open all day for €2. The structure you see now is the rebuilt 1588 version, though some kind of castle has stood here for considerably longer. Heading south from here, the town's **archaeological museum** (Tue-Sat 1000-1600, Sun 0930-1420, €3) stands at 5, Vraila. Its star exhibit is the Gorgan Medusa, originally part of a 6th-century BC Temple of Artemis.

Another star attraction of the town is the church of **Agios Spiridon** on Agiou Spyridonos. Inside, you'll find a silver coated coffin containing the body of St Spyridon — the island's patron saint. This is ritually paraded about the town on the saint's feast day.

If you've some time here, perhaps one of the quirkiest places to visit is the **Serbian War Museum**, on Moustoxidi. Unfortunately, it's open only on request — telephone the Moraitis School of Languages (☎ 035 615) for an appointment. Inside, you'll find memorabilia mainly from the bitter WWI struggle between the Serbs and the invading Austro-Hungarian and German forces, a campaign that forced the Serbian army almost completely out of Serbia itself and south into Greece.

Apart from all this, one of the attractions of the town is simply to walk about in its old part, getting woefully lost. There are plenty of cafés to rest up in and admire the façades, alleyways and narrow streets.

Around the island

North of town, Corfu's premier package-tourist resort status is very apparent, with extensive villa, apartment and hotel coverage extending well beyond Pyrgi. First stop on the road north then should be Kalami, the one time home of expat Brit novelists, Gerald and Lawrence Durrell. Their house, known as the White House, is now a restaurant, right on the water's edge. Up behind, the tall mountain is in fact the island's highest peak — Mt Pantokrator (906m).

Keeping north along the coast road, the stretch between Kalami and Kassiopi is one of the island's gems. The coast of Albania lies opposite, while Kassiopi itself is a cool harboured village with a reasonable beach to the west of town and a 12th-century castle up behind. After this, Sidhari is the next town of note for anything except package tourism complexes. It has infrequent boats to the neighbouring Diapondia islets as well as its own sandy beach. Further on, Agios Stefanos offers just as infrequent boats to the same islets and a less-crowded beach.

The Diapondias are some of the more deserted places hereabouts, with only three of them inhabited all year round: Ereikousa, a beach paradise, Mathraki, home to loggerhead turtles (see p24) and Othoni, the largest, yet with the pebbliest beaches. Good day-trip material, though schedules are wildly variable from Corfu Town itself, Agios Stefanos and Sidhari, a ticket going for €4-5 one way.

South of Corfu Town, the two most immediate attractions are on the Kanoni Peninsula — the area where the island's ancient capital stood and also the birthplace of Prince Philip, the husband of Queen Elizabeth II. The grounds of his manor, **Mon Repos Villa**, are open 0800-2000 every day. Further south in the village of Gastouri is another aristocratic legacy, the late 19th-century **Ahillion Palace**, one-time summer residence of the empress of Austria-Hungary. The gardens are also open to the public, from 0900-1600, with an admission fee of €5.

The island becomes flatter and narrower as you head south, with a number of major resorts taking advantage of the sandy terrain. On the west coast try Mirtiotisa Beach, almost due west of Corfu Town, which is also nudist, or south of there, Glifada, Pelekas and Agios Gordis. Pelekas is also good for the village of the same name inland, which is overshadowed by the **Kaiser's Lookout**, signposted from the village square and giving some spectacular views.

Further north lies **Paleokastritsa**, a major resort but still breathtakingly beautiful thanks to its coast, which includes high mountains falling to a pebbly chain of beaches in secluded coves.

PRACTICAL INFORMATION
Orientation
Corfu Town is dominated by its two fortresses to the east and west of town. It also divides north–south with the northern section forming the old part. Ferries dock here and it is a short walk into the labyrinth of old streets containing most of the sights.

Services
The **tourist office** (EOT; ☎ 037 520, 🖳 www. corfu-greece.biz/), on the corner of Voulefton and Mantazarou, is open Mon-Fri 0800-1400. It has maps and accommodation lists. The **tourist police** (☎ 030 265), 4, Samartzi, are based in the police station, open 24hr. The main branch of the **post office** is on Alexandras, open Mon-Fri 0730-2000, Sat 0730-1400, Sun 0900-1330. **Internet access** is available at Netoikos, 14, Kalogeretou, near the cricket pitch.

For **books** in English, try Xenoglosso, 45, Markora.

International **newspapers** are readily available, if a day late. The local **English-language magazine**, *Corfiot*, published monthly (€1.50), has plenty of useful ads, expat notices and recipes for Zacynthos bean soup.

Ferries   [see p450 for full details]
Domestic ferries Services to and from **Igoumenitsa** and **Patras** are operated by ANEK, Blue Star (not Igoumenitsa), and Minoan and leave from the New Port. There are also regular ferries to and from the neighbouring island of **Paxi**.

Get tickets for the above from the ferry building on Xenofontos Stratigou, the harbour road or any of the dozens of travel agencies in town.

The port authority is on ☎ 039 513.

International ferries Ferries from Corfu go to Italy (**Bari**, **Bríndisi**, **Trieste** and **Venice**), though most are the Patras–Italy or Igoumenitsa–Italy boats calling in.

The ferry agents here are Ferry Travel (☎ 025 232), 2, Ethn Antistaseos, New Port, for Blue Star Ferries; Mancan Travel (☎ 032 664), 38, El Venizelos, for both ANEK Lines and Ventouris Ferries; and Spyros Vergis Travel (☎ 025 000, 🖳 eta-corfu @minoan.gr), 2, Ethn Antistaaseos, for Minoan Lines.

Buses
Corfu Town has regular bus connections with towns around the island (see box below); the green KTEL buses (☎ 030 672) that run these routes depart from Platia Neou Frouriou.

Local blue buses run to a city limit of 10km out of town and leave from the central Plateia San Rocco. A flat-rate €0.50 ticket will take you to Potamos, Perama, Afra, Agios Ioannis, Achillion, Kastellani or Kontokali every half an hour.

Cars and bikes
Rent-a-car agencies in Corfu Town are plentiful, as are moped hirers. Try *Autorent* (☎ 044 623), 34, Xenofondos Stratigou, for both.

❏ BUSES IN CORFU

To	Frequency	Journey time	Route
Agios Gordios	4 times a day	45 minutes	via Sinarades
Agios Stefanos	5 times a day	1½ hours	via Sidari
Aharavi	4 times a day	1 hour 20 mins	via Roda
Glyfada	6 times a day	45 minutes	via Vatos
Kavos	10 times a day	1½ hours	via Lefkimmi
Loutses	4 times a day	1¼ hours	via Kassiopi
Messongi	7 times a day	45 minutes	
Paleokastritsa	7 times a day	45 minutes	
Pyrgi	9 times a day	30 minutes	via Ypsos

ADRIATIC SEA

Planes

Corfu has an international airport just south of town, though no airport bus. Local bus No 3 stops on the main road outside, however, and takes you to Plateia San Rocco in town. The airport also has Olympic Airways domestic flights to Athens three times a day and to Thessaloniki three times a week. Olympic Airways (☎ 038 694) is at 11, Polyla, Corfu Town.

Where to stay

Corfu Town   Accommodation can be arranged at the EOT office (see p269).
Hotel Ionian (☎ 030 628), 46, Xenofondos Stratigou, on the seafront. Cheap and cheerful; €30/45 sgl/dbl.
Hotel Europa (☎ 039 304), 10, Yitsaiali. One of the oldest budget venues; €25/40 sgl/dbl.
Hotel Constantinople (☎ 048 716), 1, Zavitsianou, in the old town. Now considerably more upmarket than it used to be; €50/75 sgl/dbl.

The nearest **campsite** is *Dionysus Camping Village* (☎ 091 417), Dhassia, some 8km to the north. Alternatively, head for the beaches on the west coast, with *Vatos Camping* (☎ 094 505), in the village of Vatos, a good option.

Around the island In Agios Gordios, the west coast resort, *The Pink Palace* (☎ 053 103) is something of an island institution for backpackers – a budget hostel doubling as a bar/nightclub; sgl/dbl for €20/30.

Where to eat

Corfu Town The southern end of the old town is a good place to dig for budget eateries, notably *Taverna O Giogas*, 16, Guilford, with inexpensive mezedes, or *Restaurant Arpi*, 20, Giotopoulou, which is a little more pricey, though a full meal should still be around €10. Up a notch or two is the *Falirak*i, on the corner of Arseniou and Kapodistra, which has authentic Corfu cuisine — a rare mix given the variety of occupiers who left behind a few culinary tips while lording it over the island.

Around the island In Kinopiastes, *Tripas*

Tavern (☎ 056 333), 5km south of Corfu Town has served a variety of celebrity guests in its time including Francois Mitterand and Jane Fonda. On separate occasions, of course. Big menu, though with big prices at €20 a head.

Entertainment

Corfu has more bars and clubs than it seems possible to enumerate, but recommended are the simple people-watching pleasures of the cafés on the Liston in Corfu Town, or the swimming pool in the *Hippodrome nightclub*, north of the new harbour.

Igoumenitsa

AREA CODE: ☎ 2665 POPULATION: 6800
While itself not much to reckon with, Igoumenitsa has come through in recent years as a key port for Adriatic shipping and a major transit place for Greek trade with the rest of Europe. From here, international ferries ply across to Italy, while local boats also go to neighbouring Corfu.

The town is also a fair base for exploring the surrounding mainland, the Epirus, which is one of Greece's less well-known yet spectacularly beautiful regions. Containing the snow-capped Pindus Mountains as well as the lake of Ioánnina, for many years this was wild border country, running over into Albania to the north. It was used to making its own rules, and for many years was run as a separate kingdom by the Albanian Muslim chieftain, Ali Pasha. It was in these mountains, too, that modern Greece experienced one of its finest hours — defeating the 1940-41 Italian fascist invasion — but also one of its worst: it was here that the Greek Civil War came to its bloody conclusion in 1948, with the first recorded use of napalm, dropped from US planes on the pro-Communist Democratic Army making its last stand amongst the sometimes unforgiving mountains of the Epirus.

Now, though, the region is opening up to tourism, and affords an increasingly rare opportunity to savour a disappearing

ADRIATIC SEA

Greece. In its mountain villages and small communities, it may seem a long way from the pictures of Greece that adorn the brochures; and indeed, that's because it is.

WHAT TO SEE
The town has no real sights, so if you are have some time on your hands, trips out are well advised. First off, there's Corfu, lying an hour and a half offshore, then there's Ioánnina, the regional capital, back inland. South-west of that is Dodona, one of ancient Greece's most important oracles, while south of Igoumenitsa, along the coast, is another — the Oracle of the Dead on the River Acheron, and the entrance to Hades — the underworld — itself (see box p272).

PRACTICAL INFORMATION
Orientation
Igoumenitsa is no great size, with everything within walking distance. The main

bus station is a block back from the waterfront road and has four buses a day to Athens (8 hours, €30), and one a day to Thessaloniki (8 hours, €28).

The bus from Thessaloniki arrives around four in the morning, so if you arrive on this, you'll be obliged to stay the night. For this, head to **Egnatia Hotel** (☎ 023 648), 2, Eleftherias, in the square to the right as you come out of the bus station. Singles/doubles go for €30/40 with bathroom.

Other than that, your choices are limited to waking up the slumbering owner of one of the *domatia* — rooms in people's houses — around the port.

Ferries [see p450 for full details]
Igoumenitsa is a major port for ferries to Italy, though alas the coastal boats up to Albania no longer run.

Igoumenitsa to Corfu
On the ferry out from Igoumenitsa, the sea seems somehow different from the usual Aegean waters. Something more animated, more fractured, with the lines of waves across the green-blue strait separating the harbour from Corfu following a swirl of contradicting paths.

On this day, to the north, the larger, more ungainly looking *Adriatica* ship pulls out heading for Bari, while our smaller ferry heads on for the long shadow of the island. Behind, Igoumenitsa is a pretty unprepossessing place for Greece's key Adriatic port, consisting largely of a harbour whose associated buildings spread slightly beyond the port limits and one day got classified as a town.

Yet Corfu Town – that's something quite different.

After crossing the narrow strait, the ferry follows along the whole stretch of the coast where the Town's castles, old and new, stand out above rows of Italianate houses, terraces of wooden-shuttered apartments. Street openings run back inland at angles from the seafront road. The ferry journey becomes almost a panoramic tour of the Town, before the boat docks, the other side of everything.

Corfu seems from the water to be Italy already, such a short distance and yet such a long way from the hardy, Northern Epirus that you've just left – home of Hades and the last bitter struggles of a lost, curiously 19th-century Greece. Here, the sea calms again, an Italian sea, with a town laid out to recollect a softer life, *la dolce vita*. Yet here, too, is also Greece, a fact which seems odd, somehow, especially since it's also a Greece that plays cricket.

From here though, you can look north to the Adriatic and west to the Italian coast. Accustomed to being on the edge of every map, perhaps Corfu would like to remind its visitors, at a moment like this, that really it's slap bang in the middle, the natural stepping stone from East to West. Food for thought, though maybe not too much, as you eat your souvlaki in the shade of an Italianate piazza.

ADRIATIC SEA

To Italy ANEK, Minoan and Superfast have services to **Ancona**. Minoan, Superfast and Ventouris operate to **Bari**, and Agoudimos Lines, Blue Star, Fragline, HML and Maritime Way go to **Bríndisi**, Blue Star and Minoan have regular sailings to **Venice**. Finally, ANEK goes daily to **Trieste**.

The main agents are: Giogiakas Travel (☎ 024 252), 62, Ethn Antistaseos, for Blue Star Ferries; Revis Travel (☎ 024 235), 34, Eth Antistasis, for both ANEK Lines and Fragline Ferries; Makridis Travel (☎ 022 952, 🖳 eta-igoumenitsa@minoan.gr), 58A, Ethn Antistaaseos, for Minoan Lines; Milano Travel (☎ 023 565), 11b, Agion Apostolon, for Ventouris Ferries; Marlines Travel (☎ 023 301), 42, Ethn Antistasis, for Marlines; V Pitoulis & Co (☎ 028 150), 147, Agion Apostolon, for Superfast Ferries; and Zois Shipping (☎ 025 682), 30, Ethn Antistasis, for Agoudimos Ferries.

The port authority is on ☎ 022 240.

Domestic ferries Ferries from Igoumenitsa to **Corfu Town** leave frequently and take 1¹/₂-3 hours. The main companies are ANEK and Minoan but enquire locally about other services. Services to **Patras** are also frequent and are operated by ANEK, Blue Star, HML, Minoan and Superfast.

Buy your ticket from one of the travel agents on the harbour-front road or at the portacabin inside the port next to where the ferries depart. The boat takes you to the New Port, west of the town's fortress. The ferries return from there too.

Ioánnina

AREA CODE: ☎ 2651 **POPULATION:** 56,496
The capital of the Epirus, the modern city has lost some of its older charm but still has an astonishing setting in the Pindus

---

The River Acheron and Hades

Heading south from Igoumenitsa along the coast, after some 50km you'll find the River Acheron flowing down to the sea near the village of Mesopotamo. Next to this lie the ruins of the 4th-century BC Necromanteion, the Oracle of the Dead.

Back then, the flat lands around here formed a shallow, reedy lake, known as Acherousia. The ancient Greeks believed that in its mists and marshlands, surrounded by rocky gorges and caves, lay the entrance to the underworld — Hades. Here was where Hermes would bring the souls of the dead before handing them over to Charon, the ferryman, who would take them down into the depths of the Lake itself.

The idea behind the Necromanteion was therefore to communicate with these dead souls. In the crypt lie the remains of a kind of crane, used to raise statues of the dead up from the depths, as if in resurrection, while the priests who lived there also built for themselves vast networks of secret passages to enable them to pop up at unexpected moments, doubtless amongst much fire and brimstone, and freak out the lamenting hordes who'd come to try and communicate with their departed. Homer describes the visit of Odysseus here, though the Romans were less impressed and burnt the place down in 167BC. A monastery of St John the Baptist was then built on the site in the 18th century.

There is still a good deal to see, however, and the setting is decidedly eerie, especially out of season. It's open 0900-1500, €2.50, with the best way of getting there being a boat trip from Igoumenitsa in season, which runs down the coast and upriver to the site for €10. Otherwise, the Preveza bus runs through Mesopotamo, though pretty infrequently.

ADRIATIC SEA

Mountains next to Lake Pamvotidha. The medieval Kastro, or citadel, is the high point, its fortifications the most obvious surviving testament to Ioánnina's most charismatic ruler, Ali Pasha, the 'Lion of Janina', as Ioánnina was once called.

Starting out in the mid-1700s, Ali Pasha had taken over the family business — banditry — from his mother, Khamco, and proved a rip-roaring success. Through murder, assassination and blackmail he ascended the slippery slope to become virtual emperor of much of northern Greece and southern Albania — despite the fact that these territories were nominally part of the Ottoman Empire.

Both the British and French treated him as an independent ruler, which perhaps contributed to the Ottoman sultan's decision in 1819 to kill him. Ioánnina was besieged and Ali Pasha murdered. In his time though, Ioánnina was something of a centre for barbaric glamour, with his huge harem and massive bodyguard – an orientalist fantasy come to life. He also protected his Greek community better than the Ottoman rulers who came after him, who clung on to Ioánnina until 1913.

WHAT TO SEE
In the Kastro you'll find signs to the **Byzantine Museum** (daily 0800-1900, free) with some good silverware, and the **Municipal Art Museum** (daily 0900-2000, free), which has some interesting costumes and artefacts from the town's long-gone Jewish community.

Down from the Kastro there is also the bazaar area, which has a respectably shambolic collection of Ottoman-era buildings, and the **Archaeological Museum** (Tue-Sun 0830-1430, €1.50). The high point in this is the collection of tablets on which are inscribed requests to the Oracle of Zeus at neighbouring Dodona, one of the most important in the ancient world.

Dodona is also worth a visit, lying 22km south-west of Ioánnina. There are three buses a week there, or get a cab for around €17 return. The site of the ruins (daily, summer 0800-1900, winter 0800-1700, €2.50) include an enormous 3rd-century BC ancient theatre, heavily restored in the 19th century.

In ancient times, the priestesses of the Oracle here would make predictions and offer their wisdom according to interpretations of sounds — the wind rustling in the sacred trees, or the sound made by a large brass gong continuously vibrating in the breeze. This last gave rise to a Greek expression still in use — *Khalkos Dodones* ('Brass of Dodona') — to describe someone who blathers on without really having anything to say.

PRACTICAL INFORMATION
Services
The **tourist information office** (☎ 025 086) is at 39, Dhodhoni. It's open mornings only, Mon-Sat 0930-1230.

Buses
The main bus station is at 4, Zozimadhon for northern and western destinations such as Igoumenitsa, while 19, Bizaniou is the bus stop for Dodona.

Planes
Flights between Ioánnina Airport and Athens leave daily, while those to Thessaloniki go weekly. Try the tourist office for details.

Where to stay
Hotel Esperia (☎ 024 111), 3, Kaplani, between the bazaar and the central square. Sgl/dbl €25/35.
Hotel Metropolis (☎ 026 207), 2, Krystálli, in the same area. €30/45 sgl/dbl.
Limnopoula campsite is 2km north on the airport road and on the lake shore.

Where to eat
Try around the Kastro entrance and the bazaar area for cheap eats.

ADRIATIC SEA

Patras

AREA CODE: ☎ 261 **POPULATION:** 160,010
The second busiest port in Greece after
Piraeus, and the country's third largest city,
Patras (Patra) is otherwise remarkable only
for the speed in which most people pass
through it. Transport is the main idea here,
with boats to the Ionian Islands and Italy
heading west, while trains and buses depart
east to Athens and northern Greece via

Corinth. To the south lie the Peloponnese,
where there are some of Greece's greatest
ancient monuments, including Olympus,
the site of the first Olympic games.

Otherwise, a day trip to the island of
Kefalonia — of *Captain Corelli's Mandolin*
fame — is possible. Indeed, given that
there's no ferry linking up all the Ionian
Islands at the present moment, Patras has
become the only port serving the southern
part of this group.

HISTORY
Named after the Achaean chief, Patreus, the
city has a long and distinguished history,

Lepanto
Fought off Patras on 7 October 1571, Lepanto has gone down in history as a decisive battle in the age-old struggle between Ottomans and Europeans,
Muslims and Christians. Until then, so popular belief has it, the conflict had been one
of almost continuous Islamic expansion and Christian retreat — after then, though,
the boot was on the other foot. However, you may be surprised to find out that actually almost none of the above is true.

The battle, fought entirely at sea, came about as part of a combined Christian
effort to try to prevent the Ottomans from taking Cyprus, at that time a besieged
Venetian stronghold. Venice cobbled together an alliance with the Pope, Pius V, and
Philip II of Spain, at that time the most powerful Christian kingdom in the world.
Philip's half-brother, Don John of Austria, was put in command of a combined fleet
of around 200 ships, assembled at Messina.

However, by the time the fleet was ready, the war was in fact almost over. The
Ottomans had landed on Cyprus, captured Nicosia and were besieging Famagusta.
Meanwhile, their fleet had entered the Adriatic and was moored off Patras, cutting off
any attempt the Venetians might make to send reinforcements to Cyprus.

Don John set off to confront this fleet, which was commanded by Ali Pasha.
After four hours of fighting, the Christian forces were victorious, capturing some 117
Ottoman galleys and taking thousands of prisoners, including Ali Pasha himself.

But when the smoke cleared, Famagusta had fallen and Cyprus, the main point of
the campaign, was in Ottoman hands. The losses sustained by the Ottoman navy were
enormous, yet the empire was still strong enough and rich enough to have another,
even larger, fleet built within a matter of months. Lepanto then, was really more of a
consolation prize for Christendom, a tactical victory in the midst of an overall defeat.

Nonetheless, this victory of the combined Christian fleets over the Ottomans was
hailed in Europe as a moment of true deliverance. Painted by Titian, Tintoretto and
Veronese and celebrated by the author of *Don Quixote*, Miguel Cervantes, who actually took part, it was the subject of much bell-ringing and prayer-chanting throughout
Christendom at the time.

Furthermore, despite the overall defeat, it did at least give a psychological boost
to the Ottomans' enemies, while also being an early example of the power of good
PR. With some of Italy's finest painters showing the great victory, and the Pope himself branding it a turning point, who in Europe could possibly disagree?

Patras

IROON POLITEHNIOU

AGIAS SOFIAS

ATHINON

KONSTANTINOUPOLEOS

Ferries
to Italy

FAVIEROU

Camping
Rion

Ferries to
Ionian Islands

(i) Tourist
Info

KAROLOU

0   100   200m

Bus
Station

ZAIMI

Railway
station

Hotel
Splendid

MESONOS

KANAKARI

AGIOU NIKOLAOU

Kastro

OTHONOS AMALIAS

★ TRAILBLAZER

Pension
Nicos

Mezedopolio
Mouries

AGIOU ANDREOU

GOUNARI

KORINTHOU

Plateia
25 Martiou ● Odeon

YERMANOU

TRION NAVARHON

GOUNARI

Cathedral of
St Andrew

HILONOS PATREOS

ADRIATIC SEA

though regrettably little of this is still visible, save for the Kastro. St Andrew, the town's patron saint, is said to have been crucified here, and by the 13th century it was a Latin archbishopric, following the establishment of mainly Frankish control over mainland Greece. Venice and the Ottoman Empire fought over the town for centuries, with one of the most famous battles of the medieval period — Lepanto — being fought out on the Gulf in front of town (see box on p274).

Finally, it was here in 1821 that the Greek War of Independence broke out, with most of the city being burnt down in the fighting that followed. What you see now is the post-independence rebuild.

WHAT TO SEE
This usually doesn't take too long. South-west of the port looms the Cathedral of St Andrew, which has amongst its holy knick-knacks the head of the saint himself. Cut inland from here towards the Kastro, and a restored amphitheatre, the Odeon, comes into view on Plareia 25 Martiou.

The walled fortress (Kastro) is just behind this, accessed by steps from the top of Agiou Nikolaou. The walls are mainly Venetian, as Venice occupied the Peloponnese — which it called the Morea — on and off for many years, with Patras and Nafpaktos (Lepanto), across on the other side of the gulf, two fortresses that could control the entrance to the Gulf of Corinth on the one hand, and the sea lanes down the Greek coast via the Ionian Islands on the other. Unfortunately for Venice, this powerful strategic position ended up in Ottoman hands, with dire consequences for the city republic's empire.

PRACTICAL INFORMATION
Orientation
Patras is built on a regular grid plan, with the harbour area along the main corniche, Othonos Amalios. The railway station is on this road by the harbour too, along with the main inter-city bus station. Othonos becomes Iroön Politehniou as it curves north, and on this stretch you'll find most of the wide variety of shipping agencies. Up

behind and inland is the Kastro, the Byzantine-Turkish-Venetian fortress built on the site of the ancient acropolis. Everything you'll want to see is within walking distance.

Services
The EOT tourist office (☎ 0620 3539), at the international ferry terminal, is open Mon-Fri 0800-2000.

The tourist police station (☎ 045 1833), also based at the international ferry terminal, is open daily 0730-2300. The main branch of the post office, on the corner of Zaïmi and Mezonos, is open Mon-Fri 0730-2000, Sat 0730-1400. Internet access is available at Rocky Racoon, 56, Gerokostopoulou.

Ferries   [see p451 for full details]
Patras has good connections for Italy (Ancona, Bari, Bríndisi, Trieste and Venice) and for Corfu, Ithaca and Kefalonia. Ticket agencies lie around the port, particularly at the northern end. Shipping companies and agencies operating from here include: Aquarius Travel (☎ 0421 5000), 4, Athinion Ave, for Minoan Lines and GA Ferries; Express Shipping Agencies (☎ 022 2958), 81, Othonos Amalias, for Ventouris Ferries; Filopoulos Th-K Parthenopoulos SA (☎ 062 2500), for Superfast Ferries; Telonis-Tsimaras (☎ 062 2602), 14, Othonos Amalias, for Blue Star Ferries; and United Ferries Agencies (☎ 022 6053), 25, Othonos Amalias, for ANEK and Hellenic Mediterranean Lines (☎ 045 2521).

The port authority is on ☎ 034 1024.

Trains
Patras is a four-hour train journey from Athens, with some eight trains a day, the first around 0600, the last around 2200. The cost is around €10.

Buses
There are buses to Athens every 30 minutes (3 hours, €14).

Where to stay
Pension Nicos (☎ 062 3757), 121, Agiou Andreou, at the south-western end of the harbour, has economical rooms for €25/35 sgl/dbl.

Hotel Splendid (☎ 027 6522), on the corner of Othonos Amalias and Koloktroni. Has waterfront views for €30/45 sgl/dbl.

For camping, *Camping Rion* (☎ 099 1585) lies 7km north of Patras on the beach.

Where to eat
Unfortunately, Patras has developed a reputation for being one of the worst places in Greece to eat out, so try *Mezedopolio Mouries*, in Papadiamatopoilou St, opposite the Kastro entrance, for some well-made meze for around €1.50 a plate, or try one of the gyro/souvlaki buffets around the international ferry terminal.

Kefalonia

AREA CODE: ☎ ARGOSTOLI 2671, SAMI ☎ 2674 POPULATION: 33,000
The second largest of the Ionian Islands and a neighbour to Ithaca — the one time home and destination of Odysseus — Kefalonia now has something of a literary feel to it, as thousands of copies of one of the Aegean's most inescapable books, *Captain Corelli's Mandolin*, fill up its beach hampers, backpacks and bookshelves. The recent movie has also added to its tourist appeal, but it is still largely one of the more untouched Greek islands, with its mountainous interior, dominated by the snow-capped 1628m Mount Aenos, and beautiful coasts making it a real gem.

It also has several ports. It's most likely you will arrive at Sami, on the eastern coast, while the capital is at Argostoli in the west.

HISTORY
Starting out as a significant settlement in Mycenean times, Kefalonia was an ally of Athens, the losers in the Peloponnesian wars. It then surrendered, revolted and was destroyed by the Romans in 189BC, before later being seized by the Norman adventurer Robert Guiscard. Robert himself was killed in a revolt in 1085, leading to alternate Venetian and Neopolitan rule, with a brief Ottoman interlude between 1479-99.

Revolutionary France took over in 1797, before decidedly unrevolutionary Britain snapped it up in 1809. It became a part of the little remembered British Ionian Protectorate until 1864, when it was given to Greece.

In WWII it was occupied by the Italians. That was, until 1943, when Italy surrendered to the Allies. It was then taken over by the Germans, who had until then been on Italy's side. However, resistance to the German takeover by the 9000 strong Italian garrison led to a massacre. All but 33 of the Italian troops were slaughtered. Louis de Bernieres' *Captain Corelli's Mandolin* tells this story, and of the postwar devastation wrought on the island by the 1953 earthquake which reportedly either destroyed or damaged every single building on Kefalonia.

Nowadays, it is an island slowly waking up to its tourism potential, though with traditional industries — boat-building being one — still intact.

WHAT TO SEE
Argostoli is unlikely to win any Mediterranean beauty contests despite its magnificent setting. The earthquake clearly destroyed much of the town, and what stands today is largely modern concrete blocks. However, it does have a busy atmosphere, with some lively goings-on along the waterfront and the British-Protectorate-era causeway linking across the lagoon to the rest of the island.

The **Archaeological Museum** (Tue-Sun 0830-1500, €2.50), on Rokou Vergoti, has a small collection of antiquities, while further up on the same street is the **Historical and Cultural Museum** (Mon-Sat, 0900-1400, €2.50) with a nice collection of costumes and pictures of what the town used to look like before the quake.

Outside Argostoli, one of the main sights is the Venetian **Kastro**, 9km to the south-east. This was the capital of the island during Venetian rule, and its castle, Agios Georgios (0800-1500, free), has some well-worth-the-climb views. Up into the interior from here is the Monastery of Agios Gerasimos, the island's patron saint. South of town is also where you'll find two good

ADRIATIC SEA

sandy beaches, around 5km out, at Makrys Gialos and Platys Gialos, connected by frequent bus services (€1).

Some of the island's main attractions are subterranean. **Drongarati Cave** lies 4km south-west of Sami (€2 entrance), with **Melissani Cave** (€2.50 entrance) close by on the Sami–Agia Efimia road. For a glimpse of what many of the towns and villages looked like before the quake, however, head for the northern port of Fiskardo. Lined with Venetian buildings with pretty squares and an excellent waterfront, it's a fine place to stay too, looking over at the island of Ithaca. Café Tselenti is also supposedly the model for the Drosoula Taverna in *Captain Corelli's Mandolin*.

Kefalonia is also a centre for loggerhead turtles (see box on p24). They hit the southern sands of the island around June to lay their eggs, so many beaches are closed off. Check with the tourist information office to find out what the latest developments are.

PRACTICAL INFORMATION
Orientation
Boats from Patras arrive at Sami, with buses meeting the ferries and taking you on the short ride to Argostoli. The bus station is at the southern end of the harbour, near the causeway. Running along the waterfront in Argostoli is the main road, known as Ioanou Metaxa at its southern and northern ends but as Antoni Tristi in the middle.

Services
The **EOT** (☎ 2671-022 248), on the southern dock of the quay in Argostoli, is open Mon-Fri 0730-1430, and can help with accommodation. The main branch of the **post office** is on Diad Konstantinou; the OTE **phone office** is on Georgiou Vergoti.

Ferries   [see p451 for full details]
The main companies operating to **Bríndisi** from here are HML, Maritime Way and Med Link Lines; Blue Star, Fragline and GA Ferries go to **Ithaca** and HML and Med Link Lines to **Patras**.

If you aim to venture to any of the other islands round here, ferries depart from an unsettlingly varied number of different ports and portlets. For **Lefkada** or **Ithaca**, you want the port of Fiskardo, connected by two buses a day with Argostoli (€3). Also for **Ithaca**, try Sami. For **Zakynthos**, try Pessada, which regrettably isn't on the bus route, though you could try the twice-daily Skala bus and get off about 1km from the town at the Pessada turn off.

Agents in Sami: Sami Travel (☎ 2674-023 050) for Four Island Ferries and GA Ferries; Marketou Shipping Agency (☎ 2674-022 055) for Blue Star Ferries; while Schinari-Pessada Local Lines (☎ 2675-023984) does not have an office.

Buses
Buses leave for Platys Gialos and Sami every half an hour or so (€1.50, 10-15 mins); three times a day to Poros (€2.75, 1 hour); twice a day to Skala (€2.50, 45 mins); and twice a day to Fiskardo (€2.75, 1½ hours).

Planes
The airport is 9km south of town and there's no airport bus. A taxi should be around €10. There's one flight a day to Athens; the Olympic Airways office (☎ 2671-028 808) is at 1, Rokou Vergoti.

Where to stay
Hotel Kefalonia Star (☎ 2671-023 181), 60, Ioanou Metaxa, Argostoli. Has waterfront views, with sgl/dbl €40/60.
Vivian Villa (☎ 2671-023 396), 9, Deladetsima, Argostoli. Well appointed and clean; €35/50 sgl/dbl.
Regina's Rooms (☎ 2671-041 125), Fiskardo. €30/40 sgl/dbl.
Argostoli Camping (☎ 2671-023 487), 2km north of town on the coast.

Where to eat
Kalafatis, on Andoni Tristi in Argostoli. Has good wholesome food for €10 a head.
Patsouras Taverna, opposite the ferry dock, Argostoli. Has good local produce for €10-12.
Lagoudera, in Fiskardo.Another fine establishment for local specialities; budget €10-15.

ADRIATIC SEA

Ithaca

AREA CODE: ☎ 2674 POPULATION: 4000

Unspoilt and rocky, Ithaca today seems quite an easy place to believe in ancient Greek legends. It was here that Odysseus finally returned at the end of Homer's *Odyssey*. Or at least, that's what most people think. Neighbouring Kefalonia also has a claim to being Odysseus' final destination, while several other Mediterranean islets have thrown their hats into the ring at various times too. Whatever, though, Ithaca today — known as Ithaki — has maintained a good off-the-beaten-track feel to it, though partly this is to do with its lack of sandy beaches or ancient sites to live up to its literary reputation.

The main settlement is Ithaca Town (also known as Vathy) where the ferries from Kefalonia and Patras come in. One kilometre west of here is the island's main current highlight — the Cave of the Nymphs, where Odysseus is supposed to have stashed piles of loot given to him by the Phaeacians, who had returned him to the island. No one has ever found Odysseus' palace though, with current archaeological thinking placing it near Stavros, on the island's north-west coast. Stavros also has a good, if rocky, beach, while the fishing village of Frikes, on the northern tip, is a gentle, quiet retreat.

The island's bus service runs three times a day from Vathy to Kioni, a pleasant harbour village with a beach 1km east of Frikes (€1.75).

PRACTICAL INFORMATION

Services

The **tourist police station** (☎ 032 205) in Vathy is on Evmeou; open Mon-Fri 0800-1300. The **post office** and **bank**, on the central square, are both open mornings only, Mon-Fri.

Where to stay

Hotel Odysseus (☎ 032 381), on Georgiou Gratsou in Vathy, south-east of the waterfront. Sgl/dbl for €28/40.
Vasiliki Vlasopoulou Domatis (☎ 032 386), south of the quay. €25/35 sgl/dbl.

Where to eat

The harbour front in Vathy has many decent cafés and restaurants — try *Kantouni* for good fish dishes, €10 a head, or work back from the water for cheaper eats — *O Nikos*, one street back, serves the island's own wine; €8.

Ferries   [see p451 for full details]

Blue Star, Fragline and GA Ferries have daily services to **Sami** and **Patras** from Vathy. Fragline also operates to **Lefkada** from Frikes and Schinari-Pessada goes daily to **Zakynthos**.

ADRIATIC SEA

PART 7: AEGEAN SEA

Introduction

From the coast of Thrace in the north to Crete in the south, and from Greece in the west to Turkey in the east, the Aegean is a sea knee-deep in history and, during the summer months, also knee-deep in tourists. Yet, while taking off as a major vacation venue last century, it still has a much rougher edge to it than anywhere in the western Med, with enough of its scattered islands and crenellated coasts to provide the traveller with somewhere far from the maddening crowd.

It's also a place long-famed for its light. There's a strength to its colours too, and to its culture, factors which bring Greeks and Turks much closer together than might be expected. Yet the contrasts too are exhilarating, from the unmistakable skyline of İstanbul to the cradle of Western civilization in Athens.

Much of the route outlined in this guide also brings contact with other cultures that have shaped the Aegean's present: the Italians, who for many years ruled the Dodecanese; the Venetians, who held Crete as their most precious possession; or the European religious union of the Knights of St John, which built its castles and fortresses up and down the Anatolian coast.

Travelling around, if you arrive at İstanbul, you can head south to İzmir by boat, or make the bus trip to Ayvalık, a wonderfully ramshackle old Greek town on the Turkish coast opposite Lesbos. From either place, ferries over to Greece are available, and it's possible to then continue south, hopping back and forth between the two countries and taking in the best of both.

Making for Athens, the whole Aegean is at your disposal. One idea is to cross from there south to Crete, an island in a world of its own, before going over to Rhodes, a great base for heading back up through the Dodecanese to İstanbul, or further east, to Cyprus, the transport hub for the Eastern Med.

If you want to go back west though, Thessaloniki is a worthy stop off, while a short overland journey will bring you to the Ionian sea ports of Igoumenitsa, off Corfu, and Patras. From here, regular ferries take you over to Italy, to begin a tour of either the Adriatic or, with a short ride across the toe of Italy, the Tyrrhenian Sea.

TRAVELLING AROUND THE AEGEAN

When it comes to ferries, the Aegean is also the best served region of the Mediterranean. Hundreds of boats depart daily from Athens' harbour, Piraeus, heading for all the Greek islands, while the Turkish coast has in recent years become increasingly hooked up by sea to its neighbour.

SUGGESTED ITINERARIES

Athens to İstanbul

This route means you'll be doing something that until recently was almost unheard of – hopping between historic foes, Greece and Turkey. What you may find too, is how both share far more than is commonly thought, with the Aegean coast of Anatolia an astonishing treasure house of ancient Greek cities and sights. Athens is a place most people either love or hate but either way it should be part of the itinerary of any Aegean trip, not least because its port is pivotal to the services operating in the region. The island of Rhodes, like Athens, has remains from many civilizations, particularly in Rhodes Town. On the Turkish side, Marmaris is most notable for its setting whereas Bodrum offers perhaps the liveliest nightlife in Turkey. Kos is home to one of the region's most important archaeological sites – the Asklepion – and some excellent beaches. Samos also has some lovely beaches and mountains as well as the remains of some significant temples. Kuşadası is the nearest port to Ephesus, one of the Mediterranean's top five ancient Roman cities. İzmir has enough of interest for a day or so but the main incentive must be to move on to İstanbul, a city whose strategic location has given it an important role in the history of the Mediterranean and a place which, unlike Athens, almost everyone loves.

Athens/Piraeus to Rhodes (daily, 18 hrs); Rhodes to Marmaris (daily, 2hrs); Marmaris to Bodrum (daily, 2hrs); Bodrum to Kos (daily, 20 mins); Kos to Samos (Pythagorio; daily, 3¹/₂hrs); overland to Vathy; Vathy to Kuşadası (daily, 60 mins); overland from Kuşadası to İzmir; ferry (weekly, 19hrs) or bus to İstanbul.

Circuit of the Aegean

Iraklio is a good base for anywhere on Crete, particularly the ancient Minoan palace at Knossos. For those wanting a less touristy atmosphere Sitia is preferable

---

❑ **Aegean – the highlights**
● **İstanbul** – One time capital of three different empires, with one of the most emblematic skylines in the world, the city has boomed in recent years into a giant megalopolis. It's also boomed in terms of its modern attractions with a great entertainment centre, Beyoğlu, and one of the greatest of all Mediterranean boulevards in İstiklal Caddesi.
● **Athens** – Recovering from its Olympic facelift, Athens still manages a good mix of new and trendy with old and gritty. With Piraeus still the greatest of all Mediterranean ferry ports, the city's ancient pedigree is surpassed by few.
● **Ayvalık** – On Turkey's northern Aegean shores, this marvellous mesh of old alleys and arty people is also a great jumping-off point for the region.
● **Kalymnos** – Seems to have been bypassed by much of the Aegean tourist traffic, giving it the feel of a Greek island out of time, with a harbour-front of hand-painted signs and friendly ouzeria.
● **Nisyros** – Both weird and beautiful, try being there around the Feast of the Assumption in mid-August, when a strong mysticism captures this strange volcanic island of black-sand beaches and sulphurous interior.

The Aegean Sea
FERRY ROUTES

.... Ferry route   ----- Currently no service   - - - Mini-Cruise

GREECE

Thessaloniki

Kavala

Skiathos
SKIATHOS

Myrina
LIMNOS

AEGEAN

Psara
Town
PSARA

Olinousses
Town

CHIOS

Chios
Town

Cesme

LESBOS

Ayvalik

Mytilini

Izmir

Kusadasi

T U R K E Y

TURKEY

ISTANBUL

AEGEAN SEA

0   50   100   150km

APPROX SCALE

AEGEAN SEA

To Limassol, from Rhodes

To Limassol, from Piraeus

Gelibolu
Marmaris
Kormen
Symi Town
SYMI
Rhodes Town
RHODES
Megisti
KASTELORIZO
Bodrum
Kos
KOS
Kardamena
Karpathos Town
KARPATHOS
Nimborio
CHALKI
Diafani
Livadia
TILOS
Agia Marina
KASSOS
Vathy
Pthagorio
SAMOS
AGATHONISI
Ag. Marina
LEROS
Lipsi Town
LIPSI
ARKI
Mandraki
NISYROS
Masti hari
Kalymnos Town
KALYMNOS
Lakki
Astypalea Town
ASTYPALEA
Karlovassi
Fourni Town
FOURNI
Evdilos
IKARIA
Ag. Kyrikos
Skala
Patmos Town
PATMOS
Katapola
AMORGOS
Ios Town
IOS
Athinios
SANTORINI
Sitia
Spinalonga
Agios Nikolaos
SEA
MYKONOS
Mykonos Town
Naxos Town
NAXOS
Iraklio
CRETE
Paros Town
PAROS
Tinos Town
ANDROS
Gavrio
TINOS
Ermoupolis
SYROS
Milos Town
MILOS
Adamas
Rethymno
Marmari
Karystos
Rafina
ATHENS
Piraeus
Souda
Kissamos/Kastell
Egina Town
EGINA
Skala
ANGISTRI
Hydra Town
HYDRA
Spetses Town
SPETSES
Potamos
ANTIKYTHIRA
Agia Pelagia
KYTHIRA
GREECE

To Ancona & Brindisi from Cesme

To Venice, from Izmir

The population exchange

Visit almost any village, town or city on Turkey's Aegean coast or on the neighbouring Greek islands and a short ramble is usually enough to tell you something's wrong. Abandoned houses, crumbling churches and mosques, sections of the old town in states of great disrepair – the present-day remains of a tragic episode from over 80 years ago: the 1923 population exchange.

Go back to the beginning of the 20th century and you'll find that the Aegean region was ethnically quite different from today. While Greece was by then independent, much of its present territory was still part of the Ottoman Empire. Meanwhile, much of present-day Turkey was inhabited not by Turks but by Greeks. İstanbul itself had an enormous Greek-speaking population, with around half the city non-Muslim. Further south, İzmir had a Christian majority, while many of the villages and towns of the Anatolian coast were almost exclusively Greek.

Across the water, too, most present-day Greek islands had Turkish-speaking populations. Crete, for example, was around a third Muslim – a proportion roughly similar to the island of Cyprus today. Inland, too, most Greek towns and villages had mosques as well as churches, while some had Turkish majorities.

This was the combined legacy of the Byzantine Empire, which had spread far across Anatolia, and the Ottoman Empire which had conquered it. For centuries, these two populations lived side by side, albeit under the dominance of the Turks.

That came to an abrupt end with WWI and its aftermath. Seeking to take advantage of the collapse of the Ottoman Empire and re-establish the old Byzantine realm, Greece staged an invasion of Anatolia, starting from İzmir and pushing ever eastwards. Countering this was a resurgent Turkey under the command of its greatest leader, Mustafa Kemal Atatürk. After a decisive battle on the River Sakarya in 1923, the Greeks were repelled, retreating back to İzmir and then across the Aegean.

The episode is referred to in Greece as the 'Asia Minor Disaster', while in most Western countries it's the Greek–Turkish War, and in Turkey, the War of Liberation. Whatever it's called, the result was a deal between Greek and Turkish governments (with the British and French involved too) that fixed the boundaries of both states.

It also followed the prevailing principle of the time: nationalism. What this meant in this case was that there was no longer any room for Greeks in Turkey, or Turks in Greece. Hundreds of thousand of people were suddenly uprooted from their ancestral homes and forced into exile in lands they had never seen before. It is not known how many were killed in the process, or died en route, but within a short time the entire Greek-speaking population of Anatolia had been sent to Greece, while the entire Turkish-speaking population of Greece travelled the other way.

Under the terms of the agreement – the Treaty of Lausanne – the Greeks of İstanbul were spared, along with the Turks of Thrace. The Turks of the Dodecanese Islands were also spared, as these islands were then under Italian rule. All the rest had to leave, often being settled in the houses the others had vacated. Ayvalık, for example, was for centuries a Greek town, yet its Greek inhabitants were forced to leave and settle on Lesbos. Meanwhile, the Turks of Lesbos were forced to leave and settle in Ayvalık. The numbers swapped were never an exact match, though, with more Greeks uprooted than Turks. This left many buildings, and in some places entire villages, to fall into ruin.

Despite the intervening years, there are still some who can just about remember the old days. Sometimes you can see them too, wandering slowly the old streets of their childhood towns. What happened to them was not the first, and certainly not the last, example of ethnic cleansing – nor was it one of the more violent – yet it has certainly left its scars on both sides of this long, troubled sea.

to Agios Nikolaos though both have places of interest. The well-preserved buildings in Rhodes Town are good to stroll around but the Acropolis at Lindos should also be visited. Nisyros is one of the most mystical islands in the Dodecanese, whilst Kalymnos is often overlooked in favour of Kos. Patmos, a holy island due to St John's revelation there during his exile, has some wonderful beaches. Chios, one of the biggest islands in the Aegean, offers fishing villages and the Nea Moni monastery, a World Heritage listed building. The long journey to Thessaloniki is particularly worthwhile if you are interested in archaeology (there is an excellent museum there) and good nightlife.

Note: It would be hard to fit the circuit outlined below into two weeks but it could easily by shortened by returning to Piraeus from any of the places en route.

Piraeus to Santorini (daily, 9hrs); Santorini to Iraklio (daily, 4hrs); overland to Agios Nikolaos/Sitia; Agios Nikolaos/Sitia to Rhodes (3-4 per week, 9-11hrs); Rhodes to Nisyros (4 per week, 2hrs); Nisyros to Kalymnos (3 per week, 2^1/2hrs); Kalymnos to Patmos (daily, 2hrs); Patmos to Chios (weekly, 5^1/2hrs), Chios to Thessaloniki (weekly, 16^1/2hrs); Thessaloniki to Piraeus (weekly, 26 hrs).

Aegean Sea – ports and islands

Thessaloniki

AREA CODE: ☎ 231 **POPULATION:** 475,000
Set on a long, slightly-curving waterfront at the head of the Gulf of Thermaikos, Thessaloniki is Greece's second city, a major national and international transport hub, and was even the European City of Culture back in 1997.

Like Athens, it is also a city on which the Balkans, Asia Minor and the Aegean have all left major imprints, with all the turbulent history that that implies. Unlike Athens, though, it was never a great ancient Greek city, coming into its own only in Roman times. As a result, it lacks the grand spectacle of a Parthenon but still has a number of recommendable sites from antiquity and an excellent archaeological museum.

Trade, though, is what Thessaloniki has always been about, a fact you can still see in the bustle of streets back off the waterfront and the busy harbour – the commercial and industrial workings of a great city. It also has a lively nightlife and some excellent

restaurants, along with good connections to elsewhere in Greece — either by train, bus or ferry — and to neighbouring Macedonia, Bulgaria and Turkey. It's also the main access point to Halkidiki, the peninsula to the south-east that contains the Greek Orthodox version of the Vatican City, the Monastic Republic of Mt Athos — an independent, men-only finger of land dotted with the Church's most sacred monasteries.

Another local-ish sight, and a bit more female friendly, is the 2917m Mt Olympos, home of the Greek gods, which rises some 100km to the south-west, off the Athens road. Otherwise, the region around is one of Greece's less well known, stretching along a narrow coastal plain to the Turkish border. Indeed, there is still a substantial ethnic Turkish population in Komotini and Xanthi.

HISTORY
The name of the city — which is also referred to as Salonika, or Saloniki — originally came from one of Alexander the Great's sisters, yet it was no great city until Roman times when, in 146BC, it was made

capital of the province of Macedonia.

It was a major stop on the Via Egnatia, the main Roman road heading west out of Constantinople (İstanbul) to the Adriatic coast and hence to Italy. This was clearly a major boon to local business, and the city grew to such prominence that St Paul even wrote two letters to its early inhabitants.

As with many successful cities though, prosperity attracted its fair share of adventurers, freeloaders and, ultimately, downright barbarians, with the 6th and 7th centuries AD being particularly rough for attacks by Avar and Slavic tribes. Internal trouble within the Byzantine Empire then followed, with the Thessalonians taking the 'pro-icon' side in the iconoclastic period of the late 8th century – a decision that must have angered the powers in Constantinople. In the ensuing centuries, successive Norman, Arab and Bulgarian attacks followed. Restored to Byzantine rule in 1246, it remained so until 1423 when, in an effort to keep the Ottomans out, it gave itself away to Venice. The Venetians didn't do too good a job of defending it, though, and it soon fell to Sultan Murad II's forces in 1430.

The 1492 pogrom in Spain, in which the Jews of the Iberian Peninsula were forced to leave or be slaughtered by their new Catholic rulers, Isabel and Ferdinand, proved a bonus for Thessaloniki. In a rare example of medieval humanitarianism, the Ottomans invited the Spanish Jews to come and settle in their empire, with large numbers of them arriving in Thessaloniki. From then until WWII, when the occupying Nazis sent almost the entire Jewish population to the death camps, Thessaloniki was one of the most important Jewish cities in the world.

With this new population and the prosperity Ottoman rule gave, the city continued to grow and gained a remarkably cosmopolitan character. Greeks, Jews and Turks lived here together, with one of the most famous of the latter being Mustafa Kemal, later known as Atatürk, the founder of modern Turkey. He was born here and did a fair amount of intriguing in its officers' clubs with other Young Turks — the Ottoman Empire's would-be reformers. The

city stayed outside Greek control until the First Balkan War of 1912, after which it was ceded to Athens. A short while later, it was the scene of the assassination of the Greek king, George I, in 1913.

In WWI, Thessaloniki was the base for Allied operations against both Turkey and Bulgaria, during which someone must have been very careless with matches, as a fire in 1917 destroyed many of the harbour front buildings and most of the commercial district. The population exchange with Turkey in 1923 (see box on p284) brought in many Greek-speaking Anatolians, though the Turkish minority in this region was allowed to stay. With the extermination of the Jewish population in 1941, the city thus emerged into the second half of the 20th century with a radically different population than the one it had started out with. An earthquake in 1978 also inflicted major damage.

Yet despite such travails, the city is still a thriving metropolis, the building and rebuilding leaving it with a distinctive character, its grid plan streets, lined with a combination of 19th- to 20th-century city blocks and Byzantine churches, all rising up behind the waterfront and on into the hills beyond.

WHAT TO SEE

Ancient Thessaloniki was bisected by the Via Egnatia, which ran from the Vardar Gate in the west to the Kalamaria Gate in the east. Modern Thessaloniki is basically the same, and to make things still easier, the central east–west avenue is still called **Egnatia**. For a look around, it's an idea to begin at the western gate — or at least, **Plateia Dimokratias**, the square that now occupies the site of the Vardar Gate. Heading south towards the waterfront from here will take you through a maze of warehouses and workshops before you emerge by the ferry terminal on the main corniche, **Nav Koundouriotou**. Walk along here as far as **Plateia Aristotelous**, a grand square with a road heading straight inland lined with arcaded buildings modelled on the street that stood here before the 1917 fire. Keep on going to the other end of the waterfront road though for Thessaloniki's main landmark, the **White Tower** (Tue-Sun,

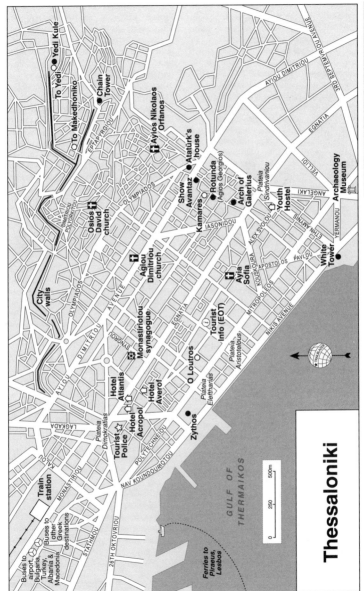

Thessaloniki

AEGEAN SEA

To Yedi
Yedi Kule
Chain Tower
To Makedhoniko
EFTAPYRGIOU
Ayios Nikolaos Orfanos
Atatürk's house
AYIOU DIMITRIOU
3RD SEPTEMVRIOU AVENUE
EGNATIA
VELLIDI
DIMITRIOU POLIORKITIOU
Osios David church
Show
Avantaz
Rotunda (Agios Georgios)
Arch of Galerius
Plateia Sindrivaniou
Archaeology Museum
OLYMPIADOS
Kamares
Youth Hostel
ANGELAKI
ERMANOU
IASONIDOU
AEX SYOLOU
City walls
Agiou Dimitriou church
EGNATIA
ETHN AMYNIS
Ayia Sofia
Plateia Sindrivaniou
APOSTOLOS PAVLOU
White Tower
TERMANOU
OLYMPIADOS
AVENUE
SYGNROU
MTROPOLEOS
KOUSKOURA
NIKIS AVENUE
DIMITRIOU
Monastiriotou synagogue
Tourist Info (EOT)
Plateia Aristotelous
AYIOU
Hotel Atlantis
O Loutros
LAGKADA
Hotel Averof
Plateia Elettharias
Hotel Acropol
Tourist Police
Zythos
Plateia Dimokratias
KALOU
POLYTECHNEIOU
NAV KOUNDOUROTOU
GULF OF THERMAIKOS
MONASTIRIOU
Train station
Buses to airport, Bulgaria, Turkey, Albania & Macedonia
Buses to other Greek destinations
STATHMOU
26TH OKTOVRIOU
Ferries to Piraeus, Lesbos

0   250   500m

0800-1430, free). This is the last of the medieval towers that once encircled the city. It is no longer white, and now contains a small collection of Byzantine art.

From here, turning up Yermanou past the State Theatre brings you to the **Archaeology Museum** (Mon 1230-1730, Tue-Sun 0830-1500, €5), housing a fine and extensive collection of antiquities, with gold and silver exhibits from the royal tomb of Philip II of Macedon the star attraction. Allow plenty of time for a good look round.

Strolling back inland up Angelaki to Plateia Sindrivaniou, turn left and on your right you'll see the AD303 **Arch of Galerius**, a Roman construction that once stood over the Via Egnatia, and was the city's main eastern gateway. The carvings on it commemorate Emperor Galerius' victories over the Persians in Armenia and Mesopotamia.

Immediately north of here is perhaps the most impressive ancient structure in the city, the **Rotunda** (daily 0830-1500, free). Built around AD306, this was intended as a pantheon-cum-mausoleum by Galerius but appears to have never been used, having quickly been converted into a church: Ayios Georgios. During Ottoman times it was converted into a mosque, hence the minaret that stands by its side today, but which strangely fails to appear on any of the official pictures of the place. The effect inside of this tall, barrel-like building is at once eerie and uplifting.

North again from here brings you to the east–west Ayiou Dhimitriou Avenue. Cross over, turn left then quickly right and you'll arrive at **Atatürk's house**, now in the gardens of the Turkish consulate. Inside is a museum dedicated to the great man, born here in 1881. Viewing is by arrangement with the consulate; 0930-1200 is the best time to ask. Still further north, up Apostolos Pavlou, is the 14th-century **Ayios Nikolaos Orfanos** (Tue-Sun 0800-1430, free). The frescos of Christ's passion inside are the best preserved in the city.

The church lies in the old Turkish quarter, the Kastra. The streets here are more twisting, and the houses have the distinctive overhanging upper floors of Ottoman architecture. You're also close to

the surviving sections of **city walls**, built during the reign of Roman Emperor Theodosius I between AD379-395, though subsequently reinforced and restored on numerous occasions. These run north-west to the **Chain Tower**, a corner bastion, then on to **Yedi Kule** ('Seven Towers' in Turkish), the remains of the main northern defensive stronghold of the city.

Further west in this jumble of streets, on Dimitriou Polyorkitou, is the **Osios David** (Mon-Sat 0800-1200, 1700-1800, free). This 15th-century church has a fine mosaic of Christ, appearing in a vision to Old Testament prophets Ezekiel and Habakkuk. Thessaloniki's other main Christian sites are the 8th-century **Church of Ayia Sofia**, in the square of the same name, and the 5th-century Ayios Dimitrios, named after the city's patron saint and located, naturally enough, on Ayiou Dimitriou. The former is notable for its design, representing a transition from the domed basilica – it's modelled on the most famous of these, Aya Sofya in İstanbul (see p385) — to the later cross plan. The dome has a beautiful 9th-century mosaic in the ceiling depicting Christ's Ascension.

Ayiou Dimitrios (Tue-Sun 0800-1930, free) is built on the site where the saint was martyred and is the largest church in Greece. The mosaics inside next to the altar are original, 7th-century work, and are almost all that survived the 1917 fire. The church you see now is a reconstruction, undertaken between 1926 and 1948.

One other site worth seeing is the **Monastiriotou synagogue** on Syngrou, one of the few surviving reminders of the city's Jewish past. It's open to worshippers but not the general public unless by appointment. Contact: the Rabbinate of Thessaloniki at 24, Tsimiki (☎ 0221124).

PRACTICAL INFORMATION
Orientation
Thessaloniki's shape is relatively straightforward, a series of parallel lines running east–west stacked up behind the waterfront with streets running up and down between them to form the grid. The **train station** is at the western end of this pattern, along with the **departure point for buses** to the

airport, Athens and Igoumenitsa. To the north-west are the buses heading towards Turkey and Bulgaria. The main ferry port is midway along the waterfront, while the archaeological museum is at the waterfront's eastern end.

Thessaloniki is quite walkable, though city-buses regularly plough the main avenues, with a flat €0.45 fee for a ticket, bought onboard.

The airport is 16km south-east of town, a regular bus, No 78, taking you from there to the stop by the train station for (first bus around 0600, last around 2300) and back again. A taxi costs about €9.

Services

The **Greek Tourist Information Authority office** (EOT; ☎ 022 1935), 8, Plateia Aristotelous, is open Mon-Fri 0900-2100, Sat 1000-1800, Sun 1000-1700.

The **tourist police** (☎ 055 4871) at 4, Dodekanisiou, is open daily 0730-2300. The main branch of the **post office**, 26 Aristotelous, is open Mon-Fri 0730-2000, Sat 0730-1415, Sun 0900-1330. The **telephone office** (OTE), 27, Karolou Dil, is open 24hr. For **internet access** try the Link, 50, Gounari, or Globus, 12, Amynda.

Ferries   [see p460 for full details]

Ferries go from Thessaloniki via **Limnos**, **Lesbos** and **Chios** to **Piraeus** and via **Skiathos** and **Syros** also to **Piraeus**. At present there are only domestic ferry routes, though with the recent Greek–Turkish rapprochement, plans are being mooted to open up a link to İzmir; check with the port authority (☎ 053 1504-5).

The following agencies have offices in town: Crete Air Travel Ltd (☎ 054 7407), 1, Ionos Dhragoumi, for Minoan Lines; Karacharisis Travel (☎ 051 3005), 8, Koundouriotou for NEL Lines, Hellas Flying Dolphins.

Trains

Domestic There are 10 trains a day to and from Athens, the first leaving Thessaloniki around 0700, the last around 2300 (€12.50 one way). Going east, there are regular trains to Drama, Xanthi, Komotini, Alexandroupolis and Ormenia, the last stop before Bulgaria. Heading west, trains also depart for Edessa and towards the Macedonian border regularly.

Thessaloniki railway station can be reached on ☎ 051 7517-8; Athens on ☎ 21-0823 7741.

International There is one train a day through to İstanbul, via Alexandroupolis, costing €50 and taking anywhere between 12 and 24 hours. A more leisurely way of getting there is to take the Lesbos ferry, then the boat over to Ayvalık, from where buses go to İstanbul. This route, however, could take around two days.

There is also one train a day to Sofia (9 hours, €30), though this cannot be recommended as delays are routine at the border. The daily train to Skopje in Macedonia takes 5 hours and costs €15.

Buses

The Athens–İstanbul bus passes through Thessaloniki bus station, next to the railway station. The fare from Thessaloniki is €48 one way, taking around 12 hours.

The Athens–Sofia bus also passes through, costing €19 and taking 8 hours to Sofia on a good day at customs.

Planes

Thessaloniki is on several international air routes plus many domestic ones. The Olympic Airways office (☎ 023 0240) is at 3, Nav Koundouriotou. There are daily flights to Limnos, hourly ones to Athens, three a week to Corfu and two a week to Chios.

❑ **Visiting Mount Athos**
Men only are allowed in the Monastic Republic. You need a permit from the Mount Athos Pilgrims' Office (☎ 086 1611), 14, Konstantinou Karamanli, open Mon-Sat 0830-1330. Take your passport and be ready to specify a day on which you wish to go there.

AEGEAN SEA

Where to stay

The main area for budget accommodation is at the western end of Egnatia, near Plateia Dimokratis.

Youth Hostel (☎ 022 5946), 44, Alex Svolou, has dorm beds for €8.50 a night. It's open only March-November, though.

Hotel Acropol (☎ 053 6170), 4, Tantalidou, is in a side street off Egnatia, with sgl/dbl for €20/28.

Hotel Atlantis (☎ 054 0131), 14, Egnatia, is on the main drag; €20/30 sgl/dbl.

Hotel Averof (☎ 0538 840), 24, Leontos Sofou, is on another side street off Egnatia; €22/35 sgl/dbl.

The nearest **campsite** is at Ayia Triada, 24km away to the south of Thessaloniki round the bay.

Where to eat

O Loutros, 5, Koundoura, lies outside an old Ottoman hamam. It's a touch pricey, but there's excellent food. €15 a head.

To Yedi, next to the Yedi Kule fortress, open evenings only, an *ouzeri* (see p302) with fine *mezedes*; €10.

To Makedhoniko, Portara Gate. Popular 'youthy' ouzeri with cheap eats (€7.50).

Kamares, 11, Ayiou Georgiou, serves good wholesome dishes; €10.

Entertainment

Thessaloniki has long been in competition with Athens to claim top spot for rebetiko music (see box on p292). Try ***Show Avantaz***, 156, Agiou Dimitriou, for some, or for more contemporary sounds try the main bar and club area, Ladhadhika, west of Plateia Eleftherias near the port. ***Zythos***, 5, Plateia Katouni, is one of this district's favourites. For cafés and people-watching the waterfront road, Nikis, is lined with establishments.

Athens

AREA CODE: ☎ 21 POPULATION: 4 MILLION

Rising up amongst the hills north of the port of Piraeus, Athens is definitely a love/hate metropolis. To those who enjoy narrow streets and ancient temples, top flight bars and spit-and-sawdust tavernas, it's a hard place to leave. For others, disappointed by its pollution, traffic jams, seedy central district and boiling summers, the city's most welcome sights remain the airport, the train station and any other exit.

Yet, love it or hate it, Athens is clearly unmissable. Towering amongst the giants of Mediterranean cities, it has a recorded history going back several millennia, and for many years could feasibly lay claim to being the centre of Western civilization. Some of its inhabitants would say that it still is, too.

But what gives it its distinct character, apart from the postcard favourites of the Acropolis and its other ancient relics, is the fact that it contains both Western and Eastern currents and styles. It is at once a Balkan, Asian, Mediterranean and global city, with Ottoman houses next to Hellenic temples, and steel and glass business centres next to 19th-century Italian-designed apartment blocks. The crowds in its cafés and bars, clubs and pubs are also both strongly Greek and often strongly international. Athenians themselves are often particularly well travelled, with a diaspora ranging across all corners of the globe.

Yet, apart from the Acropolis, Athens remains strangely faceless. Built away from the sea between hills, its centre seems somehow difficult to grasp. Its narrow streets mean there are few grand boulevards, few parks, and monuments tend to be lost amongst the squeeze of buildings. Yet this, of course, is also the city's true charm. Going there just to see its ancient sites is to miss much, for the more memorable moments are likely to be encounters not with the far flung past, but the vibrant present.

With 2004 seeing the Olympics finally return to the land of their birth, much of the city is in even more chaos than usual. With the clock ticking and the roof only just on the Grand Olympic Stadium, the Games have given many Athenians much to gripe about – particularly when the Metro system, the roads and many other vital arteries of the city have become clogged with Olympic activity. Yet when the dust finally settles, the Olympics will most likely have transformed the city in many important ways, bringing a more stylish, up-to-date and western European look to many old quarters. As usual, this has both pluses and minuses.

HISTORY

The Acropolis, or at least the land on which it is built, is where the city's history starts. Pottery shards going back to neolithic times have been found there, and it's on this hill that the city's first building work can be traced as well — Cyclopean walls dating to around 1200BC. By this time, Athens was already an important regional power.

In the 6th century BC the city underwent rapid and massive expansion. The Acropolis changed from being a fortified camp to a religious sanctuary, as the city spread out beyond and across the valley floor. During the rule of Peisistratus and his sons (around 560-510 BC), major stone temples began to be constructed on the Acropolis, with the first temple to Athena built in 580BC. In 566BC, Peisistratus also organized the first Olympics. (The games, of course, returned in 2004.)

However, in 480BC the city was captured by the Persians and burnt to the ground. Little was done to rebuild it until peace returned in 448BC, after which, financed by Athenian enterprise on the high seas and some handy silver mines up in the Lavrion hills, lavish reconstruction could begin, including the Parthenon.

Athens was at the height of its power during this period, which lasted up to the Peloponnesian Wars with neighbouring Sparta. Begun in 432BC, these were resolved only in 402BC and the defeat of the Athenians. The city was slow to recover but nevertheless remained the vital cultural and artistic centre of the ancient Mediterranean world. The 4th century BC saw a flourishing of philosophical schools, and, also the arrival of Alexander the Great and his successor rulers, most of whom donated monuments to the city.

With the Romans arrival in 86BC, however, the city was once again sacked. On the ruins they created, the Romans then rebuilt, with the emperors Augustus, Hadrian and Valerian all commissioning

major architectural projects. New defences were also built, but these proved to no avail when the city was taken by the Germanic Heruli tribe in AD267. Rebuilt again, Athens survived as a centre for paganism in the newly Christianized Roman Empire, with its philosophical schools continuing to give it cultural weight until they were closed by the Emperor Justinian in AD529.

From then on, Constantinople became the undisputed centre of the Hellenistic world, right up until Greek independence in 1834, while from the 6th century AD Athens became a provincial Byzantine capital, captured and sacked yet again in 1204 by the Crusaders who began a protracted Latin occupation of the whole of the Peloponnese. Around the city they established the Duchy of Athens, which flourished under the Burgundian La Roche family until 1308 and the arrival on the scene of the Catalan Company. This band of mercenaries first fought on the side of the Duchy, but then turned against it, occupying Athens in 1311. They remained in charge until 1388, when they were forcibly ejected by another band of Iberian 'soldiers of fortune', the Navarrese Company.

In 1394, the Venetians jumped into the fray and occupied the city, staying only until 1402 when they too were ejected by the Florentine lord of Corinth, Nerio Acciaiuoli. His relatives ran Athens until the Ottomans finally took it in 1458, after a two-year siege. Two hundred years later the Venetians once again returned as part of their 1684 invasion of Greece. During their capture of the city the Parthenon was badly damaged when a Venetian shell blew up an Ottoman powder magazine hidden within it. The Venetians continued to rule until 1715, when the Ottomans returned to take charge.

Their rule was interrupted repeatedly by a succession of attempts by Greek nationalists to win back the city, most noticeably (and successfully) in 1821. With Greek independence in 1834, Athens was declared the new capital.

Following the Greek defeat in the post-WWI Turkish War of Independence a century later, mass deportations of Turkish Greeks to Turkey and Greek Turks to Greece

❏ Rebetiko

'My roll burns,
I smoke it slowly.
Istanbul is good,
but its owners are too tricky.'

Artful and wistful and deeply illusive, the music of rebetiko can sometimes be as hard to grasp as a curl of cigarette smoke — then suddenly, it can hit you like a slap. Its origins are obscure, yet began in poverty, and always with a certain *attitude*.

Back in 1821, according to the Greek musical theorist Elias Petropoulos, a social underclass known as *rebetes* began to emerge. The word comes from Turkish and means something like 'rebel', 'tough nut' or 'outlaw'. The original rebetes were unemployed, disaffected and often half-starved, living in Ottoman cities such as Athens, İstanbul and İzmir. Liberation from Ottoman rule brought little real change for many of the lower-class Greeks, and it was amongst these that rebetiko developed.

It was always protest music, yet without any overtly political forms. The instruments were the *bouzouki* and the *baglamas*, stringed instruments that were as much Turkish as Greek, while the melodies themselves were a blend of everywhere — Jewish, Bulgarian, Black Sea and Aegean. The musicians, too, belonged to no one single race or nation either, as the names of some of the most famous early performers, such as Rosa Eskenazi, or the violinist Semsis, testify. The main venues for a performance back then were the prison or the hash house — dope-smoking teahouses known as *tekes* after the Turkish word for a lodge. These were a major feature of İzmir, then known as Smyrna, and in other big Ottoman and Greek cities.   *(Continued opposite)*

took place, filling Athens with thousands of refugees from Asia Minor, while emptying its dozens of mosques — again changing the city's character. In WWII, though occupied by the Germans, Athens suffered relatively little bomb damage, though its population was badly affected by both near starvation and anti-resistance reprisals.

Modern times

Post WWII, the country and the city went through a bloody civil war between the leftist, communist-dominated Democratic Army and the rightist central government, which was backed up first by British troops and then by US aircraft. By 1948, the leftists had lost. Yet stability still proved elusive. In 1967, army commanders staged a coup and established the so-called Colonels' Junta. This lasted until 1974 when an abortive attempt to seize Cyprus backfired. In the aftermath of the defeat, the colonels were ousted and the conservative New Democracy party was elected to office, to be replaced in 1981 by the leftist PASOK party

as Greece entered the EU. With the exception of a brief period in the early 1990s, PASOK has remained in power ever since.

Currently, the government of Prime Minister Costas Simitis has been pushing for rapid integration with the EU, meaning wide-ranging political and economic reform. This has brought the government into conflict with the church — over removal of information on religion from ID cards in line with EU policy — and with the unions over privatization. Neither of these conflicts is anywhere near over. Meanwhile, Simitis has backed up a policy of tentative rapprochement with neighbouring Turkey.

In 2004, Athens held the Olympic games again. In preparation, the city underwent a major face lift. In its colossal history, this will not be the first time such a rebuild has taken place; nor, most likely, will it be the last, either.

WHAT TO SEE

Most of Athens' sights and its places to stay are within a small section of the city. Using

❏ **Rebetiko** *(Continued from p292)*
In Piraeus the Trumba area was notorious for them; in Thessaloniki it was Barra district. Throughout the latter half of the 19th century and into the 20th, rebetiko stayed as the music of the disadvantaged. Yet that was to change with the 'Asia Minor Disaster' of 1923. With the defeat of the Greek army's attempt to seize Anatolia from the Turks, vast numbers of Greeks were uprooted (see box on page 284) and descended en masse to a Greek state that was already impoverished by years of warfare. Unemployment in cities such as Athens and Thessaloniki became colossal, with the underclass of the rebetes swelling tenfold in consequence. The refugees also brought with them an extra layer of wistfulness: the longing for a home now gone forever. In this period, rebetiko came out of the teke and started to move mainstream. The bouzouki became increasingly identified as a Greek instrument and rebetiko as the essential Greek music. Yet, as Petropoulos adds, 'The bouzouki is not synonymous with Greece, but with rebetiko'. By the 1930s, rebetiko was being made into records by HMV.

Post-WWII, and post-Greek Civil War, the music was further developed with the introduction of the electric bouzouki and the addition of an extra string, making it tune up just like the first four strings of a guitar. All this aided its promotion, with the great rebetiko composers and performers of the 1950s and 1960s — such as Vassilis Tsitsanis and Manolis Chiotis — ironically also presiding over the music's eventual decline during that period, to the point where, today, rebetiko is the preserve more of the music critic or the intellectual in much of Greece. Nonetheless, it is still possible to get a hint of that lost world in some of the cafés of Athens, or, ironically enough, in İstanbul's Beyoğlu district, across the water in neighbouring Turkey.

the Acropolis as a focal point, in its shadow to the north lies first Plaka, then Monastiriaki, with Syndagma to its east and Psiri to its west, and finally Omonia, with Exarhia to its east. An old saying has it that Syndagma is the heart of Athens, while Omonia is the heart of Greece. Today though, Syndagma is where the government is, along with many foreign embassies, while Omonia is a pretty seedy place, with many of its older *ouzeria* gone. All this is set to change though, with a major redevelopment plan for the district underway. As for the other districts, Plaka lies immediately around the Acropolis and is known for its ancient sites and restaurants, plus some of the nicest old houses, while Psiri has a good bar and café scene. This is also true of Exharia, which has recently blossomed as an entertainment district due to its high student population.

Plaka and the Acropolis
A good place to start exploring is **Plaka**, with Monastiriaki metro station a useful focal point. At present, this is largely a building

site (though hopefully it will be ready by the Olympics), but head south from here amongst the duck boards and automatic drills and you'll find yourself on Areos, a winding street that heads up the hill towards the Acropolis. On the way you'll pass the **Museum of Traditional Greek Ceramics** (Wed-Mon 1000-1400, €2), housed in the 1759 Mosque of Tzistarakis. The area around here was once the Turkish bazaar, with the narrow streets and flea markets of Monastiriaki a continuing testimony to this eastern tradition. Next to the museum are the ruins of the **Library of Hadrian**.

Keeping straight on up the hill after the library, the second street is Polygnotou, a street leading on the right to the ancient **agora** or market-place (Tue-Sun 0800-2000, €4). This was where much of the action took place in the ancient city, and indeed in Western civilization too, with Socrates, Plato and many of the other founders of Western thought engaging in lengthy open-air debate here. The site also contains a museum housed in the Stoa of

Attalos, the Temple of Hephaestus and an 11th-century Church of the Apostles.

Heading back the way you came and continuing up the hill, the next sight you'll come to is the ruined **Roman Agora**, built by the Emperor Augustus as an extension of the existing Greek one. Inside here is one of

the city's most intriguing sights — the 1st-century BC **Tower of the Winds** (see p300). From here, turn south up Panos and head right to the **Paul & Alexandra Kanello-poulos Museum** (Tue-Sun 0800-1430, €2), a wonderfully restored 19th-century mansion. East of here is the **Museum of the**

The Greeks
With an astonishing list of gifts to humanity, stretching from drama to dredging, politics to metalwork and just about everything else besides, the ancient Greeks seem almost unassailable as the pre-eminent Mediterranean civilization.

Divided into several different city states, these ancients roamed the sea, establishing colonies from one end to the other and out into the Black Sea beyond. They achieved spectacular success in spreading their language, customs, religion, art and pattern of social organization, heavily influencing the Romans and almost everyone thereafter. By around 4000BC, it seems that the Aegean was dominated by three groups — the Minoans on Crete, the Myceneans in the Peloponnese and the Cycladic civilization on the islands now bearing their name. Earthquakes and tidal waves eventually put paid to the Minoans, while around 1400BC a wave of invasions from the north brought in a number of different tribes. These were the Aeolians, Dorians and Ionians, who spread across to the Anatolian coast – modern-day Turkey.

The Aeolians controlled their territory from the River Gediz northwards towards Troy, while the Ionians ruled the coastal strip south of this as far as the River Büyük Menderes, the ancient River Meander. Further south were the Dorians, including the island of Rhodes. These states included both coast and neighbouring islands, which were natural trading hubs for all the goodies coming up out of Anatolia along its Aegean-bound rivers.

Inland were a number of other civilizations, many of whom possessed a legendary wealth. The Phrygian King Midas famously turned all he touched into gold, while the Lydians, who lived in south-western Anatolia, were also thought by the Greeks to be fabulously wealthy. The last Lydian king was Croesus, another Midas-like character in Greek history, with tons of gold at his disposal. He also appeared in Ephesus, a city founded by the Dorians on a 7th-century BC Mount Rushmore — a set of relief-decorated pillars of the world's most famous people, which was one of the Seven Wonders of the Ancient World. His place in this hall of fame was assured by the fact that he paid for the whole thing himself.

Eventually the Lydians were taken over by the Persians, and from 546 and 334BC the region was dominated politically by the Achaemenian Persian Empire. Yet also at this time, the Greek city states began to develop a sense of common cultural identity as Hellenic states, with their influence expanding within Anatolia. The southern coastal regions of Caria, around Bodrum, and Lycia, around Kaş, became Hellenized at this time, while, back in the Peloponnese, Athens, Sparta and Corinth were emerging as powerful rivals — both of each other and the Persians.

In 490BC, after overrunning the Greek cities of Anatolia, the Persian king Darius I sent a huge expedition to attack Athens and Sparta, who were compelled into alliance against the invader. Darius' army was famously defeated at the Battle of Marathon.

(Continued opposite)

University (Tue, Thu and Fri 0930-1430, Mon & Wed 1430-1900, free). For some time, this Venetian building was, in fact, the university, and its collection commemorates the history of this seat of learning

From here, a winding path takes you around the mildly wooded hill of the Acropolis to its western end, where the main entrance is located. The **Acropolis** (daily 0800-2000, €12) you see now is largely the work of ancient Greek architect and city planner Pericles, an army of slaves, millennia of weathering, a ton of Turkish gunpowder and, finally, British archaeological loot-

AEGEAN SEA

❏ The Greeks

(Continued from p294) News of the Greek victory was brought to Athens by a runner – literally the first marathon runner, from whose adventure the Olympic sport is derived.

The Persians returned again in 481BC under King Xerxes I. His huge army crossed the Dardanelles on a bridge of boats, occupying and destroying Athens after overwhelming a brave Spartan rearguard at Thermopylae. However, the Athenians in turn destroyed the Persian navy at the battle of Salamis, forcing Xerxes to flee.

Thus began the Golden Age of Athens. The architect, statesman and polymath Pericles commissioned a complete rebuild of the city, while Athenian commerce and maritime skill made them rapidly the leading Greek state. A clutch of Greek playwrights also emerged during this Athenian renaissance, including Sophocles, Euripides and Aristophanes, while great philosophers such as Socrates and Plato could be seen debating in the Athenian agora.

All this success and culture was, however, beginning to grate with neighbouring Sparta. The ensuing, lengthy Peloponnesian War ended in 404BC with a Spartan victory. The Athenians then allied themselves with the Persians to exact revenge. But by now the focus of the Hellenistic world was Macedonia. From here, Alexander the Great charged forth in 334BC, pulling the Greek city states behind him in an epic journey of conquest, taking the banner of Hellenism all the way to modern-day Pakistan.

This empire was as brief as it was enormous. On his death from poisoning in 333BC, his conquests were divided among his generals. Back home, Athens and Sparta were no longer major powers, while Lycia and Caria became part of the generals' newly gained territories. Much of the rest of the Anatolian coast became Seleucid territory (Seleucus being one of Alex's generals amongst whom the Great man's territory was divided on his death). Central control had become rather frayed though, and in the 3rd century, all the coastal states enlarged their power, with Pergamum becoming a major Anatolian power as well as an Aegean one. The centre of Greek culture also shifted from the Peloponnese southwards across the Med, to Alexandria, a dominance that was to last until the rise of Constantinople — İstanbul — some six centuries later.

The rise of the Roman Empire in some ways saw the eclipse of Greek culture, but in others saw its successful survival. By 188BC, the whole Aegean and Anatolian region was under the rule of Rome. In conquering the Greeks, the Romans also appropriated and adapted much of their culture. The Greek gods, for example, were translated into Latin. With the Emperor Constantine the Great making Constantinople — a Greek city — the capital of his empire, the survival of Hellenism was ensured. And while the official language of the empire remained Latin, in the provinces of the eastern Mediterranean and Anatolia the language the 'Romans' spoke was most definitely Greek. Indeed, the Greek-speaking population of İstanbul continues to be known by the Turks as 'Rum' — Romans.

Meet the Gods

Hera, Athena, Aphrodite, Europa, Apollo, Zeus, Poseidon, Priapus –
there's a huge range of gods available in the ancient Greek pantheon. Subject to fits
of rage, compassion, lust and remorse, all were different from (and more human than)
the single God of Judaism, Christianity and Islam, and all were part of a sophisticated religion that saw everything — from a sudden gust of wind to a poor harvest — as
the responsibility of a different god.

For the ancient Greek home, there was a god of doors, Janus, whose two faces
looked in and out, and a goddess of the hearth, Hestia, who was invoked before each
meal. Outside, gods and goddesses were responsible for the water of the local spring,
the growth of the crops and the passage of the seasons. As such, all had to be honoured, with their own temples and shrines.

The gods were, however, subject to a certain hierarchy. At the top were the
Olympians, the horrifically dysfunctional family of Zeus. He was the possessor of
absolute power, having survived an early attempt by his father, Cronos, to eat him.
An event traumatic for any new-born, it's no surprise that Zeus then spent 10 years
confronting his father. At the end of this, Zeus was given the heavens, Poseidon the
sea and Hades the underworld.

Yet, perhaps due to his upbringing, Zeus' adulthood was characterized by a string
of failed relationships — with both goddesses and mortal women — producing a
small army of children. Among these was Athena, whom Zeus fathered with the goddess Metis. She was a strong, warrior woman who supported the Greeks in the siege
of Troy. She also became the focal point of a cult behind the city of Athens, of which
she became the Greek equivalent of a patron saint.

Zeus also had a sister, Hera, whom he married, producing a number of offspring.
These included Ares, the god of war, who was disliked by both parents. Hera was also
repeatedly and publicly jilted by Zeus, leading her to pursue her rivals with a frightening tenacity. One of these rivals was Aphrodite, the goddess of love, who had a
fling with Zeus that produced a son by him, Priapus. In furious jealousy, Hera made
Priapus extremely ugly, leading Aphrodite to reject her own son and cast him out.
However, the boy did have an uncommonly large penis, and representations of him
usually showed this, the god being used as a symbol of fertility. This was ironic, since
it's said that Priapus himself was unable to ejaculate. Statues showing him as a small,
bearded character were used to guard orchards in ancient times, perhaps the precursor of that blight of suburbia, the garden gnome.

Another example of Hera's furious temper occurred during her discussion with
Zeus over whether women or men got more pleasure out of sex. Zeus claimed women
did, Hera the opposite, and in an attempt to resolve the issue they asked Tiresias, a
gender-bender who'd been both. His answer that women experienced ten times more
pleasure than men caused Hera to attack Tiresias, blinding him forever.

The chaotic existence of the gods of ancient Greece found an echo in the lives of
the people who worshipped them. Without the modern pantheons of science, many
events defied any explanation, and life itself was brief — the life expectancy for your
average Greek at the time of Alexander the Great was no more than 35. Meanwhile,
earthquakes shook the ground, volcanoes arose out of nowhere, and the sea, the great,
blue vista beyond, was full of sudden storms, freak waves and bizarre monsters.
Perhaps by giving each of these its own god, the Greeks found a more comforting way
of dealing with them. And who knows, one day you might be caught in a sudden white
squall on the restless Aegean — a quick appeal for Poseidon's mercy wouldn't hurt
then, would it?

ing. Its principal building, the **Parthenon**, served first as a sanctuary for the Goddess Athena, then later as a cathedral (complete with belltower during the Catholic Crusader occupation of the city) and later still, during the period of Ottoman rule, as a mosque (complete with minaret).

Entrance to the site is through the monumental Propylaia, constructed in 437BC, in front of which stands the Temple of Athena Nike, which overlooks Piraeus and the Saronic gulf below. A frieze in the temple depicts the Athenians' victory over the Persians at the Battle of Plateia. Ascending from the Propylaia, the Panathenaic Way leads you past the Parthenon by the Porch of the Caryatids, six sculpted maidens who hold up the roof of one wing of the Erechtheion, a major place for worshipping both Athena and Poseidon. One of these maidens was taken by Britain's Lord Elgin, along with a major frieze from the Parthenon itself, in 1801. He later sold these to the British Museum where they are now better known as the Elgin Marbles; Greece, understandably, would very much like to have them back.

'Parthenon' actually means 'Virgins' Chamber' and originally referred to only one section of this colossal, 449-438BC work of architectural brilliance — the part consisting of the high priestess's chambers. When it was completed, it also contained a huge, 11m-high gold and ivory statue of Athena, long since vanished, but with numerous copies still extant. In Athens, the National Archaeological Museum houses a Roman version.

From the hilltop you can also see two ancient theatres built into the Acropolis' southern slopes. The larger is the **Theatre of Dionysos** (Tue-Sun 0830-1430, free entry with Acropolis ticket, entrance in Dhionysiou Arepayitou), rebuilt in the 4th century BC and the place where many of the plays of Aeschylus, Sophocles, Euripides and Aristophanes were first performed. The smaller of the two theatres is the later, Roman, **Odeion of Herodes Atticus**, nowadays open only for performances during the summer city drama festival.

Back on Dhionysiou Arepayitou, turn east for the **Temple of Olympian Zeus** (Tue-Sun 0830-1500, free entry with Acropolis ticket). Sixteen columns out of the original 104 are still standing in this structure dedicated to the god by the Roman Emperor Hadrian in AD131. Opposite, as the road swings round up Leoforos Amalias, stands **Hadrian's Arch**, which marked the boundary of the classical city. On your right here you'll see the **National Gardens**, which surround the parliament building on Plateia Syndagma. From this square, one of the city's most famous streets, Ermou, leads you back to where you started at Monastiriaki.

The other great place to go for Athens' ancient past is the **National Archaeology Museum** (Tue-Fri 0800-1900, Sat, Sun & holidays 0830-1500, Mon 1230-1900, €6), 44, Patission. Very crowded in summer, if you do manage to elbow your way in you'll find the Mycenaean hall is a highlight, with the gold Mask of Agamemnon on display.

PRACTICAL INFORMATION
Orientation
Athens has a spanking new airport, Eleftherios Venizelos, 25km east of the city. The metro is scheduled to link up with it in time for the Olympics, but until then the E94 bus runs every 15 minutes, 24 hours a day, to and from Ethniki Amina, the nearest metro stop. The total cost of the bus/metro trip into the town centre is €2.90. The E96 runs every 40 minutes, 24 hours a day to and from Plateia Karaiskaki in Piraeus port and costs the same. Keep hold of the ticket, too, as you can use it on any Athens metro or bus for the rest of the day. Bus journey times are horrific: $1^1/_2$-2 hours in daytime. A taxi will set you back around €20 to Syndagma — make sure the meter is on.

Arriving at Piraeus by ferry, travel into Athens is easiest via the metro. Line 1 runs straight to Monastiriaki from its terminal on Akti Kalimassioti on the eastern side of the Great Harbour. Bus No 40 runs 24hr a day from Zea Marina to Syntagma, and No 49 travels from the Great Harbour to Omonia.

Note that in 2004 the new 'central' railway station at Arharnon, 18km north of the

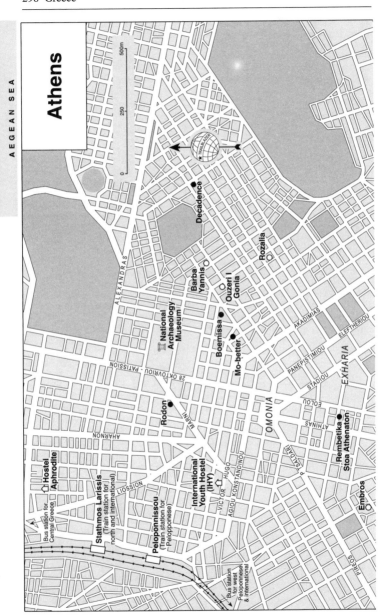

AEGEAN SEA

Athens

500m

250

0

Decadence

Rozalia

Barba
Yannis

Ouzeri I
Gonia

ALEXANDRAS

National
Archaeology
Museum

Boemissa

Mo-better

AKADIMIAS

ELEFTHERIOU

28 OKTOVRIOU - PATISSION

PANEPISTIMIOU

STADIOU

EXHARIA

MARNI

Rodon

EOLOU

OMONIA

AHARNON

ATHINAS

P ISADRI

Rembetika
Stoa Athenaton

LIOSSION

Hostel
Aphrodite

Stathmos Larissis
(Train station for
north and international)

International
Youth Hostel
(IHY)

VICTOR
HUGO

AGIOU KONSTANDINOU

Peloponnissou
(Train station for
Peloponnese)

Bus station for
west Peloponnese
& international

PIREOS

Embros

Bus station for Central Greece

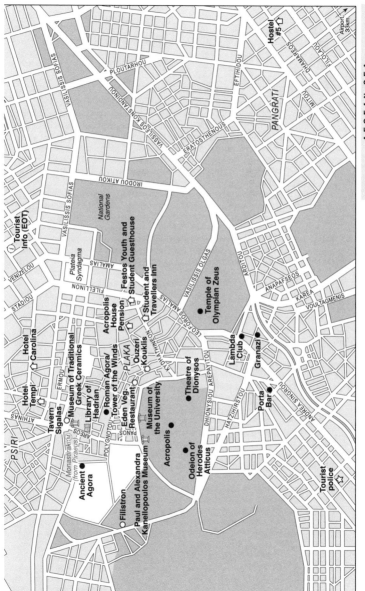

AEGEAN SEA

Airport, 33km

Hostel #5

PANGRATI

Tourist Info (EOT)

National Gardens

Plateia Syndagma

Festos Youth and Student Guesthouse

Student and Travellers Inn

Temple of Olympian Zeus

Hotel Carolina

Acropolis House Pension

Museum of Traditional Greek Ceramics

Hotel Tempi

Library of Hadrian

Tavern Sigalas

PSIRI

Roman Agora/ Tower of the Winds

Eden Veg. Restaurant

PLAKA

Ouzeri Kouklis

Lambda Club

Granazi

Museum of the University

Theatre of Dionysos

Monastiraki (M) (from Piraeus)

Ancient Agora

Acropolis

Porta Bar

Paul and Alexandra Kanellopoulos Museum

Filistron

Odeion of Herodes Atticus

Tourist police

city will open. Until then, the main station for northern and international trains is Stathmos Larissis, 11km north-west of Omonia and on Metro line 2 from Plateia Syndagma. Just next door is the Peloponnissou train station, for trains to the Peloponnese, as its name

suggests. Larissis is connected to Plateia Syndagma by bus No 57.

The main bus station for coaches to and from abroad, northern and western Greece and the Peloponnese is at 100, Kifissou, accessed by city-bus No 51 from the corner

The Tower of the Winds

Amongst the rubble of the Roman Forum in Athens, a much older building still stands — the eight-sided Tower of the Winds. Built around the 1st century BC, it remains to this day an octagonal testimony to Athenian maritime prowess.

Before the discovery of the magnetic compass, mariners would often use the prevailing winds to tell them in which direction things lay. This was particularly true in the Aegean, as it's the only region of the Mediterranean which has regular summer winds. These always go in a north to south direction and are known locally as the *meltemi*. So, for example, if you were on Chios and wanted to go to Samos, you'd know you'd want this wind almost directly behind you. Likewise, if you wanted to head west, you'd need to keep it to starboard.

The meltemi undoubtedly played a vital role in the development of Greek culture and civilization. It enabled ancient Greek mariners to sail south from island to island and then on to Crete — never for long out of sight of land — before continuing to the North African coast. There, they would trade with the ancient Egyptians and lay up until the spring, when the wind turned and a warm southerly, known in Arabic as the *Khamsin*, would be behind them, bowling them along back home.

Today you can still feel the meltemi's power. It usually starts up around midday in summer, blowing, as always, from north to south. In neighbouring Turkey it's known as the *meltem*, which is also a girl's name. Further west, it changes its signature slightly, with the Maltese calling it the *Majjistral*, a name similar to that given to it in France: Le Mistral. This wind, bellowing out of the north and into the Gulf of Lions, is still something of a menace, particularly to smaller vessels, and can blow your hat off as far south as Majorca.

As time went on, the Greeks began to identify a number of other winds too. There was the Boreas, a cold wind also coming from the north and well known outside the Aegean, particularly in the Adriatic, where it's called the *Bora*, a gale force north-easterly. Another potentially hazardous wind, at least to mariners, is the Gregale, which blows across the southern end of the Adriatic into the Ionian Sea in winter from its home in the Balkan mountains. This north-easterly can churn things up as far away as the North African coast, in ancient times disrupting east–west trade altogether. Other winds include the Notus, a warm southerly, and the Africus, another breeze from the south, this time off the Libyan desert. Yet, as troublesome as these winds may on occasion be, they are also responsible for blowing the seeds of Mediterranean civilization from one shore to another; not a bad achievement for nothing more than thin air.

As for the tower itself, by the time the astronomer Andronicus got permission to build it, eight winds had been given official recognition. At the top of each side of the tower is a relief showing a figure personifying one of them. In the old days, a revolving statue of Triton also stood on top, acting as a weather vane by pointing his trident in the direction of the wind.

of Zinonos and Menandrou, near Ominia, (or take a taxi, €4). Buses to and from central Greece go from Gousiou, on bus No 24's route from Plateia Syndagma and north of the train stations. Get off the bus at the 260, Liossion stop and turn right for the terminal.

Ferries

See Piraeus, p304.

Trains

The offices of the Greek national railways (OSE) are at 17, Filellinon, 6, Sina, and 1, Karolou, all of which can sell you tickets, distribute timetables and give you directions for the new railway station (see p300). While schedules change, there are generally eight trains a day to Patras, four of them express ($3^{1}/_{2}$ hours, €10), and 10 a day to Thessaloniki, with five of them express (6 hours, €20). One of these goes through to İstanbul (24 hours, €65) via Alexandroupolis (12 hours, €50). The train is rather dismal, has no sleeping cars or couchettes and experiences long delays at the border, where you must change onto a Turkish train. See the İstanbul section (p391) for the unappealing truth about travelling the other way. There are no trains to Igoumenitsa — for this, you must take a bus.

Buses

There are three buses a day to Igoumenitsa (8 hours, €28), and buses every half hour to Patras (3 hours, €11.50). Ten coaches a day go to Thessaloniki (8 hours, €30).

Bus schedules and tariffs can be found at all EOT offices in the city, the main one being at 2, Amerikis (see Services below). Buy tickets at the bus stations.

Local buses are everywhere. Buy tickets from kiosks by the stops, with a flat €0.45 fee in operation regardless of distance. These tickets must also be franked in an orange franking machine onboard the bus when you get on. The bus service also halts at midnight, starting at around 0500.

Planes

Olympic Airways (☎ 0926 7663) has its most convenient office at 15, Filellinon, near Syndagma. Olympic flies to dozens of

Greek destinations, particularly to the islands. Flights are often booked up well in advance, though, so it is good to think well ahead if you intend using this service.

The metro

Given the frequent and epic traffic jams, the metro is by far the best way to move around town, with tickets costing €0.70 or €3 for a one-day pass; buy these at the stations from slot machines or ticket windows. Metro tickets should also be franked in the orange franking machines as you go onto the platform and before you board the train. At the time of writing there were three lines, though the blue line is being extended west from Monastiraki. The newly refurbished stations are almost worth a visit for their own sakes. Services run from 0500-midnight.

Taxis In comparison to most EU cities, these are pretty cheap. The official ones are yellow with red letter number plates and are all metered. Luggage costs extra if it goes over 10kg, at €0.25 a piece.

Services

The **EOT** office (☎ 0331 0561/2, ✉ gnto@eexi.gr), 2, Amerikis, is open Mon-Fri 0900-1900 and Sat 0900-1200. The staff give out free maps and help with accommodation and transport, including ferries. A website worth looking at is ✉ www.athensguide.org.

The **tourist police station** (☎ 0924 2700), 77, Dimitrakopoulou, is open 24hr.

Internet access is available at Sofokleous.com, 5, Stadhiou; Downtown Internet, 10, Platia Omonia; and Museum Internet Café at 46, Patisson. For English-language **books** try Eleftheroudhakis, 17, Panepistimiou, or Iy Foliatou, Vivliou 25, Panepistimiou. The main branch of the **post office**, at 100, Eolou, Omonia, is open Mon-Fri 0730-2000, Sat 0730-1400.

Where to stay

EOT tourist information offices can help with hotel accommodation but not hostels. Athens is a premier tourist destination so it helps to book in advance during the summer months.

AEGEAN SEA

Hostels *Hostel Aphrodite* (☎ 0881 0589), 12, Inardhou, on the corner with 65, Mihail Vodha, near Plateia Viktorias. Comes complete with a travel agency; dorm beds €8.

International Youth Hostel (☎ 0523 4170), 16, Victor Hugo. Official HI hostel, located in Omonia; €9 per person for members.

Festos Youth and Student Guesthouse (☎ 0323 2455), 18, Filellinon. On the edge of Plaka; €10 for a dormitory bed.

Hostel #5 (☎ 0751 9530), 75, Dhamareos, in Pangrati, on trolley bus No 2/11 route. €9 for a dorm bed.

Hotels *Acropolis House Pension* (☎ 0322 2344) 6-8, Kodrou. Beautiful 19th-century house; €50/70 sgl/dbl.

Student and Travellers Inn (☎ 0324 4808) 16, Kydhathineon, in the centre of Plaka. Dorm beds for €15, sgl/dbl €35/45, all with shared bathrooms.

Hotel Tempi (☎ 0321 3175, ☐ www.travelling.gr/tempihotel), 29, Eolou. Nicely situated in Monastiraki; €25/35 sgl/dbl.

Hotel Carolina (☎ 0324 3551), 55, Kolokotroni. Near the Tempi, but more upmarket; €35/55 sgl/dbl.

Campsites include *Varkiza* (☎ 0897 4329), some 27km south in the beach suburb of the same name. It's near the water and accessed by bus from Plateia Syndagma. There's also *Nea Kifissía*, which is closer in and has a swimming pool. Take bus No 528 from Omonia or the metro to the last stop, Kifissia, and bus No 528 from there to the site.

Where to eat

Greek cookery is justly famous and there are a variety of places in which you can try it. In brief, there are *ouzeri*, which used to serve just ouzo and light snacks known as *mezedes* but now often run to bigger meals and other drinks; *taverna*, which are full-blown restaurants; and places which call themselves restaurants, and which are sometimes more expensive than the other two. There are also dozens of cheap snack-food places selling *gyros* or *souvlaki* — kebabs — which can be a filling meal in themselves. Vegetarians are less well catered for, although plenty of mezedes are meat free.

Tavern Sigalas (☎ 0321 3036), 2, Monastiriraki Square. Located in an alley off the square, this wonderful taverna is decorated with dozens of pictures of the owner shaking hands with famous visitors. Head outside for gyros and souvlaki at €2 a go, or inside for a meal costing around €10 for salad, main course and a beer.

Ouzeri Kouklis, Tripodon 14, Plaka. Has wooden ceilings and excellent mezedes, though not main meals. However, the mezedes are substantial enough; €8 should fill you up.

Eden Vegetarian Restaurant, 12, Lyssiou, Plaka. Does good veggie versions of Greek staples, with €10 enough for a good meal. Closed Tuesdays.

Rozalia, 58, Valtetsiou, in Exharia. Taverna with good seafood and house vino, and you can eat outdoors in summer; allow about €10 a head.

Embros, 4, Plateia Agion Anargyron in Psiri. Has a good range of mezedes and is set in a trendy area. Allow €15.

Ouzeri I Gonia on the corner of Emanual Benaki and Arahovis in Exharia. This district's high student population brings the prices down, though the quality is still good. Serves mezedes only, but €7.50 should ensure a full stomach.

Barba Yannis, further up at 94 Emanual Benaki in Exharia. Has some outdoor seating, with a full meal costing around €10.

Filistron, 23, Apostolou Pavlou in Thissio. An ouzeri with excellent Acropolis views and meals for around €15.

Bars, cafés and clubs

Athens has an excellent nightlife with Exharia and Psiri the main venues for bars and cafés, while clubs are more often to be found down on the coast along the Posidonos road in Kalamaki. Taxis back from there are around €8. These clubs tend to be venues where dress style is everything; furthermore, men unaccompanied by women are unlikely to get in. Both *The Venue*, which serves up Latin and jazz as well as house music, and *+Soda* have the least stringent door policy and are both on the Posidonos road. Expect to pay €12-15 a head to get in. For the latest information there are two listings mags, *Odyssey* and *Athenorama*, or try *Athens News*.

As for bars, try ***Decadence***, in Exharia, on the corner of Chrisolora and Voulgaroktonou. A beach-party theme here once had tons of sand filling the bar, and ordinarily it has a seriously bohemian feel. On a Friday or Saturday night you'll get charged an entrance fee of €7, which includes one free drink.

Also in Exharia is ***Mo-better***, located on Messolongiou and Koleti streets, which has good indie music. For rock, try the ***Rodon***, 24, Marni, north of Omonia.

Away from the centre, a good place for cafés is Pangrati, with the main drag, Imitou, playing host to a string of café bars in a variety of styles, though black clothing seems de rigueur among the clientele.

Gay bars include ***Granazi***, 20, Lembesi, and ***Lamda Club***, 15, Lembesi. Lesbians could try ***Porta Bar*** 10, Falirou.

Rebetiko fans should head to ***Boemissa***, 19, Solomou, in Exharia, or ***Rembetika Stoa Athanaton***, 19, Sofokleous, though this shuts during the summer season.

Festivals

Athens hosts a major international festival from June to September, with many cultural events organized by the city authorities. For details, try the festival box office (☎ 0322 1459) 4, Stadhiou. There's also the Athens Film Festival in August/September (ask at the EOT office for details) and the Athens Rock Wave festival, also in August, though dates vary; again, the EOT office (see p301) will be able to give you details.

Around Athens

PIRAEUS

AREA CODE: ☎ 21 **POPULATION**: 180,000

Possibly the most famous harbour in the Mediterranean, it was from this deep-water port that Athenian power was born. Connected to the ancient city by the long walls, which meant that it could continue to supply Athens even when the city was under siege, it is nowadays part of the capital's urban sprawl. You're most likely to visit it only when catching a ferry, though it does have the worthy **Maritime Museum** (Tue-Sun 0900-1400, €2) at Akti Themistokleous in Zea Marina. It's tricky to spot though, as it's actually under the road. Inside, there are many model ships and diorama depicting the exploits of the *Averoff*, the Greek navy's most famous warship. To get there from Athens, try bus No 40 from Plateia Syndagma; from Piraeus, Zea Marina buses go from outside the Metro station on Alipedou. You can also walk it in about 20 minutes by going over the hill along Vasileos Georgiou and turning down Labraki.

The **Great Harbour** itself is excellent for ticket agencies, moneychangers and hustlers of all descriptions, particularly along the waterfront road, Akti Kalimassioti. There are also some cheap eateries around the market area, located around Plateia Themistokleous.

Sounion

Some 70km south-east of Athens stands one of the greatest of ancient Greek temples, the **Temple of Poseidon** at Sounion (open daily, 1000-sunset, €3). Standing on a headland overlooking the Gulf, it is probably the most classic classical building bar the Parthenon in Greece, given its spectacular setting, particularly at sunset. There are also some half decent beaches, several less crowded coves and regular buses (every 30 mins, 2-hour trip, €10) from the main terminal at Mavromateon in Athens.

The temple is also noted for an example of early English hooliganism — the poet Lord Byron scratched his name on a column back in the 1820s. The temple is the centrepiece of a complete sanctuary to the sea god, constructed in the time of Pericles.

Practical information
Ferries   [see p457 for full details]

Piraeus is the Mediterranean's busiest ferry port, with continuous traffic in and out of the harbour. For the most up-to-the-minute information on arrivals and departures, try the Port Authority (☎ 0451 1310–17) or Zea Marina (☎ 0459 3144).

Ferries go from Piraeus to nearly every port and island in Greece, with space not permitting a full list here. There are ferries to Crete, Thessaloniki, Lesbos, Chios, Samos, Kos, Rhodes, the rest of the Dodecanese and the Cyclades. There are also ferries through to Cyprus. Practically the only place they don't go is round the corner to the Ionian islands. For these, you have to travel overland to Patras and Igoumenitsa.

Allow plenty of time to find your ferry — check with the ticketing agency exactly where it goes from as the port is vast and not designed in any way whatsoever for walking around in a hurry with lots of luggage.

The information listed on p457 should be seen as a mere guide only, as the schedules change year to year and even sometimes day to day as boats break down, get sold off or change routes. The only really accurate ferry timetable you're likely to find is the one in the Great Harbour on the day. Otherwise, see the internet section (p433) for some useful addresses.

The main ferry companies are: ANEK ☎ 0419 7410; DANE Sea Lines ☎ 0429 3240; LANE Sea Lines ☎ 0411 0231; Hellas Flying Dolphins ☎ 0619 8340; Minoan Lines ☎ 0419 9900; Angistri-Piraeus Lines ☎ 011 3108; GA Ferries ☎ 0419 9100; ANEN Lines ☎ 0419 7420; NEL Lesbos Maritime ☎ 2251-026 299.

International services   Two shipping companies handle ferries to **Cyprus** and **Israel**: Poseidon Lines (☎ 0965 8300) and Salamis Lines (☎ 0429 4325). Both follow the same route, Piraeus–Rhodes–Limassol –Haifa; however, at the time of writing services for both companies were suspended.

AEGINA

AREA CODE: ☎ 2297 POPULATION: 11,000

A welcome break from the bustle of Athens is the neighbouring island of Aegina, the largest of the Saronic Gulf group. Ferries depart from Piraeus every hour, take 1½ hours to get there and cost €5. Hydrofoils also leave hourly, take 35 minutes and cost €8.50. They connect with Aegina Town, on the western coast of the island, which is flanked by two acceptable beaches at Faros and Kolona. There are also the remains of an **ancient harbour** north of the ferry dock, and an **Archaeological Museum** (Tue-Sun 0830-1500, €2) and **Temple of Apollo** on the northern headland. Sadly, the latter is now reduced to just one column.

The main ancient attraction, though, is on the other side of the island — the 480BC **Temple of Aphaia** (Mon-Fri 0830-1900, Sat & Sun 0830-1500, €2.50). Buses run there every 45 minutes from Aegina Town; tickets can be bought from the kiosk on

---

Milos

Overview   Originally home of the celebrated Venus de Milo – a 4th-century BC statue of Aphrodite (now in the Louvre, Paris), Milos is the Cyclades' most western outpost. With many secluded beaches – most accessible only by boat – and a bizarre volcanic landscape, its capital, Plaka, is a classic whitewashed town. Just north-east of Milos lies the smaller island of Kimolos, for an even more away-from-it-all experience.

Where to stay   Most accommodation lies around the island's port, Adamas, with a **campsite** 6.5km east at Arhivadolimni. In season, finding a room can be tricky, with the website ⌨ www.milostravel.com a good one for booking ahead. Prices range from €30-60 for a double.

Ferry connections   There are ferries from Piraeus (see p458), Santorini, Crete (see p453, p459) and Karpathos.

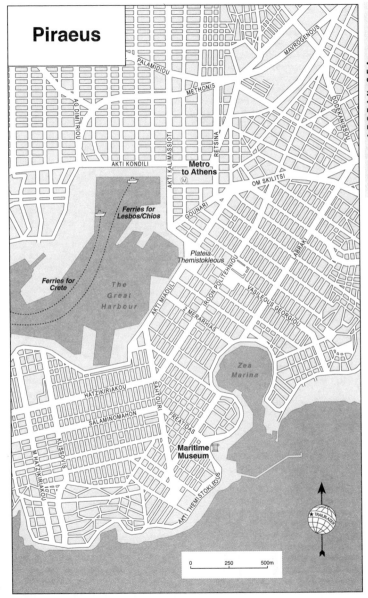

Piraeus

AEGEAN SEA

PALAMIDIOU

MAVROGENOUS

METHONIS

DODEKANISSOU

AG. DIMITRIOU

AKTI KONDILI

AKTI KALIMASSIOTI

RETSINA

Metro to Athens
Ⓜ

OM SKILITSI

GOUNARI

Ferries for Lesbos/Chios

Plateia Themistokleous

LAMRAKI

Ferries for Crete

The Great Harbour

IROON POLITEHNIOU

VASILEOUS GEORGIOU

AKTI MIAOULI

2. MERARHIAS

Zea Marina

HATZIKIRIAKOU

SAHTOURI

SALAMINOMAHON

FREATIDAS

KLISSOVIS

M. HATZIKIRIAKOU

Maritime Museum 🏛

AKTI THEMISTOKLEOUS

★ TRAILBLAZER

0   250   500m

Kythira

Overview A mysterious and highly symbolic place for many Greeks, as in the Angelopolous film *Voyage to Kythira* the island represents the end of the line, the last stop, off the southern coast of the Peloponnese. More Cyclades-like than Ionian, it is nonetheless one of the least spoilt and least visited islands. With its capital at Chora, its interior holds a number of monasteries, with Moni Myrtidion one of the most impressive.

The island's best beaches are to be found near Paleopoli in the south-east. Elsewhere, Mylopotamos has the Cave of Agia Sofia, while the south also has a 19th-century English bridge, an architectural left-over from the little-known time when the island was a British protectorate.

Where to stay In Chora, pensions go from €25-60, while Agia Pelagia, the main ferry stop, also has a cluster of budget options near the quay, from €30-50.

Ferry connections There are ferries from Neapoli and Gythio on the mainland, and from Piraeus via Crete (Kissamos, see p455) and Antikythira.

Kazantzaki, the main road by the port. Set among pine woods, it is one of the only temples in Greece to have preserved some of its interior columns. Aphaia herself was a minor ranking goddess, a daughter of Zeus.

In ancient times, Aegina was an important naval power, thanks to its controlling position in the Gulf. This didn't impress the Athenians much and they invaded and subjugated this neighbour-cum-rival in 459BC. Its other claims to fame are that in 1829 it was briefly the capital of Greece, that Nikos Kazantzakis wrote *Zorba the Greek* here, and that it is now the country's pistachio capital — try some of them.

If you fancy staying here rather than merely seeing it on a day trip, try *Hotel Plaza* (☎ 025 600), on Kazantzaki, which has singles/doubles for €18/25, or the *Avra* next door (☎ 022 303) which is much the same. For something to eat, try *Restaurant I Agora* behind the fish market at 47, Pan Irioti. A full meal should set you back around €10.

Because of its proximity to Athens, the island does fill up at weekends in summer; book ahead if you're aiming to stay. Also get your return tickets in advance if you find yourself on the island in high season and have to get back to Athens to catch any ferries or planes, as the boats fill up too.

RAFINA

AREA CODE: ☎ 2294 **POPULATION:** 10,000

Located on Attica's eastern coast, Rafina is set to take over much of the northern Aegean ferry traffic from Piraeus in years to come. It is something of a transit town, with little reason to visit except to go somewhere else. Between 0545 and 2215 it is connected by frequent buses to Athens' Mavromateon terminus, the trip taking an hour and costing €2.

Practical information

Ferries   [see p458 for full details]

Ferries from Rafina tend to be slightly cheaper than their equivalents from Piraeus, and for northern destinations are more rapid. For the most up-to-the-minute information on departure times, call the port authority on ☎ 028 888/022 481.

For the contact details of ferry companies serving Rafina (Blue Star, HFD, Karystia and Kiriakoulis), see pp433-7. In addition, try Karystia Shipping: ☎ 0453 7930 and Blue Star Ferries: ☎ 0422 5000.

Where to stay If you find yourself trapped here, try *Hotel Avra* (☎ 022 781), overlooking the port and with sgl/dbl for €35/45 with breakfast, or *Corali* (☎ 022 477) on Plateia Plastira, with sgl/dbl for €20/30.

Crete

Lying way south of the Greek mainland, and shielding the southern approaches to the Aegean, Crete has long cut a fiercely independent path through the crowded millennia of Mediterranean history. The fifth largest island in the Sea, and Greece's largest, it wasn't until 1913 that it finally became united with the mainland. One of the first Mediterranean civilizations, the Minoan, started out here, while just about every other major player in the Med's history has ruled the mountainous land at one time or another.

Nowadays, the northern shore is the most developed, with the major cities and ports ranged along it. Meanwhile, inland Crete is a mountainous place, the interior far from the tourist developments, while large areas of the southern coast, too, remain untouched by package complexes.

There are also many stark contrasts about this island. The terrain is rugged, yet some of the beaches are the softest and most tranquil in the eastern Med. Its people have a refreshing, if not sometimes slightly alarming, directness, yet images that are also likely to linger include the charming, febrile faces of Minoan frescos, or the mystical odysseys of Crete's greatest writer, Nikos Kazantzakis.

Take your time here — it will be well worth it.

HISTORY
While the island shows evidence of human habitation going back to neolithic times, the real story begins around 3000BC and the emergence of the Minoans. It is thought these originally came from Anatolia, but as with much of their story, little is really certain. But whatever their origins, they were clearly a powerful mercantile state, trading as far away as Afghanistan and Scandinavia. Regrettably, although they kept copious records in a script known as 'Linear A', no one has to date been able to decipher any of

it, a fact that has been a curse to archaeologists, but a blessing to many a fantasist.

From the evidence of their palaces, though, which were grand and lavish affairs, plus the stunning fluidity and colour of their art, it does seem reasonable to conclude they weren't short of a penny or two, Their art seems marvellously celebratory, too, with little obvious religious or even hierarchical significance. What gods they had seem to have been based around a matriarchal, rather than patriarchal, divinity. They were also probably the first civilization in the old world with proper drains.

However, they also seem to have spawned their eventual nemesis — the Mycenans, who probably started out as Minoan colonists on the mainland of Greece and other islands, but who grew increasingly antagonistic towards the Minoans and invaded repeatedly after 1500BC. The gods themselves then joined in and detonated the volcanic island of Strongphyle, which blew up in an explosion equivalent to 600 to 700 tons of TNT (or, to put it another way, the equivalent of a 600 kiloton atomic bomb) somewhere between 1500 and 1450BC. The explosion created the caldera island of Santorini, while earthquakes cracked out around the Aegean resulting in a massive tidal wave which probably drowned most of the coast of Crete.

By the 5th century BC, the island had broken into warring city states in much the same way as the rest of Greece. In 67BC the island fell to the Romans, who joined it administratively with the North African province of Cyrenacia – present-day Libya — rather than with Greece. Part of the emerging Byzantine Empire, Crete continued to be ruled from Constantinople until the Venetians annexed it in 1210, turfing out their great rivals the Genoese, who had slyly taken control of parts of it from under the noses of the Byzantine emperors.

The Venetians called the island Candia, and for many years it was the jewel in the crown of their Mediterranean empire. Trade was Venice's major weapon, and the Great Island, as the Greeks called it, sat conveniently astride all the possible routes from the Adriatic and the Western

AEGEAN SEA

Mediterranean through to Cyprus and the Levant, over to Egypt or up into the Aegean and the Black Sea beyond. The Venetians fortified their prize heavily, both to withstand attacks from other Mediterranean powers and to help control rebellions by the Cretans themselves, who rose up on some 27 different occasions against their Catholic, Latin masters.

This arrangement lasted around 450 years until the Ottomans finally took the island in 1669, following an epic siege of Iraklio which lasted 25 years — one of the longest in history. The Cretans continued to rebel, however, and in 1898 a massive uprising left the Ottomans severely weakened and allowed in the Great Powers, which prised the island away from Ottoman rule and left it a British protectorate, independent from Greece. This situation continued until 1913 when, following the Balkan wars, it was finally united with the mainland.

The island re-emerged onto the pages of world history again in WWII when German forces, led by an airborne assault, invaded the island in May 1941. Another epic battle resulted, with Greek and British, Australian and New Zealand troops defending. After a decisive battle at Maleme, near Hanía, the Germans emerged victorious and the island stayed in their hands until the end of the war. During this time, though, the Cretan Resistance fought on; the conflict proved to be brutal, and the reprisals severe.

Since the war, Crete has developed as a centre for tourism while continuing as an agricultural mainstay for the Greek republic.

ORIENTATION

Ferries arrive at one of five ports — Souda (for Hanía), Iraklio, Rethymno, Agios Nikolaos (Lasithi) or Sitia. The airports are at Iraklio and Hanía. There are no railways on the island but there are frequent buses along the northern coast, which connect the major towns and cities. Less developed roads cut south through the mountains, and there is a road running east–west along the southern coast between Rethymno and Sitia. Hitching is perhaps the best way to get around the mountain areas for, as on most Greek islands, public transport withers

as the terrain gets rougher. Scooters and hire cars are also strong options.

HANÍA

AREA CODE: ☎ 2821 POPULATION: 55,000
On 1 December, 1913, the Greek flag was raised above the fortress of Hanía to mark the island's reunion with the mainland, so it could be said that this is where modern Crete really began. However, it's also one of the island's oldest settlements, and was, from 1898 till 1971, the capital. Minoan tablets have been found round here, as back then this was the important settlement of Kydonia. Nowadays, it's best appreciated round its harbour area and the old Venetian quarter where, at sunrise and sunset, the buildings glow a pinkish hue, and the jumble of architectures — from Byzantine to Italian to Ottoman — contrive to make the town much prettier than the new island capital, Iraklio.

From here you're most likely to head east to the other Cretan cities, or south to the 18km-long Samaria Gorge, Europe's longest and a mecca for hikers. North-east lies the Akrotiri Peninsula, home to a NATO airbase, while to the west some of the less developed parts of the island are still to be found.

What to see

The place to start is on the seafront at the 1645 **Mosque of the Janissaries**, now largely a café and souvenir market. This area was the site of ancient Kydonia. From here, head west along the seafront and you'll soon come across the fortress bastion holding the **Naval Museum** (daily 0900-1600, €2, 🖳 www.forthnet.gr/mar-museum-crete). This holds a splendid collection of maritime memorabilia, including an effective display on the WWII battle for the island. For more of the same there is also **Hanía War Museum** (0900-1300, no charge), south-east of the harbour area at 23, Tzanakaki. Back at the Naval Museum, follow the headland road round, then go back towards town down Theotokopolou, the main street of the old Venetian quarter. This has been well restored and is a charming place to wander round and stay in, except in the height of season when it becomes too crowded.

The town's **Archaeological Museum**, 30, Halidhon (Tue-Sun 0830-1430, €2), is in the 16th-century Venetian Church of San Fransesco. The star acts are the painted Minoan sarcophagi and the courtyard Ottoman fountain, preserved from the church's later incarnation as a mosque.

Practical information

Orientation The ferries don't dock in Hanía harbour but some 7km away at the port of Souda. There are buses linking the two places, with the first leaving Souda at 0620, the last at 2300 (cost €1). The bus stop is outside Souda port gate, on the left, and you'll be set down in Hanía by the main market on Gianari, some five minutes' walk from the harbour which is reached by turning right down Mousouron, and not at the town bus station, which is on Zymvrakidon (and has a left-luggage store).

The airport is 14km away on the Akrotiri Peninsula, and there's no bus. A taxi should be around €14.

The rest of the town lies laced round the harbour, the old Venetian port. Stretches of the **Venetian walls** also ring this area, enclosing most of the town's sights. The main waterfront drag is Akti Kountourioti, with the old Venetian quarter and the museums on the west side. Everything is easily walkable.

Services The **EOT** (☎ 092 624), 40, Kriari, has lists of accommodation. Open Mon-Fri 0730-1400, it's one of the most friendly in Greece.

The **tourist police station**, 23, Irakliou, is also open Mon-Fri 0730-1400.

The **post office** at 3, Tzanakaki is open Mon-Fri 0730-2000, Sat 0730-1400. **Phones** are next door at the OTE, open daily 0730-1000.

For **internet access** try Café Vranas on Ag Deka, next to the cathedral.

Ferries   [see p459 for full details]
From Souda there is a boat every day to **Piraeus**, taking 6-9 hours.

The port authority is on ☎ 0821-98888

and the ferry operator is ANEK Lines, whose office is next to the food market in Hanía; call ☎ 027 500–4.

Other destinations are served from Kissamos, a one-hour bus trip west of Hanía. Buses leave from the main bus station every hour and cost €3.50.

Ferries **from Kissamos** go to **Antikythira** and **Kythira** twice a week and to **Piraeus** once a week (see p455).

Buses Island buses leave from the main bus station for the following destinations: Iraklio (2½ hours, €11), Hora Sfakion (2 hours, €4.75), Kissamos (1 hour, €3.50), Lakki (1 hour, €2.50), Moni Agias Triadas (30 mins, €1.50), Omalos/Samaria Gorge (1 hour, €5), Paleohora (2 hours, €5.50), Rethymno (1 hour, €6), Sougia (2 hours, €4.75), Stavros (30 mins, €1.50).

Tickets are bought in the bus station.

Planes There are four flights a day to Athens, and two a week to Thessaloniki, the Olympic Airways office being at 88, Tzanakaki in Hanía.

Where to stay Around the harbour there are plenty of affordable options, though it's a good idea to book in advance if you're coming in summer.

George's Pension (☎ 088 715), 30, Zambeliou. Located in an antique house, with sgl/dbl for €18/25.

Pension Fidias (☎ 052 494), 8, Kalinikou Sarpaki. Has rooms for €18/25 sgl/dbl and dorm beds for €11.

Pension Lena (🖳 lena@travellingcrete.com), 60, Theotokopoulou, near the Maritime Museum. Has excellent sgl/dbl for €25/40.

Monastiri Pension, 18, Markou, next to the ruined Monastery of Santa Maria de Miracolioco. Has sgl/dbl for €20/30.

Where to eat *Taverna Tamam*, 51, Zambeliou, in the old Turkish hamam, serves good all-round dishes with a full meal for around €10 a head.

Doloma Restaurant, 8, Kalergon, is a good budget eatery, with a student clientele and a full meal for around €8.

The Samaria Gorge

Some 18km long, the Samaria Gorge is a mini Grand Canyon that has become so popular with walkers that in the height of summer it can be reminiscent of a stroll down Oxford St, London, rather than a get-away-from-it-all commune with nature. As such, perhaps the only time to go is early spring/late autumn — the area is closed from 1 November to 30 April. The gorge is spectacular stuff, narrowing to just 3m at one point, while its towering sides rise up to half a kilometre above the valley floor. The total hike from one end to the other takes about six hours, so set off early, as the gorge is the centre of a national park that opens only from 0800-1500. From 1500-sunset visitors can enter but are allowed to go only 2km inside before heading back.

Hanía is the best base camp for the walk, with regular buses making the one-hour trip from the town bus station on the Omalos bus, which also takes you to the entrance to the gorge at Xyloskala. Having paid your €5 entrance fee, you then descend sharply to the spring at Neroutsiko. A more gradual descent then follows to Riza Sykias and Agios Nikolaos, the 2km limit. Heading on from here, you pass the abandoned village of Samaria, cleared when the national park was established, then follow the course of the riverbed until reaching the narrowest part of the gorge at Sideropontes, the Iron Gates. Four kilometres later, you emerge at Agia Roumeli, on the coast, a pebble-beach resort with a hotel, the *Agia Roumeli* (☎ 091 232) with singles/ doubles for €20/30 for weary travellers. Note that you are not allowed to camp in the gorge.

The other point to note about Agia Roumeli is that it has no roads leading to it, so your only option for a getaway is by boat. Fortunately, there are three of these every day to Hora Sfakion, taking an hour and costing €5. They connect with the buses back to Hanía. Hora Sfakion's main claim to fame, apart from being a transit point for gorge walkers, is that it was from here that the British navy evacuated the remnants of the allied forces defending the island from the 1941 German invasion.

To Karnagio, 8, Katehaki, is a must for authentic Cretan food; allow €10 a head. Budget eateries are also to be found around the food market on Plateia Markopolou.

RETHYMNO

AREA CODE: ☎ 2831 POPULATION: 23,500
Dominated by the island's largest Venetian fortress and with a harbour area comprising a jumble of Ottoman and Italianate houses along meandering narrow streets, Rethymno is a bit like Hanía, only more so. It also has one major advantage over its western rival — a good beach right in the middle of town.

On either side of Rethymno there has been one of the most rapid tourist developments on the island, yet the town itself has been largely spared, as have many of its old minarets — put up during Ottoman times when several of the town's churches were converted into mosques. This gives Rethymno a more eastern skyline than other Cretan towns and is a reminder, too, of the oft-neglected contribution of Islamic culture to the fabric of Aegean culture.

The town was inhabited back in Minoan times but only really came into its own under the Venetians, who built the heavy fortifications as part of their Fortress Crete policy to keep out the Ottomans. Eventually, the policy failed though, and the town stayed under Ottoman rule until 1897, when the Russian navy arrived and took it over as part of the so-called Great Power takeover of the island, leading to the start of the protectorate. In WWII it was not bombed as heavily as Hanía, accounting for the better state of preservation of its harbour area.

What to see
The **1574 fortress** (daily 0800-2000, €3) is the natural place to start. Originally the ancient Acropolis, the Venetians built this stronghold, known as the Fortezza, in order to fend off both pirate attacks and the Ottomans. In its prime it contained a town in itself, though now all that remains are ruins and a church, once converted into a mosque.

Tucked in below the eastern walls of the Fortezza is the **Archaeology Museum** (Tue-Sun 0830-1500, €1.50). The most prized exhibits are the coins, for in its ancient heyday Rethymno minted its own. Outside and all around here is the **old town** quarter, with some excellently preserved and/or restored buildings, including a Venetian loggia – a meeting place for the town council – on Paleologou, and the Rimondi Fountain on Mesologiou, which is of 17th-century origin.

There's also the **1572 Porta Goura** on Ethnikis Antistaseos, the one surviving gateway to the Venetian town and the only surviving relic of the town defences, as the walls themselves have long vanished. Relics of the Ottoman period are many, but try the **Nerandzes Mosque** on Vernardou, as its minaret is climbable and has some great views. Further round, there's the **Kara Mustapha Paşa Mosque** off Plateia Iroun. There's also the **Historical & Folk Art Museum** at 30, Vernardou (1000-1400, €2.75) and, by the side of the main harbour corniche, El Venizelou, the **beach**, a great place for a welcome swim.

Practical information
Orientation The town occupies a thumb-like promontory, jutting out into the Aegean, with the fortress the thumbnail. Ferries from Piraeus leave from the harbour next to the old port, along with smaller coastal boats to Agia Galini and Preveli. Buses call in at the bus station on the junction of Igoum Gavril and Sintagmatos, on the western coast of the headland. You can easily walk everywhere.

Ferries (see p459) From the harbour there are daily ferries in summer to **Piraeus**, but only four a week out of season. The boats are run by ANEK Lines, 250, Arkadiou, ☎ 002 9221. The port authority is on ☎ 055 150.

Buses Frequent services operate to Haniá (60 mins, €6) and Iraklio (1½ hours, €7). During the summer there are also buses to the Monastery of Moni Arkadiou (30mins, €2), which is open daily 0800-1300 and 1530-2000 (admission free). Set in the mountains, it has a special place in Cretan history as a symbol of resistance, as it was here in 1866 that hundreds of villagers sheltering inside blew themselves up rather than surrender to the Ottoman forces besieging them.

Services The **EOT** (tourist information) office (☎ 029 148), on the beach side of El Venizelou, is handy and helpful and open Mon-Fri 0800-2000.

The **tourist police** (☎ 028 156) office, in the same building as the EOT, is open daily 0700-1000.

The **post office**, 21, Moatsou, is open Mon-Fri 0730-2000. The **OTE**, 28, Kountouriotou, is open Mon-Fri 0730-1400.

Internet access is available at Net C@fe, 2, Venieri, behind the Elina Hotel

Where to stay *Olga's rooms* (☎ 054 896), 57, Souliou. Has good clean rooms in the heart of town for €25/35 sgl/dbl.
Lefteris Papadakis Rooms (☎ 023 803), 26, Plastira. Has sea views; sgl/dbl €25/35.
Rent Rooms Seafront (☎ 051 062), 45 ,El Venizelou. The name says it all; sgl/dbl €22/36.
Youth Hostel (☎ 022 848), 41, Tombazi. Has dorm beds for €7.50.
Elizabeth Camping (☎ 028 694), is 3km east at Myssiria Beach. The Iraklio bus drops you there, and the site comes complete with taverna and shop. Price: €10 per night.

Where to eat *Kyria Maria*, 20, Diog Mesologiou. The town's best, a taverna near the Rimondi Fountain which even has a veggie dish or two. Allow €10 a head.
Gounakis Restaurant, 6, Koroneou, has live traditional music in season and a good menu; €15.

Mykonos

Overview Something of a Greek island holiday cliché, Mykonos is the place for clubbers and partygoers and is known for its gay scene. Other than that, it has some decent beaches and is a Cyclades transport hub, with good connections to the other islands. It also makes a good place to visit the ancient sacred island of Delos, a few kilometres off the west coast.

The capital, Mykonos Town, is a warren of tourist-packed streets and white-washed houses, with the island's global status providing a vast array of places to stay. As for beaches, the film *Shirley Valentine* was partly filmed on Agios Ioannis, while Psarou, east of Ornos, is relatively uncrowded, though small. Ano Mera is the only inland settlement and features the 6th-century Moni Panagias Tourlianis monastery.

Neighbouring Delos is the mythical birthplace of Apollo and Artemis, with famous sanctuaries to a number of gods and the much-photographed Terrace of the Lions. This was one of the most important religious sites of the ancient world. Visiting can be done only on day trips from Mykonos, as Delos lacks any accommodation.

Where to stay Mykonos is relatively expensive – the main town has pensions and hotels spreading upwards from €50 for a double. It is also highly recommended you book ahead between June and September.

Ferry connections There are ferries from Amorgos, Andros, Ios, Ikaria, Naxos, Paros, Samos (Karlovassi, p455), Santorini, Skiathos, Syros, Tinos, Crete (Iraklio, p454), Piraeus (p458), Rafina (p458), Thessaloniki (p460).

Stella's Kitchen, 55, Souliou, has snacks as well as main meals; allow €5-10.

IRAKLIO

AREA CODE: ☎ 281 **POPULATION:** 125,000
Jumbling up over the hill behind the port before sprawling down into great suburbs beyond, Iraklio is not only the island's capital but the richest city, in per capita terms, in Greece. However, arriving in the port area, you find yourself confronted with a crumbling, peeling seafront, and your first thoughts are likely to be that the city's wealthy inhabitants must keep most of their loot for something other than painting and decorating. But persevere, as venturing up the hill to the pedestrianized areas beyond presents a quite different town of international stores and a warren of bars, cafés and restaurants.

Wartime bombing and post-war developments have scarred Iraklio's architectural fabric severely, yet it still manages to preserve a number of impressive sights — the Venetian arsenal and the bastions of the old fortifications being two — plus it has the best archaeological museum in the country outside Athens. It's also the major jumping-off point for one of Crete's must-dos, the Minoan palace at Knossos, as well as being the island's main transport hub. International travellers arrive and depart in frightening numbers during the summer months, both from the nearby airport and from the harbour, which has ferries running out to Piraeus as well as the Cyclades.

Originally known as El-Khandak when it was run by the Arabs, a Byzantine reconquest led to a name change to Khandakos, while during the Venetian rule it was rechristened once again, this time as Candia — the same name the Venetians, rather confusingly, gave to the whole island. So how it ended up as Iraklio is anyone's guess ... but so it did following the end of Ottoman rule in 1898.

What to see

A good place to start is the **Lion Fountain**, a 1628 construction commissioned by Franscesco Morosini while he was Venetian governor. On the other side of the road is the 17th-century **Loggia**, the Venetian town hall that also served as a social centre for the ruling nobility. Behind the Lion Fountain is **El Greco park**, containing a bust of the painter himself, who was born here in 1541. In those days the island — and Iraklio in particular — was something of an artistic centre, largely due to the arrival here en masse the previous century of many talented Byzantine refugees from Constantinople, which had fallen to the Ottomans in 1453. El Greco grew up in a Venetian city, and later moved to Venice to continue his studies under Titian. He then moved on to Spain, at that time the major West European power, where he settled until his death in Toledo in 1614.

The only El Greco on the island nowadays hangs in the **Historical Museum of Crete**, 7, Lysimahou Kalokerinou (Mon-Fri 0900-1700, Sat 0900-1400, €3, 🖥 www.historical-museum.gr/kazantzakis). Located on the northern waterfront road, the museum also contains the library of the writer Nikos Kazantzakis, most widely known for the novel *Zorba the Greek*. He was Cretan-born, died in Iraklio in 1957 and is buried in a tomb in the town's Martinenga bastion. There is also a section on the 1941 Battle of Crete, more of which can be found at the **Battle of Crete Museum** on the corner of Doukos Dofor and Hatzidaki.

Iraklio's fortifications are still impressive. The main part of town is still within them as well. The old harbour seems well guarded by the **Rocca al Mare**, the Venetian fortress, (Mon-Sat 0800-1800, Sun 1000-1500; €2), while the cathedral-like boatyards of the arsenal still loom across the harbour road. Rather akin to U-boat pens, inside these boatyards the defenders could refit and repair the pride of St Mark — the Venetian galleys that for centuries dominated trade in the eastern Med.

All this aside, if you have no more than a day here it's best you should spend most of it in just one place — the **Archaeology Museum** (Tue-Sun 0800-1900, Mon 1230-1900; €6). Located on Plateia Eleftherias, it contains the best collection of Minoan artefacts anywhere, as well as a pretty lavish spread of ancient Greek and Roman relics. It is, however, very crowded, even in the low season, so start early. Downstairs, Room 3 contains a highly mysterious object — the Phaestos Disc. Spirals of as-yet undeciphered hieroglyphs cover both sides and theories abound as to their significance. In Room 4 is the world-famous bull's head, a beautifully executed miniature sculpture of an acrobat and two fine snake goddesses. Unfortunately, there is no labelling worthy of the name on many of the exhibits, nor

AEGEAN SEA

Naxos

Overview   A central Cyclades hub, this is the largest island of the group and also one of the most fertile. This makes it a favourite for hikers, particularly in the cooler spring and autumn months, with the vegetation of its valleys standing in marked contrast to its rocky mountains. The Chora, or Naxos Town, is the capital and also the port, with an unfinished Temple of Apollo on the islet of Palatia connected to the harbour by a short causeway.

Agia Anna, south of the capital, is the best of the beaches, with sandy strips continuing from there to Pyrgaki. Another highlight is the Tragaea region, in the heart of the island, with its string of monasteries and churches. On the north coast lies Apollonas, with a giant 7th-century BC *kouros* (see p350) statue abandoned in an ancient quarry just outside the village.

Where to stay   Chora is the accommodation hub, with a large number of pensions and hotels ranging from €10-60. Campsites are clustered near the town's beaches.

Ferry connections   There are ferries from Amorgos, Anafi, Diafani, Fourni, Ikaria, Ios, Samos (Karlovassi, p455), Koufonisia, Mykonos, Paros, Santorini, Schinousa, Skiathos, Syros, Tinos, Crete (Iraklio, p454), Piraeus (p458), Thessaloniki (p460).

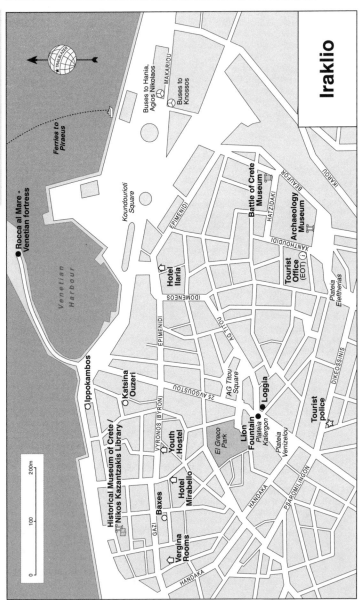

Iraklio

AEGEAN SEA

Ferries to Piraeus

Rocca al Mare - Venetian fortress

Venetian Harbour

Koundourioti Square

Buses to Hania, Agios Nikolaos

MAKARIOU

Buses to Knossos

Battle of Crete Museum

HATZIDAKI

Archaeology Museum

XANTHOUDIDI

Tourist Office (EOT)

Plateia Eleftherias

BEAYOR

IKAROU

EPIMENIDI

Hotel Ilaria

IDOMENEOS

EPIMENIDI

AG TITOU

AG Titou Square

DIKEOSSINIS

Ippokambos

Katsina Ouzeri

25 AVGOUSTOU

Loggia

Tourist police

VYRONOS (BYRON)

Youth Hostel

Lion Fountain

El Greco Park

Plateia Kalergon

Plateia Venizelou

Historical Museum of Crete / Nikos Kazantzakis Library

Baxes

Hotel Mirabello

HANDAKA

PSAROMILINGON

GAZI

Vergina Rooms

HANDAKA

200m

100

0

> ## Amorgos
>
> **Overview** Mountainous and sparsely inhabited, Amorgos is a get-away-from-it-all tadpole of an island, situated in the eastern Cyclades near the Dodecanese. The main settlements, the ports of Aegiali and Katapola and the medieval capital, Amorgos, are supplemented by a string of spectacular monasteries. Principal among these is **Panagia Hosoviotissa**, which is embedded into the cliff face near the beach of Agia Anna. This beach was the location for some of the scenes of the movie the *Big Blue*, while other beaches include **Levrossos**, a nudist venue, and **Maltezi**, near Katapola port.
>
> Elsewhere, **Amorgos Town** (Chora), is a warren of narrow streets, Byzantine churches and whitewashed houses around a Venetian castle.
>
> **Where to stay** There are no hotels, but a decent pension can be found in Amorgos Town/Chora, along with *domatia* (rooms for rent).
>
> **Ferry connections** There are ferries from Piraeus (p457), Naxos, Mykonos and Santorini.

(margin: AEGEAN SEA)

any explanatory notices. It is as if developments in museum theory since Sir Arthur Evans uncovered these treasures back in 1900 have entirely passed Iraklio by. Nonetheless, the lack of texts does mean you end up concentrating on the forms themselves — a marvellous experience given the sheer beauty of Minoan art. This is also much to be appreciated in the frescos upstairs. These are all from Knossos and at once confirm that the Minoans were a radically different culture from what came later. There appear to be no gods, no emperors nor any scenes of martial triumph. Instead, the frescos are characterized by scenes of celebrations in vibrant colours, as well as a certain grace to the figures depicted — something that can also be seen in the pottery and sculpture downstairs. Room 14 also holds the sarcophagus from Agia Triada, a richly decorated stone coffin considered by many to be one of the greatest triumphs of Minoan art.

After this, the later Greek and Roman exhibits downstairs look decidedly clunky. Clearly, a great deal was lost when this civilization finally disappeared.

Practical information
Orientation Ferries arrive at the modern port, east of the old one yet still comfortably close to the town centre. Buses arrive at more or less the same place, the main terminal, which is on Makariou and serves up buses to Knossos as well as other long-distance destinations. Arriving here can at first appear a little daunting as you survey the buildings rising up the slope, with most of them looking strangely derelict. Have no fear and boldly stride up the dozens of steps by the cavernous Venetian arsenal into the old town itself. The central square is Plateia Kalergon, which stretches out past the most famous landmark, the Lion Fountain, to Plateia Venizelou. From here, most of the pensions and sights can be easily found, and all the places you're likely to want to go to are within easy walking distance.

Services The **EOT** (☎ 022 8225), on the north side of Plateia Eliftherias, directly opposite the Archaeological Museum, is open Mon-Fri 0800-1400, and has maps.

The **tourist police office** (☎ 028 3190), 10, Dikeosynis, is open daily 0700-2300.

The main **post office**, Plateia Daskalogiani, is open Mon-Fri 0730-2000, Sat 0730-1400. The **OTE** is at Theotokopoulou, El Greco Park, open daily 0730-2300.

Internet access is available at Net C@fe, 4, Odos 78. For **car/scooter rental** try Blue Sea (☎ 024 1097), 7, Kosma Zotou.

Ferries [see p454 for full details]
Iraklio is not poor when it comes to names,
being referred to on timetables as either
Iraklio, Iraklion, Heraklio or even Heraklion
– so watch out.

There are boats to **Piraeus**, **Santorini**,
Ios, **Naxos**, **Kasos**, **Karpathos** and **Rhodes**.
Most travel agencies are on 25 Augustou.
The port has ferries operated by ANEK Lines
(☎ 022 2481), 33, 25 Augustou, and Minoan
Lines (☎ 033 0301), 78, 25 Augustou, GA
Ferries and Hellas Flying Dolphins (HFD).
The port authority is on ☎ 024 4956.

Buses Buses leave hourly for Rethymno
(1¹/₂ hours, €7) and Hanía (3 hours, €11),
every half hour for Agios Nikolaos (1¹/₂
hours, €5.50) and every 10 minutes to
Knossos (20 mins, €1).

Planes The airport is on the bus route
from Plateia Eleftherias in town (20 mins,
€1). The airport has frequent international
and domestic flights. Olympic Airways (☎
022 9191), 42, Plateia Eleftherias, has four
planes a day to Athens, three a week to
Thessaloniki, four a week to Rhodes and
two a week to Santorini. Aegean Airlines
(☎ 033 0475, office at the airport) flies
three times a day to Athens and daily to
Thessaloniki.

Where to stay *Youth Hostel* (☎ 028
6281), 5, Vyronos. Has dorm beds for €8.
Vergina Rooms (☎ 024 2739), 32, Hortat-
son. Spacious rooms for €12/25 sgl/dbl.
Hotel Mirabello (☎ 028 5052), 20, Theotokopoulou. A good bet; €30/45 sgl/dbl.
Hotel Ilaria (☎ 022 7103), 1, Ariadnis.

KNOSSOS
Over a century after its discovery by British archaeologist Sir Arthur
Evans, the Minoan palace of Knossos still arouses controversy. One of the main reasons for this is Evans himself, who decided to reconstruct parts of the palace, a practice frowned upon deeply by professional archaeologists ever since. Yet for many visitors to the site the painted, fake tapering columns and rebuilt walls are undeniably a
big boost to the attractiveness of what could otherwise be simply a huge pile of
stones.

Whatever the case, this is a premier Mediterranean archaeological site. Over centuries, several different palaces were constructed here, each one meeting a sudden
and, it seems, violent end. Mystery surrounds Knossos' final destruction too, and
there is also some uncertainty as to whether or not it was in fact what Evans was looking for — the palace of the legendary King Minos.

According to ancient Greek myth, Minos was a powerful ruler of Crete who was
once given a sacred white bull by Poseidon, the sea god, to sacrifice in his honour.
Minos refused, which so angered Poseidon that he decided to make Minos' wife,
Pasiphae, fall in love with the animal. Suffice to say that some time later, Pasiphae
gave birth to a creature that was half man, half bull — the Minotaur.

Meanwhile, Minos' son, in an apparently unrelated incident, was killed by the
Athenians, who were relatively minor characters back then in comparison to the
Cretans. Minos demanded reparations, which involved a tribute of Athenian youths
who would be fed to the Minotaur. The creature had been imprisoned beneath the
palace in a labyrinth, constructed by Minos' chief craftsman, Daedalus. Deciding to
flee, Daedalus and his son Icarus escaped the palace by flying, using wings made of
wax and feathers that Daedalus had built. Unfortunately, however, Icarus flew too
close to the sun, the wax in his wings melted, and while Daedalus made it all the way
to Sicily, Icarus crashed on the island of Ikaria and died.

(Continued opposite)

More upmarket than most, with a roof terrace; €35/50 sgl/dbl.

The nearest **campsite** is at *Creta Camping* (☎ 041 400), Kato Gouves, some 18km away. Buses for Hersonissos will let you off here. These depart from the main bus station by the port.

Where to eat *Baxes*, 14, Gianni Chroaki. Good wholesome stews and other Cretan fare at around €10 a head.

Ippokambos, on Sofokli Venizelou, at the junction with 25 Augustou. Good fish dishes and good value. Allow €8.

Katsina Ouzeri, 12, Marinelli. For fine mezedes and a good atmosphere.

For even cheaper eats, try any of the *souvlaki* and *gyro buffets* around the Lion Fountain, where a couple of kebabs and a beer won't cost more than €5.

AGIOS NIKOLAOS
AREA CODE: ☎ 2841 POPULATION: 8500

While over-crowded come summer, with heaving crowds on its main pedestrianized thoroughfares, 'Ag Nik' as it is sometimes called does have a certain something. Positioning is a lot — being a headland town with the port on one side and the commercial harbour on the other. The tourist bonanza has also added plenty of bars, restaurants and clubs, and it can also be a useful centre of operations for exploring the more unspoilt areas of eastern Crete.

A word of warning though — if you do intend to stay here during the peak summer months, book well in advance — it does get very crowded.

❏ KNOSSOS

(Cont'd from p316) As for the Athenians who were to be sacrificed, one of their number, Theseus, killed the Minotaur and found his way out of the labyrinth by using a ball of thread given to him by King Minos' daughter, Ariadne. Escaping Crete, Theseus married Ariadne but left her on Naxos and returned to Athens. However, on approaching the harbour he forgot to give a pre-arranged signal to his father to say that he was still alive. Thinking his son dead, Theseus' father then killed himself from remorse.

The site

The bus from Iraklio puts you down outside the main entrance, which is crowded with souvenir shops. The site is open daily 0800-1900 in summer, 0800-1700 out of season; entrance is €6.

Evans kept digging here for years, gradually disinterring the extraordinary site you see today. The first palace was constructed on this site around 1900BC, but was largely destroyed in an earthquake around 1700BC. A rebuild on this is what you now see. This was partly destroyed again in around 1500BC, was reinhabited for half a century more and then burnt to the ground. The size of the site is impressive, with its multi-storeyed buildings connected together with staircases and passages that could have you wandering for hours. Look out for the **Royal Road**, to the left of the entrance, which was Europe's first paved roadway. Also look for the drainage system, the like of which wouldn't be seen anywhere in the Med for centuries after the destruction of this civilization. In the **Queen's bathroom**, there's even a toilet that flushes.

While the palace consisted of store rooms, royal chambers, ceremonial areas and religious places, it was also the centre of a great bureaucracy, as the dozens of records recovered from here show. Seek out the **Hall of the Double Axes** too. The double axe was a Minoan symbol, and the Minoan word for it was *labrys*, a clear connection to the word labyrinth that begs a number of questions. But this is often the result of a visit to Knossos, for it seems sometimes that Evans' attempt to make the site clearer through reconstruction has in fact made everything still more mysterious.

AEGEAN SEA

What to see

The town was originally known as Lato before the Venetians renamed it St Nicholas, a name translated into its present form when the island joined Greece. The town lacks any historical ruins but does have an **archaeological museum** (Tue-Sun 0830-1500, €2) at the port end of Paleologou. The finds inside are mainly Minoan artefacts from around the region.

Outside the museum there's the town's other attraction, **Lake Voulismeni**. This lagoon was reputedly bottomless – though is in fact only 55m deep – nor is it any longer a lake, since the construction in 1902 of a trench to connect it to the sea. The road passes across this channel to the main harbour square – with a good people-watching spot at the Café Asteria – and continues straight on up and over the hill to the town beach, Kitroplatia. It's really not recommended, however, and if it's sand you're after, head 1km south for Almyros Beach, after the Municipal Beach Club.

Otherwise, the town holds little except shops to while away the time — 28 Octovriou and Roussou Kounouriou are the main drags. The principal activity once this has been done is leaving. This can be done on a day trip basis or more permanently, with the former constituting a number of good options.

Spinalonga The site of a protracted last stand by Crete's Venetian occupiers, the fortress island of Spinalonga held out some 30 years longer against the Ottomans than the rest of Crete, finally surrendering in 1715 along with two other Venetian-held lumps of rock, Gramvoussa and Souda Island.

Spinalonga — which means 'Long Spine' — was coincidentally also the *first* place the Venetians occupied on Crete, and was an important bulwark in their defensive network. The Ottomans also used it as a fortress, while under Greek control it became a leper colony, the last inhabitant dying there in 1955. Now it is abandoned — except for the thousands of tourists who visit during the summer months. Visited in winter, though, it has quite a different aspect, and the central redoubt, the Castello

degli Spiriti ('Castle of the Spirits') seems to live up to its name very well.

You can get to the island by boat from Agios Nikolaos by day trip (€20), with boat owners advertising their services there in the harbour. Alternatively, you can go from Elounda (€7), 11km north of Ag Nik. This is the better option, as Elounda itself is an attractive fishing village, a bit swamped by tourism but still charming. Buses for Elounda leave Ag Nik every half hour, take 20 minutes and cost €1.

The Lasithi Plateau Some 900m above sea level, this giant table-top of orchards and fields way up in the island's eastern mountains is an excellent destination for walkers. It's also windmill territory, with an estimated 7000 of these sprinkled across the landscape. Located west of Ag Nik, it centres on the village of Psyhro, which itself lies next to the Dikteon Cave. This particular grotto has a key role in the story of Zeus, as it was here that Rhea hid the baby Zeus from Chronos, the supergod's dad, who was disturbingly fond of eating his own children.

The cave is open daily 0800-1600, admission €3; bring a torch and some good shoes if you intend going in. There are some worthwhile hikes around here too, notably over to the plateau's main town, Tzermiado, an hour and a half's walk away.

To get to the grotto without your own transport is tricky, as buses go to and from the plateau on Mondays, Wednesdays and Fridays only. Hitching is a reasonable option, though, with traffic infrequent but reliable for lifts whenever it does appear.

Practical information

Orientation Buses arrive south of the marina at the bottom of Sofias Venizelou. Head up this for most things — from shops to places to stay. Ferries arrive and depart from the port, which is handily right in town. Nowhere is more than a stroll away, including the local town beaches.

Services The **EOT** (☎ 022 357), on the harbour-front, just over the bridge from 28 Octovriou, is open daily in season, 0830-2130, and has accommodation lists.

The **tourist police office**, 34 Kondogianni, is open daily 0730-1430.

The **post office**, 9, 28 Octovriou, is open Mon-Fri 0730-1400 The **telephone office**, on the corner of 25 Martiou and K Sfakianaki, is open daily 0700-2300.

Café Peripou, 25, 28 Octovriou is an **internet café**.

Ferries [see p453 for full details] Agios Nikolaos is the main ferry port for the eastern end of the island, with ferries to/from **Karpathos** (via **Kassos**), **Sitia**, **Milos**, **Piraeus**, **Rhodes** and neighbouring **Spinalonga**. The ferry to Rhodes goes via Sitia, Kassos and Karpathos. The ferry to Piraeus goes daily at 18.00, the ferry to Milos on Wed, Sat and Sun at 15.30.

The main ferry line is LANE, at Sitia (☎ 025 555). Most ticket agencies are around the harbour area and the port authority is on ☎ 022 312.

Buses Buses depart for Elounda (20 mins, €1, 20 per day), Iraklio (1¹/₂ hours, €5, 12 per day) and Sitia (1¹/₂ hours, €5, 5 per day).

Where to stay *Green House* (☎ 022 025), 15, Modatsou. Popular, with a garden courtyard and variety of rooms; sgl/dbl €15/25. *Rooms Aphrodite* (☎ 028 058), 27, Koritsas. Rooms sgl/dbl €15/25. *Hotel Doxa* (☎ 024 614), 7, Idomeneos. Well-appointed rooms and a nice atmosphere too; €35/50 sgl/dbl.

AEGEAN SEA

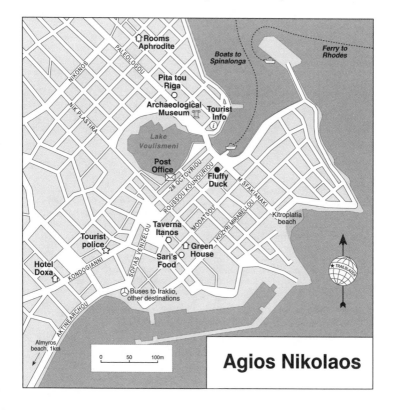

Agios Nikolaos

AEGEAN SEA

Campers should try **Gournia Moon Camping** (☎ 093 243), 19km south-east at Gournia and the site of an old Minoan settlement. The Sitia bus can drop you off there.

Where to eat The central area is full of restaurants, most of which cater for package tourists and charge unusual prices.

Try **Sari's Food**, 15, Kyprou, for budget eats at around €8 a head, or, farther along at 1, Kyprou, the **Taverna Itanos**, with larger meals for €10. Otherwise, on Paleologou there are a number of places selling kebabs, including **Pita tou Riga**, which does 'Arabic fillings' including a vegetarian hoummus offering.

For a decent pint, try the **Fluffy Duck** at 2, 25 Martiou, which has Guinness on draft.

SITIA
AREA CODE: ☎ 2843 POPULATION: 8000
In many respects, Sitia is preferable to Agios Nikolaos as a place to stay on the eastern side of the island, given its pretty whitewashed houses and Venetian castro. It also has good-ish beaches within easy walking distance and a much less touristy atmosphere.

Unfortunately, it doesn't have the transport connections of Agios Nikolaos, although ferries do leave here for Karpathos and Rhodes, even if they are usually the same ones as from Ag Nik. The last week in August is the town's main celebration, a sultana festival that's perhaps more famous amongst visitors due to the copious amounts of local wine on offer during it.

You can also head out from Sitia to the very eastern tip of the island and one of Crete's star attractions, the sandy beach of Vai, fringed by Europe's only natural palm forest. Now a national park, the trees of the palmery are a species native only to Crete.

Sitia plays host to a decent **archaeological museum** (Tue-Sun 0830-1500, €2.75), located on the Ierapetra road and with a focus on locally discovered Minoan artefacts.

The **fortress** on the hill behind the town was originally built in 1204, then expanded by the Venetians before falling to the Ottomans in 1651.

Practical information
Services The **EOT** (☎ 028 430), on the sea-front road, just off Plateia El Venizelou, opens daily 0900-2100 and has lists of accommodation.

The **post office** is on the corner of Papanastassiou and Therissou.

The OTE **phone office** is on the corner of Kapetan Sifi and I Kondilaki.

Santorini
Overview Something of an iconic travel destination, Santorini is the spectacular remnant of a gigantic volcanic explosion, with the island's curve of rock the remains of a crater rim. The bay in which both cruise liners and ferry boats arrive is the result of the sea flooding in to the detonated volcanic cone and is one of the deepest in the Mediterranean. The eruption, around 1650BC, is thought to have caused a tidal wave that wiped out the Minoan civilization on Crete.

Boats tie up at the foot of the cliff, with a cable-car and a staircase up to Fira, the island capital. In summer, the island is densely crowded. Ancient Akrotiri, a Minoan outpost, contains some impressive 16th-century BC remains, while Moni Profiti Ilia monastery on the island's highest point, at 567m, has excellent views.

Where to stay Most accommodation is in Fira; hotels and pensions range from €30-80. Camping is possible 400m east of the main square.

Ferry connections There are ferries from Mykonos, Anafi, Amorgos, Naxos, Paros, Ios, Crete (Iraklio, p454) and Piraeus (p458).

Ferries [see p459 for full details] Boats leave for **Karpathos** (via **Kassos**), **Agios Nikolaos, Milos, Piraeus** and **Rhodes**. The main ticket agency is Tzortzakis Travel (☎ 022 631), 150, Kornarou. The port authority is on ☎ 027 117. The main ferry operator is LANE (☎ 025 555).

Buses There are buses to and from Iraklio (3¹/₂ hours, €10, 5 per day), Ag Nik (1¹/₂ hours, €5, same 5 per day) and Vai (1 hour, €1.50, 5 per day).

Planes Sitia has a small domestic airport 1km out of town, with Olympic Airways flights to Athens once a week. The Olympic agent is Tzortzakis Travel (see above). There's no airport bus; a taxi should be around €4.

Where to stay *Youth Hostel* (☎ 022 693), 4, Therissou. Communal kitchens and dorms for €8, doubles for €15.
Hotel Archontiko (☎ 28 172), 16, Kondilaki. A good terrace; both guests and rooms are well looked after; sgl/dbl for €17/22.
El Greco Hotel (☎ 023 133), 13, Arkadou. A notch up in both quality and price; €25/35 sgl/dbl.

Where to eat *Kali Kardia Taverna*, 20, Foundalidou, just along from an ouzeri of the same name at No 28, has good value grub for €7.50 a head.
Mixos, 117, Kornarou, serves great kebabs, with dishes for €5-8.

Rhodes

POPULATION: 43,000
One of the Mediterranean's bigger islands, Rhodes has often loomed large on the historical stage and has certainly also blossomed on the international tourist circuit too in recent years. Lying so close to the Anatolian shore, it dominates the south-east Aegean, with the view from its central

mountains — rising in some places to over 1200m — stretching all the way to Crete.

Its main sight is undoubtedly Rhodes town, a labyrinth of medieval streets enclosed within Disney-like castle walls. In its warrens you'll find traces of just about every civilization to have ever set sail in the Mediterranean, and several days can easily disappear by just wandering these ancient, cobbled streets.

Yet the island has plenty else to offer. Lindos, on the eastern coast, is a classic of Acropolis-dominated towns with white-washed buildings round a sleepy bay. There are also two important, ancient city sites and a fair deal of forest and hill country in the interior. The island is also important for travellers as it is a major ferry hub for the Greek islands and mainland, Turkey and beyond. From Rhodes town, the ferry leaves for Cyprus, and on to the Levant.

HISTORY
The first settlers on Rhodes are thought to have been Minoans from Crete. The arrival of the Dorians in around 1100BC led to the establishment of the island's three major ancient city states: Lindos, Ialyssos and Kamiros. According to myth, Rhodes was the bride of Helios, the god of the sun, and the three Dorian cities were each named after the three sons of this marriage. This myth does have some basis in reality, too, as Rhodes receives the most hours of sunshine of any Greek island — 300 a year, according to the tourist board.

The history of Rhodes, however, is a good deal stormier than its climate. Rhodian cities fought with Athens against Persia in 490BC, then with Persia against Athens in 480BC. They then joined Athens against Sparta in 478BC, but again went over to Sparta against Athens in the subsequent Peloponnesian wars, before rejoining Athens against Sparta in 394BC. Just to confuse matters still further, they then joined up with the Persians against Alexander the Great soon after that, only to join Alexander the Great against the Persians a few months later.

After Alexander's death, Rhodes ended

up siding with one of his successors, Ptolemy. This heralded the start of the island's golden age. Rhodes had the largest navy in the region, was a centre of international trade and went through an artistic renaissance too, with the Rhodian school of sculpture outshining even that of Athens. Its most famous sculptor was Pythocretes, whose rock-carved *trireme* — an ancient warship — can still be seen in the Acropolis at Lindos.

The Romans brought that era to a close, however, and the island was devastated by the soldiers of Cassius, one of the contenders for Julius Caesar's power after he had been assassinated. After AD70, Rhodes became part of the Roman Empire, where it stayed

until that empire split. Part of the Byzantine province of the Dodecanese, it then changed hands repeatedly, with the Persians, Arabs, Seljuks, Crusaders, Genoese, Knights of St John and finally the Ottomans enjoying varying degrees of control over the island at some stage. Ottoman rule continued until, along with the rest of the Dodecanese, Italy took over in 1912. They stayed until 1943, when Rhodes was occupied by the Germans, before passing to the British at the war's end in 1945.

The British continued in occupation till 1947, when the Dodecanese were finally handed over to Greece, making the Rhodians some of the Hellenic republic's newest citizens.

The Knights of St John
Founded amidst the rubble of Jerusalem following its conquest by the forces of Christian Europe in the First Crusade, the organization of the Knights of St John was to have an impact on the Mediterranean far in excess of its tiny size.

Starting out in 1113 as a holy order charged with looking after the sick and wounded, they graduated quickly to become the élite foreign legion of medieval Europe, a multi-national army of fundamentalist believers dedicated to perpetual warfare against Islam. Many young nobles from France, Italy, Spain, Germany and England thought that dedicating their lives and property to such an idea was a thoroughly righteous act and swelled their ranks. For crusading, initially at least, was seen as a worthy cause, rather than a grab for someone else's land and property.

Recruits to orders such as St John would join as monks, renouncing worldly goods and pleasures in an effort to contain their own sinfulness. Fighting was part of this religious devotion. While the Knights might work as 'nursing brothers' to try to save others, or fight the Muslims to 'save the holy places', the bottom line was that both were activities designed primarily for them to save themselves. As such the Knights of St John, with their banner, the eight-pointed cross (now the flag of Malta), played an important role in all the Crusades. the primary aim of which was to secure the Holy Land — Palestine — for Christianity. However, as these ventures proved less and less successful, culminating in final defeat at Acre in 1291, the Knights were obliged to move out. First, they settled on Cyprus, then, in 1309, they moved to Rhodes.

The order was organized according to langues — language groups — under the authority of the grand master. Building the mighty fortress of Rhodes town, still there today, the langues — Auvergne, France, Provence, Aragon, Castile, England, Germany and Italy — were each given a different section of the wall to defend.

By this stage, despite the vows of poverty undertaken by the individual Knights, the order was fabulously wealthy. Partly this was because the Knights had to give most of their estates to the order when they died. As a result, the Knights of St John acquired enormous estates throughout Europe. They also developed a powerful navy, their flagship being the *Great Carrack*. *(Continued opposite)*

WHAT TO SEE
Rhodes Town
AREA CODE: ☎ 2241

Next to St Catherine's Gate/Port Gate, near where the old harbour ferry docks, is Pindarou, with the ruined **Our Lady of the City Church** right in front of you. Turn right and after 75m you'll enter Plateia Evreon, lined with restaurants and cafés. Head straight on, with the street curving to the right, where it becomes Aristoteleous. Follow this past the souvenir shops and snack bars to Plateia Ippokratous, which has in its centre a famous **Ottoman fountain**.

This town was originally built according to the plans of Hippodamos of Miletus in 408BC to a standard Hellenistic grid pattern.

By now though, you'll be aware that this regularity has long since disappeared. Passing on from here to the right, Ermou takes you to a crossroads with Apelou. Right here brings you into the main tourist destination – the Knights Quarter.

Following Roman then Byzantine rule, Rhodes was taken by the Arabs until the Crusaders came along in 1204. They handed control on to the Knights of St John a century later, in 1309 (see box, below). The Knights left an indelible mark on the city, which became their headquarters, by building and rebuilding the walls you see today. The Knights also withstood the advance of the Ottomans twice, in 1444 and 1480, but in the end they succumbed to the armies of

AEGEAN SEA

❏ The Knights of St John

(Continued from p322) This was a giant fighting ship that was widely thought unsinkable. With this at its head, the Knights' navy marauded up and down the sea lanes of the eastern Mediterranean, attacking any Muslim ship it found. The booty taken also added to the order's growing wealth. Some of this went towards building fortifications along the Anatolian coast to further hamper Muslim trade routes.

Later, when the Knights had been forced to withdraw from Rhodes after a lengthy siege by the Ottomans, they settled on Malta. There they perfected a system of religious piracy known as the Corso. Under this, corsairs (see p92) could receive the protection of the Knights' navy and use Malta's harbours, provided they attacked Muslim ships only. As a result, Malta's slave market became one of the busiest in the Mediterranean.

Given this behaviour, it comes as no surprise to find that the Ottomans decided to try to finish off the order once and for all in 1565, and sent an enormous fleet to Malta in an effort to take the island. This was to prove the Knights' finest hour though, with a successful defence that was to pass into legend. The Ottoman defeat showered them in glory, securing their place on the island for a further couple of centuries.

Yet the order grew increasingly at odds with the times. Christianity was itself riven with disputes, as counter-reformation followed reformation, and the old feudal aristocracy on which the whole organization of the Knights was based began to collapse. The final end came with the arrival of Napoleon's troops on the island in 1798. However, even this was not the complete end of the story, for as late as 1827 the French langue tried to set out again for the eastern Med, having struck a deal with Greek nationalists fighting the Ottoman Turks. In return for the Knights' support against the old enemy, the Greeks had promised them a new island base. But the agreement was never fulfilled on either side, with the Knights unable to raise sufficient cash for the expedition despite floating themselves on the London Stock Exchange.

However, London remains the place where there is still some echo of the Knights' noble past today. They continue there and throughout Britain as the St John's Ambulance service, handing out tea and bandages at many a football match or village fête. It's perhaps not an unwelcome return to their earlier, more caring, sharing role.

AEGEAN SEA

Süleyman the Magnificent. After a lengthy siege in 1522 the Knights surrendered but were allowed safe passage out by Süleyman, known to Turks as Süleyman the Just, with the survivors retreating to their new headquarters on Malta.

Passing down Apelou, on the immediate left of the wide cobbled street is the **Archaeological Museum** (☎ 027 657, open Tue-Sun 0830-1500, €3), housed in the old Knights' hospital. Nowadays, it is more famous for its ancient Greek statues, including the *Aphrodite of Rhodes*, showing the goddess drying her hair after bathing. There's also the 4th-century *Aphrodite of Thalasia*, a statue worn down after centuries of being submerged but still attractive enough for the British writer Lawrence Durrell to use for the title of his book *Reflections on a Marine Venus*. Going back outside the museum, right opposite is the rather ruined **Inn of England**, a shell of a building that once housed the English Knights of St John, contrasting strongly with the immaculate condition of the inns belonging to the other langues, which can now be seen by turning right into the slowly ascending **Street of the Knights**, the centrepiece of the old town.

With its pebbled roadway leading up between two terraces of well-preserved and restored medieval buildings, first on the right up the street is the Inn of Italy, built in 1519. Then there's the Palace of Villiers de l'Ile Adam, named after the knight who arranged the final evacuation of the Knights of St John from the town. Next door is the Inn of France with its chapel next door. Opposite, on the left at this point, is a bit of an intruder amongst all this — the Turkish garden. This is well worth a visit, with its small, shaded courtyard containing an 18th-century fountain and stairs which lead up to an Ottoman house, the Villaragut mansion, now a museum.

Continuing on up the street, the next sight on the right is the Inn of Provence, opposite which is the Inn of Spain. All of these have been well restored with finance coming either from their respective countries or EU grants; though regrettably, none is open to the public. One place that is,

though, and which is another must-see, is the **Palace of the Grand Master**, the final port of call at the very top of the street. This museum (Tue-Sun 0830-1500, €5.50) is a grand, Disney-like castle, betraying the fact that it's not really the grand master's at all by its overdone, 20th-century film-set style. In fact, the original palace was blown up in 1856 when a gunpowder magazine left behind by the Knights was abruptly rediscovered by some unfortunate throwing away a match. What you see now was in fact built during the Italian fascist occupation as a holiday home for Mussolini. He never came but in the lobby, you can still see a carved stone plaque dedicating the place to him.

Inside, the furnishings include a number of Roman and ancient Greek mosaics from Kos, plus many fine examples of medieval craftsmanship — particularly carved wooden furniture. It's also a good place to get out of the sun, as its many rooms are light and airy. In the basement there's also an exhibition on the history of Rhodes from its foundation in 408BC to the beginning of the Ottoman period.

Due south of the palace, down Panetiou, is the towering **Süleymaniye Mosque**. It was built immediately after the victorious Süleyman the Magnificent's troops had taken the town. Opposite the entrance, on Apollonian, is the restored 18th-century **Ottoman library**, where the poet Namik Kemal wrote while serving as Ottoman governor at the end of the 19th century. It opens irregularly, with a sign on the door giving the latest schedules.

Turning right from here down Socratous — a good place for souvenir shopping — and then immediately right again to head south along Ippodamou, you'll pass the Church of Aghii Apostoli on the left and Agia Paraskevi on the right, before coming to the turning for Arhelaou on the left. Follow this for 15m or so and you'll come to a small square containing the minaret-less **Mustafa Mosque**. This is now used as a community centre by the island's Turkish Greeks, and if you're lucky you might catch a wedding in full swing. Next to the mosque is the 18th-cen-

Rhodes Town

AEGEAN SEA

0   250   500m

Windy beach

GEORGIOU PAPANIKOLAOU

Restaurant Ellinikon

Airport

MANDRAKI

Plateia Vas Georgiou II

Hotel Anastasia

26TH OKTOVRIOU

PAPAGOU

ELEFTHERIAS (HARBOUR ROAD)

VENIZELOU ELEFTH

West side buses

New Market

East side buses

Tourist Info (i) (EOT)

Ferries to Nisyros

Ferries to Marmaris

Ferries to Cyprus, other destinations

RIGA FEREOU

MELA PAVLOU

Palace of the Grand Master

Archaeological Museum

STREET OF THE KNIGHTS

OLD TOWN

Ottoman fountain

St Catherine's Gate/ Port Gate

Suleymaniye mosque

SOCRATOUS

PANETIOU

APELOU

ERMOU

ARISTOTELEOUS

Alexis Restaurant

Marine Gate

PINDAROU

Ottoman Library

ARHELAOU

Mustafa mosque/ hamam

Plateia Ippokratous

Fisherman's Ouzeria

Plateia Evreon

Our Lady of the City church

Aghii Apostoli church

AGIOU FANOURIOU

Paradosiako Kafeneio

PITHAGORA

Hotel Spot

TARISOFOU

Synagogue

HIPPODAMOU

OMIROU

Pension Andreas

Hotel Via Via

EFTHIMIOU

DIMOKRATIAS

St John's Gate

VYRONOS

MEGALOU KONSTANTINOU

KODRIKTONOS

KANADA

VENETOKLEON

PALEOLOGOU

tury **hamam** (Tue 1300-1900, Wed, Thu and Fri 1100-1900, Sat 0800-1800, €2). Leaving the square at its lower end, a few metres on you'll come to Agiou Fanouriou. Turn right, and head along for about 100m to the junction with Omirou. Here turn left and after about 150m, turn right, which will bring you to the medieval splendour of **St John's Gate**. Go through here and you find yourself overlooking the town moat, a vast defensive earthwork that stretches all around the old town. You can get down into it further east, about 50m down Efthimiou, where a long tunnel takes you under the walls and up into this grassy arena. However, we advise you to take in the view and then head back the way you came in, as the next exit isn't for some kilometres.

From St John's Gate, head east, hugging the inside of the walls until you come to the right-hand turn into Tavrisrou. This is the town's old Jewish quarter and there's a **synagogue** in Dossiadou, which Tavrisrou merges into after about 20m. It's not easy to spot but stands in some disrepair next to an equally-battered Ottoman fountain. From here, carrying straight on will bring you back to the Plateia Evreon, near where you began your journey.

The new town, clustered around Mandraki Harbour, is where you'll find the usual Western chain stores and an extensive collection of umbrella shops, strange given that the island receives more sunshine than any other island in Greece. In addition, while not to everyone's taste but increasingly trendy architecturally, is the Italian fascist architecture of the administrative district, gathered around the Plateia Vas Georgiou II at the end of the main harbour front road, Elefthekias. There's also a piece of classic, fascist-period, orientalist fantasy in the **New Market**, the colonnaded collection of shops and restaurants at the old town end of Elefthekias.

Elsewhere, keeping on Elefthekias and walking round the headland brings you onto the western side of the new town, and to a very passable beach, the pebbly **Windy Beach**. The new town also contains most of the package hotels.

Mandraki Harbour may seem modern enough but it in fact has a very ancient pedigree. In ancient times, Rhodes established itself as the premier Greek city after beating off the troops of one of Alexander the Great's successors, Demetrius, in a famous siege of 305BC. This battle left the Rhodians with some useful equipment — including two giant siege engines abandoned by the fleeing enemy. These the townsfolk sold to raise cash for the building of the city's awesome Colossus of Rhodes. This 35m giant stood, according to some stories, across the mouth of the entrance to Mandraki harbour and was a precursor in design to New York's Statue of Liberty. One of the Seven Wonders of the Ancient World, it was a monument to the sun god Helios and carried a torch, while the head was surrounded by a fiery halo.

Unfortunately, the statue collapsed in an earthquake soon after its 290BC construction. However, its remains continued to lie about for over nine centuries until AD653 when the island came under Arab rule and the rubble was carted off to Aleppo in Syria. No trace has been found of them since.

Lindos and eastern Rhodes

AREA CODE: LINDOS / MONOLITHOS ☎ 2244/ 2246

Heading down the east coast, the first stop is **Kalithea** (16 buses per day, 10km, 15 mins, €1.25), an old Italian occupation-era spa full of crumbling 1920s' and 1930s' orientalist buildings set in small parks next to a rocky beach. Some 5km further on, **Faliraki** (18 buses per day, 20 mins, €1.30) has a good, wide sandy beach and plenty of nightlife. **Ladiko** is the next beach along (10 buses per day, 25 mins, €1.70), where WWII-action movie *Guns of Navarone* was filmed. From here on the beaches in order of appearance are: **Kolymbia** (10 buses per day, 30 mins, €2), **Tsambika** (10 buses/day, 35 mins, €2) and **Stenga** (10/day, 40 mins, €2.50). All three are good spots, with the latter the least crowded, reached via a path from the village of Archangelos, where the bus stops. Archangelos also has a 1467 Knights of St John castle and a 1377 Byzantine church, the latter decorated with some excellent frescos.

Lindos is a stunningly situated town of whitewashed, flat-roofed houses clustered around an impressive Acropolis. The bus (10 per day, one hour, €3.50) drops you off away from the town centre (though it does pick up passengers from the central square on its return journey) leaving you with a 5-minute walk to the shaded square overlooking the bay — the ancient grand harbour. Down the hill from here through the usual seething crowds, you'll pass a donkey station where you can hire a beast of burden to take you right up to the Acropolis (€4 one way). Walking up to the Acropolis from town takes around 10 minutes, though in the summer heat it's advisable to take longer and carry plenty of water.

At the top you'll have a breathtaking view, which gets better when you enter the **Acropolis complex** itself (Tue-Sun 0800-1830, Mon 1230-1800, €6). Pythocretes' rock-carved trireme is on the right, while the steps take you up further to a Knights of St John tower. Leaving this, immediately to your left is the Byzantine Church of Agios Ioannis. Carrying straight on up the hill along the inside of the wall, you arrive at the 348BC Temple of Athena Lindia. Not a lot of the original is left and, as with other parts of the site, some Italian occupation era 'restoration' has not helped. But the site was the centre of religious worship back to the 10th century BC when the first tributes to the goddess Athena took place here (See Meet the Gods box on p296). Down the hill from the temple is the Propylaea, the formal gateway to the temple precinct, and beyond this the monumental stairway leading down to two lower terraces, on the last of which is the site of a later Roman temple.

The town beach is a good place to head for next, with its shallow, tepid sea below the Acropolis hill.

Western Rhodes

Ancient **Ialyssos** is some 10km out of town, but isn't so easy to get to without your own transport. Your best bet is to get one of the regular west-coast buses to the village of Trianda (12 buses per day, 10 mins, €1). This is still 5km from the site, so you'll have to hitch or walk the remaining distance. The site is built on Philerimos Hill, with excellent views of the surrounding countryside. On the hill you'll find two monuments — a 3rd-century BC temple of Athena and a much later church built by the Knights of St John. There's not much of the city itself left but the strategic worth of the site is obvious. It was here that Süleyman the Magnificent set up his headquarters during the siege, the hill offering such a clear view of the battle.

Some 5km further down the main highway from Trianda is the turning for **Butterfly Valley**, or Petaloudes. There are no buses here so if you don't have your own transport you'll have to hitch or go on an organized tour. Where the road ends there's a cliff-top restaurant surrounded by thick forest. A path leads you to the entrance to this nature reserve (daily, 0800-1700, €4), where millions of tiger moth butterflies congregate. A small display at the entrance helps you identify them, though there are plenty flitting about anyway, even in the restaurant. The reserve has a number of well-marked paths to follow though you're advised not to set off too late if you want to do some serious trekking.

Some 15km further south along the highway, **Kamiros** has more to see than Ialyssos and is much easier to get to. Buses from town go right to the entrance once a day (€3). You can also catch the more regular buses to Monolithos (3 per day, €3.25) and get off at the Kamiros bus stop, 1km from the site. Kamiros was inhabited from Mycenaean times but the ruins on display now are of the later Hellenistic city and its Roman additions. After going through the entrance gate you pass down into a large square, the ancient Agora, or marketplace, with the 3rd-century BC Temple of Apollo on your left. Pass next to this and you enter Fountain Square, which once had a number of springs around it, probably used for sacred purposes. A row of columns has been reconstructed here as well and passing to the side of them, up some steps, you come to the city's main street. As this ascends the hill there are the remains of many Hellensitic houses on either side, some with the ruins of their inner courtyards still visible.

The street eventually finishes at the stoa, the ruins of a huge, 200m-long portico that used to cover the city's cistern. Behind this is the ruined 3rd-century BC Temple of Athena. From here, the view into the interior of the island is breathtaking, with woods and hills stretching all around.

Some 20km on from here is **Monolithos**, with its spectacular 15th-century **Knights of St John Castle**. Situated at the top of a 240m headland, it has compelling views across the water to the neighbouring island of Halki. Access is via a dirt track out of the town square. Walking further along this takes you to a fork, with the shingle Fourni Beach to the left and the monastery of Moni Georgiou to the right.

PRACTICAL INFORMATION
Orientation

Rhodes International Airport is some 8km south-west of Rhodes Town and linked by frequent buses, which drop you off at the west side bus station in Mandraki, the new harbour/town north of the old, walled Rhodes Town. Ferries dock in the old town harbour, before the medieval walls, and arriving at sunset is a real gem. A narrow harbour-front road leads round the old port, and then on to Mandraki. Off this are several gates into the old town, which is all pedestrianized (though there are plenty of scooters about). The quickest way in is through St Catherine's Gate, to the east of the harbour, or the Marine Gate, a classic twin-towers-style portal in the centre of the battlements.

Inside is a maze but it roughly breaks down into an area of souvenir shops close in to the walls, an area of mainly residential and more run-down houses behind that, and the old Knights Quarter, to the north-west, where most of the museums and sights are.

The rest of the island is divided into east and west sides. Buses serve the main destinations on each from two different stops in Mandraki. The west side is next to the kiosk on the north-western corner of the New Market, while the eastern side is served from the bus stop on Papagou, just along from the tourist information office. The main roads go down each coast, with a few branches heading off inland. The neighbouring islands of Halki and Symi are served by frequent local boats from Rhodes Town.

Services

The **EOT** (☎ 023 255), in Plateia Alexandrias, next to the bus stops for the east side of the island and opposite the New Market, has useful brochures and maps (open Mon-Sat 0800-2000, Sun 0800-1300. A good website is 🖳 www.rodosnet.gr. The **tourist police** (☎ 027 423) is nearby on Makariou and Papagou. There is a **post office** in Mandraki (Mon-Fri, 0730-2000) and a **phone office** at 91, Amerikis. Cosmonet (☎ 036 951, 🖳 cosmonet@aias.gr) in Plateia Evreon, No 45B, offers **internet access**.

Ferries [see p459 for full details]

Rhodes has ample domestic ferry services. Agencies in Mandraki around the New Market area are plentiful. Ferry lines are: GA Lines and Kalymnian Shipping at Kydon Tourist Agency (☎ 023 000); LANE at Zorpidis Tourism (☎ 020 625); Kiriakoulis Maritime at Kiriakoulis Maritime (☎ 078 052). Also operating are DANE Lines (☎ 077 070), 95, Amerikis. The port authority is on ☎ 022 220.

Boats go to **Agios Nikolaos** and **Iraklio** on Crete, via **Halki**, **Karpathos** and **Kassos**, while also going east to **Kastelorizo** and north to **Symi**, **Nisyros**, **Kos**, **Kalymnos**, **Tilos** and **Patmos**. Ferries also leave for **Piraeus** and the Cyclades, via **Naxos**.

To Cyprus/Israel
Salamis Lines, at Kydon Tourist and Shipping (☎ 027 900), 14, Ethn, Dodekanisos, and Poseidon Lines at Kouros Travel (☎ 022 400), 34, Kartpathou, deal in tickets for Limassol, Cyprus. The same boats also continue to Haifa in Israel. However, at the time of writing services were not operating.

To Turkey
Daily ferries go to Marmaris; tickets are available from Triton Holidays (☎ 021 657) or from any of the large number of ticket agencies in the new town around the New Market. There is a hydrofoil link to Bodrum (Turkey) in the summer. Again, passports should be handed in the night before.

Kastelorizo

Overview Lying just off the Turkish coastal town of Kaş, Kastelorizo is the Latin name for the island the Greeks optimistically call Megisti, or 'Large Island'. It is also known as the 'Last Island' as it lies the furthest east of any Greek territory. Quiet even in the high season, the main port and village is now being restored by mainly overseas Greeks, particularly from Australia and the US. The town museum stands next to an Ottoman-era mosque and in the ruins of a Crusader-era castle, while walking up the 400 or so steps behind the town takes you to the roof of the island and a cluster of deserted monasteries. The Italian film, *Mediterraneo*, was filmed on this island; many of the locals are still more than willing to tell you all about it.

Where to stay Most of the lower-priced options are around the town waterfront, with prices running from €20-50 for a double.

Ferry connections There are ferries from Kaş, Turkey, and Rhodes (p459).

AEGEAN SEA

Buses
Buses for the west of the island go from the north-west corner of the New Market in Mandraki, east side from near the tourist office on Papagou: see the text for details.

Planes
There are five flights a day to and from Athens with Olympic (☎ 024 571), whose office is at 9, Ierou Lohou. The airport is about 10km out of town but 21 buses a day travel there and back from the west side bus station in the new town, costing €1.40.

Where to stay
It's advisable to try booking accommodation in advance during the summer season, which runs from June through to October.

There are plenty of options, but it pays to hunt around.

Rhodes Town *Hotel Anastasia* (☎ 021 815), 46, 28 Octovriou, in the New Town. Set in an old, characterful Italian villa; €30/40 sgl/dbl.
Hotel Via Via (☎ 027 895), 2, Lisipou, near Pythagora. Spotless rooms; €25/45 sgl/dbl.
Pension Andreas (☎ 034 156, 🖳 andreasch @otenet.gr), 28D, Omirou, Old Town. Upmarket; €55/65 sgl/dbl.
Hotel Spot (☎ 034 737), 21, Perikleous, Old Town. Long established hotel, with pleasant rooms; €25/35 sgl/dbl.

Faliraki *Cannon Bar Pension* (☎ 085 596), Greek-American owned, good clean sgl/dbl for €25/35.

Lindos With around 500,000 tourists visiting every year, accommodation can be a problem unless booked many moons in advance. It's also a more expensive resort than Rhodes.
Pension Electra (☎ 031 266), follow the path for the Acropolis for about 150m from the town square. €30/45 sgl/dbl.
Pension Katholiki (☎ 031 445), opposite Electra. €30/45 sgl/dbl, shared bathroom.

Monolithos *Hotel Thomas* (☎ 061 291). The only hotel in town, but a good, clean place with sgl/dbl for €25/40.

Where to eat
Rhodes Town The *Fisherman's Ouzeri*, Sofokleous. Budget eats, with excellent quality fish; €5.
Alexis Restaurant, on Sokratous. Another top of the range seafood haunt; €10-15.
Restaurant Ellinikon, 6, Papanikolaou. Good quality traditional dishes; €10-15.
Paradosiako Kafeneio, 45, Aristofanois. Italian-influenced fare; €15-20.

Those on a tighter budget should try the restaurants around the New Market in the new town, where plenty of gyro and souvlaki buffets serve at all hours.

Symi

Overview Lying just off Marmaris, on the Turkish coast, Symi is an often-overlooked gem, largely patronized by day-trippers from nearby Rhodes. The island's main settlement, Symi Town, is picturesque, with many once-abandoned houses now being restored. Walking tours and boat trips to small coves around the coast are the main highlights of a laidback visit.

Where to stay Symi's main accommodation centre is the town, with prices a touch higher than other islands. Expect to pay €50-75 a double.

Ferry connections There are ferries from Rhodes (p459), Kos (p456), Kalymnos (p455) and Nisyros (Mandraki, p456), and to Kormen, Datça, Turkey, in the summer.

AEGEAN SEA

Lindos *Restaurant Aphrodite*, near the Electra. Offers good quality Greek food at reasonable prices; €10.

Marmaris

AREA CODE: ☎ 0252 POPULATION: 25,000
Set at the head of a long and beautiful inlet, Marmaris town somewhat makes up for its lack of impressive historical sights or architectural aesthetics by its location and usefulness as a base for exploring the local area, the picturesque Reşadiye Peninsula. This long, finger-like strip of land is a world all of its own. Hilly, pine covered and possessing a seemingly endless series of bays, it lends itself well to hiking as well as sunbathing, to sailing as well as snorkelling.

The peninsula divides into three — the northern shore of the Gulf of Gökova, the southern promontory just outside Marmaris town and the narrow strip of land to the west leading out to Datça.

HISTORY
In ancient times, Marmaris was known as Physcus, a colony of the Dorian League. Later, it formed the most important city of the 'Rhodian Peraea', the name given to the peninsula back then, as it belonged to the three united cities of Rhodes.

Little trace of this now remains and the town slumbered for centuries until Süleyman the Magnificent took advantage of its magnificent harbour to assemble his troops

here for the invasion of Rhodes in 1522.

After that, the record thins again until 1798, when the famous British admiral, Horatio Nelson, assembled his fleet here before defeating Napoleon's ships at the Battle of the Nile.

Nowadays, Marmaris town's only claim to fame is as the birthplace of General Kenan Evren, who led Turkey's 1980 military coup and then became president. His local boy status is etched on the town's maps, with Kenan Evren Bulevard and a local private school bearing his name.

WHAT TO SEE
Atatürk's statue, surfing in out of the bay at the end of the town's main drag, Ulusal Egemenlik Bulvarı, is a good place to start exploring. Go left along the Kordon for the castle and the marina, or right along Atatürk Caddesi for the long seafront road round to Uzunyalı Beach and beyond.

Heading south along the Kordon, the entrance to the bazaar area also leads up to the town's castle. On the way, down at the bazaar end of the alley, you'll pass an old **Menzilhane**, a kind of medieval express mail office, built on Süleyman the Magnificent's orders. The **castle** (0800-1200, 1300-1700; US$1) was also built by Süleyman the Magnificent, after he'd returned from defeating the Knights of St John on Rhodes (see box on p322). It was built on top of a much older Byzantine castle. The area immediately around here is the Kaleiçi district, a small warren of streets that still survive from the old Marmaris — even if it is now surrounded by a fan of restaurants and bars that spread out onto the harbour corniche and the marina beyond.

For the nearest beach, İçmeler is connected to Marmaris by frequent dolmuş. With many hotels, parks and wide streets, this tangerine-tree-lined beach resort has a pleasant, garden-town atmosphere. For nightlife, Marmaris is still the place to go but dolmuş run most of the night during the summer between the two places.

You could also try **Cennet 'island'**, which looks separate from the mainland, with the Yalancı Boğazı ('Fake Channel') apparently running between them. This area is a favourite for day trips by boat, but it is also possible to walk across the natural causeway. Along the route to Datça there is also **Günnücek**, a forest and beach area where, for a week in summer, a small stream also runs.

The Gulf of Gökova

One of the most popular day trips from town takes you straight to the end of this gulf, north of the peninsula, for a short boat trip over to Sedir Adası. The more romantic name on the leaflets is Cleopatra's Isle. Whatever it's called, it has certainly got one of the best beaches around. In ancient times, this was Cedreae, an important city of the Rhodian Peraea, and a fortification wall and ancient theatre can still be found among the cedar trees. The story runs that the sand on the beach was brought here on the orders of Cleopatra, who wanted a decent beach on which to frolic with Mark Antony. There's no evidence historically for this whatsoever,

but it is geologically odd that this type of sand appears nowhere else in the region.

Getting there under your own steam is tricky as there are no direct dolmuş to Camlı, from where the ferries leave. All the travel agencies on Ulusal Egemenlik Bulvarı offer this one though, so shopping around should find a good price. There's also a US$4.25 entrance fee, payable to the island's park attendant.

Some 11km north of Marmaris is Ingliz Limanı – 'English Harbour'— a gorgeous fjord near Karacasogut (Karacaköy on some maps). This is also accessible only by sea and gets its name from WWII, when a damaged British warship ran for cover here, these being neutral waters at the time. Karacasogut itself is accessible by land, though, with a local dolmuş going from Marmaris bus station (25 mins, US$1).

South of Marmaris

Boarding a dolmuş going to **Orhaniye** (20 mins, US$1) on Ulusal Egemenlik Caddesi will bring you to a small hamlet on a wonderful bay, an anchorage for yachties and also a destination for lunch. The **Kiz Kumu Plaji** ('Girls Sand Beach') features a handy restaurant, while the sea gives you the chance to fool the folks back home with a picture of yourself apparently walking on water. This is due to a long sand spit, much of which lies just beneath the waves, which stretches out into the bay. Local legend has it that a young girl, smitten with a boy living on the other shore, filled her skirts with sand and every night filled in just a little bit more

---

Tilos

Overview Well off the beaten track, some 65km west of Rhodes, Tilos has high cliffs, abandoned villages and verdant valleys in its interior. The capital and port, Livadia, is the only functioning settlement, with two abandoned villages – Megalo Horio and Mikro Horio – evocative places inland. This adds up to a good walking tour destination, while the 18th-century monastery, Moni Agiou Panteleimona, 5km from Megalo Horio, has some fine frescos.

Where to stay Accommodation stretches from **camping** on the beaches west of the island – Eristos being a good one – to pension rooms in Livadia for €20-40/double.

Ferry connections There are ferries from Rhodes (p459), Kos (p456), Kalymnos Town (p455), Nisyros (Mandraki, p456) and Leros.

AEGEAN SEA

of a path across to his waiting arms. She must have been a well-built lass considering the tonnage of sand transported. With its glittering waters, the green trees of the cliffs and the boats at anchor, the bay is beautiful.

Further on is **Selimiye**, reached via the same dolmuş (30 mins, US$1.25). Here, an Ottoman fort overlooks another bay, along with a number of restaurants and pensions. Further on is Bozburun (40 mins, US$1.50) at the end of the peninsula, a yachtie haven which looks across the waters at the Greek island of Symi.

The next valley over is the hamlet of **Sogut**. A dolmuş takes you from Bozburun to the hilltop village of **Taslica**, 5 mins from Bozburun (US$0.25), from where a four-hour hike through the coastal hills takes you to **Loryma**, another ancient Rhodian city where the crumbling ruins of its fort look out over another gorgeous bay. Down in it is **Bozukkale**, which has a number of small restaurants, and the occasional boat round the coast back to Bozburun (30 mins, US$5).

Datça

Some 60km west of Marmaris on a newly resurfaced and expanded highway, Datça — reached by regular bus from the Marmaris otogar (station) for US$4 — can be a bit of an anticlimax. The town is useful for boats to Bodrum in summer but apart from the charm of Eski Datça (Old Datça) and the nearby site of ancient Cnidos, there's not much of interest.

Datça is basically a long high street running between two bays. At the furthest bay (south-west) from the main dolmuş halt is the place where you can get tickets for a ferry to Bodrum. **Eski Datça** is 3km inland from the new town centre and has some good examples of old Ottoman houses — some in the process of renovation — along with twisting, characterful streets.

Cnidos (0800-1900, US$2) is 35km further west, at the very tip of the peninsula. Getting there can be difficult, though, as there are no buses or dolmuş, and a taxi will set you back US$30 for the round trip with one hour at the site. Cheaper and more pleasant is to go by tour boat from Datça, a trip of around an hour, with the boat costing around US$10. Cnidos was once a city rivalling Ephesus on this coast, back in the days of the Dorian Hexapolis, though this league of city states shrank to a Pentapolis when Halicarnassus (Bodrum) left. Thus it remained the only Rhodian city on the mainland of Anatolia, taking full advantage of its strategic location. The Cnidians also set up colonies far away on the coast of North Africa in the 6th century BC, while later they developed a medical school to rival that at the Asklepion on Kos. The city was also home to the ancient astronomer Eudoxus, who studied the motion of the planets from his observatory here in the 4th century BC.

However, the place was really famous for something far more tabloid friendly — it was famous as a sanctuary for the worship of Aphrodite, the goddess of love. In a temple dedicated to her, a famous 4th-century BC statue of the goddess stood. This was the first ancient Greek sculpture to depict a goddess nude, and was later copied all over the ancient world. Made by the sculptor Praxiteles and modelled on his mistress, the courtesan Phryne, it had such notoriety that it made Cnidos into a major place of pilgrimage for Aphrodite worshippers. What happened to the statue is unclear, except that it was taken to Byzantium much later and then vanished from the pages of history. There are claims that her head turned up much later still — in the vaults of the British Museum — but in Turkey, archaeologists are still continuing to look for this missing gem.

Nowadays, there's not much evidence of glamour, though the headland where the city stood is still covered with a jumble of walls and ruined houses, temples and fallen columns. The view is spectacular both out to sea and back along the narrow peninsula.

If you do need to stay the night in Datça, try *Huzur*, ☎ 712 3052, on the hill separating the town's two bays. US$10/15 sgl/dbl.

PRACTICAL INFORMATION
Orientation

Marmaris town is something of an urban sprawl these days, but generally, buses arrive at the otogar, some 25-minutes' walk from the seafront, but only 10- to 15-minutes' walk from the ferry terminal for boats to Rhodes. Dolmuş serve the otogar, taking you into town, while from the ferry stop things are a touch more difficult. Taxis can be extortionate here, so it may be worth hiking in through the marina to your left, which brings you eventually to the town's waterfront centre.

Many dolmuş for the surrounding area are easily caught along the waterfront road — Atatürk Caddesi — or, heading inland, on Ulusal Egemenlik Bulvarı.

What's left of the old town and castle is hidden among a jumble of other buildings, restaurants and the start of Marmaris' own bar street, next to the old ferry stop and the harbour headland.

AEGEAN SEA

Santa's coming to town

It may come as something of surprise but Santa Claus, alias Father Christmas, alias Nicholas of Bari, alias Nicholas of Myra, does not in fact come from some snowbound polar waste. Rather, he hails from a much warmer climate — Demre, a town some 150km east of Marmaris in what is now south-western Turkey.

He would probably therefore find a thick red coat, boots and a long, white beard a little sweaty to wear about town. Little is known of the life of Saint Nicholas. He was most likely bishop of Myra, the ancient city bordering Demre, in around the 4th century AD. Local legend has him born at Patara, the town's seaport, from where he travelled to Palestine and Egypt in his youth. He was also reportedly imprisoned during the Roman Emperor Diocletian's persecutions of Christians, but released by the Emperor Constantine, who himself converted to the new religion. He also attended the Council of Nicea in AD325, a meeting of the church's top bishops called to hammer out just what was and was not to be officially recognized as 'Christianity'. The resulting Nicene Creed is still a central part of the Christian rule book.

When he died, Saint Nicholas was buried in his church in Myra, which became an important shrine by the 6th century. Around then, as a further mark of his importance, the Emperor Justinian had a church dedicated to him in Constantinople. However, in 1087, with Christendom split between Western and Eastern churches, a bunch of Italian sailors showed up in Myra one day and promptly ran off with his corpse.

They took it to Bari, where Nicholas' bones were interred in the church which still bears his name, San Nicola. The new tomb also became a major centre of pilgrimage.

Nicholas' reputation is built on his legendary acts of kindness and generosity. One story goes that he gave marriage dowries to three local girls in Myra and thus saved them from a life of prostitution. Another tells how he somehow reassembled and brought back to life three children after they'd been hacked up by the butcher, and dunked in a tub of brine.

He thus became the patron saint of unmarried women, children and, for some reason, pawnbrokers. Cities as far away as Moscow and Freiburg in Switzerland also took him as their patron saints, while his feast day, 6 December, was celebrated throughout Europe. This was done with a particularly unusual custom. A boy from the neighbourhood would be elected local bishop and run the church's affairs until Holy Innocents' Day, 22 days later.

In Holland, he later became venerated as Sinterklaas, a Dutch version of the name Saint Nicholas, which was later Anglicized to Santa Claus. His legend became entangled with various Nordic folk tales of a kindly old man who handed out gifts to good little boys and girls. The stage was thus set for the arrival of the modern festival of consumption, celebrated around the Nordic, pagan midwinter of 25 December.

Which, it has to be said, is all a long way from the beach at Patara.

Visiting many of the peninsula's sights is best done by boat, though. The harbour is usually a forest of rigging for tour boats offering day trips to most of these locations, usually with lunch thrown in and plenty of swimming breaks.

Services

The **tourist information office** (☎ 412 1035), on the Kordon, under the castle, is open daily in summer, 0800-2000, winter Mon-Fri 0800-1200, 1300-1700.

Lin Net at 38, Atatürk Caddesi is a good **internet café**.

Europcar (☎ 412 2001), 12, Kordon Caddesi, is useful, but all the major international **car rental** companies operate here, mostly with branches on Kordon or Ulusal Egemenlik Caddesi.

Ferries   [see p456 for full details]

Ferries to and from Rhodes arrive and depart from the international quay in Marmaris town, which is south-east of the marina and some 20-minutes' walk from the centre of town. A taxi should cost US$2 from Atatürk Meydanı. The quay is not so far from the otogar though, and a taxi there should be no more than US$1.

Tickets for ferries to Rhodes can be bought from Yeşil Marmaris at 11, Barbaros Cad (☎ 412 2290), or Engin Turizm at 10, Kordon Cad (☎ 412 1082). In season two hydrofoils a day make the one-hour trip and there's a car ferry once a week— phone in advance to book and check prices. Passports should preferably be handed in the night before.

Tickets for the daily ferry from Datça to Bodrum are available at Karya Tour, ☎ 712 1759, at 13, Karantina Caddesi, Datça. The ferries actually depart from Kormen, a 15-minute bus ride away, but the tour company lays on a service bus. The boat sails from the end of June to the end of September.

Buses

Marmaris bus station is well out of town, though regular dolmuş link the two — go to the dolmuş rank nearest the bus station entrance to catch one out, or pick one up heading inland on Ulusal Egemenlik

Caddesi marked 'otogar'. It takes five minutes and costs US$0.50. The town has regular inter-city coaches from the bus station to İzmir, Bodrum, İstanbul, Ankara, Kaş and Antalya.

The best way to get one, though, is to book at one of the ticket offices around the Tansas supermarket on Ulusal Egemenlik Caddesi in town, as they will also take you out to the otogar for free.

Planes

The nearest airport is at Dalaman, 100km east, which has regular THY flights to İstanbul and Ankara. The THY office is on 26-B, Atatürk Caddesi, ☎ 412 3751. A service bus serves these flights to/from the THY office. In summer, plenty of package tour operators also use Dalaman, as it serves the other south coast resorts as well.

Where to stay

Interyouth Hostel (☎ 412 3687), 45, 42 Sokak, in the bazaar. Has dorms and couldn't be more central; US$6-10 for a bunk.
Hotel Nadir, behind Tansas supermarket. Has nice clean rooms at US$10/17 sgl/dbl.
Marina Motel (☎ 412 6598, 🖳 www.turquaz-guide.net), 37, Barbaros Caddesi. Good value at US$13/20 sgl/dbl.

Campsites lie out of town, with *Dimet Camping* (☎ 413 3905), 1.5km east, and *Karya Mocamp* 8km south at Acmeler village.

Where to eat

Yeni Liman Restaurant, Kemeralti Sokak in the bazaar area. One of the few in this quarter not to be overpriced; US$10 a head.
Kircicegi, Kubilay Alpagun Caddesi, behind the bazaar area. Has good food in good surroundings for US$10-12.
Turhan, Atatürk Cad, west of the harbour towards Uzunyalı. Good Turkish food, US$10.

Bars

Bar Street, along the side of the bazaar, has evolved as a smaller replica of the one in Bodrum, with similar sets of dazzling white teeth on show from the gyrating waiters and the invitation to dance on the tables till dawn. It's pretty pricey, though Panorama on the castle hill at least offers a good view.

Bodrum

AREA CODE: ☎ 0252 POPULATION: 35,000
Standing out some way above Turkey's other Aegean resort towns, with its white-washed, flat-roofed houses laced with jasmine and brightly-coloured flowers, Bodrum is, for all its commercialism, still a place of some character. A ban on tall buildings and an insistence that new buildings follow a certain style were good decisions by the locals who have, after all, been entertaining tourists for around 2500 years.

This was Halicarnassus in ancient days, home to Herodotus, the father of history, and of another of the region's Seven Wonders of the Ancient World — the Mausoleum. Bodrum also lies at the end of a peninsula that contains some of the most beautiful coves, beaches and hills anywhere in the Aegean. It also has some of the liveliest nightlife in Turkey.

HISTORY
Bodrum was founded probably about 5000 years ago by the Carians. In the 11th century BC, the Dorians arrived from the Peloponnese and colonized the area. They linked the town together with Kos, Knidos and the three Dorian cities on Rhodes — Lindos, Kamiros and Ialyssos. This gathering was known as the Dorian Hexapolis, though Bodrum was expelled from the Hexapolis in about the 6th century.

Herodotus was born in 484BC during the rule of the Persians, though he later fled due to the increasingly oppressive rule of Lygdamis II, a Persian overlord whose dynasty continued during the following century with King Mausolos — not himself a Greek, but a big fan of Greek style. He established the town as the capital of a powerful Carian kingdom that included Rhodes, Kos and Chios. He also began work on his own mausoleum, though died before finishing it. This was ultimately left up to his brother-in-law, Idreius, who completed what became known as one of the Seven Wonders of the Ancient World and much later gave English the word 'mausoleum'.

Alexander the Great was next, causing such carnage here with a two-month siege in 334BC that the town never fully recovered. It continued as capital of Caria, under Queen Ada, then the Ptolemites of Egypt, the Seleucids of Syria and finally the Romans. Later, the town was sacked in AD654 by the Arabs, then passed to the Seljuks in 1071, and in the 13th century was captured by the Menteseoglu Turkmen, who later became part of the Ottoman Empire. Things stayed that way until 1402 when the Knights of St John, the militant Christian order established on Rhodes to fight the Ottomans (see box on p382), sneaked over, grabbed the town and built the castle.

It is probably from this fortress that the Turkish name 'Bodrum' comes from — meaning 'cellar' or, more likely, 'dungeon', a place of fear for many Ottoman subjects, both Greek and Turkish, who then lived along the coast.

When the Ottoman sultan Süleyman the Magnificent's troops captured Rhodes in 1522, part of the resultant peace treaty was that the Knights also abandon Bodrum, and so Ottoman troops finally took over in 1523.

In common with most other towns of the coast — whether on the islands or the mainland — Ottoman Bodrum was of mixed Turkish and Greek population, with the Greeks settled mainly in the Kumbahçe district and the Turks between the castle and Azmakbasi. The town's small Jewish population lived around the town hall. WWI saw some skirmishes, while the Turkish War of Liberation which followed saw the end of the mixed citizenry, the population exchange swapping the Greek inhabitants for Turks from Crete. In WWII, Turkey's neutrality meant no involvement in the hostilities save that a damaged British destroyer sheltered here in 1944. However, the coast was secretly used by British commandos on a number of occasions as a launch pad for raids on the German and Italian-held Greek islands (see box on p356).

In the 1960s, Bodrum was rediscovered as a hang-out for a bohemian crowd of Turkish writers and artists. They arrived in a

AEGEAN SEA

AEGEAN SEA

town which already had a cult writer in residence — Cevat Şakir Kabaagacli, otherwise known by his pen name of the Fisherman of Halicarnassus. From this more liberal environment, Bodrum grew rapidly as a tourist resort, finally achieving a status as Turkey's premier international holiday destination and the most popular domestic resort.

WHAT TO SEE

The **Castle of St Peter** (Tue-Sun, 0830-1200, 1300-1700, US$7) is entered via the west gate, on the harbour front, near a collection of souvenir shops and a café next to the walls. Ascending the castle steps, you'll notice the coats of arms of various Knights carved in stone, along with odd bits of masonry taken by the Knights from the ancient Mausoleum. At the end of the steps you'll emerge in the lower courtyard, where a number of peacocks amble about, and on the right is the old chapel, converted into a mosque by the Ottomans. The castle towers and buildings house a variety of museums — the **Underwater Archaeology Museum** has a collection of objects recovered from various ancient wrecks found off the coast here, while the **Glass Wreck Hall** (1000-1100, 1400-1600, US$2.50 extra) has part of a Byzantine ship found off the coast near Marmaris. There's also the **Carian Princess Hall** (1000-1200, 1400-1600, US$2.50 extra). Here, you can see a video of Princess Ada's face being reconstructed by University of Manchester specialists.

Further round the harbour and back inland, the ruins of the **Mausoleum** (Tue-Sun 0830-1200, 1300-1730, US$2) are still impressive, if not a little melancholic. There's a well-presented exhibition put together by Danish archaeologists to the left of the entrance. The Mausoleum was originally around 60m high and had a 39 square metre base. On the summit was mounted a statue of Mausolos and his wife Artemisia in a chariot — now to be found in the British Museum.

Up on the town's main ring road is the **amphitheatre**, another Mausolos initiative, this one finished off by the Romans. At one time it could take a crowd of 13,000. It's now used for the town's festival every September. About 200m further along the road away from town is the **Mydas Gate** — the only real remains of Mausolos' city walls.

Heading back to the Belediye Meydanı, turn left when you get there and into the pedestrian zone of Kale Caddesi. Here you'll find a labyrinth of covered streets packed with shops and restaurants, as well as the beginning of one of Bodrum's institutions — Bar Street. Otherwise known as Cumhuriyet Caddesi, this long drag contains dozens of bars and cafés plus a narrow stretch of sandy beach. The street runs the whole length of this bay, finishing up at a slight headland on which sits another Bodrum institution — the Halicarnassus nightclub. Behind here you'll also find Zeki Muren Sokak, named after the famous transvestite pop singer who died in 1996 and whose villa is also here.

Beaches and bays

Some 2km further along the peninsula's southern shore, **Gumbet's** 600m-long grit sand beach makes it the closest place to the town to sprawl in the sun, a dolmuş to get there from the otogar taking about five minutes and costing US$0.25. Another couple of kilometres further on, **Bitez** has a more upmarket feel and some pretty new hotels, apartments and pensions built in the traditional whitewashed, flat-roofed style. The beach is grit sand and seems to have become a favoured hangout for windsurfers. Dolmuş from Bodrum otogar take about 10 minutes and cost US$0.40.

Ortakent, aka Musgebi, is around 5km west of Bodrum and is connected to Yalısı Beach, a lengthy strand on the coast some 2km away. Just outside the village is the Mustafa Paşa Tower, a 17th-century fort, while Ortakent also acts as a centre for local agricultural produce, helping to preserve some sense of the region's pre-tourism identity. At **Yalısı Yali**, you'll find a long stretch of beach with a jumble of pensions and beach bars alongside. Dolmuş from Bodrum otogar take 10-15 minutes and cost US$0.45 — make sure you choose a dolmuş continuing to Yahsi if it's the beach you're after.

Near the southern tip of the peninsula and 22km from Bodrum, **Akyarlar** has a long history, some of the area's best places to eat and some convenient neighbouring beaches. You get there via Ortakent and the village of Gürece, where a left turn takes you along the coast past two more beach areas, Bagla and Karaincir. The former of these has some excellent soft sand while the latter is just as good, and both share some clear, sparkling waters. Akyarlar itself was once a Greek harbour, known as Kefalouka, and before that was ancient Arhialla. From here, the island of Kos looks close enough almost to touch. Akyarlar is very popular with Turkish tourists, making it a good place to find Turkish food at reasonable prices. A dolmuş from the Bodrum otogar takes around 30-40 minutes and costs US$1.80.

On the peninsula's western end, **Turgutreis** has two major historical claims to fame — the first as the birthplace of Turgut Reis himself (see box on pirates,

p92), one of Turkey's most famous mariners, and, secondly, as the first place in the country to have time-share villas. Take a dolmuş from Bodrum (45 mins, US$1.80).

Gümüşlük, some 3km south-east of Turgutreis, was well known in ancient times as Myndos, though this ancient city was located some 3km to the south-east on the hilltop at Bozdag. Part of Mausolos' Carian kingdom, it successfully defended itself against Alexander the Great, but once Halicarnassus had fallen to the Macedonian, it then fell to Queen Ada.

Nowadays it is a favourite for yachts, with a wonderful sheltered deep anchorage in the lee of Tavsan Adaşi — Rabbit Island. It makes for a more relaxing and quieter option than many of the peninsula's other destinations, with a clutch of pensions and restaurants along its sand and gravel beach. To get there, take a dolmuş from Bodrum otogar (40-45 minutes, US$2.50), or one of the frequent day trips by boat from Bodrum.

AEGEAN SEA

Blue cruises

One of the most popular ways of seeing the Aegean coast — and the Mediterranean too — is by taking a 'Blue Cruise'. These come in a variety of forms but generally involve a boat known as a *gulet*. These are the big wooden ships you'll see lined up in Bodrum harbour — where many of them are made — and in many other Turkish Aegean ports.

There are two main ways of securing a cruise. Either you can join a pre-planned trip to a variety of places along the coast, getting a cabin on one of these gulets, or you make up a group and hire the whole thing. With the former, you'll join whoever else thought this was a good idea at the time, and follow a route set out by the captain. You pay a fee for your cabin and usually have to pay for food while onboard, which the crew cook for you. The latter arrangement gives some more control over where you go and how long for, as the group can — all being well — decide on its own route. Again, you pay a fee for hiring the whole boat, plus have to buy food along the way which, again, the crew cook. One variant of this is 'bare board', whereby you hire the whole boat and, provided you or one of your group has the necessary qualifications, you captain the boat yourselves.

The name Blue Cruise is another legacy of the Fisherman of Halicarnassus, who coined the term for a voyage of his own, conducted down the Turkish Aegean coast just after the war. It's at times a blissful experience, and certainly allows you to visit many bays and islets inaccessible from shore. There are also shorter-term variants of the cruises: day trips to the surrounding area, which usually operate like dolmuş — setting off when they're full. This is not a problem in the high season, but at other times you could be waiting a long time.

AEGEAN SEA

PRACTICAL INFORMATION
Orientation
The town is mainly arranged around the crescent-shaped harbour, with the hills forming an arc behind. Expansion has also happened eastwards, along another crescent-shaped bay, and further inland. The castle is a distinctive landmark, with the main harbour front drag, Neyzen Tevfik Caddesi, at right angles to Cevat Şakir Sokak, which leads up to the town bus and dolmuş stop. The airport is a 45-minute car journey away but a service bus connecting with THY flights drops you at the THY office in a square just off Cevat Şakir Sokak. Getting around town is easy enough on foot, while the surrounding region is well served with dolmuş from the town bus station.

Services
The **tourist office** (☎ 316 1091), just next to the ferry dock and by the castle walls, is open Mon-Sat 0800-2000. The **post office**, at the bottom end of Cevit Şakir, is open 0830-2400. **Phones** are outside.

Try Palmiye **internet café** (🖳 www. bodrum-bodrum.com), 196, Neyzen Tevfik Caddesi, opposite the Marina.

For **car hire** try Oxygen Tours (☎ 313 3343), 28, Cevat Şakir Cad, or for a jeep try Highland Jeep Adventures (☎ 316 8924), 2, Seldir Seyh Cad.

Ferries   [see p453 for full details]
Ferries to and from **Kos** use the ferry port in front of the castle. The customs post is also there. Bodrum Express Lines (☎ 316 4067, office at Custom Area Kale Cad, No 18) run hydrofoils daily in summer to Kos. Out of season though, the service gets patchier, so ring first for details. There is also a daily ferry to Kos. As usual, for both services it is preferred if you can give your passport in to the ticket agency the day before. The same company also run a hydrofoil to **Marmaris** and **Rhodes**, and a hydrofoil/ferry service to **Datça** (June to September).

Buses
There are regular and frequent services to İstanbul (12 hours, US$18), İzmir (4 hours, US$10), Ankara (12 hours US$18) and other destinations up and down the coast from the otogar, which is at the top of Cevat Şakir Sok, around 500m from the waterfront

Planes
THY has regular flights to Bodrum-Milas airport, with service buses (trip takes 45 mins, US$5) connecting with their flights and leaving in town from the THY office at Neyzen Tevfik Cad (☎ 313 3172), in a square just off Cevat Şakir Sok. You can go by taxi, but it's a real budget breaker.

Where to stay
Durak (☎ 316 1564), 8, Rasathane Sokak. Well looked-after rooms; sgl/dbl US$12/15.
Emiko (☎ 316 5560), 11, Uslu Sokak, off Atatürk Caddesi. Japanese-run and has a good standard; US$10/17.50 sgl/dbl.
Bahçeli Ağar (☎ 316 1648), 4A, 1402 Sokak, near the marina. Has a shared kitchen; US$12.50/17.50 sgl/dbl.

Where to eat
Zetas Ocakbasi, Atatürk Caddesi. One of Bodrum's few quality budget eateries; US$10 a head.
Gemibasi, opposite the marina on the corner of Firkateyn Sokak and Neyzen Tefvik. Has quality food for less than the restaurant above; US$7.50 a head.
Amphora On Neyzen Tefvik. A useful venue with good-quality Turkish fare; US$10.

Kos

AREA CODE: ☎ 2242 **POPULATION:** 26,000
A 45km long, fish-like stretch of land, swimming towards the Turkish coast, Kos is one of the Aegean's most developed tourist destinations and contains one of the region's most important ancient sites — the Asklepion — along with many good beaches. With a long ridge of mountains along its southern side and a flatter, coastal plain to the north, Kos is also an easy place to travel round, with a good, well-surfaced highway that speeds along to Antimahia, the island's central crossroads, from where the

three other main towns can be reached — Mastihari to the north, Kardamena to the south and Kefalos to the south-west. Kos Town, Kardamena and Mastihari are also all ferry ports, making the island a major hub of Aegean ferry traffic.

HISTORY

By the time of the siege of Troy, Kos was rich enough to send 30 ships with the attacking fleet. The island had been settled by the Dorians and was a major player in the Dorian Hexapolis, linking Kos to the Rhodian cities of Lindos, Kamiros and Ialyssos. The Persians later moved in, while in 477BC it joined the Delian League. Soon after this, one of its most famous sons was born: Hippocrates. He was one of the world's first 'modern' doctors, advocating a methodical approach to medicine, along with the boiling of drinking water, a massively important idea for preventing sickness. His memory was honoured by the building of a medical school at the Asklepion, the sanctuary also built around this time. The famous Hippocratic oath is also attributed to him.

Alexander the Great then arrived, while after him Kos became part of Ptolemaic Egypt — with Ptolemy II himself being born on the island. In 130BC, the Romans took over, expanding Kos Town. With the rise of the Byzantines, the island became a bishopric and continued its role as an important intellectual and religious centre for the region, despite a major earthquake in AD554. However, in the 11th century, it was plundered by the Arabs and later occupied in 1215 by the Knights of St John. This militant Christian order (see box on p322) built the town's fortress as part of their network of castles up and down the Aegean designed to try and control shipping and block Ottoman movements.

However, in 1523, the Ottomans took the town after three sieges, along with the rest of the island. It then became a prosperous Ottoman possession, known as Istanköy, with a large Turkish population. The town stayed Ottoman for nearly 400 years until occupied by Italy in 1912, along with the rest of the Dodecanese. An earthquake in 1933 destroyed much of Kos Town's old Turkish quarter. In WWII, the island stayed under Italian occupation until Mussolini's defeat in 1943. Briefly occupied by the Germans, the British took over at the war's end but instead of leaving, stayed until 1947 before handing the island over.

WHAT TO SEE
Kos Town

From the ferry docks on the southern stretch of Akti Kountouriotou, with the castle looming on your left, head first into Diakon which brings you out after 20m or so at the square, **Plateia Eleftthekias**. Here you'll find the **Deftedar Mosque** and one major landmark of the Italian occupation, the building housing the town's **archaeology museum** (Tue-Sun, 0830-1500, €2.50). This contains a statue of Hippocrates and a fine mosaic from the Roman Agora.

The entrance to the **Agora** — the ancient market — is on the eastern side of the square. A massive area bounded by the old city walls, it has within it the remains of a shrine to the goddess Aphrodite, a temple of Hercules and a Byzantine Christian basilica.

Leaving the Agora into Plateia Platanou, you'll find the square is dominated by the 1786 **Gazi Hasan Paşa Mosque** — whose minaret towers over both an old Ottoman fountain and the **Plane Tree of Hippocrates**, under which, local legend has it, the great doctor himself lectured medical students. The tree isn't actually that old, but it's a good story anyway.

From here, a short path leads across a narrow stone bridge to the entrance of the **Castle of the Knights of St John** (Tue-Sun, 0830-1500, €3.50). Originally built in the 13th century, but refortified after an earthquake in 1495 by the grand masters d'Aubusson and d'Amboise, it also had a moat separating it from the mainland, now taken up by Finikon. Inside, you'll find the Knights weren't shy when it came to using whatever local resources came to hand in their construction work. Plenty of Roman and ancient Greek stone from the Asklepion can be found in these castle walls, which were thick enough to withstand two sieges by major Ottoman armies and navies.

Back inland, the **Casa Romana** — a restored, luxurious 3rd-century AD Roman villa (Tue-Sun 0830-1500, €3) — is another example of how the island's one-time Italian occupiers tried to assert their claim to the place by reviving its Roman past. Opposite is a 3rd-century Temple of Dionysos, while walking further west along Grigoriou, you'll see on the right-hand side a shelter protecting more 3rd-century exhibits — **mosaics from the House of Europa**, so-called because the mosaics themselves show scenes from the abduction of Europa by Zeus disguised as a bull. A section of the old Roman town's main street, the Dekumanus Maximus, runs round from the mosaics to the nymphaeum and the xysto, ancient Roman latrines and a Hellenistic gymnasium respectively. On the other side of Grigoriou from here you'll also see the **Odeion**, a similarly restored ancient theatre.

The Asklepion

A major archaeological site, the Asklepion (Tue-Sun, 0830-1500, €4) was a kind of ancient medical college and is a testimony to the island's past importance as a centre of learning. The god of medicine after whom the Asklepion is named was a son of Apollo and yet another victim of Zeus' green-eyed jealousy. Zeus feared that Asklepios would end up curing every disease and maybe even death itself, thus making all men immortal, something which he himself had conspicuously been unable to achieve. So, in a familiar tantrum of the gods, he had the poor Asklepios struck down by a thunderbolt.

However, in one way, Asklepios has managed to survive down to the present day: when painted or sculpted, he was usually depicted holding a staff, around which was coiled a serpent — a symbol still used by medical practitioners the world over to represent their craft.

Some 4km south of Kos Town, the site was founded a century after the death of Hippocrates in 357BC. In the ancient world, it was not only a major centre for medicine, but also for architecture and culture. It functioned up until the 6th century AD, long after the Roman (then Byzantine) Empire had

converted to Christianity, and was finally closed only after an earthquake. It then lay in ruins for centuries, gradually disappearing beneath the earth and prompting a major archaeological expedition to try to find it in 1896, which failed to turn up anything until 1902, when it was pinpointed by the English archaeologist WR Paton. A Greek archaeologist, GE Zaraphtis then began excavating, but the Italian fascist occupation halted this, though Mussolini's archaeologists did begin rebuilding parts of it.

The complex consists of four terraces. On the lower level, along from the entrance, athletic contests were held in ancient times, while around the edges stood statues of the gods — some torsos of these still remain at the top left-hand corner of the terrace. Continuing straight up from here, a flight of 30 steps takes you to the second terrace and — straight in front of you — the Great Altar of Asklepios, dated to the 4th century BC. To the right of this is the Temple to Asklepios and to the left, a later, Roman addition, the Temple of Apollo (with the columns re-erected much later still by Mussolini's men). Going forwards from here, another flight of steps leads up to the third terrace. But before mounting them, look to your right and you'll see the ruins of the Priests' Quarters. The priests would offer medical services to the sick, with sacred waters being a large part of their cure, along with the practice of sleeping in the temple, as it was supposed that the god Asklepios affected cures of the sick in dreams.

On the fourth terrace, straight ahead up the steps, are the ruins of the 2nd-century BC Large Temple of Asklepios. This was the main building of the whole complex, with black marble used for its lower steps. Behind here, a sacred wood runs up to the edge of the terrace, but take the path immediately behind the temple, follow it as it turns to the left, and after 70m or so you'll find another temple ruin, this time dedicated to an unknown god, resting amid the shade and flickering light of the surrounding pine trees.

Platanos

Worth a detour on your way to the Asklepion, Platanos village is a touch of

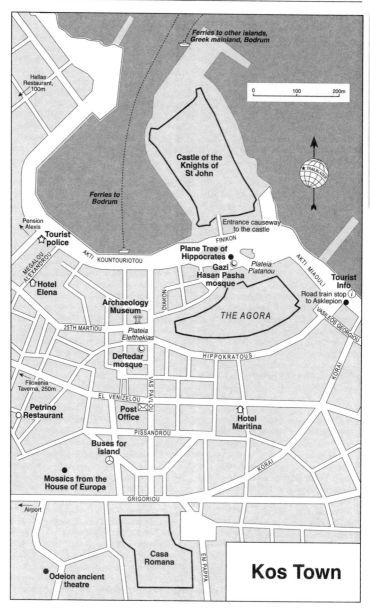

AEGEAN SEA

Ferries to other islands,
Greek mainland, Bodrum

Hellas
Restaurant,
100m

0   100   200m

Castle of the
Knights of
St John

★ TRAILBLAZER

Ferries to
Bodrum

Pension
Alexis

Tourist
police

Entrance causeway
to the castle

FINIKON

MEGALOU ALEXANDROU

Hotel
Elena

AKTI KOUNTOURIOTOU

Plane Tree of
Hippocrates

Plateia
Platanou

AKTI MIAOULI

Tourist
Info

Gazi
Hasan Pasha
mosque

DIAKON

Road train stop
to Asklepion

Archaeology
Museum

THE AGORA

VASILEOS GEORGIOU

25TH MARTIOU

Plateia
Eleftthekias

KORAI

HIPPOKRATOUS

Deftedar
mosque

Filoxenia
Taverna, 250m

VAS PAVLOU

EL VENIZELOU

Petrino
Restaurant

Post
Office

PISSANDROU

Hotel
Maritina

KORAI

Buses for
island

Mosaics from the
House of Europa

GRIGORIOU

Airport

EM PAPPA

Casa
Romana

Odeion ancient
theatre

Kos Town

Turkey in the middle of a Greek island. Approaching from Kos Town, you'll see the Muslim cemetery on the outskirts and a couple of mosques. In the village's central square there are also a number of cafés and restaurants run by Turkish Greeks, part of a community here that goes back five centuries. As Kos was Italian controlled when the population exchange between Greece and Turkey took place in 1923, the island's Turkish community remained unaffected — as elsewhere in the Dodecanese — and survives to this day, the inhabitants officially known as 'Muslim Greeks'.

Local beaches
The nearest beach outside Kos Town is **Lampi**, 4km to the north. **Tigaki**, 11km away, is less crowded and has a long, pale sandy stretch and a sea that's also good for windsurfers. Some 4km further west is the similar **Marmari Beach**. South of town, head for **Empros Thermae**, which, as the name suggests, has thermal springs which heat up the sea-water roundabout. The beach is 11km south, accessed via the same road that passes by **Psalidi** (3km) and **Agios Fokas** (7km) beaches, both of which are fine, if crowded.

Mastihari
On the island's north-west coast, 30km from Kos Town, Mastihari is set amongst wide, sandy beaches and is much more low key than Kos Town. It has harbour connections north to Kalymnos and Pserimos, a small local island with a huge sandy beach that makes a good day trip for an alternative sunbathing venue. Mastihari has little to offer in the way of sights, though, and has fairly infrequent bus connections elsewhere. Those that there are run from the stop by the ferry port.

Kardamena
Some 27km from Kos Town, this has become something of a package tour spot, with plenty of bars, cafés and discos trying to compete with the island capital.

It's also from here that the boats to Nisyros go, the most likely reason you'll end up here.

Kefalos/Paradise Beach
Out in the island's south-western fishtail and 43km from Kos Town, **Kefalos** is a pleasant village of twisting streets and traditional houses, something seen fairly infrequently elsewhere on the island. It also has a spectacular view over Kefalos Bay, with a long curving arc of sand, **Paradise Beach**, stretching out below. The village is also the last stop before some of the island's most rugged territory — the mountainous headland that stretches south-west from here and which contains two spectacularly located monasteries: **Moni Agiou Theologou** (4km away) and **Moni Agiou Ioanni** (7km away). These can be accessed only by car, trail bike or foot, but offer magnificent views and, running between them, a sand and pebble beach. There, the Restaurant Agiou Theologou is a welcome last post before the sea.

PRACTICAL INFORMATION
Orientation
Kos International Airport is 26km south of Kos Town, the settlement with the most connections on the island. Boats go from here to Turkey as well as a number of Greek islands and the mainland. The town is built around a small, lagoon-like harbour, with a narrow channel leading out to sea beneath the castle walls. The south side of the harbour-front road, Akti Kountouriotou, is where the ferries dock, with most of the sights in this corner of town.

The road train (see p343) up to the Asklepion departs from outside the tourist information office on Akti Miaouli, south-east of the castle on the seafront, while the bus station for other island destinations is at 7, Kleopatris, south of the harbour. The town itself is pretty extensive, but walkable, with the nearest beach along Akti Miaouli, past the tourist information office.

Services
Kos Town   The **tourist office** (☎ 024 460), on Akti Miaouli/ Vasileos Georgiou, is open Mon-Fri 0800-2000, Sat & Sun 0800-1500. The **tourist police** (☎ 022 444) are in the police station opposite the ferry stops. There's a **post office** on Vasileos Pavlou, with **phones** at 6, Vyronos.

Internet access is available at Status at 55, Navarinou. Prices go from €10-20 basic **bike/scooter rental**, and a good deal more for **cars and jeeps**. Try Kos One (☎ 028 837) at 17A, Themistokleous for bikes, Safari Rent a Car (☎ 027 918) on the corner of Harmilou and Karaiskaki streets for cars.

Ferries   [see p455 for full details]
Kos Town, Mastihari and Kardamena are the main ferry ports. Kos Town is the venue for the majority of ferries; services for **Kalymnos** go from Kos Town and Mastihari, and for **Nisyros** from Kos Town and Kardamena.

Amongst others, services go to **Bodrum**, **Halki**, **Kalymnos**, **Nisyros**, **Patmos**, **Piraeus**, **Rhodes** and **Samos**.

In Kos Town, the main ferry companies are: DANE Lines, at Rhodos Tours (☎ 023 962); GA Lines and Kalymnian Shipping at Exas Travel (☎ 028 545); and Kiriakoulis Maritime (☎ 025 920). Kalymnos-Mastihari Kos Lines, also at Exas, operate from Mastihari.

For the port authority call ☎ 026 594.

Ferries to Turkey There are daily boats to Bodrum, and in high summer there are often several leaving every day. The trip takes one hour. The port tax (€10) is payable at the customs post on the New Quay.

Buses
The main bus station for green (island) buses is at 7, Kleopatris (☎ 022 292). There are 10 buses a day to Tigaki (15-20 mins, €1), five to Mastihari (45 mins, €1.75), six to Kardamena (45 mins, €2), five to Pyli (30 mins, €1), six to Kefalos — via Paradise Beach — (1 hour, €2.75) and three to Zia (30 mins, €1).

To the Asklepion there is the Mini Train, a road train that runs from outside the tourist information office up to the Asklepion and back for around €1, taking about 15-20 minutes.

Planes
Kos Airport handles three flights a day to and from Athens with Olympic (€83). Their office (☎ 028 330) is at 22, Vasileos Pavlou.

Plenty of package tour flights also arrive throughout the year.

The airport is 26km south, but an airport bus (€3) leaves the Olympic office two hours before each of their departures and should leave for Kos Town just after their arrivals, too. A taxi should be around €18.

Where to stay
Kos Town *Hotel Maritina* (☎ 023 241), on the busy corner of El Venizelou and Mitropoleos (yet quieter than most). Sgl/dbl for €23/30.
Hotel Elena (☎ 022 740), 7, Megalou Alexandrou. A more central location; €22/29 sgl/dbl.
Pension Alexis (☎ 028 798), 9, Irodotou. Highly recommended, the owner is a font of local knowledge; €22/29 sgl/dbl.

Mastihari *Hotel Faenareti* (☎ 051 395), near the main square. A good standard hotel, with air conditioning and TV; sgl/dbl for €22/30.
Hotel Arant (☎ 051 167/8), also near the main square. Clean and friendly; rooms have air conditioning, TV and en-suite bathrooms; €22/30 sgl/dbl.
Rooms to Rent (☎ 059 005), near the Thomas minimarket. €20/30 sgl/dbl.

Kefalos *Hotel Kordistos* (☎ 071 251), near the beach. Nice rooms all with TV, air conditioning and en-suite bathroom; €25/35 sgl/dbl.
Petros and Maria Rooms (☎ 071 306), on the main road from Antimahia, 50m from the Agios Stefanos bus stop. €20/26 sgl/dbl.

Where to eat
Kos Town *Filoxenia Taverna*, on the corner of Pindou and Alikarnassou. A good traditional Greek place; €10-15 a head.
Hellas Restaurant, Amerikis. Popular local haunt; €10-15.
Petrino Restaurant, 1, Theologou. Beautiful garden dining with superb dishes. €10-15.

Platanos *Serif Restaurant*, in the main square under the trees. Good Turkish food in a friendly atmosphere; €10 a head.

AEGEAN SEA

Mastihari *Kali Kardia Restaurant*, on the central square. A deserved reputation for its fish; €10-15 a head.

Kefalos *Restaurant Agiou Theologou*, on the beach between Moni Agiou Theologou and Moni Agiou Ioanni monasteries. A great place for sunsets, and the restaurant's traditional cakes are renowned; €10 a head.

Nisyros

AREA CODE: ☎ 2242 **POPULATION:** 900
Some 20km south-east of Kos, Nisyros is one of the most mystical islands the Dodecanese has to offer. It's basically a volcano, a round cone that still smells of sulphur in its wide inner crater, a lunar landscape that from the sea lies concealed behind the island's olive-tree-covered cliffs.

The main settlement, Mandraki, is a thin ribbon of buildings, widening at one end into a warren of beautiful whitewashed houses beneath an ancient headland monastery. If you're there on the Feast of the Assumption, in August, when the monks chant above the sound of the waves and boats rest at anchor in the harbour, silently burning flares and sparklers, it can seem a truly magical place.

HISTORY
Around 12 million years ago three giant underground volcanic explosions pushed this lump of rock straight up out of the ocean floor. In Greek mythology, though, the great war of Giants versus Titans was to blame for the island's creation, when Poseidon, the god of the sea, hurled a huge lump of rock that he'd scooped up out of Kos at the giant, Polyvotis. This covered the giant, and it is his sighs that you now hear, hissing from beneath the volcanic crater floor.

Later on, Carians, from Anatolia, colonized the place, followed by Minoans from Crete around 1400BC. The Phoenicians then took over, with Nisyros becoming an important place for purple-red dyes, after which the island may be named. The island

then followed much the same history as the rest of the region, as Greeks, Persians and finally Romans held sway. In 1312, the Knights of St John took over, but five years later the Venetians were in charge. The Catalans then took over in 1471 and stayed until the Ottomans arrived in 1522. They stayed nearly 400 years, until the Dodecanese were handed over to the Italians in 1912. In WWII, the island continued under Italian rule till 1943, when the Germans took over, then in 1945 the British, who finally handed the island over to Greece in 1947.

Like many of Greece's Aegean Islands, Nisyros has suffered major population loss over the years, with some settlements now abandoned. Some 7000 Nisyrians live in other countries, mainly in the US, and it's not uncommon to hear more Brooklyn English than Aegean Greek in the cafés of old Mandraki.

WHAT TO SEE
Mandraki's highlight is the 14th-century headland **Monastery of Panagias Spilianis**, the Virgin of the Cave (daily 1030-1500, admission free). In addition to excellent views, the monastery has a well-turned altar frame, from 1725, and is set in what was once a Venetian castle built in 1315. From here you can also visit the **Paleokastro**, the ancient town, whose Cyclopean walls still stand in parts.

Otherwise, the main event is the **volcano**. Tour buses depart from the port to the volcano's crater, the island's hollow heart, twice daily, for €8 return. This trip is well worth it if you don't have time to walk or take the normal island blue buses, as the tour coaches take you right down into the colossal crater itself — which really takes up the whole centre of the island. Most of this area is flat farmland now but in the centre are five smaller craters which still give off that distinctive, odious sulphurous smell, hissing away beneath your feet.

Meanwhile, up around the crater are the shattered walls of the volcano, and on the rim perch two villages, Emboreios and Nikea. The former is practically deserted now and the latter is almost empty too. A blue bus still connects them to Mandraki, with Nikea a beautiful place, washed in blue and white with decorative pebbled squares — all overlooking the lunar landscape of the crater floor below.

The island's best beach is the ironically named **White Beach**, actually covered in black volcanic sand, some 2km east of Mandraki. Alternatively, in Mandraki, follow the lower headland path round the base of the monastery to Kokkaki Beach, which is nearer to hand but covered in dark round super pebbles. Take care here when swimming, too, as the waves whip in at a fair speed round the headland.

PRACTICAL INFORMATION
Orientation
Ferries arrive in Mandraki harbour, a five-minute walk down a narrow road from the town itself, which is no real size at all and easily walked around. For the rest of the island, buses for the crater floor leave from the port, where there are also several blue buses a day to the island's other settlements. However, hitching is recommended, as services are few.

The island's main festival is the Feast of the Assumption, on 15 August. For nine days before, the island is in some state of preparation for this so it can be difficult finding accommodation at this time. Book well in advance if you can.

Services
The **tourist office** (☎ 031 204) at the port is open daily 1000-1300 and 1800-2000, at least in theory. In practice, Enetikon Travel on the main street in town is more reliable.

Ferries   [see p456 for full details]
The main ferry operators on the island are DANE, Kalymnian Shipping, and Kiriakoulis Maritime, all of whom are at Diakomichalis Shipping, ☎ 031 459, and GA Lines, at Kendri Shipping, ☎ 031 227. For tickets try Enetikon Travel, ☎ 031 180, on the main street in Mandraki, as the ferry line offices are seldom open.

In season, there are daily **tour boats** to and from Kardamena on Kos. There are also regular ferries to **Kos** and **Rhodes**.

Buses
There are blue island buses to Emboreios (25 mins, €1) and Nikea (30 mins, €1.70), which go to and from the town harbour quay four times a day.

Where to stay
Hotel Romantzo (☎ 031 340), left of the quay. Has clean rooms for €22/34 sgl/dbl.
Hotel Nisyros (☎ 031 107), right below the monastery in town. All rooms en suite; €20/25 sgl/dbl.

Where to eat
Tony's Tavern, on the main street, back towards the port. Has good value eats for €10 a head.
Taverna Panorama, in the town square. Good selection of mezedes for about €10.

Kalymnos

AREA CODE: ☎ 2243 POPULATION: 18,000

Kalymnos is something of an overlooked gem in the Dodecanese. Major tourist developments have largely passed it by, giving it a slightly old-fashioned air in the painted signs of its harbour-front ouzeria and cafés and the jumble of low-lying houses that makes up its capital, Pothia. Next to the hustle of Kos, this is quite a different world — one with a strong sense of place and an identity all its own.

HISTORY
It's generally thought that the first civilization here was the Dorian, who colonized much of this region. The island minted its own coins and was an ally of Athens in the 5th and 4th centuries BC, before being taken over by the Persians and then the Macedonians under Alexander the Great. The Romans then made it part of their Asian province, and as a Byzantine island it was taken by the Venetians in 1310. The Knights of St John then ran it until 1522, when it fell to the Ottomans.

After the Italo-Turkish war of 1911-12, the Dodecanese were given to Italy, under whose control they stayed until the Italian surrender in 1943, when they came under German occupation, then, in 1945, became British occupied until 1947.

Throughout all this time, the island has been the 'sponge capital' of the Aegean, with sponge-fishing a major industry here — as it is on the Turkish coast too. The island's sponge fleet journeys as far as the North African coast come spring and summer, a practice continued since ancient times.

As with many other Greek islands, depopulation is a real problem these days, as Kalimniot youngsters are wont to try their luck elsewhere. Australia has long been a favoured destination, along with the US.

WHAT TO SEE

Pothia town sponge factory, on 25 Martiou, is open to tourists in the mornings and demonstrates just how the dozens of sponges covering the harbour-front stalls were collected and processed. There's also an **archaeological museum** (daily 0800-1400, €2) west of Plateia Kyprou, containing relics from many of the only-partially excavated sites around the island.

However, most of the things worth seeing are out of town, accessed from the green bus stop on Plateia Ethnikis Antistasis. **Petra Kastro** is worth a look, though it does entail a steep climb from the present-day village of **Chorio**, the former island capital. Petra Kastro is being gradually restored and is a fortified settlement, complete with walls, gates and nine chapels, built this high up in order to ward off pirates, who were a great problem on the island for centuries.

From Chorio, keep west for some fine, semi-deserted shingle beaches at **Plia Yialos**, **Panoromos** and further round, where the island's only road chunters on up the western shore to **Emboreios** and a tree-lined pebble strand.

Heading the other way, buses go to **Vathy**, a small harbour settlement at the head of a narrow and picturesque inlet. Behind the village, a valley of fruit trees and fields, kept behind high whitewashed walls, runs into the foothills of the island's central mountain.

Pothia harbour is where boats leave on day trips for **Kefalas Cave**, a wonderful sea cavern full of stalactites and stalagmites where Zeus is said to have lurked while plotting the murder of his father. Frequent boats go during the season, with some taking in the neighbouring islet of **Nera**, with its small monastery and quiet beach. The usual deal is to combine Nera and the cave on a day trip for €18, including lunch. Other boats go to the **Daskalio Caves**, around the headland near Vathy, yet inaccessible from there. These tours are roughly similar in price and length.

PRACTICAL INFORMATION
Orientation

Most boats arrive at Pothia, the main town, which is at the head of an inlet and on one side of the island's narrow waist. There is really only one road, which snakes across from the northern village of Emboreios to a string of settlements opposite the island of Telendos on the western coast, before heading inland to cross to Pothia. After the capital, it wriggles around the north-eastern coast to Vathy, before finally heading up into the foothills of Mt Profitis Ilias, at 690m, the island's highest point.

Pothia itself is easily navigated, being a collection of shooting-gallery-like streets heading inland off the harbour-front road, 25 Martiou. Up these race the town's over-large scooter population, making for some scary encounters at the many blind corners. The main island road comes in at the east side of the harbour before heading off north.

Services

The **tourist information office**, behind the statue of Poseidon on the main harbour-front road, is open summer only, 0930-1330.

There's an **internet café** right on the harbour-front road, on the corner of Plateia Elefthekias and Georgiou Oikonomou.

Ferries [see p455 for full details]

Kalymnos is well connected to other islands and the Greek mainland, with boats to **Kos**, and to **Samos** via **Patmos** and **Leros** and on to **Piraeus**. Alas, though, there are no direct boats to Turkey. For these, head up to Samos

Astipalea

Overview Lying some 23 nautical miles off Kos and with just over a thousand inhabitants, Astipalea is a place for peace and quiet. A narrow 100m strip of land unites the two parts of Astipalea, with island life centring on the ancient Chora, with its Venetian castle and two churches, Panagia of Castro (the Holy Virgin of the Castle) and Agios Giorgios. Near to Chora is the village of **Livadi**, known for its orchards and its beach. However, the island's best beaches are at Kaminakia and Vatses which can be reached by small boats from the villages of Pera Yalos and Maltezana.

Where to stay On arrival at the port beneath the Chora, known as Skala, pension and domatia owners meet the boats. Prices here range from €20-60 for a double in a hotel or pension, with **camping** possible 3km east along the coast.

Ferry connections There are ferries from Kos; see p455 for details.

or down to Kos. The main shipping agencies are DANE Lines and Kiriakoulis Maritime at Kalimnia Yacht Club (☎ 024 083); GA Lines, at Magos Shipping Agency (☎ 028 777); Kalymnian Shipping (☎ 029 612). The port authority is on ☎ 029 304.

Buses

There are buses from Plateia Ethniki Anistasis on Pothia to Masouri (2km, 10 mins), which you'll need to take to reach both the beaches on the west of the island and Petra Kastro (1km, 5 mins), a fortress village in the middle of the island. To Vathy, catch buses from round the corner, they take 30 mins and cost €1.50.

Where to stay

Pension Greek House (☎ 029 559), located up from Georgiou Oikonoumou near the Astor Sponge Factory. Has sgl/dbl for €15/25 and a friendly owner who also owns two other pensions of a similar quality round this area.

Archontiko Hotel (☎ 024 149), next to the ferry stops. €30/40 sgl/dbl.

Where to eat

Eating in Pothia is never a problem, with a harbour-front lined with great, characterful restaurants, while the *Xefteries Taverna*, off Venizelou behind the Plateia Ethnikis Antistasis, is also a great local haunt at €10 a head.

Patmos

AREA CODE: ☎ 2247 POPULATION: 2500
Some 50km south-west of Samos is the holy island of Patmos — one of the most famous Christian sites in Greece. A spread of low-lying, crenellated land around the sudden hilltop of the main Hora, it has numerous bays and some wonderful beaches. This is also where St John, banished from Ephesus, had a particularly unpleasant revelation. This then became the Biblical book of the Apocalypse — the end of the world — a favourite of gothic horror films ever since.

WHAT TO SEE

The **Monastery of St John** (daily 0830-1300, admission free, but €3 to look in the Treasury; visitors must also dress with legs covered — long skirts or trousers required) was founded in AD1088, and grew into its present fortress-like construction in response to repeated attacks by pirates. Inside are a series of priceless frescos, plus the Treasury, which contains some 890 medieval manuscripts, including several illuminated versions of the *Apocalypse* and a 6th-century *Gospel of St Mark*.

From here, a path dating back to Byzantine times leads down the hill to the

Monastery of the Apocalypse (opening times as above). This walk takes about 25-30 minutes along a stone track, mostly in shade. The monastery itself sits above the cave, in which there is now a small chapel. The monks give short lectures on the Revelation and the story of St John, regrettably only in Greek. It's a very atmospheric place, the dark stone of the cave walls decorated with icons and candles.

North of town, the **beaches** begin at Meloi, followed by Agriolivado and then Kambos. Continuing over the hill from here brings you to one of the least-visited beaches, Lampi, which is noted for its multicoloured pebbles. From Skala to Lampi it's about 8-9km. The best beach, though, is to the south at Psili Ammos, best reached by boat from Skala harbour. These boats go every morning, returning in the evening, and are advertised on the quayside.

PRACTICAL INFORMATION
Orientation
The main harbour, Port Skala, is where you'll turn up by ferry, and from here, in the main square, there are regular buses (seven a day, 15 mins, €0.75) up the hill to the Hora and the monasteries. North of town is the main beach area, with a string of places round to Kambos Bay, some 2km away. That's about it, with the whole island no more than 10km from end to end.

Services
There's a **tourist office** (☎ 031 666) on the waterfront, opposite the ferry docks.

The **tourist police office** (☎ 031 303) is behind the dock passenger transit building.

Blue Bay Hotel, east of town, has **internet** facilities.

Ferries   [see p457 for full details]
Patmos has ferries to **Samos** and **Ikaria**, **Leros** and **Kos**. There are also through ferries to Rhodes and Piraeus. The main agents are: GA ferries at Astoria Travel (☎ 031 205); DANE and Kalymnian Shipping at Konstantas Shipping (☎ 031 314); and Kiriakoulis, at Apollon Travel, (☎ 031 724). Miniotis ferries and Hellas Flying Dolphins also operate from here – try the agencies by

the harbour for tickets. The port authority is on ☎ 031 231.

Buses
From Skala, there are seven buses a day to the monasteries (€0.75), five to Grikos (€0.75) and four to Kambos (€0.75).

Where to stay
Warning Patmos fills up to more than capacity in season, and is usually pretty heavily booked out of season too. If you're depending on staying here, book a place well in advance.
Pension Maria (☎ 032 152), up on the Hora road. Sgl/dbl for €15/20.
Hotel Rex (☎ 031 242), opposite the passenger transit building. €20/35 sgl/dbl.
Pension Sydney (☎ 032 118), in Skala. €20/35 sgl/dbl.

Where to eat
On the harbour front in Skala you'll find a collection of mainly overpriced restaurants. Head a block inland and the prices drop, though frankly, the quality is not particularly good anywhere. Try *To Hiliomohdi*, towards the Hora, a seafood ouzeri at €10 a head, or *Vangelis*, a taverna on Plateia Levias, for €12 a head.

Samos

AREA CODE: ☎ 2273 POPULATION: 31,000
Covering almost everything from sandy beaches to serious mountains, Samos is definitely something of a world of its own. A major site in ancient times, it has the remains of some significant temples — the Sanctuary of Hera, or Hereon, being one of the Seven Wonders of the Ancient World. It's also well connected to other islands, Turkey and mainland Greece. The main settlement, Vathy, or Samos Town, is a workaday port with plenty of places to stay and visit, while neighbouring Pythagorio — the ancient island capital and birthplace of Pythagoras — is much more touristy, but has still preserved a great deal of charm.

HISTORY

Settlement on the island goes back to neolithic times around present-day Pythagorio, which until 1955 was known as Tigani. As with most of this coast, the Ionians arrived in the 11th century BC and established a major trading colony for the Aegean. In 540BC, Polycrates took over as 'tyrant' — sole ruler — and, as with many dictatorships since, he quickly became obsessed with grandiose public works schemes. This led to the Hereon, a massive religious complex, along with the Evpalinos Tunnel and a huge harbour jetty in Tigani.

It was also during Polycrates' time that another local, Pythagoras, came up with the since much-used rule that the square on the hypotenuse of a right angled triangle is equal to the sum of the squares of the other two sides. From this, logarithms evolved, the basis of much higher maths until the arrival of the pocket calculator. The island also produced Aesop, of fable fame, Epicurus, the much misunderstood philosopher, and Aristarchus, who believed that the earth revolved round the sun, an idea that was way out of fashion for the time. There was also a celebrated mariner from Samos, Kolaios, who in 650BC was the first Greek to sail a ship out beyond the Rock of Gibraltar into the Atlantic.

In 522BC, the Persian ruler, Darius, captured the island, which then see-sawed back and forth between Persian, Athenian and Spartan control until in 189BC it was made part of the Roman district of Pergamum. Under the Byzantines it was headquarters for the Aegean military district, but was then handed over to the Genoese in the 13th century. The Ottomans arrived in 1453, finding the island largely depopulated and settled large numbers of Albanian Muslims here.

While Greece became independent in 1832, the new kingdom was obliged to accept a frontier in the Aegean Islands which excluded Samos. The Samians, however, refused to accept this. Out of their resistance was born within the year one of the Mediterranean's more peculiar microstates – the Principality of Samos.

Under this, the Samians were ruled by a prince of their own religion — although these were appointed at short intervals by the Ottomans, mostly from old Greek and Rumanian Phanariot families (these were families from Constantinople's Phanar District who were appointed as princes by the sultan — the appointments going to the highest bidders — and whose power within their respective principalities was absolute).

As time went on, successive disorders led to further reforms, and by 1905 they had a senate of eight annually elected members and an Assembly-General of 39, plus the archbishop. Wealthy emigrés endowed a new cathedral. There was still a small Turkish garrison, though, and old photographs show a villainous looking Greek gendarmerie of 150 men. The principality also had its own flag — actually two flags, as the prince had his own personal one as well.

The principality endured until the Italians occupied the island in 1912 as part of their attempts to force the Ottomans to give up Libya, and Samos' status remained undetermined when the Aegean was swallowed up in WWI. It was still shown as a separate principality in atlases in the early 1920s.

ORIENTATION

Vathy, or Samos Town, is the main port for arrivals, though both Pythagorio and Karlovassi on the north-west coast also have ferry services. The airport is 4km west of Pythagorio, with no bus connections. A taxi from/to the airport to/from Vathy should be around €10, or to/from Pythagorio, €5. Vathy is the main centre for buses, though in fact there are precious few of these, hitching being your main option short of car or scooter hire. The bus station in Vathy is really just a street where the buses stop, a café on the corner of Kanari street serving as the place to find out when the buses leave.

VATHY/SAMOS TOWN
What to see

One of the first major buildings you'll see off the ferry in Vathy is the **Roman Catholic Cathedral**, right on the waterfront, some 100m from the ferry stop. Parallel to the harbour-front road is Lykourgou Logothethi, a narrow, bazaar-like street of souvenir shops, cafés and restaurants, which ends at the central square of Plateia Pythagora. Vathy's **archaeology museum** (Tue-Sun 0830-1500, €3) is at the end of Kapetan Katavani and behind the municipal gardens. This is well laid out, with the most striking exhibits the tall *kouros*, one of which is about 4.5m high. These mythological beings are from the sanctuary of Hera — the Hereon — located in the west of the island.

From the museum, head inland again, up Ioannou for about 20m, where the road forks. Take the right-hand road if you are feeling energetic, as it will take you to the wonderfully undisturbed backstreets of the old town — **Ano Vathy** — which spreads a patchwork of red-tiled roofs across the steepening hillside.

Practical information
Orientation The town is largely a series of streets running parallel to the harbour-front drag, Themistokelous Sofouli, with busy markets and a wide, arcing bay out front that goes on for over a kilometre. Ferries dock at the northern end of the harbour, where you'll also find the main collection of ticketing agencies.

Services The **tourist information office** (☎ 028 530), located in the last of the side streets off Lykourgou before Plateia Pythagora, is open summer only, 0830-1300.

The **tourist police** (☎ 027 980) are at 129, Themistokleous Sofouli.

For **car hire** try Autoplan (☎ 023 555), 17, Themistokleous Sofouli.

Ferries [see p460 for full details]
GA Ferries and Hellas Flying Dolphins are at Grigoriou Shipping (☎ 080 600); Kiriacoulis Maritime at Ship, Travel & Shipping (☎ 080 445); Miniotis Lines at Kritikos Shipping (☎ 025 133). The port authority is on ☎ 027 890.

There are ferries to **Chios**, **Fourni**, **Kos**, **Lesbos**, **Lipsi**, **Naxos**, **Paros**, **Piraeus** and **Rhodes**.

Ferries to/from Turkey There are two boats a day (45-60 mins) to Kuşadası in summer from Vathy, one a day out of season. The port tax (€10), must be paid at the customs post in Vathy harbour. For this reason, it's best to turn up about an hour before departure.

Many of the harbour ticket agencies also organize excursions, such as day trips with a visit to Ephesus thrown in. These are usually around €25-35, but you must come back with them the same day.

Buses From Vathy bus station, on Kanari, there are 13 buses a day to Kokkari (20 mins, €1), 13 a day to Pythagorio (25 mins, €1.10), eight to Agios Konstantinos (40 mins, €1.50), seven to Karlovassi (one hour, €2.50), and six to the Hereon (25 mins, €1.50).

Planes In season, there are four daily flights to and from Athens (€70 one way) and two to/from Thessaloniki (€125 one way) with Olympic. Their office (☎ 027 237) is on the corner of Kanaris and Smyrnis streets in Vathy. The island is also a destination for many European package-tour operators. It is advisable to book any of these flights well in advance if you're travelling in summer, as they fill up rapidly.

Where to stay *Pension Ionia* (☎ 028 782), 5, Manoli Kalomir. Clean, basic accommodation; €18/25 sgl/dbl.
Paradise Hotel (☎ 023 911, 🖳 paradise@ gemini.diavlos.gr), opposite the bus station on Kanari. €30/50 sgl/dbl.
Pension Avli (☎ 022 939), on the corner of Areos and Manoli Kalomiri. A former Catholic convent; €25/dbl.
Samos Hotel (☎ 028 377, 🖳 hotsamos @otenet.gr), next to the ferry stop on Themistokleous Sofouli. €35/45 sgl/dbl.

Where to eat *To Katoi Ouzeri*, behind the museum, on the corner of Sahtouri and Svaronou streets, has good mezedes and main dishes, €10-15 a head.
Taverna Grigoris, On Smyrnis, near the post office, has good food and atmosphere, with a lucky draw sometimes, the winner eating for free. Otherwise, €15-20.

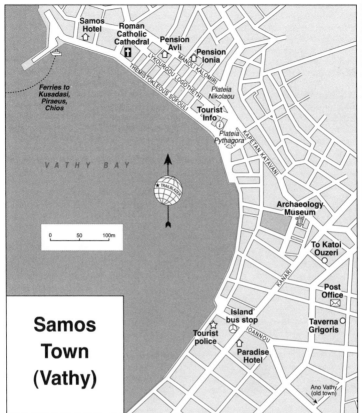

Samos Hotel
Roman Catholic Cathedral
Pension Avli
Pension Ionia
LYKOURGOU LOGOTHETI
MANOLI KALOMIRI
THEMISTOKLEOUS SOFOULI
Ferries to Kusadasi, Piraeus, Chios
Plateia Nikolaou
Tourist Info
Plateia Pythagora
KPETAN KATAVANI
VATHY BAY
AEGEAN SEA
★ TRAILBLAZER
0   50   100m
Archaeology Museum
To Katoi Ouzeri
KANARI
Post Office
Island bus stop
Taverna Grigoris
IOANNOU
Tourist police
Paradise Hotel
Ano Vathy (old town)

Samos Town (Vathy)

PYTHAGORIO

The island's main tourist destination, with a pretty harbour and an adequate beach, Pythagorio also serves as an embarkation point for many of the ferries heading south for the Dodecanese, and is a useful jumping-off point for the island's main archaeological sites. There are also plenty of nice hotels, pensions and rooms, as well as cafés, bars and restaurants, with the whole ambience much more of a tourist town than Vathy.

What to see

West of the harbour is the **Castle of** **Lykourgos Logothetis** (always open, free admission). Built in 1824 during the island's first brief period of independence, it is named after a local nationalist hero. Another local boy made good is **Pythagoras**, who is commemorated by a statue on the other side of the harbour, just before the town beach.

The other sights are really out of town. The **Evpalinos Tunnel** (Tue-Sun 0815-1400, €4), is a good 2.5km out above Pythagorio and accessed via an old amphitheatre, and the medieval **Moni Panagias Spilianis**, both on the same path. The tunnel is pretty impressive — named after its architect, it was built in 524BC and is a very early example of municipal plumbing. Dug through the hillside, it channelled fresh water into the city below. It was also dug simultaneously from both ends, with the two meeting in the middle— a considerable achievement for the time.

Practical information

Orientation Pythagorio lies on steepish hills behind a hook-like harbour. The ferries south leave from alongside the long concrete harbour mole that juts out towards the Turkish coast. The main street, Logothetou, runs at right angles to the waterfront, back inland, where after 200m it divides — the right-hand road heading back up the hill and over to Vathy, while going straight on takes you to the airport and, beyond that, the Hereon. This junction is also the point where the buses to and from Vathy stop.

Services The **tourist information office** (☎ 062 274), is open daily 0800-2200.

The **tourist police** (☎ 061 100) are on Lykourgou Logotheti.

Autoplan (☎ 061 096) offers **car hire**.

Ferries [see p458 for full details]
The agencies are Kalymnian Shipping, Kiriakoulis Maritime at Ship Travel & Shipping Agency (☎ 062 285), Miniotis (☎ 030 880). The port authority is on ☎ 061 225.

Ferries leave here for **Kos**, via **Patmos**, **Leros** and **Kalymnos**. There are

two services a day to Patmos, taking 70 mins, which continue to Kalymnos (total journey time 3hr) and Kos (4hr).

There are also three Kiriakoulis ferries to Fourni a week, taking an hour, and a daily service to Lipsi.

Where to stay *Delphini Hotel* (☎ 061 205), north end of the harbour, on the quayside. €25/40 sgl/dbl.
Hotel Alexandra (☎ 061 429), corner of Metamorfosis Sotiros and Despoti. €17/25 sgl/dbl.
Pension Arokaria (☎ 061 287), opposite Hotel Alexandra, has a shady garden. €17/25 sgl/dbl.

Where to eat *Restaurant Remataki*, by the town beach. Has some mezedes and main courses. €10 a head.
Taverna ta Platania, on the southern side of Plateia Irinis; well-prepared food in a good value restaurant. €10-15.

KARLOVASSI
The island's third port, 30km north-west of Vathy, Karlovassi's golden age was in the 19th century. Ferries bound for Athens and points west still call here, so you may find yourself in what is largely an industrial mess.

Practical information
Orientation The town is in three parts — Neo Karlovassi, Meso, and Palaio Karlovassi. The last two are the more

---

The Hereon
Some 8km west of Pythagorio, this one-time Wonder of the Ancient World is next to a village of the same name and is connected by regular buses to Pythagorio and Vathy.

The Hereon (Tue-Sun 0830-1430, €3) was the sacred sanctuary to the goddess Hera (see box on p296). It once consisted of a massive complex and a temple of 99 columns — four times larger than the Parthenon. There was also the very boat in which Kolaios, in 650BC, became the first Greek to sail a ship out beyond the Rock of Gibraltar into the Atlantic.

Now though, only one pillar remains standing, and much of the rest of the site requires some imagination to grasp. The remains of temples to Aphrodite and Hermes can also be seen, along with the stone base that used to support Kolaios' ship.

attractive, particularly as they are closer to a decent sand and pebble beach at Potami, some 2km further west.

Ferries   [see p455 for full details]
The main ferry agencies are GA Ferries, at Charlambakis Ferry Agency (☎ 032 320); Hellas Flying Dolphins, at Diakogeorgiou Shipping (☎ 033 695); Miniotis Lines at Soutos Tours (☎ 030 880). The port authority is on ☎ 030 888.

Ferries leave here for **Ikaria**, **Piraeus**, **Chios**, **Fourni**, **Syros**, **Mykonos**, **Naxos**, and **Paros**.

KOKKARI

Ten kilometres north-west of Vathy, the town of Kokkari lies at the start of a run of good beaches along Samos' northern coast. Served by regular and frequent buses, it has also become a favourite place in itself for many package tourists, though has maintained a very laidback, village like atmosphere.

The area consists of two headlands, with curving beaches between them and on either side. Those to the west — Tsamadou, Lemonaki, Avlakia and Platanakia — are pebbly, with the last some 5km off but still on the Vathy–Karlovassi bus route.

AEGEAN SEA

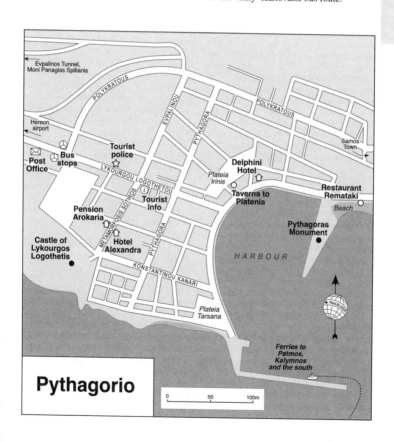

Pythagorio

Evpalinos Tunnel, Moni Panagias Spillianis

POLYKRATOUS

Hereon, airport

Post Office   Bus stops

Tourist police

EVPALINOU

PYTHAGORA

POLYKRATOUS

Samos Town

LYKOURGOU LOGOTHETOU

Plateia Irinis

Delphini Hotel

Restaurant Remataki

Tourist Info

Taverna to Platenia

Beach

Pension Arokaria

METAMORFOSIS SOTIROS

Hotel Alexandra

PYTHAGORA

Pythagoras Monument

Castle of Lykourgos Logothetis

KONSTANTINOU KANARI

HARBOUR

Plateia Tarsana

Ferries to Patmos, Kalymnos and the south

0   50   100m

Practical information
Where to stay *Pension Eleni* (☎ 092 317), near Dionysis Garden restaurant. €13/25 sgl/dbl.

Where to eat
Paradisos Restaurant, located at the road turn off for Manolates. Excellent quality and good prices; €8-10.

Kuşadası

AREA CODE: ☎ 0256 POPULATION: 51,000
Kuşadası is not the sort of place that many people dream of. In many ways a poor man's Bodrum, it has mushroomed spectacularly over the last few years, mostly sprouting endless concrete-block hotels and apartment houses. This is largely thanks to its location as the nearest harbour to Ephesus, one of the Mediterranean's top five ancient Roman cities, which has made Kuşadası a regular stop for Mediterranean cruise ships. It has also got boats to Samos, and is only 70km from İzmir Airport, making it a well-equipped place to get away from, which is probably what most visitors will want to do fairly rapidly.

HISTORY
As almost everyone you meet here will tell you, Kuşadası means 'Bird Island', named after the small islet out in the bay, which is in fact Güvercin Adası, or 'Pigeon Island',

and which has a small 14th- to 15th-century Genoese-built fort on it, now in use as a restaurant-cum-nightclub and connected to the mainland by a causeway.

The history of the town does go further back than that, although exactly when it started no one seems to know. Around 3000BC, this area was settled by the Carians, who came from the Anatolian hinterland, but by the 12th century it was part of the Ionian League. The area here was known as Panionia and contained three settlements: Phygale, Marathesion and Neopolis. It was in these that assemblies of the League were held, until 546BC when the Persians arrived to conquer the whole coast.

By 200BC, however, the conquerors were Roman and Kuşadası was part of their Asian province. Then Byzantine rule followed and as the port of neighbouring Ephesus silted up, Neopolis gained in significance. With its natural harbour, the town attracted many merchants, with the Venetians and Genoese naming this port Scala Nouva. The Seljuks swept through here briefly in 1071, with the town finally going to the Ottomans in 1413.

Öküz Mehmet Paşa, Grand Vizier to sultans Ahmet I and Osman II, had its fortifications strengthened, a karavansaray built and a hamam and mosque put up. The old town had large Jewish, Genoese and Venetian areas, as well as Greek, up until WWI. Then, as with the rest of the coast, the population transfers left it with a population of native Turks supplemented by refugees, mainly from Crete. Today, most

---

Fourni
Overview Lying just between the islands of Ikaria and Samos, Fourni is another tranquil, quiet escape, consisting of a main island, Korsi, and a cluster of even smaller, rocky outcrops. The Monastery of Agios Ioannis is on one of these, Thymaina, while the island group's other pleasures tend to be simple, namely away-from-it-all beaches and tiny tavernas in the main town, Fourni.

Where to stay The only place with accommodation is Fourni Town, on the main island, with rooms going for €25-60. Kampi Beach, a 15-minute walk away, also has some similarly-priced options.

Ferry connections There are ferries from Ikaria, Samos (Karlovassi, p455), Patmos (p457), Paros, and Piraeus (p457).

of that town has gone too, with Kuşadası a lively international resort.

WHAT TO SEE

A good place to start for a tour of the town's highlights is the **tourist information office** (daily 0800-1800, ☎ 614 1103) at 13, Liman Caddesi. From here, you'll also see the big stone walls of the **Öküz Mehmet Paşa Kervansaray** — now the Hotel Kervansaray — at the junction of Liman Caddesi and Barbaros Bulvarı. Built in 1618, the kervansaray was the main stop for visiting traders in medieval times, acting as a kind of hotel, stock exchange and department store for merchants. It is now an excellent place to rest up in, with the shade of its inner courtyard a cool respite from the streets in the heart of summer.

Keep on the pedestrianized Barbaros Bul and after about 50m from here on the left you'll see the **Kaleiçi Camii**, also built by Öküz Mehmet Paşa's workmen. Behind this you'll find the **Kaleiçi hamam**, the Turkish bath. Back onto Barbaros, continue another 10m and you'll come to the crossroads with Sağlik Caddesi. On the left-hand corner, there's a tower — part of the remains of the **old town walls**.

As for **beaches**, the most popular is Kadinlar Denizi (Ladies' Beach), 3km south-west of town and accessed by dolmuş from Atatürk Caddesi, heading south. The trip takes five minutes and costs US$0.30. Tusan Beach, 5km north and in front of the Tusan Hotel, is less crowded, with the frequent Kuşadası–Selçuk dolmuş taking 5-10 minutes and costing US$0.50. Further north still is Pamucak Beach, some 15km out of town at the mouth of the Kucuk Menderes river. To get there, take a Tamsa Otel dolmuş from Atatürk Caddesi, with the trip taking about 15-20 minutes and costing US$0.80. The beach has around 4km of sand, though is best visited when there's little wind as it is a bit exposed.

The **Dilek Yarimadasi Milli Parki** (Dilek Peninsula National Park), 30km south of Kuşadası, is a more natural setting for some long, pebbly beaches. Thanks to preservation orders, the park is still home to a number of rare species, including lynx

and wild cats. The unusual climatic conditions here also mean juniper, oak and cypress trees are in abundance. The park is open daily 0800-1800 (US$0.50 per person, US$3 for a car), with camping forbidden. Dolmuş from the otogar take around 45 minutes (US$1).

PRACTICAL INFORMATION
Orientation

Ferries dock in the heart of town, while the bus station is on the town's southern edge. There are dolmuş from the bus station to the centre, though it's not far to walk. The bus station is also the place for a dolmuş to Ephesus. The town itself is focused around largely pedestrianized areas next to the harbour and is easy to get around on foot.

Ferries [see pp455, 458, 460 for details]

There are two boats a day to **Samos** between 1 July and 31 August, falling off to one a day for the rest of the year. Services go to all the main ports on Samos. Ferries leave from Liman Caddesi, and it's good to get there early in season as queuing is hectic.

Tickets can be bought from Azim Tour (☎ 614 1553) on Liman Cad, Yayla Pasaji, or Diana Tours (☎ 614 4900) on the corner of Kibris Cad and Guvercinada Cad.

Buses

Most coach companies have regular direct services to Kuşadası from İstanbul (9 hours, US$35), İzmir (1 hour, US$5) and Ankara (9 hours, US$35). Catch all from the main bus station.

Services

The **tourist office** (☎ 614 1103), 13, Liman Caddesi, is open daily 0800-1800.

The **post office**, on Barbaros Hayrettin Bulevard, is open 0800-midnight.

Where to stay

Sammy's Palace (☎ 614 5711, 🖳 www.hotelsammyspalace.com), 14, Kibris Caddesi. A firm backpacker favourite, with sgl/dbl for US$12/20.

Golden Bed (☎ 614 8708), 4, Uğurlu Çikmazi, off Asanlar Caddesi. Caters for a similar market at similar prices to Sammy's.

Territorial waters

The past 50 years have seen Turkey and Greece almost permanently at loggerheads over rival claims to territorial waters in the Aegean. Most recently the two almost went to war over a group of small islets near the Dodecanese, long assumed to be Turkish, but over which in 1996 Greece decided to declare sovereignty.

There was nothing inevitable about this confrontation. Although Greece now occupies the majority of the Aegean Islands this was not always the case. When the Ottoman Empire was divided up after WWI, the Dodecanese Islands, which boasted sizeable Turkish-speaking Muslim communities, were handed not to Greece or Turkey but to Italy. Even during WWII, the islands' future was far from clear. In 1941 the British foreign office discussed a plan to offer the islands to Turkey in return for Turkey entering the war on the Allied side, but dropped it for fear of Soviet opposition.

However, bribe or no bribe, while Turkey failed to join the Allies until the dying days of the war, it did play a vital role in the Allied campaign in the Eastern Med, helping not only British and American forces but also the Greek resistance.

Turkish support began in 1941 when it accepted thousands of Greeks escaping the German invasion as well as hundreds of Greek and British soldiers.

British soldiers and airmen reaching Turkey were allowed to travel on by train to rejoin British forces in Palestine. Germans and Italians were not so lucky, finding that Turkey impounded them for the duration of the war.

More significantly, the British and later the Americans were allowed to set up bases on the Turkish coast from where they launched covert operations against German and Italian forces in the Dodecanese and Greece. These began in 1941 with a small number of Greek fishing caiques manned by British troops and Greek resistance fighters which made forays into occupied waters to rescue captured British aircrew. Operations were launched from bases at Bodrum and Kuşadası.

With the capitulation of Italy in 1943, the Allies were able to use these bases to invade the Dodecanese in the hope of replacing the surrendering Italians.

It was not to be, with a newly arrived German force proving more than a match for the invaders. Again, Turkish help was to prove invaluable in facilitating the escape of thousands of British and Greek troops as well as over 1500 Greek civilians, 3000 Italian troops that had opted to join the Allies and even a number of Jewish refugees.

Subsequently, in 1944 Allied activities out of Turkey became more daring, with groups of commandos succeeding in capturing – and bringing back to Turkish waters — a German supply boat, and of blowing up German warships anchored off Leros.

While German diplomats issued protests at the highest levels in Turkey, their weakened military position ensured that they went unheeded.

Hotel Liman (☎ 614 7770, 🖳 hasandegirmenci@superonline.com), 4, Buyral Sokak. Has good views plus some dorm space. US$12/20 sgl/dbl.

Campers should try *Onder*, just behind the yacht marina, for reasonable prices.

Where to eat

Ada Restaurant Plaj Café is perhaps the only waterfront eatery without intergalactic prices, US$15 a head for fish and mezes on Pigeon Island.

Melamet Sofrasi, in the Kale area near the mosque, has reasonable fare for US$10. *Onder*, at the **campsite**, is a popular restaurant with good prices (US$10).

Finally, *Oz Urfa*, also in the Kale district, on Cephane Sokak, has good kebabs (US$7.50).

İzmir

AREA CODE: ☎ 0232 **POPULATION:** 3 MILLION
Once one of the most important ports on the Mediterranean, İzmir still has a major role in the Turkish economy, as well as in the country's cultural and political life. A mixture of styles and periods, the city has an atmosphere and an appearance quite unlike any other in the country, with its wide, palm-tree-lined boulevards running down to the sea. There they intersect with one of the Mediterranean's most famous seafront roads — the Kordon.

HISTORY
In ancient times, the coast of this region was known as Ionia, an area settled by ancient Greek colonists around the 10th and 9th centuries BC. They founded 12 cities here and dozens more around the Mediterranean. Wealthy and prosperous, they also became a vital centre for ancient Greek philosophy and culture. However, they soon became victims of their own success. Expansion inland brought them into conflict with their neighbours, and in particular the Lydians. After repeated battles, most of their territory finally came under Lydian rule during the reign of King Croesus, around 560-546BC. The Lydians were in turn defeated by the Persians, who made Ionia one of their provinces. In an effort to throw off the Persian yoke the Ionians launched a major, and totally unsuccessful, revolt against the Persians in 499BC.

At times Ionia did become briefly liberated from the Persians, only to finally fall under Roman rule in 133BC, when it became part of the province of Asia. During this era cities such as İzmir (known as Smyrna) and Ephesus boomed and flourished. Passing into Byzantine hands, there then followed a period for the region during which Arabs, Seljuks, Genoese and Crusaders took it in turns to invade, followed in 1402 by Tamerlane the Great. He destroyed İzmir completely, leaving it a smouldering ruin for the Ottomans when they arrived in 1415.

Things began to improve after that, with the region regaining its importance as a centre of Mediterranean and international trade. In 1535, Süleyman the Magnificent permitted foreign traders to live within the Ottoman Empire and many settled in İzmir and its surroundings, giving the city a certain cosmopolitan sophistication.

However, with WWI and the subsequent Greek–Turkish War, the region was changed completely. A large part of İzmir was destroyed and many of the surrounding towns and villages which had Greek majorities were emptied by the population exchange. New settlers then arrived — Muslim, Turkish speakers from what is now northern Greece and from various Aegean Islands. For many years, İzmir struggled to pull itself back together, a task largely achieved thanks to the resilience of its people and its strategic location. It became the headquarters for NATO South-eastern Command following WWII, and is now a huge metropolis, and one that's still growing. It is also Turkey's third largest city.

WHAT TO SEE
Konak Meydanı is a good place to start, with its distinctive clocktower, the **1901 Saat Kulesi**. This is now the municipal emblem and commemorates Sultan Abdulhamid's 25th year on the throne. Next door is the **Konak Camii**, which has a fine façade of decorative tiles from the Ottoman tileworks at Kutahya.

South of this square are nearly all the city's museums, plus the municipal and state cultural centres. Leaving Konak Meydanı and turning right down Milli Kutuphane Caddesi brings you to the Ottoman art deco doors of the **Devlet Opera ve Balesi** (State Opera and Ballet theatre), renowned for its wide tastes, stretching from classical to pop. Tickets can be bought from the building's ticket office on the day of the performance.

Keep on straight down this street and you'll come out in parkland fronting the city's **Archaeological Museum** (daily 0830-1730, US$2.50). (*Continued on p360*)

AEGEAN SEA

Ephesus

The ancient city of Ephesus (daily May-Sept 0830-1830, Oct-April 0830-1730; US$10) is Turkey's second most-visited spot after Sultanahmet in İstanbul. This isn't too surprising when you realize it's also one of the greatest ancient cities anywhere, and stands in a remarkable state of preservation.

The main Kuşadası–Selçuk highway runs near to the site, and the dolmuş will put you down on it at a small junction by Tusan Motel. Follow this turn-off on foot — unless you fancy hiring a horse and carriage, which can take you to the site entrance for around US$5. Ephesus has a number of different entrances, but the main one — the Lower Entrance — is straight on, past the motel. After about 150m, you come to a large car park area ringed with souvenir shops, and the gate where you can get your tickets.

Although nowadays the sea is some 5km away, back in ancient times it came right up to the city walls. Initially, Ephesus was the site of a shrine to the Mother Goddess, Cybele, later co-opted by the Ionians when they arrived here around 700BC. They turned her into Artemis and built a massive temple to her here, known as one of the Wonders of the Ancient World. Ephesus was not only a port, but also commanded the western end of one of the great trade routes from Europe into Asia — the Cayster Valley. The city's location also gave it good access to both the Hermus (Gediz) and the Maeander (Büyük Menderes) rivers. These were vital trade routes into the Anatolian interior and from there into Asia via the fabled Silk Road.

This made Ephesus one of the richest cities in the ancient world and attracted a lot of unwanted attention as a result. First it was the Carians, who attacked in the 7th century BC, then the famous Lydian King Croesus took Ephesus in the 6th. The Persians then took it from him, followed by various Greek states, then Alexander the Great in 334BC. The city then fell to the Romans in 133BC.

As the capital of Roman Asia, the city was visited by St Paul in AD51, preaching and proselytizing, actions which resulted in his imprisonment and then deportation. In the early days of Christianity the city was also famous as the place where St John died — in the early years of the 2nd century AD — and, so it is believed by many, as the place where Mary, Jesus' mother, lived out her old age. Later on, under Byzantine rule, Ephesus also became the site of two Church Councils. However, by this stage the city was fast losing its status as a trade centre due to the perennial problem of silting in the harbour, as the sea gradually backed away towards its present location. Arab attacks in the 7th and 8th centuries didn't help much either, and the population began drifting away. Many moved to a neighbouring hill where the Byzantines had built the Church of St John. Over time, this became the beginning of the town of Selçuk, with the Seljuks themselves settling here in the 14th century. The Ottomans then moved in after 1426, by which time Ephesus was largely an abandoned ruin.

Looking around the site, you begin at the Arcadian way, a street up from the ancient harbour. Turn left and then right along Marble Street, a shiny, paved thoroughfare that is lined by the remains of houses and the huge **amphitheatre**, set into the hill on your left. It has been partly rebuilt as a stage for concerts and operas and contains some 20,000 seats. The theatre retains some outstanding acoustics, the bowl of the hill acting as a natural amplifier for those on stage. On the other side of the street you'll see the **Lower Agora**, or marketplace, with the **Temple of Serapis** behind it. These are currently off limits, but can be viewed from the street, allowing you to imagine the ancient scene. The market and temple would have been bustling with Egyptian traders, the cult of Serapis being special to them, and the masts of their boats in the ancient harbour would have seemed like a forest.

(Continued opposite)

❏ **Ephesus** *(Continued from p358)*
Moving on a few metres, you'll come to a junction with Curetes Street. On the left-hand corner, look out for a footprint and a female head carved into one of the stones. This, so the story goes, was the sign for a brothel. Inside, there are a number of fine mosaics still in situ which portray the four seasons.

To the right, looms one of Ephesus' most famous places — the **Library of Celsus**. This has been wonderfully restored by Austrian and Turkish archaeologists and is quite an imposing building. Originally put up by the Roman consul, Gaius Julius Aquila, between AD110 and 135, it is both library and mausoleum, as Gaius' father, Celsus Polemaeanus, is buried in its western wall. Here some 12,000 scrolls were stored under the watchful eyes of the four intellectual virtues, statues of which — or rather, contemporary copies of which — are still in place on the main façade. To the right of the library is the also-impressive triple Gate of Mazaeus and Mithridates, named after a wealthy Ephesus trader.

Turning back up Curetes Street (the *curetes* were priests of the temple of Artemis) head up the hill and, a few metres on the left, there is another popular site — the **Roman public lavatories**. Next door, incongruously, is the **Temple of Hadrian**, which was built in AD118 in honour of the city, Artemis and the Emperor Hadrian. Some steps to the right-hand side of this take you behind to the **Baths of Scholastica**, dedicated to a 5th-century Byzantine woman, a statue of whom — minus the head — stands at the entrance.

Back on the street, opposite the Temple of Hadrian, another stepped path leads you to the Terraced Houses. These were off limits at the time of writing but when open give a valuable insight into Roman dwellings, with a number of fine mosaics still in place. Back on Curetes Street, keep heading up the hill and on the left you'll pass **Trajan's Fountain**, then the **Gate of Hercules**, with a stone relief of the man himself dressed in a lion's skin. Take a right here and you'll find yourself amongst the tumble of **remains of Domitian's palace**. Inside the lower floor here was the Museum of Inscriptions, which regrettably is also closed off. (It seems some of the closures are due to archaeological work, while others are due to shortages of staff, a result of the country's financial troubles.)

Above the palace, you'll find yourself in the **main Agora**, or market-place. On its left edge stand the remains of the Prytaneum, in which the eternal flame of the city was kept, along with two statues of Artemis now in the Selçuk Museum. From here, continuing on the path leads you past the Odeon, the city's parliament, and the baths of Varius — now closed. After this, you'll find yourself at the exit. The city still continues beyond this though, with the huge east Gymnasium on the left and the Magnesia Gate a few metres further on, which marks the true edge of the old city.

A 5km walk from the exit will then take you to a sacred Christian shrine — the **House of the Virgin Mary** (known as Meryemana). This shrine may also be visited by taking a cab from the exit gate, which shouldn't cost more than US$5. While many theologians contend that Mary died and was buried in Jerusalem, another school maintains that she came here with St John in the middle of the first century. Many centuries later, in the 18th, a German nun, Catherine Emmerich, had a dream in which she saw a vision of the place Mary died, a vision that was actively researched by priests from İzmir in 1891. They stumbled across this small chapel, Panayia Kapili, and declared it the very place. The Pope visited in 1967 and now it is a place of pilgrimage for many Christians — and Muslims. Outside the house (dawn–dusk, US$2) you'll see many scraps of cloth tied to the bushes — wishes from Muslim pilgrims, who also see Mary as a saint (see box on p259).

AEGEAN SEA

Selçuk

Just up the road from Ephesus — a 15-minute walk — Selçuk has come on in recent years as an alternative place to stay while visiting the site — it's remarkably untouristy, yet also has some sights of its own worth visiting. The town's **archaeology museum** (Tue-Sun 0830-1200, 1300-1730, US$3) is some 200m back down the main Kuşadası road from the bus station, and opposite is the handy **tourist information office** (May-Sept daily 0830-1200, 1300-1730; Oct-April closed at weekends; ☎ 892 6945) on Ugur Mumcu Sevgi Yolu. In the museum, you'll find one of the most famous statues of Artemis — the original of millions of copies you'll notice in the souvenir shops. For a long time, the goddess was thought to be portrayed with dozens of breasts, but apparently current thinking is that they're testicles...

Turn left out of the museum and head up **Turgutreis Sok** for about 250m and take another left. You'll see ahead of you the Gate of Persecution, a bit of a misnomer it would seem. The Byzantines gave it this name after a relief of Achilles that used to be above the entrance that they misinterpreted as a depiction of Christians being eaten by the lions in Ephesus amphitheatre. Go through the gate and ahead you'll see the remains of the Basilica of St John. Until Tamerlane's troops destroyed it in 1402, it was one of the greatest churches in the world, the burial place of St John, and constructed on the Emperor Justinian's orders in the mid-6th century.

From here, turn left again and head down the hill to the **Isa Bey Camii**, a classic 14th-century Seljuk monument with an architecturally innovative courtyard and Roman pillars on the inside. Regrettably, it's also usually closed, but worth a look for its transitional style, between Seljuk and Ottoman. The mosque is also on a square and heading straight ahead here, back towards the Kuşadası road, brings you to the last of Seljuk's monuments, the Artemision, the site of the original temple of Artemis that gave Ephesus its Wonder of the Ancient World. Nowadays, though, it is hard to see what the fuss was about from what little remains. A solitary column amongst the rubble, the site is also partially flooded in winter. A melancholic and slightly disappointing place, then, its glory long since confined solely to the history books. The site is open daily 0830-1730, admission free.

If you want to stay the night here two places worth trying are: *Artemis Guest House 'Jimmy's Place'* (☎ 892 1982, 💻 www.artemisguesthouse.com) at 2, 1012 Sokak, which has good sgl/dbl for US$12/20; and *Vardar Pansiyon* (☎ 891 5451), east of town at 9, S DD Caddesi, which has sgl/dbl for US$7.50/13 (no en suite).

For a meal, *Old House: Deniz Topel Caddesi*, has alcohol and reasonable prices, US$10 a head. Otherwise, try the centre of town for cheap eats.

(*Continued from p357*) The Archaeological Museum contains some excellent ancient statues including a Hellenistic statue of Eros with a veil, presumably torn, clenched in his teeth. On other floors you'll find some interesting Roman mosaics, Bronze Age pottery and Ionian seals.

Housed in a late Ottoman building that was previously a hospital, the neighbouring **Ethnographic Museum** (daily 0830-1200, 1300-1730, US$1.50) contains mock-up rooms from a traditional Turkish house and from a Levantine merchant's villa. There are also rooms dedicated to weaving and other crafts and a display on one of the Aegean region's most popular sports — camel wrestling.

From here, head back towards the coast and Mithatpaşa Caddesi, where you'll find the **Painting and Sculpture Museum** (ground floor open daily 1000-1800, upper floors open weekdays only 1000-1700, free admission). The collection isn't that special but does contain upstairs some hundreds of paintings by republic-era Turkish artists.

After all this high culture, go north again along Mithatpaşa Caddesi for the junction with Anafartalar Caddesi and turn down it to the right. This brings you into the bazaar area, **Kemeralti**. The bazaar divides into a number of streets, each specializing in one or other commodity: Anafartalar Caddesi is the place for clothing, shoes and jewellery; the alleyways south of Fevzipaşa Bulevard are good for leather goods, while if it's carpets you're after, try the recently-restored 16th-century Kizlaragaşi Hani, next to the 1592 **Hisar Mosque**. It is one of the bazaar's only major historical buildings and a bit touristy, but worth a look nevertheless.

Near here to the east lies the **Ancient Agora** (daily 0830-1730, US$2), which can be reached by turning off Anafartalar Caddesi into 943 Sokak, then west into 816 Sokak — the route is signposted. These are the remains of a 2nd-century AD Roman colonnade, though the site itself is much older — probably 2nd century BC.

To reach the castle, **Kadifekale**, head up 985 Sokak then Haci Ali Efendi Caddesi from where steps lead up to the top. The walk takes you to fortress walls that date from Byzantine and Ottoman times, though both are built on Hellenistic foundations. At twilight, the view from the walls of the city, twinkling into night, is worth the hike up.

İzmir's other main area for tourists is the northern district of **Alsancak** — which is also where you'll find the main international ferry terminal. Alsancak was the European quarter in the old days and largely survived the conflagration of 1922. To view it, start out at Cumhuriyet Meydanı on the seafront and amble north along Birinci Kordon, or Ikinci Kordon, which runs parallel just behind the main harbour-front promenade. The Kordon was always lined with luxury and still is today, with the city's most expensive apartment blocks lined along it, together with the residences of the foreign diplomatic corps.

At 248, Birinci Kordon (also known as Atatürk Cad) is the **Atatürk Museum** (Tue-Fri 0830-1700, US$0.50) in a building where Atatürk used to stay on his visits to the city.

From here, the sightseeing turns very architectural, with 1469, 1480, 1481 and 1482 sokaks all lined with fantastic 18th- and 19th-century mansion houses. Back then the area was known as Punta, and still is by some of the more Levantine of its residents. It's also a good area for bars, cafés and restaurants.

PRACTICAL INFORMATION
Orientation
For the visitor, the city nowadays spreads along the coast from Alsancak in the north to Konak in the south. In the centre, slightly inland, lies Dokuz Eylül Meydanı, a large roundabout joining İzmir's main traffic arteries. North of here is the vast Kültürparkı, home to the city's yearly international trade fair.

From Dokuz Eylül Meydanı, two major boulevards head straight for the seafront — Gazi Bulvarı and Fevzipaşa Bulvarı — with traffic on both pretty intense. At the coast they join the corniche, Birinci Kordon, which runs right from Alsancak to Konak. The bus station is 2km north of town, with the Alsancak train station the only rail link out of the city.

Services
Tourist information is available at the airport, from the office (☎ 483 5117) in Konak Meydanı, or the office (☎ 0232-445 7390) next to Büyük Efes Hotel on 1344 Sokak (all open daily 0800-1900). The PTT (**post office**) on Cumhuriyet Meydanı is open 24hr. Chat **Internet Café** is in Alsancak, 14a, 1453 Sokak, but there are dozens of others around town.

Ferries   [see p454 for full details]
There are Turkish Maritime Lines (TML) ferries from İzmir to **İstanbul** and **Venice**. The İstanbul boats are weekly and take 19 hours. The Venice ferries are also weekly and take 63 hours. Both ferries depart from the dock at Alsancak, where the main TML office is located (☎ 421 0094).

Trains
Services are poor, but there is a daily train to Ankara from Alsancak and Basmane sta-

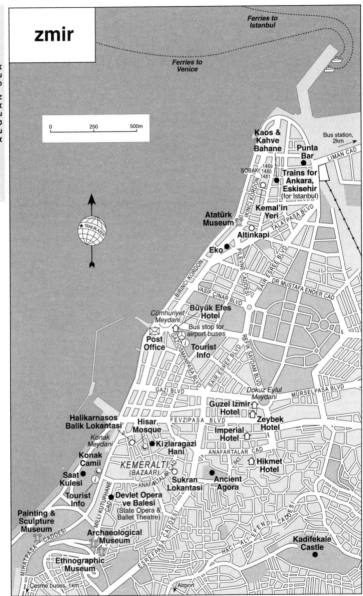

zmir

AEGEAN SEA

Ferries to
Istanbul

Ferries to
Venice

0   250   500m

TRAILBLAZER

Kaos &
Kahve
Bahane

Punta
Bar

Bus station,
2km

LIMAN CAD

1469
SOBAK 1480
1481

Trains for
Ankara,
Eskisehir
(for Istanbul)

İKİNCİ KORDON

Atatürk
Museum

Kemal'in
Yeri

ALATPASA BLVD

Altinkapi

Eko

PLEVNE CADDESI

ŞAIR EŞREF BLVD

DR MUSTAFA ENDER CAD

BIRINCI KORDON

VASIF ÇINAR BLVD

Cumhuriyet
Meydani

Büyük Efes
Hotel

Post
Office

Tourist
Info

Bus stop for
airport buses

GAZIOSMANPASA BLVD

ŞAIR EŞREF BLVD

REFIK SAYDAM BLVD

GAZI BLVD

Dokuz Eylul
Meydani

MÜRSELPASA BLVD

Halikarnasos
Balik Lokantasi

Hisar
Mosque

Guzel Izmir
Hotel

FEVZIPASA BLVD

Zeybek
Hotel

Konak
Meydani

Kizlaragazi
Hani

Imperial
Hotel

ANAFARTALAR CAD

Konak
Camii

KEMERALTI
(BAZAAR)

Hikmet
Hotel

ANAFARTALAR CAD

Saat
Kulesi

Tourist
Info

Sukran
Lokantasi

Ancient
Agora

Devlet Opera
ve Balesi
(State Opera &
Ballet Theatre)

MILLI KUTUPHANE CAD

Painting &
Sculpture
Museum

CADDESI

ESREFPASA CADDESI

HACI ALI EFENDI CADDESI

Archaeological
Museum

MIHATPASA CADDESI

Kadifekale
Castle

Ethnographic
Museum

Cesme buses, 1km

Airport

tions. Get it as far as Eskişehir and change there for İstanbul.

Buses

There are frequent and regular buses to every Turkish destination from the main bus station, 2km north-east of town. Take the No 53 local bus to get there from Konak; a taxi will cost US$5.

Planes

İzmir Airport is 18km south-east of İzmir. There is a Havaş service bus to and from the city centre, but it runs to service Turkish Airlines (THY) flights only. This means that if you arrive by another airline, you may have to wait a while for a THY flight to come in. The Havaş bus takes half an hour and costs US$2. A taxi should be around US$10-15 to central İzmir. Havaş buses to the airport leave from outside the THY office on the ground floor of the Büyük Efes Hotel on Gaziosmanpaşa Bulvarı. There are several daily THY flights to and from İstanbul and Ankara; try THY central reservations on ☎ 425 8280.

Where to stay

The area around Basmane train station is best for budget accommodation, with clusters of pensions in the Akinci and Çankaya districts.

Hikmet Hotel (☎ 484 2672) in Akinci, 25, 945 Sokak. Good value at US$10/20 sgl/dbl.
Imperial Hotel (☎ 484 9771), 54, 1296 Sokak, also in Akinci. Budget value at US$15/25 sgl/dbl.
Zeybek Hotel, 5, 1368 Sokak in Çankaya. More upmarket, with TVs in most rooms; US$15/30 sgl/dbl.
Guzel Izmir, 8, 1368 Sokak, in Çankaya. Has a sound reputation; US$15/25 sgl/dbl.

Campers should try *OBA Dinleme Tesisleri* in Guzelbahçe; it has a swimming pool and chalets for rent but is some 20km out of town.

Where to eat

The most atmospheric places are in the bazaar area, while most central streets can do you a fair-priced kebab or mixed grill for US$4-5.

Halikarnasos Balik Lokantasi, junction of 870, 871 and 873 sokaks. A fish restaurant with good value food for US$7 a head.
Sukran Lokantasi, 61, Anafartalar Caddesi, has an inner courtyard with fountain and is popular on summer nights; US$10-12.
Altinkapi, 14/A, 1444 Sokak, in Alsancak, has traditional meat dishes for US$7.
Kemal'in Yeri, 20/A, 1453 Sokak, has excellent fish dishes and gets crowded in season; US$15.

Bars

The Alsancak district is the venue for most bars, with the area developing quite a trendy aspect in recent years. *Eko*, on the corner of Pilevne Bulevard and Cumhuriyet Caddesi, does light snacks. *Kaos*, along with the neighbouring *Kahve Bahane*, are popular budget haunts in 1482 Sokak. *Punta Bar*, 26, 1469 Sokak, is one of the more established venues.

Çeşme

AREA CODE: ☎ 0232 **POPULATION:** 75,000
At the very end of a long peninsula extending out into the Aegean south of İzmir, Çeşme is a pleasant-enough place in itself and a good base camp for some picturesque villages and excellent beaches, all blown by the gentle, cooling breeze of the Imbat, a westerly summer wind. İzmir is easily within reach, while neighbouring Ilıca has become a full-on international resort in recent years.

HISTORY

Meaning 'drinking fountain' in Turkish, Çeşme is not a place of great historical dramas except for the year 1770, when the Ottoman navy came to grief at the hands of the Russians out in the straits at the Battle of Navarino. A monument to the Turkish sailors killed back then, known as the Cezayirli Hasan Paşa monument, stands on the present-day seafront road.

Mainly Greek inhabited, the town was of some importance during Ottoman times as a trading post bringing Aegean produce to the mainland — and as a guard post for the approaches to İzmir. This region is well known for its gum mastic trees, which produce the chewy resin used nowadays in making chewing gum. Its more traditional application in Çeşme was as a basis for making a mastik ice-cream and mahalebi, a milky dessert. Both are worth trying.

WHAT TO SEE

Çeşme's sights are fairly easily covered in a one- or two-hour walk. Starting at the top of Inkilap Caddesi, follow the road down to the **Ayios Haralambos Art Gallery**, which takes its name from the old Greek church in which it's located. Hours of opening are highly variable, though, so chances are you will have to admire it from the outside. Keeping to the same road, you then come out by the side of the castle and in front of the harbour. Here there are a clutch of open-air cafés and restaurants, while the **castle** (daily 0830-1200 and 1300-1730, US$2) was originally built by the Genoese, but extensively rebuilt and strengthened by Ottoman Sultan Beyazit I. This was done in order to protect the town against attack by the Knights of St John of Jerusalem, who raided much of the Anatolian Aegean coast from their base on Rhodes during the 15th and 16th centuries (see box on p322).

Inside the castle there is a small **museum**, which contains some finds from the nearby ancient city of Erythrae.

Carrying on south from here, you'll soon see the **Öküz Mehmet Paşa Kervansaray**, an impressive Ottoman building dating from 1528 — the time of Süleyman the Magnificent. Nowadays, it is Cesme Kervansaray Hotel, but non-guests can still take a stroll inside, with its cool inner courtyard a good place to relax out of the summer sun.

PRACTICAL INFORMATION
Orientation

The town is split by a central, mainly pedestrianized street called Inkilap Caddesi. This will probably give you your first impression of the town, particularly if you arrive by bus, as this will deposit you at the head of the street. A line of souvenir shops and travel agencies awaits you on your way down this road to the harbour, but head off south of this and within a few steps you will have entered a quite different town. The main bus station is some way out to the south-east, and has regular direct services to İzmir and İstanbul.

Services

The **tourist information office** (☎ 712 6653), on the harbour, is open daily 0900-1200, 1300-1700. The **post office**, on the harbour front road, north of the customs house, is open daily 0800-2400. Try Emre **internet café** at 11, Kutludal Sok.

Ferries   [see p454 for full details]

There are daily boats to **Chios**. Tickets are available from Erturk (☎ 712 6768), located opposite the tourist information office and just next to the castle, or Karavan (☎ 712 7230) at 3, Belediye Dukkanları Liman. They will take your passport – you collect it from customs before boarding. The trip takes about half an hour.

Tickets for ferries to **Ancona** (Apr to Nov) and **Brìndisi** (June to Sep) in Italy are available from Karavan (☎ 712 7932), Tamer Tur, at 15, Beyazıt Caddesi, or Herkul Turizm (☎ 712 1818), 9/F, Turgut Özal Bulvarı.

Buses

To/from İzmir Çeşme and İzmir are linked by an 80km toll highway. From Çeşme, buses depart every half-hour from the bus stop at the top of Inkilap Caddesi. You must buy a ticket in advance from the kiosk there – at least a day in advance in season. The İzmir–Çeşme trip takes about 1½ hours and costs US$2. The buses go to Uckuylar, which is 6km south-west of İzmir city centre.

If you are travelling on to other Turkish destinations by bus from İzmir, your best bet is to buy a ticket from one of the bus company offices in Uckuylar, as they have service buses to the main İzmir bus station, where most of them leave from

Excursions from Çeşme

Alaçatı Some 9km east of Çeşme, Alaçatı lies just off the main highway to İzmir. Its Greek past is still evident in the houses and former churches, while its location, at the top of a long inlet running south into the Aegean, is superb. Dominated by a row of five restored but non-operational windmills, a central street leads to a market area where you'll find the former town church, known as **Ayios Konstantinos**, turned into a mosque by Bosnian Muslims who came here after the population exchange. Its portico is now the central meat market, giving it the title of the Bazar Cami.

Around here are also a number of antique shops and cafés, with a pleasant hour or two to be spent among them. However, many visitors these days are here for something quite different — windsurfing. The inlet south of the town extends for about four kilometres and was, pre-WWII, an important secondary harbour for İzmir. Now, though, it provides an ideal area for windsurfers to test their skills. Try the website 🖳 www.alaca tli.com for the latest on this sport's possibilities, or contact Alaçatı Beach Club on ☎ 716 6161.

To get there from Çeşme, take the regular dolmuş to Ilıca (8km, 10-15 mins, US$0.50), then change to a dolmuş for Alaçatı (2km, 5 mins, US$0.40).

Altınkum A string of excellent beaches, Altınkum — or 'Golden Sands' — certainly lives up to its name. Spread along the southern tip of the Çeşme Peninsula, and some 9km from Çeşme itself, the beaches are easily reached by regular dolmuş. These depart from next to the tourist information office in Çeşme, in front of the castle by the harbour customs post. The trip takes around 15 minutes and costs US$0.50.

Dalyan A short, 10-minute dolmuş ride north of Çeşme, Dalyan has rapidly developed into an alternative resort town to Çeşme — and looks set to take over much of the yachting overspill from its larger neighbour. Set at the end of a river-like inlet, it is also still the fishing village that it has been for centuries, with a clutch of old Ottoman Greek houses at its core. It has a number of appealing fish restaurants, a small beach area and not much else, but is a nice place for an extended lunch or dinner away from Çeşme.

Dolmuş for Dalyan leave from the top of Inkalp Caddesi, where there is a roundabout marking the end of the street's pedestrianized section. Look out for the 'Dalyan' markings on one of these and hail it down. The trip costs around US$0.75 and the service both ways is frequent and reliable.

Ilıca and Sifne Named after a series of local thermal springs, Ilıca has grown into the area's main international tourist resort, with a string of package-tour hotels as well as hundreds of holiday flats for the more well-to-do İzmirians. It's also only 4km east of Çeşme and easily accessible, with regular and frequent dolmuş from the roundabout at the top of Inkalp Cad. The journey takes around 10 minutes, costing about US$0.50.

There is also an excellent 1km stretch of sandy beach at Ilıca, which runs beside a shallow sea that comes complete with a sea breeze — most welcome in the height of summer. What is probably not so useful at that time of year are the thermal springs themselves, located at the village of **Sifne**, some 3km further east. Also accessible by the same dolmuş that runs from Çeşme to Ilıca, the springs are part of an old German spa. Try the municipal Termal Otel for a hot bath, or head for the top of the village's inlet for a mud bath if the mood takes you. (Continued on p366)

AEGEAN SEA

AEGEAN SEA

❏ **Excursions from Çeşme**
(Continued from p365)
Ilidir/Erythrae Further on from Sifne, along the coast road heading for Balikliova and 27km from Çeşme lies the village of Ilidir and the site of ancient Erythrae. Again, it's the same dolmuş to Ilidir that takes you to Ilıca and Sifne, but the cost increases to around US$1 and the time to get there to around half an hour. Erythrae was once one of the most important Hellenic and Roman sites on the Aegean coast. This was due to it being the place for some popular religious cults: one dedicated to Hercules, and the others to two local sibyls, or soothsayers — Herophile and Athenais. Temples were built in honour of them all but nothing of them remains today. Instead, you'll find a crumbling 19th-century Greek church, an amphitheatre, walls, and the remains of several Roman-era houses, including a villa. Admission to the site is free.

What it's really all about though, is the view. From the top of the old Acropolis some 28 islands and islets lie in front of you in the bay, a scattering that stretches right over towards Chios. The closest takes about 15 minutes to get to for a fit swimmer. The view the other way — to the north — is also particularly good, revealing the hills and mountains of the Karaburun Peninsula.

and which is some 2km north-east of the city centre. There are also some daily direct buses to İstanbul, Ankara and Antalya from Çeşme main bus station.

Getting from İzmir to Çeşme, the No 53 local bus marked 'Konak' goes from İzmir main bus station to the centre of town, where you must change to another city-bus marked 'Uckuylar' for the Çeşme bus stop. Most bus companies offer more frequent services to and from İzmir, rather than direct to Çeşme. The İstanbul–İzmir route takes around eight hours and costs about US$10. Truva buses go via Ayvalık.

Where to stay
Avrupali Pansiyon (☎ 712 7309), 12, Sag Sokak. A pleasant guesthouse with some long-stay apartments; sgl/dbl at US$15/25.
Alim Pansiyon (☎ 712 8319), 3, Muftu Sokak. Has a choice of garden views; US$15/25 sgl/dbl.
Yalcin Hotel 38, Kale Sokak. Has good value rooms with baths; US$20/30 sgl/dbl.

Where to eat
Try *Kordon Pide*, next to the post office, for Turkish pizza, or for something more upmarket, *Korfez*, in the marina. Along Inkalp there are a number of places for reasonable eats, though few are memorable.

Chios

AREA CODE: ☎ 2271 POPULATION: 53,000
Roughly speaking, Chios Island, one of the largest in the Aegean, divides into three zones, north, central and south, each of which has something different to offer. In the north, amongst the jagged peaks of Mt Pelineo, Mt Oros and Mt Amani, there's the town of Volissos, said to be the birthplace of Homer; the pretty fishing port of Limnos; Vrontados and its Daskalopetra, or 'Teaching Rock', where Homer was supposed to have hung out and, off the north-eastern tip, the island of Oinousses — a beautiful but virtually uninhabited land that, bizarrely, is the birthplace of a vast number of Greece's most successful shipping magnates. In the central zone, the high spot is undoubtedly the Nea Moni monastery, a World-Heritage-listed building. Further on, there are also a number of nice beaches along the western edge of the island. In the south, there is one of the island's greatest highlights: the mastic villages of the Mastihohoria, centred on the town of Pyrgi. These wonderfully decorat-

ed settlements are worth a trip to the island in themselves.

At the centre of it all is Chios Town, which has a quite different buzz than neighbouring Çeşme or Lesbos. Here, off the ferry you'll be hit immediately by a wave of sound: of motor scooters, chattering crowds and cars and vans barrelling along the seafront road. The town contains plenty of rewarding sights, though, as well as being the best base for visiting the rest of the island. The ferry docks immediately in front of the old town, one of the island's best-kept secrets, which is surrounded by thick medieval walls and contains the old Ottoman Turkish quarter — a district well worth spending time in. There are also a number of museums and market areas, plus a seafront corniche of cafés and restaurants where you can eat and drink well into the night.

HISTORY

Like neighbouring Çeşme, Chios was part of Ionia in ancient times and also suffered a similar fate when the Persians took over the region in 546BC, becoming part of one of their western provinces. With the later Greek defeat of Persia, the island joined the Athenian alliance known as the Delian League. However, the islanders rebelled against their mainland allies in 412BC and again in 354BC, when their independence was finally recognized.

Under Roman rule, the island flourished, as it did under Byzantine, when it became a major centre for the Aegean wine trade. The Seljuk Turks occupied it briefly between 1089 and 1092, while the Venetians occupied it three times — between 1124-25, in 1172, and between 1204-25. Byzantine rule was then re-established, only for the island to be handed over to the Genoese Giustiniani family in 1344.

The Genoese stayed much longer but eventually gave way to the Ottomans who took over in 1566. Some islanders insist that during this time Christopher Columbus was born on the island, making Chios the home of the discoverer of America. You'll find the case put in various local publications on sale in the island's bookshops.

After the Genoese, there then followed centuries of mainly peaceful Ottoman rule, disastrously punctuated by one of the darkest spots in Aegean history — the massacres of 1822, when in reprisal for supporting Greek independence, the island was devastated by Ottoman troops. It was not to join Greece until after the 1912-13 Balkan Wars.

CHIOS TOWN
What to see

The **tourist information office** (see Services p368) is very helpful and a good place to start your tour. From here, head north towards the old town, or **Kastro**, along the street that runs up the right-hand side of the town hall. In a couple of minutes you will come to the **Porta Maggiore** — the main gate — of the old walled town. Walk through this and you emerge into daylight again next to **Giustiniani Palace** (☎ 022 819, Tue-Sun 0800-1900, €2) — which is not really a palace at all but an early 16th-century Genoese guardhouse. Restored in the mid-1980s, the building is now home to a rotating series of exhibits, along with a permanent display of 14th-century wall paintings from the dome of Panayia Krina Church in Vavyloi.

A stretch of the old town wall is quite easily accessible from the palace courtyard. While not for vertigo sufferers, it is quite possible to climb up here and walk along for about 100m — giving some excellent views out over the walled town's jumble of red tiled roofs.

The Plateia Frouriou on the left of the palace contains a small **Ottoman graveyard**. A collection of 20 or 30 tall, narrow gravestones still stands behind an iron railing fence, this being the **Kara Ali Mausoleum**. Look around here and you will already feel a long way from Genoa. The Turkish quarter runs in all directions from this square, the streets winding and twisting past some gorgeous Ottoman houses, many in a sorry state of disrepair.

Next to the graveyard you'll also see the tall, square walls of the **Bayrakli Camii**, the Islamic crescent still rising from the rooftop. The mosque is empty now, save for occasional use as a warehouse, but still has a *sura* inscribed above the door. The street in which it stands, Agiou Georgiou Frouriou, contains the old **Ottoman paşa's mansion**, which like the mosque today lies derelict, used as a warehouse by local fruit and veg traders.

Walk another 50m and you'll see on the left the **Church of Ayios Georgios**, 'Kenchri', after which the road bends a little to lead straight to the northern bastion of the fortress. Keep on, and as the houses break up into a rough jumble of bushes and ruins just inside the wall, you'll see another familiar Aegean shape — the domes of the old **Turkish hamam**.

Back in Plateia Plastira, another Ottoman relic is the 19th-century Mecidiye Camii, today housing the town's **Byzantine Museum** (Tue-Sun 1000-1500, ☎ 026 866, free admission). In the museum courtyard are numerous Ottoman and Jewish gravestones, along with a single Armenian one, attesting to the cosmopolitan nature of the town in Ottoman times. You'll also find here the stone sarcophagus of Ottuboni Giustiniani and a clutch of Genoese coats of arms.

Head off south into Aplotarias and the bazaars, a checkerboard of small shops, alleys and streets, many with old-style shopfronts and hand-painted signs in the windows. Continue on south, and the street becomes pedestrianized and more like a standard, Western shopping street, with international chains and window displays.

After about 200m, take the right-hand fork — Stefanou Tsouri — and on the left at No 20 you'll see the impressive town house of the Pateras family — now the **Chios Maritime Museum** (Mon-Sat 1000-1300, ☎ 044 139, free admission). With an impressive and lengthy seafaring history to illustrate, the museum does well, with written guides in English, French and German available to the Greek-labelled exhibits. Outside is a monument to the sailors of Chios killed in WWII.

From here, go back the way you came to the fork in the road and continue on down Aplotarias for about 10m before making a right down Argenti Korai. You'll soon see the **cathedral**, and next to this the **Philip Argenti Museum** (☎ 023 463, Mon-Thu

0830-1400, free admission). This is a tribute to the wealthy Argenti family and occupies the same building as the **Korais library**, one of the largest, reputedly, in Greece. From here you can continue south to the town's **archaeology museum** (Tue-Sun 1000-1300, ☎ 044 239, free admission), appropriately enough in Museum Street. The exhibits are not the most riveting though, and it's one for the enthusiast only.

Practical information
Orientation Ferries dock along the northern edge of the harbour, disembarking onto a portside road called Neorion, which heads off to the left and then makes a right-angled turn south to become the main corniche, Leoforos Egeou. Some 120m along this you'll come to a junction with Roidou, which heads off inland to the southern end of the Plateia Plastira — the main town square. This is where you'll find the taxi rank, the tourist information office and the Byzantine Museum. The stops for the blue town buses are on the north edge of the park on Dimokratias, while out-of-town buses leave from the station on the other side of the park; see p370.

North of Dimokratias lies the Kastro — the fortress containing the old Turkish quarter — while south of the Plateia Plastira, the main shopping area lies on and around the pedestrianized Aplotarias. Following this will also take you into the southern suburbs to the town's naval museum.

Both Neorion and Leoforos Egeou have a number of ferry-ticket agencies for tickets to Çeşme as well as to other Greek destinations, including Athens, Limnos, Lesbos, Samos, Kos and Rhodes.

Services The **tourist information** office (☎ 044 389, ✉ tourismos@chi.forthnet.gr), 18, Kanari, just off Plateia Plastira, is open Mon-Fri 0700-1430, 1730-2200, Sat 1000-1300, Sun 0700-1000.

The **tourist police** (☎ 044 427/8) are at the north-east end of Neorion.

The **post office** is on Rodakanaki, with the **phones** opposite the tourist office. Try **Enter Internet Café** (☎ 041 058, ✉ www.entercafe.gr), 98, Leoforos Egeou Ave.

Ferries   [see p454 for full details]
There are ferries to and from Çeşme in
Turkey, along with Greek domestic boats to
Thessaloniki via Lesbos and Limnos, to
Piraeus and Samos.

For tickets, try Manos Centre, 2,
Aegeou Ave (☎ 020 002, 🖳 mano2@ote
net.gr) or the Miniotis Brothers, 21, Neorion (☎ 024 670).

Boats for Çeşme leave daily, usually
around 1800, and take 45 minutes.
Passports can be presented at the customs

post on Leoforos Ergeou an hour before
departure. You must pay the port tax sepa-
rately at the kiosk by the entrance to the
customs post in euros (about €11).

The main ferry operators for Greek
domestic routes are: Kiriakoulis Maritime
Holding at Michalakis Tours (☎ 022 304);
NEL Lines, Chios-Oinousses Lines (☎ 025
074) and finally Miniotis Lines, 21, Neorion
(☎ 041 073).

The port authority is on ☎ 044 433.

AEGEAN SEA

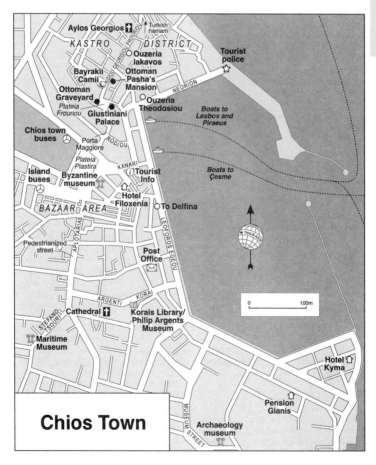

Chios Town

AEGEAN SEA

Bus The bus stops for the blue, Chios Town area buses are 15m up the north edge of the park on Dimokratias. The main out-of-town, green bus station is on the other side of the park, a similar distance up Polytechneiou. See the Buses section on p371 for details.

Planes Chios Airport is 4km from town and has no bus connections. A taxi should cost €3 to the town centre. The airport has five flights daily to Athens (€60), two a week to Thessaloniki (€80) and two a week to Lesbos (€45). These are with Olympic Airways which has its main office at Leoforos Egeou (☎ 020 359) in town.

Where to stay *Hotel Kyma* (☎ 044 500; 🖳 kyma@chi.forthnet.gr), 1, Evgenias Handris. Set in a 19th-century mansion at the harbour's far southern tip; sgl/dbl €40/55.
Pension Gianis (☎ 027 433), 48, Livanou. Set in an old Ottoman house, it has 24-hour opening — useful for late-night boat arrivals — plus a nice garden and kitchen; €15/30 sgl/dbl (€20/45 in July/Aug). Shut 31 October to 1 May.
Hotel Filoxenia (☎ 022 813), 2, Ralli (corner of Rodiou). All rooms come with TV, air con and shower; €20/35 sgl/dbl.

Where to eat *Ouzeri Iakavos*, 20, Agiou Georgiou Frouriou. An old-town institution specializing in seafood; €15 a head.
To Delfina, 25, Leforoos Egeou. A bit touristy but reasonably priced and good quality; €15.
Ouzeri Theodosiou Neorion, opposite the ferry stop. A good place to watch the boats come in, a traditional-style ouzeri attracting quite a crowd. Expect to pay €10-20 per head for a full meal, with meze around €2-5 each.

For budget eats, along Venizelou there are a number of cheaper, **buffet-style places** offering kebabs of various kinds for €2-3 a go.

CHIOS ISLAND
What to see
The north The north of the island presents some spectacular mountain scenery, along with tiny hillside villages and rocky coasts

edged by some hair-raising stretches of road. It's also the least visited part of the island, making it ideal for quick getaways from the crowds.

Volissos, some 30km north-west of Chios town, is a jumble of low, one- or two-storey houses grouped around an old Genoese fort. In this place, local legend has it, Homer was born, though others would have it that he (she?) just lived hereabouts. Historians do agree, however, that the island was the home of a school of bards known as the Homerids.

A kilometre further on is the small fishing port of **Limnos**, from where small boats, known as caiques, sometimes depart for the islet of Psara, 25km offshore. **Psara** has a long history going back to Mycenean times and is the birthplace of Admiral Kanaris, an important figure in the Greek independence struggle. Sailors from Psara were widely known for their seamanship, and still are today, even though few remain on this isolated rocky outcrop.

Over on the north-eastern side of the island, a rival claimant for Homer's birthplace is **Kardamyla**, another pretty village above the harbour town of Marmoro. About 2km further up the coast here is **Nagos**, the most popular beach area in the north of the island. All this coast feels the brush of the *meltemi*, a word you might come across in Turkey too as a girl's name — Meltem — meaning a cool, seaborne breeze (see box on p300).

Off the coast here lies the island of **Oinousses**. This is also the name of the only real settlement on the island, which boasts a number of large mansions belonging to the disproportionate number of shipping magnates born there. From the ferry stop on the island, turn left and walk by the water's edge to Plateia Antoniou P Lemou. Turn right from here to the Plateia tis Naftsynis, then right again and take the steps opposite the small café. This will bring you to the centre of the village where there is a bank, a post office and a **Maritime Museum** (☎ 055 182, open daily 1000-1330, €1.50). The latter has many models and photographs of ships belonging to the great maritime families living hereabouts. Some 2km west of town is **Kastro Beach**, a good sandy strand.

Vrondatos, once a separate village from Chios Town, is now part of the same coastal sprawl. Here you'll find the Daskalopetra, a rocky promontory on which lies the alleged stone chair of Homer. Privately though, most agree the stone in question is actually the base of a temple to Cybele, the goddess of nature.

The centre The 11th-century **Nea Moni** monastery (open daily 0800-1300, 1600-2000, admission free) is some 14km west of Chios Town. The approach is quite breathtaking, with the road out of town suddenly ascending into the mountains to bring you to a narrow valley thick with pine trees, with the monastery buildings themselves at the head looking down to the sea in the east.

Founded by the Byzantine emperor Constantine Monomachus, according to legend the monastery marks the spot where a miraculous icon of the Virgin Mary was discovered. In the centuries that followed, the Saracens ransacked the monastery in the 13th century, a feat repeated by the Ottoman army in 1822. Finally, an earthquake in 1881 toppled the eastern tower and damaged some of the interior too.

The frescos and mosaics are exceptional. The best of these is in the domed inner narthex — a mosaic of Christ washing his disciples' feet and an impressive representation of Christ's betrayal by Judas. As for the miraculous icon, that is to the right of the sanctuary entrance on the church iconostasis. You'll also see in the adjacent Chapel of the Holy Cross — which is tended by half a dozen nuns — a particularly ghoulish display of skulls in a glass cabinet. These are the remains of the monks killed at the monastery in the 1822 massacre.

The south The gum-mastic villages of southern Chios are closely knit groups of flat-roofed houses clutching defensively to the hilltops — mainly as a protection in the past against pirates.

They are also some of the Mediterranean's most decorative fortresses. Every house in the centre of some of these villages is wonderfully decorated with geometric grey and white designs, made by a technique known as *sgraffito* where the outer layer is scratched to reveal the colour of the under-layer. This involves first coating the wall in a mixture of cement and black volcanic dust, then affixing a coat of white lime on top, before parts of this latter layer are scraped off to form the geometric patterns. The warrens of narrow alleys and tunnels that burrow between these high, patterned walls make for some great exploring.

The most impressive of the villages is **Pyrgi**, 24km south-west of Chios Town. In its centre is a large, relatively modern church and in a small alley off the east side of the square is the tiny 12th-century Agios Apostolos. Inside this you'll see some fine frescos of the apostles Peter and Paul.

Around 6km south of Pyrgi is the village's old port, **Emboreios**, which lies just above **Mavra Volia Beach**, with black volcanic pebbles and a good place for a swim.

Practical information
Buses
● **To Volissos** Twice a week (45 minutes, €2). Given the infrequency, a better option might be to hitchhike or rent a car or scooter.

● **To Kardamyla** Six green buses a day (45 mins, €2).

● **To Vrondatos** Regular blue city-buses go here from the bus station on Demokratias. The journey north takes around 10 minutes and costs €0.50.

● **To Nea Moni** Take the green Anavatos bus from the bus station on Polytechneiou in Chios Town that leaves three times a week in season, twice a week at other times. Check with the bus station or tourist information office as the times change every year (around 15 mins, €1.50).

● **To Pyrgi/Emboreios** Eight green buses a day (45 mins to Pyrgi, €2, 55 mins to Emboreios, €2.10 — it's the same bus).

Where to stay *Hotel Kardamyla* (☎ 023 353) in **Kardamyla**. Most rooms €50/70 for sgl/dbl; cheaper rates off season.

Hotel Thalassoporos (☎ 055 475), in **Oinousses**. Your only choice on the island, located in the village; €22/35 sgl/dbl, though rates fall in the low season.

Rooms to Let Nikos (☎ 072 425), in **Pyrgi**. Has sgl/dbl for €15/20 and a kitchen with a fridge.

Where to eat *Restaurant Pateroniso*

Oinousses' oldest eatery, serves well-made traditional local food. €10 a head. Located in the square.

I Manoula, located in **Pyrgi**'s central square, is the chief eating place. Good, straightforward local food; €10.

Ifestio Taverna, in **Emboreios'** main square and with a livelier atmosphere than its neighbours; €15.

Lesbos

AREA CODE: ☎ 2251 **POPULATION**: 89,000
The third largest Greek island, Lesbos is also one of the least touristy. On a dusky summer's evening the colours of the land and sea here are soft and dark, well away from the harsh brightness of the south Aegean. Off the boat, you'll also be struck first by the strong smell of aniseed wafting from the town's ouzo manufacturers — ouzo from Lesbos is some of the finest and most popular in Greece.

The main town, Mytilini, possesses some decent shops and is the centre for what there is of the island-wide public transport system. It's also from Mytilini that the ferries depart for elsewhere in Greece, including a useful overnight ferry to Athens/Piraeus and an island-hopping service south to Chios and beyond.

The town is the best base for exploring the rest of the island, with the beautiful town of Mithymna/Molivos a must, while Eresos is the home of the ancient poet Sappho, and nearby Skala Eresou has excellent beaches, as does Vatera.

HISTORY
The town of Mytilini has a story going back to the start of Greek literature — with Homer's *Odyssey* describing how it was

attacked by Achilles and Odysseus during the 10-year siege of Troy. The whole island was probably taken over by Aeolian colonists from modern-day Thrace around the 10th century BC, while the town is one of six cities on the island listed by Herodotus.

Boom time for the town and the island was to come in the 6th century BC and the rule of the benevolent dictator Pittacus. He established an advanced education system on the island, including classes for girls and women — something of a novelty in those days. This island renaissance produced two of ancient Greece's finest lyric poets — Alcaeus from Mytilini and Sappho from Eressos — and won for Pittacus a spot as one of the Seven Sages of Greece.

Aristotle and Epicurus both also lived and taught in the town for a while, which later passed into Roman hands after an invasion led by Julius Caesar in 88BC. Byzantine Mytilini was repeatedly devastated by Saracen invasions between AD800 and 1100 but in 1354 things picked up a little when the Byzantines gave the island as a dowry to the Genoese. They spent some cash rebuilding the fortress above the harbour and kept the place relatively safe until 1462, when the Ottomans took over.

In keeping with the island's sea-going tradition, it was also here that the most famous Ottoman admiral of all time, Khair-ed-din or Barbarossa (see box on p92), was born to Greek parents. Mytilini stayed under Ottoman rule — along with the rest of the island — until 1912 when, following the Balkan War, it was handed over to Greece.

MYTILINI
What to see
Mytilini town's **Archaeology Museum** is divided in two parts: the older is at 7, Arg Ephtalioti (Tue-Sun 0830-1500, €3 for entry to both old and new parts), while the newer is a five-minute walk up the hill from there along 8 November (Tue-Sun 0800-1900). The older part has an informative display on the island's classical religious practices, particularly worship of the 'lesbian trinity': Zeus Antiaos, goddess of suppliants, Aioleia, glorious goddess of things born, and the colourful-sounding Kemelios Zonnysos,

associated with the 'orgiastic Dionysus cult' and an 'eater of raw flesh'. The new museum houses some fine 3rd-century AD Roman mosaics excavated from a Roman villa discovered in town and known as the Meander House owing to the depictions of Orpheus and Meander, a 3rd or 2nd century BC Greek poet, in some of the mosaics. Orpheus has strong connections with Lesbos, as legend has it that after his head was bitten off by the Maenads, it was washed up on the shores of this island, along with his lyre — thus bringing lyric poetry to Mytilini.

From the new museum it is then but a short hike to the **castle** (0830-1500, €2). This was first built in Byzantine times, rebuilt by Francesco Gattilusio of Genoa in the 14th century and then given a makeover once again by the Ottomans.

On the south-eastern slopes of the castle is a **pay beach** (€2), with little going for it. If you do fancy a quick swim we recommend you keep going further round to the left and look out for a cluster of parked scooters by a hook in the cliffs. Walking down to the sea at this point you'll find a much more popular **free beach**.

Back in town, the northern head of Ermou, the town's principal street, was Mytilini's old Turkish quarter. Halfway down on the left-hand side is a ruined mosque, the **Yeni Camii**, and the houses round about here have a distinctly Ottoman look. About 500m south down Ermou, though, is the town's main Christian landmark, **Ayios Therapon**. This pineapple-domed basilica, the largest church on the island, has a dark interior full of ornate carvings and icons, with the latter also much in evidence in the **Byzantine Museum** (☎ 028 916, Mon-Sat 1000-1300, €1.10) in the church courtyard. St Therapon was a one-time bishop of Cyprus from the iconoclastic era. The building was begun in 1850 but not completed till 1935.

Practical information
Orientation Ferries arrive and depart from the main port of Mytilini, right in town, while the island also has an airport 8km to the south, with a taxi to town costing about €4. The town is spread around the harbour,

with the fortress on a headland and the main street, Ermou, running across the neck of this. The bus station for trips around the island is next to Ayios Eirinis Park. These green buses are cheap but infrequent.

The best way to get around the island is either with your own transport or by hitching. Mytilini town is small enough to walk round easily, as are the island's other settlements.

Services The **tourist office** (☎ 042 511), 6, Aristarhou, is open daily 0830-1800.

The **tourist police** (☎ 042 511) are in the main port building.

There's a **post office** on Vournazon, west of the harbour. **Phones** are just west of the post office. Nova, on Samou near the urban bus centre, is an **internet café** with pool table; it opens afternoons and evenings only, shutting around midnight.

Ferries [see p456 for full details] Mytilini has good connections to **Thessaloniki**, via **Limnos**, and **Piraeus** via **Chios** as well as regular boats to **Ayvalık** in Turkey. The main domestic companies are: NEL Lines, at 5, El Venizelou (☎ 025 800); and Kiriakoulis Maritime, at Dimakis Tours (☎ 020 716).

The port authority is on ☎ 024 115.

For boats to **Ayvalık**, try any of the agencies along the harbour front. Departures are daily May to October. Boats leave at 0830, but you must check in at the port at 0800. You will have to pay port tax of around €10 at customs before departure. Passports should be handed in to customs the day before you go – your ticket agency usually arrange this.

Several agencies offer day-trip packages with a visit to Pergamon thrown in. Try around the harbour for the best deals.

Buses Local buses (blue) leave from Kountouriotou at the top of the main, south harbour for destinations within the town area.

Buses to out of town destinations (green) leave from the **bus station** (☎ 028 873) next to Ayios Eirinis Park. They are infrequent and usually depart only once a

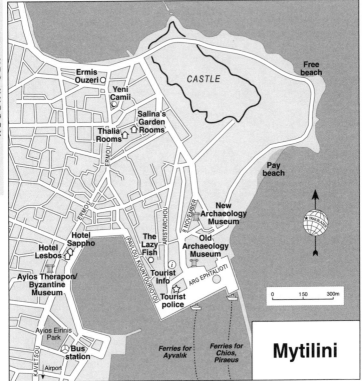

Mytilini

day, returning in the evening. To Mithymna, there are five buses a day, taking two hours, price €4, going via Petra. To Skala Eresou there are three buses (2½ hours, €6, going via Eresos).

Planes Olympic Airways fly to Lesbos from Athens (5 per day, €70) and Thessaloniki (1 per day, €85). There are also services to Chios (2 per week, €35) and Limnos (1 per week, €45).

Olympic airways office (☎ 028 659) is at 44, Kavetsou, the southern extension of Ermou. In summer, as with all island services, it is a good idea to book plane tickets well in advance, as many planes — particularly the small jets — fill up quickly.

Where to stay *Hotel Sappho* (☎ 028 415), 31, Kountourioti, on the waterfront road. Has sgl/dbl for €30/50.
Hotel Lesbos (☎ 022 037), almost next door, 27a, Kountourioti. Has sgl/dbl for much the same prices.
Salina's Garden Rooms (☎ 042 073), 7, Fokeas. In the old Turkish quarter; €20/30 sgl/dbl.
Thalia Rooms (☎ 024 640), 1, Kinikiou. An extension of Salina's Garden Rooms, with the same prices.

Where to eat *Ermis Ouzeri*, 2, Kornarou, is characterful and has good value mezes and main dishes; €10 a head.
The Lazy Fish, 5, Imvrou, nearer to the

port in a small backstreet. Greek food at reasonable prices — look out for the black wall lamps marking its entrance; €10.

There are also a string of small *cafés* serving gyros and souvlaki, along with hamburgers and other fast-food variants, at the southern end of Ermou and on the harbour road itself.

MITHYMNA/MOLIVOS

AREA CODE: ☎ 2253 **POPULATION:** 1000

Situated on a headland jutting out north towards the Turkish coast some 62km north-west of Mytilini, this town's dark grey stone, red-tiled houses and cobbled streets have been a protected area since 1965. On the horizon in Turkey rises Mount Ida, an important venue in classical Greek mythology, and watching the sun rise behind it is quite a draw.

Mithymna/Molivos has just as long a history as Mytilini, with the poet Arion amongst its famous former residents. Arion is credited by some as having written the first lyric poems with a personal, individual slant (as opposed to the epic tales of the gods that had been so prevalent before him). Others, however, credit this change to Sappho (see p372). Where the fortress stands now was, at that time, the city Acropolis. The walls still standing today

are a much later addition, however, and were designed by Francesco Gattilusio, the Genoan, in the 14th century.

Coming by bus, you'll alight at the bottom of the promontory, near an open-air cinema. Take the right-hand fork, the road marked Kastrou, to start the ascent. The other branch continues flat around the headland for some 500m to a small harbour, from where impressive views of the fortress and town up above can be had. Also, from here during the summer excursion boats leave for the neighbouring beaches of Eftalou, Skala Sykaminias, Petra and Anaxos, departing usually around 1000 and costing €2-3.

The **castle** (daily 0830-1700, €2) is worth a visit and in summer is the venue for a drama festival; details from the tourist information office (see below) near the bus station.

Practical information

Services The **tourist information office** (☎ 071 347) on 17 Novembriou is open summer only 0800-1500, 1830-2030.

For **internet access** try the café next to the open-air cinema near the bus stop.

Where to stay The *Nassos Guest House* (☎ 071 022), on Arionos, off 17 Novembriou, charges €20/30 sgl/dbl.

Limnos

Overview With its strategic location opposite the mouth of the Dardanelles in the northern Aegean previously making it something of a front-line island in Greek–Turkish confrontations, Limnos nowadays is emerging as an off-the-beaten-track haven. Myrina, the island's port and capital, is a lively place, if not a good looking one, though its castle has some excellent views towards the Greek mainland to the north.

The west of the island holds some of the best beaches, with those below the village of Platy recommended. The island's main ancient site is the Sanctuary of the Kabeiroi in the north-east of the island. For Gallipoli buffs, Limnos was the headquarters of the Allied forces during the WWI campaign and holds a large Commonwealth cemetery at East Moudros, and another at Livadohori, in the centre of the island.

Where to stay Myrina is the place for pensions and hotels, with the harbour-front road holding a string of options from €25-60 for a double.

Ferry connections There are ferries from Chios (p454), Piraeus (p458), Thessaloniki (p460) and Lesbos (Mytilini, p456).

AEGEAN SEA

Where to eat *Captain's Table* Located in the small harbour and with a great and deserved reputation for its mezes. Run by a Greek Australian couple; €10-15 a head.

ERESOS/SKALA ERESOU

Travelling to the western end of the island brings a transformation in the landscape from the olive groves and fertile lands of the east. Here Lesbos is at its most barren, with volcanic rocks in strange, twisted shapes and hillsides devoid of vegetation. Yet once the town of Eresos is reached, a more fertile zone follows the River Chalandra down to the sea and Eresos' beach extension, Skala Eresou.

While Eresos itself is charming enough, it is this beach that most people head for. Indeed, in ancient times Skala Eresou *was* Eresos, and the birthplace of the poet and lesbian/feminist icon, Sappho. There are also around 4km of fine sandy beaches here, some of the finest on the island. Beach lovers tend to divide up, with nudism beyond the river and lesbians around the river mouth.

Skala Eresou also holds the town **archaeological museum** (Tue-Sun 0830-1500, free entry) which contains a variety of Roman and Greek finds, including a large number of coins. From here, too, many travel agencies offer a trip to the local **petrified forest**, a dozen or so tree stumps that could be anything from half a million to 20 million years old. Worth skipping unless you have a lot of time on your hands.

Where to stay

Hotel Galini (☎ 053 138) in the centre of town. Nice terrace and a bar-cum-restaurant; sgl/dbl €30/50.
Sappho Hotel (☎ 053 233) on the waterfront, €30/50 sgl/dbl and women only. The women who go here are a lively crowd.

Where to eat

Egeo has a central waterside location and good local food with plenty of fine mezes. €10 a head.

VATERA

Accessed by bus from Mytilini via the town of Polychnitos, Vatera has a 9km beach, with far smaller crowds thronging the coast at Plomari, further east. It also has a number of world-class sites for dinosaur bones, back up off the beach. Some of the finds are on display in the nearby museum at Vrissa. With excavations continuing, it is also possible, if you're lucky, to view some of these dinosaurs *in situ* — enquire at the local hotel for the latest.

Where to stay and eat

Hotel Vatera Beach (☎ 061 212, 🖳 hovatera @otenet.gr) Greek-American owners and a relaxed atmosphere; €40/60 sgl/dbl with shower. Also does top Greek home cooking for around €10 a head.

Ayvalık

AREA CODE: ☎ 0266 POPULATION: 50,000
Ayvalık is a rambling, gorgeous old town, with shaded narrow streets and cobbled roadways meandering amongst markets, churches and mosques, grand old merchants' dwellings and warehouses of long forgotten trades. For centuries a Greek town, ironically, most of the older Turks who now live here are from families that before the population exchange of the 1920s lived opposite, on the now-Greek islands, or in Crete, hundreds of kilometres to the south.

In addition, many younger Turks have now made this their home, with Ayvalık an increasingly trendy venue for arty İstanbulus and İzmiris looking for the quiet life. This has led to a welcome restoration of many of the town's crumbling old houses. Ayvalık makes a good jumping-off point for the Greek islands and for the Turkish coast, with the ancient city of Pergamum to the south (see box on p294), ancient Troy to the north and, beyond that, the Gallipoli battlefields. It's also the kind of place in which you can end up spending much more time than you planned, its wistful, late afternoon atmosphere being particularly seductive.

HISTORY

Ayvalık means 'Place of Quinces' in Turkish, which is what its ancient Greek name, 'Kydoniae', also means. Back in Hellenistic times the town was one of four settlements in the area — along with Nesos (present-day Cunda), Chalkis and Pordoselene. Grouped together with the islands, the region was known as Hecatonisso, which gives a link to the god Apollo whose nickname was Hecatos. Some ancient sources also refer to the region as the Apollo Islands. This region, the north Aegean coast, was known as Aeolia in ancient times, settled by Aeolian Greeks (see history box on p294).

In Roman times, the main settlement was on the Cunda side of the present causeway and was known for its thermal healing springs, mentioned by Pliny the Elder. Later, under the Byzantines, it shifted to more or less where it is now. But little is known of the place up until the 16th century, by which time it had established itself as one of the most prosperous Ottoman Greek towns of the entire Anatolian Aegean coast.

Granted a great deal of local autonomy by the Ottomans, the town seems to have boomed. By 1803 it had its own college, was exporting its olive oil and soap to ports as distant as Marseille and Odessa, and in 1809 its own printing press also swung into action. Then came the Greek War of Independence in 1821, and the destruction of much of the town in the fighting. The early 19th century continued to be difficult for many of the inhabitants once they had returned. Many turned to smuggling and the town's architecture, with its narrow alleyways, was deliberately built to make defence easier. The houses themselves, too, took on more solid, musket-ball-proof shapes.

By the dawn of the 20th century the town had regained much of its former stature and a number of foreign consulates opened — including the French 'Union de Paris', which still stands at Maresal Cakmak Caddesi, Street 5, House 6. Under the population exchange of 1923, though, the Greeks of Ayvalık were removed — many of them only a short distance to neighbouring Lesbos. After that, an earthquake in 1944 caused major damage, but the town has continued since with its olive oil, soap manufacturing and fishing.

WHAT TO SEE

From Iskele Meydanı, head north along Inönü Caddesi some 300m until you come to the junction with Maresal Cakmak Cad. Turn right and head inland and, after about 200m, you'll come to the 130-year-old **Taksiyarhis Kilisesi** (Taksiyarhis Church). Unusually never converted into a mosque, it has been undergoing long-term restoration in preparation for opening as a museum, but is currently closed since some of its priceless portraits — painted on fish skins — were stolen. From here, follow the street round for another 150m and you will come to the **Çınarlı Camii**, the 'Mosque of the Plane Trees' and formerly a church, Ayios Yioryos, which lies up the hill from the clocktower. These days you would be hard pressed to find a plane tree anywhere near it. From here, head back towards the coast down the road running alongside the mosque and after around 100m, make a sharp right. This will bring you to the distinctive tower of the quirky **Saatli Camii**, the 'Clocktower Mosque', or formerly, the 19th-century Church of Ayios Ioannis. Closed for restoration at present, it is something of a symbol of Ayvalık with its mix of Muslim and Christian design.

Around Ayvalık, Cunda – or Alibey – Island is a must, despite its rapid transformation into a concrete box by eager developers. Now connected by a causeway to Ayvalık, it's a short car journey or a 10-minute bus ride from Iskele Meydanı. However, easily the best way to visit is by boat, with half-hourly ferries leaving from the quay alongside Atatürk Caddesi. The trip takes about 20 minutes and costs around US$1.

Previously, Cunda was known by the Greek name, Moskhonissi, 'Fragrant Island'. It has eight Greek Orthodox monasteries, all now in ruins, with Ayios Dimitrios ta Selina (known as the 'Moonlight Monastery') still the most impressive. This is located on the north side of the island — a region known as Patrice or Paterica.

Patrice itself is an abandoned old Greek village. There you will find a local institution, **Biyiklinin Yeri** ('The Moustachioed One's Place'; ☎ 327 1768). At this restaurant it's more or less compulsory to try the giant mussels, called *pina*, though with a snorkel it's also possible to collect your own in the shallow waters off the island.

The better beaches are 6km south of Ayvalık at Sarimsakli, with Altinova Beach the best, having several kilometres of fine sand. You can get to both here and Sarimsakli by regular bus or dolmuş from Iskele Meydanı. On the way there you'll pass Seytan Sofrasi, 'The Devil's Table', a volcanic plateau that's particularly good as

a sunset- or sunrise-watching spot. Local legend has it the Great Satan himself used to party here every evening with a bunch of lesser devils for company. An iron cage covers an alleged 'Devil's footprint' at one point, and this, too, is a sacred symbol, as shown by the pieces of cloth — wishing ribbons — to be found tied to it.

Visiting the dozens of other islands near here is very feasible, with frequent boat trips put on by the tour operators down along the quayside by Atatürk Caddesi. Most have set routes, but will also make detours if there is any particular island you'd like to visit.

The race to Lesbos

After a long, slow afternoon in Ayvalık, the departure of the two small ferries to Lesbos came as quite an event. Leaving at around five in the afternoon, the crowd around customs was mainly composed of Greeks who'd popped over for the day and late-season Ozzie backpackers heading south.

With a lot of engine revving and the clank of winches pulling up the landing-craft-like back doors on the single-deck ferries, the two boats set off, heading straight for the sound. Behind, the town slowly shrank away, while along the coast over to Alibey Island the impressive ranks of Turkish summer houses faded gradually into the horizon.

The ferries then began to speed up. The sound out of Ayvalık narrows past a string of low-lying islands, some uninhabited, others with the odd, tumbledown house perched on a stony shoreline. The *Jale*, our rival, had fallen behind until now, but as the strait widened out, with the lighthouse on Ciplak Island off to the south, it began to catch up fast.

The accommodation on the ferry I was on consisted of little more than a medium-sized saloon room, with the captain perched in a small cabin on top. Around the saloon, on the outside, facing the sea, ran a wooden bench, and it was here that most of the passengers gathered. There, it was time for a glass of ouzo and a plate of fruit, brought out by one of the crew — or was it one of the passengers? At times it was hard to tell the one from the other, as they were all locals and maybe even from the same family. Why did these Greek islanders come to Ayvalık? For a haircut, said one: it's cheaper in Turkey. Others pointed to bags of shopping, one opening a bag of silvery, slight fish — anchovies brought from the Ayvalık quayside fishermen.

But the *Jale* was definitely gaining now, as the two ships pulled to port to head south, parallel with the distant cliffs of Lesbos, their dark blue fading to a darker green far off above the foaming water. They were all going home, these Greeks, after a day in town – never mind that it was home in a different country. The ferry was the local bus, chuntering back across the narrow strait between Greece and Turkey. It seemed the most natural thing in the world, to lie back, a glass of ouzo in one hand and some fruit from the orchards of Anatolia in the other, and just enjoy the setting sun.

And who cares which boat won?

❏ **The need for euros**
Remember that you cannot change Turkish Lira in Greece. It's better to change any you have for euros in Ayvalık. Failing that, there is a cash point/ATM next to the port building in Mytilini, Lesbos that takes all types of cards. Euros are, of course, most welcome in Turkey.

PRACTICAL INFORMATION

Orientation
The bus from İstanbul drops you off at a roadside service stop some 2km out of town. A minibus then takes you to the town otogar, some 500m from the centre on Inönü Caddesi. The town is basically a long strip down along a bay containing 23 islands. The ferry to Lesbos departs from the central Gümrük Square, which is also where you'll find the ticket agencies and customs house. Other than that, everything you need is within walking distance and strolling amongst the town's old streets is really Ayvalık's main pleasure. The main banks are all around Iskele Meydanı, as is the main shopping street, Talat Paşa Caddesi.

Here, if the banks are shut, it is possible to change money in one of the bazaar's many jewellers, off to the left and right of this street.

Services
The **tourist information office** (☎ 312 2122), Çamlık Cad, opposite the marina, is open 0800-1200, 1300-1700. The **post office**, on Inönü Caddesi, is open 0830-1230. **Phones** are next door.

Internet access is available at Sehir Otel (☎ 312 1569), Vehibey Mhl, 2, Gazinolar Cad (open 0800-2400) and Star Internet, 39, Atatürk Cad.

Ferries [see p453 for full details]
The ferries to Mytilini on Lesbos run daily in season. The journey takes around 75 minutes.

Two companies deal with the ticketing: Jale Ayvalık Tur Shipping Agency (☎ 312 2740) in Gümrük Caddesi, by the ferry dock, and Yeni Istanbul Tour (☎ 312 6123) in Cumhuriyet Meydanı.

Miniotis is planning to start a service to Mytilini so check locally.

Buses
From İstanbul Truva bus company has the only direct service. The journey takes 8-10 hours, going via Çanakkale, and costs US$10.

Otherwise, many bus companies going to İzmir travel via Balikesir, from where the 127km to Ayvalık can be covered by another bus or dolmuş. From İzmir, take the Truva Seyhat bus through Bergama and Dikili to Ayvalık.

From Gallipoli/Çanakkale/Troy These places are served by the İstanbul bus, so services are pretty regular. Journey takes around 3 hours, US$4.

Where to stay
Taksiyarhis Pansiyon (☎ 312 1494), 71, Ismetpaşa Mhl, Marasal Cakmak Caddesi. Next to the church of the same name, two beautiful old houses knocked together, with a variety of rooms and friendly staff; sgl/dbl US$15/30; dorm beds US$7.
Chez Belize (☎ 312 4897), 28, Marezal Cakmak Caddesi, near the seafront. US$10/20 sgl/dbl.
Atun Pansiyon (☎ 327 1554), in Cunda's main square. US$10/20 sgl/dbl.

Where to eat
Balikci Barinagi, in Cunda, is good for seafood, plus some Cretan specialities; US$10 a head.
Osmanli Mutfagi, on Talat Paşa Caddesi, has good traditional fare; US$10.

Otherwise, *Tenekeciler Sokak* is Ayvalık's main place for eateries. It's located in the market area between Marsal Cakmak and Talat Paşa caddesis.

AEGEAN SEA

Troy

The ruins of Troy (Truva) may be high on the tourist agenda but visiting them can be disillusioning. There's a modern 'Wooden Horse' on the roadside to remind you of how the Greeks tricked their way into the besieged Trojan city. A guide will explain the ruins from the nine 'Troys' each originally built, the one upon the other. From the late 19th century archaeologists have worked on the site, the seventh Troy (c1250BC) discovered by Heinrich Schliemann in 1871 being now acknowledged as the Troy of Homer's *Iliad*. Although there is not much to see at the site itself there are superb views over the plains.

Troy is about 20km from Çanakkale and you can get here by dolmuş (US$1.50; 45 mins). You can also get here from Ayvalik (see p379) which is about 50km south of Troy. The site is open daily from 8am to 5pm (7pm in summer). Entry is US$7.

İstanbul

AREA CODE: ☎ 0212 (EUROPEAN SIDE), ☎ 0216 (ASIAN SIDE) **POPULATION:** C12 MILLION.

Known simply as 'The City' to the Greeks, *der Saadet* ('Seat of Bliss') to the Ottomans, Tzarigrad ('City of the Emperors') to the Slavs, and the setting for dozens of orientalist fantasies for Western Europeans, İstanbul has clearly got something going for it that no other city has. Set on both sides of the Bosphorus — a narrow channel joining the Black Sea to the Marmara and thus on to the Aegean — the city has a recorded history going back millennia and an imperial pedigree hard to beat. Not just one but three empires ruled much of the Mediterranean from these cluttered shores. Its strategic location has also made it a much coveted place, as its massive, still-standing walls can testify.

It has also long been a highly cosmopolitan, multicultural city, and up until the early 20th century was also very multi-religious. While justly famous for its Islamic sites, it still continues to be the centre of the Greek Orthodox faith. And while also famous for its Eastern ways, nowadays it also has the most lively Western-style bar and club scene in the eastern Mediterranean.

The city has also mushroomed in size over the last 20 years and now spreads out into a smog-filled horizon along both its Asian and European shores. Nonetheless, for visitors it remains an easy city to get around, with most of the major historical sites clustered together in the Sultanahmet district, which is also where the majority of budget accommodation lies. The entertainment district is also not so far away being mainly in Beyoğlu, the other side of the Golden Horn, the ancient natural harbour that divides the European part of the city in two.

İstanbul is a maritime city first and foremost. The Bosphorus is criss-crossed daily by dozens of ferries, while tankers and freighters lumber up and down it, passing beneath its two towering bridges. The city's buildings put on their best faces for the water, looking out proudly on the busy traffic from their hilly shorelines. For this reason, arriving in İstanbul by sea is highly recommended, providing spectacular views of ancient palaces and a skyline of minarets.

HISTORY

While artefacts going back to neolithic times have been found round about here, the city's story is said to begin with a Greek sailor by the name of Byzas, who founded a colony on the headland now known as Seraglio point, the site of Topkapı Palace, around 650BC. Thus Byzantium began, though other more banal theories have it that the name relates to an ancient word meaning 'a crossing place for cattle'. Whatever the case, in one of those bizarre ironies of history the pagan Greek city-state of Byzantium took as its symbol the star and crescent, a symbol now repeated on the flag of Islamic Turkey.

Byzantium's strategic value — a crossroads of crossroads with overlapping routes between Europe and Anatolia, the Black Sea and the Aegean — allowed the city to accumulate some serious wealth, but also serious enemies. Persians, Athenians, Spartans, Macedonians, everyone had an attempt at taking the place; yet surprisingly the city kept its independence one way or another until Roman times, when the Emperor Septimus Severus sacked it in AD196.

Yet by the 4th century AD, the city had re-established itself to such an extent that the Emperor Constantine, seeking to reorganize the empire, declared it his new capital. Nova Roma was the official new title yet Constantinople was how it came to be known. In keeping with its new status as the centre of the Roman universe, a massive building programme was begun, and continued by Theodosius I who extended the city out to the walls you see today.

Under Constantine, the Roman Empire also officially became Christian, although Constantinople itself remained largely pagan for many years. As the Roman emperors in the west died out during the 5th century, the city and the Eastern Roman Empire that remained took on even more importance as the surviving nucleus of the old empire. By now though, it was largely Greek-speaking, and Constantinople had reverted to its old Greek name of Byzantium by the time Justinian became emperor in 527. His was to be the Roman Empire's final fling as he launched a campaign of reconquest that returned much of the West to imperial control by the time of his death. He also had one of the city's greatest landmarks built, the Church of St Sophia, which still stands today. All this conquering came to nothing though, as the 7th century saw the sudden appearance of Arab armies fighting under the standard of Islam. They swept into the Mediterranean basin and took most of Justinian's gains with them in a matter of a few years.

From then on, the city was the capital of a gradually vanishing Byzantine Empire, though the process of change was a glacially slow one. For centuries, Byzantine emperors continued to rule over much of the Aegean, the Balkans, southern Italy and Anatolia from this city. However, in 1204 the Fourth Crusade inflicted the first of many near fatal blows to Byzantium. This military expedition by the Western Europeans, supposedly against the Muslims, was turned into an attack on the Byzantines by the Venetians. Venice was the emerging power at the time in the Christian world and wished to see its rival for control of the Aegean and eastern Mediterranean trade routes crushed. The Crusaders besieged Byzantium and finally took it, desecrating its holy sites and sacking it far more ruthlessly than its later Ottoman conquerors.

Yet after a brief period of Venetian rule, the Byzantines managed to retake their own capital in 1261. However, out in Anatolia, a major shift had occurred. This was the rise of the house of Osman among the Turkish tribes that had been moving into the region over the previous few centuries. Sultan Osman I was able to unite most of these groups and together they embarked on a campaign across Anatolia that slowly but surely tightened the noose around Byzantium. In 1394, the Ottomans — for such were Osman's descendants now called — first laid siege to the city. They failed in their attempt, but returned in 1400, 1422, 1442 and finally in 1452 (see box on p382).

Established in their new capital, the Ottomans then began a building programme of their own, converting many of the churches into mosques and also constructing anew. In the process, they produced some of the finest — some might even say, *the* finest — examples of Islamic architecture anywhere. Work on Topkapı Palace was begun, and by the reign of Süleyman the Magnificent (1520-66), the city was clearly worthy of an empire that now stretched from the gates of Vienna to the Indian Ocean by way of Ukraine, the Crimea and Caucasus, the Persian Gulf and North Africa.

In the heart of all this was İstanbul. In those times, it was world renowned as a city of great beauty, its wooded shores dotted with magnificent kiosks, or villas, and its

A E G E A N   S E A

The Ottomans

Bursting out of Central Asia and onto the Mediterranean scene in the 9th-10th century AD, the Ottoman Turks were to become rulers of an empire that stretched from the gates of Vienna to the Persian Gulf and from Central Asia to the Atlantic. A dynasty founded by Osman I, these highly mobile and martial people were initially spurred into Anatolia by the attacks of Gengiz Khan and the Mongols, even further to the east. This westward shift brought them into immediate conflict with the Byzantine, Eastern Roman Empire, which then ruled much of the eastern Mediterranean from its capital of Constantinople. The two powers were to battle it out for centuries, with the Ottoman Turks continually having the upper hand, from their decisive victory at the Battle Of Manzikurt in 1071 to Mehmet the Conqueror's capture of Constantinople itself in 1453. The Ottomans had by now taken over from the earlier Arab and Moorish empires as the pre-eminent Muslim entity. Their power thus spread throughout the Middle East and along the North African coast, bringing the sultans of Constantinople — now İstanbul — untold wealth and power.

The Arab invasions of the Mediterranean in the 7th and 8th centuries AD had met with lightning success. One of the tenets of Islam was that no Muslim could be a slave, thus offering hope to the millions enslaved in the empires of Rome and Byzantium — provided they converted. As such, the Arabs were able to make some astonishingly rapid gains, not only in terms of territory but also in terms of the numbers of people who converted to their new religion. However, the wave broke when it came across kingdoms that were organized somewhat differently — the feudal European states.

These kingdoms thus became the ones the Ottomans spent centuries fighting against, although it was hardly ever a straightforward struggle between Christians and Muslims, as European powers often sided with the Ottomans in order to gain an advantage over each other. Meanwhile, within the Ottoman Empire itself, different Muslim states, such as Persia and Egypt, often also fought İstanbul for control.

Yet for almost six centuries, from Manzikurt in 1071 to 1683 and the decisive failure to capture Vienna, the Ottomans proved to be impressively successful at expansion. The reign of Süleyman the Magnificent was their high point in terms of territory and economic wealth, with many of the empire's most impressive buildings constructed at this time. The expansion of Islam continued west and northwards through Greece and the Balkans during the 16th century, as well as around the Black Sea and through modern Ukraine and the Crimea. *(Continued opposite)*

markets — the grand bazaar in particular — known for fabulous wealth. It also lay at the end of the Silk Road, the almost mythical land route across Central Asia to China along which the imagination of many Westerners ran riot for centuries. These were also times of great success for the military, when, with their élite corps of Janissaries — professional soldiers — they repeatedly got the better of any army Christian Europe could throw at them.

But, as with all such things, this arrangement proved transient. With the Ottomans' shock defeat in an abortive siege of Vienna in 1683, another period of glacial decline for the city began. The advances in science and social organization that had gripped Europe during the Enlightenment passed İstanbul by, while at the same time, stripped of victories against foreign enemies, the Janissaries began to turn on their bosses back home. Palace coups in Topkapı became frequent.

Belatedly, efforts were made to reform the empire and make it more like its European rivals, which were by now chewing up Ottoman possessions at a great rate of knots. The Austro-Hungarians were

❏ The Ottomans

(Continued from p382)

In doing so, the empire also ended up with large numbers of non-Muslim, Christian or Jewish subjects.

As a result, within their boundaries, the Ottomans exercised a form of government that was quite unlike any other, before or since. The Sultan's subjects were organized not according to their ethnicity or race, but according to their religion. The Greek Orthodox Patriarch — the head of the Greek Orthodox Church — was established in İstanbul and charged with administering the affairs of the Greek Orthodox community. As time went by, Serb Orthodox, Bulgarian Orthodox, Jewish and Catholic communities were also given official recognition. The law was divided along religious lines too, with a Christian court trying Christians and a Muslim court trying Muslims. Christians and Jews were also excluded from military service, paying higher taxes instead.

For many centuries, the system produced a strange symbiosis between the empire's majority Muslims — who continued to control the army, the treasury and all the functions of imperial government — and the minority Christians and Jews, who came to control much of the empire's commerce. Greek merchants would sail under an Ottoman flag to trade with French and Italian ports, while the empire's Jewish subjects built Ottoman Thessaloniki into one of the Mediterranean's greatest entrepôts. Another group of merchants that were to have an impact well out of proportion to their size were the Levantines, Ottoman subjects of Italian descent, who established powerful trading and business dynasties in İzmir and İstanbul.

Yet relations were not always so good. The minorities still had no real political power and there were frequent revolts, often put down brutally. However, the wheels didn't really fall off until the 19th century, with the rise of nationalism and European and Russian imperialism. The Ottomans were also slow to adopt the changes of the industrial revolution, a major drawback for any imperial power in the age of iron and steam. By 1878, the Russian army had advanced through the Balkans as far as San Stefano (Yeşilköy), the İstanbul suburb where the present-day city airport now stands. Forced to withdraw, they nonetheless took great chunks of Ottoman territory with them. WWI saw the final dismemberment, the last Sultan leaving İstanbul at dead of night on a British warship in 1923, never to return.

Out of the ashes, the Turkish republic emerged, its modern, secular and nationalist shape in many ways at odds with its traditional, religious and polyglot past.

AEGEAN SEA

pushing down through the Balkans, as were the Russians, while the French and British helped themselves to chunks of nominally Ottoman territory in North Africa and the Middle East. Greece also broke away after a bitter war of independence, and nationalism spread rapidly amongst the empire's other subjects.

Mahmut II was brought up in Western style by his French mother who had been captured for the harem by Turkish corsairs. A great reformer, he broke the power of the Janissaries with his well-trained troops led by French officers. Then Abdul Mecit (1839-61) instituted the more liberal Tanzimat reforms. He moved the court to the Western-style palace of Dolmabahçe. By now the district of Beyoğlu, long the European quarter, had become a hive of activity, Western banks and companies moving in and buying up the Ottoman economy as the Empire sank into debt.

Russian victories in the Balkans also contributed to the city's — and the empire's — decline. After 1878 and the Russian's advance to Yeşilköy (see box above), the city — and the empire — became little more than bargaining chips between the various competing great powers. The two Balkan Wars of 1912-13 further diminished the empire's status, though they did bring the Young Turks — army-based reformers — to office. Their leader, Enver Pasha, then made the quite historic blunder of allowing the empire to be manoeuvred into joining the losing German-Austro-Hungarian side in WWI.

The war ended with İstanbul occupied by Britain, France and Italy. The Ottoman Empire ceased to exist in all but name, though the last sultan, Vadettin, continued as a puppet of the British until 1923, when he was whisked away aboard a British battleship for Malta, eventually spending his exile in Italy. The Turks finally managed to rally themselves under the leadership of an extraordinary man, Mustafa Kemal Atatürk, who led them first to victory over the Greeks, French and Italians, who had invaded much of Anatolia, and then the British, whom he manoeuvred out of İstanbul in 1923. Under Atatürk though, things would never be the same. Also a moderniz-er, he was a strong Turkish nationalist who saw no future in any religion-based state. As part of his measures, therefore, Atatürk moved the capital of his new country — Turkey — away to Ankara, in the heart of Anatolia, a move designed to emphasize that the new, secular, Turkish republic was far removed from the old, religious, cosmopolitan empire. It was a move that proved to be quite devastating for many İstanbulus though, who had been accustomed to seeing themselves as quite a cut above the 'Turks' of the rest of the country — a feeling many of them still have today.

The 1920s was also a period of mass migration, when many thousands of White Russians, fleeing the Bolshevik Revolution, settled in the city, along with thousands of Turks and other Muslims from Greece, forced out under the population exchange (see box on p284). İstanbul's Greeks were allowed to stay, however, and for many years continued to constitute a large minority within the city (in 1900, the population of İstanbul had been roughly 50% Muslim, 50% Christian or Jewish).

In WWII, Turkey was neutral, which gave the city something of a reputation for spying, with German, British, French and Italian agents lurking behind the potted palms in many a hotel lobby. The war over, the city gained a windfall from Cold War politics, with Turkey's membership of NATO leading to some US aid, much of which was spent on developing the city by the 1950s' prime minister Adnan Menderes. This involved widespread destruction of much of the İstanbul's old fabric and its replacement with roads and car parks. Menderes is also thought to have been behind the anti-Greek riots of the mid-1950s that led to the rapid departure of the city's large Greek community. Menderes himself ended up executed by the army, who launched a coup to remove him in 1960.

Instability followed, with violence common practice in daily political life. Another coup in 1971 did little to change things, and by the end of the 1970s, gun battles between left and right were daily occurrences, particularly around İstanbul University. In 1980, the military intervened again, arresting over 100,000 people. Many were tortured and killed in detention, their story still largely untold; indeed, officially at least the 1980 coup is still described as being 'welcomed by the broad mass of the population'.

The city underwent another major convulsion in the mid-1980s with the start of partial civilian rule. Under President Özal, a get-rich-quick policy was followed, with some largely uncontrolled and almost entirely unaudited market liberalization. Those around Özal grew enormous fortunes and built enormous hotels, housing estates and shopping centres — mostly without planning permission. The results of this are still there for all to see.

In the 1990s, the city continued to grow exponentially, as vast numbers of Anatolian Turks moved in looking for a way out of the growing rural poverty. Along with them came large numbers of Kurds, displaced by the war in the south-east of the country between Kurdish nationalists and the Turkish army. The result is a city that at times can seem perilously out of control. Yet it still functions as a city with a highly educated, technologically advanced and

Western-oriented élite, living amongst a largely rural-minded and poverty stricken majority. Its contradictions are wildly obvious yet, for all that, the fabric still somehow clings together. The people also still manage to be among the friendliest of any major urban settlement on Earth, and the crime rate is minimal.

And for a moment too, crossing the Bosphorus at sunset or looking down through the trees of Yildiz Park at the dark water below, it is also still possible to see that older city stretched along these ancient trade routes, and realize why it might once have deserved that title, *der saadet*, 'The Seat of Bliss'. For now, though, in amongst its urban growl and mass of buildings, perhaps the Greeks had it right after all: for this is very much The City.

WHAT TO SEE

What better place to start exploring İstanbul could there be than the centre of the world itself? The **Million Stone** marks the very spot at the bottom of Divan Yolu, the main drag up the hill from Aya Sofya square through Sultanahmet and beyond. Put up when Constantine declared this the new capital of the Roman Empire, it marked the central measuring point for everything else on the globe. East of it stands **Aya Sofya** (Tue-Sun 0930-1630, US$10), dedicated to Emperor Justinian in AD537, though with numerous add-ons now propping up its central dome. This was for centuries the greatest church in Christendom, the span of the central cupola — 30m — only beaten a thousand years later by the Süleymaniye Mosque — which is also in İstanbul.

Entering the building through what was once the Hall of the Warriors, the place where the emperor's bodyguards would line up while he was attending mass, you'll be stunned by the sheer enormous height of the building. The eye is pulled right up by the dome, floating high above and, less exhilaratingly, by the enormous amount of scaffolding now dominating the place. There is a column on the left-hand side as you enter which has magical, wish-fulfilling powers, rendered by way of putting your hand in a niche in its side. Look out, too, for the

mosaics, all only relatively recently uncovered. At the east end of the south gallery is an 11th-century working of Christ with the Byzantine Empress Zoe and her husband, Constantine IX, on either side.

While serving as a cathedral for most of its life, Aya Sofya — the Church of the Holy Wisdom — suffered great indignities at the hands of the knights of the Fourth Crusade, who trashed the place when they took the city in 1204. They also reputedly used it as a brothel, but presumably cleaned all that up when the Venetian doge, Enrico Dandallo, who had masterminded the assault on the city, had himself buried here a few years later. When the Byzantines reconquered the city his tomb — which is to the left of the entrance — was in turn trashed and his decomposed body thrown to the dogs.

Aya Sofya was also the place where the Byzantine Empire — and the Roman Empire too — was finally extinguished. On 29 May, 1453, when the Ottoman army of Mehmet the Conqueror had finally broken through the city's defences, the petrified population fled here, barricading themselves in behind the huge wooden and iron doors. It was a Sunday, and while the crowds packed in around the priests, they reputedly continued with their morning matins. Legend has it that when Ottoman soldiers finally broke down the doors and poured in, slaughtering most of the cowering inhabitants, the priests calmly collected up the sacred icons and chalices and vanished into the wall behind the altar. They're due to reappear when the building goes back to being a church and Byzantium rises again.

This, however, is unlikely to be any time soon, so ghostly apparitions are not to be feared. Instead, look now at the huge names of Allah, Mohammed and the prophets hung around the dome on shields by the Ottomans, who converted the place into a mosque, adding the four minarets outside and burying a number of eminent Ottoman sultans in the environs. Aya Sofya is thus a sacred site for Muslims, too, a fact which prompted Atatürk to call it quits and make it into a museum in 1934.

Back at the Million Stone, head for the municipal-lavatory-like building next door.

This is the entrance to the underground **Yerebatan Saray** (daily May-Oct 0900-1730, Nov-April 0930-1630, US$5), perhaps the most spectacular — and certainly the most accessible — of the network of huge water cisterns dug beneath the city streets of Constantinople to keep the population supplied with fresh water. This one was built in Justinian's time, yet lay forgotten after the Ottoman conquest, being rediscovered only in 1545 by the Frenchman Peter Gyllius. There are 336 columns, with the ones at the far end the most revealing — giant Medusa heads have been used as base plinths, probably ransacked by Justinian's men from even older pagan temples. The cistern is also the venue for concerts during summer, when its cool air is a welcome break from the furnace up above.

Opposite Aya Sofya is one of the city's other famous landmarks, the 1603 **Blue Mosque** (daily 0900-1700, free). Also known as the Sultanahmet Mosque, from the outside it is a building of wonderful grace and beauty — something architecturally lacking on the inside, given its huge supporting pillars. Nonetheless, it is still an impressive sight, with some marvellous decorative Iznik tile-work and the stone near the rocket-like pulpit, or mimbar. Legend has it that it is in fact two stones, brought here from separate corners of the empire and which miraculously slotted perfectly together.

The Blue Mosque is also the venue for a Sound & Light show at dusk, the programme available in the waiting area outside. To the right of the mosque's main entrance is the **Hippodrome**, the main venue in the Roman and Byzantine cities for games, chariot races and riots. The looping roadway runs along the same course as the ancient track, and at the western end some of the stadium's walls can still be seen. In the central spina, now a park, are a number of monuments — starting with a fountain presented by the German Kaiser Wilhelm I at the Aya Sofya end. There's also an Egyptian column taken from the Temple of Karnak; the Serpent column, a twister of bronze stolen from the Temple of Apollo at Delphi and hacked in two by a

drunken Polish nobleman a couple of centuries back; and the Column of Constantine, looking a lot the worse for wear after its coating of precious metals was ripped off by the Fourth Crusaders.

On the northern side of the Hippodrome is the **Museum of Turkish and Islamic Art** (Tue-Sun 0900-1630, US$3), housed in the 16th-century palace of Ibrahim Pasha, Grand Vizier to Süleyman the Magnificent. This is a well-planned and labelled affair, particularly interesting for its carpet displays that show the development from the chunky Seljuk kilims to the elaborate and ornate late Ottoman pieces.

Moving on, down the hill on the seaward side of the Blue Mosque, at 103 Torun Sokak, is the **Mosaic Museum** (Tue-Sun 0930-1630, US$2.50). Inside is a massive decorative pavement from the Great Palace — the Roman/Byzantine complex that once sprawled all over the southern side of the Sultanahmet Peninsula. This mosaic, dating from Justinian's time and covered with animals and mythological scenes, is one of the few major survivors of this once mighty ruin. A large part of the palace's ruins, buried under the ground for centuries, have been destroyed by developers in only relatively recent times.

Keep going west from here and in Kücük Ayasofya Caddesi you'll find the delightful **Little Aya Sofya Mosque** — which prior to 1453 was the Church of St Sergius and Bacchus, the patron saints of the Christianized Roman army. Inside is a fine frieze featuring Justinian and the Empress Theodora.

A short hop from here down the hill towards the water leads you back onto the water-front road through remains of the old sea walls. Follow these back towards Aya Sofya and cut back through the walls up Ishak Paşa Caddesi for the Imperial Gate, the entrance to another of İstanbul's must-sees, **Topkapı Palace** (Wed-Mon 0930-1600, US$8, US$6 extra for the harem).

Built between 1459 and 1465, this palace was the centre of the empire for around four centuries. Within its walls, sultans, valide sultans (mothers of sultans)

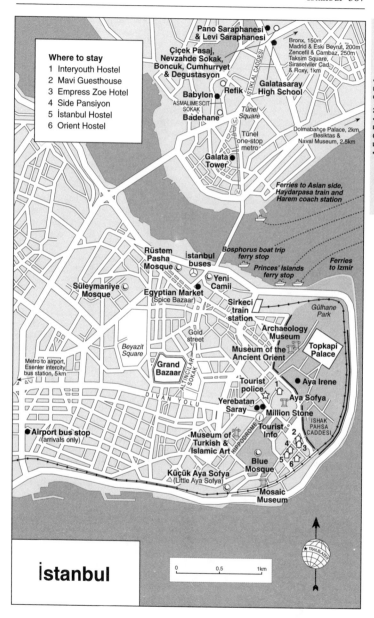

AEGEAN SEA

Where to stay
1 Interyouth Hostel
2 Mavi Guesthouse
3 Empress Zoe Hotel
4 Side Pansiyon
5 İstanbul Hostel
6 Orient Hostel

Pano Saraphanesi & Levi Saraphanesi

Çiçek Pasaj, Nevzahde Sokak, Boncuk, Cumhurryet & Degustasyon

Bronx, 150m
Madrid & Eski Beyrut, 200m
Zencefil & Cambaz, 250m
Taksim Square,
Siraselviler Cad,
& Roxy, 1km

Babylon

ASMALIMESCIT SOKAK

Refik

Galatasaray High School

İSTIKLAL CADDESI

Badehane

Tünel Square

Tünel one-stop metro

Dolmabahçe Palace, 2km,
Besiktas &
Naval Museum, 2.5km

Galata Tower

Ferries to Asian side,
Haydarpasa train and
Harem coach station

Rüstem Pasha Mosque

İstanbul buses

Bosphorus boat trip
ferry stop

Princes' Islands
ferry stop

Ferries
to İzmir

Süleymaniye Mosque

Yeni Camii

Egyptian Market
(Spice Bazaar)

Sirkeci train station

Gülhane Park

Gold street

Archaeology Museum

Museum of the Ancient Orient

Topkapi Palace

Beyazit Square

ALTINCILAR SOKAK

Grand Bazaar

Tourist police

Aya Irene

Aya Sofya

Metro to airport,
Esenler intercity
bus station, 5km

DIVAN YOLU

Yerebatan Saray

Million Stone

IŞHAK PAHSA CADDESI

Airport bus stop
(arrivals only)

Tourist Info

2

Museum of Turkish & Islamic Art

HIPPODROME

4

3

5 6

Küçük Aya Sofya
(Little Aya Sofya)

Blue Mosque

Mosaic Museum

İstanbul

0   0.5   1km

TRAILBLAZER

AEGEAN SEA

black and white eunuchs, grand viziers, harem girls, admirals, generals and janissaries all plotted, schemed and, more often than not, murdered their way either to greater glory or to a usually gruesome end. It is also a classic of Ottoman architecture and features some of the most spectacular of the empire's treasures, including some of Mohammed's whiskers.

First of all though, on passing through the main gate, on your left is **Aya Irene**, the only church in the city not to have been converted into a mosque after the Ottoman conquest. Nowadays it is sadly open only for concerts and other functions, but if you're lucky enough to be there when its great doors are open, try and slip inside. Built at the same time as Aya Sofya, for many years after the conquest it was used as an arsenal by the janissaries.

For the main palace, head straight on though for the ticket offices and the entrance through the Gate of Salutations. Note the Executioner's Fountain by the ticket office. The chief executioner washed his sword here after a morning's work, the pillars around the fountain being display areas for severed heads.

The Second Court on the other side of the Gate is bounded on the right-hand side by the Palace Kitchens, home now to a display of ceramic work. The Harem is off on the left, with a separate ticket office. You have to pay a US$6 supplement to enter this area and can do so only as part of a guided tour. Inside, you'll find an exhausting 300 rooms, along with courtyards, fountains and the very essence of the phrase 'gilded cage'. Most of the harem women were Christian or Jewish slaves, often given as gifts or tributes to the sultan. The Valide presided over choosing which were to be presented in the Sultan's bedchamber, with pregnancy a possible way for them to secure their position — provided they produced a son. However, as only one son could succeed to the throne, all the others were effectively living on borrowed time. On accession, in the early centuries the new sultan's brothers would all be ritually strangled. Later on, things became at least different, if not really more civilized, with the rival brothers confined to 'The Cage', a prison within the palace. Some would remain there for decades, brought out into the daylight, blinking and often half-mad, only on the assassination or death of the sultan.

The next gate, the Gate of Felicity, leads through to the Audience Chamber, where visiting delegations, foreign ambassadors and petitioners would present themselves. The neighbouring Imperial Treasury is also a must see, containing as it does the famous Topkapı dagger, along with handfuls of precious stones all encrusted on Korans, chain mail and swords. Opposite is the Chamber of the Mantle of the Prophet, containing many holy relics swiped by Selim the Grim after his 1517 invasion of Egypt. There is a mantle given by Mohammed to the poet Ka'b ibn Zuheyr, along with the Prophet's main battle flag and a letter from Mohammed to the Egyptian Coptic ruler, Carih bin Metel Kibti. There are also a set of Mohammed's footprints and two of his swords.

Continuing to the final courtyard, the views open out, with the Bosphorus running down the right-hand side and the Golden Horn spurring off to the left. From the Baghdad Kiosk the sultans could look out on the city, an often hostile place in truth, and it's worth doing the same from the terrace. This is the only place in İstanbul where the Golden Horn becomes such a central feature of the view, underscoring the different perspective the imperial court would have had from that of ordinary mortals. On the other side of the terrace, the Mecidiye Pavilion is now a restaurant, with a great terrace.

Down the hill from Topkapı is the city **Archaeology Museum** (Tue-Sun 0900-1630, US$4) and the **Museum of the Ancient Orient** (Tue-Sun 0900-1630, US$2). The main attraction at the former is the collection of sarcophagi from the royal necropolis at Sidon in modern-day Lebanon. These date from the sixth to the fourth centuries BC, peaking with the 4th-century BC Alexander Sarcophagus, a beautifully worked tomb showing Alexander the Great's victory at the 333BC battle of Issus on its sides. The Museum of the Ancient Orient recently reopened following a face lift and now holds a well thought out, if small, collection of artefacts from Anatolia and beyond.

From here, the road curves down through **Gülhane Park** and on to the waterfront at Sirkeci. This is where ferries depart for the Asian side, the Bosphorus boat tour (see p391) and for the Princes' Islands (see p390). Follow the Golden Horn up from here to the **Yeni Cami**, the New Mosque, which was started in 1598, but not finished until 1663.

Next door is the **Egyptian Market**, also known as the Spice Bazaar, constructed at the same time as the Yeni Cami and an atmospheric collection of aphrodisiac sellers and spice specialists. West of here lies **Rüstem Paşa Mosque**, a delight of Iznik tiles inside, while up the hill is the densely-crowded and totally essential bazaar area. This warren of streets sells everything from jeans to shotguns, and pirate VCDs to Turkish Delight. Finding your way around is well nigh impossible, but try to keep going upwards for the **Grand Bazaar** itself, known as the Kapalı Çarşı, the Covered Market.

Within this are the Old Bedestan and the Sandal Bedestan, 15th-century strongholds around which the rest of the market developed. This was once the richest market in the Mediterranean, and in most of the Western hemisphere too, with traders coming from China, Africa, Europe and South Asia to bargain and barter. Now, it's also a strongly atmospheric place. Look out for the **Altincilar Sokak** entrance. This holds a tiny street down which Turkey's currency market operates. In the days of recent financial crisis, billions of dollars were traded by the brokers here, far outstripping the activities of the official financial market.

At the top of the hill, the market gives out onto **Beyazıt Square**, the former Forum Tauri, the main market area of the Roman city. Here is the grand 19th-century gateway to İstanbul University, formerly the site of the Ottoman War ministry, and before that the Eski Saray, the pre-Topkapı Ottoman headquarters. Behind here you'll find the city's greatest architectural wonder though, the **Süleymaniye Mosque**. Finished in 1557, this is the master-

work of Mimar Sinan, the empire's most gifted architect. Its dome surpasses Aya Sofya's in size, but the most important achievement here is that the whole thing is held up by only four columns — freeing up much more space and getting away from the cramped feel of previous domed efforts. The effect here is marvellous, with a light airiness to the interior that makes it all look easy — a mark of real genius; it's also a great place to rest what by now are probably extremely weary feet.

Galata, Beyoğlu and Beşiktaş

Across the Golden Horn, the city's old European quarter rises up the hill around the 1348 Genoese **Galata Tower** (daily 0900-1900, US$4). This was the kingpin of the old defences of Galata and thus dates from a time when this area was independent of Byzantium, just across the water; it remained neutral, for example, during the 1453 siege.

The view from the top is worth seeing, while a stroll in the streets from the tower up towards Tünel Square reveals many relics of this district's once-vibrant multi-ethnic community. Another way to get from the Golden Horn to Tünel is via the one-stop, 1876 underground railway. The entrance is on Yuzbasi Sabahattin Evren Caddesi, with jetons used as tickets bought from a ticket office inside.

Emerging at the top, you are at one end of a great İstanbul institution, **İstiklal Caddesi**. Once the grand rue de Pera, this is a pedestrianized, Ramblas-style street, with 19th-century trams running its length. Here you'll find a thousand and one bars, restaurants, clubs, cinemas and bookshops, with the street heaving on a weekend or evening. At the other end is Taksim Square, with a monument to the victory of Atatürk and the new republic, along with a local bus station and the stop for the airport coaches.

At the eastern end of the square, at the top of Gumussuyu Caddesi, dolmuş run down the hill to Dolmabahçe and Beşiktaş. **Dolmabahçe Palace** (Tue, Wed & Fri-Sun 0900-1600, US$8 Selamlik, US$8 harem, or US$12 for both) was built at a time when the Ottoman Empire was well advanced in

AEGEAN SEA

terms of its decline and when 19th-century architecture was at its heaviest and most unappealing. Nevertheless, it remains a notable place to visit simply because of its fruit-trifle-with-all-the-trimmings excess. Here the final drama of the empire was played out, as the last sultan was whisked away from its jetty to exile by the British in 1923, the British themselves leaving from here a few months later.

Divided by high walls into a selamlik for the men and a harem for the women, guided tours are compulsory, a spectacularly unedifying experience as each of its hundreds of almost identical rooms is painstakingly described to you. The one room of interest is that in which Atatürk died, in 1938, an event still commemorated by the blowing of sirens on the Bosphorus ferries on the anniversary.

From here, it's a short hop to Beşiktaş and the **Naval Museum** (Wed-Sun 0930-1230, 1330-1730, US$1). The main building contains Barbarossa's battle flag (see box on p92), interesting for its combination of Christian cross, Jewish Star of David and Muslim Crescent. Outside in the grounds is the mangled hulk of a WWI German U-boat, while in an adjoining building are several graceful caiques, barges used by sultans and the wealthy to ferry themselves about the city behind banks of oarsmen.

The Princes' Islands
Known as Prinkipio in Byzantine times, this scattering of small islands lying in the Marmara off İstanbul represents a welcome break from the hustle of the big city. Ferries from Sirkeci go several times a day, calling at each of the main islands before returning. The trip takes about an hour and costs US$4.

The largest island is **Büyükada** which, like the others, still maintains a strong Greek and Armenian presence. Its beautiful old wooden mansions are best looked around by horse-drawn phaeton — there are no cars allowed on any of the islands. Take one of these up to the foot of the island's main hill and walk for about 20-25 minutes to the top. There you'll find **St George's Monastery**, with spectacular views of the sea and a great restaurant. On the way up,

notice the thousands of pieces of cloth and string tied to the bushes — each is a wish, and if you try this walk in the heat of summer, you might want to make one or two yourself. Büyükada was also home to Russian revolutionary Leon Trotsky, exiled here by Stalin in 1929. His house is at 55, Çankaya Caddesi.

Of the other islands, **Burgazada** is recommended, particularly the walk round from the port to the far side, with the road terminating in an excellent restaurant with good views out over the sea. This eatery also has a statue of the writer Sait Faik, who lived here towards the end of his life. Swimming is possible on the leeward side of these islands, which are somewhat sheltered from the pollution churned out by the city.

PRACTICAL INFORMATION
Orientation
Most people arrive in İstanbul by air. The **airport**, named after the ubiquitous Atatürk, is some 25km west of the city centre at Yeşilköy. Options for getting to the city centre are: taxi (20-25 mins, around US$15) to Sultanahmet — try to round up a group to share one if you can — or service bus, 30-40 mins, US$4. The latter (operated by Havaş) leaves every 30 minutes from in front of the arrivals hall and goes to Bakırköy, then Aksaray (for Sultanahmet), Sishane and Taksim. The first bus to the airport from Taksim leaves at 0600, the last bus out 22:50. If you arrive after that, still head for the Havaş bus stop as, if there's enough of you, they may lay on an extra service.

It's some distance to the main city-bus station at Esenler, though Havaş service buses go there from the airport once an hour (US$3), starting around 0600 and finishing around 2300. Otherwise, a taxi will get you there for around US$8. At Esenler there are dozens of ticket agencies ready to sell you a seat on coaches to almost anywhere in Turkey.

Arriving by **train** is less problematic, as the railway station, Sirkeci, is right at the bottom of the hill leading up to Sultanahmet. There's a tram going up the hill, with tickets available from the kiosk next to the stop outside the station. They cost a flat US$0.50. A taxi up there should be no more than US$1, though the taxi drivers outside Sirkeci station are rip-off merchants, marginally eclipsed in their tourist gouging only by those hanging round outside Aya Sofya.

Arriving by boat, you'll dock just inside the spectacular entrance to the Golden Horn and right beneath the walls of Topkapı Palace. From here, it's a 5-minute walk to Sirkeci (see above), or a longer, 15-minute walk in the opposite direction, round the headland and into Sultanahmet. A taxi this way should be no more than a dollar.

İstanbul is a relatively easy city to get around in for the tourist. If you're staying in Sultanahmet, all the main historical sights and most of the museums are within a 10-minute walk of each other. To the east, the Golden Horn divides the district off from Galata, Beyoğlu and Taksim, the main entertainment district, while to the south the Bosphorus and the Marmara divide it off from the Asian side.

Most of the city ferry services dock around Sirkeci and neighbouring Eminönü, from where boats leave for Beşiktaş, the Bosphorus boat tour, the Princes' Islands and the Asian shore. They're frequent, reliable and a real city institution, being mostly old 1950s' Glasgow shipyard relics. A flat US$0.60 fee buys you a jeton, a metal disc, which you use in the machines to get onboard, with these valid for every trip except the Bosphorus tour and the islands (see the relevant section for details).

There's also the **city-bus** system, which covers the whole metropolis, day and most of the night, again on a flat US$0.60 fee basis. Tickets can be bought from newspaper kiosks or special IETT portacabins in the main bus stations. There's also the dolmuş, a shared minibus, which departs when full. These charge a variety of prices depending on the distance to be covered.

There are also now two metros. One, the world's shortest, runs from Taksim but doesn't go anywhere useful for tourists but is quite funky. A second one now goes from the airport to Aksaray. Typically, the two lines don't join together.

Services
The **tourist information** office (☎ 518

8754), on Divan Yolu, Sultanahmet Square, is open daily 0900-1700. The **tourist police** (☎ 527 4503), Yerebatan Caddesi (opposite the cistern), are open 24hr. For a **post office** look for the sign PTT; the main one (worth a visit just for the late Ottoman design), on Yeni Postane Caddesi, Sirkeci, is open daily 0900-1730. Buy **phone cards** from newspaper kiosks of PTTs — they are far cheaper than the numerous private telephone offices around town.

Turkey has probably more **internet cafés** per head of population than anywhere else in the Mediterranean. There are thousands, though most are filled wall-to-wall with blokes blasting monsters. Try Blue Internet Café, 54, Yerebatan Cad, or in Tünel, Yagmur, 18, Seyh Bender Sokak, near Babylon.

Both Haydarpaşa and Sirkeci railway stations have **left-luggage** facilities. Look for the sign Emanet.

Most kiosks in the areas mentioned here have the *Turkish Daily News* and its rival the *Turkish News*, both **English-language papers**. The monthly *Time Out* is the İstanbul branch of the London/New York listings guide and does an English-language supplement. Otherwise, there's the *İstanbul Guide*, which comes out quarterly and similarly provides **listings** as well as a few features. For up-to-the-minute **news** on Turkey, try the website 🖳 www.ntvmsnbc. com, updated several times a day and with a news in English section.

Ferries   [see p454 for full details]
Boats run back and forth across the Bosphorus every 10 or 20 seconds, but for more major excursions there are a number of useful vessels.

First of these is the Turkish Maritime Lines (TML, ☎ 244 0207) ferry to **İzmir** (weekly, 19 hours). TML also go to **Avsar** (weekly, 6 hours, US$4) and from June to September to **Armutlu** (weekly, 3 hours, US$2). TML also run out to the Black Sea ports — Samsun, Trabzon and Rize (weekly, 15 hours to Samsun, 30 hours Trabzon, 34 hours Rize, US$10 Pullman to Trabzon, US$15 cheapest bunk, meals not included). All these ferries depart from Saraybrunu, beneath Topkapı Palace at the entrance to the Golden Horn.

Also handy are the fast **catamaran services** from Yenikapi, known as sea buses or Deniz Otobus (☎ 516 1212). These go every few hours to Yalova and Bandirma on the Asian side of the Marmara, with the latter useful as Bandirma has a regular bus service south to İzmir.

One other must-do of İstanbul is to catch the **Bosphorus ferry**, which departs daily from Eminönü, stops at Beşiktaş and then ping-pongs up the channel to Anadolu Kavaği at the mouth of the Black Sea. There it stops for three hours before heading back. The trip takes around three hours and costs US$6.

Trains

From Haydarpaşa, the Asian-side railway station, trains leave for Pamukkale every day, but not really anywhere else useful for this guidebook. Bizarrely, the Pamukkale train goes within a few miles of İzmir, but does not stop there. Instead, to get to Turkey's third largest city, catch the Eskişehir train and then transfer onto the Ankara–İzmir express. This isn't really recommended for anyone other than ardent rail buffs, though, as the inter-city buses are quicker and much more frequent. Tickets are reliably available only from the stations.

Buses

The city has two inter-city bus terminals. For destinations in Europe, Esenler is the main venue, while for places in Anatolia, Harem, near Kadıköy on the Asian side, is the place. Turkey has easily the best coach service of any country in Europe or the Middle East, with buses departing for just about everywhere day and night. Prices are usually pretty low too. Tickets can be bought from the travel agents on Sultanahmet, or from the offices of the bus companies themselves. Try the top end of Gumussuyu Caddesi in Taksim for most, or at the bus stations. Esenler is on the metro from Aksaray, a ticket costing US$0.60. Most companies run service buses out to the stations from their in-town ticket offices. To get to Harem, catch any of the Kadıköy or Uskudar ferries

and it's a short hop by taxi — about US$1 from either. It is possible to get buses to Asian destinations from the European side too, but if you catch them at Harem you cut out the possibility of spending hours in traffic jams as the coach attempts to cross the Bosphorus bridges. Esenler is also the venue for buses to the Balkans and Greece, with direct routes to Sofia, Skopje, Pristina, Sarajevo, Belgrade and Athens, the latter via Alexandroupolis and Thessaloniki.

Planes

Turkish Airlines (THY) operate regular and frequent domestic services to İzmir, Bodrum, Dalaman and Antalya, while along with Cyprus Turkish Airlines they fly to northern Cyprus. Tickets are available from any of the travel agents in Sultanahmet along Divan Yolu; try Pacific Travel, next to the tram stop, ☎ 512 3050. THY's main reservation service is on ☎ 663 6300.

Where to stay

There are dozens of pensions and hotels in the Sultanahmet district, particularly down the hill towards the sea from the Blue Mosque. Prices are usually negotiable, with large reductions possible out of season.

Interyouth hostel (☎ 513 6150, 🖵 www.yucelhostel.com), 6/1, Caferiye Sokak. Official HI hostel near Aya Sofya, with dorm beds for US$7.50.

Side Pansiyon (☎ 517 6590, 🖵 www.sidehotel.com), 20, Utangaç Sokak. Has good sea views and sgl/dbl from US$20/30.

Mavi Guesthouse (☎ 516 5878, 🖵 www.maviguesthouse.com), 3, Kutlugün Sokak, off Ishak Paşa Caddesi. A favourite with backpackers; US$15/25 sgl/dbl and space on the terrace for US$5.

Istanbul Hostel (☎ 516 9380, 🖵 www.istanbul-hostel.com), 35, Kutlugün Sokak. A friendly place; US$10/15 sgl/dbl.

Orient Hostel (☎ 517 9493, 🖵 www.hostels.com/orienthostel), 13, Akbıyık Caddesi. Has a women-only dorm, along with an excellent terrace and backpacker clientele. Dorm beds for US$8, sgl/dbl US$19/35.

Empress Zoe (☎ 518 2504), 10, Adliye Sokak, is a cut above the others, with higher prices but beautiful décor and a cool roof bar — good for a cold beer and a view even if you're not staying there; US$55/75 sgl/dbl.

Camping is for masochists only given the low price of hostel and pension accommodation but if you insist try **Londra Camping** (☎ 560 4200), next to the lorry park in Londra Asfalti, after Ataköy, 16km from Taksim Square on the No 73 bus route.

Where to eat

The best places for liveliness and low prices are around Beyoğlu. The Cicek Pasaj, opposite Galatasaray High School, is worth wandering through but don't stop till you get to Nevzahde Sokak, round the back. There you'll find several streets jammed with tables where you can sample the fine institution of the *meyhane*, a restaurant serving mezes, main courses and alcohol. Prices and menus here are much the same, but some slightly different ones are:

Boncuk, one of the oldest, also serving traditional Armenian mezes; US$7.50 a head.

Degustasyon, back in the Balık Pazar area of the pasaj — the fish market at the bottom end. Popular with expats and locals, and starring a Turkish TV celebrity chef. Again, around US$7.50.

Cumhuriyet, next door to Degustasyon. One of the oldest round here and a venue for republicans since later Ottoman days, now popular with more aged media hacks and '68 generation oldies; US$10 a head.

Elsewhere around Beyoğlu you'll find that rarity — vegetarian restaurants. **Zencefil**, 3, Kurabiye Sokak, has fine salads and soya beans for around US$10. Opposite, try **Deep** — not for veggies, but for an excellent fish and chips (US$10 a head).

Back towards Tünel, Asmalimescit Sokak is the main street nowadays for eats; try **Badehane**, in an alley near Tünel Pasaj 5, General Yazgan Sokak, for some interestingly improvised fare, maybe US$5 a head, amongst an arty, bohemian crowd. **Refik**, 10-12 Asmalimescit is also arty, but a more traditional meyhane at US$10 a head.

Fast food is also everywhere, with many kiosks, buffets and small stalls selling kebabs for around US$1. Also try gozleme,

another street dish, a square of pastry stuffed with potato, cheese or meat and sold for around a US$1.

Bars

Again, you're looking at Beyoğlu for the real thing. There are so many bars in the district now, a full list of even the good ones would take many pages, so here are some highlights:

Madrid, 16, Ipek Sokak, is a major institution, with a divey atmosphere, loud music and lots of beer drinking. Popular with students, English teachers and anyone else short of a few bob.

Eski Beyrut, 28/2, Imam Adnan Sokak, similar to the Madrid.

Cambaz, 2, Haci Ahmet Sokak; go up the unsignposted stairs to the third floor for a lively bar and in summer to the roof for an equally lively terrace.

Pano Saraphanesi, 8, 1368 Sokak, is opposite the British consulate. If it's too crowded there's a duplicate version a few doors back towards Galatasaray at the Levi saraphanesi. Pricier than the above, with stand-up, beer-hall décor in a 120-year-old, former Greek wine house.

Clubs

Siraselviler Caddesi, off Taksim Square, has a fine crop of these clubs, while the rest of Beyoğlu is also pretty good for music, drinking and dancing.

Babylon, off Asmalimescit Sokak at 3, Seybender Sokak. Dead pricey club/venue and also hip, with some excellent acts and world-class DJs.

Bronx, in Yeşilcam Sokak, round the corner from the Sinepop and Emek cinemas. Entrance fee (US$3.50) includes a drink. Friday and Saturday nights in particular are good for live bands with a hard, punky edge.

Roxy, 113, Aslanyatagi Sokak, off Siraselviler. US$5 to get in, but usually good music and atmosphere.

AEGEAN SEA

Introduction

For Europeans, the Eastern Med was long one of the world's most exotic regions, the mysterious Levant. Caravans carrying precious cargoes from Asia and the Far East would arrive at its coastal entrepôts, with fortunes to be made from trade and adventure. It was also for many centuries the border zone between the Muslim world and the Christian one. As such, it has also long been fought over, from the Arab invasions of the 7th and 8th century to the Crusades, a disputed land between European empires, and in more recent times, the scene of terrible conflicts in Cyprus, Lebanon and Palestine.

Yet for all that, it is usually safe for tourists, has some of the best sights in the Mediterranean open to the visitor, along with some of the best beaches and most exhilarating cities.

TRAVELLING AROUND THE EASTERN MEDITERRANEAN

Historically, Cyprus has been of crucial importance when it comes to travelling by sea around the Levantine coasts. However, ferry services in the Mediterranean are very much affected by politics. As an example, the civil war in Lebanon in the 1970s-80s led to the opening of a regular ferry route from Limassol to the Christian ports north of Beirut, as the airport was unsafe. With the war's end, though, the service was cancelled and the only ferry services currently operating from its ports are those from Girne/Kyrenia (Northern Cyprus)

❑ **Eastern Mediterranean – the highlights**
● **Beirut** – Fast and furious in rebuilding and forgetting, expensive and often annoying but somehow always compelling, Beirut is a stunning blend of cultures and characters.
● **Alexandria** – The Grand Old Lady of the 19th-century Eastern Med. Little of its ancient grandeur remains, though a stroll along the corniche with people-watching breaks in an Egyptian coffee house, French café or British bar is still a must-do.
● **Girne/Kyrenia (Cyprus)** – An unexpected gem on the Northern Cypriot coast, its tiny harbour of old Venetian houses and sturdy British colonial architecture gives it a distinctive air.
● **Karpaz Peninsula (Cyprus)** – One of the few really unspoilt coastlines on the island. Get there before the developers to savour miles of sandy beaches, abandoned coves and rolling hills.
● **Beka'a Valley (Lebanon)** – With the temples of Baalbek and the getaways of Zahle and Aanjar, the valley is a great place for both ancient history and modern gastronomy. Lebanese wine is also worth a shot, with the vineyard of Ksara the oldest and best.

to Alanya and Taşucu (Turkey). Even the long-running Piraeus–Rhodes–Limassol–Haifa ferry service has been suspended at the time of writing due to the situation in Israel. As a result, the main options for sea travel round this region are the many mini cruises from Limassol to Egypt, Lebanon and the Greek islands. It is hoped, however, that the ferry services will start up again during the life of this book – it is always worth checking.

Because of the limited ferry services we have not suggested any itineraries for the Eastern Med, for it is likely that forms of transport other than boats and ferries will feature prominently in any tour of this region. It is possible to travel by land from Beirut through Syria to Turkey, though you need a Syrian visa before going to Lebanon, and from Syria you can head south to Jordan and from there to Israel and Palestine, from where you can go east into the Sinai and Egypt. Furthermore, from both Cairo and Beirut there are regular flights to most other Mediterranean capitals.

Eastern Mediterranean – ports and islands

Alanya

AREA CODE: ☎ 0242 **POPULATION:** 250,000
Sprawled out on either side of a rocky headland, Alanya has grown rapidly in the last two decades from a sleepy backpacker venue to a tourist megalopolis. With two fine sandy beaches and good weather guaranteed most of the year, it's still a fine place to stay for a while. It's also on a regular summer ferry route to North Cyprus, and well connected by bus to the rest of the country.

HISTORY
Known in ancient times as Coracesium, Alanya was once a centre of piracy. The corsairs were so successful hijacking ships that they even caused a famine in what was then Roman Anatolia (now largely modern-day Turkey) to an extent that the Roman Consul sent Pompey to drive them out in 67BC, before a lovestruck Mark Antony gave the place away to Cleopatra and her offspring. Many Egyptian warships were built from the pine forests along Alanya's shores.

In Byzantine times the town was known as Kolonoros, which means 'Beaut-

iful Mountain' in Greek, probably after the headland which the Seljuks subsequently fortified when they took the town in the 13th century. The Seljuk sultan Alaattin Keykubat renamed the place after himself. It grew in importance, being on a strategic trade route through to the Seljuk capital of Konya. It was also a favoured holiday place of the Seljuk sultans.

Under the Ottomans, the town continued as a port. In modern times, it was briefly part of Italy's largely unclaimed post-WWI Anatolian dominions, while in the later decades of the 20th century it came to be renowned as a tourist resort once again. Now it is becoming Antalya's main Mediterranean Turkey rival.

WHAT TO SEE
The main sight in Alanya is undoubtedly the **castle**. It's quite a walk to the top, particularly in summer when you should take some water for the one-hour trek. Alternatively, you could take the bus (hourly) from the tourist information office. A taxi costs around US$5. The road winds round and up out of the town and then through the still-inhabited old quarter of the fortress. Here, Ottoman houses lurk among

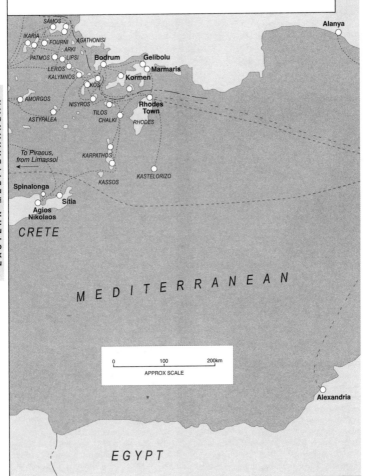

The Eastern Mediterranean

FERRY ROUTES

········· Ferry route   ---- Currently no service   -- -- Mini-Cruise

EASTERN MEDITERRANEAN

SAMOS
IKARIA
FOURNI   AGATHONISI
ARKI
PATMOS   LIPSI
Bodrum
Gelibolu
Marmaris
LEROS
KALYMNOS
Kormen
KOS
Alanya
AMORGOS
NISYROS
ASTYPALEA
TILOS
CHALKI
Rhodes Town
RHODES
To Piraeus, from Limassol
KARPATHOS
KASTELORIZO
KASSOS
Spinalonga
Sítia
Agios Nikolaos
CRETE

MEDITERRANEAN

0   100   200km
APPROX SCALE

Alexandria

EGYPT

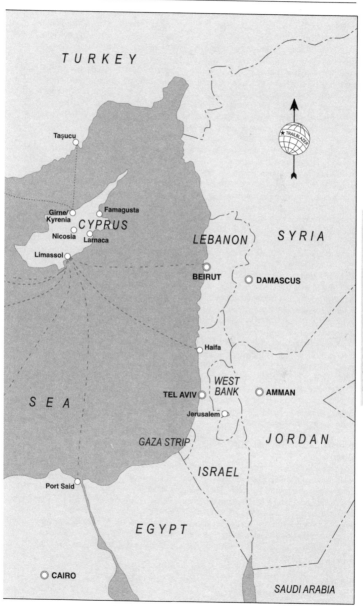

the bushes and trees before everything turns to scrub and the walls appear. The castle entrance (daily 0800-sunset, US$5) leads into the 1226 fortress. There you'll find the fortifications running out in several directions all over the peninsula, while within them is a Byzantine church, converted to a mosque by the Seljuks, and a cistern. The views are amazing. The **Adam Atacagi Tower** is some 250m above sea level, and it was from here that some prisoners were thrown to their deaths. These days it's known as a place to make a wish while throwing a small stone over the edge.

Down in the town, the main aim of most visitors is to get to a beach, the best of which is Kleopatra to the north-west. This long sandy stretch is lined with hotels and apartment houses but still makes a fine place to sprawl out in the sun. The other main tourist attraction is the **Damlatas Cave** (daily 0600-1000 for asthma sufferers only, 1000-sunset for the rest, US$1.50). This is behind the Damlatas restaurant just near the tourist information office on the western side of the headland. The cave is noted for relieving asthma sufferers, thanks to its damp, warm climate; it also has some fine stalactites and stalagmites.

Down in the port, visit the **Red Tower**, built in 1226 as part of the castle defences. Inside it is **Alanya Museum** (daily 0800-1200, 1330-1730, US$1) and next door is the **Tersane**, the shipyards Sultan Alaattin Keykubat built here two years after the Red Tower. These are the only Seljuk shipyards to have survived down the ages.

PRACTICAL INFORMATION
Orientation
The city unfolds on either side of the large, rocky headland, with Kleopatra Beach to the north and the harbour to the south. The roads mainly curve round the landward side of the headland, with only one going up to the top. Most of the places to stay, eat and see are in the central area of the headland. The bus station is 3km west of this centre, with regular dolmuş going to the centre (US$0.50).

Services
The **tourist information office** (☎ 513

1240) at Carsi Mahallesi, Kalearkasi, across from the Alanya Museum, has maps and some information on accommodation. For an **internet café** try Iskele Caddesi.

Ferries   [see p460 for full details]
From July to September there are three ferries a week to Girne/Kyrenia in Northern Cyprus. Contact Sun Tur (☎ 511 1527) or the tourist information office for details.

Buses
There are hourly buses to Antalya (2 hours, US$5), the main junction for other Turkish destinations. There are direct services to İstanbul (14 hours, US$20) daily, or indirect ones via Antalya. From Antalya you'll also find buses to Kaş, Marmaris, Bodrum and beyond. Unfortunately, you have to buy a new ticket each time you change buses so you can't book ahead. Getting a bus to your destination is usually not difficult as services are generally good across the country.

Heading east, there are eight buses a day to Adana (10 hours, US$15), via Taşucu, Silifke and Mersin. In Adana, there are daily connecting buses to Aleppo (Haleb in Turkish; 12 hours, US$30), in Syria. From Aleppo there are regular buses to Damascus and Beirut. Be advised that the nearest place to obtain a Syrian (and Lebanese) visa is Ankara, so it's probably better to sort this out before leaving home.

Planes
The nearest airports are Antalya and Adana, both of which have regular Turkish Airlines flights to Ankara and İstanbul.

Where to stay
Pension Best (☎ 513 0446), 23, Alaaddinoglu Sokak. A friendly stop near the centre, with sgl/dbl for US$10/17.50.
Pension Alanya (☎ 513 1897), 4, Nergis Sokak. Similar to the Best.
Hotel Oba (☎ 513 2675), 8, Meteoroloji Sokak. Further up in the direction of Kleopatra Beach; US$15/25 sgl/dbl.

Where to eat
Alanya's **bazaar area**, east of the centre around Hulumet Caddesi, has some good

options, though many get very busy with tourists, with prices escalating accordingly. There are many kebab shops for US$2 a go. Otherwise, try *Buhara*, on Kuyular Onu Sokak (US$7.50), or for a fish and seafood blow-out, *Mahperi Restaurant* (US$12) on the front by Gazi Paşa Caddesi.

Taşucu

AREA CODE: ☎ 0324 POPULATION: 10,000
There isn't a lot to say about Taşucu other than the Cyprus ferry docks here and it is a pleasant-enough place to while away a few hours before getting the bus or ferry out; its main venues are the bus station and the jetty. The Peace Park commemorates the 1974 Cyprus landings, in which Taşucu played a part as an embarkation point for Turkish troops.

PRACTICAL INFORMATION
Orientation
Once you've made it through customs you'll see the bus station immediately to the left of the terminal. The town itself is more to the right, with the Peace Park stretching along the shore. There's a small strip of beach, but keep walking away from the port as it gets less rubbish-strewn the further you go.

Ferries   [see p461 for full details]
There are daily hydrofoils to Girne/Kyrenia on Northern Cyprus. Tickets are on sale at the Kibris Express office in Taşucu's main square or from Ermal Denizcelik (☎ 741 4782). You will have to pay various miscellaneous items (such as port tax etc) and generally go through some formalities before getting on board. Keep a supply of million lira notes handy. The port authority is on ☎ 741 4004.

Buses
There are direct buses to İstanbul twice a day (16 hours, US$25) and Antalya four times a day (8 hours, US$15), via Alanya. To head east, catch one of the half-hourly dolmuş to Silifke bus station and then take an Adana-bound coach; these depart roughly every half-hour, take about two hours and cost US$5. From Adana there is a daily coach to Aleppo in Syria, from where there are connections to Damascus and Beirut.

Where to stay
Almost everyone leaves as soon as they can but a pleasant place to stay is *Lades Motel* (☎ 741 4008), 89, Atatürk Caddesi. Complete with swimming pool, it'll do you a decent B&B for US$25/35 sgl/dbl.

Where to eat
Denizkizi (Mermaid) Restaurant in the town square. For some good-value Turkish staples; US$5 a head.

Cyprus

To arrive in Cyprus is to set foot in a land of contradictions and stark contrasts, of fractured histories and beautiful land and seascapes. Part Greek, part Turkish, it has strong traces too of many old empires, from the Roman to the Venetian and the British. Looking at the map, it also becomes clear why so many people have coveted it over the years. Strategically located between Anatolia, the Middle East and North Africa, it has long been a vital way-station on the trade routes between Europe and the Levant.

At times, this has given Cyprus great wealth and power, while at others it has left it conquered and forlorn. Now de facto divided between the Greek-Cypriot dominated South and the Turkish-Cypriot North, it has increasingly become two countries, united only by a fading memory and a certain historical bitterness.

Yet at the same time, it remains a major tourist destination, at least in the South while the North has a strangely unspoilt quality, suspended in a diplomatic never-never land since a few hot and terrible days in the summer of 1974. However, all that may now be set to change, with membership of the European Union for the Greek south granted in May 2004. This has

EASTERN MEDITERRANEAN

put pressure on the North to reach a settlement and reunite the island, with some hope (as this book went to press) that this may happen soon. The result of this pressure is now visible in the North where, for the first time since 1974, signs in Greek have begun reappearing, along with long car convoys of Greek Cypriots taking advantage of a recent relaxation in the rules to visit their old birthplaces in the North.

HISTORY

The earliest settlements found on the island date back to 6800BC, making Khirokita, between Limassol and Larnaca, one of the oldest neolithic sites in the world. Later on, the island became known as a source for copper, the name Cyprus being derived from the ancient Greek/Latin words for this flexible metal. Greek colonists arrived during the 15th century BC, first from Mycenea, then

The Girne–Taşucu ferry

If you've ever wondered what happened to those mad game designers who came up with the ideas for the 1970s' TV series *It's a Knockout*, then you might be surprised to hear that the answer may lie on the route of the Girne–Taşucu ferry.

When the BBC finally decided it had had enough of foam baths and greasy racetracks, bizarre obstacle courses and giant inflatable jokers, these out-of-work designers must surely have found a new home in the Turkish and Turkish Cypriot customs departments. At least, that's how it has always seemed to me taking this hydrofoil, a craft that is otherwise perfectly seaworthy, fast and efficient.

Leaving Girne, it heads north-east for the 3-hour crossing, most often across a largely flat sea, with the last hour or so in sight of the Turkish coast. This it follows a few miles offshore, running along the ochre cliffs to the small, unassuming port of Taşucu.

Some years ago, I travelled this way. It happened to be the day of Princess Diana's funeral. During the whole voyage, the TVs in the main cabin had been relaying the Westminster Abbey service live – to the rapt attention of the passengers, who were mostly poorer Turkish families travelling to meet relatives and friends on the mainland.

By some quirk of fate, we arrived at the harbour, and the doors of the hydrofoil were flung open, just at the very point when the cathedral bells were rung. Not a single passenger moved, with the exception of myself, never a loyal fan of the royal family. Outside, I found the quayside deserted; a pretty empty experience in a small place like Taşucu. Then I realized that all around – from back on the boat, from the customs house at the end of the jetty and from the houses clustered up beyond – I could hear the bells as Westminster Abbey, over a thousand miles away, rang out the funeral toll. It was perhaps the first time this stretch of Anatolian coast had heard such an intrinsically Christian sound in centuries.

Yet perhaps it wasn't just fascination with the British royal family that had kept everyone glued to the screen back on board, for the Taşucu customs post is a scene straight from *Jeux Sans Frontières*. It goes like this: first, turn up with your ticket at the normal-looking entrance. Then get this stamped and proceed to the second kiosk; here, you must buy a small plastic token. Why? Because you need this plastic token to put in the turnstile, the turnstile that allows you along a narrow, iron-bannistered walkway to kiosk number three. There, you have to show that you have bought one of these plastic tokens by pointing to the relevant stamp in your documents (documents? You ask, what documents? WRONG! Back you go!

(Continued opposite)

later from Achaea. But the island had already embarked on its troubled career by then, with the Phoenicians, Egyptians and Persians all invading at one time or another before Alexander the Great took over in 333BC.

The Romans arrived in 58BC, with Christianity following a century later in the form of St Paul and St Barnabas, who converted the locals in AD45. With the collapse of the Western Empire, the island came under Byzantine rule until an Arab invasion in 647 began three centuries of Islamic rule. Recaptured finally in 963 by the Byzantine Emperor Nikiphoros Phocas, rule from Byzantium lasted until England's Richard the Lionheart, on his way to the Third Crusade, conquered in 1191. However, while conquering and slaying may have been Richard's forte, finance wasn't, and he found himself broke by 1192 and sold the

---

❏ The Girne–Taşucu ferry

(Continued from p400)

Of course, you now have to go back down the walkway, against the flow of people coming the other way. Then, of course, there's the turnstile. Naturally enough, it only turns one way, so there's no escape. By now, too, the flood of people carrying suitcases, bundles of clothes, chickens, chests of drawers and other paraphernalia is in full surge. The only way not to be swept back up the walkway to kiosk three is to climb up onto the iron bannister and swing round, jumping the turnstile and landing full square in front of a posse of disgruntled customs officials.

What you've done is, of course, simply not allowed. Under some arcane ruling of the 1922 criminal code, it may even be classed as an attempt to undermine Turkey's secular republic, carrying a fine that inflation has now reduced to the equivalent of £2.50, or 35 years (unaffected by inflation!) in jail: so grovel intensely.

If you're lucky, you just buy another plastic token and this time make sure you have the pieces of paper to say so. Then, back to kiosk number 3. By this time, any head start you may have had is but a bitter memory. Pushing and shoving amongst the surging crowd, you are after another piece of paper, naturally with a small fee attached, but you can finally and triumphantly head up the sloping concrete walkway to what appears to be the final hurdle. Yet at kiosk four, which involves circling snake-like along and around a series of other pathways, at one point bringing you back to within a few inches of where you started (but on the other side of an oh-so-important white tape) the quest is still not over.

You now, of course, require a visa. Stamps for this are available only from the visa issuing office, deep in the heart of the sinister looking warehouse – on the other side of the queue lines. It's one of those moments where some may simply break down and weep. To do so could be fatal though, as the crowd is surging around you and falling would lead inevitably to you being trampled under foot. The only way back is to look sharp for any watching customs officers, take your life in your hands, and duck nimbly under the white tape.

In the customs warehouse, the visa office is easy to spot thanks to the line of dodgy-looking foreigners queuing outside. By now, though, there is something almost relaxing about being amongst a bunch of Ukrainian hookers, Russian mafiosa and visa-tripping English teachers. Calmly, after handing over your £10 for the small pink visa sticker, a bored official slowly writes your name in a giant ledger, using an almost illegible biro. You're in. *Hoşgeldiniz.*

Such experiences can be rather character forming, I've heard some say.

EASTERN MEDITERRANEAN

island to the Knights Templar. They enjoyed no more success either, and sold it on to the recently made kingdomless Crusader king of Jerusalem, Guy de Lusignan. All these real estate deals were, naturally enough, conducted without any involvement from the people who actually lived there, the Greeks.

Guy did, however, found a dynasty that was to rule the island for the next three centuries. Nicosia became the capital, while Famagusta experienced a boom in trade that was to make it one of the richest cities in the world by the mid-Middle Ages. The key to its success was the thwarting of the papal rule following the fall of Acre in 1291 that forbade trade between Europeans and Muslims. The Christian Syrians were thus perfectly positioned to buy merchandise, and Famagusta, the closest port to the Syrian coast, was perfectly positioned to act as a halfway house for selling the goods on. Lusignan Cyprus flourished, or at least, the merchants and feudal Frankish lords did.

But the line eventually died out, with the last Lusignan, Queen Catherine Cornaro, manoeuvred into handing the island over to the Venetians in 1489. For the next 89 years, the banner of St Mark flew over an island that was about to prove that the power of Venice was no longer the force of old. Despite the Venetians building the awesome battlements and other defences around Nicosia and Famagusta, they could not stop the Ottomans, who took the island in 1571.

Under Ottoman rule, the island's strategic significance as the essential trading go-between vanished. It became just another of the Sultan's possessions in an eastern Mediterranean that was entirely Ottoman. The front line had shifted several hundred kilometres further west to Malta, while the opening up of the New World to European merchants was beginning to downgrade the status of Levant trading altogether. Cyprus went into a kind of hibernation, while at the same time the Ottoman colonial policy of physically settling Muslim, mainly Turkish, populations on captured soil led to the creation of the island's Turkish Cypriot population, moved onto the island from Anatolia.

Thus things remained until the Ottoman Empire itself began to collapse in the 19th century. In exchange for British help in repelling a Russian threat to İstanbul in 1878, Cyprus was leased to Britain, who saw it as a potentially useful base from which to guard the approaches to the Suez Canal, 350km to the south. With Britain and the Ottomans at war in WWI, Britain annexed the island, formally making it a colony in 1923.

The expectation among the Greek population was that Britain would then give the island its independence. Yet on the war's successful conclusion, the British found the island far too important to hand over. Agitation for independence continued among the Greek population and an armed struggle broke out in 1955.

Leading this were the right-wing Greek nationalist guerrillas of EOKA. Led by General Grivas, a hero of Greece's anti-communist forces during the Greek civil war, they embarked on a campaign of assassination and sabotage that would continue for the best part of five years. Its aim was to force the British out and join Cyprus to Greece. These aims were not widely supported by the island's Turkish Cypriot population who feared ethnic cleansing if EOKA got its way. By 1960, the British withdrew, while maintaining the 'Sovereign Base Areas'. The island became the independent Republic of Cyprus.

From the beginning though, the new country was unstable. EOKA had fought to join Greece (a plan known as 'enosis'), not to set up their own state. For their part, the Turkish Cypriot population had little faith in the new regime and complained of discrimination, while some agitated for partition of the island between Greece and Turkey. By 1964, these stresses and strains had broken out into open warfare, resulting in UN intervention and a ceasefire.

Despite this sobering background, a kind of peace then came that allowed the Cypriot economy to grow strongly, with places such as Famagusta taking off as international holiday resorts. But the underlying political tensions remained, breaking to the surface a decade later.

In July 1974, the Greek military government of the time sponsored a coup against the Cypriot leader, Archbishop Makarios, aimed at deposing him and joining the island to Greece. Carried out by an ultra-right wing Greek Cypriot group, EOKA-B, the coup was botched, with an attack on the archbishop's palace in Nicosia failing as the wily archbishop scrambled out of a back window and escaped.

A bloodbath followed, with fighting between pro and anti-coup Greek Cypriots, an attempt by EOKA-B to ethnically cleanse the Turkish Cypriots and then, finally, a Turkish invasion.

Thousands of Greek Cypriots who had lived in the north, where the Turkish troops landed, fled to the south, while thousands of Turkish Cypriots who had lived in the south fled to the north. UN troops established a ceasefire, and until 2003, this was largely how things stood. In 1983, the north declared independence as the Turkish Republic of Northern Cyprus, though only Turkey recognized it.

However, after dozens of UN plans aimed at reunification had failed, in 2003 the Turkish Cypriots opened the border to all Cypriots, allowing many to visit homes they had last seen 29 years before. In 2004, negotiations began to try and finally end the division, which were still in progress as this book went to print.

ORIENTATION

The Northern (Turkish) third of the island is divided from the South by the Green Line, the unofficial border. The name comes from the colour of the pencil used by a British army officer to map the final ceasefire line in 1974. Crossing this line from North to South is forbidden by the Greek Cypriots, though you are permitted to cross from the South to North, but only for a limited period (usually 12 hours), only via the Hotel Ledra Palace border gate in Nicosia and only if you take no luggage with you.

Otherwise, getting around within each part is relatively straightforward. In both the South and North there are frequent dolmuş between all the main towns, the difference being that in the North you go to the dolmuş, while in the South the dolmuş comes to you. Hitch-hiking is easy in both parts, and the roads are generally in good condition. Hiring scooters and cars is also an option.

In the South, ferries depart from Limassol, planes from Larnaca. In the North, the ferry port is Girne/Kyrenia, and the airport Ercan, east of Nicosia. There are no bus services to or from either airport so you'll have to take a taxi or hitch; Ercan is particularly difficult in this regard as it's miles from anywhere, so a taxi can be very expensive (US\$20 to Girne) but hitching from the airport entrance is very easy.

LIMASSOL (GR: LEMESOS)
AREA CODE: ☎ 25 **POPULATION:** 82,000

Known in Greek as Lemesos, this ancient and venerable port lies on the great arching bay of Akrotiri in the south-west of the island. As a port of arrival from Rhodes, Beirut, Haifa or Port Said, it is a fairly low-rise introduction to the island, with a long sprawl of buildings heading east from the harbour, 5km from town. Up behind and some way inland are the Trodos Mountains, while the bay curves south-west to the pancake-flat Akrotiri Peninsula where there is a British air force base and a large salt lake.

History

A small market town between the major Greek and Roman settlements at Curium and Amathus, Limassol came to the limelight in 1191 when Richard the Lionheart landed here to conquer the island (the Third Crusade). Defeating the forces of the Byzantine ruler, Isaac Angelus of the House of Commeni, he married Berengaria of Navarre (in the chapel of the town fortress) to cement his alliance with Philip of France.

With the collapse of Crusader fortunes in the Holy Land and the fall of Acre in 1291, Limassol came under the guardianship of evacuee Knights Hospitaller and Templar (see p402). They then left, after which the Genoese levelled the place in 1373, with just enough time for a rebuild before the Arabs levelled it again in 1426. Earthquakes also added their share of woe, reducing the place to virtual insignificance by the time the Ottomans landed in 1571. Nonetheless, it

EASTERN MEDITERRANEAN

was still a useful anchorage, located on the routes to and from the Levant, though these too grew less and less significant from the 19th century. In 1815 the population was down to 150.

Under British control, the port did begin a revival thanks to its usefulness as a stopping-off place before the Suez Canal, the British Empire's lifeline to its Indian and eastern colonies. With the loss of Famagusta to the Turks in 1974, Limassol then became the South's main port and supply line. The war in Lebanon during the 1980s also meant much of the Levantine trade passed through here instead of Beirut, while the closure of Beirut Airport meant ferries from Limassol were one of the only ways Christian Maronite Lebanese could get in and out of the country.

Limassol's surrounding beaches have also added to the town's prosperity, making it a draw as a tourist destination, with resorts spreading out along the coast during the 1980s and 1990s.

What to see
The town's main ancient relic is the **medieval castle** which now houses the **Cyprus Medieval Museum** (Mon-Fri 0900-1700, Sat-Sun 1000-1300, C£1). This is at the south-western end of 28 October, one street back. Despite all the hype, this is not the place where Richard and Berengaria married; that was destroyed by an earthquake in the early 14th century. The Venetians also pulled much of the castle down in 1525, after it had been taken over by Turkish pirates. It was then used as a prison by the British until their departure in 1960. The museum has a good collection of medieval arms and armour, along with exhibits on the island's history up to the Ottoman invasion.

The main Greek Orthodox church, the **Church of the Holy Handkerchief of St Veronica**, is a relatively recent construction, built in 1903. Head north-east from here to the old Turkish quarter, with its half-demolished mosques and Ottoman houses off Bayazit St, making this the most interesting part of town to look around.

The **beaches** are a good place to head

for, with the town stretch reasonable enough once you go half a kilometre north-east up 28 October where the waters get clearer and the crowds less dense. This waterfront road is also a good place to meet hundreds of Filipinos. Why this is so is a mystery.

Kolossi Some 14km west of Limassol, off the Paphos road, the castle of Kolossi is a distinctive and intriguing landmark of South Cyprus. A blunt, square keep is largely all that remains of this 1454 construction, once the residence of the grand master of the Knights of St John (see box on p322). After the fall of Acre in 1291, the order fled to Cyprus, setting up headquarters here. They stayed until the start of the 16th century, when the castle passed to Queen Cornaro.

Inside the tower you'll find a number of rooms, one of which bears the coat of arms of the Knights' Grand Commander on Cyprus, Louis de Magnac, while the third floor has the rooms of the Grand Master himself, Jacques de Milli, who is further commemorated by an elaborate coat of arms above the north door. The views are magnificent from the roof, particularly south to the great salt lake and the RAF base. Next door is a large barn, the Knights' quarters; ironically it was Murad Paşa, the second Ottoman governor of Cyprus, who was responsible for the plaque commemorating the restoration of these in 1591. There's also an aqueduct to bring water into the castle grounds, where the Knights must have had their vineyards; their wine, known as *commanderia*, was noted.

To visit, get the Paphos bus from Limassol (2 per hour, C£1), getting off after about 14km and walking a few hundred metres to the site, which is clearly visible.

Kourion The ancient city of Kourion is some 13km west of Limassol, on the hourly Paphos-bus route. Legend has it that the city was founded on an easily-defended cliff-top site in 1595BC by Koureus, a Greek from Argos in the Peloponnese: those who defiled the city's Sanctuary of Apollo were cast into the sea below. This 8th-century BC sanctuary and the neighbouring 2nd-century AD stadium have been partially reconstructed, an

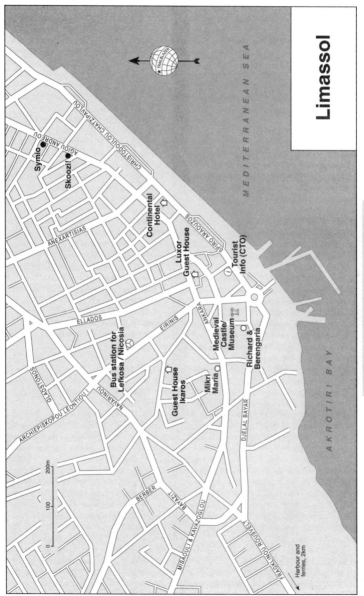

Limassol

MEDITERRANEAN SEA

AKROTIRI BAY

Harbour and
ferries, 2km

earthquake most likely having destroyed the later Roman city. A 2nd-century BC theatre is also on site, along with a House of the Gladiators and a House of Achilles. Note the mosaics inside. The site is open daily June-Sept 0800-1915, Oct-May 0800-1700, C£0.80. Nearby, there's also a museum (Mon-Wed & Fri 0730-1430, Thu 1500-1800, C£1) with a good display of artefacts recovered from the site.

The Trodos mountains   North of Limassol are South Cyprus's main mountain range, the Trodos. These offer good opportunities for hiking, whether as a day trip or longer. The hills are never too steep, with good tracks winding among isolated monasteries, pine trees and streams.

A good place to start trekking is Pano Platres, from where it's a half-hour walk up to the Caledonian Falls, a pretty waterfall set amongst the trees. The icy water is sometimes a relief to stand under in high summer, though we don't advise drinking it. The nearby village of Pedhoulas is also a popular destination, as it contains the 15th-century Church of Archangelos. The frescos inside are from 1474.

Some 20km west is Kykkos Monastery, which dates from the 12th century, although it has been largely restored and rebuilt over the years. The mosaics and frescos are also new, but the monastery derives its fame from possessing one of only three icons officially recognized as painted by the apostle St Luke himself. This is a Virgin Mary given to the monks by the Byzantine Emperor Alexis Comnenos. Archbishop Makarios was a novice here and is buried 3km away at the village of Throni.

Every day except Sunday, Kyriakos/Karydas service taxis go to Pano Platres (1 hour, C£1). Phone ☎ 0364 114 if you want them to pick you up in Limassol, or go to their office at 2, Thessalonika St. Coming back is a problem as the service taxi and bus both leave first thing in the morning. It is easy enough to hitch.

Practical information
Orientation   Limassol is a ribbon-like place stretching along the coast with a pleasant beach by the side of the main road, 28 October. The town's other roads mostly run parallel behind this, with the ferry port some 5km to the south-west. Take the half-hourly No 30 bus, or a shared taxi/dolmuş, to get between the port and the town centre. The ferry port is pretty big, so allow time if you're walking to your ferry; the Beirut boat in particular docks a good 10-minute walk from the customs building.

The bus station is 400m north of the castle on Eirinis St. On either side of the rather nebulous centre are the better beaches: Dhassoudi is 3km east on the No 6 bus route, while Ladies' Mile Beach is just west of the port on the No 1 bus line. In town, you won't need buses at all as the sights are all within easy walking distance.

Services   The **Cyprus Tourist Office** (CTO; ☎ 0362 756), 15, Spiro Araouzos, is on the waterfront east of the castle. It opens Mon-Fri 0815-1430, 1600-1830 (Wed 0815-1430) and Sat 0815-1315. There is also a branch at the harbour.

For **internet access** try Cybernet café, 79, Eleftherias St.

Ferries   [see p461 for full details] At the time of writing, services from Limassol are mostly mini-cruises operating at the weekend. The boats have cabins only, but are excellent value as the price includes all meals and a triumphantly-tacky onboard show. Most routes are run by Louis Lines (☎ 0363 161).

It *is* possible to get a one-way ticket but these go on sale only at the last minute (the company trying to fill as many cabins as possible with people buying the whole package). If it's only one-way you want, put your name down in advance, then see if anything's available closer to departure.

To get a one-way ticket for the boat to Lebanon, you must have a visa for Lebanon (see p65) and an onward ticket from there. Otherwise, without a visa you'll have to take a return trip, the ship keeping your passport and Lebanese customs issuing you with a special one-day pass only. With no other ferries leaving Beirut for anywhere else at the time of writing, this is your only option.

The Limassol to Port Said and Limassol to Alexandria boats are much easier to use, as Egyptian visas can be obtained on arrival. However, there are no boats out of Egypt heading further on up the African coast, or to Haifa, Beirut or beyond. This means you are effectively obliged to return to Cyprus if you want to travel by sea, or alternatively, have to take a bus or plane out (see Egypt, p50, for details).

Buses KEMEK (☎ 0747 532) operates five buses a day to Nicosia (C£1, 1 hour) on weekdays, three on Saturday and none on Sunday. There are also two a day to Paphos (C£1, 45 mins); take this service for Kolossi and Kourion. They all go from the main bus station, north of the castle. There are also three a day to Larnaca (C£1.50, 1 hour) operated by Kallenos and leaving from outside the CTO.

Shared taxis These are a feature of South Cyprus and provide the fastest and most useful way of getting between the big towns, though they are more expensive than the bus.

The way it works is either you go to the office and pay in advance for a place in a shared taxi leaving at a specific time, or you phone (or get your hotel to phone) and they come and pick you up.

The Kyriakos/Karyadas service taxi company (☎ 0364 114), 21, Thessalonikos St, operates shared taxis to Pano Platres Mon–Sat for C£1.50.

Acropolis Taxis (☎ 0366 766), 65, Spyros Araouzou St, has half-hourly cabs to Nicosia (C£2), Larnaca (C£2) and Paphos (C£2).

Where to stay *Continental Hotel* (☎ 0362 530), 137, Spiro Araouzos. Conveniently situated on the waterfront; sgl/dbl C£15/30.
Luxor Guest House (☎ 0362 265), 101, Ag Andreou. In the older part of town, east of the castle; C£6/11 sgl/dbl.
Guest House Ikaros (☎ 0354 348), 61, Eleftherias. Quirky but reliable; C£6/12 sgl/dbl.
Governor's Beach Camping (☎ 0632 300). 20km to the east, but seems to be the only option for **campers**.

Where to eat *Mikri Maria*, 3, Ankara St. A local favourite, has good-value traditional fare for C£5 a head.
Richard and Berengaria, by the castle. Has good Turkish/Greek fusion food; C£5.
Skoozi!, 292, Agiou Andreou. A good bar for music with some tasty snacks.
Symio, on the same street but at No 248. More arty and has a lively atmosphere.

LARNACA
AREA CODE: ☎ 24 POPULATION: 76,000
Site of the South's main airport and of an ancient city, Larnaca is beach-holiday land, lying next door to another British military base and a base for Agia Napa, birthplace of Aphrodite, goddess of love. It is also now the scene of the Mediterranean's largest parties. There is not much to do here unless you are interested in beaches.

History
Much of the present town lies on top of the ancient city of Kition, founded by Mycenean colonists in the 13th century BC. It was later the birthplace of the philosopher Zeno, founder of Stoicism. Its Greek name comes from the words for 'funerary urn', as there were so many burial places. Its later Turkish name, however, Iskele, 'port', refers more directly to its modern role. This was how it was developed by the Ottomans, a role ironically extended once the 1974 Turkish invasion had cut off Famagusta and the Greek Cypriots had to develop alternative harbours. Likewise, Larnaca Airport was given a boost when Nicosia International Airport fell into the UN buffer zone under the 1974 ceasefire, taking it out of operation ever since.

The town has thus developed quite an important transport and communications role. One of its other large employers is the British military, whose Dhekelia Sovereign Base Area (SBA) employs many locals. Tourism has boomed since 1974, with many resorts stretching along the coast.

What to see
The town's highlights begin with **St Lazaros Church**, recently rebuilt over the 9th-century original and said to contain the tomb of

EASTERN MEDITERRANEAN

Lazaros himself. He it was whom Jesus brought back from the dead. The Byzantines later took the body to Constantinople but the empty tomb remains, reached by steps on the right of the iconostasis.

The **Archaeology Museum** (Mon-Sat 0730-1330, C£0.75) contains a number of finds from ancient Kition, an excavated part of which lies just up the road off Archiepiskopou Kyprianou. This is part of the ancient acropolis and is open the same hours and costs the same as the museum. Kition has been rebuilt several times since its foundation in the 13th century BC, notably by the Phoenicians in the 9th century.

Back on the waterfront, south of the harbour and located in the old Turkish quarter, is the 1625 **fort** (Mon-Sat 0730-1930, C£0.75). Built by the Ottomans, it has good harbour views and a small collection of Kition artefacts, plus a number of items from the Hala Sultan Tekke. This is one of the holiest Muslim sites in South Cyprus, or indeed anywhere, and is some 3km west of town, just after the airport. The mosque there now lies over the tomb of Umm Haram, an aunt of the Prophet Mohammed, who died here during an Arab attack on the island in 694 after falling from her mule. Beautifully situated by the Larnaca salt lake and surrounded by palms, it is still the destination for many Muslim pilgrims.

Practical information

Orientation The No 19 bus (C£1) goes from the airport (3km out of town) to St Lazaros Church at the southern end of town.

From there a series of parallel streets run north–south along the shoreline, with the harbour in the centre. Athens Avenue is the main harbour-front road, with Makarios III Avenue up behind. Getting around on foot is easy.

Services The **CTO** (☎ 0654 322), 2, Plateia Vasileos Pavlou, is open Mon-Fri 0815-1430, Sat 0815-1330.

Buses There are regular buses to Nicosia (C£1), Limassol (C£1.50) and Agia Napa (C£1) from the bus stop on the waterfront, though only the Agia Napa service operates on a Sunday.

The main longer-distance bus stops are outside the Chinese restaurant on the waterfront.

Service taxis Try Acropolis (☎ 0652 929) on Leoforos Archiepiskopou Makariou III, for a service taxi to Nicosia (C£2) or Limassol (C£2.50).

Taxis to the airport cost C£3.

Planes There are regular flights to European and international destinations as well as to Greek airports. However, the latter tend to be heavily booked, so try reserving as far in advance as possible.

Where to stay *HI Hostel* (☎ 0621 188), 27, Nikolaou Rossou St, east of St Lazaros Church, has bunks for C£4 a night. *Hotel Pavion* (☎ 0656 688), also across from the church, has sgl/dbl for C£10/17.

Campers should try **Forest Beach Camping** (☎ 0644 514), open June to Oct, 8km along the road to Agia Napa.

Where to eat *Militzis Restaurant* South of the fort on the waterfront road. Good local fare for C£5 a head.

NICOSIA (GR: LEFKOSIA, TR: LEFKOSA)

AREA CODE: ☎ 02 **POPULATION:** 180,000

The world's last divided capital, and the island's main city since the 10th century, Nicosia is today a sprawling, dynamic place, overspilling the battlements of its old core to head off south towards the Trodos Mountains. Jumbled as much with skyscrapers as with old Venetian, Ottoman and Orthodox buildings, it is in most senses a modern European city — yet with a major scar down its middle. The Green Line is at its narrowest here, with the border sometimes no more than an alley wide. With smart, pedestrianized shopping streets and old bazaars, it represents all the island's contradictions at once, along with a great deal of its fascination.

History

Located almost in the middle of the island, the site on which Nicosia now stands has long been inhabited. Neolithic remains have been found in the locality, while by the 7th century BC the city of Ledra, located under the modern metropolis, was a kingdom in its own right. Later, the Romans were here, with the city having its own bishop by the 4th century AD. From then on, it shared the history of the rest of the island, being Byzantine, then Lusignan, Venetian, Ottoman, British, Cypriot – and now a divided city.

Under the Lusignans, it developed a reputation for enormous wealth. The kings had their palace here, as did the bishops, all of whom reportedly had a great passion for hunting wild rams with their pet leopards. The defensive walls are largely Venetian upgrades of Lusignan originals, a sad waste of money as the Ottomans had little trouble taking it in 1570.

Under their rule, many of the cathedrals and churches were converted into mosques, producing one of Cyprus's great hallmarks: a Gothic cathedral, identical in design and construction to hundreds of others across northern Europe, with two minarets tacked on the sides and reconsecrated to Allah. An earthquake in 1741 damaged many of these new minarets but, apart from that, Ottoman rule seems to have been largely uneventful.

Under British rule, the city grew, though one of the long-standing complaints was that very little in the way of resources was given to the island by its new masters. The city remained divided into Greek and Turkish quarters, though some of the newer, middle-class suburbs were a little more mixed. When EOKA began its military campaign against the British, the city also became the scene of a number of atrocities. These included assassinations of civilians on the 'Murder Mile', then Victoria St, which runs south from the Kyrenia Gate (in the Turkish sector) to the Green Line before continuing nowadays as a pedestrianized stretch in the Greek sector. In addition, the prison became the scene for a number of executions as the authorities attempted to suppress the rising.

With the British gone, the city became the capital of the Independent Republic of Cyprus in 1960. However, intercommunal violence at the end of 1963 led to the deployment of UN troops. In 1974, fighting was particularly intense in the city with the besieged Turkish Cypriot population, supported by Turkish paratroops, holding out against Greek Cypriot soldiers and militias until the Turkish army broke through. The ceasefire line was drawn through the city's centre, meaning that the border today almost exactly corresponds to the positions of the two armies at the hour the shooting halted.

On the Greek Cypriot side, the war damage has been almost all repaired, with people living right up to the line itself. On the Turkish Cypriot side though, a different military strategy has meant the creation of a buffer zone of bombed-out buildings and bullet-spattered walls, gradually collapsing as the years go by. In the city's heart, at the Ledra Palace Hotel, UN troops and diplomats continue their efforts at reconciliation. The future of the city thus depends on the future of the Green Line, which has sealed off the two Nicosias from each other for over a quarter of a century.

What to see

Start inside the walls, entering from Plateia Eleftherias, just east of the bus stops on Plateia Solomou. The main pedestrianized route, Lidras St, heads off north. After 200m, the **Woolworth's Tower** on the right has an observatory (0830-1730, free) on its top floor and an exhibition of the city's history from the Greek-Cypriot perspective. The observatory has powerful binoculars offering panoramic views, including the North and the Besparmak Mountains, now under Turkish-Cypriot control and featuring a giant Turkish flag etched into the hillside.

Back on Lidras, head north to the **Green Line**, where a street-level observation post allows you to look across the short stretch of no-man's land to the Turkish Cypriot lines. The posters show faces of those missing since the 1974 events. Greek Cyprus holds the Turkish Cypriots and Turkey responsible for their disappearances and this is one of the most controversial issues still dividing the two sides. The Turkish Cypriots claim that most of those missing were in fact killed by the rival Greek-Cypriot factions in the coup against Archbishop Makarios.

Head east along the Green Line and you'll be wandering amongst the run-down garages and workshops of what was once a much larger bazaar area; on the other side of the line, the streets are much the same. Ahead lies the **Famagusta Gate**, once the main entrance to the city and now a very imposing cultural centre. Turn down Nikiforos Phocas and then turn right into Thiseos St; the **National Struggle Museum** (closed for renovation at the time of writing) is down the first road on the left and is next door to the **Cyprus Folk Art Museum** (Mon-Fri 0900-1700, Sat 1000-1300, C£1). However, of more interest is **Agios Ioannis Cathedral**. Built in 1662, it has some marvellous frescos from the 18th century. Next to this is the **Archbishop's Palace** while inside is the **Byzantine Museum** (Mon-Fri 0900-1630, Sat 0900-1300, C£1) where there's a vast collection of Byzantine icons and a small exhibition area illustrating the damage done to the palace in the abortive coup of 1974. Outside is a giant statue of Archbishop Makarios.

From Plateia Archipiskopou Kyprianou, where you now find yourself, head for the **Liberty Monument** at the bottom of Korais. Symbolizing liberation from British rule, the EOKA fighters are depicted releasing the population from a cage, the Turkish Cypriots heading one way, the Greek Cypriots the other: a sustained symbolism

Go back west, along by the walls, before returning to the centre along Ayios Antonios. Turn left along Patriarch Grigorios to the **House of Hadjigeorgakis** (Mon-Sat 0730-1330 in summer, 0730-1400 in winter; 0730-1300 Sundays, C£0.75), an 18th-century Ottoman building, once the home of the grand dragoman, the chief Turkish court interpreter. A little further along is the **Omeriye Mosque**. This was once an Augustinian church but, on the city's capture by the Ottomans in 1570, the victorious general Mustapha identified it as the place where the Prophet Omar had slept on a much earlier visit to Cyprus.

You should also visit the **Leventis**

Municipal Museum, in Hippocrates St, (Tue-Sun 1000-1630, free). This has exhibitions of the city's story from prehistory to the present day.

To cross into the North, go west round the outside of the city walls, from Plateia Eleftherias, heading for Leoforos Markou Drakou, which takes you to the Ledra Palace Hotel checkpoint. Continue further west for the **British High Commission** and the **old prison**, in which there is a museum dedicated to the EOKA fighters executed by the British (daily 0900-1330, C£1).

On a cheerier note, also outside the city walls, on Museum St, is the **Cyprus Museum** (Mon-Sat 0900-1700, Sun 1000-1300, C£1) where you'll find an excellent collection of 7th-century BC terracotta figurines and a wonderful mosaic of Leda and the Swan found at Aphrodite's Sanctuary at Kouklia.

Practical information

Orientation It is simple to walk round the southern part of the city, the main attractions being within the old city walls. Buses and shared taxis arrive and depart from just outside the fortifications, at Plateia Solomou, one of the old town entrances.

To get into the North, you must go to the Ledra Palace hotel checkpoint. Sometimes the border is closed completely but usually it is possible to cross without luggage between 0800 and 1300, but you must return before 1700. These regulations are subject to change as relations between North and South thaw or freeze, so it is best to check at the tourist information office for the latest regulations. You walk through the grounds of the hotel, now occupied by UN troops, and arrive at the Turkish-Cypriot checkpoint where you must present your passport. Ask them to stamp a special visa paper rather than your passport, as having a TRNC stamp can make it difficult to enter Greece or southern Cyprus on another occasion.

Services The **CTO** (☎ 0674 264) is in Laiki Yotonia, just inside the city walls from Plateia Eleftherias. It's open Mon-Fri 0830-1600, Sat 0800-1400.

Buses The KEMEK bus stop is at 3, Omirou St; there are five buses a day to Limassol (C£1.50), one to Paphos (C£2.25), and one to Pano Platres (C£2). Another bus company, Kallenos, operates from Leoforos Salaminos and has five buses a day to Larnaca (C£1.25).

Service taxis Try A Makris (☎ 0466 201) at 11, Leoforos Stasinou, and Kypros (☎ 046 4811) in the same street but at No 9. A shared cab to Limassol should be C£3, to Larnaca C£1.50.

Where to stay *HI Hostel* (☎ 0674 808), 5, Hadjidakis St, off Themistokli Dervi. Nice place, with bunks for C£5 a night. *Sans Rival* (☎ 0474 383), 7c Solonos 3. A long-time staple, with sgl/dbl for C£14/25. *Tony's Bed & Breakfast* (☎ 0466 752), 13 Solonos. Also in the thick of things and Tony is helpful; C£17/30 sgl/dbl.

Where to eat *Savvi Xara Iampous*, 65, Solonos. Has a good selection of local food for C£5 a head. *Zanettos Taverna*, 65, Trikoupi. One of the oldest restaurants in Nicosia and excellent value; C£5. *Acropolis*, 14-16 Leonidou. Outside the walls near Plateia Eleftherias. Serves a fine suckling pig, or sheep's head if available. C£7.

NORTH NICOSIA (GR: LEFKOSIA, TR: LEFKOSA)

AREA CODE: ☎ 022 POPULATION: 50,000
North Nicosia is certainly quite a different world from the city's South. While the Greek Cypriot economy has boomed, the North has stayed well behind, leaving the north of the city a low-rise jumble of old streets, many of which have a dusty, neglected air. Along the Green Line itself there are many bomb-damaged buildings, and walls of dirt-filled oil barrels blocking off streets. It's also where most of Turkey's 30,000 troops stationed on the island go for their days off, making it thick with squaddies.

Yet it also contains some remarkable monuments and a sense of how *all* the old

city used to look – a look that has now been lost in the South.

Here you might still see an old 1960s' British car chugging along, while there isn't a chain store in sight. If you're here on a day-pass from the South, there are better places in the North to spend time on, and a quick dash round for an hour should give you a glimpse of most of the city's finer points.

What to see
A good place to start is the **Saray Hotel** in Atatürk Square, the North's equivalent of the Woolworth's Building and, at five floors, the tallest structure north of the Green Line. Take the lift up to the top floor, where there is a restaurant and a view of the whole city, leading off to the Trodos Mountains to the south. In the square below, note the British colonial architecture of the central police station and the post office opposite before heading south. The street narrows and brings you into the bazaar area which, followed round, takes you to the well-restored **Büyük Han**. This was built by the Ottomans in 1572 as a caravanserai, a meeting place and rest house for merchants. Now it houses a number of arty workshops while in the centre is a small mosque, built to allow guests to pray between deals.

Along from here is the **Selimiye Mosque**, formerly St Sophia Cathedral. Construction of this began in 1209 under the Lusignans, the French style being obvious in the high arches and marvellous sculpted porch. The minarets were added after the Ottoman conquest, since when it has remained a mosque. Inside, you'll see that it has been twisted round from the Christian arrangement so that the faithful can face towards Mecca while praying.

Next door is the **Bedestan**, the Ottoman covered market, which was built in the ruins of two churches. Now, though, the ruins of the churches are all that remain standing, the market having long gone. Returning eastwards, you'll wander through many streets that have seen better days before reaching the **Büyük Hamam** (Turkish bath). Once again, this was originally a church, as the entrance porch shows. St George of the

EASTERN MEDITERRANEAN

Latins was the original name, but now it's a very well-known hamam, charging US$3.50 for the whole restorative process of steaming, sweating and massage.

The **Dr Kucuk Museum** on Girne Caddesi, near the dolmuş office, was the home of the first leader of the Turkish Cypriot community following independence. Open Tue-Sat 1000-1330, US$1, it has a collection of his memorabilia, including the calling cards of his Greek Cypriot lawyer. Elsewhere, the Green Line can best be seen west of Atatürk Square. Go south down Mahmut Paşa Sokak (formerly Victoria Rd) and you will come to a series of bombed-out streets leading round to Paphos Gate. This is on the other side of the line, but go through the small park in the bastion there and you'll be able to look down, through the wire on the street below, onto the republic. It is forbidden to take photographs around here, so be careful.

Practical information

Orientation The north of the city is largely within the walls of the old town and is easily covered on foot. In any case, taxis charge an exorbitant US$5 flat fee to take you anywhere in the city limits so they should be avoided. Girne Caddesi is the main road from Girne Gate to Atatürk Square; it continues to the Green Line and in the South becomes Lidra St.

Services The helpful **tourist office** is hidden inside Kyrenia Gate (Mon-Fri 0900-1600, Sat & Sun 0900-1300). The staff at **Rustem Bookshop**, on Girne Caddesi south of Atatürk Square, are very friendly and helpful too. Something of an institution, the collection of books there seems left behind from 1974, with 'brand new' beach-holiday thrillers fading on the racks. It also has a good collection of English-language material on the Cyprus problem, written from the Turkish perspective.

Buses/taxis Buses are not much use for visitors; better are the dolmuş (shared taxis) which can be found for Girne/ Kyrenia at A Cavus Sokak, east of and parallel to Girne Caddesi and about 100m south of Girne

Gate. You can get a taxi to the airport (usually around US$10) from the Girne dolmuş office. Dolmuş for Famagusta leave from the stop on Cemal Gursel Caddesi to the east of Girne Gate. Dolmuş for Girne leave when full, while those for Famagusta require you to buy a ticket for a specific time; usually they leave every 30 minutes.

Planes The only direct international flights to Ercan are from Turkey. Both Turkish Airlines and Cyprus Turkish Airlines have flights, with a return trip to İstanbul costing US$140.

Note: Ercan Airport is in the middle of nowhere, so you must either get a taxi (see above) or hitch. To hitch to the airport from Lefkosa, head to Atatürk Caddesi, north of the old town, and hitch east on the main Famagusta road. The turn for Ercan is on the right after about 15km, from where it's another 10km to the airport.

Where to stay If you are going to stay in the North it's worth moving on to Girne or Famagusta as they are much nicer. But if you're stuck here, try *Saray Hotel* which sometimes has singles/doubles for as low as US$22/38. Otherwise *Palmiye Hotel* (☎ 87 733), on Mecidiye Sokak, has singles/doubles for US$14/25.

Where to eat Try the *Saray Hotel rooftop restaurant*, which has fixed menu lunches for US$8. Girne Caddesi has many cheap places to eat, but most are unbearably hot in summer. A finer venue is the *Boghjalian Konak Restaurant*, in the restoration area south-west of Saray Hotel. Expect to pay around US$10 a head.

GIRNE (GR: KYRENIA)
AREA CODE: ☎ 081 POPULATION: 8000

With easily the prettiest harbour in Cyprus, North or South, Girne is a hidden gem. Backed up by the dramatic mountains of the Besparmak ('Five Finger') range and with some beautiful coast on either side, it's easy to see why it was one of the most popular tourist destinations in the days before 1974. Even now it's the North's main tourist attraction and has the highest concentration of hotels and restaurants in Turkish Cyprus, along with a large-ish expat population, mainly from Germany and the UK, with the latter often referred to as the ancient Britons since so many retire here.

It's also the place for the ferry to and from Turkey and for trips to some spectacular castles along the coast. Rare turtles also come ashore around here (see box, p24), making parts of it an important protected habitat.

What to see

The place to start is the **old harbour**, a delightful place, curving round by the side of the **castle**. The fort, originally Byzantine, now houses the **Shipwreck Museum** (daily 0800-1700, US$2). The Lusignans and Venetians both strengthened the castle considerably, though it didn't hold out long against the Ottomans when they arrived in 1570, the Venetian commander surrendering without a shot being fired. Above the inner gateway is a well-preserved Lusignan coat of arms: three lions on their hind legs. Also look out for the tomb of Sadik Paşa, the Ottoman commander who captured it, and a small Byzantine chapel by the northwest tower. Most impressive, however, is the Shipwreck Hall. Here is the hull of a 2300-year-old Greek trading ship, along with its complete cargo. Discovered by a sponge diver in 1965, it was painstakingly restored by a team from the University of Pennsylvania. There's also an exhibition on the various occupants of the castle over the centuries, from Roman through to British.

Just behind the castle is the pleasant **Anglican Church of St Andrews**, while the **Cafer Paşa Mosque** is to the east. Wandering in the back streets up from the harbour here is a good way to spend some time, with the **Folk Museum** (daily 1000-1700, US$1.50) now housed in an old carob warehouse perched above the smart waterside restaurants. Also worth a look is the **Icon Museum**, housed in the old Greek Orthodox Church of the Archangel Michael (Tue-Sun 1000-1700, US$1.80). The icons here are from many of the churches in the North now abandoned since most of the Greek-Cypriot population fled in 1974.

Back on the harbour, the customs house is a British colonial period addition, housing the tourist information office. The quay alongside is also a relatively late British addition, as is the Dome Hotel, west along the harbour-front road, a classic 1930s' construction. You can swim here from a concreted area among the rocks behind.

However little time you have here, your priorities should be Bellapais Abbey and the Castle of St Hilarion, both some way out of town. **Bellapais Abbey**, 10 minutes by taxi (US$5) inland from Girne, is an Augustinian monastery built by monks fleeing the collapse of Crusader fortunes in Palestine in 1187. The view from the terrace is spectacular, right along the coast and across the dark sea to Turkey, a faint line along the horizon. Set in gardens with lemon trees, Bellapais was for a long time the home of British writer Lawrence Durrell who wrote his memoirs *Bitter Lemons* here at the start of the EOKA guerrilla war. His house is in the village, south of the abbey and up from the massive plane tree, the Tree of Idleness, around which Greek peasants used to snooze away the hot afternoons. Now the inhabitants are all Turkish Cypriots, mainly refugees from villages in the South.

The castle is a rather longer taxi ride away (US$10); the cab will leave you for an hour before taking you down again. The **Castle of St Hilarion** must have been one of the most dominant defence fortresses in Christendom, set right on the top of a high mountain peak, 3km up behind Girne. The view on a clear day is awesome but watch the weather out of season as the castle is high enough to be surrounded by clouds some of the time. Crenellated battlements and half-collapsed halls, royal apartments and smoke-blackened refectories, this is the island's most romantic fortification, built largely by the 11th century Byzantines and reinforced periodically ever afterwards. The last time it was fought over was in 1974, as the many bullet holes will testify.

Practical information

Orientation Everything worth seeing in town is easily reached on foot. The main street, Hurriyet Caddesi, runs parallel to the

EASTERN MEDITERRANEAN

coast. The harbour by the castle is the place for chilling out, drinking or eating, while some 1.5km to the east is the port. Transport is centred on the square formed by the junction of Hurriyet and Ecevit Caddesi, with shared taxis, known as *kombis*, leaving from here for Nicosia and Famagusta.

Services The **tourist office** (☎ 52 145), in the former British customs house in the old harbour, is open around 1000 most days, an usually in the evening too in summer.

Ferries [see p460 for full details] There are daily hydrofoils between Girne port and Taşucu (3 hours), and from July to September, three services a week to Alanya (5 hours), both on Turkey's southern coast. Check departure times with port information on ☎ 56 001.

Allow plenty of time before boarding, as the bureaucracy involved is astonishing. Several queues operate simultaneously so check up with a few others in the line to ensure you're in the right one and take a good book to pass the time, particularly if you are waiting for the opening of passport control. You have to pay departure tax (this varies but is usually around US$2) and get a piece of paper stamped to say that you have. Getting off at the other end in Taşucu is even worse (see box pp400-1).

Buses/kombis Kombis (shared taxis) are more useful for visitors than buses. The kombi stop is on Ecevit Caddesi, just before the square, and they go to Nicosia and Famagusta. In season, you may be lucky enough to find one going to St Hilarion but at other times the kombi office can probably sort out a taxi for you and can be bargained with. Famagusta kombis are much less frequent than Nicosia ones, so a faster way may be to hitch: walk south-east along Cumhuriyet Caddesi for the signs to Famagusta (known as Gazimagusa, or just Magusa in Turkish).

Car hire Try Bros Rent-a-car, whose garage is out of town on the Lefkosa road but who will drive in to meet you if you call (☎ 59 207, mobile ☎ 0542 851 2936).

Expect to pay around US$30 a day rental, with petrol expensive at around US$1.20 a litre. A word of warning though – always hire a jeep, as North Cyprus's roads are abysmal out of the towns and off the main highways: if you intend to visit any of the castles, you'll probably find your off-road skills severely tested.

Where to stay Out of season, prices can be well below their usual levels, so see what you can bargain for. In season, you may have to shop around if you want somewhere by the water, as demand can be high. *Ergenekon Hotel* (☎ 54 677), on the harbour front. Has good views and friendly owners; US$22/38 sgl/dbl. *Bingol Guest House* (☎ 52 749), at the top end of Hurriyet Caddesi, by the square. US$17/28 sgl/dbl. *New Bristol Hotel* (☎ 56 570), further down Hurriyet. US$13/25 sgl/dbl.

Where to eat Girne has a wide range of restaurants (Chinese to French, to Indian), with some of the best in the region. However, prices are high for quality, and usually written in British pounds. The cheaper options are all around the kombi stop on Ecevit Caddesi, where kebabs, fish and chips and other staples will cost around US$5 a head.

If you are flush for cash, the T-Bone at the *Greenhouse Restaurant*, some 250m down Ecevit Caddesi on the left, is probably the best steak in the eastern Mediterranean but will set you back US$15-20.

As for **bars**, try back up off the harbour front, where several expat hang-outs have a cheerful aspect, including the *Irish bar* and the *Fisherman's Inn*.

FAMAGUSTA (TR: GAZIMAGUSA/ MAGUSA; GR: AMMÛKHOSTOS

AREA CODE: ☎ 036 POPULATION: 20,000

Once the envy of the world for its opulence and power, Famagusta today is surely one of the most melancholy cities in the Mediterranean. Once said to have a church for every day of the year, these grand Gothic buildings now lie scattered like stranded whales amongst the crumbling houses and sprouting palm trees of the old town. Yet this makes for a memorable visit, as does a tour out to the edge of town to the borderline around the forbidden city of Magusa. This was once Cyprus's premier tourist resort, but is now a empty ghost town. Nevertheless go there.

This is a place where much of the Eastern Mediterranean's history was shaped, and traditionally the 'seaport in Cyprus' from where Shakespeare's *Othello the Moor of Venice* planned to embark to 'battle the turbaned Turk'.

What to see

Entering the old town across the moat through the **Land Gate**, note the huge ramp used by the Venetians to roll cannon up onto the walls. The fortifications you see now are largely the result of their restoration just prior to the Ottoman attack in 1570. This was an epic siege, with a tiny Venetian garrison, led by Mark Antonio Bragadino, holding out for some 10 months against a huge Ottoman army led by Mustafa Paşa. The defenders eventually surrendered, having been promised safe passage if they did so. However, an argument then broke out allegedly over the execution of many Ottoman prisoners and a massacre of the defenceless Venetians ensued, with Bragadino himself flayed alive.

Many centuries later, these walls were once again to take on their defensive role. In 1974, the old town housed most of the city's Turkish Cypriot population, while the modern suburbs were Greek. For some days, the Turkish Cypriots held out behind these walls as Greek Cypriot artillery shelled the town and snipers traded fire across the moat. The arrival of the Turkish army lifted the siege, while the defenders were given the prefix 'Gazi' ('Defender of the Faith') thus making the modern Turkish name, Gazimagusa.

Keep to the main street ahead, İstiklal Caddesi. This leads down to the main square and the **Lala Mustafa Paşa Mosque**, the former St Nicholas Cathedral. Built by French architects in the early 14th century to resemble the cathedral at Rheims, it is a distinctive construction, not least for the asymmetry of the minarets

stuck on the old towers. Inside, the conversion into a mosque leaves the imagination working hard to picture the scene here when Famagusta was in its heyday. Back then, the Lusignan kings and queens were crowned here amidst much pomp and ceremony.

Opposite the mosque are the ruins of the late 15th-century **Venetian palace**, once Bragadino's headquarters and home. The arches are now covered in graffiti, while inside is a small park, off which is a museum to the Turkish nationalist poet Namik Kemal, who was imprisoned here by the Ottoman government in the mid-19th century (daily 1000-1700, US$1).

Heading east from the square brings you to the sea walls and the impressive bulk of **Othello's Tower** (daily 1000-1700, US$1). This was the citadel, the fort within a fort, and the entrance is covered by a Venetian Lion of St Mark. Inside, you can climb up onto the ramparts and view the port below and the Famagusta skyline around, noting the numerous churches, most now converted into mosques. Below is the Great Hall, mentioned in *Othello* as a scene of great quaffing and revelry. Shakespeare's Moor may have been based on an historical character, Sir Cristoforo Moro. He was Venetian governor of Cyprus in the early 1500s, and reputedly killed his wife, Desdemona, in a jealous rage.

Heading west from here will take you to the famous **Martinengo Bastion**. The walls are some 4-5m thick and capable of withstanding a direct hit from the cannon of the time. Such was its reputation that the Ottoman army apparently made no attempt to attack it during the 1570 siege, instead concentrating on the **Canbulat Bastion** in the south-eastern corner, which was the Venetian arsenal. Canbulat was the Ottoman officer whose kamikaze-style attack enabled his men to break through by his putting out of action the fiendish Venetian rotating sword defence machine on this bastion approach.

Outside the walls, go south-east along Hava Senturk Caddesi for the **Palm Beach Hotel**. The road curves around the former small harbour, now marked by a rather lost-looking dolphin statue, and past various military barracks to the hotel entrance.

EASTERN MEDITERRANEAN

Continue a short way and follow the footpath to the public beach. Here, look south at the lines of apartment buildings and hotels along Cyprus's most golden and gorgeous sands. Everyone of these has stood empty and crumbling since 1974. A line of rusting **barbed wire** across the beach marks the edge of this forbidden zone, the resort of Varosha, occupied by the Turkish military, but left deserted as a bargaining chip in negotiations over the future of the island. Parties of journalists are occasionally allowed to look round it, where they find a retro time capsule, a city the size of Marbella or Torremolinos frozen on the day in July 1974 when it was evacuated.

Practical information

Orientation Famagusta is basically in two parts: the medieval walled city, and the modern tourist suburbs to the south and north. The dolmuş drops you just by the main entrance to the old town; all the important historical sites are within this. The port is east of the old town but there are currently no ferry services. Everything is easily reached on foot, though walking to Palm Beach Hotel and the border takes around 15 minutes from the dolmuş stop.

Services The **tourist information office** is just outside the city walls to the south (Mon-Fri 0900-1700, Sat & Sun 0800-1700). Again, they are very helpful.

Shared taxis (kombis) The kombi office is by the side of Lefkosa Yolu, just west of the Monument to Victory roundabout. Kombis go to Girne (US$1.50) and Nicosia (US$1) roughly every half hour.

Where to stay *Panorama Hotel* (☎ 65 880), on Ilker Karter Cad in the new town. Has budget sgl/dbl for US$10/17.50.
Altun Tabaya Hotel (☎ 65 363), 7, Kizilkule Yolu in the old town. US$17.50/30 sgl/dbl.

Where to eat Try the cafés on İstiklal Caddesi for some good-value breakfasts. Otherwise, the *DB Café*, in the square in front of Lala Mustafa Pasha Mosque, serves great pizzas and has a cluster of tables outside in summer. Expect to pay around US$5 for a pizza, with beers for US$1-2. The *Palm Beach* also has a standard lunch menu for US$7.50.

Beirut

AREA CODE: ☎ 01 POPULATION: 1.5 MILLION
A great emblematic city, Beirut stretches along the Mediterranean coast and across a turbulent history. For many years the scene of a bitter conflict, it is now a peaceful, dynamic place, where rebuilding and reconstruction continue at a furious pace. Meanwhile, though, the city still has retained its old allure — the jewel of the Levant and a hotchpotch of different religions and cultures.

It's also well located for exploring top-class ancient sites such as Baalbek and the unexpected beauties of the Beka'a Valley. Since Israel's withdrawal from southern Lebanon, this area also makes an interesting place to visit, easily accessible from Beirut itself. Also easily accessed is Damascus, provided you've sorted out a Syrian visa in advance as there's no Syrian consulate in Lebanon. Note that it is impossible to cross from Lebanon into Israel and vice versa. The only way through is to go to Syria, cross into Jordan and then come round into Israel. However, see pp59-61 about Israel.

HISTORY
Ignore the jackhammers and hard hats of modern Beirut, now under reconstruction, and cast your mind back 4000 years beyond the time of Abraham to the second millennium when it is mentioned in Egyptian papyrus, its name probably derived from the Canaanite word Be'erot, meaning 'Wells'.

The coast on either side was the birthplace of the ancient Phoenician civilization, a crucial link in the evolution of the entire Mediterranean. These seafarers, based in Tyre, Sidon and Byblos, developed amazing maritime skills, establishing trade routes and bases even as far away as Britain.

In 14BC the port became a Roman colony. Under the rule of the Caesars a famous law school was established and trade prospered, but all this came to a sudden end in AD551 when a series of earthquakes launched a tidal wave against the city, destroying much of it.

When the Arabs arrived in 635, Beirut was largely a ruin. They began to rebuild, as directed by neighbouring Baalbek, their regional capital. But Beirut was never much more than a fortified harbour until the 10th century when Syria (with Beirut at the time part of this most powerful Arab province in the region) came under the control of the Egyptian Fatimid rulers. This revived the port's importance as a trading centre in the Eastern Med.

In 1110 the army of the First Crusade arrived and captured it, putting it under the control of the Latin kingdom of Jerusalem. Connected to Genoa and other western European cities, Beirut boomed, though this wasn't helped by an almost constant struggle for its control. Local Druze tribesmen attempted to take it, as did Saladin, the great Saracen leader, more successfully in 1187. The Crusaders came back 10 years later, but the Mamluks (aka Mameluks or Mamlukes) finally drove them out in 1291.

As the chief port for Syria, Beirut continued to prosper until the next conquerors, the Ottomans, came along in 1516. Time and circumstance had moved on decisively by this stage, as the Portuguese Vasco da Gama had rounded the Cape of Good Hope to Calicut on the West Indian coast, gradually undercutting the overland spice routes that passed through Syria and Beirut.

The Lebanese merchants turned to the production of silk that they'd previously got overland from China. This they exported to France and Italy, reviving the city's fortunes. The French connection was also important to the city's large Maronite Christian majority, powerful and influential when the provinces of Lebanon passed from Ottoman control to local Druze and Maronite emirs in the 18th century.

The Russo-Turkish war of 1768-74 left the town in a period of slump, but its importance was restored after the Egyptian ruler,

Mohammed Ali, conquered Syria in 1832. By 1842 Beirut had re-established itself as a premier port and industrial city, with the Christian population swelled by many co-religionists fleeing the now Muslim-dominated hinterland. France also declared itself the protector of the Lebanese Catholics, while Russia supported the Lebanese Orthodox. Several foreign universities were established in the late 19th century; some are still there. By the dawn of the 20th century, the city had become the cradle of modern Arabic literature, and of Arab nationalism.

World War I saw Beirut occupied by the victorious Allies and the collapse of Ottoman rule. Lebanon became part of the French Mandate of Syria. The French then expanded the Christian-dominated Mount Lebanon area (Beirut and its environs) to the current Lebanese borders. This gave the largely pro-French Christians more territory, but also gave them a Muslim population larger than their own.

The creation of the state of Israel in 1948 also added to Lebanon's problems. Thousands of Palestinians were forced to flee Palestine in the face of Israeli occupation, and many settled in Lebanon, creating huge refugee camps around Beirut. Tensions blew up in 1958, then again in 1975, which marked the beginning of 15 years of warfare in the city.

The conflict was never just between Christians and Muslims, though. In 1982, the Israeli army invaded Lebanon and fought the Palestinian Liberation Organization (PLO) on Beirut's streets. Meanwhile, in the late 1980s, much of the fighting was between rival Christian groups, while rival Muslims also fought each other. In the end, the Syrian army moved in and forced a ceasefire. Some 130,000 people had been killed and the city was devastated.

Since then there has been a lot of rebuilding to do. The Green Line — the border between Muslim West Beirut and Christian East Beirut — has been officially lifted, and access is now free. However, the psychological and cultural divides are still pretty evident. A massive programme of reconstruction — known as Solidere — is now nearing completion in the gutted central district.

The political balance also seems to be holding. Syrian troops withdrew from Beirut itself in 2002, though Damascus is still a major influence on events. Meanwhile, the citizenry seem to have embraced the rebuilding with zeal, and a frantic effort to move on seems to be underway. The Lebanese gift for business has stood them in good stead so far, and the hope is that surely, tomorrow cannot be far away now.

WHAT TO SEE

Up from the harbour, your first port of call is the **Sursock Museum** (daily 0800-1400, 1600-1800 for exhibitions, free) in rue Sursock. The building is a gem of Italian/Lebanese architecture built for the wealthy Sursock family. Regular exhibitions are held here, usually of Lebanese art, with the grounds a delight to stroll round.

From here, head south for place Sassine, then down rue Sassine to rue Badarq and the **National Museum** (daily 1000-1700, US$3.25) on ave Abdullah Yafi. The museum is one of the best in the Eastern Mediterranean and certainly one of the most recently restored. The exhibits include many well lit and labelled ancient finds, including a number of statues, a good coin collection and the first-known inscription of the Phoenician alphabet. The sarcophagi and the mosaics from Baalbek are amazing. A free video shows how the museum curators preserved many of the exhibits during the civil war; the sarcophagi being stored in their own 1.5m thick concrete sarcophagi to prevent bomb damage. The museum was pummelled with bullets during the fighting, so much so that the columns outside virtually disappeared.

The other main museum is the **AUB Archaeology museum** (Mon-Fri, summer 0900-1430, winter 0900-1600, free) in the American University. This has a significant collection of archaeological finds from Beirut and many neighbouring digs, both in Lebanon and Syria. It's on rue Bliss, a lively street with student snack bars, and is a good introduction to the Hamra district. Rue Hamra is a popular shopping street and the

neighbouring district of Verdun is the home of many of the rich and famous. Walking down to the sea, you'll find the corniche, the ave du Charles de Gaulle, which sometimes acts as an outdoors exhibition area, with students displaying artwork. Continue round and you'll come to Pigeon Rock, a pretty landmark of sea-hollowed limestone, around which there are several *nargileh* cafés.

Cafés of a different kind are also much in evidence nowadays in the Solidere development area. Sodeco Square has been lined with some very fancy post-modern variants on late-19th-century themes, a development worth looking around. Rebuilding work has also uncovered a number of **archaeological sites**: one site already open is an ancient tell, which contains parts of a Bronze Age city gate, a Phoenician defence-wall, an ancient Greek tower and parts of a Crusader castle.

From Solidere, walk up place des Martyrs and follow the road inland, the war-damaged buildings sometimes so shot-up that no wall still stands. You'll also now see a contemporary Lebanese phenomenon; expensive boutiques and café-bars in the ground floors of buildings that have otherwise been literally blown apart.

Heading into West Beirut from here, the architecture changes again, with narrow streets much more reminiscent of Cairo than Marseille. The Hizbullah graffiti and posters of the Iranian Ayatollah Khomeni may be a little off-putting but the people are friendly and usually very pleased to see visitors. The maze of streets eventually brings you back out on the seafront, so head north for the nearest café with beer, up by Pigeon Rock.

PRACTICAL INFORMATION
Orientation

Ferries arrive at the harbour in East Beirut, about 5-10 minutes' walk from the Central District, the meeting place of the city's two halves. This is largely a blank space now, lined with bomb-damaged buildings, but these are being restored at speed, or demolished and replaced by reproduction work of various kinds. The central area has now begun to revive as a venue for trendy — and expensive — cafés and restaurants. Avenues lead away from the sea through the centre of the city, while others traverse this route between the two sectors.

The district of Hamra, situated on the headland of West Beirut (Ras Beirut) is dominated by the American University plus the smarter shopping and residential areas. Not far from them are the poorer Muslim quarters, while running round the seafront is ave du General de Gaulle, the main corniche. Orientation can be tricky in Beirut as street names often have several variations, and while usually written in French and Arabic, they're sometimes not written at all.

Likewise, maps usually bear only a nominal relationship to reality. It may well be time to practise your French if lost in East Beirut, or whatever comes to hand in West Beirut.

Services

The **tourist office** (☎ 343 073) is in Hamra at the intersection of rue de Rome and Central Bank St. It's open Mon-Fri 0800-1600, Sat 0800-1300, and is very useful with lots of maps and brochures.

The **tourist police** (☎ 343 286) share premises with the tourist information office above; the office is open 24hr.

Naufal Booksellers, on rue Sourati has a wide selection of English-language material. For **internet access** try PC Club on rue Mahatma Gandhi, off rue Bliss, or Web Café in Hamra on rue Makhoul.

Ferries   [see p460 for full details]

One-way tickets are available on the Louis Lines ferry to Limassol (15 hours) but only at the last minute as the company fills as many berths as possible with people doing the round trip. Keep trying if they say they are full as they'll probably squeeze you in. There are no deck- or Pullman-class tickets, the price being for a cabin only. Ask at the tourist information office for details.

Buses

Inter-city buses go from a number of different terminals and depart only when full, so timetables are rare. For Baalbek (3 hours, US$4.75), Tyre (3½ hours, US$3.50, known in Arabic as Sur) and Sidon (2 hours, US$0.75, known in Arabic as Sa'ida) you need the terminal at Cola Bridge, at the end of rue Borj Abi-Haidar. For Damascus (3½ hours, US$7) or Tripoli (2 hours, US$1.50), you need Charles Helou, on ave Charles Helou, up behind the port.

The fare for city-buses is a flat US$0.35. To catch one, stand on the road on the side for your destination and wave all of them down, shouting out the destination until one of the drivers beckons you on board. They stop running around 2000.

Service taxis

Service taxis (shared taxis), look a lot like normal taxis, so again, wave all of them down (provided they have an official red number plate), then shout 'Service?'. If you get the nod, jump in. For destinations within the city, you should pay less than US$2; ask the other passengers how much they are paying before asking the driver.

There are service-taxi terminals at Cola Bridge, Charles Helou bus station and Dawra.

Planes

Middle East Airlines is the national carrier and has flights to most international destinations. Many other airlines also fly here.

The airport (☎ 629 065) is 3km south of town; a taxi there costs US$7.50.

Where to stay

Pension Home Valery (☎ 362 169), rue Phoenicia. In the 'Ain Mreisse' district, 100m on the right from Hard Rock Café; bunks for US$5.

YWCA (☎ 367 750), just round the corner from the Valery. For women only; bunks for US$15, rooms for US$25/30 sgl/dbl.

Mushrek Hotel (☎ 345 773), on rue Makdissi in Hamra; US$19/25 sgl/dbl.

University Hotel (☎ 365 391), at the American University in Hamra, just off rue Bliss. Good location and US$20 per person, or student-only stays of US$150 a month.

EASTERN MEDITERRANEAN

EASTERN MEDITERRANEAN

Where to eat

Cheap food can be found around the American University in Hamra, where snack bars are thick on the ground. Otherwise, Beirut offers the range of international cuisine common to most big cities worldwide, with everything from Chinese to Mexican. Finding Lebanese food is not so easy but generally worth the search.

Hamadeh Snack, on the corner of rue de Rome and Central Bank St. Has good local food for US$5 a head.

Al-Amadouli, on the junction of rue Makdisi and rue Nehme Yafet. Charges extra (US$0.75) for live music on Wed and Sun evenings; good food at US$10.

Café de Paris, on Hamra St. Excellent for coffee and snacks and a chance to browse through the *Journal du Liban*.

Bars and clubs

Beirut took off in the late 1990s as a venue for dance-and-trance parties, with a number of ultra-decadent clubs springing up. Most are very expensive but the following might be worth a splurge. Otherwise, bars are good around Hamra and the university campus.

Orange Mechanique, Sin al-Fil south-east of the port near the Beirut River and 300m north of Beirut Hall. Beirut's best-known venue; open Thu-Sat, a techno haven, with drinks at US$7.50 a go.

Blue Note, on rue Makhoul, in Hamra. Eating here is expensive but the local beers are a relatively low US$3.

Henry J Bean's, rue Madame Curie. OK, it's seriously non-local, but it does have Guinness.

Baalbek

An essential trip inland from Beirut, Baalbek is one of the best-preserved ancient cities in the Mediterranean. Some 86km to the east, its Roman temple area is amazing

---

The Phoenicians

Hailing from the coast of modern-day Syria and Lebanon, the Phoenicians were a great maritime people and centuries before Galileo invented the telescope they established colonies and founded ports right across the Mediterranean, from Tangier to Marseille, Sicily to Cyprus.

However, despite giving the world its first phonetic alphabet – a script way more advanced than the hieroglyphs of ancient Egypt – almost nothing of their own writings remain. This has had a detrimental effect on their reputation, for it has meant that most of what we know of them comes from the accounts of their enemies – and is thus usually less than flattering. For example, we have their great early rivals, the Greeks (who nicked their alphabet and improved it), describing them in derogatory terms as 'purple men', which is what the word 'Phoenician' means. This is probably because they traded in, amongst other things, purple dye.

Their influence was founded on their skill as sailors. Their ships were way in advance of anything the Greeks had. Their homeland, Lebanon, gave them some natural advantages too in boat building, providing plenty of oak, pine and cedar wood for construction. Starting out from Tyre and Sidon and using a square-rigged central sail, banks of oars and a horse-head figurehead, their vessels managed to successfully circumnavigate Africa several millennia before it was ever done again. They were also the first to establish regular trade, notably with Britain.

And trade was really the name of the game for the Phoenicians, who were never known for their martial prowess. Instead, they hired armies of mercenaries to fight their wars for them, a practice continued by their offspring empire, Carthage, the Tunisian city they founded and which went on to challenge Rome for dominance of the Mediterranean.

and the surrounding Beka'a Valley is also very beautiful. To get there, take the bus (3 hours, US$4.75) or a service taxi (2½ hours, US$4) from Cola Bridge. Alternatively, some of the tour agencies arrange trips; if you've come on the Louis Lines ferry you can sign up for a coach tour while on board.

The archaeological site is a short walk from the town, which is the headquarters of the Hizbullah movement. Don't be alarmed, though, as they are perfectly happy to see tourists wandering round. A little sensitivity to local mores is required though, so dress appropriately.

HISTORY

Baalbek was founded by the Phoenicians as a sacred site for the worship of their deity, Baal, the God of War and Thunder. He was a colourful character, part man, part bull calf. Thanks to Baal's protection, the Phoenicians had no worries putting to sea, while their crops also received a divine guarantee. However, to secure the latter, Baal himself had to die every year before being resurrected to continue the cycle.

In 64BC the Romans brought their own gods; Baal became Jupiter, and Astarte, the Phoenician goddess of fertility, became Venus, and huge temples to both were erected in Baalbek c16BC.

After the gradual conversion of Rome to Christianity, Emperor Constantine shut these, while Emperor Theodosius tore down the altars to Baal and used the stone for his basilica, the remains of which can still be seen inside the longer-lasting Temple of Jupiter.

Under the Arabs, the temple area was turned into a fortress, subsequently used by the region's other conquerors until the early 20th century, when a German restoration team set to work, their job being continued by the French after WWII.

WHAT TO SEE

The site is open from 0800 to sunset, admission US$6.50. On entering, you are immediately at the foot of a staircase leading to the *propylaeum* (the entrance hall), next to which is the hexagonal court. Here you'll see two famous statues: Jupiter bearing lightning in one hand and a whip in the other, and Mercury with two bulls at his feet. On the west side, three gates lead into the sacrificial courtyard in front of the remains of the Temple of Jupiter. The six remaining columns of this temple make you realize the size of the original structure: at 22m, it's the tallest Roman temple in the world.

The Temple of Bacchus (probably a misnomer, as many archaeologists believe it was actually dedicated to Venus/Astarte), is the best preserved of the sites, being almost intact. Its doorway leads into a richly carved and decorated interior, with vine leaves,

Zahle

If you've a little more time to spare, on your way to or from Baalbek stop off at Zahle, at the southern end of the Beka'a Valley. Here, the River Bardouni rushes cool and clear besides a largely Ottoman-era town that is known for its wine and for being the birthplace of the 'Egyptian' actor, Omar Sharif.

The Ksara winery is around 2km from town and is one of the region's best. Originally run by Jesuits, it is now under private ownership and has a good reputation. The winery has a complex of over 2km of underground tunnels, believed to date back to Roman times, which provide the perfect temperature for ageing wine; some half a million bottles are stored down there. A tour and a tasting costs about US$5.

Back in Zahle, try any of the restaurants alongside the river for an excellent meal, accompanied of course by a bottle of the local vintage, *araq*. If this all proves too much and you need a bed in a hurry, try *Hotel Akl* (☎ 08-820 701) on rue Brazil for US$19/40 sgl/dbl.

EASTERN MEDITERRANEAN

sheaves of corn and other symbols of fecundity much in evidence. There's a small museum which shows reconstructions of what it looked like in its heyday, along with finds from pre-WWI German excavations.

PRACTICAL INFORMATION
Orientation
The site is along the road to the left of the Palmyra Hotel in Baalbek, which is at the intersection of rue Abd el-Halim Hajar and boulevard Ras al-'Ain. The Palmyra (built in 1874) is worth a look: Kaiser Wilhelm II, Kemal Atatürk and Charles de Gaulle have all stayed there.

Services To **change money**, try the offices on rue Hajar in town, or use cards at Fransabank on Ras al-Ain blvd.

The **post office** is a long walk down Ras al-Ain blvd, so it might be an idea to send your postcards from Beirut.

Where to stay
Baalbek doesn't have much of a choice in terms of accommodation, there being only three places to stay. Returning to Beirut may therefore be a good option, as transport is frequent and not expensive.

Pension Shuman (☎ 370 160), on boulevard Ras al-Ain. Near the ancient site; sgl/dbl for US$8/12.
Ash-Shams Hotel (☎ 373 284), rue Hajar. Offers a similar deal.
Palmyra Hotel (☎ 370 230), by the ruins. A great institution, with a wonderful guestbook (see Orientation above) that you can look at. Rates (US$45/65 sgl/dbl) are quite a bit higher at this Victorian haunt.

Where to eat
Try the *snack bars* on rue Hajar (US$1-2 a sandwich), or the Palmyra Hotel restaurant for a fuller meal at US$8 a head.

Haifa

Sprawling down the steep slopes of Mt Carmel, Haifa (*Hefa* in Hebrew) has long been Israel's main sea gateway. However, that's been both a blessing and a curse as the city has often been little more than a transit hub for travellers and traders heading on to Tel Aviv or Jerusalem.

In recent years it has developed a few

Elijah and the prophets of Ba'al
Mt Carmel is of great importance to Jews and Christians thanks to a dramatic story recounted in Kings I Chapter XVIII. The mount is where the prophet Elijah brought the Children of Israel back to their faith in the Lord after King Ahab, abetted by Jezebel, had taken them 'whoring after false gods'. In his presence, Elijah challenged the 450 priests of Ba'al to call fire down from their gods to consume their sacrifices as a sign that they would bring rain to the parched land. All day the Ba'alim prayed for the rain, but to no avail.

For his part, Elijah had but the one altar on which he laid his sacrifice, soaking it and the ground around with water. At the time of the evening sacrifice he prayed long and passionately to the Lord who sent down fire that consumed not only the sacrifice but also the drenched altar and wood around.

Having seen how the Ba'al prophets had failed, the people fell on their faces and acknowledged their true God. To ensure that they would never again turn to these prophets, Elijah ordered the people to take the 450 prophets of Ba'al to the brook of Kishan, where he slew them. Elijah then went to the top of Mt Carmel and prayed, sending his servant to look at the sea for signs of rain. At the seventh time of asking the servant saw a cloud no bigger than a man's hair. Soon after the skies were black and there was a great rain.

tourist attractions, from the fabulous Baha'i shrine to a great Carmelite monastery and the German Colony, a bit of Bavaria in the middle of the Middle East.

It also has a reputation for religious tolerance absent in most other Israeli cities, with a corresponding lack of the violence that sadly characterizes much of the rest of the Jewish state.

HISTORY

Eusebius, an early Christian theologian and biblical topographer, referred to the port as Sykaminos, a classification that was then changed by the Crusaders when they invaded in 1100. Renaming it Caiphas, they built a number of monasteries in the hills to honour Elijah, before losing it back to the Muslims. The port was not officially founded until 1761, when the ruler of Galilee, Daher El Omar, gave it its charter. It continued as part of the Ottoman Empire till the end of WWI, with the exception of a brief occupation by Napoleon in 1799 and by the Egyptian general Ibrahim Pasha in 1839. In 1918 it was occupied by the British and became part of the British Imperial Mandate of Palestine in 1922.

As Palestine's chief port during the WWII era and its aftermath, Haifa became a focal point for hundreds of thousands of Jews fleeing Europe after the Holocaust. A guerrilla war between British colonial forces and radical Zionist groups continued until 1948, when Britain pulled out and Israel was created.

Fighting then broke out between Palestinians and Jewish settlers, with the latter victorious. The majority of the Palestinian population fled the city, the Muslim population dropping from 50,000 in 1947 to 3000 by 1949. Many of those who fled and their descendants still live as refugees in neighbouring Lebanon, Jordan and the Palestinian territories.

Since then, Haifa has prospered as Israel's leading port, despite the closing of much of its natural hinterland in southern Lebanon because of the continuing conflict between Israel and its Arab neighbours. Now the city's focus is towards the south and across the narrow land to Jerusalem.

WHAT TO SEE

With Haifa such a vertical city and summer temperatures running high, it's usually best to start at the top and work down. The last stop on the Carmelit metro is **Gan Ha-Eim**, a park area with the zoo and a few missable museums; more interesting are the botanical gardens. From there, wander down to the **Museum of Japanese Art** (☎ 838 3554, Mon, Wed, Thu 1000-1700, Tue 1000-1400, 1700-2000, Fri 1000-1300, Sat 1000-1400, free), 89, Ha-Nassi Ave, for some oriental distraction, then head for the **Baha'i Shrine** (☎ 835 8358, daily 0900-1200, gardens 0800-1700) on Ha-Tzimonut Avenue.

The shrine commemorates the first Baha'i prophet, Sa'id Ali Muhammed, known as Al-Bab. He was exiled from his native Persia and stayed on this spot on his way to Akko. Much later, in 1909, his remains were brought here and interred inside the shrine. Since then, Haifa has been an important point of pilgrimage for followers of the Baha'i faith, with the shrine and surrounding gardens a great architectural testimony to Baha'i belief in concord and harmony.

Heading west you come to the **German Colony**, founded in 1869 by German members of the Templar Society. They were not the first, nor the last, of the many messianic groups to have settled in Palestine over the years. They believed that the Messiah would soon return and only those who had gathered in the Holy Land and who had followed the Christian teachings of the society's founder, Christoph Hoffman, would be saved.

During WWII, however, as a result of their support for Nazi Germany's policies, members of the colony were rounded up and deported by the British authorities.

For a good tour round, head down Ben Gurion Boulevard from the junction with Hagefen St. On your left is the Colony Restoration Project headquarters, which has handy maps. Number 24 Ben Gurion Boulevard is a whole complex of Templar buildings. The Templar houses are notable for their blends of architectural styles; everything from Bauhaus to Baghdad. The community was once the richest in the city,

EASTERN MEDITERRANEAN

with Haifa owing much of its past power to their influence and skill.

Go west along Allenby Rd and you'll come to the **National Maritime Museum**, (☎ 853 6622; Mon, Wed, Thu 1000-1700, Tue 1000-1400, 1700-2000, Fri 1000-1300, Sat 1000-1400, free), at No 198. Inside is an exhibition of '5000 years of shipping', complete with a multitude of ships from ancient to modern periods, alongside a collection illustrating marine mythology.

Continue on down Allenby for the **Clandestine Immigration and Naval Museum** (☎ 853 6249, Sun-Thu 0830-1600, free), at No 204. While making a refreshing change to see illegal immigration embraced and celebrated rather than feared and condemned, the museum tells the story of the efforts by the Zionist movement to flood Palestine with Jews in the 1930s and 1940s and thus enable the creation of the State of Israel. It also contains a run-down on the history of the Israeli navy.

Still on Allenby, **Elijah's Cave** (☎ 852 7430, Sun-Thu 0800-1745, Fri 0800-1245, free) is a shrine sacred to Judaism, Christianity and Islam: the Jews believe that Elijah hid here and the Christians that Mary, Joseph and their child Jesus took refuge on their way back from Egypt to Galilee. The Muslims honour Elijah as Al-Khadar (the Green Prophet).

Retrace your steps a little for the **Rakbal cable-car** up to the **Carmelite monastery** (☎ 833 7758, daily 0830-1330, 1500-1800, free). This was originally founded here under the auspices of the Knights of St John as Christian monks were forbidden to live in Elijah's Cave: a 12th-century Latin monk, Berthold, set up the Carmelite order here. The original monastery survived until 1291, when it was destroyed by Sultan Baybars. What you see now is an 1836 reconstruction on the site of an ancient Byzantine chapel and a Greek church. Naturally, it is crowded on 20 July, the feast day of St Elias (Elijah).

PRACTICAL INFORMATION
Orientation
Haifa's layout is all about the mountain, with height a definite advantage. The further up

you go, the wealthier the districts become, with the Carmelit metro a great asset for a trip to the top. The city is built on three distinct terraces, with the port at the bottom of the northern slope and the mountain a promontory jutting into the eastern sea.

From the port's passenger hall, the railway runs parallel to the seafront and Ha-Atzma'ut, the main harbour-front road. West along this about 1km is the central bus station and railway station in the Bat Galim district.

A kilometre on from there along Ha-Hagana lies Elijah's cave and the cable-car to the Carmelite monastery. The old city is right in front of the passenger hall, up the hill, with the German Colony a little to the west of this. Herzl St is the main road, running east–west through the terraced Hadar district further up the mountain.

Above that is Carmel Centre, the district for the most exclusive restaurants, hotels and mansions.

Services
The main **tourist office** (☎ 853 5606) is at 48, Ben Gurion St. You'll be treated to a free film showing you the town's highlights, plus there's a good selection of maps and general information.

Try **Beverley's Books**, 18, Herzl St, for English-language material. There's a good stock of second-hand volumes too.

The **police**, 28, Jaffa St, deal with tourist problems.

Ferries
At the time of writing no ferry services were operating from Haifa. Should they resume, there are likely to be boats to Cyprus and Greece, with Poseidon Lines and Salamis Lines traditionally the two companies providing services.

Trains
Israel Railways (☎ 830 3133) run regular services down the coast to Tel Aviv (US$5) from Haifa Central, and on from there to Ashdod. You can get a 10% discount with an ISIC card and timetables are available from any of Haifa's three mainline stations and from the tourist information office.

Buses

The central bus station (☎ 851 2208) is at Jaffa Rd and Rothschild Blvd. There are buses every 15 minutes to Tel Aviv (1½ hours, US$5), every 45 minutes to Jerusalem (2-3 hours, US$9), to Nazareth every hour (1½ hours, US$5), to Ben Gurion airport every half an hour (2 hours, US$7) and Tiberias every hour (1½ hours, US$6). Roadblocks may add time to the journey.

Planes

The nearest airport is Ben Gurion, which also serves Jerusalem.

El Al, the national airline, has flights to many international destinations and is the most security-conscious airline in the world.

Where to stay

Lev Haifa (☎ 867 3753), 61, Herzl St. Has doubles for US$35 and a good location.

Eden Hotel (☎ 866 4816), 8, Shmaryahu-Levin St. A Haifa institution, with doubles for US$38.

Where to eat

The bargain-meals district is the Kikkar Paris area, while prices go up with altitude. *Tzimzhonit Hayim*, 30 Herzl St, is a long-established favourite, with a range of vegetarian food also available. Budget on US$5 for a main course.

Port Said

AREA CODE: ☎ 066 **POPULATION:** 450,000
Gateway to the Suez Canal, and thus the most important port in Egypt, Port Said has had a chequered history yet nowadays has emerged as a duty-free mecca for Egyptian shoppers, as well as a handy starting point for exploring Sinai and the rest of the country.

It's also a place of unexpected charm. Walk along Palestine St at dusk by the banks of the canal and there's a real buzz as the lights come on and the giant ships glide past out into the Mediterranean or down into the Red Sea and beyond.

HISTORY

Port Said's history is intimately linked to the history of the canal. The place didn't even exist until the first share certificates of the Suez Canal company had been printed, with the official foundation taking place in 1859. It was a flat, sandy strip running between the sea and Lake Al-Manzilah next door. The giant breakwaters were added in 1868, a marvel of engineering in a time of marvels, as a year later the canal itself was completed.

The idea of a channel between the Med and the Red Sea is almost as old as civilization itself, with both ancient Greeks and Romans considering it, as much later did Napoleon. It was not till the mid-1800s, however, that the engineering technology required and the vast sums of capital necessary became available. That money was raised by the Suez Canal Company and, with the permission of the Khedive of Egypt, Sa'id Pasha, they employed a Frenchman, Ferdinand de Lesseps, to start work. The canal was opened in 1869 but it was not France but Britain who gained control of it when the prime minister, Disraeli, financed by fellow Jews, the Rothschilds, bought the bulk of the company's shares from the almost bankrupt Khedive Ismail, simultaneously increasing British influence in Egypt.

The opening of the 195km-long canal changed the entire history of the Mediterranean. With the discovery of routes round Africa, not to mention the lucrative trade of the New World, the Med had been in decline for some time as an international export–import channel. Thanks to the canal, though, the boat once more came in. Port Said itself benefited dramatically from this, booming thanks to its massive dry docks and coal bunkers, vital fuel for ships of the steam age.

Thus Britain's route to her Indian territories and colonies in the Far East had been dramatically shortened. Furthermore, France could not win the ensuing diplomatic conflict with Britain for supremacy in Egypt, still nominally an Ottoman state, or over the strategically-located waterway. Egypt continued to be ruled by khedives, later kings, but these were guided by Britain. Despite riots and protests, the British didn't depart from the rest of Egypt until 1936. Gamel

EASTERN MEDITERRANEAN

Abdel Nasser dethroned Farouk in 1952. Ownership of the canal was still predominantly British, however, though France had some stake in it too. So Nasser nationalized the Suez Canal Company in 1956. Britain and France invaded the Sinai to force Nasser to back down but he refused to capitulate and after the UN had forced the European powers to withdraw Nasser became a national hero – and the canal finally came under Egyptian control.

During the 1967 Arab–Israeli war the canal was blocked, the eastern bank becoming the Israeli frontline. The blockage had one permanent spin-off: the supertanker. Having to ship oil round Africa once again, international petroleum companies invested in ever bigger tankers to cut transportation costs. When peace between Egypt and Israel was agreed in 1975, the canal was cleared but the supertankers remained, posing big questions for the canal's future. With a canal depth of 15m at most, these giants of the seas cannot pass through: so should the canal be widened and deepened, and if the answer's yes, how much would that cost?

Meanwhile, the declaration of Port Said as a free port in 1975 rapidly transformed it from a gigantic dockyard into a haven for many a Middle Eastern shopper.

WHAT TO SEE

Regrettably, the giant statue of the canal's founder, Ferdinand de Lesseps, was destroyed in the 1956 invasion, but **Port Said National Museum** (Sat-Thu 0900-1700, Fri 0900-1200, 1400-1700, E£20) at Palestine St's northern end gives some idea what it looked like. Also on display is the carriage the khedive rode in to the official opening back in 1869, plus an excellent collection of finds from ancient Egypt and other periods of the country's history.

There's also a **military museum** (Sat-Thu 0900-1700, Fri 0900-1200, 1400-1700, E£15), on 23 July St, which contains many items of equipment as well as exhibits on the Suez invasion and the Arab-Israeli wars, the last of which the Egyptians seem strangely convinced they won.

Other than that, there's not much else to visit except for the shopping arcades and the beach. For the former, try the streets around El-Gomhoriyya, an avenue running parallel to Palestine St one block back. The latter is a shell-covered stretch north of town, with the crowds thinning the further west you go.

Remember that this is not bikini country: Egyptian women at the beach are likely to spend their time fully dressed under a sunshade, while the men cavort in the waves in skimpy G-strings.

PRACTICAL INFORMATION
Orientation

The city is built on a regular grid pattern, with the area containing the sights a slightly tilted over right-angled triangle. Along the hypotenuse runs the Mediterranean sea, with a long sandy beach, while the harbour, Palestine St and the Suez Canal run along the shorter, eastern side. The longer side runs along Sa'ad Zaghloul St, the main boulevard. The train station is south of Sa'ad Zaghloul, on Mustafa Kemal St, while Superjet buses to Cairo and Alexandria depart next door. The other inter-city bus station is at Salah ad-Din St, on the northern side of the Ferial Gardens.

Getting round on foot is easy, with wide pavements and streets that you should savour before the narrower and more chaotic streets in Cairo and Alexandria.

Services The **tourist office** (☎ 235 289), 5, Palestine St, is open Sat-Thu 0900-1400.

The **tourist police** (☎ 228 570) are in the otherwise empty old post office on El-Gomhoriyya St.

Buy **phone cards** from street vendors or from the **phone office** on Palestine St, north of the tourist information office.

Ferries [see p461 for full details]
The only service from Port Said is the Louis Lines ship to Limassol; however, this is marketed as a mini-cruise so you will have to wait until the last minute if you want a one-way ticket.

Trains

Port Said station has three trains a day to Cairo (4½ hours, E£30), via Isma'ilia (1½ hours, E£14).

Port Said station seems pretty chaotic but works reliably and quite efficiently.

Buses
There are two bus stations: the West Delta company has its services based on Salah ad-Din St on the northern side of Ferial Gardens. From here there are hourly buses to Cairo (4½ hours, E£30) and Isma'ilia (1½ hours, E£8), 4 a day to Alexandria (4 hours, E£40) and Suez (2½ hours, E£15).

The Superjet station is next to the train station on Mustafa Kemal St. They have 10 buses a day to Cairo (3 hours, E£30) and one a day to Alexandria (4 hours, E£45).

Service taxis
These leave from next to the Superjet bus station and the train station and can be hired to take you anywhere in the city, or indeed the country. Haggling is obligatory. If you're going any distance make sure you give the vehicle a good once-over. If it can't get out of the parking lot, the chances of it reaching the Siwa Oasis are pretty slim.

Where to stay
Youth Hostel (☎ 228 702), Muhammad es-Sayed Sirhan St, 20 minutes' walk from the city centre. Official HI hostel; E£25 a bunk.
Akri Palace Hotel (☎ 221 013), 24, El-Gomhoriyya St. Victorian-era and atmospheric; sgl/dbl for E£30/60.
Hotel de la Poste (☎ 224 048), 42 El-Gomhoriyya St. E£65/100 sgl/dbl.

Where to eat
As in all Egyptian cities, it is possible to eat very cheaply from street vendors, who serve tasty falafel snacks (also good for vegetarians) for a few cents. However, make sure it all looks fresh and that the locals are keen on it too, as otherwise you could be in for some lengthy lavatory time. Best of all, go to some of the places listed below if you've got a few extra dollars.
El-Borg, on Port Said's northern beachside road. Good seafood/fish dishes at reasonable prices; about E£50 for a full meal.
Galal Restaurant, 60, El-Gomhoriyya St. Serves good Egyptian fare for E£30 a head.
Lord's Pastry, near the junction of El-Gomhoriyya and 23 July St. A classic patisserie; around E£5 each.

Alexandria

AREA CODE: ☎ 03 **POPULATION:** 5,067,000
One of the Mediterranean's most ancient and venerated ports, Alexandria still somehow manages to retain enough of its past glamour to keep its soul from expiring under the weight of modern development. It's a tough act, but one that's well worth seeing.

The city's ancient reputation as a seat of learning has recently received a boost with the completion of the new Library of Alexandria, while its more recent past reputation as a city of intrigue and colonial skulduggery still lingers in the Victorian grandeur of some of its hotels, French cafés and British bars. For Egyptians, Alex is also a place of relative liberalism and freedom from social mores as witnessed by the wider prevalence of Western fashions, women and wine. Most of all, though, this is a busy, working Mediterranean port, a gateway to the River Nile thanks to a connecting canal, and the major centre for the Nile Delta, Egypt's main agricultural area.

In summer, it can also be a lifesaver for Cairenes, who descend here in hordes for the cooler sea breezes away from the furnace-like heat of the desert capital. A modern fast train connects the two cities, as do a number of buses. The city is also a good base for going west, with the tourist resort of Marsa Matrouh on the coast, and further on the spectacular oasis of Siwa in the Western Desert, close to the Libyan border.

HISTORY
There had been a Greek colony on this site for around 1200 years when Alexander the Great came in 332BC seeking a new Egyptian capital and a major Eastern Med naval base before launching his invasion of Persia. Recognizing the potential of what was then the fishing village of Rakotis, he founded the city around what is now the peninsula of El-Anfoushi, but which was

EASTERN MEDITERRANEAN

then the island of Pharos. Alexander never got to rule from here, though, having died of a sudden fever in Babylon, but his body was brought back to the city for burial: what happened to it is unknown, though the site of his tomb reportedly somewhere off the present-day Nabi Daniel St, which was then one of the city's main roads.

Under the rule of Alexander's satrap of Egypt, the first Ptolemy, a new religious cult developed round the composite god, Serapis, a fusion of the old gods, Osiris and the bull-god Alpis, with the attributes of a number of Hellenistic gods; thus it was acceptable to the Greeks and worship of Serapis became widespread, nourished as it was in the Serapeum, the important centre of learning that gave Alexandria the key role as the original melting pot of Oriental and Occidental thought. Ptolemy's successors established the Mouseion, the world's first research centre, where Euclid, Archimedes, Plotinus the philosopher and the geographers Ptolemy and Eratosthenes studied. The first translation of the Old Testament from Hebrew to Greek, the Septuagint, was also produced here.

Under the power of Rome, the last effective member of the Ptolemite dynasty, Cleopatra, had been restored to the throne of Egypt by Julius Caesar following the death of Pompey, her Roman guardian. She claimed after the murder of Caesar that he was the father of Caesarius, her son, and she became involved in vicious political manoeuvres. Mark Antony, sent to censure her, dallied with her in Alexandria and she bore him twins. They married and Mark Antony divided parts of the Eastern Roman Empire between her and her children, telling the Senate that he was installing client rulers. By giving Roman territory to outsiders (Cleopatra and her offspring were of Greek ancestry) Rome declared war on Egypt and Octavian, brother of Mark Antony's Roman wife, defeated him at Actium. Mark Antony committed suicide and Cleopatra followed suit, preferring death to a Roman triumph.

However, Alexandria's location made it a city that could not be ignored, and it rapidly re-established its pre-eminent position in the ancient world. The arrival of Christianity added to this, with St Mark himself turning up in around AD62 to convert the population. At this time, Christianity was still prohibited and there were major persecutions in the city up until Emperor Constantine converted in the 4th century and Christianity became the official Roman religion.

Yet that was not the end of it. The city continued as a hot bed of inter-faith and intra-faith rivalry, with heated arguments breaking out over the nature of Christ. The first of these between two Alexandrian bishops, Athanasius and Arius, led to full-scale rioting. In AD325, Constantine convened the Council of Nicea, near Constantinople, the new Roman capital. The council ruled that Arius' contention that Christ, as a man, was lower than God was heresy, hence the Athanasian Creed.

Meanwhile, in 391, religious fervour, partly encouraged by Emperor Theodosius, led to the destruction by a Christian mob of what remained of the great Mouseion library, home to over 500,000 manuscripts. Also burnt down was Ptolemy's Serapeum. In 415, other Christians murdered the neo-Platonist female philosopher Hypatia, egged on by the city's Bishop Cyril. The city's Jewish and Christian communities also staged regular massacres of each other's followers.

In 451, a new church council, at Chalcedon (today's Kadıköy in İstanbul) met to sort out another heresy originating in Alexandria, Monophysitism — in some ways the opposite of Arianism in that this time, Christ was seen as not man at all, but completely divine. Despite the efforts of the church rulers in Constantinople, the Alexandrian Christians persisted in this belief, breaking from Constantinople and founding the monophysite Coptic Church, which still has some five million followers in Egypt.

All this bad faith left Alexandria and Constantinople seeing each other more as enemies than as parts of the same empire, so when the Arabs arrived in 642 with the new Islamic religion, the city fell without significant resistance being offered.

However, the Arabs not only had a new religion, but also a new geographical framework. Their capital of Egypt was to be Al-Fustat, way to the south of Alexandria and now part of Cairo's urban sprawl. Alexandria continued as an important naval base under both the Fatimids and Mamluks. It was a centre for the spice trade until the European discovery of a route round Africa to India and the Far East. The Ottomans then invaded in 1517 and had no real use for a port that rivalled their own in Anatolia. The canal to the Nile silted up, trade died and by the time Napoleon invaded in 1798, Alexandria had already gone back to the fishing-village status it had had when Alexander the Great first saw its potential.

However, things were about to turn around again. With French and British armies and navies coming and going as they pleased during the Napoleonic Wars, in 1805 the Ottomans, who still nominally held the place, appointed as viceroy of Egypt an Albanian, Mohammed Ali, with a brief to pull the place together again. He built a new canal linking Alex with the Nile, the Al-Mahmudiyyah, and brought in foreign traders through a system known as the Capitulations. This gave foreign communities resident in Alexandria the right to live according to the laws of their own countries, rather than Ottoman law, and also bestowed attractive benefits on foreign investment. The result was an economic boom and the location of many new industries in the city.

The introduction of cotton to Egypt in the 1820s was also a good investment. Supplying the mills of Britain and France became a lucrative business, particularly when Egypt's main cotton rival, the US, saw the American Civil War Unionist blockade cut off supplies from the Confederate south. The Cairo–Alexandria railway was opened in 1856, while the Suez Canal opening in 1869 also led to a boom in Egyptian ports.

With such a lot of cash around, and such vital strategic concerns, the European imperial powers all developed a strong interest in Alexandria and Egypt. Rivalry between Britain and France for control ended with a British bombardment of the city in 1882, ostensibly to put down an Egyptian nationalist revolt, but which in fact led to de facto occupation of Egypt by Britain.

This was also a time when the city underwent a minor cultural renaissance, with its foreign community some 100,000 strong. The Greek poet Constantine Cavafy was an Alexandrine, while British writers EM Forster and Lawrence Durrell also lived here, the latter writing his epic, *Alexandria Quartet*, in the city. Alexandria was also the country's summer capital, with entire diplomatic missions and government departments moving here from Cairo to escape the heat. The result was a kind of cosmopolitan glamour that still lingers.

In WWI and WWII Alexandria was the Allies' chief Eastern Mediterranean naval base. In the latter conflict, it became a vital base for the British war effort in North Africa against the German Afrika Korps of General Rommel. In 1941, the German forces came within a few kilometres of taking the city, occasioning the 'Alexandria flap' when panicking residents began fleeing and columns of smoke rose over British headquarters as thousands of documents were burnt. The decisive Battle of El-Alamein, only a short distance west of the Alexandrian suburbs, turned the tide.

While British troops left Alexandria in 1946, London continued to exercise control over Egypt via King Farouk, a pro-British monarch. However, nationalist forces under Gamal Abdel Nasser overthrew the king in 1952, with Alexandria the port from which the deposed monarch fled. After the abortive Anglo–Franco–Israeli Suez invasion of 1956, nationalization of foreign property drove out many foreign investors and residents of the city. Nasser's government also embarked on a major 'Egyptianization' campaign, giving jobs previously held by foreigners to Egyptians.

With Nasser's defeat by the Israelis in the 1967 Six Day War, the Suez Canal was closed. This benefited Alexandria as it took on the trade of Port Said, the main canal harbour. The introduction of open-door trade in 1974 also led to a flood of imports into the country, mainly through Alexandria. As the 1970s wore on, new petrochemical industries were founded, as well as iron and steel plants. While not so pretty to look at, all this has had spin-offs in terms of civic projects. Major archaeological work in the harbour during the 1990s revealed many fascinating remains of the ancient city, as did construction work in the old quarter. In 2000, the rebuilt Mouseion, now named the Bibliotheca Alexandrina, was opened, which, despite its difficulties, holds great promise for the city's future.

WHAT TO SEE

From the western harbour, the promontory north, once the island of Pharos, is dominated by two buildings. The first, **Fort Qaytbey** (daily 0900-1600, E£20), is built on the foundations of the ancient lighthouse that was one of the Seven Wonders of the Ancient World. The fort is an Islamic Mamluk-era construction from 1480 and houses a collection of debris from the French fleet sunk by British Admiral Horatio Nelson in the Battle of the Nile, which took place in Abu Qir bay, just east of Alexandria. Just south of here is **Al-Mursi Abu Abbas Mosque** (daily 0500-2200, women admitted to the back only, closed to non-Muslims during prayer times). With four domes, it's the city's largest and is named after a 15th-century Andalucían Muslim preacher. Built in the style of Al-Andalus, albeit in a 20th-century version, it now stands over El-Abbas' tomb.

On the western side of the promontory are the **Anfushi Tombs** (daily 0900-1600, E£20), built sometimes in the 3rd century BC for Greek citizens of the city who had converted to the pharaonic Egyptian religion. The tombs are located underground around an open light well and are probably just the tip of a crematorial iceberg that extends under the present-day streets around.

Heading south from here you come to the **Catacombs of Kom esh-Shoqofa** (daily 0900-1600, E£25). Descending three floors below ground, they are a classic example of the kind of mix and matching that went on in religious practice during the 2nd century AD. In particular, note that the heads of Egyptian gods are depicted with Roman bodies, and vice versa. At the entrance, Medusa heads and winged serpents beckon you down, with most of the main tombs on the second level. Watch out, too, for a jackal-headed Anubis and a sarcophagus engraved with Egyptian gods and Roman flourishes. An Anubis dressed as a Roman legionary also stands guard next to an Anubis disguised as a serpent. Anubis with his jackal's head was the ancient Egyptian deity responsible for guiding souls into the underworld. The Roman god Mercury had a similar function, which is why he is at the entry to the catacombs.

Nearby is **Pompey's Pillar**, named as such by the Crusaders, though it has no actual connection to the Roman civil war general, Pompey. In fact, this is the only remaining connection to Ptolemy's Serapeum. The pillar was put up in the Serapeum in AD297 by a citizenry grateful that Emperor Diocletian had spared them from a massacre.

From here, head east over towards the station in El-Gomhoriyya Square and a block further on you'll find the **Roman Amphitheatre** (daily 0900-1600, E£15). This is the only one of its kind in Egypt and is an acoustically perfect example of the art. Behind it there are excavations of a Roman bath and villa complex. Not far to the northeast is the **Graeco-Roman Museum**, at 5, El-Mathaf Er Roumani St (Sat-Thu 0900-1600, Fri 0900-1130, 1330-1630, E£20). This is the city's principal archaeological museum, with exhibits on display from a variety of sites around the city. Good for mosaics and stuffed, mummified crocodiles, it also now holds finds from the site of the ancient Pharos lighthouse and the underwater digs out in the eastern harbour.

Going seaward you pass through the district of Chatby with its fine old colonial-era European apartment blocks before coming to the hieroglyphic-covered façade of the new **Library of Alexandria**. This massive complex, surrounded by a man-made lake, is next to the university buildings on Lisan al-Silah St. With some four million books and 50,000 maps, it is a fine addition to the Alexandrian waterfront.

Head east from here, though, for a more ancient landmark, the city's oldest catacombs, the **Tombs of Chatby** (daily

0900-1600, E£15). On Port Said St, these date from the 4th century BC.

Returning to the west, take in the **Coptic Orthodox Patriarchate** on Elah Abad St (daily, free). There has been a church on this site since AD67, though what you see now was built in the 1950s. Nevertheless, there are some wonderful mosaics and stained-glass windows. Look out, too, for the ostrich eggs hanging above the altar; these are a symbol of the Resurrection and are unique to Coptic churches. St Mark, who is credited with introducing Alexandria to Christianity, is also buried here in a chapel to the left of the iconostasis.

Off Nabi Daniel St at 4, Shari Sharm el-Sheikh is another Alexandrian shrine, the museum dedicated to the Greek poet of the city, Constantine Cavafy. **Cavafy Museum** (0900-1600, E£10) was his house, containing the original furniture and copies of his books. Born in 1863, perhaps his greatest work was the haunting poem *The City*, which contains as some sobering thoughts for travellers, such as 'You won't find a new country, won't find another shore/This city will always pursue you.' Alexandria certainly pursued Cavafy, his house situated between a brothel and a church, his homosexuality practised in one and condemned in the other.

From here, it's a short walk through the crowded streets back to the waterside **Corniche**. This street is one of Alexandria's greatest monuments and strolling along it a real pleasure. Head for Sa'ad Zaghloul Square, and by the Cecil Hotel you'll see a number of the city's older French cafés — excellent places to rest some weary limbs.

PRACTICAL INFORMATION
Orientation
The city nowadays is a long stretch of a place, with the centre and most of the monuments up at the western end. A promontory sticks out at this point, joining the coast to what was once a separate island. On either side of this promontory are the two harbours, with ferries docking in the western one. The downtown area is east of the promontory and stretches back inland from the waterside road, the original Corniche. This leads round

to the new library and beyond. The main station is south of the eastern harbour in Gomhoriyya Square, from where the ancient main road, Nabi Daniel St, heads north to the waterfront and Sa'ad Zaghloul Square. The other main focal points are to the west at Orabi Square and Tahrir Square, where you'll find most of the old diplomatic missions and summer residences.

Practically all you need to see is in this area and within easy walking distance, though the nearest beaches are a bus ride away from Sa'ad Zaghloul Square. Buses depart from the station at 15 May Square. From the airport, south of town, catch local bus No 203 or minibus 703 to Orabi Square. Most of the budget hotels are in the central district west of Sa'ad Zaghloul Square.

Services
The main **tourist office** (☎ 484 3380), on the corner of Nabi Daniel St and Sa'ad Zaghloul St, is open 0830-1800 daily. There's also a branch at the Maritime Station, open 0800-1700. Both are good for free literature and maps. The **tourist police** are above the tourist office in Sa'ad Zaghloul.

Try branches of Bank Misr for **ATMs**, the branch on Tala'at Harb St having a couple. The branch on Sa'ad Zaghloul St gives Visa and MasterCard **cash advances** (Sun-Thu 0800-1400).

For **English-language publications** try Al-Ma'aref at 44, Sa'ad Zaghloul St or the Used Book Market near Misr Station at the southern end of Nabi Daniel.

Ferries   [see p460 for full details]
There are weekly Louis Lines mini-cruises to Limassol; check with the company about the availability of one-way tickets or get general information from the Maritime Station in the harbour (0800-1700 or on boat arrivals/departures, ☎ 480 3494) or at the tourist information office.

Trains
Misr Railway Station has inter-city expresses to Cairo: either the fast Turbini trains, which go five times a day (2½ hours, E£45 first class, E£35 second), or the slightly slower French trains (3 hours, E£40 first

EASTERN MEDITERRANEAN

class, E£25 second) which go eight times a day. Buy tickets at the station.

Buses

Superjet fast buses make the run to Cairo (3 hours, E£40 to downtown Cairo, E£45 to Cairo Airport) every 30 minutes from the bus station at 15 May Square behind Sidi Gabr train station. They also have a daily bus to Port Said (4½ hours, E£42). Alternatively, West Delta operate hourly buses to Cairo from the same place (3 hours, E£40) and four a day to Port Said (5 hours, E£30 without air con, E£45 with – in summer, definitely go for the latter).

Planes

Egypt Air (☎ 482 5937) at 19, Sa'ad Zaghloul St, Lufthansa (☎ 482 2607) at 6, Tala'at Harb St, and Olympic (☎ 482 1014) also on Sa'ad Zaghloul, east of Egypt Air; have regular flights out, the last two to Frankfurt and Athens respectively.

Where to stay

Hotel Normandy (☎ 480 6830), 4th floor, 8, Gamal ed-Din Yassin St. Near the waterfront, an old-established backpacker haunt; sgl/dbl E£35/45.

Hotel Gamil (☎ 481 5458), in the same building as the Normandy. Again, a backpacker haunt, with sea views from some rooms; rooms E£45, or E£60 for a triple.

Hotel Acropole (☎ 480 5980), 27, Gamal ed-Din Yassin St. Sgl/dbl range from E£30-50/E£60-70 depending on the view from the window.

Hotel Ailema (☎ 484 7011), 7th floor, 21, Amin Fikhry St. E£45/60 sgl/dbl.

Where to eat

Elite, 43, Sa'ad Zaghloul St. An Alexandrian classic, run by an impressive ancient Greek and decorated by a big fan of Matisse; E£50 a head.

Trianon, on the corner of Sa'ad Zaghloul and Ramleh Station Square. Another Alexandria institution from colonial times. Excellent French, Greek, and Egyptian fusion cuisine served in art-deco surroundings; E£60.

Muhammad Ahmed Fuul, 17, Abd el-Fattah el-Hadari St. Popular local dive for Egyptian cuisine; E£35.

Restaurant Denis, 1 Ibn Bassam St, near the Corniche. Has excellent seafood, the full spread settling you back E£60.

Bars and *ahwas* (coffee houses)

Spitfire, 7, rue Bourse el-Hadema, between Sa'ad Zaghloul Square and Orabi St. No visit to the city is complete without a trip to this haven; live music in the back room and a lively atmosphere in the front. Local beer only, for E£15 a glass.

Sheik Ali, off Sa'ad Zaghloul St. Has a fine selection of mezes to go with the drinks.

Sofianopoulo Coffee Shop, on Sa'ad Zaghloul St. Another classic city venue.

Ma'mura, on the Corniche. Open till late with coffee and *sheesha* (water pipes).

APPENDIX A: FERRY COMPANIES

● **Adriatic Shipping Co** (ASC Ltd, La Valletta, Malta, part of the Agestea group; 🖳 www.agestea.com) Has a service from Dubrovnik to Italy (Bari, Ortona).

● **Adriatica** (🖳 www.adriatica.it). Part of the Tirrenia group and operates passenger and vehicle services between Italy and Albania, Serbia/Montenegro and Croatia. UK agent: SMS Travel & Tourism (🖳 www.sms.com.mt, ☎ 020-7244 8422).

● **Agestea** see Adriatic Shipping Co.

● **Agistri-Piraeus Lines** Operates between Agistri and Piraeus via Aegina.

● **Agoudimos Lines** (🖳 www.agoudimos-lines.com). Has services from Greece (Igoumenitsa) to Italy (Bríndisi) and from Italy (Bari) to Albania (Durrës); online reservations. UK agent Viamare (☎ 08704 106040, 🖳 www.viamare.com).

● **Algerie Ferries** (🖳 www.algerieferries.com, in French only) Operates ferries between Marseille/Alicante and Algeria.

● **Alilauro** (🖳 www.alilauro.it; website in Italian only). Has services from Naples around the Italian coastline including to Ischia, Capri, Sorrento, the Aeolian Islands, the Pontine Islands, Positano, Amalfi and Salerno.

● **Aliscafi** See SNAV

● **ANEK Lines** (🖳 www.anek.gr). Has services within Greece from Piraeus/Patras to Crete (Iraklio, Haniá/Souda, Rethymno) and Corfu, and internationally from Patras/Corfu/Igoumenitsa to Italy (Ancona, Trieste); online reservations. Camping on board (see p16) permitted. UK agent Viamare (☎ 08704 106040, 🖳 www.viamare.com), French agent Navifrance (🖳 www.navifrance.net).

● **ANEM** Runs between Kalymnos and Mastihari (Kos).

● **ANEN Lines** (🖳 www.anen.gr, but in Greek only). Operates between west Crete, Kythira and the Peloponnese. ANEN, ANEK, DANE, LANE and NEL are all affiliated.

● **Arkadia Lines** See Hellas Flying Dolphins p435.

● **ASC Ltd (La Valletta Malta)** See Adriatic Shipping Company.

● **Baleària (Eurolines Maritimes**; 🖳 www.balearia.net, in Spanish only). Has services between the Balearics (Mallorca, Ibiza, Menorca, Formentera) and the Spanish mainland

---

❏ **General ferry information websites**
● 🖳 **www.ferries.gr** and 🖳 **www.paleologos.gr** For all Greek ferries plus connecting routes between Greece and Italy
● 🖳 **www.greekferries.gr** General route information for ferries from Greek ports
● 🖳 **www.greekislands.gr** General route and ferry information for the islands
● 🖳 **www.gtp.gr** Includes ferry schedules within Greece
● 🖳 **www.traghettionline.net** Will suggest the best company in terms of deals and rates for your chosen route from the main companies operating in the Mediterranean; you can then book online.
● 🖳 **http://uk.geocities.com/my_ferries** General Mediterranean-wide ferry information
● 🖳 **www.evasions.com/ferries.htm** General route and shipping company information though not for the Western Mediterranean.
● 🖳 **www.andalucia.com/ferry/home.htm** Details about ferry routes between Spain and Morrocco
● 🖳 **www.informare.it** Information about the ferry companies operating in the Mediterranean and their services (particularly international ones).

(Barcelona, Denia/Valencia) as well as between Algeçiras and Tangier. UK agent Viamare (☎ 08704 106040, 💻 www.viamare.com).

● **BEL** See Bodrum Express Lines.

● **Blue Line** (💻 www.sem-ferry.com/eng). Also known as SEM Maritime Company. Operates services from Italy (Ancona) to Croatia (Split, Zadar, Hvar); online reservations.

● **Blue Star Ferries/Strintzis Lines** (💻 www.bluestarferries.com). Has international services from Greece (Patras, Igoumenitsa) to Italy (Ancona, Venice, Bríndisi) and domestic ones from Piraeus to Crete, Corfu, Patmos, Leros, Kos, Rhodes, Syros, Mykonos, Amorgos (Katapola) and from Patras to Kefalonia (Sami), Ithaca (Ithaca Town/Vathy) and Corfu. Also has many routes in the Cyclades. Online reservations. Some rail passes are accepted on the Bríndisi route. Blue Star and Superfast are part of the Premium Alliance so some Blue Star services are operated by Superfast ferries. Camping on board (see p16) permitted on most international services. UK agent Viamare (☎ 08704 106040, 💻 www.via mare.com).

● **Bodrum Express Lines** (BEL; 💻 www.bodrumexpresslines.com). Has services from Bodrum to Kos, Rhodes, Marmaris, Datça and Dalyan.

● **Caremar** (💻 www.caremar.it or www.gruppotirrenia.it/caremar). Part of the Tirrenia group, Caremar has hydrofoils and ferries between the Italian mainland (Sorrento, Naples) and islands in the Bay of Naples including Capri, Ischia, Procida Ponza and Ventotene.

● **Caronte & Tourist** (💻 www.itraghetti.it/caronte.htm). Operates between Messina (Sicily) and Salerno (Italy).

● **CFSF** See Corsica Ferries.

● **Chios-Oinousses Lines** See Miniotis Lines.

● **Comanav** See Compagnie Marocaine de Navigation

● **Comarit** (💻 www.comarit.com; in Spanish). Operates between Algeçiras and Tangier.

● **Compagnie Marocaine de Navigation** (Comanav; 💻 www.comanav.co.ma, in French only). Has services from Séte to Tangier and Nador, Genoa to Tangier, Algeçiras to Tangier and Almería to Nador.

● **Compagnie Méridionale de Navigation (CMN)** See La Méridionale.

● **Compagnie Tunisienne de Navigation/Tunisia Ferries** (CTN; 💻 www.tunisienet. com/ctn/anglais.html or www.ctn.com.tn). Operates between Tunis and Genoa (Italy) and is part of the Tirrenia group. UK agent: Southern Ferries (☎ 020-7491 4968, 🖷 020-7491 3502, 💻 southernferries@seafrance.fr).

● **Corsica Ferries Sardinia Ferries** (CFSF; 💻 www.corsicaferries.com) has services from France/Italy to Corsica, Italy to Sardinia, and between Corsica and Sardinia; online reservations. Special Jackpot fares (car plus two people for a return journey) are offered on some routes. UK agent Viamare (☎ 08704 106040, 💻 www.viamare.com).

● **Corsica Marittima** Has services between Italy and Corsica; see SNCM.

● **CTN** See Compagnie Tunisienne de Navigation/Tunisia Ferries.

● **DANE Sea Lines** (💻 dane@otenet.gr). Operates within Greece, from Piraeus to Thessaloniki via Patmos, Rhodes and Mykonos.

● **Dodekanisos Express** (💻 www.12ne.gr.English). Operates from Rhodes to Kos, Kalymnos and Leros regularly. Services go less regularly to Patmos, Lipsi, Symi and Kastelorizo.

● **Enermar** (💻 www.enermar.it; in Italian only). Services between Genoa and Palau & Palau to La Maddalena. Tris Ferries are now part of Enermar, which in turn is part of Tirrenia Group.

● **Euroferrys** (💻 www.euroferrys.com). Operates between Algeçiras and Ceuta/Tangier.

● **Ferrimaroc** (💻 www.ferrimaroc.com). Has services between Almería and Nador.

● **Ferrys Rápidos del Sur** (FRS; 💻 www.frs-maroc.com/eng). Has services between Tarifa, Algeçiras and Gibraltar and Tangier. Online reservations. UK agent: Viamare (☎ 08704 106 040, 💻 www.viamare.com).

● **Four Islands Ferries** Operates services from Sami, Ithaca.

● **Fragline** (🖥 www.fragline.gr). Has services from Igoumenitsa/Corfu to Bríndisi. UK agent Viamare (☎ 08704 106040, 🖥 www.viamare.com).

● **FRS** See Ferrys Rápidos del Sur

● **GA Ferries** (🖥 www.gaferries.com) Has services from Piraeus all over the Aegean. Online reservations.

● **GNV** See Grandi Navi Veloci

● **Gozo Channel Company Ltd** (🖥 www.gozochannel.com). Operates between Malta (Cirkewwa, Sa Maison) and Gozo (Mgarr). The Sa Maison route is geared to cargo but passengers and cars are accepted when there is space.

● **Grandi Navi Veloci** (GNV; 🖥 www.gnv.it). Operates cruise-style ferries between Genoa and Barcelona, Palermo, Porto Torres, Olbia and Tunis (via Malta); also Livorno to Palermo, and Civitavecchia to Palermo. UK agent: Viamare (☎ 08704 106040, 🖥 www.viamare.com).

● **Grecia Maritime Ltd** (www.ts.camcom.it/english/oranave_albania.htm). Operates between Trieste (Italy) and Durrës (Albania).

● **Grimaldi** (🖥 www.grimaldi.it). Grandi Navi Veloci is part of the Grimaldi Group.

● **Hellas Flying Dolphins** (HFD; 🖥 www.dolphins.gr). Has services from Piraeus, Rafina, Iraklio and Lavrio doing round-trips to the Cyclades. Online reservations. Formerly known as Minoan Flying Dolphins. The company has also taken over Arkadia Lines.

● **Hellenic Mediterranean Lines** (🖥 www.hml.gr). Has services from Igoumenitsa, Patras, Kerkyra (Corfu), Kefalonia, Paxi and Zakynthos to Italy (Bríndisi). Holders of Eurail, Eurail Selectpass, Europass or Inter-rail cards can travel on their Italy-to-Greece services for free (see p14). Online reservations.

● **HFD** See Hellas Flying Dolphins.

● **Iscomar** (🖥 www.iscomarferries.com). Operates between Barcelona, Denia and the Balearic Islands.

● **Jadrolinija** (🖥 www.jadrolinija.hr). Croatia's main ferry company with services along the Adriatic coast (Rijeka, Zadar, Split, Dubrovnik, Hvar, Korčula, Mljet, Brijuni Islands), also to/from Ancona and Bari. UK agent: Viamare (☎ 08704 106040, 🖥 www.viamare. com); French agent Euromer (🖥 www.euromer.net).

● **Kalymnian Shipping** Operates services from Kalymnos around the Dodecanese.

● **Karystia Shipping** (🖥 www.gtp.gr). Has services between Rafina and Marmari (Evia).

● **Kiriakoulis Maritime** (🖥 www.travelpoint.gr). Operates services in the Aegean.

● **LANE Lines** (🖥 www.forthnet.gr; both in Greek only). Has services from Agios Nikolaos/Lissithi and Sitia on Crete to Piraeus and Rhodes and some other small islands, particularly the Dodecanese.

● **Linea dei Golfi** (🖥 www.lloydsardegna.it). Operates between Italy (Livorno and Piombino) and Sardinia (Olbia and Cágliari).

● **Linee Lauro** (🖥 www.lineelauro.it; part of the Medmar Group). Has services from Naples to Palau, Porto Vecchio and Tunis, La Spezia to Tunis, Palau and Porto Vecchio, Palau to Porto Vecchio, Trapani to Tunis, and Sète to Palma. Online reservations. UK agent Viamare (☎ 08704 106040, 🖥 www.viamare.com).

● **Linee Marittime Partenopee** (🖥 www.consorziolmp.it/). Has regular services from Naples to Sorrento and Ischia, and from Sorrento to Capri.

● **Louis Lines** (🖥 www.louiscruises.com). For mini-cruises/trips from Cyprus (Limassol) to Lebanon (Beirut), Rhodes, and Egypt (Alexandria, Port Said); online reservations. UK office: Louis (UK) Ltd (☎ 0800-018 38830 or ☎ 020-7383 2882).

● **La Méridionale** (🖥 www.cmn.fr) Has services from France (Marseille) to Corsica and from Corsica to Sardinia; online reservations.

● **LaRivera** (🖥 www.lariverabus.it). Hydrofoil service from Termoli/Vasto (Italy) to Dubrovnik and some Croatian Islands.

● **MA.RE.SI Ferries** (🖳 www.sms.com.mt). Operates from Malta (Valletta) to Sicily (Catania) and also from Valletta to Reggio di Calabra (Italy). UK agent SMS Travel & Tourism (🖳 www.sms.com.mt, ☎ 020-7244 8422).

● **Maritime Way/My Way** (🖳 www.maritimeway.com). Has services between Italy (Bríndisi) and Greece (Igoumenitsa, Patras, Corfu, Kefalonia). UK agent: Viamare (☎ 08704 106040, 🖳 www.viamare.com).

● **Marlines** (🖳 www.marlines.com). Operates from Italy (Bari) to Montenegro (Bar and Kotor) and to Albania (Durrës). UK agent Viamare (☎ 08704 106040, 🖳 www.viamare.com).

● **Maritime Company of Lesvos-NEL** Has services from Piraeus to Mytilini (Lesbos).

● **Marmara Lines** (🖳 www.marmaralines.com). Has services from Turkey (Cesme) to Italy (Venice and Bríndisi).

● **Marmaris Shipping** Daily catamaran and weekly car ferry between Marmaris and Rhodes.

● **Med Link Lines** (MLL; 🖳 www.mll.gr). Has services from Bríndisi to Patras, Cesme and Kefalonia. MLL is associated with NEL Lines.

● **Medmar Linee Lauro** See Linee Lauro.

● **Minoan Flying Dolphins** See Hellas Flying Dolphins

● **Minoan Lines** (🖳 www.minoan.gr). Routes from Italy (Ancona, Bari, Venice) to Greece (Athens, Crete, Patras, Thessaloniki and the Cyclades). Online reservations and various special offers such as midday discounts and a free ticket for every five bought in a six-month period. Camping on board (see p16) permitted on most ships. UK agents Viamare (☎ 08704 106040, 🖳 www.viamare.com) and Magnum Travel (☎ 020-8360 5353).

● **Miniotis Lines** (🖳 www.miniotis.gr; includes Chios-Oinousses Lines). Has services from Chios to Cesme, Karlovassi, Vathy and Inousses, and from Lesbos to Ayvalık.

● **MLL** See Med Link Lines.

● **Moby Lines** (🖳 www.mobylines.it). Operates between Italy (Genoa, Livorno, Civitavecchia, Piombino), Corsica (Bastia, Bonifacio), Sardinia (Olbia, St Teresa di Gallura), and Elba (Portoferraio). Online reservations. Camping on board (see p16) permitted between April and October on services to/from Livorno. Services from Livorno depart from both Stazione Marittima and Varco Galvani. UK agent: Viamare (☎ 08704 106040, 🖳 www.viam are.com) and SMS Travel & Tourism (☎ 020-7244 8422, 🖳 www.sms.com.mt).

● **My Way** See Maritime Way

● **Navigazione Generale Italiano** (NGI; 🖳 www.cormorano.net/ngi). Has services from Messina to Reggio di Calabria, and from Milazzo to the Aeolian Islands.

● **Navigazione Libera del Golfo** (NLG; 🖳 www.navlib.it/). Operates ferry and fast ferry services from Naples to places in and around the Bay of Naples.

● **NEL Lines** (🖳 www.nel.gr, but only in Greek). Associated with Maritime Company of Lesvos, has services from Piraeus to Rafina to the Cyclades.

● **NGI** See Navigazione Generale Italiano.

● **NLG** See Navigazione Libera del Golfo.

● **Poseidon Lines** (🖳 www.greekislands.gr). Services are suspended until further notice but they generally operate between Italy, Cyprus, and Israel.

● **Prekookeanska plovidba** (🖳 www.visit-montenegro.com). Services from Bar to Bari.

● **Roditis Shipping** Has hydrofoil and ferry services between Rhodes and Turkey (Bodrum and Marmaris); also to Kos, Kalymnos, Leros, Patmos, Tilos and Nisyros.

● **Salamis Lines** Services were suspended at the time of writing but when operational they go between Greece (Piraeus, Patmos and Rhodes), Cyprus (Limassol) and Israel (Haifa). UK agent: Viamare (☎ 08704 106040, 🖳 www.viamare.com).

● **Sardinia Ferries** See Corsica Ferries Sardinia Ferries.

● **Saremar Lines** (🖳 www.traghettilivorno.it/ or www.saremar.it). Has services between Italy, Sardinia (including La Maddalena) and Corsica.

● **Saronikos Ferries** Has a hydrofoil and ferry service from Piraeus to Aegina.

● **Schinari-Pessada Local Lines** Operates from Agios Nikolaos/Ithaca.

● **SEM Maritime Company** See Blue Line.

● **Siremar** (Sicilia Regionale Maritima; 🖳 www.gruppotirrenia.it/siremar). Has services between Sicily and Naples, and to the Aeolian Islands. Part of the Tirrenia group. UK agent SMS Travel & Tourism (🖳 www.sms.com.mt, ☎ 020-7244 8422).

● **SNAV Ferries** (🖳 www.snav.it/eng). Operates in the Adriatic particularly between Ancona and Split and also in the Tyrrhennian between Italy (Naples) and Sicily, the Aeolian Islands and also to the Pontine Islands. UK agent Viamare (☎ 08704 106040, 🖳 www.viamare.com).

● **SNCM** See Société National Maritime Corse Mediterranée below.

● **Société National Maritime Corse Mediterranée** (SNCM; 🖳 www.sncm.fr). Services from France (Marseille, Nice, Toulon) to Algeria, Tunisia, Sardinia (Porto Torres), Corsica (Porto Vecchio, Propriano, L'Ile Rousse, Ajaccio, Calvi, Bastia); online reservations. Most services from Marseille are overnight ferries, those from Nice are fast ferries. UK Agent: Southern Ferries (☎ 020-7491 4968, 🖹 020-7491 3502, 🖳 southernferries@seafrance.fr).

● **Strintzis Lines** See Blue Star Lines.

● **Superfast Ferries** (🖳 www.superfast.com). Operates between Italy (Ancona, Bari) and Greece (Patras, Igoumenitsa). Check their website for train and ferry special offers including train travel in Greece or Italy. Online reservations. Superfast and Blue Star are part of the Premium Alliance so some Superfast services are operated by Blue Star ferries. UK agent: Viamare (☎ 08704 106040, 🖳 www.viamare.com).

● **Tilos 21st Century Shipping Company** Operates routes from Tilos in the Aegean.

● **Tirrenia Ferries** (🖳 www.tirennia.it). Operates between the Italian mainland (Genoa, Naples) and Sardinia, Sicily and Tunisia. Tirrenia Group includes Adriatica, Caremar, Enermar, Saremar, Siremar, and Toremar. UK agent: SMS Travel & Tourism (☎ 020-7244 8422, 🖳 www.sms.com.mt).

● **TML** See Turkish Maritime Lines.

● **Tomasos Transport Tourism** (TTT; 🖳 www.fun.informare.it/ferry/ttt). Operates between Naples and Catania (Sicily).

● **Toremar** (🖳 www.toremar.it). Has services between Piombino and Elba, and from Livorno to Gorgona and Capraia, and Porto St Stefano to Giglio.

● **Tras** See Trasmediterránea.

● **Trasmediterránea** (Tras; 🖳 www.trasmediterranea.es). Operates services within Spain (from Valencia and Barcelona to the Balearics) and between Spain and Morocco. UK agent Southern Ferries (☎ 020-7491 4968, 🖹 020-7491 3502, 🖳 southernferries@seafrance.fr).

● **Tris Ferries** See Enermar.

● **TTT** See Tomasos Transport Tourism.

● **Turkish Maritime Lines** (TML; 🖳 www.tdi.com.tr/eng). Has services between Bríndisi and Cesme, Venice to İzmir, and from İstanbul to Marmara, Avsa and İzmir. Online reservations. UK agent Alternative Travel and Holidays (☎ 020-7241 2687).

● **Umafisa Ferries** (🖳 www.umafisa.com). Operates between Barcelona and Ibiza.

● **Ustica Lines** (🖳 www.usticalines.it). Has services from Naples to Ustica and Ustica to Trapani as well as from Trapani to the Egadi Islands off the western coast of Sicily (Levanzo, Favignane, Marettima) and to Pantelleria.

● **Vektar** (🖳 www.visit-montenegro.com). Has services from Montenegro (Bar) to Bari.

● **Venezia Lines** (🖳 www.venezialines.com). Operates catamarans in the summer from Venice/Trieste to ports along the Istrian coast.

● **Ventouris** (🖳 www.ventouris.gr). Has services between Greece (Corfu, Igoumenitsa,) Albania (Durrës) and Italy (Bari, Bríndisi); camping on board (see p16) permitted on some services; online reservations. UK agent Viamare (☎ 08704 106040, 🖳 www.viamare.com).

● **Virtu Ferries** (🖳 www.virtuferries.com). Has services from Valletta (Malta) to Sicily (Pozzallo, Catania). UK agent: Viamare (☎ 08704 106040, 🖳 www.viamare.com).

● **Yeni İstanbul** Operates a car ferry between Ayvalık, Turkey, and Mytilini, Lesbos.

APPENDIX B: FERRY SERVICES

Fares
● Fares quoted are for an adult; children aged under 4 often travel free and are half price if aged between 5 and 12. However, policies vary so it's always best to check.
● The fares quoted are one-way; most companies offer a wide variety of discounts so it's also worth checking what you might be entitled to.
● The price range quoted reflects variations in season and class of travel. Some companies have only two seasons, some four or more so it is always worth checking.
● Passenger fares given are generally for deck class and a Pullman seat (an airline-style seat). Cabin fares are given for journeys over eight hours.
● Vehicle fares quoted are car, motorbike and bicycle. Fares for trailers, caravans etc are available on the relevant company's website (see pp433-7) or through an agent.
● Port taxes are not included in the prices quoted but are generally €5-15 per person.

Miscellaneous
● Some companies describe the more modern ferries as 'high-speed', others as 'fast'; for consistency the latter is used in the text.
● Services operate year-round unless specified but again it is always worth checking as service frequency is affected by many different factors.
● Where a company operates both regular and fast-ferry services the former often operate year-round, the latter in summer only.
● Some companies offer a free bus service from their office to the port.
● Some companies have agencies which will be able to provide full information about the services. Most agencies are in Europe; some are listed in the list of ferry companies (see pp433-7) but are also available on most ferry companies' websites.
● For ease of use the ferry companies are listed in alphabetical order; the list is purely for information and is not meant to be a recommendation of any one company over another.

WESTERN MED ROUTES
Alcudia (Mallorca) to   [see p98]
Barcelona BALEÀRIA, daily, weekend service direct (3hrs), Mon to Fri via Ciutadella 5-5½ hrs; ferry €47-69, fast ferry €58-142, car €137-226, motorbike €20-37, bicycle €10.
Ciutadella BALEÀRIA, 1-2/day, Mon to Fri only, 60 mins, fast ferry €42-84, car €100-121, motorbike €19-32, bicycle €10; ISCOMAR, 1-2/day, 2½hrs, ferry, Pullman €31, car €75, motorbike €26, bicycle free.
Maò/Mahón BALEÀRIA, 2/week (at weekends), 2hrs, fast ferry, Pullman €42-84, car €100-121, motorbike €19-32, bicycle €10.

Algiers (Algeria) to
While travel to Algeria is becoming easier, both in terms of getting a visa and the overall security situation in the country, check with your consulate for the latest advice as the situation there remains volatile.
Alicante ALGERIE FERRIES, one every two weeks, up to 2/week in the summer, 12hrs, Pullman €113-149, cabin €149-268 (meals included), car €376.
Marseille ALGERIE FERRIES and SNCM operate a service between April and September, 1-6/week, 20hrs, but neither company's schedule is regular; €162 Pullman (no meals), €250 cabin (meals included), car €376.

Algeçiras (Spain) to   [see p113]
Ceuta EUROFERRYS, ferry, 5/day, 90 mins, Pullman €21-4, car €62, motorbike €16-20; TRASMEDITERRÁNEA, ferry 2-6/day, 90 mins, fast ferry (passengers only),12/day, 40 mins, €21-24, car €34-94, motorbike over 500cc €17, bicycles free.

Tangier BALEÀRIA, 4/day, 1hr, fast ferry €25, car €40-110, motorbike free €15; COMANAV, every 60-90 mins, fast ferry 70 mins €24, ferry 2¹/₂hrs €18-22, hydrofoil 2/day Mon-Sat 90 mins, car €55-70, motorbike €17-22; COMARIT, 4/day, €23-28, car €72, motorbike €27; EUROFERRYS, 12/day, 60-90 mins, €28, car €72-105, motorbike/bicycle €22; FERRYS RÁPIDOS DEL SUR, 70 mins, 4-5/day, €24, car €72-105, motorbike €22, bicycle €15; TRASMEDITERRÁNEA, ferry up to 14/day 2¹/₂hrs, fast ferry 2/day 1hr, ferry €24-38, fast ferry €25-29, car €33-105, motorbike over 500cc €223, bicycle free.

Alicante (Spain) to
Algiers see Algiers

Almería (Spain) to   [see p105]
Melilla TRASMEDITERRÁNEA, 6/week, Jun to Sep, 6-9¹/₂hrs, departure times vary, Almería to Melilla mostly at night, Melilla to Almería both day and night, deck €24, Pullman €27-70, cabin €45-113, no cars.
Nador COMANAV, up to 3/day, 5-10hrs, Pullman €29-66, car €130+; FERRIMAROC, 1-3/day, Nov to Sep, 6-8 hrs, Pullman €29, cabin €40-66, car €130-175, motorbike €35; TRASMEDITERRÁNEA, up to 6/day, Jun to Sep, 6-8hrs, Pullman €29, cabin €44-67, no cars.

An-Nadûr (Morocco) to see Nador

Barcelona (Spain) to   [see p91]
Alcudia see Alcudia
Ciutadella BALEÀRIA, Mon to Fri only, 1/day, 3hrs, ferry €47-69, fast ferry €58-142, car €137-226, motorbike €20-37, bicycle €10.
Genoa GNV, 2-3/week, 18hrs, Pullman €59-100 (no deck class), cabin €76-183, small car €93-166, motorbike €43-88.
Ibiza Town TRASMEDITERRÁNEA, 1-6/week (ferry/fast ferry), 8¹/₂-11hrs, Pullman €36, cabin €59-151, car €113-202, motorbike €34; UMAFISA, June to Sep only, at least 1/day, Pullman €47, cabin €54-167, car €131, motorbike €38, bicycles free.
Maó/Mahón BALEÀRIA, 1/day, via Alcudia at weekends, fast ferry 5hrs €58-142, direct daily ferry 9hrs, €47-69, car €137-226, motorbike €20-37, bicycle €10; TRASMEDITERRÁNEA, 1/day, 9¹/₂hrs (Barcelona to Maó/Mahón usually at night, Maó/Mahón to Barcelona both night and day services), Pullman €36, cabin €59-151, car €113-202, motorbike €34.
Palma ISCOMAR, 3/week, Apr to Feb, 8hrs, Pullman €24, cabin €28-110, car €162, motorbike €33; TRASMEDITERRÁNEA 5-7/week; fast ferry (3³/₄hrs, Pullman €56-116, car €125-211, motorbike €39), ferry (6-7hrs, Pullman €36, cabin €59-151, car €113-202, motorbike €34).

Ceuta (Spanish protectorate) to   [see p114]
Algeçiras see Algeçiras.

Ciutadella (Menorca) to   [see p98]
Alcudia see Alcudia
Barcelona see Barcelona.

Denia (Spain) to
Ibiza Town BALEÀRIA, fast ferry 6/week 2hrs €58-142, ferry daily 4hrs, €47-69, car €137-226, motorbike €20-37, bicycle €10; ISCOMAR, 6/week, 4¹/₂hrs, ferry, Pullman €30, car €160, motorbike €35, bicycle free.
Palma BALEÀRIA, direct 1/week at weekends 3¹/₂hrs, daily ferry via Ibiza Town 9³/₄hrs (Denia to Palma night service, Palma to Denia day service) ferry €47-69, fast ferry 5hrs €58-142, car €137-226, motorbike €20-37, bicycle €10; ISCOMAR, 6/week, 10hrs via Ibiza, ferry, Pullman €30, car €160, motorbike €35, bicycle free.

Gibraltar (Gibraltar) to   [see p110]
Tangier FERRYS RÁPIDOS DEL SUR, daily, 80 mins, €24, car €49-75, motorbike €15, bicycle €8.

Ibiza Town (Ibiza, Spain) to   [see p98]
Barcelona see Barcelona.
Denia see Denia.
La Savina BALEÀRIA, daily, frequent, fast ferry (25 mins, €14, car €85-115, motorbike €11-38), ferry (60 mins, €9.50, car €43-58, motorbike €5-19).
Palma BALEÀRIA, ferry (daily 4½hrs, €32-48), fast ferry (6/week 2hrs, €42-84), car €100-121, motorbike €19-32, bicycle €10; ISCOMAR, daily 4½hrs, Pullman €20, car €30, motorbike €20, bicycle free; TRASMEDITERRÁNEA, 6-7/week fast ferry, 2hrs, €36-73, car €65-110, motorbike €20.
Valencia BALEÀRIA, 6/week, 3½hrs, ferry €47-69, fast ferry €58-142, car €137-226, motorbike €20-37, bicycle €10 (note that Baleària services go from Denia but include the bus fare to/from Valencia); TRASMEDITERRÁNEA, 6-7/week, fast ferry, 3hrs, Pullman €56-116, car €125-211, motorbike €39.

La Savina (Formentera, Balearics) to   [see p98]
Ibiza Town see Ibiza Town.

Maó/Mahón (Menorca, Balearics) to   [see p98]
Alcudia see Alcudia.
Barcelona see Barcelona.
Palma TRASMEDITERRÁNEA, weekly, June to Sep only, 5½hrs, Pullman €20, cabin €31-77, car €62-101, motorbike €17.
Valencia TRASMEDITERRÁNEA, weekly via Palma, 13-15 hrs, Pullman €36, cabin €59-151, car €113-202, motorbike €34.

Málaga (Spain) to   [see p108]
Melilla TRASMEDITERRÁNEA, June to Sep, 6-7/week (generally one ferry and one fast ferry a day), ferry (7½-8hrs, €24, car €72-218, motorbike over 500cc €44-49, bicycle free), fast ferry (4hrs, €28, car €91-255, motorbike over 500cc €59, bicycle free).

Melilla (Spanish protectorate) to   [see p107]
Almería see Almería; **Málaga** see Málaga

Nador/An-Nadûr (Morocco) to
Almería see Almería.
Sète COMANAV, June to Sep, every four days, 36hrs, cabin €130-420, car €209-386, motorbike €86-110.

Palma (Mallorca, Balearics) to   [see p98]
Barcelona see Barcelona
Denia see Denia
Ibiza Town see Ibiza
Maó/Mahón see Maó/Mahón
Sète MEDMAR, 3/week, Mar to Dec, 14-15hrs, deck €40-48, Pullman €45-55, couchette €55-66, cabin €60-169, car €120-157, motorbike €35-40, bicycle free (20% discount if you book a journey to Ibiza or Menorca with Iscomar or Baleària).
Valencia BALEÀRIA, direct 1/week (at the weekend) 4¾hrs, via Ibiza inc bus from Valencia to Denia 6/week, 6¼hrs, ferry €47-69, fast ferry €58-142, car €137-226, motorbike €20-37, bicycle €10; TRASMEDITERRÁNEA, daily fast ferry 5¾hrs (most services go via Ibiza), ferry 6/week 7¼hrs, ferry (deck €36, car €113-202, motorbike €34, bicycle free), fast ferry (deck €56-116, car €125-211, motorbike €39, bicycle free).

F E R R I E S

Sète (France) to
Nador see Nador.
Palma see Palma.
Tangier COMANAV, alternate days, 36hrs, Mar to Jan (services stop in February for maintenance), basic cabin €152-228, car €184-344, motorbike €74-253.

Tangier/Tanja (Morocco) to   [see p115]
Algeçiras see Algeçiras.
Genoa see Genoa, Tyrrhenian Sea.
Gibraltar see Gibraltar.
Sète see Sète.
Tarifa FERRYS RÁPIDOS DEL SUR, 2/day, 35 mins, fast ferry, deck €24, car €72-105, motorbike €23, bicycle €15.

Tarifa (Spain) to
Tangier see Tangier.

Valencia (Spain) to   [see p103]
Ibiza Town see Ibiza Town.
Livorno see Livorno (Tyrrhenian Sea)
Maó/Mahón see Maó/Mahón.
Palma see Palma.
Salerno see Salerno (Tyrrhenian Sea)

TYRRHENIAN SEA ROUTES
Aeolian Islands (Sicily, Italy) to   [see p186]
Messina SNAV, daily hydrofoil service (no cars) year-round between all the islands (from Lipari 80 mins, Vulcano 100 mins, Salina 2hrs 10 mins, Panarea 2½hrs, Stromboli 2hrs, €17-20; from Filicudi, 4hrs, €28.
Milazzo NAVIGAZIONE GENERALE ITALIANO (ferry and hydrofoil), 2-4/day, Salina to Lipari (55 mins), Lipari to Vulcano (25 mins), Vulcano to Milazzo (2hrs); weekly Panarea to Salina (70 mins), Stromboli to Panarea (2hrs), Filicudi to Salina (70 mins), Alicudi to Filicudi (60 mins); SIREMAR (night) ferry service 3-7/week year-round, a fast ferry (from Lipari only), and a 3-7/week year-round hydrofoil service; SNAV, 2-6/day from Vulcano (45 mins, €11), Lipari (1hr, €12), Salina (90 mins, €13), Panarea (1hr 50 mins, €14), Filicudi (2hrs, €18), Stromboli (2hrs 10mins, €18) Alicudi (2½hrs, €22).
Naples ALILAURO, once daily calling at Stromboli (4hrs, €57-63), Panarea (4hrs 25mins, €65-72), Salina (4¾hrs, €71-78), Vulcano (5¼hrs, €75-83) and Lipari (5½hrs, €77-86; SIREMAR, ferry service year-round (4-5/week in summer, 2-3/week in winter) as well as a daily hydrofoil (no cars) in the summer months; SNAV daily hydrofoil (no cars) in the summer months, frequency, duration and cost similar to Alilauro above; service also from Filicudi 10hrs €87 and Alicudi 10½hrs, €89.
Palermo SNAV, ferry 4/week, 1-3/day hydrofoil (no cars) in summer from Alicudi (90 mins, €30), Filicudi (2hrs 20mins, €26), Salina (3hrs, €31), Vulcano (3½hrs, €32), Lipari (4hrs, €32), Panarea (7hrs, €37), Stromboli (8hrs 20 mins, €42).
Reggio di Calabria SNAV, daily hydrofoil (no cars) from Alicudi (4½hrs, €36), Filicudi (4hrs, €34), Stromboli (3½hrs, €19), Salina (2hrs 40 mins, €25), Vulcano (2¼hrs, €18), Panarea (2hrs 10 mins, €20) and Lipari (2hrs, €18).

Ajaccio (Corsica, France) to   [see p145]
Marseille SNCM daily, 10-12hrs overnight, €35-52, car €49-99; the *Napoléon Bonaparte* (see p143) is used for some services on this route and is recommended.
Nice CFSF, 7-8½hrs, cruise ferry, weekly, deck €20-33, Pullman €28-46, cabin €51-135, day cabin €20, car €40-142, motorbike €23-58, bicycle €3; SNCM, weekly Jan-Mar,

F E R R I E S

3/week Apr-June and Oct, daily Jul-Sep, 2/month Nov and none in December, 4hrs, deck €30-40, car €40-107.
Toulon CFSF, 4/week, 4³/₄-5³/₄hrs express, deck €20-33, Pullman €28-46, car €40-142, motorbike €23-58, bicycle €3.

Arbatax (Sardinia) to
Cágliari TIRRENIA, 2/week, 5¹/₄hrs, deck €20-24, Pullman €21-29.
Civitavecchia TIRRENIA, 2/week, 10¹/₂hrs, deck €22-26, Pullman €26-39 via Cágliari.
Fiumicino TIRRENIA, 2/week, 5¹/₂hrs, deck €34-58.
Genoa TIRRENIA, 2-3/week, overnight 14-17hrs, deck €25-50, Pullman €28-69, cabin €41-115, car €60-108, motorbike €29-040, bicycle €10.
Olbia TIRRENIA, 2/week, 3-5hrs, deck €20-25, Pullman €22-29.

Bastia (Corsica) to   [see p138]
Genoa MOBY, late May to late Sep, daily, 4¹/₂hrs, deck €15-28, Pullman seat free but not bookable, car €31-113, motorbike €29-40.
Livorno CFSF, shuttle service (1-4/day, 4hrs), express (weekly, June to Sep, 2³/₄hrs), deck €16-29, no Pullman seats, €20 for a day-crossing cabin, cabin €30-92, car €32-120, motorbike €30-48, bicycle €3; MOBY, Apr to Sep, 4-7/week, 3hrs, deck €15-28, car €31-113, motorbike €29-40, bicycle free (if a day departure is fully booked between July and Sep Moby will operate an additional night service, 4hrs).
Marseille SNCM, daily, 10-12hrs, deck €35-52, car €49-99.
Nice CFSF, 6-7/week, 4³/₄hrs express, 7-8¹/₂hrs cruise ferry (July-Sep), deck €20-33, Pullman €28-46, cabin (cruise ferry) €41-135, day cabin €20, car €40-142, motorbike €23-58, bicycle €3; SNCM, weekly Jan-Mar, Nov-Dec, 3/week Apr-May and Oct, daily June-Sep, 3³/₄ hrs, €30-40, car €40-107.
Savona CFSF, 5-7/week (up to 3/day Jun to Sep), 3¹/₄-4¹/₄hrs express, 6-8hrs cruise ferry, deck €20-33, Pullman €28-46, cabin €49-135 night crossing, €20 day cabin, car €40-142, motorbike €23-58, bicycle €3.
Toulon CFSF, 4-7/week, cruise ferry 8¹/₂ hrs, deck €20-33, Pullman €28-46, cabin €49-135, car €40-142, motorbike €23-58, bicycle €3.

Bonifacio (Corsica) to   [see p148]
Santa Teresa di Gallura MOBY, 4-10/day, Apr to Sep, 60 mins, €8-12, car €21-50 (€10 if you travelled to Corsica/Sardinia on a Moby service), motorbike €11-21, bicycle €3; SAREMAR 4-8/day year-round, 60 mins, €7-9, car €20-33, motorbike €8-10, bicycle free (special fare of €29 for two passengers and a car on certain crossings if you travelled to Corsica/Sardinia on Corsica Ferries Sardinia Ferries).

Cágliari (Sardinia) to   [see p157]
Arbatax see Arbatax
Civitavecchia CFSF, 4/week, June to end Sep only, 13hrs overnight, Pullman €31-52, car €50-82; TIRRENIA, daily, 14¹/₂-17hrs, deck €26-32, Pullman €31-41, cabin €37-73, car €61-94, via Arbatax.
Genoa TIRRENIA, July to Sep, 2/week, 20hrs, deck €45, Pullman €53, cabin €60-92, car €72-88.
Livorno LINEA DEI GOLFI, weekly, Apr to Sep, 19hrs, night service €26, bunk €28-45, car €35-51, motorbike €30, bicycle free.
Naples TIRRENIA, 1-2/week, 16¹/₄hrs, deck €26-32, Pullman €31-41, cabin €39-80, car €61-94, motorbike €29-40, bicycle €10.
Palermo TIRRENIA, weekly, 13¹/₂hrs, deck €24-31, Pullman €29-39, cabin €38-74, car €61-94, motorbike €30-40, bicycle €10.
Trapani TIRRENIA, weekly, 11hrs, deck €24-31, Pullman €29-39, cabin €38-74, car €61-94, motorbike €30-40, bicycle €10, boat continues to Tunis.

Tunis Tirrenia, weekly via Trapani, 24hrs, deck €49-58, Pullman €51-59, car €80-103, motorbike €30-40, bicycle €10.

Calvi (Corsica) to   [see p142]
Marseille SNCM, weekly, 11½hrs, Pullman €25-53, compartment €8-18, cabin €28-90, car €40-141, motorbike €21-59, bicycle €14.
Nice CFSF, 2-5/week, 3-3¾hrs express, 5¼hrs cruise ferry, deck €20-23, Pullman €28-46, cabin €41-135, day cabin €20, car €40-142, motorbike €23-58, bicycle €3; SNCM, 2¼hrs, deck €30-41, compartment €8-18, cabin €28-90, car €40-179, motorbike €21-59, bicycle €14.
Savona CFSF, 1-3/week, 3-4hrs express, cruise ferry 8hrs Jun to Sep, €16-33 day, €23-33 night, €20 day cabin, cabin €49-135, car €40-142, motorbike €35-57, bicycle €3.

Capri (Italy) to
Ischia Alilauro, 1/day, €12.
Naples Caremar, 40-60 mins, fast ferry €11, ferry €6, different departures daily; NLG, 4/day, 40 mins, €12; SNAV, up to 7/day, 40 mins, €11, no cars.
Sorrento Caremar, 4/day, 25 mins, €6, car €16-24; LMP, ferry 7/day €7, fast ferry 12/day €9.50 ; NLG, 6/day fast ferry 25 mins €9.50, ferry 5/day 40 mins €7.

Catania (Sicily) to   [see p181]
Naples Tomasos Transport Tourism, 4/week, 9-11½hrs.
Reggio di Calabria Ma.Re.Si Ferries, 1/week.
Valletta Ma.Re.Si Ferries, 2/week, 13hrs, Pullman €55, cabin €80-130, car €95, motorbike €35, bicycle €18; Virtu Ferries, express hydrofoil weekly Nov-Feb, 2/week Mar-June and Sep-Oct, 3/week July, 4/week Aug, 3hrs, €70-83, car €130, motorbike €78, bicycle €16.

Cirkewwa (Malta) to
Mgarr Gozo Channel Co Ltd, RoRo service, daily, every 90 mins, 25 mins.

Civitavecchia (Italy) to   [see p161]
Arbatax see Arbatax.
Cágliari see Cágliari.
Golfo Aranci CFSF, May to Oct, 3-7/week, 3½-4hrs express, deck €29-54, car €44-145, motorbike €28-70, bicycle €3; cruise ferry 5-10hrs, €17-44 day, €24-44 night, Pullman €31-54, cabin €30-105; Tirrenia, up to 4/day, 4hrs day, 10hrs night, deck day €21-22, deck night €17-18, Pullman €22-23, cabin €30-65, car €65-101.
Olbia Moby, 4-7/week Apr to Sep, 5hrs, deck €25-52, Pullman €28-55, car €37-140, motorbike €27-65, bicycle free; Tirrenia, daily, ferry 8hrs, deck day €21-22, night €17-18, car €65-85, motorbike €30-40, bicycle €10-13; fast ferry, daily May to Sep only 4hrs, €27-70, car €73-118, motorbike €35-50, bicycle €10-13.
Palermo GNV, 2-3/week, 12 hrs, Pullman €38-40, cabin €61-138, car €76-90, motorbike €33-44, bicycle free.

Fiumicino (Italy) to
Arbatax see Arbatax.
Golfo Aranci Tirrenia, daily in summer, 3½hrs, fast ferry €30-61, car €73-114, motorbike €34-50, bicycle €13.

Genoa (Italy) to   [see p129]
Arbatax see Arbatax
Barcelona see Barcelona
Bastia see Bastia
Cágliari see Cágliari.

FERRIES

Olbia GNV, daily Jun to Sep, 10hrs at night, 8hrs day, Pullman (no deck class) €41-82, cabin €59-165, car €84-149, motorbike €40-77, bicycle €15; MOBY LINES, late May to late Sep, daily, 9½ hrs, deck (night) €30-53, Pullman €37-60, cabin €58-165, car €47-137, motorbike €36-52, bicycle free; TIRRENIA, up to 2/day, 9-13½hrs, deck €28-38, Pullman €29-45, cabin €35-79, car €61-106, motorbike €29-40, bicycle €10.

Palau ENERMAR, daily Jun-Aug, weekly at other times, 11-13hrs (day and night services), Pullman €35-39, cabin €30-200, car €60-135, motorbike €36-55, bicycle €10-15.

Palermo GNV, 6-7/week, 20hrs, Pullman €74-119, cabin €95-204, car €111-202, motorbike €57-111, bicycle €28.

Porto Torres GNV, 6-7/week, 11-12hrs, Pullman €33-82, cabin €59-165, car €84-149; TIRRENIA, 1-2/day, 8-10hrs, deck €25-50, Pullman €26-70, cabin €50-115, car €70-108.

Tangier COMANAV, every 4 days June to Sep, 48hrs, cabin €213-252, car €277-372, motorbike €85-141.

Tunis CTN, 1-2/week Oct to May, 2-3/week Jun-Sep, 21-3 hrs, deck €108-196, couchettes €117-214, cabin €120-358, car €216-334, motorbike €42-89, bicycle €20; GNV, 2-3/week, Feb to Dec, 23hrs, Pullman €107, cabin €120-269, car €216-290, motorbike €44-96; SNCM, 20-24hrs, Pullman from €108, car from €216, motorbike €42-89, bicycle €20.

Valletta GNV, Feb to June and Oct to Dec, weekly, Genoa to Valletta via Tunis 39hrs, Valletta to Genoa direct 29hrs, Pullman €107-115, cabin €120-269, car €216-90, motorbike €44-96, bicycle €20.

Golfo Aranci (Sardinia) to [see p152]
Civitavecchia see Civitavecchia.

Fiumicino see Fiumicino.

Livorno CFSF, 6-7/week May-Oct (sometimes up to 2/day), 6hrs express, 8-10hrs overnight cruise ferry, day €21-48, night €30-48, Pullman (night) €37-58, cabin €58-145, car €38-142, motorbike €30-54, bicycle €3.

Ischia (Italy) to
Capri see Capri

Naples ALILAURO, frequent departures daily, to Naples Beverello and Mergellina; MEDMAR LINEE LAURO, 6/day, €6.50-7, car €27-57, motorbike €12-28.

Sorrento ALILAURO, 1/day, check locally. LMP, fast ferry 6/day via Naples, one direct.

La Maddalena (Italy) to [see p155]
Palau ENERMAR, half-hourly starting around 0700 and finishing about 1945, 20 mins, €1.60, €4 a car.

La Spezia (Italy) to
Palau MEDMAR LINEE LAURO, July to Sep, weekly, 13hrs, deck €25-50, couchette €35-60, car €20-100, motorbike €30-55, bicycle €10.

Tunis MEDMAR LINEE LAURO, Jun to Sep, weekly, 24-29hrs, deck €90-130, couchette €100-140, cabin €110-175, car €45-260, motorbike €80-120, bicycle €50.

L'Ile Rousse (Corsica) to
Marseille SNCM, weekly, 11-12 hrs, €35, car €40-121, motorbike €21, bicycles €14.

Nice CFSF, weekly Jun to Sep, 4¾ hrs, deck €20-33, Pullman €28-46, day cabin €20, car €40-142, motorbike €23-58, bicycle €3. SNCM weekly, 8½-12hrs, €30-35, car €40-123, motorbike €21, bicycles €14.

Savona CFSF, 1-5/week, Jun to Sep, 3hrs express, deck €20-33, Pullman €28-46, day cabin €20, car €40-142, motorbike €23-58, bicycle €3.

FERRIES

Livorno/Leghorn (Italy) to [see p135]

Bastia see Bastia.
Cágliari see Cágliari.
Golfo Aranci see Golfo Aranci.
Olbia LINEA DEI GOLFI, 4-5/week, Jan to Sep, 14-15hrs, deck €26, bunk €28-45, car €35-51, motorbike €30, bicycle free; MOBY, Mar to Jan, 6-7/week, 9-11hrs, deck €20-46 day, €29-46 night, Pullman €27-56, cabin €58-165, car €37-137, motorbike €29-52, bicycle free.
Palermo GNV, 3/week, 17hrs, Pullman €60-105, cabin €80-189, car €98-181, motorbike €48-97, bicycle €28.
Valencia GRIMALDI, weekly, 36hrs, berth from €93, car from €120, motorbike €52, bicycle free.

Marseille (France) to [see p123]

Ajaccio see Ajaccio.
Algiers see Algiers (Western Mediterranean).
Bastia see Bastia.
Calvi see Calvi.
Porto Torres SNCM, daily May to Sep, 3/week Oct to Apr, 17hrs, Pullman €60-70.
Tunis CTN, 1-2/week Oct-May, 2-5/week June to Sep, 20-25hrs, Pullman €78-154, car €182-364.

Messina (Sicily) to [see p184]

Aeolian Islands see Aeolian Islands.
Reggio di Calabria NAVIGAZIONE GENERALE ITALIANA, daily, frequent, 15-20 mins.
Salerno CARONTE & TOURIST, daily May to Dec, 7½hrs, deck €15, Pullman €20-25, car €52, motorbike €21, bicycle free.
Villa San Giovanni NAVIGAZIONE GENERALE ITALIANA, and tourist ferry boats, check details locally.

Mgarr (Gozo) to

Cirkewwa see Cirkewwa.
Sa Maison GOZO CHANNEL CO LTD, RoRo service geared to cargo but passengers/cars taken when space. Services once a day, Mon-Fri, 75 mins. Recommended as the boat goes round the Maltese coastline; it is also less crowded than, but just as comfortable as, the passenger boat from Cirkewwa.

Milazzo (Sicily) to

Aeolian Islands see Aeolian Islands.
Naples SNAV, daily, 5hrs, €86, no cars.

Naples (Italy) to [see p167]

Note that long-distance services leave from both Beverello and Mergellina Harbour – check which port you need before departure.
Aeolian Islands see Aeolian Islands.
Cágliari see Cágliari.
Capri see Capri.
Catania see Catania.
Ischia see Ischia.
Milazzo see Milazzo.
Palau MEDMAR LINEE LAURO, June to Sep, weekly, 13-20hrs, €35-70, couchette €45-85, cabin €45-110, car €70-150, motorbike €50-90, bicycle €10.
Palermo SNAV SICILIA JET, April to Oct, fast catamaran, daily 4hrs, €57, also ferry overnight 11½hrs, deck €47; TIRRENIA, daily, 10hrs, deck €36-41, car €67-86.

Porto Vecchio MEDMAR LINEE LAURO, June to Sep, weekly, 15-16hrs, Pullman €35-70, couchette €45-85, cabin €45-110, car €70-150, motorbike €50-90, bicycle €10.
Sorrento ALILAURO, 8/day from Beverello; LMP fast ferry 8/day, €7.30; NLG, fast ferry, 6/day, 30 mins, €7.50.
Tunis MEDMAR LINEE LAURO, 2/week, 19-21hrs, deck €80-120, couchette €90-130, cabin €95-155, car €38-200, motorbike €70-110, bicycle €50.
Ustica USTICA LINES, check locally for details.

Nice (France) to [see p127]
Ajaccio see Ajaccio.
Bastia see Bastia.
Calvi see Calvi.
L'Ile Rousse see L'Ile Rousse.

Olbia (Sardinia) to [see p152]
Arbatax see Arbatax.
Civitavecchia see Civitavecchia.
Genoa see Genoa.
Livorno see Livorno.
Piombino LINEA DEI GOLFI, 8½hrs, day ferry €16.50, night ferry €22, bunk €7, cabin €22-37, car €35-55, motorbike €30, bicycle free.

Palau (Sardinia) to [see p154]
Genoa see Genoa.
La Maddalena/Islands see La Maddalena.
La Spezia see La Spezia.
Naples see Naples.

Palermo (Sicily) to [see p175]
Aeolian Islands see Aeolian Islands.
Cágliari see Cágliari.
Civitavecchia see Civitavecchia
Genoa see Genoa .
Livorno see Livorno.
Naples see Naples.
Salerno GRIMALDI, 1-2/week, 13hrs, berth from €56, car from €55, motorbike €21, bicycle free.

Piombino (Italy) to
Bastia see Bastia.
Olbia see Olbia.
Portoferraio MOBY, 10-14/day, 60 mins, deck €7-10, car €34-59, motorbike €13-18, bicycle €5.

Portoferraio (Elba) to
Piombino see Piombino

Porto Torres (Sardinia) to
Genoa see Genoa.
Marseille see Marseille.
Porto Vecchio GNV, 2½hrs, see Genoa.
Propriano SNCM, 2-3/week, 3½hrs, May to Oct.

Porto Vecchio (Corsica) to
Naples see Naples.
Porto Torres see Porto Torres.

FERRIES

Propriano (Corsica) to
Porto Torres see Porto Torres.

Reggio di Calabria (Italy) to
Aeolian Islands see Aeolian Islands.
Catania see Catania.
Messina see Messina.
Valletta MA.RE.SI, weekly, 14hrs, €70, car €110, motorbike €40, bicycle €30.

Salerno (Italy) to
Messina see Messina.
Palermo see Palermo
Tunis GRIMALDI, weekly, via Malta, 40hrs, Pullman €93-120, cabin €93-238, car €129, motorbike €77, bicycle free.
Valencia GRIMALDI, weekly, 37hrs, berth from €129, car from €129, motorbike €77, bicycle free.
Valletta GRIMALDI, weekly, some direct 16¹/₂hrs, July to Dec via Tunis 19-20hrs, deck/Pullman on some services only €93, cabin €93-222, car €129-150, motorbike €77, bicycle free.

Sa Maison (Malta) to
Mgarr see Mgarr.

Santa Teresa di Gallura (Sardinia) to   [see p156]
Bonifacio see Bonifacio.

Savona (Italy) to   [see p171]
Bastia see Bastia; **Calvi** see Calvi; **L'Ile Rousse** see L'Ile Rousse.

Sorrento (Italy) to
Capri see Capri; **Ischia** see Ischia; **Naples** see Naples.

Toulon (France) to
Ajaccio see Ajaccio; **Bastia** see Bastia.

Trapani (Sicily) to   [see p178]
Cágliari see Cágliari.
Egadi Islands USTICA LINES operates to the Egadi Islands as well as to Pantelleria; check locally for details of services.
Tunis MEDMAR LINEE LAURO, weekly, 7-10hrs, deck €40-60, Pullman €44-51, couchette €50-70, cabin €55-85, car €20-120, motorbike €40-70, bicycle €50; TIRRENIA, weekly, 8-10¹/₂hrs, €42-50 deck, €80-94 a car. Be advised that Trapani–Tunis is a day voyage, Tunis–Trapani a night one. The boat to Trapani comes from Cágliari, and from Tunis continues to Olbia.

Tunis (Tunisia) to   [see p188]
Cágliari see Cágliari; **Genoa** see Genoa; **La Spezia** see La Spezia; **Marseille** see Marseille; **Naples** see Naples; **Salerno** see Salerno; **Trapani** see Trapani; **Valletta** GNV, see Genoa.

Valletta (Malta) to   [see p196]
Catania see Catania; **Genoa** via Tunis, see Genoa; **Pozzallo** see Pozzallo; **Reggio di Calabria** see Reggio di Calabria; **Salerno** see Salerno; **Tunis** see Tunis.

Villa San Giovanni (Italy) to
Messina see Messina.

FERRIES

ADRIATIC SEA
Ancona (Italy) to   [see p228]
Bar ADRIATICA, weekly, 15-16¹/₂hrs, deck €44-50, Pullman €56-61, cabin €70-99, car, €70-74, motorbike €35-41, bicycle free.

Brbinj JADROLINIJA, weekly (continues to Zadar), 5¹/₂-6hrs, deck €50-60, cabin €99-151, car €67-80, motorbike €26-39, bicycle free.

Cesme MARMARA LINES, weekly, Apr to Nov, 56hrs, Pullman €155-185, cabin from €165, car €155-185, motorbike €35-50, bicycle free; fare includes breakfast.

Durrës ADRIATICA, 4/week, 18hrs, deck €64-85, Pullman €69-82, cabin €87-134, car €92-103, motorbike €33-36, bicycle free.

Hvar Town BLUE LINE, July to Sep, 4/week, 10hrs, deck €37, Pullman €40, car €40, motorbike €20, bicycle free.

Igoumenitsa ANEK, 6-7/week, 15hrs, deck €52-68, Pullman €66-86, cabin €104-316, car €66-98, motorbike €28-36, bicycle free; MINOAN, daily, 15hrs, deck €55-78, dorm €93-122, cabin €95-286, car €68-102, motorbike €30-37, bicycle free; SUPERFAST, daily, 15hrs, deck €61-96, dormitory €98-140 (no Pullman), cabin €119-380, car €78-237, motorbike €41-56, bicycle free.

Korčula JADROLINIJA, 1/week, June to Sep, 15hrs via Split and Stari Grad; fares same as to Split.

Patras ANEK, 6-7/week via Igoumenitsa, 20¹/₂hrs, deck €52-68, Pullman €66-86, cabin €104-316, car €66-98, motorbike €28-36, bicycle free; BLUE STAR, daily (direct or via Igoumenitsa), 19-21hrs, deck €58-80, dorm €93-122, cabin €95-286, car €74-133, motorbike €34-66, bicycle free; MINOAN, daily via Igoumenitsa, 19hrs, deck €54-72, Pullman €72-94, cabin €107-318, car €68-102, motorbike €30-37, bicycle free; SUPERFAST daily direct 19hrs, via Igoumenitsa 21hrs, deck €61-96, dormitory €98-140 (no Pullman), cabin €119-380, car €78-237, motorbike €41-56, bicycle free.

Split ADRIATICA, 2-4/week, 8¹/₂hrs, deck €38-44, Pullman €44-49, cabin €55-93, car €36-46, motorbike €23-26, bicycle free; BLUE LINE, Apr to Oct, 6/week, 11hrs, deck €37, Pullman €40, car €40, motorbike €20, bicycle free; JADROLINIJA, 3-6/week, 10hrs, deck €54-64, Pullman €61-74, cabin €174-200, car €70-84, motorbike €28-41, bicycle free.

Stari Grad BLUE LINE, 2/week, 13hrs, July to Sep, via Split, deck €37-43, Pullman €40-50, car €45-55, motorbike €10-25, bicycle free; JADROLINIJA, 2/week, June to Sep, 12¹/₂hrs via Split; fares same as to Split.

Zadar BLUE LINE, June to Sep, 3-4/week, deck €38, Pullman €43, car €52, motorbike €20, bicycle free; JADROLINIJA, 1-4/week, 8hrs, deck €50-60, cabin €99-150, car €67-80, motorbike €26-39, bicycle free, some services go via Brbinj. There is also a hydrofoil service, June to Sep, 3-7/week, 3-3¹/₂hrs, some direct, some via Bozania, €60 to €80.

Bar (Montenegro) to   [see p249]
Ancona see Ancona.

Bari ADRIATIC SHIPPING CO, 2/week, 10hrs, deck €44, Pullman €50, car €60; MARLINES, 3/week, 8¹/₂ hrs, deck €39, Pullman €44, cabin €52-120, car €61, motorbike €24; PREKOOKEANSKA PLOVIDBA, 5/week, 9-10hrs, and VEKTAR, 3/week, 10hrs.

Bari (Italy) to   [see p258]
Bar see Bar.

Corfu Town MINOAN, June to Sep, 2-3/week, 7¹/₂hrs (boat continues to Igoumenitsa and Patras), deck €34-56, Pullman €50-66, cabin €82-108, car €36-118, motorbike €20-30, bicycle free; VENTOURIS, 4-7/week, 11¹/₂hrs, deck €22-45, Pullman €37-56, car €22-56, motorbike €10-23, bicycle free.

Dubrovnik ADRIATIC SHIPPING CO, 9hrs, 2-3/week, July to Sep; deck €43-48, Pullman €48-56, cabin €81-170, car €51-58, motorbike €20-35, bicycle free; JADROLINIJA, weekly Oct to May, 4-5/week June to Sep, 9hrs, deck €35-45, Pullman €40-50, car €40-50.

Durrës ADRIATICA, daily, 8¹/₂hrs, deck €46-58, Pullman €54-61, cabin €64-104, car €81-90, motorbike €26-29, bicycle free; AGOUDIMOS, 3-5/week, 9hrs, deck €42-56, Pullman €47-62, cabin €55-90, car €75-93, motorbike €14-22, bicycle free; ASC, daily, 8hrs, €49-59 deck, Pullman €54-64, cabin €67-108, car €85-92, motorbike €28-30, bicycle free; VENTOURIS, 4-7/week, Feb–Nov, 8-9hrs, deck €42-57, Pullman €49-60, car €75-95. Note: a passenger-only catamaran operates during the summer, 4hrs, 2/day, €65, check locally.

Igoumenitsa MINOAN, June to Sep, daily, 9hrs, deck €34-56, Pullman €50-66, cabin €82-108, car €36-118, motorbike €20-30, bicycle free; SUPERFAST, daily, 9¹/₂hrs, deck €48-68, Pullman €67-81, dorm €79-101, cabin €100-301, car €49-207, motorbike €25-36, bicycle free, continues to Patras; VENTOURIS 4-7/week, 12¹/₂hrs, via Corfu, deck €22-45, Pullman €37-56, car €22-56, motorbike €10-23, bicycle free.

Patras MINOAN, June to Sep only, daily via Igoumenitsa, 3/week via Corfu, 15hrs, deck €34-56, Pullman €50-66, car €36-67, motorbike €20-30, bicycle free; SUPERFAST, daily via Igoumenitsa, 15¹/₂hrs, deck €48-68, Pullman €67-81, dorm €79-101, cabin €100-301, car €49-207, motorbike €25-36, bicycle free.

Rijeka JADROLINIJA, 1-4/week, 33hrs via Dubrovnik, Mljet, Korčula, Stari Grad, Split and Zadar, deck €74-83, Pullman €83-99, couchette €109-130, cabin €130-305, car €109-131, motorbike €46-57, bicycle free.

Brač (Croatia) to
Supetar see Supetar

Brbinj, Dugi Otok (Croatia) to
Ancona see Ancona.
Dubrovnik JADROLINIJA, July to Sep, weekly, 14¹/₂-15hrs.
Korčula JADROLINIJA, July to Sep, weekly, 10hrs.
Rijeka JADROLINIJA, July to Sep, weekly, 5¹/₂hrs.
Stari Grad JADROLINIJA, July to Sep, weekly, 6¹/₂hrs.
Zadar JADROLINIJA, daily, 1¹/₂hrs, deck €3, car €14, motorbike €4, bicycle €3.

Brijuni Islands (Croatia, Brioni) to
Pula use an excursion boat that stops on the islands as not all do, 5hr round trip.

Bríndisi (Italy) to   [see p262]
Cesme MARMARA LINES, weekly, June–Sep, 28-30hrs, Pullman €90-110, cabin bed from €110. Breakfast inc for cabin passengers, car €145-165, motorbike €25-40, bicycle free.
Corfu Town BLUE STAR, 3-7/week, 6-8¹/₂hrs, deck €33-54, no Pullman, cabin €60-110, car €32-55, motorbike/bicycle free; FRAGLINE, end Mar to end Sep only, daily, 7¹/₂hrs, deck €26-44, Pullman €37-55, car €28-48; HML, June to Sep, 6-7/week, 6-9hrs, deck/cabin €30-118, car €29-82, motorbike free; MARITIME WAY, Mar to Sep, deck €30-50, Pullman €40-60, car €28-52, motorbike free; MED LINK LINES, 8hrs, daily, June to Sep; SNAV, 4/week Oct to June, daily July to Sep, 12¹/₂hrs.
Igoumenitsa AGOUDIMOS LINES, 6-7/week, Feb-Dec, 8hrs, deck €22-37, Pullman €28-48, car €27-45; BLUE STAR, 3-7/week, 9¹/₂hrs, deck €33-54, no Pullman, cabin €60-110, car €32-55, motorbike/bicycle free, via Corfu; FRAGLINE FERRIES, daily end Mar to end Sep, 9hrs, deck €26-44, Pullman €37-55, car €28-48; HML, 4/week, Oct to June, daily July to Sep, 11¹/₂hrs, deck €25-45, Pullman €35-55, car €22-43; MARITIME WAY, Mar to Sep, deck €30-50, Pullman €40-60, car €28-52, motorbike free.
Kefalonia HML, June to Sep, 2/week, via Corfu and Igoumenitsa/Paxi, 9-11hrs, €30-160, car €28-56, motorbike free; MARITIME WAY Mar to Sep, alternate days, deck €30-54, Pullman €40-65, car €28-56; MED LINK LINES, direct, June to Aug, 11hrs, alternate days, deck €40, Pullman €50, car €35, motorbike €18, services go to Sami.
Patras HML, 3-4/week, Oct–June, daily July-Sep, 13-18¹/₂hrs, deck €25-45, Pullman €35-55, car €22-43; MARITIME WAY via both Igoumenitsa and Kefalonia, Mar to Sep, alternate

days, deck €30-54, Pullman €40-65, car €28-56; Med Link Lines, 15hrs, alternate days, deck €40, Pullman €50, car €35, motorbike €18.

Corfu Town (Corfu, Greece) to [see p265]
Bari see Bari.
Bríndisi see Bríndisi.
Igoumenitsa ANEK, 3hrs, 1-6/week, deck €27, Pullman €27, car €74, motorbike €15, bicycle free; Minoan, 3-6/week, 1½hrs, deck €6, car €24, motorbike €8.
Patras ANEK, 7-8hrs, 1-6/week, deck €27, Pullman €27, car €74, motorbike €15, bicycle free; Blue Star, 4/week, 7hrs, deck €21, Pullman €21, car €75, motorbike €15-23, bicycle free; Minoan, 3-6/w, 6-7hrs, Pullman €26, car €76, motorbike €23, bicycle free.
Trieste ANEK, 1-6/week, 22-3hrs, deck €52-68, Pullman €66-86, cabin €104-316, car €66-98, motorbike €28-36, bicycle free.
Venice Blue Star, 2-4/week, 26-27hrs, deck €44-60, Pullman €57-72, cabin €94-285, car €61-77, motorbike €31-35, bicycle free; Minoan, 3-6/week, 21hrs, deck €57-75, cabin €112-134, Pullman €76-96, car €70-110, motorbike €34-40, bicycle free.

Dalmatian Islands (Croatia) see Dubrovnik. [see p241]

Drvenik (Croatia) to
Sugcuraj Jadrolinija, 4-10/day, 30 mins, €1.50.

Dubrovnik (Croatia) to [see p234]
Note: other ferry companies also operate services between Dubrovnik and the Dalmatian Islands; check locally.
Bari see Bari.
Brbinj see Brbinj.
Hvar (Hvar Town) Jadrolinija via Korčula, Jul to Sep, 4/week, 7½-9hrs, deck €16-19, Pullman €19-23.
Korčula (Korčula Town) Jadrolinija, 2-4/week, 3½hrs direct, 6hrs via Sobra, deck €28-33, Pullman €36-41.
Mljet (Sobra) Jadrolinija, daily, 2hrs, deck €7.
Ortona Adriatic Shipping Company, 2/week, 12hrs, July to Sep, deck €49-59, Pullman €55-69, cabin €89-180, car €65-80, motorbike €25-45, bicycle free.
Rijeka Jadrolinija, 2-4/week, 22hrs, deck €39-45, Pullman €46-57 via Korčula, Stari Grad, Split and Zadar.
Sipan (Sipanska Luka) Jadrolinija, daily, 1¾hrs, €15.
Split Jadrolinija, 2-4/week, 11-12hrs, deck €17-21, Pullman €21-28, via Sobra (1/week), Stari Grad and Korčula.
Stari Grad Jadrolinija, 2-4/week, 7½hrs, deck €16-19, Pullman €19-23.
Zadar Jadrolinija, 2-4/week, 15-17hrs, deck €19-25, Pullman €36-44 via Korčula, Stari Grad, and Split.

Durrës (Albania) to [see p251]
Ancona see Ancona.
Bari see Bari.
Trieste Grecia Maritime Ltd, 2/week, 24hrs.

Hvar Town (Hvar, Croatia) to [see p246]
Ancona see Ancona.
Split Jadrolinija, 3-7/week (service comes from either Vis, or Lastovo and Vela Luka), 1-2hrs, €8; SEM, 2-7/week, 2¼hrs, €5.
Termoli LaRivera, 2-3/week June-Sep, 4-5hrs, catamaran €80 (some go via Bol and Vasto)
Zadar Aliscafi, June to Sep, hydrofoil daily, 3hrs, €24; SEM, 2/week, 15½hrs, €23.

Igoumenitsa (Greece) to   [see p270]
Ancona see Ancona.
Bari see Bari.
Bríndisi see Bríndisi.
Corfu Town see Corfu Town.
Patras ANEK, 4-6/week, 6-10hrs (direct or via Corfu) deck €27, Pullman €27, cabin €42-60, car €74, motorbike €15, bicycle free; MINOAN, daily, 5-10hrs (direct or via Corfu), deck €25, car €76, motorbike €23; SUPERFAST, 2/day, 5-6hrs, deck €27, Pullman €27, cabin €42-73, car €74, motorbike €15, bicycle free.
Trieste ANEK, 4-6/week, 21-23hrs, deck €52-68, Pullman €66-86, cabin €104-316, car €66-98, motorbike €28-36, bicycle free.
Venice BLUE STAR, 2-4/week, 23-25hrs, deck €44-60, Pullman €57-68, cabin €95-286, car €61-112, motorbike €31-35, bicycle free; MINOAN 4-6/week, 22hrs, deck €57-85, Pullman €76-96, cabin €112-134, car €70-110, motorbike €34-40, bicycle free.

Ithaca (Greece) to   [see p279]
Kefalonia BLUE STAR, FRAGLINE, GA FERRIES, daily, 35 mins, €2, from Ithaca Town/Vathy to Sami. Also from Fiskardo to Frikes.
Lefkada FRAGLINE, daily, 2¹/₂hrs, €2.50, from Frikes to Nidri.
Patras BLUE STAR, FRAGLINE, GA FERRIES, daily from Ithaca Town/Vathy.

Izola (Slovenia) to
Venice Occasional day trips, summer only – check locally.

Kefalonia (Greece) to   [see p277]
Bríndisi see Bríndisi.
Ithaca see Ithaca.
Patras HML and MED LINK LINES, 2-6/week, 3hrs, €9.50.
Zakynthos SCHINARI-PESSADA, daily, 1 hour, €3.

Korčula Town (Korčula, Croatia) to   [see p244]
Ancona see Ancona.
Brbinj see Brbinj.
Dubrovnik see Dubrovnik.
Rijeka JADROLINIJA, 2-3/week, 14¹/₂-19hrs, via Stari Grad and Split, deck €25-38, Pullman €44-55.
Split JADROLINIJA, 2-3/week, 3¹/₂hrs direct, 6hrs via Stari Grad, deck €16-20, Pullman €19-27.
Termoli LARIVERA, Jun to Sep, 3/week, 4¹/₂hrs some via Lastovo, €80.
There are also services to other local islands in summer – check locally.

Lefkada (Greece) to
Ithaca see Ithaca

Mljet (Sobra) to   [see p242]
Rijeka JADROLINIJA, July to Sep, weekly via Korčula, Split, Zadar and Brbinj, 21hrs, deck €34-41, Pullman €42-51.

Ortona (Italy) to
Dubrovnik see Dubrovnik.

Patras (Greece) to   [see p274]
Ancona see Ancona.
Bari see Bari.
Bríndisi see Bríndisi.
Corfu Town see Corfu.
Igoumenitsa see Igoumenitsa.

FERRIES

Ithaca see Ithaca.
Kefalonia see Kefalonia.
Trieste ANEK, 4-6/week, 31-2hrs, deck €52-68, Pullman €68-86, car €66-98, motorbike €28-36, bicycle free, via Corfu and/or Igoumenitsa.
Venice BLUE STAR, 2-4/week, 33hrs, deck €44-47, Pullman €57-71, cabin €94-285, car €61-112, motorbike €31, bicycle free; MINOAN LINES, 4-6/week, 33hrs, deck €57-75, cabin €112-134, car €70-110, motorbike €31-40, bicycle free; both services go via Igoumenitsa and Corfu.

Piran/Pirano (Slovenia) to [see p217]
Venice VENEZIA LINES, 2/week, May to Sep, 2½hrs, €42-52, bicycle €7, no cars.

Poreč/Parenzo (Croatia) to [see p219]
Trieste VENEZIA LINES, May to Sep, 1/week, 1hr 20 mins, €40-50, bicycle €7, no cars. The boat comes from Rovinj.
Venice VENEZIA LINES, May to Sep, 3-7/week direct 2½hrs, others via Piran, Umago or Pula, 4-5hrs, €42-52, bicycle €7, no cars; occasional summer-only excursion boats; check locally.

Pula (Croatia) to [see p222]
Brijuni Islands see Brijuni Islands.
Venice VENEZIA LINES, 2/week, May to Sep, 2hrs 50 mins, €42-52, bicycle €7, no cars.

Rijeka (Croatia) to [see p224]
Bari see Bari.
Brbinj see Brbinj.
Dubrovnik see Dubrovnik.
Korčula see Korčula.
Mljet see Mljet.
Split JADROLINIJA, July to Sep, 2-3/week, 11hrs, deck €28-33, Pullman €33-40.
Stari Grad JADROLINIJA, July to Sep, 2-3/week, 15hrs, deck €30-36, Pullman €36-44.
Zadar JADROLINIJA, July to Sep, 2-3/week, 6hrs, deck €28-33, Pullman €33-40.

Rovinj/Rovingo (Croatia) to [see p221]
Poreč see Poreč.
Trieste VENEZIA LINES, May to Sep, 1/week via Poreč, 2hrs 20 min, €40-50, cycle €7, no cars
Venice VENEZIA LINES, May to Sep, 3/week, 2hrs 40 mins, €42-52, bicycle €7, no cars.

Split (Croatia) to [see p230]
Note: other companies also offer services to the Dalmatian Island destinations; check locally.
Ancona see Ancona.
Dubrovnik see Dubrovnik.
Hvar Town see Hvar Town.
Korčula Town see Korčula Town.
Rijeka see Rijeka.
Stari Grad JADROLINIJA, 1-3/day, 2hrs, €5.
Supetar JADROLINIJA, 5-7/day, 1hr, €2.
Zadar JADROLINIJA, 2/week, 5hrs, €10.

Stari Grad (Hvar, Croatia) to [see p230]
Ancona see Ancona; **Brbinj** see Brbinj; **Dubrovnik** see Dubrovnik; **Rijeka** see Rijeka.
Split see Split.

Sugcuraj (Hvar, Croatia) to
Drvenik see Drvenik.

Supetar (Brač, Croatia) to [see p247]
Split see Split.

Termoli (Italy) to
Hvar see Hvar
Korčula see Korčula

Trieste (Italy) to [see p214]
Corfu Town see Corfu Town; **Durrës** see Durrës; **Igoumenitsa** see Igoumenitsa; **Patras** see Patras; **Poreč/Parenzo** see Poreč/Parenzo; **Rovinj** see Rovinj.

Venice (Italy) to [see p206]
Corfu Town see Corfu; **Igoumenitsa** see Igoumenitsa; **İzmir** see İzmir (Aegean); **Izola** see Izola; **Patras** see Patras; **Piran** see Piran; **Poreč/Parenzo** see Poreč/Parenz; **Pula** see Pula; **Rovinj** see Rovinj.

Zadar (Croatia) to [see p226]
Note: there are services to many of the Dalmatian Islands from Zadar; check locally.
Ancona see Ancona; **Brbinj** see Brbinj; **Dubrovnik** see Dubrovnik; **Hvar Town** see Hvar Town; **Rijeka** see Rijeka; **Split** see Split.

Zakynthos (Greece) to
Ithaca see Ithaca.

AEGEAN SEA
The routes shown below are the main ones of the many operating in the Aegean. The majority operate year-round but some run in the high season only, which is generally from April or May to the end of September or October. Check before planning your itinerary.

It is best to make advance reservations for journeys within the Aegean during the summer months, particularly at weekends. At other times tickets can be obtained at the port on the day, though you should be there at least an hour before departure.

The word 'Town' after a place name means the island has the same name as the port. Places are listed under the most familiar name (this may be the island or a town on the island) with the port name in parenthesis if it is different from the island's name.

The fare shown (an adult one-way ticket deck class) should be used as a guideline only as fares vary depending on the season, time of day, company, and whether you take a ferry or a catamaran/hydrofoil.

Agios Nikolaos (aka Lasithi, Crete) to [see p317]
Tour boats go to Spinalonga daily.

Halki (aka Chalki, Nimborio, via Sitia, Kassos and Karpathos)	3/week	11½ hours	€16	LANE
Karpathos Town (via Sitia and Kassos)	4/week	6 hours	€15	LANE
Milos Town	3/week	7 hours	€19	LANE
Piraeus (via Milos Town)	daily	12 hours	€28	LANE
Rhodes Town (via Sitia, Kassos, Karpathos Town and Halki)	3/week	11 hours	€22	LANE
Sitia (Crete)	5/week	1½ hours	€9	LANE

Ayvalık (Turkey) to [see p376]
Mytilini YENI İSTANBUL, 3-5/week, May to Oct, 75 mins, car ferry, €60.

Bodrum (Turkey) to [see p335]
Kormen/Datça BEL, June-Sep, daily hydrofoil to Kormen then bus to Datça (40 mins, €10) daily ferry,1½-2hrs, deck €8, car €22.50.
Kos Town BEL, hydrofoils daily May to Sep, 20 mins, €25; ferry daily May to Sep, 3/week Oct to April, 50 mins, deck €20, car €100, motorbike €40.

Gelibolu/Marmaris BEL, hydrofoil to Gelibolu then bus to Marmaris, 4/week, June to Sep, 1$^{1}/_{2}$-2hrs, €25 one way.
Rhodes BEL, hydrofoil, 2/week, 2$^{1}/_{4}$hrs, €50.

Cesme (Turkey) to [see p363]
Ancona see Ancona, Adriatic.
Bríndisi see Bríndisi, Adriatic.
Chios MINIOTIS, May to Oct, daily 30-45 mins, €40, car €45-100, motorbike €40.

Chios Town (Chios / Hios) to [see p366]

Cesme see Cesme above				
Lesbos (Mytilini)	2/day	3 hours	€24	Kiriakoulis, NEL Lines
Limnos (Myrina, via Lesbos)	3/week	9$^{1}/_{2}$ hours	€19	NEL Lines
Oinousses Town	daily	1 hour	€7	Kiriakoulis, Miniotis
Piraeus	1-2/day	8 hours	€24	NEL Lines
Psara Town	3/week	3$^{1}/_{2}$ hours	€11	Miniotis
Samos (Karlovassi)	4/week	1$^{1}/_{2}$-3$^{1}/_{2}$ hours	€21	Kiriakoulis, Miniotis
Samos (Vathy)	4/week	2-3$^{1}/_{2}$ hours	€21	Kiriakoulis, Miniotis
Thessaloniki (via Lesbos and Limnos)	weekly	16$^{1}/_{2}$-21 hours	€28	NEL Lines

Crete see Agios Nikolaos, Iraklio, Kissamos, Rethymno, Souda (for Haniá), and Sitia.

Datça (Kormen, Turkey) to
Bodrum see Bodrum

Iraklio (Crete) to [see p312]

Ios Town (via Santorini)	4/week	2$^{1}/_{2}$hours	€12	HFD
Mykonos Town (via Santorini and Paros Town)	daily	6$^{1}/_{2}$ hours	€26	HFD, Minoan
Naxos Town (via Ios and Santorini)	6/week	6$^{1}/_{2}$ hours	€23	HFD, Minoan
Paros Town (via Santorini)	daily	7$^{1}/_{2}$ hours	€26	HFD, Minoan
Piraeus	daily	6-9 hours	€32	ANEK Lines, Minoan
Santorini (Athinios)	daily	1$^{3}/_{4}$-4 hours	€18	HFD, Minoan
Skiathos (via Santorini, Paros, Mykonos, Tinos)	1/week	18 hours	€39	Minoan
Syros (via Santorini, Naxos or Paros)	1-2/week	9 hours	€24	Minoan
Thessaloniki (via Santorini, Naxos or Paros, Mykonos, Syros or Tinos and Skiathos)	1-3/week	21 hours	€45	Minoan
Tinos Town (via Mykonos, Paros, and Santorini)	4/week	10$^{1}/_{2}$ hours	€27	Minoan

İstanbul (Turkey) to [see p380]
Bosphorus Ferries operate regularly across the Bosphorus – check locally.
İzmir TML, weekly, 19hrs, €10 Pullman no meals, bunk (in the cheapest cabin) inc all meals €20, car €110-130.

İzmir (Turkey) to [see p357]
İstanbul see İstanbul
Venice TML weekly, 63hrs, Pullman €230, bunk (in lowest-class cabin) €360, car €230.

Kalymnos Town / Pothia (Greece) to [see p345]

Kos Town	2/day	1 hour	€12	DANE Lines, GA Ferries, Kalymnian, Kiriakoulis, NEL Lines
Leros (Lakki)	2/day	1½ hours	€14	DANE Lines, GA Ferries, Kalymnian, Kiriakoulis
Lipsi Town	daily	3 hours	€14	Kalymnian, Kiriakoulis
Nisyros (Mandraki, via Kos)	3-4/week	2½-3 hours	€9	DANE Lines, GA Ferries, Kalymnian
Patmos (Skala, via Leros)	2/day	2-4 hours	€18	DANE Lines, GA Ferries, Kalymnian, Kiriakoulis
Piraeus (via Leros and Patmos)	daily	14 hours	€24	DANE Lines, GA Ferries
Rhodes Town (via Kos Town)	2/day	5 hours	€28	DANE Lines, Dodekanisos, GA Ferries, Kalymnian, Kiriakoulis
Samos (Pythagorio, via Leros and Patmos)	3-4/week	3½ hours	€23	Kalymnian, Kiriakoulis
Symi Town (via Kos)	3/week	7 hours	€24	GA Ferries, Kalymnian, Kiriakoulis
Tilos (Livadia, via Kos)	3/week	3 hours	€12	DANE Lines, Kalymnian

Kardamena (Kos) to [see p342]

Nisyros (Mandraki)	daily	45 mins	€9	ANEK

Karlovassi (Samos) to [see p352]

Chios Town	4/week	1½-3½ hours	€21	Kiriakoulis, Miniotis
Fourni Town	5/week	1¼ hours	€11	HFD, Miniotis
Ikaria (Agios Kyrikos)	daily	1hr 40 mins	€14	GA Ferries, HFD, Miniotis
Mykonos Town (via Ikaria)	2/week	5½ hours	€17	GA Ferries, HFD
Naxos Town	2/week	5 hours	€16	GA Ferries, HFD
Paros Town (via Naxos)	2/week	7 hours	€18	GA Ferries, HFD
Piraeus (via Ikaria)	6/week	10 hours	€21	GA Ferries, HFD
Syros (Ermoupolis) via Mykonos and Ikaria	3-4/week	6½ hours	€18	GA Ferries, HFD

Kissamos / Kasteli (Crete) to

Antikythira (Potamos)	2/week	2 hours	€10	ANEN
Kythira (Agia Pelagia, via Antikythira)	2/week	4 hours	€16	ANEN
Piraeus (via Antikythira and Kythira)	1/week	10 hours	€22	ANEN

Kos see Kardamena, Kos Town, Mastihari

Kos Town (Kos) to [see p338]

Astipalea (Chora, via Kalymnos)	2/week	3hrs 40 mins	€13	DANE Lines, GA Ferries
Bodrum see Bodrum				
Halki (aka Chalki, Nimborio, via Nisyros and Tilos)	weekly	4 hours	€23	Kiriakoulis
Kalymnos Town	2-3/day	60 mins	€12	DANE Lines, Dodekanisos GA Ferries, Kalymnian, Kiriakoulis

FERRIES

Leros (Agia Marina, direct or via Kalymnos)	3/day	60-90 mins	€16	DANE Lines, Dodekanisos GA Ferries, Kiriakoulis
Lipsi Town (via Kalymnos and Leros)	daily	1½-3hours	€16	Dodekanisos, Kiriakoulis
Nisyros (Mandraki)	4/week	50-80 mins	€14	DANE Lines, GA Ferries, Kalymnian, Kiriakoulis
Patmos (Skala, via Kalymnos and Leros)	2-3/day	2-4 hours	€20	Blue Star, DANE Lines, GA Ferries, Kiriakoulis,
Piraeus	daily	13-18 hours	€30	DANE Lines, GA Ferries
Rhodes Town	2-3/day	2-3 hours	€24	Blue Star, DANE Lines, Dodekanisos, GA Ferries, Kalymnian, Kiriakoulis
Samos (Pythagorio, via Leros, Lipsi and Patmos)	2/day	3½ hours	€22	Kiriakoulis
Samos (Vathy)	weekly	4 hours	€23	GA Ferries
Symi Town	4/week	90 mins	€19	DANE Lines, GA Ferries, Kalymnian, Kiriakoulis
Tilos (Livadia, via Nisyros)	4/week	2 hours	€16	DANE Lines, Kalymnian, Kiriakoulis

Kuşadası (Turkey) to [see p354]

Samos (Vathy)	daily	45-60 mins	€34	check locally

Lesbos see Mytilini

Mandraki (Nisyros) to [see p344]

Kardamena (Kos)	daily	45 mins	€9	ANEK
Kalymnos Town (via Kos Town)	3-4/week	2½-3 hours	€9	DANE Lines, GA Ferries, Kalymnian
Kos Town	4/week	50-80 mins	€14	DANE Lines, GA Ferries, Kalymnian, Kiriakoulis
Leros (Lakki, via Kos Town)	weekly	4 hours	€11	DANE Lines
Patmos (Skala, via Kos Town and Leros)	weekly	6 hours	€13	DANE Lines
Rhodes Town (via Tilos)	4/week	2-3 hours	€20	DANE Lines, GA Ferries, Kalymnian, Kiriakoulis
Symi Town	2/week	4 hours	€11	Kalymnian
Tilos (Livadia)	5/week	45 mins	€13	Kalymnian, Kiriakoulis

Marmaris (Turkey) to [see p330]

Rhodes MARMARIS SHIPPING, daily catamaran May to Oct, 60 mins, €45, car ferry 1/week (2 hrs), cars charged according to size.

Mastihari (Kos) to

Kalymnos Town	daily	1 hour	€12	ANEM

Mytilini (Lesbos) to [see p372]

Ayvalık	see Ayvalık			
Chios Town	2/day	3 hours	€24	Kiriakoulis, NEL Lines
Kavala Town (via Limnos)	2/week	10 hours	€23	NEL Lines
Limnos (Myrina)	3-4/week	6 hours	€17	NEL Lines
Piraeus (via Chios)	daily	12 hours	€24	NEL Lines
Rafina (via Chios)	2/week	12 hours	€20	NEL Lines
Samos (Vathy, via Chios)	2-3/week	5 hours	€28	Kiriakoulis
Thessaloniki (via Limnos)	2/week	13 hours	€28	NEL Lines

Nisyros to see Mandraki

Patmos (Greece) to   [see p347]

Fourni Town via Ikaria	2/week	90 mins	€14	Kiriakoulis
Ikaria (Agios Kyrikos)	2/week	60 mins	€14	Kiriakoulis
Kalymnos Town (via Leros Agia Marina/Lakki and/or Lipsi)	2-3/day	2-4 hours	€18	DANE Lines, Dodekanisos, GA Ferries, Kalymnian, Kiriakoulis
Kos Town (via Leros, Lipsi and/or Kalymnos)	2-3/day	2-4 hours	€20	Blue Star, DANE Lines, GA Ferries, Kalymnian
Leros (Agia Marina)	2/day	50 mins	€13	Dodekanisos, Kiriakoulis
Leros (Lakki)	2/day	1 hour	€13	Blue Star, DANE Lines, GA Ferries, Kalymnian
Lipsi Town	2/day	30 mins	€11	Dodekanisos, GA Ferries, HFD, Kalymnian, Kiriakoulis, Miniotis
Nisyros (Mandraki, via Leros, Kalymnos and Kos)	2/week	5-6 hours	€21	DANE Lines, GA Ferries
Piraeus	daily	10 hours	€28	Blue Star, DANE Lines, GA Ferries, HFD
Samos (Pythagorio)	2/day	3 hours	€20	Kalymnian, Kiriakoulis, Miniotis
Rhodes (via Leros, Kalymnos and Kos)	daily	7-7^1/$_2$ hours	€34	DANE Lines, Dodekanisos, GA Ferries, Kiriakoulis

Piraeus (Greece) to   [see p303]

Aegina/Egina Town	hourly	30-90 mins	€9	Saronikos Ferries
Agios Nikolaos (Crete, via Milos)	daily	12 hours	€28	LANE
Amorgos (Katapola)	weekly	8-9 hours	€19	GA Ferries
Angistri (Skala)	daily	1 hour	€8	Angistri-Piraeus
Astypaleia Town (direct, or via Paros, Naxos and Amorgos)	2/week	10-15 hours	€29	DANE Lines, GA Ferries, HFD
Chios Town	daily	8 hours	€24	NEL/Maritime Company of Lesvos
Fourni Town (via Paros and Ikaria)	2/week	10 hours	€22	GA Ferries, HFD
Haifa (no service operating at the time of writing)				
Hydra Town	daily	3^1/$_2$ hours	€12	HFD
Iraklio (Crete)	daily	10 hours	€27	ANEK Lines, Minoan
Ikaria (Agios Kyrikos)	daily	9 hours	€22	GA Ferries, HFD
Ios Town (direct or via Paros, Naxos and/or Santorini)	daily	4-7^1/$_2$ hours	€22	Blue Star, GA Ferries, HFD
Kalymnos Town (via Patmos and Leros)	daily	12-14 hours	€28	DANE Lines, GA Ferries
Kissamos (Crete, via Antikythira and Kythira)	1/week	10 hours	€20	ANEN
Kos Town (via Patmos, Leros and Kalymnos)	daily	13-18 hours	€30	Blue Star, DANE Lines, GA Ferries
Kythira (Agia Pelagia)	4/week	4 hours	€37	ANEN, HFD
Leros (Lakki, via Patmos)	daily	11 hours	€26	Blue Star, DANE, GA Fer's
Lesbos (Mytilini, via Chios)	daily	12 hours	€26	NEL Lines
Limassol (no service operating at the time of writing)				

Limnos (Myrina via Lesbos and Chios)	weekly	13 hours	€27	NEL Lines
Milos (Adamas)	daily	7 hours	€21	HFD, Lane
Mykonos Town (via Syros)	daily	5½ hours	€21	Blue Star, GA Ferries, HFD, NEL Lines
Naxos Town (via Paros)	2/day	3½-6 hours	€19	Blue Star, HFD
Paros Town	3 daily	4-5 hours	€21	Blue Star, GA Ferries, HFD NEL Lines
Patmos Town	daily	10 hours	€28	Blue Star, GA Ferries, HFD, NEL Lines
Rethymno (Crete)	4-7/week	9½-12 hrs	€27	ANEK Lines
Rhodes Town (via Patmos, Leros, Kalymnos and Kos)	2/day	16-18 hours	€35	Blue Star, GA Ferries, HFD, LANE
Samos (Karlovassi, via Syros, Mykonos, Agios Kyrikos or Evdilos, Fourni)	6/week	12-14 hours	€21	GA Ferries, HFD, NEL Lines
Samos (Vathy, via Syros, Mykonos, Agios Kyrikos or Evdilos, Fourni and Karlovassi)	4-7/week	13-15 hours	€26	GA Ferries, HFD, NEL Lines
Santorini (Athinios, via Paros)	3/day	9 hours	€24	HFD, NEL Lines
Sitia (Crete, via Agios Nikolaos and Milos)	5-7/week	14 hours	€21	LANE
Souda (Crete, port for Haniá)	daily	6-9 hours	€20	ANEK Lines, Blue Star
Spetses Town (via Hydra)	daily	4½ hours	€11	HFD
Syros (Ermoupolis)	3/day	2¾-4 hours	€15	Blue Star, GA Ferries, HFD, NEL Lines
Thessaloniki (via Chios, Lesbos and Limnos)	weekly	26-30 hours	€40	Minoan, NEL (via Chios and Lesbos),
Tinos Town (via Syros)	daily	4½ hours	€16	GA Ferries, HFD, NEL Lines

Pythagorio (Samos) to   [see p351]

Fourni Town	3/week	1 hour	€15	Kiriakoulis, Miniotis
Kalymnos Town (via Patmos and Leros)	3-4/week	3-3½ hours	€23	Kalymnian, Kiriakoulis
Kos Town (via Patmos Lipsi, Leros and Kalymnos)	2/day	3½ hours	€23	Kiriakoulis
Leros (Agia Marina, via Patmos)	2/day	2 hours	€18	Kalymnian, Kiriakoulis
Lipsi Town (via Agathonissi and Arki)	daily	3 hours	€15	Miniotis, Kiriakoulis
Patmos Town	2/day	70 mins	€14	Miniotis, Kalymnian, Kiriakoulis

Rafina (Greece) to   [see p306]

Andros (Gavrio)	daily	2 hours	€12	Blue Star, HFD
Karystos	3/day	2 hours	€10	Kiriakoulis
Marmari	daily	1 hour	€13	Karystia Shipping
Mykonos Town (direct, or via Andros and Tinos)	4/day	2½ hours	€16	Blue Star, HFD
Paros (via Tinos and Mykonos)	2/day	3 hours	€18	Blue Star, HFD
Tinos Town	3/day	2-4 hours	€16	Blue Star, HFD

Rethymno (Crete) to   [see p310]
Piraeus   4-7/week 9$\frac{1}{2}$-12 hrs   €27   ANEK Lines

Rhodes (Greece) to   [see p321]

Agios Nikolaos (Crete, via Halki, Karpathos, Kassos and Sitia)	3/week	12 hours	€23	LANE
Halki (Nimborio, aka Chalki)	3/week	2 hours	€15	LANE
Haifa, Israel (no service operating at the time of writing)				
Kalymnos Town (via Kos)	2/day	3-5 hours	€28	DANE Lines, Dodekanisos, GA Ferries, Kiriakoulis, Kalymnian
Karpathos (Diafani or Karpathos Town, both via Halki)	3/week	3$\frac{1}{2}$ hours	€17	LANE
Kastelorizo (Megisti)	4/week	4 hours	€16	DANE Lines, Dodekanisos, GA Ferries, Kalymnian
Kos Town	2-3/day	2-3 hours	€24	DANE Lines, Dodekanisos, GA Ferries, Kiriakoulis, Kalymnian, Roditis
Leros (Lakki, via Kos)	6/week	6 hours	€30	DANE Lines, Dodekanisos, GA Ferries, Kiriakoulis
Limassol, Cyprus (see Eastern Mediterranean)				
Marmaris see Marmaris				
Nisyros (Mandraki, via Tilos, or Symi and Tilos)	5/week	4-7 hours	€20	DANE Lines, GA Ferries, Kalymnian, Roditis, Tilos Shipping
Patmos Town (via Kos and Leros)	daily	7-7$\frac{1}{2}$ hours	€34	DANE Lines, GA Ferries, Kiriakoulis
Piraeus (via Kos, Kalymnos Patmos and Leros)	2/day	16-18 hours	€29	Blue Star, DANE Lines, GA Ferries, LANE
Samos (Vathy, via Kos)	weekly	7$\frac{1}{2}$ hours	€28	GA Ferries
Sitia (Crete, via Halki Karpathos and Kassos)	4/week	9 hours	€21	LANE
Symi Town	4/week	60 mins	€13	DANE Lines, Dodekanisos, GA Ferries, Kiriakoulis, Kalymnian
Tilos (Livadia)	daily	80 mins	€20	DANE Lines, GA Ferries Kalymnian, Roditis, Tilos

Samos to see Karlovassi, Pythagorio and Vathy

Sitia (Crete) to   [see p320]

Agios Nikolaos (Crete)	daily	1$\frac{1}{2}$ hours	€9	LANE
Karpathos (Karpathos and Diafani, via Kassos)	3/week	4-5$\frac{1}{4}$ hours	€15	LANE
Milos (Adamas, via Agios Nikolaos)	5/week	9$\frac{1}{2}$ hours	€19	LANE
Piraeus (via Agios Nikolaos and Milos)	5/week	15 hours	€25	LANE
Rhodes (via Karpathos and Kassos)	4/week	9 hours	€21	LANE

Souda/Hanía (Crete) to   [see p308]
Piraeus   daily   6-9 hours   €220   ANEK

FERRIES

Thessaloniki (Greece) to   [see p285]

Chios Town (via Limnos, and Lesbos)	2/week	20 hours	€28	NEL Lines
Iraklio (Crete, via Syros, Mykonos, Naxos and Santorini)	2-5/week	21 hours	€40	GA Ferries, Minoan
Limnos (Myrina)	2/week	7 hours	€20	NEL Lines
Lesbos (Mytilini, via Limnos and Chios)	2/week	13 hours	€28	NEL Lines
Mykonos Town (via Tinos, or via Skiathos and Tinos)	3/week	12-14 hours	€33	Minoan
Naxos Town (via Syros and and Mykonos)	2/week	15 hours	€31	Minoan
Paros Town (via Tinos and Mykonos)	3/week	14 hours	€33	Minoan
Piraeus (via Limnos, Lesbos, and Chios)	weekly	26-30 hours	€44	NEL Lines
Santorini (Athinios, via Syros, Mykonos and Naxos)	3-5/week	19$\frac{1}{2}$ hours	€36	Minoan
Skiathos Town	3/week	4-6 hours	€15	Minoan
Syros (Ermoupolis)	2/week	12 hours	€31	Minoan
Tinos Town (direct, or via Skiathos)	3/week	12-14 hours	€33	Minoan

Vathy/Samos Town (Samos) to   [see p349]

Chios Town	4/week	2-3 hours	€21	GA Ferries, Miniotis, NEL Lines
Fourni Town	4/week	2-4 hours	€14	GA Ferries, Miniotis
Kuşadası	daily	45-60 mins	€34	check locally
Lesbos (Mytilini, via Chios)	2-3/week	6-7 hours	€28	GA Ferries, NEL Lines
Kos Town	1-2/week	4 hours	€24	GA Ferries
Lipsi Town (via Patmos)	weekly	4 hours	€20	GA Ferries
Naxos Town (via Ikaria, or via Karlovassi, Fourni and Ikaria)	5/week	3-7 hours	€18	GA Ferries, NEL
Paros Town (via Karlovassi Fourni, and/or Ikaria and Naxos)	5/week	4-8 hours	€16	GA Ferries, NEL Lines
Piraeus (via Karlovassi and Ikaria, or via Fourni, Ikaria, Naxos, Paros)	4-7/week	7$\frac{1}{2}$-14 hours	€26	GA Ferries, HFD, NEL Lines
Rhodes Town (via Kos)	2/week	7$\frac{1}{2}$ hours	€28	GA Ferries

EASTERN MEDITERRANEAN

Alanya (Turkey) to   [see p395]
Girne/Kyrenia SUN TUR, 3/week, July-Sep, 5 hrs, €35.

Alexandria (Egypt) to   [see p427]
Limassol LOUIS LINES, weekly, Nov to Mar only, two nights, from €174; mini cruise includes a trip to Cairo and entertainment on board. A one-way trip is possible at the last minute if there is availability.

Beirut (Lebanon) to   [see p416]
Limassol LOUIS LINES, weekly mini-cruise, year-round, two nights, from €122. A one-way trip is possible at the last minute if there is availability.

Girne/Kyrenia (North Cyprus) to   [see p412]
Alanya see Alanya
Taşucu ERMAL DENIZCELIK, daily hydrofoils, 3 hours, €12.50.

Haifa (Israel) to   [see p422]
Cyprus/Greece POSEIDON and SALAMIS but at the time of writing services were suspended.

Limassol (South Cyprus) to   [see p403]
Most services from Limassol are mini cruises rather than ferry services, therefore the price quoted is for a round trip.
Alexandria see Alexandria
Beirut see Beirut
Greek Islands LOUIS LINES operates a variety of itineraries between April and October including places such as Kos, Santorini, Samos, Salonica, Corfu, Mytilini, Iraklio, Rhodes, Naxos and Mykonos; from €333. A one-way trip is possible at the last minute if there is availability. Check details direct with the company.
Haifa POSEIDON and SALAMIS but services are not operating at present.
Piraeus POSEIDON and SALAMIS but services are not operating at present.
Port Said LOUIS LINES, 2/week, 2 nights, from €135; a one-way trip is possible at the last minute if there is availability.
Rhodes LOUIS LINES, weekly, May to Oct, three days, from €160; a one-way trip is possible at the last minute if there is availability. POSEIDON and SALAMIS services are not operating at present.

Port Said (Egypt) to   [see p425]
Limassol see Limassol.

Taşucu (Turkey) to   [see p399]
Girne/Kyrenia see Girne.

APPENDIX C: USEFUL WORDS AND PHRASES

ARABIC

	Egyptian	Lebanese
Basic conversation		
Yes / No	*Aywa / La*	*éh or Na' am/La'*
Hello	*ahlan wa sahlan*	*marhaba*
Goodbye	*ma'a salaama*	*ma'assalama*
God willing!	*Inshallah*	*Inshallah*
Do you speak English?	*inta bititkalim ingleezi* (m)	*btiHke inglizi?*
	inta bititkalimi ingleezi (f)	
I don't understand	*ana mish faehem (m)*	*ma bif-ham*
	ana mish fashma (f)	
How much is it?	*qaddaysh?*	*addesh*
Please	*min fadlak* (m) / *min fadlik* (f)	*min fadlak* (m) / *min fadlik* (f)
Thank you (very much)	*shukran (gidam)*	*shukran (kteer), merci*
Sorry	*aasi* (m), *asfa* (f)	*assif* (m) / *asfa* (f) / *sorry*
Excuse me	*an iznaak* (m)	*bil izin, pardon*
	an iznik (f)	

Travel and directions		
Where is …?	*Wayn …?*	*Wayn ...?*
the port / ferry terminal	*mina'a*	*marfaa*
the ferry	*jenniyeh*	*markab*
the train station	*mahattat il'atr*	*m-Hattit trayn*
the bus station	*mahattat al-otobis*	*m-Hattit bas, autobis*
the tourist office	*maktab as siyaha*	*maktab alsyaha*
a hotel	*al funduq*	*hotel*
a café / restaurant	*mak-hah* / *mata'am*	*ahwé* / *mat-am*
a bank	*bank*	*bank*
a cash dispenser	*sraf alli*	*sraf alli*
a post office	*maktab al-bariid*	*bosta* / *maktab bareed*
a shop / supermarket	*mattal* / *supermarket*	*mattal* / *supermarket*
Is it far?	*Hal bai-ed?*	*b-id?*
opposite	*bwijj*	*bwijj*
next to	*hadd*	*hadd*
near to	*'urrayib min*	*areeb*
left	*yasaar*	*shmeyl*
right	*shimal* / *yemun*	*yameen*
straight on	*doughri* / *alatoul*	*dighri*
timetable	*gadwal*	*jadwal wa-it*
single ticket	*tazkara rawtta*	*btaa'a rawtta*
return ticket	*tazkara raj-a*	*btaa'a raj-a*
What time does the ferry leave?	*Emta jenniyeh yeghaader*	*Ayya se'-a ilmarkab byimshe'?*
What time does the ferry arrive?	*Emta jenniyeh yewassel*	*Ayya se'-a ilmarkab byoussal?*

Days and months

Monday	*yawm al itnin*	*(yom) ittaneyn*
Tuesday	*yawm at talata*	*(yom) ittale'ta*
Wednesday	*yawm al arbi'a*	*(yom) il-urb'a*
Thursday	*yawm al khamis*	*(yom) il-Khamees*
Friday	*yawm al jum'a*	*(yom) il-Jim-a*
Saturday	*yawm as sabt*	*(yom) il-Sabt*
Sunday	*yawm al ahad*	*(yom) il-attad*
Yesterday	*imbarih*	*m-be'ritt*
Today	*al-yom*	*il-yom*
Tomorrow	*bukra*	*bukra*
January	*Yanayir*	*kanun altani*
February	*Fibrayir*	*shbat*
March	*Marir*	*azar*
April	*Abril*	*nissan*
May	*Mayu*	*ayyar*
June	*Yunyu*	*hzayran*
July	*Yulyu*	*tammuz*
August	*Agustus*	*aab*
September	*Sibtimbir*	*aylul*
October	*Obtobir*	*teshreen al awal*
November	*Nuvembir*	*teshreen al tani*
December	*Disimbir*	*kanun al awal*

Numbers

	Egyptian	Lebanese		Egyptian	Lebanese
1	*wahid*	*wahad*	18	*tamantashar*	*tme'n-tash*
2	*ithnayn, itnaan*	*tnein*	19	*tiss'atasha*	*tisi'tash*
3	*tala'ata, tlaat*	*tle'te'*	20	*ishri'in*	*eshreen*
4	*arba'a*	*arba'a*	21	*wahid wa ishri'in*	*wahdaw eshreen*
5	*khamsa*	*khamse'*	30	*talathi'in*	*tle'tein*
6	*sita'a*	*sitte'*	40	*arba'ati'in*	*arb'een*
7	*saba'a*	*saba'a*	50	*khamsi'in*	*khamseen*
8	*tamanya*	*tméne'*	60	*sitti'in*	*sitteen*
9	*tissa'a*	*tisa'a*	70	*saba'i'in*	*sab'een*
10	*a'ashra*	*asharah*	80	*tamaani'in*	*tme'neen*
11	*ihdashr*	*hda'sh*	90	*tis'i'in*	*tiss'een*
12	*itnaysh*	*tna'sh*	100	*miyya*	*miyye'*
13	*tala'atash*	*tlét-tash*	200	*mittayn*	*miteyn*
14	*arba'ata'ash*	*arbatash*	1000	*elf*	*alf*
15	*khamastashar*	*khams-tash*	2000	*alfayn*	*alfeyn*
16	*sittashar*	*sitt-tash*	3000	*tala'athat aalaaf*	*tlet aleyf*
17	*saba'tashar*	*sab'a-tash*	1,000,000	*malaayin*	*malyon*

	Moroccan	**Tunisian**
Basic conversation		
Yes / no	*Iyeh / la*	*Iyeh / la*
Hello (peace be upon you)	*Salam a' laykum*	*Salam a' laykum*
(Response)	*malaykum salam*	*malaykum salam*
Goodbye	*b'selama*	*b'selama*
God willing!	*Insh' allah!*	*Insh' allah!*
Do you speak English?	*Wesh ket hadar linglizeeia?*	*Wesh ket hadar linglizeeia?*
I don't understand	*mafhemtsh*	*mafhemtsh*
How much is it?	*Bish-hal?*	*Bchhal?*
Please	*'afak*	*afak*
Thank you (very much)	*shokran (jazilan) / barakalaufik*	*aishek ni / barakalaufak*
Sorry	*smehli*	*smehli*
Excuse me	*smeh leeya*	*smeh leeya*

Travel and directions		
Where is …?	*Feyn ..?*	*Feyn ...?*
the port / ferry terminal	*al mersa*	*al mersa*
the ferry	*l'bato / albabuur*	*l'bato*
fast ferry	*l'bato errapid*	*l'bato errapid*
the hydrofoil	*l'bato*	*l'bato*
the train station	*mahatta dial tran*	*mahatta dial tran*
the bus station	*mahatta dial otobis*	*mahatta dial otobis*
a hotel	*al-Lotel / funduq*	*hotel / funduq*
a café / restaurant	*al-lkahoua / restaurant*	*al-lkahoua / restaurant*
a bank	*al-banka*	*al-banka*
a cash dispenser	*al-makina dial flous*	*al-makina dial flous*
a post office	*al-busta*	*al-busta*
a shop / supermarket	*al-bissri / supermarché*	*al-bissri / supermarché*
Is it far?	*Wash b'ad?*	*Wash b'ad?*
opposite	*quddem*	*quddem*
next to	*hedda*	*hedda*
near to	*kreeb*	*kriba*
left	*lisar*	*a lisar*
right	*leemen*	*a la yemeen*
straight on	*seer neeshan*	*tool*
timetable	*asaa*	*asaa*
single ticket	*allé simple*	*allé simple*
return ticket	*warka derjouaa*	*warka derjouaa*
What time does the ferry leave?	*Achmen saa l'bateau kai kalaa?*	*Achmen saa l'bateau kai kalaa?*
What time does the ferry arrive?	*Achmen saa l'bateau kai w'sel?*	*Achmen saa l'bateau kai w'sel?*

Days and months		
Monday	*nhar al-tneen*	*nhar tneen*
Tuesday	*nhar al-taleta*	*nhar ttlat*
Wednesday	*nhar al-arba'*	*nhar larb'*
Thursday	*nhar al-khamiis*	*nhar lekhmees*
Friday	*nhar al-jemaa*	*nhar jemaa*
Saturday	*nhar as-sabt*	*nhar ssebt*
Sunday	*nhar al-ahad*	*nhar lhedd*

Yesterday	*albareh*	*lbareh*
Today	*al-yuum*	*lioum*
Tomorrow	*ghaddan*	*ghadda*
January	*zhanveeyeh*	*ch'har ouahed*
February	*fevreeyeh*	*ch'har jouj*
March	*mars*	*ch'har tlata*
April	*abreel*	*ch'har rabaa*
May	*mayoo*	*ch'har khemsa*
June	*yoonyoo*	*ch'har setta*
July	*yoolyooz*	*ch'har sebaa*
August	*ghoosht*	*ch'har tmenya*
September	*sebtamber*	*ch'har t'soud*
October	*ooktoober*	*ch'har aachra*
November	*noovamber*	*ch'har h'dach*
December	*deesamber*	*ch'har tnach*

Numbers

	Moroccan	Tunisian			Moroccan	Tunisian
1	*wahed*	*wahid*	19		*tsatach*	*tsatach*
2	*itnin*	*zhoozh*	20		*'ashreen*	*eshreen*
3	*talata*	*tleta*	21		*wahed u*	*wahid u*
4	*areb'a*	*reb'a*			*ashreen*	*ashreen*
5	*khamsa*	*khamsa*	30		*tlateen*	*tleteen*
6	*setta*	*setta*	40		*reb'een*	*reb'een*
7	*seb'a*	*seb'a*	50		*khamseen*	*khamseen*
8	*tamenya*	*temanya*	60		*setteen*	*setteen*
9	*tissa*	*t'sa'a*	70		*seb'een*	*seb'een*
10	*'ashra*	*'ashra*	80		*tmaneen*	*tmaneen*
11	*hdaash*	*hdaash*	90		*tes'een*	*t's'een*
12	*tansash*	*tansash*	100		*mya*	*mya*
13	*teltash*	*teltash*	200		*miateen*	*miateen*
14	*arbatash*	*rebatash*	1000		*alf*	*alf*
15	*khamstash*	*khamstash*	2000		*alfayn*	*alfayn*
16	*settash*	*settash*	3000		*teltalaf*	*teltalaf*
17	*sebatash*	*sebatash*	1,000,000		*melyuun*	*melyou*
18	*tmentash*	*tmantash*				

FRENCH AND SPANISH

	French	Spanish
Basic conversation		
Yes / no	*oui / non*	*si / no*
Hello / Good morning	*bonjour (polite), 'allo (informal)*	*buenos dias / hola*
Goodbye	*au revoir*	*adiós / hasta luego*
Do you speak English?	*Parlez vous Anglais?*	*Habla usted Inglese?*
I don't understand	*Je ne comprends pas*	*No entiendo*
How much is it?	*Combien est-il?*	*Cuanto vale?*
Please	*s'il vous plaît*	*por favor*
Thank you (very much)	*merci (beaucoup)*	*(muchas) gracias*
Sorry	*pardon*	*lo siento*
Excuse me	*excusez-moi / pardonnez moi*	*pardon*
Travel and directions		
Where is ...?	*Où est ...?*	*¿Dónde esta ...?*
the port / ferry terminal	*le port / le ferry terminal / la gare maritime*	*la estacion maritima*
the ferry	*le ferry*	*el transbordador / barco*
the fast ferry	*la rapide*	*el transbordador rápido*
the hydrofoil	*le hydrofoil*	*la hidroala*
the train station	*la gare* (f)	*la estación des trens*
the bus station	*la gare routière* (f)	*la estación del autobús*
the tourist office	*le syndicat d'initiative* (m) / *bureau de tourisme*	*la oficina de tourismo*
a hotel	*un hotel*	*un hotel*
a café / restaurant	*un café / un restaurant*	*un café / restaurante*
a bank	*une banque / Credit Mutuel*	*un banco*
a cash dispenser	*un distributeur de billets*	*un cajero automático*
a post office	*une poste* (f)	*una oficina de correos*
a shop / supermarket	*magasin / supermarché* (m)	*una tienda / el supermercado*
Is it far?	*Est-ce qu'on est loin?*	*Esta lejos?*
opposite	*en face de*	*en frente*
next to	*a cote de*	*proximo a*
near to	*pres de*	*cerca de*
left	*a gauche*	*izquierda*
right	*a droite*	*derecha / recta*
straight on	*tout a droit*	*todo derecho*
timetable	*l'horaire* (m)	*el horario*
single ticket	*le billet simple*	*solo ida billete*
return ticket	*le billet aller-retour*	*ida y vuelta billete*
What time does the ferry leave?	*Le ferry part a quelle heure?*	*¿A qué hora sale el transbordador?*
What time does the ferry arrive?	*A quelle heure arrivera le ferry?*	*¿A qué hora llega el transbordador?*

Days and months

Monday	*Lundi*	*Lunes*
Tuesday	*Mardi*	*Martes*
Wednesday	*Mecredi*	*Miércoles*
Thursday	*Jeudi*	*Jueves*
Friday	*Vendredi*	*Viernes*
Saturday	*Samedi*	*Sabado*
Sunday	*Dimanche*	*Domingo*
Yesterday	*hier*	*ayer*
Today	*aujourd' hui*	*hoy*
Tomorrow	*demain*	*mañana*
January	*Janvier*	*Enero*
February	*Fevrier*	*Febrero*
March	*Mars*	*Marzo*
April	*Avril*	*Abril*
May	*Mai*	*Mayo*
June	*Juin*	*Junio*
July	*Juillet*	*Julio*
August	*Aout* (pronounced 'Aoot')	*Agosto*
September	*Septembre*	*Septiembre*
October	*Octobre*	*Octubre*
November	*Novembre*	*Noviembre*
December	*Decembre*	*Diciembre*

Numbers

	French	Spanish		French	Spanish
1	*un / une*	*uno / una*	20	*vingt*	*veinte*
2	*deux*	*dos*	21	*vingt et un*	*veinte y uno*
3	*trois*	*tres*	30	*trente*	*treinta*
4	*quatre*	*cuatro*	40	*quarante*	*cuarenta*
5	*cinq*	*cinco*	50	*cinquante*	*cincuenta*
6	*six*	*seis*	60	*soixante*	*sesenta*
7	*sept*	*siete*	70	*soixante-dix*	*setenta*
8	*huit*	*ocho*	71	*soixante et onze*	*setentiuno*
9	*neuf*	*nueve*	75	*soixante-quinze*	*setenticinco*
10	*dix*	*diez*	80	*quatre-vingt*	*ochenta*
11	*onze*	*once*	90	*quatre-vingt-dix*	*noventa*
12	*douze*	*doce*	100	*cent*	*cien / ciento*
13	*treize*	*trece*	150	*cent-cinquante*	*cien y cincuenta*
14	*quatorze*	*catorce*	200	*deux cents*	*dos cientos*
15	*quinze*	*quince*	1000	*mille*	*mil*
16	*seize*	*dieciséis*	2000	*deux milles*	*dos mil*
17	*dix-sept*	*diecisiete*	3000	*trois milles*	*tres mil*
18	*dix-huit*	*dieciocho*	5000	*cinq mille*	*cinco mil*
19	*dix-neuf*	*diecinueve*	1,000,000	*million*	*un milion*

ITALIAN AND GREEK

	Italian	**Greek**
Basic conversation		
Yes / No	*si / no*	*ne / ohi*
Hello (informal/formal)	*ciao / buongiorno*	*ya-su / ya sas*
Goodbye	*ciao / arrivederci*	*gia / andio*
Do you speak English?	*Parla Inglese?*	*Milate Anglika*
I don't understand	*non capito*	*den katalaveno*
How much is it?	*Quanto costa (*singular) / *Quanti costanno?* (plural)	*Poso kani*
Please	*per favore*	*se parakalo*
Thank you	*grazie*	*efharisto poli*
Sorry	*mi perdoni*	*lipame*
Excuse me	*mi scusi / mi scusa* (formal / informal)	*signomi*

Travel and directions		
Where is ...?	*Dov'è ...?*	*Pu ine ...?*
the port / ferry terminal	*il porto / stazione marittima*	*limani*
the ferry	*il traghetto*	*plio*
hydrofoil	*aliscafo*	*plio*
the train station	*il stazione treno*	*stathmos trenon / o sidirodromikos stathmos*
the bus station	*il stazione l'autobus*	*o stathmos leoforion*
the tourist office	*il ufficio turistico*	*to turistiko grafio*
a hotel	*un albergo*	*ena xenodohio*
a café / restaurant	*una café, un ristorante*	*ena estiatorio*
a bank	*una banca*	*ena mia trapeza*
a cash dispenser	*una macchina di cassiere automatizzata*	*ena antalaktirio hrimaton*
a post office	*un ufficio postale*	*ena tahidromio*
a shop / supermarket	*un negozi /un supermercato*	*ena magazi/supermarket*
Is it far?	*E lontano?*	*Ine makrya?*
opposite	*davanti*	*piso apenandi*
next to	*accanto a*	*dipla*
near to	*vicino á*	*konda*
left	*sinistra*	*aristera*
right	*destra*	*dexia*
straight on	*diretto*	*olo efthia*
timetable	*orario*	*pinakas dromologhion / programa*
single ticket	*il biglietto unidirezionale*	*aplo isitirio*
return ticket	*biglietto di ritorno*	*met epistrofis*
What time does the ferry leave?	*A che ora parta il traghetto?*	*Ti ora fevgi to plio?*
What time does the ferry arrive?	*A che ora arriva il traghetto?*	*Ti ora ftani to plio?*

Days and months

Monday	*Lunedi*	*Deftera*
Tuesday	*Martedi*	*Triti*
Wednesday	*Mercoledi*	*Tetarti*
Thursday	*Giovedl*	*Pempti*
Friday	*Venerdi*	*Paraskevi*
Saturday	*Sabato*	*Savato*
Sunday	*Domenica*	*Kiriaki*
Yesterday	*ieri*	*khtes*
Today	*oggi*	*simera*
Tomorrow	*domani*	*avrio*
January	*Gennaio*	*Ianuarios*
February	*Febraio*	*Fevruarios*
March	*Marzo*	*Martios*
April	*Aprile*	*Aprilios*
May	*Maio*	*Maios*
June	*Giugno*	*Iunios*
July	*Luglio*	*Iulios*
August	*Agosto*	*Avgustos*
September	*Septembre*	*Septemvrios*
October	*Ottobre*	*Oktovrios*
November	*Novembre*	*Noembrios*
December	*Dicembre*	*Dekemvrios*

Numbers

	Italian	Greek		Italian	Greek
1	*uno*	*ena*	21	*ventuno*	*ikosi ena*
2	*due*	*dio*	30	*trenta*	*trianta*
3	*tre*	*tria*	40	*quaranta*	*saranta*
4	*quattro*	*tesera*	50	*cinquanta*	*peninta*
5	*cinque*	*pente*	60	*sessanta*	*eksinta*
6	*sei*	*exi*	70	*settanta*	*evdominta*
7	*setta*	*efta*	71	*settantuno*	*evdominta ena*
8	*otto*	*ohto*	75	*settantacinque*	*evdominta pente*
9	*nove*	*enia*	80	*ottanta*	*oghdonta*
10	*dieci*	*deka*	90	*novanta*	*eneninta*
11	*undici*	*enteka*	100	*cento*	*ekato*
12	*dodici*	*dodeka*	150	*cento*	*ekato peninta*
13	*tredici*	*deka tria*		*cinquanta*	
14	*quattordici*	*deka tesera*	200	*due centi*	*diakosia*
15	*quindici*	*deka pente*	1000	*mille* (s)/	*khilia*
16	*sedici*	*deka exi*		*mila* (pl)	
17	*diciasette*	*deka epta*	2000	*due mila*	*dio khiliades*
18	*diciotto*	*deka okto*	3000	*tremille*	*tria khiliades*
19	*diciannove*	*deka enia*	5000	*cinque mila*	*pente khiliades*
20	*venti*	*ikosi*	1,000,000	*un millione*	*ena ekatomirio*

TURKISH AND CROATIAN

	Turkish	Croatian
Basic conversation		
Yes / No	*evet / hayir*	*Da / Ne*
Hello	*merhaba*	*Zdravo*
Goodbye	*Iyi gunlar* (daytime) /	*Dovidjenja*
	Iyi Akshamlar (evening / night)	
God willing!	*Inshalla*	
Do you speak English?	*Inglizdje biliyormasiniz?*	*govorite li Engleski?*
I don't understand	*Anlamiyorum*	*Ne razumijem*
How much is it?	*Nekadar?*	*Kolikos kosta?*
Please	*lutfen*	*Molim*
Thank you	*teshekurlar*	*Hvala*
Sorry	*uzur delerim*	*Pardon*
Excuse me	*pardon / afedersiniz*	*Oprostite*
Travel and directions		
Where is …?	*… nerede?*	*Gdje je …?*
the port / ferry terminal	*limana / iskele*	*luka*
the ferry	*feribot / vapur*	*brod*
the hydrofoil	*gemi kayagi*	*hidrokrilni*
the train station	*tren gar*	*zheljenichka stanika*
the bus station	*otogar*	*autobusna stanika*
the tourist office	*turizm burosa*	*turistichki ured / biro*
a hotel	*otel*	*hotel*
a café / restaurant	*café / kahvehani / restorant*	*café / restoran*
a bank	*banka*	*banka*
a cash dispenser	*bankamatik*	*bankomat*
a post office	*posta*	*poshta*
a shop / supermarket	*bakaal / supermarket*	*duc' an*
Is it far?	*Uzak ma?*	*Daleko?*
opposite	*karsha*	*suprotan*
next to	*bitishik*	*skraj*
near to	*yakin-dan*	*blizu*
left	*sol*	*lijevo*
right	*sa*	*desno*
straight on	*direkt / dum duz*	*pravo naprijed*
timetable	*tarife*	*itinerar*
single ticket	*gidish bileti*	*stoji karta*
return ticket	*gidish-donush bileti*	*povratna karta*
What time does the ferry leave?	*Feribot ne zaman kalkiyor*	*kada brod polzai*
What time does the ferry arrive?	*Feribot, ne zaman geliyor?*	*kada brod dolazi*

Days and months

Monday	*Pazartesey*	*Ponedjeljak*
Tuesday	*Sala*	*Utorak*
Wednesday	*Charshamba*	*Srijeda*
Thursday	*Pershambey*	*Chetrvtak*
Friday	*Djuma*	*Petak*
Saturday	*Djumartasey*	*Subota*
Sunday	*Pazar*	*Nedjelja*
Yesterday	*doon*	*jucher*
Today	*bugun*	*danas*
Tomorrow	*yarin*	*sutra*
January	*Odjak*	*Sijechanj*
February	*Shubat*	*Veljacha*
March	*Mart*	*Ozhujak*
April	*Nisan*	*Travanj*
May	*Mayis*	*Svibanj*
June	*Haziran*	*Lipanj*
July	*Temuz*	*Srpanj*
August	*Agusto*	*Kolovoz*
September	*Eylul*	*Rujan*
October	*Ekim*	*Listopad*
November	*Kasim*	*Studei*
December	*Aralik*	*Prosinac*

Numbers

	Turkish	Croatian		Turkish	Croatian
1	*bir*	*jedan*	21	*yermi bir*	*dvadesetjedam*
2	*iki*	*dva*	30	*otuz*	*trideset*
3	*üç*	*tri*	40	*kirk*	*cetrdeset*
4	*dört*	*chetiri*	50	*eli*	*pedeset*
5	*besh*	*pet*	60	*altmush*	*shezdeset*
6	*alta*	*shest*	70	*yetmish*	*sedamdeset*
7	*yedi*	*sedam*	71	*yetmish bir*	*sedamdesetjedam*
8	*sekiz*	*osam*	75	*yetmish besh*	*sedamdesetpet*
9	*dokuz*	*devet*	80	*seksan*	*osamdeset*
10	*on*	*deset*	90	*doksan*	*devedeset*
11	*on bir*	*jedamaest*	100	*yuz*	*sto*
12	*on iki*	*dvanaest*	150	*yuz eli*	*stopedeset*
13	*on üç*	*trinaest*	200	*iki yuz*	*dvasto*
14	*on dirt*	*chetrnaest*	1000	*bin*	*tisutchu*
15	*on besh*	*petnaest*	2000	*iki bin*	*dva tisuc'a*
16	*on alta*	*shestnaest*	3000	*üç bin*	*tri tisuc'a*
17	*on yedi*	*sedamaest*	5000	*besh bin*	*pet tisuc'a*
18	*on sekiz*	*osamnaest*	1,000,000	*bir milyon*	*jedan milijun*
19	*on dokuz*	*devetmaest*	5,000,000	*besh milyon*	*pet milijun*
20	*yermi*	*dvadeset*	1 billion	*bir milyard*	*neki rac'un*

APPENDIX D: BIBLIOGRAPHY

Abram, David *Trekking in Corsica* (Trailblazer, 2002)

Abulafia, David *The Mediterranean in History* (J Paul Getty Museum, 2003)

Aubet, Maria Eugenia, Mary Turton (translator) *The Phoenicians and the West: Politics, Colonies and Trade* (Cambridge University Press, 2001)

Blanch, Lesley *The Wilder Shores of Love* (Touchstone, 1970)

Boswell, James *An Account of Corsica* (c1765)

Bradford, Ernle *Mediterranean: Portrait of a Sea* (Hodder and Stoughton, 2000)

Bradford, Ernle *The Shield and the Sword. the Knights of Malta* (Hodder and Stoughton, 1972)

Braudel, Fernand *The Mediterranean and the Mediterranean World in the Age of Philip II* (University of California Press, 1996)

Brown, Peter *The Rise of Western Christendom* (Blackwell Publishers, 2003)

Casson, Lionel *The Ancient Mariners* (Princeton University Press, 1991)

Flower, Harriet *The Cambridge Companion to the Roman Republic* (Cambridge University Press, 2004)

Fraser, Antonia *Marie Antoinette: the Journey* (Weidenfeld & Nicholson, 2001)

Freeman, Charles *Egypt, Greece and Rome: Civilizations of the Ancient Mediterranean* (Oxford University Press, 1999)

Gatier, Pierre-Louis et al *The Levant: History and Archaeology in the Eastern Mediterranean* (Konemann, 2000)

Guerber HA *The Myths of Greece and Rome, their stories, signification and origin* (Harrap)

Hammerton, JA (ed) *Outline of World History* (The Amalgamated Press)

Horden, Peregrin & Purcell, Nicholas *Corrupting Sea: A Study of Mediterranean History* (Blackwell Publishers, 2000)

Hornblower, Simon & Spawforth, Antony *The Oxford Companion to Classical Civilization* (Oxford University Press, 1981)

Keller, Werner *The Bible as History* (Hodder and Stoughton)

Lawrence TE (trans) *Homer's Odyssey*

Liddell and Scott *Classical Greek Dictionary*

Mclynn, Frank *Napoleon – A Biography* (Pimlico, 1998)

Pryor, John H *Geography, Technology, and War: Studies in the Maritime History of the Mediterranean, 649-1571 (Past and Present Publications)* (Cambridge University Press, 1992)

Riley-Smith, Jonathan *The Oxford Illustrated History of the Crusades* (Oxford University Press, 2001)

Runciman, Steven *The Sicilian Vespers: A History of the Mediterranean World in the Later Thirteenth Century* (Cambridge University Press, 1992)

Stedman, Henry *Istanbul to Cairo Overland* (Trailblazer, 1997)

Stuart, Andrea *The Rose of Martinique* (Macmillan)

❑ TRAILBLAZER GUIDES

Adventure Cycling Handbook	1st edn mid 2005
Adventure Motorcycling Handbook	4th edn out now
Australia by Rail	4th edn out now
Azerbaijan	3rd edn out now
The Blues Highway – New Orleans to Chicago	2nd edn out now
China by Rail	2nd edn Nov 2004
Coast to Coast (British Walking Guide)	1st edn out now
Cornwall Coast Path (British Walking Guide)	1st edn out now
Good Honeymoon Guide	2nd edn out now
Inca Trail, Cusco & Machu Picchu	2nd edn out now
Japan by Rail	1st edn out now
Kilimanjaro – a trekking guide to Africa's highest mountain	1st edn out now
Land's End to John O'Groats	1st edn mid 2005
Mediterranean Handbook	1st edn out now
Nepal Mountaineering Guide	1st edn Oct 2004
New Zealand – The Great Walks	1st edn out now
Norway's Arctic Highway	1st edn out now
Offa's Dyke Path (British Walking Guide)	1st edn out now
Pembrokeshire Coast Path (British Walking Guide)	1st edn out now
Pennine Way (British Walking Guide)	1st edn out now
Siberian BAM Guide – rail, rivers & road	2nd edn out now
The Silk Roads – a route and planning guide	1st end out now
Sahara Overland – a route and planning guide	2nd edn Oct 2004
Sahara Abenteuerhandbuch (German edition)	1st edn out now
South Downs Way (British Walking Guide)	1st edn out now
South-East Asia – The Graphic Guide	1st edn out now
Tibet Overland – mountain biking & jeep touring	1st edn out now
Trans-Canada Rail Guide	3rd edn out now
Trans-Siberian Handbook	6th edn out now
Trekking in the Annapurna Region	4th edn Oct 2004
Trekking in the Everest Region	4th edn out now
Trekking in Corsica	1st edn out now
Trekking in the Dolomites	1st edn out now
Trekking in Ladakh	3rd edn out now
Trekking in Langtang, Gosainkund & Helambu	1st edn out now
Trekking in the Moroccan Atlas	1st edn out now
Trekking in the Pyrenees	2nd edn out now
Tuva and Southern Siberia	1st edn mid 2005
West Highland Way (British Walking Guide)	1st edn out now

For more information about Trailblazer and our expanding range of guides,
for where to find your nearest stockist, for guidebook updates
or for credit card mail order sales (post-free worldwide) visit our web site:

www.trailblazer-guides.com

ROUTE GUIDES FOR THE ADVENTUROUS TRAVELLER

Europe
Trekking in Corsica
Trekking in the Dolomites
Trekking in the Pyrenees
(and the British Walking Series: see p473)

South America
Inca Trail, Cusco & Machu Picchu

Australasia
New Zealand – Great Walks

Africa
Kilimanjaro
Trekking in the Moroccan Atlas

Asia
Trekking in the Annapurna Region
Trekking in the Everest Region
Trekking in Ladakh
Trekking in Langtang
Nepal Mountaineering Guide

Trekking in Corsica *David Abram*
1st edition, 320pp, 74 maps, 48 colour photos
ISBN 1 873756 63 1, £11.99, Can$26.95, US$18.95
A mountain range rising straight from the sea, Corsica holds the most arrestingly beautiful and diverse landscapes in the Mediterranean. Among the many trails that penetrate its remotest corners, the GR20, which wriggles across the island's watershed, has gained an international reputation. This guide also covers the best of the other routes.   *'Excellent guide'.* **The Sunday Times**

Trekking in Ladakh *Charlie Loram*
3rd edition, 288 pages, 75 maps, 24 colour photos
ISBN 1 873756 75 5, £12.99, Can$27.95, US$18.95
Fully revised and extended 3rd edition of Charlie Loram's practical guide to trekking in this spectacular Himalayan region of India. Includes 75 detailed walking maps, guides to Leh, Manali and Delhi plus information on getting to Ladakh.
           'Extensive...and well researched'. **Climber Magazine**

New Zealand – The Great Walks *Alexander Stewart*
1st edn, 272pp, 60 maps, 40 colour photos
ISBN 1 873756 78 X, £11.99, Can$28.95, US$19.95
New Zealand is a wilderness paradise of incredibly beautiful landscapes. There is no better way to experience it than on one of the nine designated Great Walks, the country's premier walking tracks which provide outstanding hiking opportunities for people at all levels of fitness and proficiency. Also includes detailed guides to Auckland, Wellington, National Park Village, Taumaranui, Nelson, Queenstown, Te Anau and Oban.

The Inca Trail, Cusco & Machu Picchu *Richard Danbury*
2nd edition, 288pp, 45 maps, 35 colour photos
ISBN 1 873756 64 X, £10.99, Can$24.95, US$17.95
The Inca Trail from Cusco to Machu Picchu is South America's most popular hike. Includes the **Vilcabamba Trail** to the ruins of the last Inca capital, plus guides to Cusco and Machu Picchu. *'Danbury's research is thorough...you need this one'.* **The Sunday Times**

Kilimanjaro: a trekking guide to Africa's highest mountain
Henry Stedman, 1st edition, 240pp, 40 maps, 30 photos
ISBN 1 873756 65 8, £9.99, Can$22.95, US$17.95
At 19,340ft the world's tallest freestanding mountain, Kilimanjaro is one of the most popular destinations for hikers visiting Africa. It's possible to walk up to the summit: no technical skills are necessary. This new guide includes town guides to Nairobi and Dar-Es-Salaam, excursions in the region and a detailed colour guide to flora and fauna.

Sahara Overland – a route & planning guide *Chris Scott*
2nd edition, 640 pages, 24 colour & 170 B&W photos
ISBN 1 873756 26 7 Hardback £19.99, Can$44.95 US$29.95
Fully-updated 2nd edition covers all aspects Saharan, from acquiring documentation to vehicle choice and preparation; from descriptions of the prehistoric art sites of the Libyan Fezzan to the ancient caravan cities of southern Mauritania. How to 'read' sand surfaces, using GPS – it's all here along with detailed off-road itineraries covering 26,000kms in nine countries. "*THE essential desert companion for anyone planning a Saharan trip on either two wheels or four.*' **Trailbike Magazine**

Tibet Overland – a route & planning guide *Kym McConnell*
1st edition, 224pp, 16pp colour maps
ISBN 1 873756 41 0, £12.99, Can$29.95, US$19.95
Featuring 16pp of full colour mapping based on satellite photographs, this is a guide for mountain bikers and other road users in Tibet. Includes detailed information on over 9000km of overland routes across the world's highest and largest plateau. Includes Lhasa–Kathmandu route and the route to Everest North Base Camp. '*..a wealth of advice...*' **HH The Dalai Lama**

The Silk Roads *Paul Wilson & Dominic Streatfeild-James*
1st edition, 336pp, 50 maps, 30 colour photos
ISBN 1 873756 53 4, £12.99, Can$29.95, US$18.95
The Silk Road was never a single thread but an intricate web of trade routes linking Asia and Europe. This new guide follows all the routes with sections on Turkey, Syria, Iran, Turkmenistan, Uzbekistan, Kyrgyzstan, Pakistan and China.

Trans-Siberian Handbook *Bryn Thomas*
6th edition, 432pp, 52 maps, 40 colour photos
ISBN 1 873756 70 4, £12.99, Can$26.95 US$15.95
First edition short-listed for the **Thomas Cook Guidebook Awards**. New sixth edition of the most popular guide to the world's longest rail journey. How to arrange a trip, plus a km-by-km guide to the routes. Updated and expanded to include extra information on travelling independently in Russia. New mapping.
'Definitive guide' **Condé Nast Traveler**

Trans-Canada Rail Guide *Melissa Graham*
3rd edition, 256pp, 32 maps, 30 colour photos
ISBN 1 873756 69 0, £10.99, Can$24.95, US$16.95
Expanded 3rd edition now includes Calgary city guide. Comprehensive guide to Canada's trans-continental railroad. Covers the entire route from coast to coast. What to see and where to stay in the cities along the line, with information for all budgets.

The Blues Highway New Orleans to Chicago
A travel and music guide *Richard Knight*
2nd edition, 304pp, 50 maps, 30 colour photos
ISBN 1 873756 66 6, £12.99, Can$29.95, US$19.95
New edition of the first travel guide to explore the roots of jazz and blues in the USA. ❑ Detailed city guides with 40 maps ❑ Where to stay, where to eat ❑ The best music clubs and bars ❑ Who's who of jazz and blues ❑ Historic landmarks ❑ Music festivals and events ❑ Exclusive interviews with music legends Wilson Pickett, Ike Turner, Little Milton, Honeyboy Edwards and many more.
'Fascinating' – **Time Out**

INDEX

Note: *place name* used for city/town/island

COLOUR SECTION (following pages)

● **C1 GREECE** Statue of Pythagoras, Samos ● **C2 CORSICA Top left**: Statue of Napoleon, Ajaccio. **Top right**: Bonifaccio. **Bottom**: Cliffs near Bonifaccio. ● **C3 TUNISIA Top left**: Nargile pipe seller, Tunis. **Top right**: Central Mosque, Tunis. **Bottom**: Ruins of Carthage.
● **C4 ITALY Top**: Crater, Vulcano, Aeolian Islands. **Bottom**: Detail from Trajan's Column, Rome.
● **C5 MALTA Top**: Valetta. **Bottom**: Fishing boats, Valetta harbour.
● **C6 CROATIA (Top)**: Waterfront, Split. **BOSNIA HERZEGOVINA (Bottom)**: Street chess, Sarajevo. ● **C7 GREECE Top**: Acropolis, Athens. **Bottom**: Harbourside entertainment, Kos.
● **C8 GREECE Top**: Church of the Apocalypse, Patmos. **Bottom**: Octopus in a restaurant window, Patmos. ● **C9 GREECE** Church, Nisyros. ● **C10 GREECE Top**: Beach, Samos. **Bottom**: Lion of St Mark, Lindos, Rhodes. ● **C11 TURKEY** Mehter Janissary band, İstanbul.
● **C12 TURKEY Top**: St Sophia and St Irene, İstanbul. **Bottom left**: On the ferry, Chios-Çeşme. **Bottom right**: Library façade, Ephesus. ● **C13 TURKEY Top**: Tour boat, Ayvalık-Lesbos channel. **Bottom**:Roman amphitheatre, Bodrum. ● **C14 LEBANON (Beirut) Top**: Pigeon Rocks. **Bottom left**: Reconstructed buildings. **Bottom right**: Roman columns. ● **C15 CYPRUS Top**: Anglican Church, Girne/Kyrenia. **Bottom left**: Bazaar, Lefkosia. **Bottom right**: Salamis.

C2

C5

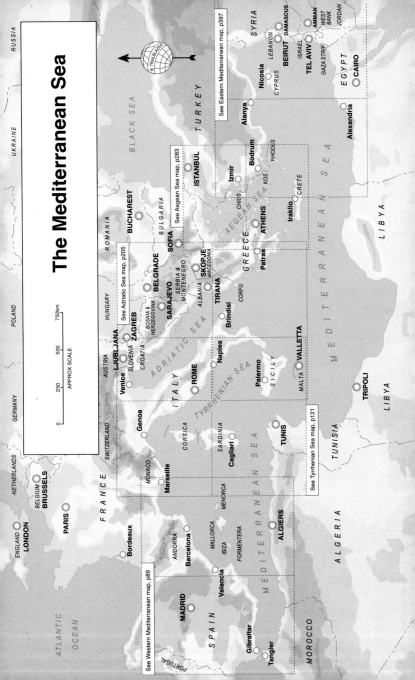

The Mediterranean Sea

See Eastern Mediterranean map, p397

See Aegean Sea map, p283

See Adriatic Sea map, p205

See Tyrrhenian Sea map, p121

See Western Mediterranean map, p89

APPROX SCALE

0   250   500   750km

ATLANTIC
OCEAN

ENGLAND
LONDON

NETHERLANDS
BELGIUM
BRUSSELS

PARIS

GERMANY

POLAND

UKRAINE

RUSSIA

BLACK SEA

ROMANIA
BUCHAREST

BULGARIA
SOFIA

HUNGARY

AUSTRIA

SWITZERLAND

F R A N C E

Bordeaux

SLOVENIA
LJUBLJANA

CROATIA
ZAGREB
Venice

BOSNIA &
HERZEGOVINA
SARAJEVO

BELGRADE

SERBIA &
MONTENEGRO

SKOPJE
MACEDONIA

ALBANIA
TIRANA

CORFÚ

Brindisi

G R E E C E

Patras

CHIOS

ATHENS
Iraklio

CRETE

T U R K E Y

ISTANBUL

Izmir

Bodrum

KOS
RHODES

Alanya

Nicosia
CYPRUS

S Y R I A

BEIRUT
LEBANON

DAMASCUS

ISRAEL
TEL AVIV
GAZA STRIP
WEST
BANK
AMMAN
JORDAN

E G Y P T

CAIRO

Alexandria

L I B Y A

MEDITERRANEAN SEA

AEGEAN SEA

ADRIATIC SEA

TYRRHENIAN SEA

I T A L Y

ROME
Naples

Palermo
S I C I L Y

VALLETTA
MALTA

TRIPOLI

L I B Y A

Genoa

MONACO
Marseille

CORSICA

SARDINIA

Cagliari

TUNIS

TUNISIA

ALGIERS

A L G E R I A

ANDORRA

MADRID

S P A I N

Barcelona

Valencia

MALLORCA
IBIZA
MENORCA
FORMENTERA

Gibraltar

Tangier

MOROCCO

PORTUGAL

MEDITERRANEAN SEA